# Time Out
# Croatia
**www.timeout.com/croatia**

**Time Out Digital Ltd**
4th Floor
125 Shaftesbury Avenue
London WC2H 8AD
United Kingdom
Tel: +44 (0)20 7813 3000
Fax: +44 (0)20 7813 6001
Email: guides@timeout.com
www.timeout.com

**Published by Time Out Digital Ltd**, a wholly owned subsidiary
of Time Out Group Ltd. Time Out and the Time Out logo are
trademarks of Time Out Group Ltd.

© **Time Out Group Ltd 2015**
Previous editions 2006, 2009.

10 9 8 7 6 5 4 3 2 1

**This edition first published in Great Britain in 2015 by Ebury Publishing.**
20 Vauxhall Bridge Road, London SW1V 2SA

Ebury Publishing is part of the Penguin Random House group of companies
whose addresses can be found at global.penguinrandomhouse.com

Distributed in the US and Latin America by Publishers Group West
(1-510-809-3700)

**For further distribution details, see www.timeout.com.**

ISBN: 978-1-84670-719-3

A CIP catalogue record for this book is available from the British Library.

Printed and bound in China by Leo Paper Products Ltd.

Penguin Random House is committed to a sustainable future for our
business, our readers and our planet. This book is made from Forest
Stewardship Council® certified paper.

**MIX**
Paper from
responsible sources
**FSC® C018179**

# Contents

170

Croatia's Top 20                          10
Croatia Today                             18
Itineraries                               22
Diary                                     28
Croatia's Best                            34

## Explore                                38

Zagreb                                    40
Istria                                    70
Kvarner                                  102
Zadar & Northern Dalmatia                140
Split & Central Dalmatia                 170
Dubrovnik & Southern Dalmatia            230

## In Context                            274

History                                  276
Food & Wine                              288
Nature & Wildlife                        294
Sailing                                  299

## Essential Information                 304

Getting Around                           306
Resources A-Z                            307
Vocabulary                               312
Further Reference                        314
Index                                    315

**220**

**248**

**268**

# Time Out Croatia

## Editorial
**Editor** Peterjon Cresswell
**Copy Editor** Ros Sales
**Proofreader** Jo Willacy
**Indexer** Patrick Davis

**Editorial Director** Sarah Guy
**Group Finance Manager** Margaret Wright

## Design
**Art Editor** Christie Webster
**Designer** Alaa Alsaraji
**Group Commercial Senior Designer** Jason Tansley

## Picture Desk
**Picture Editor** Jael Marschner
**Deputy Picture Editor** Ben Rowe
**Picture Researcher** Lizzy Owen

## Advertising
**Managing Director** St John Betteridge

## Marketing
**Senior Publishing Brand Manager** Luthfa Begum
**Head of Circulation** Dan Collins

## Production
**Production Controller** Katie Mulhern-Bhudia

## Time Out Group
**Founder** Tony Elliott
**President** Noel Penzer
**Publisher** Alex Batho

## Contributors

Revised and adapted from previous editions of *Time Out Croatia* by Peterjon Creswell, with contributions from Jonathan Bousfield (Croatia Today, Zagreb, Istria, Kvarner), Ivica Profaca (Split, Hvar, Brač, Vis, Getting Around, Resources) and Cormac Doyle (mapping assistance).

**Maps** JS Graphics Ltd (john@jsgraphics.co.uk)

**Cover Photography** Alan Copson/AWL Images

**Back Cover Photography** Clockwise from top left: M.V. Photography/Shutterstock.com, SJ Travel Photo and Video/Shutterstock.com, Ivica Drusany/Shutterstock.com, Matej Kastelic/Shutterstock.com, danilo ducak/Shutterstock.com

**Photography** pages 2/3 RnDmS/Shutterstock.com; 10/11 Ivica Drusany/Shutterstock.com; 13 (top), 26 (bottom), 40, 50, 236, 224, 269 (top), pull-out map paul prescott/Shutterstock.com; 16 (top), pull-out map Szabolcs Emich/Wikimedia Commons; 16 (bottom) stepmorem/Shutterstock.com ; 18/19 Goran Telak; 21 InnaFelker/Shutterstock.com; 22, 266/267 Sergio Gobbo/Croatian National Tourist Board; 22/23, 140/141 Croatian National Tourist Board; 23 Roberta F./Wikimedia Commons; 27 (top) Jazzmany/Shutterstock.com; 27 (bottom) andras_csontos/Shutterstock.com; 31, 140 Dario Vuksanovic/Shutterstock.com; 32 Dan Medhurst Photography; 34/35 (bottom) Ajan Alen/Shutterstock.com; 43 (left), 66, 129 Deymos.HR/Shutterstock.com; 68, 69 Damir Fabijanić; 82, 83 © manuelpaljuh2015; 88 Nenad Simunic; 98 FOTO PRIZMA; 146 (top) AlMare/Wikimedia Commons; 146 (bottom) Fratelli Alinari/Alinari Archives/Getty Images; 148 Nikolina Mimić Dujmović; 149 Tim Ertl; 150/151 Peter Skrlep; 157 Tamisclao/Shutterstock.com; 182 AFP/Getty Images; 184 Basic Marijo; 208 OPIS Zagreb/Shutterstock.com; 276 Francoise De Mulder/Roger Viollet/Getty Images; 278 Oton Iveković/Wikimedia Commons; 279 Wikimedia Commons; 281 Photo12/UIG/Getty Images; 282, 283 Mondadori Portfolio/Getty Images; 285 Heribert Proepper/AP/Press Association Images; 287 David Caulkin/AP/Press Association Images; 288/289 Isiwal/Wikimedia Commons; 294 Misalalic/Wikimedia Commons

The following images were supplied by the featured establishments: 5 (top and middle), 17 (top), 28/29, 30, 33, 37, 48, 52, 53, 60, 64, 85, 89, 108, 109, 111, 114, 115, 120, 121, 123, 124, 125, 139, 154, 164, 170, 178, 179, 181, 185, 192/193, 197, 199, 210, 211, 212, 216, 217, 220/221, 222, 226, 240, 241, 243, 248, 250, 303, 304/305

# About the Guide

## GETTING AROUND

The explore chapters contain city or town maps marked with the locations of sights and museums (❶), restaurants (❶), cafés and bars (❶) and shops (❶). In addition, there is a detachable fold-out page with street maps.

## THE ESSENTIALS

For practical information, including visas, disabled access, emergency numbers, lost property, websites and local transport, plus a vocabularly primer, see the Essential Information section. It begins on page 304.

## THE LISTINGS

Addresses, phone numbers, websites, transport information, hours and prices are all included in our listings, as are selected other facilities. All were checked and correct at press time. However, business owners can alter their arrangements at any time, and fluctuating economic conditions can cause prices to change rapidly.

In this guide, hotels have been graded as deluxe (€€€€€), expensive (€€€€), moderate (€€€) and budget (€). In Croatia, room rates vary wildly between high and low seasons. Hotel categories are based on prices of an average of €100 or below per night for budget,

€100-€175 for moderate, €175-€275 for expensive and above €275 for deluxe. For restaurants, we have categorised according to a rough average price for main courses (excluding lobster): up to €7 (€); up to €15 (€€); up to €25 (€€€), and over €25 (€€€€).

The very best venues in the city, the must-sees and must-dos in every category, have been marked with a red star (★). We've also marked sights with free admission with a FREE symbol.

## PHONE NUMBERS

The national code for all numbers in this guide is 385. Within Croatia, dial the whole number given in the guide. From outside Croatia, dial your country's international access code (00 from the UK, 011 from the US) or a + sign, followed by 385, then the number listed in this guide but omitting the initial 0. So, to reach Zagreb City Museum, dial + 385 1 48 51 361.

## FEEDBACK

We welcome feedback on this guide, both on the venues we've included and on any other locations that you'd like to see featured in future editions. Please email us at guides@timeout.com.

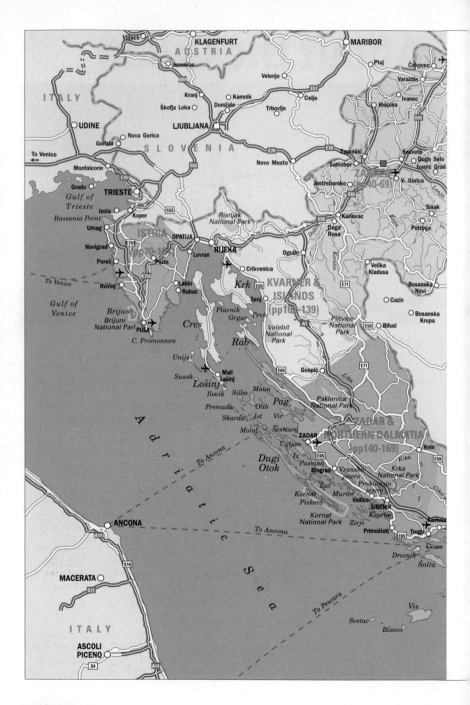

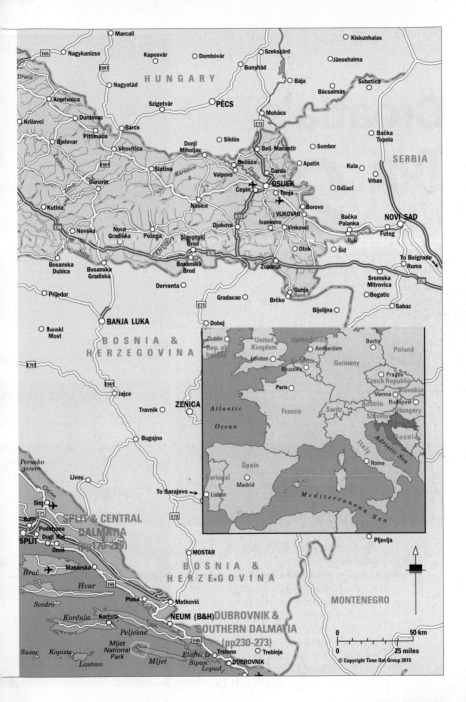

# Croatia's Top 20

*From ancient palaces to
island idylls, we count
down the country's finest.*

## 1 Dubrovnik City Walls
(page 236)

Historic, iconic and easily accessible,
the stark stone of Dubrovnik's City
Walls contrasts so dramatically with
the azure waters of the Adriatic, it was
almost invented for postcards. Stroll
round the top of the fortifications and
gaze out over the blue horizon to one side,
and the signature roof tiling of the Old
Town (and people's washing) to the other.

## 2 Zagreb Dolac market
(page 49)

Set on a raised plaza just above Zagreb's main square of Jelačić, the Dolac market has been part of the urban fabric of the city since the 1930s. Comprising a large outdoor space and covered hall, the Dolac is complemented by an adjoining fish market and is surrounded by cheap eateries that put its products to tasty and affordable use. Organic vegetables, fresh fish and cream cheese are the key items – but the Dolac is a tourist sight in itself, free to enter and endlessly fascinating.

## 3 Kornati National Park
(page 168)

Kornati is unique among Croatia's many dramatic national parks, mainly because it is only accessible by boat. It comprises an archipelago of 140 islands, none permanently inhabited – the only buildings you'll see will be the odd church erected by a grateful sailor saved from shipwreck by a handy cove. Kornati teems with marine life and yachters can take advantage of the handful of makeshift seafood restaurants set up in various bays.

⑥

## 4 Biševo Blue Cave
(page 224)

In a land filled with natural wonders and intense beauty, Biševo still stands out. On unspoiled Vis, the most distant of Croatia's island destinations, the cave of Biševo is best visited when the sun is high. This is why tourist boats leave Komiža at 9.30am – so visitors arrive some time after 11am, to catch the moment when light pours through a submerged side entrance and bathes this ethereal grotto in a fabulous blue light. Everyone then dives in to wallow in the turquoise waters for as long as nature allows.

## 5 Istrian truffles
(page 98)

One of the delicacies of Istrian cuisine, truffles are mainly found in the dense forest of Motovun. Dogs are trained to hunt out the precious fungus, and restaurants proudly place a *tartufima* sign outside, indicating that their *fuži* pastas, steaks and even ice-cream feature the tasty truffle. Around Motovun itself are specialist eateries, most notably pricey, formal Zigante, famous for its owner having discovered the world's largest white truffle.

⑤

## 6 Brijuni Islands
(page 76)

Known for their historic and prehistoric remnants, including a dinosaur footprint, the Brijuni Islands are most famous for their association with Tito. As head of Yugoslavia when it was part of the non-aligned movement after World War II, Tito would invite leaders from India, Indonesia and across Africa to visit. They would offer a gift in return – a pair of elephants, say, or a zebra or a waterbuck. Some of the beasts remain to this day, and are visible when you take the little tourist train round the main island, Veliki Brijun.

# 7 Buža bars, Dubrovnik
## (page 241)

Cut into the cliff-face, looking out at nothing but sea and horizon, Dubrovnik's two Buža bars are a short walk from the Old Town. Furnishings and comforts are minimal but that's not why you're here – you're here to take in the stunning view and linger over a drink or two.

# 8 Mljet National Park
## (page 271)

A pleasant catamaran ride from Dubrovnik, Mljet is an island idyll and national park. Its population stands at around 1,000, dotted in little villages across a territory slightly smaller than Jersey, and almost outnumbered by the mongooses brought in a century ago to rid Mljet of venomous snakes. Nature here is otherwise tranquil, with verdant forests, secluded beaches and an inland lake centrepieced by a historic monastery only accessible by boat.

# 9 Plitvice
## (page 294)

The most spectacular of Croatia's inland national parks, Plitvice is a stunning complex of 16 lakes, cascades, travertine dams and walkways from which to observe the changing shades of green, blue and grey in the water, caused by varying mineral and organism content. Among the beech, spruce and fir trees, you might spot lynx, owls and eagles, even a rare wild cat or brown bear. There are also pond turtles, lizards and more than 20 kinds of bat.

## 10 Zagreb Cathedral
(page 43)

Historic symbol of Croatia's capital, the twin Gothic towers of the cathedral rise over the main square. Built by Hermann Bollé in 1880 after a terrible earthquake hit Zagreb, the cathedral stands on the site of its fortified predecessor. Inside, a relief by renowned sculptor Ivan Meštrović is the most impressive architectural detail, offset by Neo-Gothic altars and stained glass.

## 11 Zagreb Museum of Contemporary Art
(page 67)

The most significant museum to open in Zagreb for more than a century, the MSU (as it's known locally) houses major works from Croatia and former Yugoslavia from the 1920s onwards. Occupying a striking new building, the museum focuses on the Zagreb-based New Tendencies movement of the late 1960s and 1970s, alongside photographs and films documenting the outlandish antics of contemporary performance artists.

## 12 Pula Roman Amphitheatre
(page 72)

The sixth largest Roman amphitheatre in the Empire is well preserved and still hosting cultural events – two millennia after gladiatorial contests took place. As well as a summer-long series of big-name concerts, the long-established Pula Film Festival is held here. In the tunnels, where the lions were kept, you'll find a detailed map of the Via Flavia that connected Pula with Trieste.

## 13 Poreč Euphrasian Basilica
(page 86)

Built in the sixth century – though parts of it date back to the 300s – the Euphrasian Basilica was created

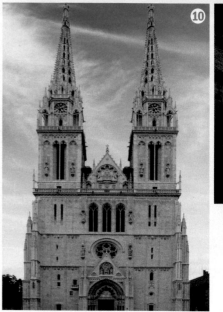

by Byzantine masters using marble from the Sea of Marmara. The bright mosaics are among the finest Byzantine examples still in existence. Supported by four marble columns, the ciborium or canopy was modelled after St Mark's in Venice and created in the late 13th century.

## 15 Zlatni Rat beach, Brač (page 206)

The best-known of the thousands of beaches that line Croatia's long coastline, Zlatni Rat ('Golden Cape') is both a tourist magnet and a natural phenomenon. This spit of land changes shape according to alterations in tide, current and wind – the south-easterly Jugo is Croatia's equivalent of the Sirocco. Close to the harbour town of Bol, Zlatni Rat attracts scores of windsurfers, who flock here during the afternoon to take advantage of the favourable westerly wind known here as the Maestral.

## 14 Diocletian's Palace, Split (page 172)

Most ancient palaces are carefully protected monuments. Not so Split's, where the Emperor Diocletian built his retirement home in the early 300s. The Diocletian's Palace is not only still a living, breathing structure, but it forms the very heart of Croatia's second city. Locals hang out their washing, cats scatter through its maze of alleyways and a whole network of bars, shops and restaurants do a roaring trade. History is always close at hand – the sphinx in the Peristil is from Ancient Egypt.

## 16 Luxury hotels, Hvar (page 221)

Luxury yachts and helicopters descend on this island close to Split all summer long, bringing film stars, playboys and millionaires to the clubs and restaurants of Hvar town. Catering for these top-dollar guests is a chain of luxury lodgings, Sunčani Hvar, which has transformed the island's previously tired hotel stock and brought high-end gastronomy and international standards of service. On the flip side, it's also priced a lot of Croatians out of Hvar during high season.

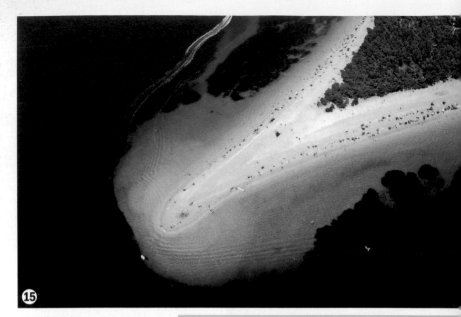

15

## 17 Pelješac wines (page 268)

Pelješac, a mountainous sliver of land north of Dubrovnik, is the place to come for Croatia's finest reds. The most notable is Dingač, named for a seven-kilometre stretch of seaside land where Plavac mali grapes grow. Only those harvested in this small area can be called Dingač. The land faces southwest – giving the grapes their full allowance of long, sunny Dalmatian days. The result is a strong, full-bodied red with a massive bouquet. The main winemakers can be visited and their wares sampled, in situ.

## 18 The Garden, Zadar (page 149)

The bar that instigated Croatia's coast-with-the-most reputation and sparked a whole raft of

16

(19)

(17)

## 19 Lešić-Dimitri Palace, Korčula
(page 257)
Representing the pinnacle of luxury on the island of Korčula, the high-end Lešić-Dimitri Palace hotel takes its decorative lead from the travels of Marco Polo, the medieval traveller who (probably) hailed from here. Suites are named after stages on the Silk Road: Arabia is hung with flowing fabrics; the Far East is full of exotic touches. All the same, the sleek, in-suite kitchens and espresso machines are very much 21st-century. Another feature of this former bishop's palace from the 1700s is the panoramic LD restaurant, a gastronomic temple to the fresh, seasonal produce of Dalmatia.

## 20 Museum of Broken Relationships, Zagreb
(page 46)
This award-winning, highly entertaining attraction started out as a playfully ironic art installation before being carted around as an international touring exhibition. Then, once it was established in Zagreb's sight-filled and somewhat staid Upper Town, it became something of a global cult. Housed in a fine Baroque mansion, the thematic display takes visitors through a series of different emotions associated with break-up, illustrated by objects donated by members of the public.

top-quality music festivals, the Garden is just that: a relaxing terrace with private cabanas. But this superbly located lounge bar also has the advantage of overlooking one of the world's finest sunsets, created by the kind of natural conditions that brought Hitchcock here to film. Set atop Zadar's Venetian battlements, the Garden provides zinging cocktails, sought-after craft beers and name DJs all summer long.

# Croatia Today

*A future model for the Mediterranean.*

**TEXT: JONATHAN BOUSFIELD**

The EU's newest member may no longer be the new kid on the block as far as Mediterranean tourism is concerned, but it still offers the allure of fresh discoveries. 'Croatia: Full of Life' is the latest marketing slogan, and there's no doubt that the country is the Med destination of the moment, with new festivals and a burgeoning bistro culture, not to mention *Game Of Thrones* tours. Visitors who already know about Dubrovnik are beginning to grasp why they need to spend more time exploring Pelješac and Korčula; press stories about hedonism in Hvar have morphed gently into press stories about the reinvigorating authenticity of the same island. And people who visited the Croatian capital, Zagreb, ten years ago are beginning to realise that the Zagreb of today is a different city entirely.

## CROATIAN COOL

Croatia's ongoing status as a perception-challenging destination might be one reason why the Croatian National Tourist Association chose 2015 as the right time to replace its 15-year-old slogan, 'The Mediterranean As It Once Was' with the new motto, 'Croatia: Full of Life'. Local wags were quick to subject the new slogan to 'my child could have thought that up' levels of derision, although professionals were equally fast in defending the choice as the most versatile, open-ended and appropriate solution available. The old slogan was very successful in drawing attention to Croatian heritage and unspoiled nature, but probably meant little to a new generation of tourists more interested in music festivals, wine bars, sleek hotels and Adriatic cool.

And where Croatia is concerned, cool is far from being an overused word. The Croatian music festival boom shows no signs of letting up; the legendary, genre-defining Garden Festival may well have packed away its turntables in 2015 for its tenth and final edition – but the Garden site in Tisno will continue to host a summer-long cavalcade of music-driven events. The other big-name festivals (Hideout at Zrće, Outlook near Pula) go from strength to strength, and new events are being added to the calendar every year.

The idea of a country that's creatively on the rise spreads to other spheres of culture too: people have been going on about Croatian design for ages and it finally looks as if there are enough products in the shops to justify the hype. The newly opened Croatian Design Superstore in Zagreb gathers together almost everything you might want to buy under one roof – it's only disadvantage is that you have to head inland to Zagreb to visit it.

Indeed it is Zagreb, long overlooked by tourists due to its landlocked position, which is brushing off its cloak of invisibility to reveal itself as Croatia's true centre of innovation. A new raft of festivals (Gourmingle, the Courtyards, and an updated, ultra-chic Advent season) have recast the city as a place of all-year outdoor happenings rather than museum visits and sightseeing trails. A new breed of bistros and café-bars has placed increased emphasis on quality local ingredients and culinary ingenuity. The emergence of a craft beer scene is the latest twist in the developing story of the city's frolicsome nightlife.

The other runaway success story of recent years is Split, where bistro culture has also gone ballistic, but here with more Mediterranean sleight of hand – think more seafood, more Adriatic olive oil, and more boutique wines from vineyards that are just a boat ride away. Split's Poljud Stadium has hosted the Ultra Festival since 2013, a hugely popular event that brings thousands of techno fans to the city for one mad weekend in July. However most summer-round visitors to Split are here for different reasons: the ancient monuments, the medieval alleyways, the legendary vivacity of the locals – and more recently, sightings of a certain Princess Daenerys from the TV smash *Game Of Thrones* in the basement of Diocletian's Palace.

*'Whatever PR strategies are dreamt up, they still can't match the free publicity generated by Game Of Thrones.'*

Zadar is another centuries-old city that continues to retune its historical appeal with chic urban improvements. The wonderful *Sea Organ* and *Greetings to the Sun* installations on the waterfront have become symbols of Croatia's contemporary identity. Trg pet bunara, 'Five Wells Square', is the latest old-town space to be treated to a thorough restoration.

And the Istrian port of Pula is increasingly making international waves on account of its *Lighting Giants*, the illuminated shipyard cranes lit up by artist Dean Škira. First switched on in 2014, the *Giants* look set to become a permanent feature. Indeed Croatia is increasingly home to the kind of iconic urban landmarks that would make many other Central European nations blush with envy: the Hotel Lone in Rovinj, the Mosque & Islamic Centre in Rijeka, the Museum of Evolution in Krapina… The country is increasingly looking like the Mediterranean as it might be rather than the Mediterranean as it once was.

Whatever PR strategies are dreamt up by the tourist authorities, they still can't match the free publicity generated by *Game Of*

Dubrovnik.

*Thrones*, the fantasy TV phenomenon that, having featured Dubrovnik as a location for the last four seasons, has now extended operations up the coast to film in Split and Šibenik as well. The media rollercoaster that surrounds the series has been gathering momentum with the screening of each season; 2015 looks like being the year when its effect will truly be felt on tourism throughout Dalmatia.

## POLITICAL CHALLENGES

All of which is more good news for a tourist industry that, in 2014, finally overtook the visitor numbers recorded in the pre-recession summer of 2007. Despite rising seasonal revenues, however, many branches of the Croatian economy still show signs of the post-recession blues. Upcoming parliamentary elections are due at some stage in 2015 although a precise date has not been fixed. Whoever wins will have a tough job on their hands. The presidential elections of December 2014 saw a shock defeat for the popular left-of-centre lawyer and composer Ivo Josipović, losing by a single percentage point to conservative rival Kolinda Grabar-Kitarović.

The intense election race and campaign produced huge public interest and a healthy turnout, demonstrating that Croatian democracy was in more robust shape than many people thought. Grabar-Kitarović, whose previous jobs include Croatian Ambassador to the USA, Croatian Foreign Minister and Assistant Secretary-General at NATO, is a widely known and trusted figure on the international stage.

## THE ENERGY QUESTION

The main challenge for the future is whether Croatia can retain its reputation as one of the cleanest, most unspoiled destinations in the Mediterranean. In December 2014, the Croatian government handed out licences to ten companies to start prospecting for oil and gas in the Adriatic Sea. While raising the possibility of Croatia becoming a major European energy supplier, it also drew a storm of protest from locals. The Croatian Adriatic is famous for being one of the cleanest seas in Europe, and the threat of even minor environmental pollution is a major worry.

Writing from the perspective of 2015, the Adriatic oil rush still looks a long way off, if indeed it ever happens at all. In the meantime, Croatia will continue to display its shape-shifting ability to mix uncomplicated authenticity with innovation and surprise.

# Itineraries

*Plot your perfect trip to Croatia with our city day planners.*

9AM

## A day in Zagreb

**9AM** Start the day off surrounded by old-style grandeur at the **Esplanade** (*p65*), which was a one-time haunt of Orson Welles, Elizabeth Taylor and Alfred Hitchcock. If it's a sunny morning, you can linger over a coffee on the terrace overlooking the classic façade of the main train station, Glavni kolodvor. From there, it's a short walk to Tomislav trg – note the statue of Croatia's medieval king of the same name – and the **Art Pavilion** (*p54*). Even if the current exhibition isn't to your liking, the building, which was shipped from Budapest in 1896, is definitely worth a gander.

**10AM** The next stop is **Strossmayer's Gallery of Old Masters** (*p55*), an excellent collection of Flemish and Italian works displayed in a neo-Renaissance palace.

10AM

**1.30PM**

**11.30AM**

Afterwards, carry on walking away from the station. You're not only heading towards the main square, you're passing along the prettiest part of the Green Horseshoe of landscaped spaces created by urban planner Lenuci in the 1800s.

**11.30AM** The **Archaeological Museum** (*p54*) is worth a look, with its Egyptian sarcophagi, Roman artefacts and the 4,000-year-old ceramic Vučedol Dove found near Vukovar. If you're out by noon, you should hear the daily cannon boom from the nearby **Lotršćak Tower** (*p42*).

**12.30PM** It's about time to

Clockwise from above: **Tkalčićeva; Strossmayer's Gallery of Old Masters; Art Pavilion; Lotršćak Tower.**

start thinking about lunch. Although fewer and fewer downtown places now serve cheap late-morning meals, many do daily specials. After a stroll around the main square, Trg bana Josipa Jelačića, and a browse of the fresh produce at the main market, **Dolac** (*p19*), behind, check the board at nearby **Kerempuh** (*p47*) for what fresh meat or vegetable dishes they've sourced at the stalls that morning. Behind you is the **Cathedral** (*p43*) – worth a quick look inside before you sit down to lunch.

**1.30PM** Walk off lunch with a stroll up one of Zagreb's most atmospheric streets, **Tkalčićeva**, perhaps stopping for a coffee at funky **Kava Tava** (*p48*), with its strong house brew.

# 3.30PM

**2PM** It's time to take in the Upper Town, reached by crossing historic Krvavi Most and scaling the steep cobbled streets to admire **St Mark's Church** (*p46*), the Croatian Parliament and the Ban's Palace. After all that history, it's time for some fun with a visit to the wonderfully quirky **Museum of Broken Relationships** (*p46*), which is devoted to what gets lost and what gets kept when couples go their separate ways.

**3.30PM** Nearby, past leafy Strossmayerovo šetalište, take the funicular down to focal Ilica, before the short stroll to the **Croatian National Theatre** (*p53*) on Trg maršala Tita and its signature fountain outside, *The Source of Life*, by Ivan Meštrović. You should still have enough energy to

take in one last museum, the **Mimara** (*p54*), which is home to the city's premier collection of fine art, with Rembrandt, Rubens and Manet all on show under one roof.

**6PM** With the Mimara closing at 7pm in summer and 5pm in winter, you should have enough time afterwards to head to the pedestrianised bar quarter around nearby Cvetni trg for an early-evening aperitif before dinner. There are plenty of options here: **Maraschino** (*p61*) is named after the cherry-flavoured Croatian liqueur that infuses many of its mixes, while **Vinyl** (*p61*) has a rambling and bohemian vibe.

**8PM** It's time for dinner. You could do a lot worse than sample the best of Zagreb's new bistro culture

at **Fotić** (*p56*), with its select menu and range of cute design touches.

**9.30PM** For a post-meal drink, you're bound to find plenty going on in the city's busy bar strip of Tkalčićeva. One choice might be the rocky **Booze and Blues** (*p51*) – even if the live music (four nights a week) isn't for you, you can tuck into the currently on-trend Istrian San Servolo beer. Admission won't cost very much.

**10.30PM** Up to you from here on in. You could either hit the hay or sample one of Zagreb's many mid-sized live-music venues, the most reliable choice being **KSET** (*p63*). It's just the other side of the train station and is a great place to catch emerging bands.

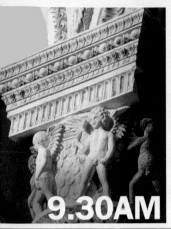

**9.30AM**

**10.30AM**

Clockwise from left:
**Croatian National
Theatre; Rector's
Palace; Pile Gate.**

## A day in Dubrovnik

**9AM** Start the day, as everyone else does, with coffee on the main drag of Stradun. The **Cele Café** (*p241*), at Stradun 1, is the perfect option, overlooking the historic square of Luža – you can also order a more substantial breakfast if your

hotel hasn't provided one. And if you're an early bird, it opens from 7am, allowing you a take a leisurely stroll round the nearby Old Port after breakfast.

**9.30AM** It's time for the first sightseeing stops of the day. The **Rector's Palace** (*p237*) is filled with artefacts relating to when Dubrovnik was Ragusa, a powerful medieval republic. Free to enter, the **Sponza Palace** (*p237*) was the former Ragusa mint and now houses

the state archives – definitely worth a quick look.

**10.30AM** Before the sun gets too high and too hot, it's time to scale the **City Walls** (*p236*) – there's a public entrance at the Old Port side of the Old Town. From here, you not only get a gorgeous view of the Adriatic, you also get a real sense of quite how powerful and canny the Ragusa republic was, fending off Venice and the Ottomans for centuries. It's up to you which direction you decide to walk in, but ideally you'll finish up at

the Pile Gate at the opposite end of Stradun.

**11.30AM** This brings you out perfectly for a visit to the **Franciscan Monastery and Old Pharmacy Museum** (*p236*), a complex of medieval cloisters surrounding one of the oldest apothecaries in Europe – which is still in operation today.

**12.30PM** It's about time for lunch. Considering its location by the Pile Gate and pedigree as a meeting place for Dubrovnik intellectuals a century ago, **Dubravka 1836** (*p237*) should be more expensive than it is – plus you get a fabulous sea view.

**1.30PM** Walking back the short distance to Stradun, maybe splashing your face along the way with water from Onofrio's Great Fountain that once supplied Ragusa, you head for Antuninska and a more contemporary sight: **War Photo Limited** (*p237*). Originally created by an expat photographer who was here during the bombardment of the early 1990s, the gallery now encompasses in visual form various world conflicts. It's a chilling visit but will give you some idea of how the Old Town looked only two decades ago.

**2.30PM** As the heat rises, take the short, calf-crunching climb to the far side of the City Walls and the station for the **Cablecar** (*p246*). As you rise up the hillside, the whole of Dubrovnik comes gloriously into view.

**3PM** It might be time for a thirst-quenching drink at the

**1.30PM**

**Panorama** café-restaurant (*p247*) at the top terminus of the Cablecar. Revived, wander up to the Imperial Fort and the **Homeland War Museum** (*p246*), with its displays relating to the shelling that took place from this very spot from 1991 onwards.

**4PM** Take the cablecar back down towards the Old Town but skirt the City Walls by strolling down Hvarska then on to the main road of Frana Supila. It's about a 15-minute walk, but worth it for a couple of hours on the city beach of Banje – it'll still be warm and slowly filling with locals who've finished work for the day. If it gets too hot, head inside the **East-West** (*p249*) for a beer or cocktail.

**6.30PM** As the sun is slowly sinking, it's the perfect time to head back into the Old Town, cross Luža and, stopping en route to admire the **Cathedral** (*p235*), saunter round to one of the two **Buža** bars (*p241*) that are cut into the cliff face

**2.30PM**

below the sea-facing City Walls. If you opt for the less polished Buža I, you can even take an early-evening dip in the Adriatic.

**9PM** It's tme for dinner. If you're looking to splash out, then you should make a beeline for **360 Degrees** (*p237*) in the bastion of Sveti Luka for high-quality Mediterranean cuisine with a view. Take your time – this is once-in-a-holiday stuff.

**11PM** If you're still up for it, Dubrovnik has plenty of places to party, and the best DJ club in town is just nearby: the **Culture Club Revelin** (*p244*). International DJs and a party vibe in historic surroundings should take you through until the early hours.

Clockwise from above: **Cablecar; Onofrio Fountain; Riva; Bačvice Beach**.

# A day in Split

Split, built around a living Roman ruin, has everything you could want from a city break and then some. Historic remains, a rash of great new bistros and the best bar crawl on the Adriatic coast – not to mention a summer-long beach party. And unlike glam near-neighbour Dubrovnik, Split is eminently affordable.

Everyone begins the day on the Riva, the palm-fringed, pedestrianised walkway lined with café terraces overlooking the Adriatic. They're all good, so take your pick – **Fro** (p180) seems to attract the chicest customers.

Diocletian's Palace, the old Roman complex that forms the heart of Split, is just behind. It's all pleasantly walkable, so it's easy to admire the Ancient Egyptian sphinx at the crossing point of Peristil, climb the tower of the **Katedrala** (p174) and visit the **Split City Museum** (p174) – all in one morning. Just wandering around the alleyways is entertaining enough. Enjoy a light lunch at one of Split's new-style bistros, such as **Uje** (p179) or the **NoStress Bistro** (p177).

The afternoon is best spent at the city beach of Bačvice, popping into seaside bars such as **Žbirac** (p193), while dipping in and out of the Adriatic. At some point, locals will probably set up a session of **picigin** (p182), a beach game involving a small ball and a group of acrobatic lads artistically jumping around in the shallows.

Take a stroll from the beach back to the Old Town and reward yourself with an early-evening cocktail at **ST Riva** (p183). From here, you can walk along the Riva to one of Split's top-notch new eateries, **Brasserie on 7** (p175), with its seafood platters and black Angus burgers.

You're now within a few minutes' walk of Croatia's finest bar crawl, around the streets and passageways of the Roman Palace. The narrow thoroughfare of Dosud is a good place to start. **Figa** (p180) is an ever-busy drinking den, but don't forget to pop into the more bohemian **Academia Ghetto Club** (p179) – part nightspot, part gallery and with a pleasant garden to boot.

Bars in the Old Town must close by 1am but it's a short walk to the harbour building and weekend DJ parties at **Imperium** (p194) – or back to Bačvice and the popular **Legends Bar** (p194).

# Diary

*Everything from sun-
drenched dancing to
open-air movies…*

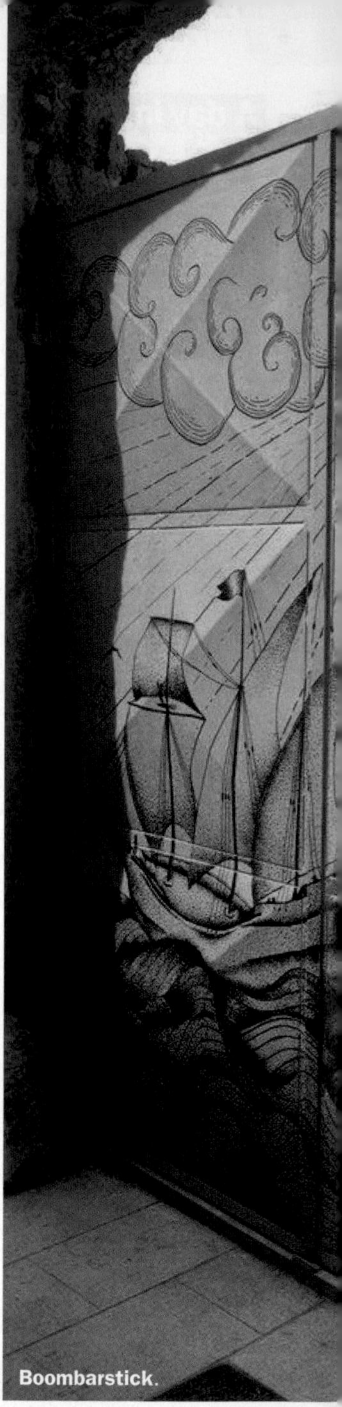

**Boombarstick.**

**C**roatia has developed a reputation in recent years as a destination for summer dance festivals, crowds drawn by Adriatic sunshine grooves and superstar DJs. But the country offers a great deal more than alfresco electronica for visitors who look good in a bikini or budgie smugglers. The devout pomp of the St Blaise's Day procession in Dubrovnik in early February provides one kind of spectacle for example – the gay pride parade in Zagreb in mid June provides another. Whether you're interested in motorbikes, traditional cuisine, Shakespeare performed in English, Baroque music, design, or top-class tennis, this nation of fewer than five million souls can deliver. And then there's film. You can hardly visit Croatia between the months of June and November without bumping into a film festival of some kind. They cover animation, documentaries, feature films and shorts – or just everything. The daddy is Zagreb towards the end of the year.

# Spring

## Boombarstick

**Vodnjan** *various venues (www.boombarstick.com).*
**Date** 1 May-1 Nov.
Boombarstick happens on the cobbled streets of Vodnjan, Istria. Originally lasting five or six days, this street art and music project now runs for a full six months, starting in spring.

## Strossmartre

**Zagreb** *Strossmayerove šetalište (www. ljetonastrosu.com).* **Date** mid May-late Sept.
This series of outdoor events kicks off in spring, lasts until autumn, and offers a varied programme of concerts, arts and crafts stalls, and unusual happenings like the best mongrel show, or the finest spritzer competition. It takes place in the lovely, leafy setting of Strossmayer Promenade in Zagreb's Upper Town.

# Summer

## Cest is d'Best

**Zagreb** *various venues (www.cestisdbest.com).*
**Date** early June.
Founded by street musicians who gained fame for their performances on Croatian TV, Cest is d'Best is a celebration of international street entertainment. Expect tons of entertaining sideshows, great music and weird sports competitions – all on open-air stages throughout Zagreb.

## Mediterranean Film Festival

**Split/Bačvice** *open-air cinemas, Split Cinematheque, Gallery of Fine Arts (fmfs.hr).*
**Date** early June.
The must-attend event of Split's early summer season. Categories range from documentaries to experimental films, with shorts and features. All screenings in the garden of the Gallery of Fine Arts are free. Afternoons are reserved for the city's smallest cinema, the colourful Cinematheque. After the show, head for Bačvice and theme parties with music ranging from film scores to 1980s nostalgia.

## Animafest

**Zagreb** *Kino Europa, Kino Tuškanac, Cineplexx (www.animafest.hr).* **Date** mid June.
Long-running Animafest promotes itself as 'Croatia's only A-list film festival'. In the world of animation, it's second only to Annecy in terms of global prestige.

## IKS International Festival of Contemporary Theatre

**Split** *Croatian National Theatre, City Puppet Theatre (www.iksfestival.eu/iks-festival).* **Date** mid June.
When young and talented dancer, choreographer and theatrical promotor Nela Sisarić started this festival a few years ago, it was a gathering of avant-garde theatre and dance writers. But her efforts in

Top: **Zagreb Pride**. Bottom: **Animafest**.
Opposite: **Victory Day**.

staging increasingly more high-profile attractions have really put the IKS Festival on the map.

### INmusic
**Zagreb** *Lake Jarun (www.inmusicfestival.com)*.
**Date** mid-late June.
*See p33* **New Waves**.

### Midsummer Scene
**Dubrovnik** *Fort Lovrijenac (midsummer-scene.com)*.
**Date** mid June-early July.
An opportunity to see *Twelfth Night* performed in English at historic Fort Lovrijenac. Performances begin at 9.30pm (with scenes set in the historic independent republic of Ragusa). Current director Helen

Tennison and the cast are British. If raining, the action moves to the Marin Držić Theatre.

### Le Petit Festival du Théâtre
**Dubrovnik** *Lazareti (www.lepetit festival.com)*. **Date** mid June.
This festival explores cultural concepts, from poetry to fashion and music, using a variety of media. From interactive workshops to art made with recycled materials, from fascinating lectures on our planet and its consciousness to live piano improvisation around a silent film, there's all kinds of things to see.

### Zagreb Pride
**Zagreb** *city centre (www.zagreb-pride.net)*. **Date** mid June.
Annual LGBTIQ celebration with a march through the city centre, starting from the House of Croatian Artists, ending at Zrinjevac park.

### Croatian Summer Salsa Festival
**Rovinj** *various venues (www.crosalsafestival.com)*.
**Date** late June.
Billed as 'sun, sea and salsa', the Summer Salsa Festival brings carefree Latin vibes to Rovinj, Istria. Dance points are set up all over the city and beach parties take place at nearby resort Amarin.

### International Children's Festival
**Šibenik** *various venues (www.mdf-sibenik.com)*.
**Date** late June-early July.
This festival has been running for more than 50 years. Suitable for both children and adults, programmes include workshops, games and shows.

### Gourmingle
**Zagreb** *Strossmayerov trg (www.zagreb-touristinfo.hr)*. **Date** late June-early Sept.
The lawns and bushes of Strossmayerov trg play host to a summer-long party-in-the-park, with Croatian food and wine as the centrepiece.

### Hideout Festival
**Pag** *Zrće beach (www.hideoutfestival.com)*.
**Date** late June-early July.
*See p33* **New Waves**.

### Istra Inspirit
**Istria** *various venues (www.istrainspirit.hr)*.
**Date** June-Sept.
Istra Inspirit offers a real insight into the history, gastronomy, architecture, culture and literature of Istria, with a series of events each Tuesday and Thursday. Themes have included the lives of miners in Labin, what connects Jules Verne to Pazin's castle, and the legend of pirate captain Henry Morgan.

## Dan D
**Zagreb** *Stara Vojna Bolnica, Vlaška 87
(www.dan-d.info).* **Date** early July.
A showcase for young designers from Croatia and
beyond, Dan D ('D Day') is held at the former military
hospital on Vlaška. The courtyard features a coffee
bar, wine booths and the odd DJ station.

## Papaya Day & Night
**Pag** *Zrće Beach (www.papaya.com.hr).*
**Date** early July.
*See p33* **New Waves**.

## Dubrovnik Summer Festival
**Dubrovnik** *various venues (www.dubrovnik-
festival.hr).* **Date** 10 July-25 Aug.
*See p250* **All Dubrovnik is a Stage**.

## Revelin Festival
**Dubrovnik** *Culture Club Revelin.* **Date** mid July.
*See p33* **New Waves**.

## Seasplash
**Pula** *Fort Punta Christo (www.seasplash-
festival.com).* **Date** mid July.
*See p33* **New Waves**.

## Split Summer Festival
**Split** *various venues (www.splitsko-ljeto.hr/
split-summer-festival).* **Date** 14 July-14 Aug.
Split's Old Town is the stage for a month of drama,
opera, ballet and music – one of the oldest performing arts festivals in Croatia.

## Stop Making Sense Festival
**Tisno** *The Garden (www.stopmakingsense.eu).*
**Date** mid July.
*See p33* **New Waves**.

## Supetar Super Film Festival
**Supetar** *www.facebook.comSupetar
SuperFilmFestival.* **Date** mid July.
Super Film in Supetar shows current European
documentaries, but also has exhibitions, concerts,
parties and workshops a step away from the beach.

## Ultra Europe Festival
**Split** *Stadium Poljud (www.ultraeurope.com).*
**Date** mid July.
*See p33* **New Waves**.

## The Courtyards/Dvorišta
**Zagreb** *Upper Town courtyards (dvorista.in).*
**Date** late July.
Some of Zagreb's most beautiful backyards are opened
up for a ten-day festival of music, food and wine.

## Croatia Tennis Open
**Umag** *Stella Maris Tennis (www.croatiaopen.hr).*
**Date** late July.
Global tennis stars flock to the Croatia Open in Umag.

# PUBLIC HOLIDAYS

**New Year's Day**
1 Jan

**Epiphany**
6 Jan

**Easter Sunday**
27 Mar 2016, 16 Apr 2017

**Easter Monday**
28 Mar 2016, 17 Apr 2017

**Labour Day**
1 May

**Corpus Christi**
26 May 2016, 15 June 2017

**Anti-Fascist Resistance Day**
22 June

**Statehood Day**
25 June

**Victory Day**
5 Aug

**Assumption**
15 Aug

**Independence Day**
8 Oct

**All Saints' Day**
1 Nov

**Christmas Day**
25 Dec

**St Stephen's Day**
26 Dec

## Motovun Film Festival

**Motovun** *various venues (www.motovun filmfestival.com).* **Date** late July.

An international movie event and five-day party all in one, the Motovun Film Festival takes over this beautiful hilltop town, 270m (890ft) above sea level, in Istria. International and Ex-Yu films are screened at a number of pop-up cinemas, indoors and out; screenings take place from early morning until around 2am. Parts of the festival also take place at the nearby town of Buzet.

## Pula Film Festival

**Pula** *various venues (www.pulafilmfestival.hr).* **Date** late July.

Running since 1953, even before Cannes, this festival is partly held in the city's historic Roman amphitheatre, which transforms into an open-air cinema and venue for the opening night and award ceremonies.

## Vanka regule

**Sutivan, Brač** *www.vankaregule.com.* **Date** late July. Since 1999, this has been a must for all extreme sports fans. *Vanka regule* is Dalmatian dialect (loosely translated as 'beyond routine') and this event is exactly that. It's a competition, but more important is the coming together of like-minded people looking for fun. Disciplines include climbing, freestyle cycling, slacklining, long-distance kayaking and stand-up canoeing. Brač is ideal for such activities, with sea, country roads, cliffs and mountains.

## Sinjska Alka

**Sinj** *www.alka.hr.* **Date** early Aug.

For the last 300 years, a jousting tournament has been held in Sinj, a small inland Dalmatian town, half an hour from Split. Commemorating a historical battle against the Ottomans, it's a popular event with local competitors in historic costumes riding around trying to hit target rings.

Below: **Soundwave**.
Opposite: **Stop Making Sense**.

## Soundwave

**Tisno** *The Garden (www.soundwavecroatia.com).* **Date** early Aug.
*See p33* **New Waves**.

## Sonus Festival

**Pag** *Zrće Beach (www.sonus-festival.com).* **Date** mid Aug.
*See p33* **New Waves**.

## Croatia Bike Week

**Pula** *Monumenti (www.croatiabikeweek.com).* **Date** late Aug.

The biggest of Croatia's numerous motorcycle meets, Pula's Twin Horn MC run this exciting and laid-back celebration. The location is interesting: an ex-Yugoslav army base long abandoned to the elements. Thousands of motorcycles of all kinds rock up; there are stunt shows and live concerts. It's not just for bikers – casual visitors pay a token entrance fee.

## Dimensions Festival

**Pula** *Fort Punta Christo (www.dimensionsfestival.com).* **Date** late Aug.
*See p33* **New Waves**.

## International Late Summer Music Festival

**Dubrovnik** *various venues.*
**Date** late Aug-mid Sept.

Hot on the heels of the Dubrovnik Summer Festival, this event was launched by the Dubrovnik Symphony Orchestra in 2013. Under the watchful eye of musical director Christoph Campestrini (he's big in Austria), the festival comprises a programme of solo and orchestral performances, and film nights.

## Spančirfest

**Varaždin** *various venues (spancirfest.com).* **Date** late Aug.

Anything and everything goes at Varaždin's annual festival, from street performance to art exhibitions, workshops or a circus. You won't be bored.

## Vukovar Film Festival

**Vukovar** *various venues (www.vukovarfilm festival.com).* **Date** late Aug.

Now approaching its tenth anniversary, this festival offers features, shorts and documentaries – judged after open-air screenings by the Danube. Indeed, only entries from the Danubian region are admissible. There's good nightlife after the showings too.

## FOR Festival

**Hvar** *various venues (for-festival.com).* **Date** early Sept.
*See p33* **New Waves**.

## Kinookus Food & Film Festival

**Ston, Pelješac** *various venues (www.kinookus.com.hr).* **Date** early Sept.

Foodies and culture fans will love this festival. Traditional cuisines are featured over four days, food documentaries are shown at various locations, and workshops for kids are laid on. There's also a market for local produce.

### Korkyra Baroque Festival
**Korčula** *various venues (www.korkyrabaroque.com)*. **Date** early Sept.
This showcases soloists and ensembles from Croatia and abroad, performing anything from their own original pieces to interpretations of traditional works.

### Outlook Festival
**Pula** *Fort Punta Christo (www.outlookfestival.com)*. **Date** early Sept.
*See right* **New Waves**.

## Autumn

### Split Film Festival
**Split** *www.splitfilmfestival.hr*. **Date** mid Sept.
One of the oldest film events in Croatia, this is dedicated to more experimental material, with new video art and non-mainstream work by arthouse masters. The only criteria is creativity. In previous years, Jonas Mekas, Béla Tarr and Lars von Trier have all been guests. Films are shown at indie cinemas around town and all screenings are free.

### Zagreb Film Festival
**Zagreb** *Kino Europa & various venues (www.zagrebfilmfestival.com)*. **Date** Nov.
Croatia's capital plays host to a week of non-stop, high-quality films, culminating in the award of the prestigious Golden Prams. There's something for everyone, with current arthouse productions, documentaries, retrospectives and after-show DJ events.

## Winter

### Advent in Zagreb
**Zagreb** *various venues (www.adventzagreb.com)*. **Date** late Nov-early Jan.
Zagreb's newly supercharged Advent embraces markets, live music and DJ sets. The main square, Zrinjevac, Europski trg and the 'Fuliranje' alley of food and drink stalls on Tomićeva are the main venues.

### St Blaise's Day
**Dubrovnik** *Old Town (www.dubrovnik.hr)*. **Date** 2-3 Feb.
Major procession that snakes through the Old Town of Dubrovnik in honour of its patron saint.

### Rijeka Carnival
**Rijeka** *various venues (www.rijecki-karneval.hr)*. **Date** week before Shrove Tuesday.
*See p109* **Rio in Rijeka**.

# NEW WAVES
*Music festivals rock Croatia all summer long.*

The **Garden** (see *p149*) has led an anything but quiet revolution in Zadar. As well as running a quality lounge bar, it instigated a major summer music festival, combining sought-after DJs and live acts with jaw-dropping locations. Having wrapped up its tenth and last annual bash in 2015, the Garden has inspired all kinds of other music events up and down the coast. At the Garden's last winning location of Tisno, near Šibenik, are **Stop Making Sense** (see *p31*) and its boat parties, with the likes of Skream and Jackmaster; and the boutique **Soundwave** (see *p32*), where a live art and film programme has recently been added to DJs such as Mr Scruff.

Further up the coast on Pag, Zrće has long been party central. Festivals are now more the rage – even the **Papaya** (see *p31*) has got in on the act. **Hideout** (see *p30*) is one of the hottest, with a younger crowd and the best DJs from Zrće's main clubs. The newer **Sonus** (see *p32*) is a bit more discerning, without losing the boat-party element.

Croatia's other prime festival site is the 2,000-year-old ruined Fort Punta Christo near Pula. There you'll find July's **Seasplash** (see *p31*), for reggae, dubstep and drum 'n' bass acts; the underground **Dimensions** (see *p32*); and **Outlook** (see *left*), a firm favourite for garage, dub step, and hip hop.

Croatia has urban festivals too. Zagreb's **INmusic** (see *p30*), near Lake Jarun, is known for big-name acts. Split's **Ultra Europe** (see *p31*) brings the likes of the Chemical Brothers and David Guetta to play the Poljud football stadium. In Dubrovnik, July's DJ-based **Revelin Festival** (see *p31*) takes place in the club (and historic sight) of the same name.

Even swanky Hvar is getting involved, with the **FOR Festival** (see *p32*). Recent line-ups have included Mark Ronson and the Klaxons.

# Croatia's Best

*There's something for everyone with our hand-picked highlights.*

Sljeme, Zagreb.

## Sightseeing

### VIEWS
**Dubrovnik/City Walls** p236
Symbol of historic Ragusa overlooking the Adriatic.
**Split/Vidilica** p192
Lookout point and a decent bar too.
**Rijeka/Trsat Castle** p106
So that naval commander Nugent-Westmeath could see Napoleon coming.
**Zagreb/Sljeme** p68
Slopes for skiing champions, hikers and picnickers, overlooking the capital.
**Brač/Vidova Gora** p206
Highest peak in the area with great views over central Dalmatia.

**Zadar/The Garden** p149
Lounge bar bathed in a sunset that Hitchcock wanted to film.
**Motovun** p95
Hilltop village with Istria all around.

### ART
**Zagreb/Mimara Museum** p54
They may have been plundered, but these Spanish and Flemish Masters still shine.
**Split/Meštrović Gallery** p188
Scores of works by Croatia's greatest sculptor, in his own house and workshop.
**Zagreb/Museum of Contemporary Art** p67
New Tendencies, EXAT 51 and other local movements.

**Marko Polo Exhibition, Korčula.**

**Korčula/Maksimilijan Vanka** p255
Works by this Expressionist painter plus summer shows.
**Zagreb/Galerija Nova** p54
All-girl foursome break new ground.

### HISTORY
**Dubrovnik/Rector's Palace** p237
How Ragusa was run, including the clock that stopped when Napoleon came knocking.
**Zagreb/Zagreb City Museum** p46
How the city came to be.
**Pula/Archaeological Museum of Istria** p72
Plenty of Roman finds plus Illyrian treasures.
**Zadar/St Mary's Church & Treasury** p144
This church is home to glittering Byzantine jewels and stunning Venetian art.
**Korčula/Marko Polo Exhibition** p256
Did the famous world traveller begin his life's journey in Korčula?
**Dubrovnik/Homeland War Museum** p246
The shelling and defending of Dubrovnik in the 1990s.
**Split/Archaeological Museum** p188
Historic finds from the Roman hub of nearby Salona.
**Zagreb/Technical Museum** p55
Pre-war locomotives and an Italian submarine you can climb inside.

### OUTDOORS
**Mljet** p270
Gorgeous National Park populated by mongooses.
**Zagreb/Maksimir Park** p66
Large expanse of green with woods, meadows and lakes.

**Rijeka/Modern & Contemporary Art Museum** p106
Leading collection of domestic art, including prints, photographs and posters.
**Dubrovnik/Museum of Modern Art Dubrovnik** p246
Four floors of local artists in the beautiful Banac Mansion.
**Split/Split Fine Art Gallery** p174
Works by Vlaho Bukovac and Ivan Meštrović, plus the odd Veneziano and Dürer.
**Grožnjan** p98
The so-called 'Town of Artists', where every other house is a gallery.
**Zagreb/Strossmayer's Gallery of Old Masters** p55
Exactly that – with plenty of Tintoretto, El Greco and Delacroix.

**Kornati** p152
Unique archipelago of
uninhabited islands.
**Plitvice** p294
Cascades, waterfalls and all
manner of birds and plants.
**Lastovo** p272
Swim in a bay all to yourself.
**Vis/Biševo Blue Cave** p224
Bathed in ethereal light at
high noon.
**Krka** p167
Roški slap, Skradinski
buk and other natural
water wonders.
**Medulin** p79
Long, indented coastline
offers watersports aplenty.
**Zagreb/Botanical
Gardens** p54
Ponds covered in lily pads
plus 10,000 plant species.

## STEEPLES

**Zagreb/Cathedral** p43
Twin Gothic towers and
a Dürer triptych.
**Zadar/St Donat's
Church** p144
Pre-Romanesque landmark
with fine acoustics.
**Split/Katedrala** p174
Climb the belltower for a
panoramic view.
**Poreč/Euphrasian Basilica
& Bishop's Palace** p86
Fabulous surviving example
of Byzantine art.
**Zagreb/St Mark's
Church** p46
National symbol in the
Upper Town.
**Dubrovnik/Cathedral** p235
Said to have been founded
by Richard the Lionheart.
**Šibenik/Cathedral of
St James** p161
Monumental basilica and
Gothic-Renaissance
masterpiece.
**Korčula/St Mark's
Cathedral** p254
Standing guard over the
Pelješac Channel.

St Mary's Church, Zadar. *See p35.*

# Eating & drinking

## BLOW-OUTS

**Dubrovnik/360 Degrees** p235
Top-drawer setting and
top-notch cuisine.
**Rovinj/Blu** p81
Swimming and fine dining
in one spot.
**Opatija/Le Mandrać** p118
Key venue in Croatia's main
gastro hub.
**Split/Noštromo** p178
Just the place for a
special occasion
**Zagreb/Zinfandel's** p59
Dine where royals and film
stars have stayed.
**Zadar/Kornat** p147
Monkfish to die for and a
spruced-up terrace.
**Novigrad/Pepenero** p92
Let a TV chef invent dinner
for you.
**Zagreb/5/4** p55
Dino Galvagno's great newbie.
**Hvar/Gariful** p215
Join the jet-set for a
fish supper.
**Opatija/Johnson** p117
Lobster's the speciality at this
LBJ-inspired eaterie.
**Dubrovnik/Nautika** p238
Book a sea-view table for Mario
Bunda's stand-out dishes.
**Rijeka/Kukuriku** p108
Superior seafood at Kastav,
outside town.

## LOCAL EATS

**Novigrad/Konoba Čok** p92
Family-run operation with fish
the focus.
**Vis/Kantun** p226
Quality lamb or amberjack
under the grapevines.
**Motovun/Konoba
Dorjana** p96
As homely as it gets.
**Split/Konoba Hvaranin** p190
Lively local spot, popular
with writers.
**Buje/Konoba Morgan** p94
Has Italians streaming
over the border.
**Hvar/Humac** p216
Classic Dalmatian cuisine
by candlelight.
**Trogir/Vanjaka** p201
The perfect fish platter in
a picturesque square.
**Rijeka/Konoba Blato** p106
Home-style seafood and
hearty grilled meats.
**Zagreb/Gostionica
Tip-Top** p57
Daily specials here are a
real delight.

## CLASSIC CAFÉS

**Split/Fro** p180
Sip espresso on the Riva –
everyone else does.
**Zagreb/Cogito Coffee** p60
Flagship outlet for local
bean-roasters.
**Zadar/Illy Bar** p150
Sassy baristas serve
Trieste's best coffee.

Opatija/**Café Wagner** p119
Habsburg-era coffeehouse
with cakes to match.
**Pula/Cvajner** p77
Arty coffeehouse amid
historic Roman surroundings.

## PUBS & BARS
**Zadar/The Garden** p149
Lounge bar par excellence.
**Zagreb/Melin** p49
Old grunge spot, now a funky
jazz haunt.
**Rovinj/Piassa Grande** p83
Every Istrian wine known to
man – plus rare Belgian brews.
**Dubrovnik/Duža I** p211
Cliff-face bar with moonlight
swimming.
**Zagreb/Sedmica** p61
Arty hangout with some
decent beers.
**Opatija/Monokini** p119
Bohemian, retro and
music-savvy.
**Grožnjan/Kaya
Energy Bar** p99
Chilled spot for quality drinks.
**Split/Academia
Ghetto Club** p179
Arty haunt in the ruined
Roman palace.
**Poreč/Epoca** p87
Sunset cocktails overlooking
the harbour.
**Dubrovnik/Hard Jazz Caffe
Troubadour** p242
Busy spot once run by a
famous pop star.
**Zagreb/Bacchus Jazz
Bar** p205
Bohemian haunt with an
indoor garden.
**Novigrad/Vitriol** p92
Italian-style mixed drinks on
a sea-lapped terrace.
**Hvar/Hula Hula Beach Bar**
p219
Swing with Hvar's party set.
**Split/Žbirac** p193
Lively spot on Bačvice beach.
**Šibenik/Godimento** p164
Fun-loving upmarket spot with
clubby music.

# Nightlife

**Hvar/Carpe Diem** p220
Landmark nightspot with
famed VIP section.
**Dubrovnik/Lazareti** p249
Great DJ venue – depending
on the agenda.
**Zagreb/KSET** p63
Quality mid-range live venue.
**Dubrovnik/Culture Club
Revelin** p244
Where Fatboy Slim spins in a
Ragusan landmark.
**Split/Imperium** p194
Get down in the ferry terminal.
**Rijeka/Karolina** p113
Seafront party tunes until the
early hours.
**Poreč/Byblos** p88
Top DJs pound the best sound
system in Istria.
**Zagreb/Sirup** p63
Stand-out nightspot with
decent DJs.
**Šibenik/Aurora** p166
Big-name Croatian DJs in a
landmark nightspot.
**Opatija/Colosseum Beach
Bar** p119
Alfresco dancing and drinking.
**Zagreb/Močvara** p68
Great venue for alternative
live acts.

**Vodice/Hacienda** p159
Top nightspot on the
Dalmatian coast.

# Shopping

**Zagreb/Bornstein** p49
Croatia's best wine labels.
**Rovinj/Atelier Devescovi** p84
Jazzy paintings in funky Grisia.
**Split/Nadalina** p185
Cult chocolate in various
groovy flavours.
**Zagreb/Take Me Home** p51
Funky accessories by local
designers.
**Rijeka/Šta Ja?!** p112
Original garments with a
Rijeka touch.
**Dubrovnik/Gundulićeva
poljana** px243
Great Old Town market filled
with fresh produce.
**Zagreb/Croatian Design
Superstore** p61
As it says on the sign.
**Split/GetGetGet** p183
Original knick-knacks by
local creatives.
**Dubrovnik/Maria
Boutique** p243
The world's top designers
under one roof.

Hula Hula Beach Bar, Hvar.

# Explore

# Zagreb

Zagreb is quickly gaining the big-city vibe of Vienna and Budapest, its Habsburg-era counterparts, while managing to hold on to its distinctive charm. Set below Mount Medvednica, where the last Alpine foothills meet the Pannonian plain, the city still feels like a big village. You can walk to most places you'd want to visit and the majority of tram routes pass through Trg bana Josipa Jelačića, the main square, making the city easy to navigate. Everything has an order common to German-speaking Europe, but with a Balkan sense of fun and – after dark – hedonism. Sightseeing may involve a hike around the cobbled Upper Town, a stroll through the greenery and grid-patterned streets of the Lower Town, or crossing the Sava river to Novi Zagreb and the Museum of Contemporary Art – the most significant cultural opening of the last decade. The Croatian capital has become a regional business and conference centre, as well as a pleasant, pretty destination with an ever-growing agenda of year-round events.

**EXPLORE**

Museum of Broken Relationships.

## Don't Miss

**1** **The Cathedral** The city's iconic twin towers (p43).

**2** **Museum of Broken Relationships** Cult attraction of genius (p46).

**3** **Esplanade Zagreb** Landmark hotel built for the Orient Express (p65).

**4** **Museum of Contemporary Art** Major collection from recent radical decades (p67).

**5** **KSET** Essential gig venue in a music-savvy city (p63).

## INTRODUCING ZAGREB

**Zagreb** grew up on the north bank of the Sava. It comprised two rival hilltop settlements, **Gradec** and **Kaptol**, the site of today's **Sabor**, or Croatian Parliament, and the **Cathedral**. After Hungarian King Ladislas founded a diocese here in 1094, it remained under the archbishopric of Hungary until 1852. Kaptol and Gradec fought for most of that millennium. A testament to their animosity can be found in the naming of **Krvavi most**, Bloody Bridge, the alley at the western end of Skalinska and scene of battles between them.

By the 17th century, with the Governor (Ban) of Croatia and the Sabor based here, Zagreb's importance overshadowed the local rivalry. By the 19th, its development reflected a growing search for a Croatian identity. Prestigious buildings such as the **Academy of Arts and Sciences** and the **National Theatre** centrepieced a neat spread of grid-patterned streets and squares between the **Upper Town** (Gornji Grad) of Kaptol and Gradec, and the new railway station. Habsburg in appearance, it gained the name of **Lower Town** (Donji Grad). A main square, Harmica, was laid out where the Upper and Lower Towns met.

But power still rested in the twin Habsburg capitals of Vienna and Budapest. With the clamour for reform, in 1848, the Croatian Ban, Josip Jelačić, led an army into Hungary. His bid failed and Jelačić died a broken man. He was honoured with a statue on Harmica, on his horse, his sword pointed in defiance. Tito had it taken down and the square named Trg republike. With the fall of Communist rule in 1990, the statue was reassembled and the square renamed **Trg bana Josipa Jelačića**.

Across the Sava, Tito built the Socialist-style housing estate of **Novi Zagreb**. Zagreb, as the second city of Yugoslavia, acquired an industrial edge. Many Socialist-era shopfronts can still be seen around the Lower Town. At the same time, an underground rock and art scene flourished and a Zagreb spirit emerged, distinct from the bourgeois atmosphere between the two world wars. It was savvy, independent, liberal, certainly not supportive of rule from Belgrade, but neither comfortable with the nationalist undercurrents of Croatian leader Franjo Tuđman and his cronies. Apart from an audacious rocket attack in 1991 on the Ban's Palace, and one on citizens in 1995, Zagreb was spared the worst of the war that attended the breakup of Yugoslavia. Its population swelled by refugees from Bosnia and the countryside, Zagreb and its outskirts did see a significant political shift to the right. This has been dissipated with the need for post-war recovery. Zagreb, in the mid-point between Mitteleuropa and the Mediterranean, knows its future lies with Europe.

The war and the economic struggle after independence in 1991 froze the city in its two seminal points in time: 19th-century Habsburg and 20th-century Socialist. More recently, shiny malls, fashionable shops and gleaming offices have sprung up, as well as a bar quarter on the pedestrianised streets around **Preradovićeva**, and a commercial district along **Savska**, south-west of the Lower Town.

All journeys start and begin with Trg bana Josipa Jelačića main square, often referred to as Jelačić plac. Nearly everything in the city centre is walkable; parking is a nightmare. For serious sightseeing, invest in a three-day **Zagreb Card** (www.zagrebcard.com; 24hr/90kn, 72hr/90kn) from the **tourist office** (*see p69*) on Jelačić plac.

## UPPER TOWN

Close to Jelačić plac, a short, steep climb away, is the well-stocked and always busy daily market, **Dolac**, and **Zagreb Cathedral**. Further over on Gradac, the other side of Bloody Bridge, is a cluster of sights around **St Mark's Church**. This group of churches and galleries is best accessed from a **funicular** (Tomićeva, every 10mins, 6.30am-9pm daily; 4kn) by Ilica, a gentrifying commercial street running west from Jelačić. The short ride takes you to the **Lotrščak Tower** (Strossmayerovo šetalište 9, 01 48 51 768, open 11am-8pm Tue-Sun, 10kn), a lookout tower reached by climbing a winding wooden staircase. Built in the 13th century, it has also housed a sweet shop and, on the first floor, Zagreb's first pool hall. Every day since 1877, a couple of loud cannon blasts from here signal noon sharp.

Leafy Strossmayerovo šetalište runs by the tower giving a lovely view of the rooftops. Nearby stands **St Catherine's Church** (Katarinski trg, 01 48 51 950, open 10am-1pm daily), built by the Jesuits in the 17th century, with a beautiful Baroque interior of pink and white stucco. Clustered around it are the **Croatian Museum of Naive Art** and **Klovićevi Dvori**. Just north of Klovićevi Dvori stands the **Stone Gate** (Kamenita Vrata), the only remaining medieval entrance to the Upper Town. It's more of a short, bendy tunnel than a gate, and is a shrine to mark a fire, in 1731, that consumed everything here but a painting of the Virgin Mary. Prayers are whispered, flowers laid and candles lit.

Passing through it, you wander around the cobbled streets of Gradec, looking into little squares, perhaps popping into a **Croatian History Museum** (Matoševa 9, 01 48 51 900, www.hismus.hr; open 10am-6pm Mon-Fri, 10am-1pm Sat, Sun; 10kn), a lovely Baroque mansion with a collection of photographs, furniture, paintings and weapons thematically relating to Croatia's development.

At the heart of Gradec stands St Mark's Church on Markov trg, a square housing the **Croatian Parliament** and the **Ban's Palace**. North, edging towards the slopes of Mount Medvednica, are the **Meštrović Atelijer**, the **Natural History Museum** (Demetrova 1, 01 48 51 700, www.hpm.hr; 10am-5pm Tue-Fri, 10am-1pm Sat, Sun; 15kn) and **Zagreb City Museum**.

Walking back through the Stone Gate, you come into Radićeva and, crossing back over Bloody Bridge, to one of the most atmospheric and lively streets in Zagreb, **Tkalčićeva**. Pastel-shaded low-rise old houses accommodate galleries, bars and boutiques. Crossing the market square, your eyes are drawn towards the spires of the cathedral, surrounded on three sides by the ivy walls of the **Archbishop's Palace**. Around it runs Vlaška, which brings you up to the park of **Ribnjak**, pleasant by day, filled with amorous teenagers after dark at weekends.

## Sights & Museums

### ★ FREE Cathedral
*Kaptol 31 (01 48 14 727).* **Open** 10am-5pm Mon-Sat; 1-5pm Sun. **Admission** free. **Map** p45 E2 ❶
The Cathedral of the Assumption of the Holy Virgin Mary (Katedrala Uznesenja Blažene Djevice Marije)

is Zagreb's principal landmark. And though much of the exterior has long been veiled behind construction sheathing, its neo-Gothic twin towers, visible over the city, are as close as Zagreb gets to an iconic visual identity. The first church was destroyed by the Tatars in 1242 and later reconstructions were damaged by fire. After an earthquake in 1880 the city hired architect Hermann Bollé, who added a monumental pair of 105m (344ft) bell towers. The interior remains austere: neo-Gothic altars, 19th-century stained glass, and an Ivan Meštrović relief that marks the resting place of controversial Croatian Archbishop Alojzije Stepinac.

### Croatian Museum of Naive Art
*Ćirilometodska ulica 3 (01 48 51 911, www. hmnu.org).* **Open** 10am-6pm Tue-Fri; 10am-1pm Sat, Sun. **Admission** 20kn; 10kn reductions. **Map** p44 D2 ❷
Housed on the second floor of the 18th-century Raffay Palace, this collection is a solid introduction to Croatian Naive Art, mostly the work of self-taught peasants from the villages of the east. The collection is frequently rotated but there are usually plenty of representations of rural life executed by the big names of the genre: Ivan Generalić, Mirko Virius and Ivan Rabuzin. Also included are international exponents like the Polish-Ukrainian Nikifor.

Cathedral.

**EXPLORE**

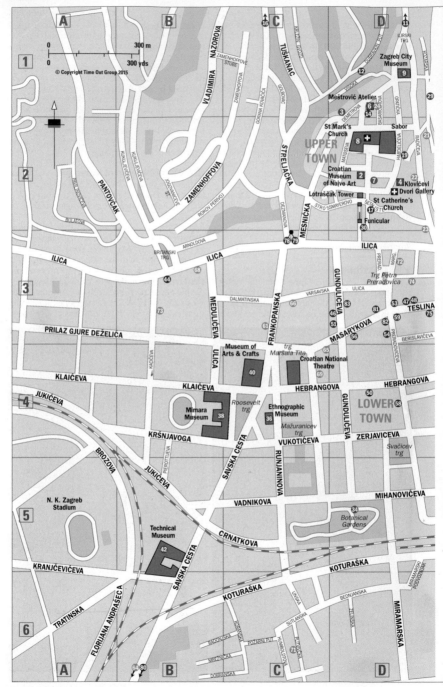

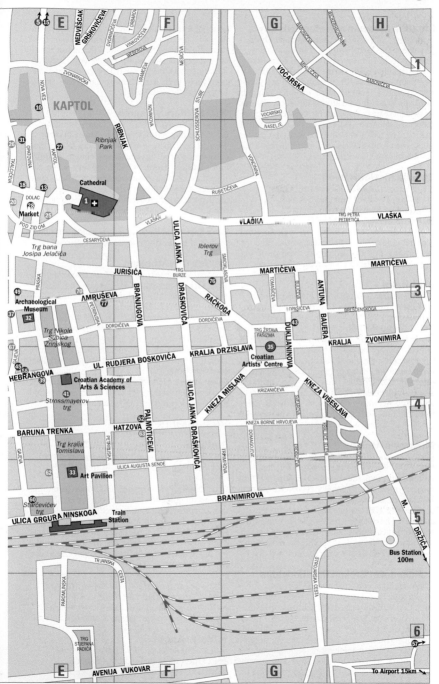

EXPLORE

## Croatian Museum of Natural History

*Demetrova 1 (01 485 1700, www.hpm.hr).* **Open** 10am-5pm Tue, Wed, Fri;10am-8pm Thur; 10am-7pm Sat; 10am-1pm Sun. **Admission** 20kn; 15kn reductions. **No credit cards. Map** p44 D1 ❸
As important a scientific institute as it is a public attraction, this museum holds exhibits including rocks and minerals from around the globe, many on permanent display. Look out for the section on prehistoric Krapina man, one of the most significant of its kind. The zoological collection features Croatian fauna; there's a botanical section and herbaria too. The museum publishes the journal *Natura Croatica*.

## Galerija Klovićevi Dvori

*Jezuitski trg 4 (01 48 51 926, gkd.hr).* **Open** 11am-7pm Tue-Fri. 11am-2pm Sat, Sun. **Admission** 20kn; 10kn reductions. **No credit cards. Map** p44 D2 ❹
This high-profile gallery, set in the stunning space of a former Jesuit monastery in Gornji Grad, is known for curating first-rate temporary exhibits of bigname local and international artists.

## Gliptoteka

*Medvedgradska 2 (01 468 6060, gliptoteka.mdc. hr).* **Open** 11am-7pm Tue-Fri; 10am-2pm Sat, Sun. **Admission** 10kn; 5kn reductions. **No credit cards. Map** p45 E1 ❺
Created by the Croatian Academy of Science & Arts to house plaster copies of famous sculptures, the Gliptoteka has expanded its activities to become a major venue for changing exhibitions of contemporary painting, sculpture design and new media art. There is still an extensive permanent exhibition of sculpture, featuring replicas of medieval tombstones, statues, and a handful of originals by famous Croatian sculptors.

## Meštrović Atelijer

*Mletačka 8 (01 48 51 123, www.mdc.hr/mestrovic).* **Open** 10am-6pm Tue-Fri; 10am-2pm Sat, Sun. **Admission** 30kn; 15kn reductions. **Map** p44 D1 ❻
Croatia's most internationally renowned sculptor, Ivan Meštrović, lived and worked in this restored trio of adjoining 17th-century mansions between 1923 and 1942. The collection here – marble, stone, wood and bronze sculptures, reliefs, drawings and graphics – grace two floors of the house, the front atrium and his atelier off the ivy-covered courtyard.

## ★ Museum of Broken Relationships

*Ćirilometodska ulica 2 (01 485 1021, www. brokenships.com).* **Open** *June-Sept* 9am-10.30pm daily. *Oct-May* 9am-9pm daily. **Admission** 25kn; 20kn reductions. **No credit cards. Map** p44 D2 ❼
Starting as a playfully ironic art installation and subsequently an international touring exhibition that became something of a global cult, the Museum of Broken Relationships has become Zagreb's prime visitor attraction since opening the

doors of its permanent home in 2010. Based in one of the Upper Town's finest Baroque mansions, the thematic display takes visitors through a series of different emotions associated with breakup, illustrated by objects donated by the public. It has previously been named 'most innovative' at the European Museum Awards.

## FREE St Mark's Church

*Trg sv Marka 5 (01 48 51 611).* **Open** 9am-noon, 5-5.45pm daily. **Admission** free. **Map** p44 D2 ❽
Two coats of arms grace the red, white and blue chequered roof of this emblematic church: Zagreb's and Croatia's. Since the 13th century when the Romanesque original was built, the church has gone through many architectural styles – note the Gothic south portal and Baroque, copper-covered belltower. Inside are hand-painted walls by Jozo Kljaković and a crucifix by Meštrović. The square outside, with the Ban's Palace and the Croatian Parliament, has been the hub of political activity since the 16th century.

## Zagreb City Museum

*Opatička ulica 20 (01 48 51 361, www.mdc.hr/ mgz).* **Open** 10am-6pm Tue-Fri; 11am-7pm Sat; 10am-2pm Sun. **Admission** 30kn; 20kn reductions. **No credit cards.** Map p44 D1 ❾
Occupying the 17th-century Convent of the Clares, the City Museum has a fine collection of 4,500 objects tracing Zagreb's history from prehistoric times. Themed sections include Iron Age finds, walk-through reconstructions of 19th-century Ilica shops, and study rooms of famous Croatian artists. Other items include old packaging and automatic music machines; many exhibits are interactive and it's all well documented in English.

# Restaurants

## Baltazar

*Nova Ves 4 (01 46 66 999).* **Open** noon-midnight Mon-Sat; noon-5pm Sun. €€€. **Map** p45 E1 ❿
**Croatian**
In a little Kaptol courtyard, this rustic restaurant attracts an upmarket clientele with impeccable service and presentation, and a pretty summer terrace. But it's the food that attracts the repeat custom: seafood and regional meats from Zagorje and Slavonia; duck, lamb and turkey also feature. With wine, the bill might creep up but carnivores won't begrudge it in the slightest.
▶ *Baltazar's twin restaurant Gašpar (01 46 66 824) is one of the best places in Zagreb to enjoy seafood, with fresh Adriatic fish grilled to perfection, and classic dishes such as škampi na buzaru (whole unpeeled scampi in wine sauce).*

## ★ Bistro Apetit

*Jurjevska 65A (01 46 77 335, www.bistroapetit. com).* **Open** 10am-midnight Tue-Sun. €€. **Map** p44 D1 ⓫ **Croatian**

Bistro Apetit offers superb standards of food, wine and service, standards imposed by Austrian chef and owner Christian Cabalier, previously of Vienna's Cantinetta Antinori. One key to its success is the location, hidden in a hedged garden on a tranquil residential street, just a short walk north of the city's Gradec old quarter. The cooking mixes the best of Croatian-Adriatic cuisine with the contemporary European mainstream. Not priced beyond the average pocket, there are always some truly outstanding dishes on the seasonally changing menu; desserts are truly heavenly.

### Dubravkin put

*Dubravkin put 2 (01 483 4975, www.dubravkin-put.com).* **Open** 11am-1am Mon-Sat. €€. **Map** p44 D1 ⓬ **Croatian/Wine Bar**
Long one of Zagreb's top addresses for seafood, Dubravkin put descended into the doldrums during the noughties before being successfully relaunched as an upscale wine bar and restaurant in late 2010. Located in a wooded dell between the Upper Town and the Tuškanac woods, it features a cool minimalist interior full of dark brown furniture and low-key lighting. Seafood remains the kitchen's strong point, and both the baked fish and a 12-course tasting menu are well worth the splash-out. Otherwise choose between exquisitely prepared and presented mains like monkfish in black olive paste, rack of lamb, or oxtail. It's also a stylish venue for an intimate drink, with hundreds of wines and a tempting menu of nibbles chalked up on a board beside the bar.

### Kerempuh

*Kaptol 3 (01 48 19 000).* **Open** 7am-11pm Mon-Sat; 7am-4pm Sun. €€. **Map** p45 E2 ⓭ **Croatian**
Kerempuh has a reputation for being an informal neighbourhood restaurant but quite the foodie venue too. It has served as something of a proving ground for culinary celebrities in recent years, with both TV chef Ana Ugarković and rising star Dino Galvagno – of the celebrated 5/4 – doing stints in the kitchen. Ingredients come from the Dolac market (see p49) first thing in the morning for the daily changing menu, which you find chalked up on the blackboard outside. Traditional central Croatian dishes such as buncek (leg of ham) and lungić (pork loin chop) form the backbone of the regular menu, although there are always a couple of attractive vegetarian options among the meat.

### Konoba Didov San

*Mletačka 11 (01 485 1154, www.konoba-didovsan.com).* **Open** 10am-midnight daily. €€. **Map** p44 D1 ⓮ **Dalmatian**
This might be one of the cosiest locales in Zagreb, on a narrow passage among the cobbled streets behind St Mark's Church and the Croatian parliament in the Upper Town. But even as quaint as this is, the food is a match. This is Dalmatian cuisine with a Neretva Valley twist. Frogs' legs with

prosciutto and eels speak of the owner's heritage – and may not be for everyone – but other choices such as pasta with snails, the veal, and baked lamb for two are also well prepared. The interior is faux Neretva village, with stone walls, red-checked tablecloths and dried tobacco leaves hanging from sturdy wooden beams above.

### Mano

*Medvedgradska 2 (01 466 9432, www.mano.hr).* **Open** noon-1am Mon-Sat. €€€. **Map** p45 E1 ⓯ **Steakhouse**
Though called an Italian restaurant in tourist brochures, Mano is actually a high-end steakhouse fit for an anniversary dinner, or the business associate you're trying to impress. A better description of Mano ('hand' in Italian, as in 'hand-made') would be a fusion tribute to the grill. Fine cuts are grilled on charcoal in a kitchen set behind glass so patrons can watch. Order the Steak Mano or T-bone and the waiter will bring the cut of meat – marinated in rosemary, olive oil and Dijon mustard – to your table with a mini-grill so that you can cook it to your own specifications. Simple, sleek and modish wooden chairs and tables sit on tongue-and-groove floors under exposed brick. The wines – a long, international list – are in a glass room for your inspection. Reservations recommended.
▶ *Mano now has a branch, Mano2, at the Green Gold Centar, Radnička cesta 50.*

### Okrugljak

*Mlinovi 28 (01 46 74 112/www.okrugljak.hr).* **Open** 10am-1am daily. €€€. **Map** p44 C1 ⓰ **Croatian**
The grande dame of Zagreb restaurants is worth the hike to reach it. Its cachet attracts old money and the new jet set, munching and mingling in the two high-ceilinged wooden-clad dining halls near Sljeme. Top-rated international and traditional dishes from the continent and the coast are prepared with special care – from juicy barbecue meats and blood sausages to super-fresh tuna fillets and delectable swordfish carpaccio. Expect to see fresh lamb roasting on spits in the yard on spring weekends. The pasta is made on the premises; the wine list has more than 100 varieties. Book ahead at weekends.

### Pod Gričkim Topom

*Zakmardijeve stube 5 (01 48 33 607, www.restoran-pod-grickim-topom.hr).* **Open** 11am-midnight Mon-Sat. €€. **Map** p44 D2 ⓱ **Croatian**
Just below the Grič cannon (hence the name), this leafy terrace is a summer evening favourite; when the weather turns the new enclosed terrace warms the mood. On offer are dishes from different regions of Croatia: octopus baked under a *peka* (a metal lid covered in charcoal), Dalmatian *pašticada*, and monkfish carpaccio. There's also Zagreb steak (filled

**EXPLORE**

La Štruk.

with ham and cheese) and *zagorski štrukli* for dessert. Portions are well sized, service is excellent, the clientele cosmopolitan. Always reserve if sunny.

### La Štruk

*Skalinska 5 (01 483 7701).* **Open** 11am-10pm daily. **€. Map** p45 E2 ⑱ **Štrukli**
The doughy parcels known as *štrukli* constitute one of the trademarks of north Croatian cuisine, and it was only a matter of time before they got their own dedicated restaurant. They come either boiled or baked – cheese *štrukli* are usually eaten as a savoury dish although sweet versions with jam are also popular. At La Štruk you get a choice. Although the classic cheese edition occupies centre stage, they also conduct regular experiments (cheese and nettle, or cheese and paprika perhaps) to demonstrate just how much potential the basic concept actually has. La Štruk's sweet *štrukli* with walnuts and honey, or apple and cinnamon, are quite simply divine.

### Trilogija

*Kamenita 5 (01 485 1394, www.trilogija.com).* **Open** 11am-midnight Mon-Thur, Sun; 11am-1am Fri, Sat. **€€. Map** p44 D2 ⑲ **International**
Trilogija sits just above the Stone Gate. Cobblestones lead from the individual landings under vaulted, brick ceilings. The cosy dining room includes a bar area where folks can snack on a steak and cheese sandwich with caramelised onions. The idea is that even if you're in a hurry you can still enjoy a quality feed and glass of wine but more time lets you sample wonderful natural ingredients. Daily specials change per artistic mood and supplies on hand. Entrées include sea bass in lobster sauce, and beefsteak in port –you won't regret the black tiger shrimp risotto with mango and spinach either.

## Cafés & Bars

### Kava Tava Tkalčićeva

*Tkalčićeva 12 (098 193 3878, www.kavatava.com).* **Open** 7am-midnight daily. **Map** p45 E2 ⑳
The menu is the same as at the open air Kava Tava on Britanski trg (*see below*) but the experience couldn't be more different: a sequence of barrel-vaulted spaces that seem to tunnel deep into this historic Tkalčićeva building. The interior designer clearly has an eye for quirky detail, with hair dryers turned into lamps, airline seating doubling as café chairs, old sewing machines perched on ledges, and – disconcertingly if you're not a Pink Floyd fan – the lyrics of 'Another Brick in the Wall' straggling across the walls. All in all, it's just another soothing place in which to tuck in to KT's trademark menu of strong coffee, breakfasts and pancakes. The terrace, perfectly situated on a curve of this pedestrianised street, comes into its own in spring and summer.
▶ *There's another branch at Britanski trg (no phone, same website; open 7am-midnight daily).*

## Melin

*Kožarska 19 (01 485 1166, www.melin.hr).*
**Open** 10am-2am Mon-Sun. **No credit cards.**
**Map** p44 D2 ㉑
Visitors accustomed to the old, grungy, rock-a-punk
version of Melin will be in for a shock. Tkalčićeva's
favourite cult bar entered 2014 in a completely new
guise. For starters, the guiding musical theme is now
jazz (with a capital J). Brassy blasts and sultry croon-
ing spew forth from the sound system and there's a
tiny stage for occasional live performances. The decor
follows the guess-what-I-bought-at-the-fleamarket
school, with misfit furnishings and hollowed-out
TVs setting a pleasingly vintage tone. The choice
of wines and spirits is excellent as well; it's less of a
beer-drinkers joint than it used to be, while your bill
arrives tucked into a paperback book. The customer
age range has risen slightly thanks to the makeover.
Its central nature means it's still a favourite of
youngish, alternative types.

## ★ MK Bar

*Radićeva 7 (01 483 0980).* **Open** 8am-1am
Mon-Sat; 9am-11pm Sun. **No credit cards.**
**Map** p44 D2 ㉒
Known by all as 'Krolo' after the writer Miroslav
Krleža who lived here, this beautiful old wooden
bar near the main square gives a flavour of pre-
1991 Zagreb. The bar staff are easy-going, inviting
the older clientele to scan the day's newspapers in a
religious fashion while the younger regulars gather
round the semicircular counter. No DJs, no hipster-at-
tracting tricks, but it's still crowded and raucous at
weekends. 'Timeless' is the word you're looking for.

## Pivnica Pinta

*Radićeva 3A (01 483 0889, www.pinta.hr).*
**Open** 8am-11pm Mon-Sat; 10am-11pm Sun.
**No credit cards. Map** p44 D2 ㉓
It simply doesn't get any more local than this. And,
you'd be hard-pressed to find a place more central.
Located in an alley just metres north and west from
the main square, this passage was once used to stable Ban Jelačić's horses. The patio spills into this
passage while inside, it's a real bar – everything
is wooden and people are there to drink. There are
pictures of old Zagreb strewn about the two rooms,
lots of beer (Kilkenny, Paulaner, Erdinger and local
draughts) and liquors to keep folks happy.

## Pod starim krovovima/Kod Žnidaršića

*Basaričekova 9 (01 485 1808).* **Open** 9am-2am
Mon-Sat. **No credit cards. Map** p44 D1 ㉔
One of Zagreb's classic watering holes, patronised
by writers and actors since the 19th century, Kod
Žnidaršića looks every inch the part, with its bare
pine floor, wooden panelling, timber-beamed ceiling and old-style stove. It's one of the few bars in
the Upper Town that has successfully held on to a
regular late-night clientele, with art exhibitions
and sporadic concerts helping to keep a bohemian

spirit. With hard-to-get Vukovarsko beer on tap, and
a handsome list of rakija and wines, it's certainly the
right place for the discerning drinker; baguette sandwiches will take care of any lingering hunger.

## Pod Zidom

*Pod Zidom 5 (098 669 690, www.facebook.com/
PodZidom).* **Open** 8am-midnight Mon-Tue;
8am-2am Wed-Sat. **Map** p45 E2 ㉕
Opened in June 2014, Pod Zidom 'Coffee, Wine &
Food Bar' has effortlessly elbowed its way to the top
of the wine bar league, offering an affordable-to-ex-
pensive mix of great Croatian wines, a range of
Mediterranean-style lunch and tapas dishes, regular
live music, and a wonderful outdoor terrace overlooking a street that's very central but also slightly
hidden from the hubbub of the main square. Done
out in greys and pale wood tones, it manages to look
smart but laid back at the same time. The weekday
'set lunches from Dolac market are a steal.

## Rakhia Bar

*Tkalčićeva 45 (no phone).* **Open** 8am-midnight
Mon-Thur, Sun; 8am-2am Fri-Sat. **Map** p45 E2 ㉖
This first-floor flat in a charming old Tkalčićeva
building has been transformed into an agreeable
warren of quirkily decorated sitting rooms, with
mix-and-match furnishings, paintings, and agree-
ably low-key lighting. There's also outdoor seating
in a slightly raised garden overlooking one of the
busiest stretches of this bar-filled street. Rakija is
the star of the show: if there's a fruit or vegetable
that you can make brandy out of then rest assured
that it will be on the menu here somewhere. Bottled
beers include the excellent Velebitsko pivo and the
boutique Visibaba range.

## Shops

### ★ Bornstein

*Kaptol 19 (01 481 2361, www.bornstein.hr).*
**Open** 9am-8pm Mon-Fri; 9am-2pm Sat.
**Map** p45 E2 ㉗ **Food & drink**
Now run by an enthusiastic and friendly young couple, Bornstein is the best wine boutique in Zagreb
and potentially in all of Croatia. It opened in 1990 on
Pantovčak, the first private enoteca in all of former
Yugoslavia, selling only wines from private producers. Some 24 years later, the store is filled with labels
from every Croatian region, and clear advice on their
qualities is offered willingly. The outlet also stocks
truffles, honey and olive oils, making it a handy one-
stop shop for quality souvenirs.
▶ *The original Bornstein is just above Britanski trg
at Pantovčak 9 (01 48 23 435, same website).*

### ★ Dolac

*Dolac.* **Open** 6am-2pm Mon-Fri; 6am-3pm
Sat; 6am-2pm Sun. **No credit cards. Map**
p45 E2 ㉘ **Market**
*See p50* **Trading Places.**

# TRADING PLACES

*Zagreb's central market, the Dolac, is its most popular living landmark.*

Overlooking the main square, and in the shadow of the Cathedral, is Zagreb's most precious resource: the Dolac ('Market', *see p49*). This is more than just a place of trade. In this fractured capital of Upper and Lower towns, the Dolac is a constant, a hub of classless social interaction, a weather vane of the local economy and Zagreb's connection with the surrounding villages, even with distant Dalmatia. Traders' voices are either distinctly urban ('*Kaj?*'), provincial, or come from the deepest south. Around the square are little bars and eateries offering *gableci*, cheap late-morning lunches. Daily from 7am, the Dolac is abuzz until the early afternoon.

After considering several locations, the city fathers had a main market built between Kaptol and Tkalčićeva, Zagreb's most atmospheric thoroughfare. Opened in 1930, it comprised a raised open square lined with stalls of fruit, vegetables and eggs. At street level was an indoor market for meat and dairy traders, then in 1933, a fish market – based on the one in Trieste – was set up alongside. This layout remains in place today, with the addition of a mezzanine in the indoor section and the bright reconstruction of the Ribarnica (the fish market). Florists now occupy the top level, where the Dolac meets Opatinova.

Entering from the street, you walk through the main hall of bakers and butchers. Pekara Dinara from Sesvete is so renowned there are queues outside its two downtown outlets. Of the butchers, Pečun-Pečun is a quality purveyor of sausages from Dugo Selo while Leka Crijeva I Zacinj allows you to make your own from the pigs' intestines they provide. To the right is a separate area for Mliječni Proizvodi, the dairy producers; for many locals this is sufficient reason for a visit.

*Sir i vrhnje* is the cream cheese that forms a definitive Zagreb staple. Sold by the plastic cup (or you can bring your own receptacle), it can be sprinkled with salt and paprika, embellished with a few diced onions, some *kružnjak* cornbread and, at a stretch, spots of *špek* ham or slices of dried sausage. The typical producer, name and address placed on each stall, is a friendly woman of a certain age: the *kumica*. A cross between 'trader' and 'godmother', the *kumica* is a much-loved figure. Shoppers have their own favourite; a *kumica* statue even stands at the market entrance.

At the back of the main hall are buckets heaped with sauerkraut. Upstairs you'll find poultry and game – with frozen goods (octopus, cod) in between – and two bars at each end, the latter where traders lay into cheap *čobanac goulash* after a hard morning's work.

Wooden cabins sell olive oil, which is best put to use on the fish on offer in the Ribarnica where pretty mosaics depict the seafood for sale. You won't find fresh fish on Mondays, or when the Jugo or Bora winds blow; also note that out of season much of what is on sale has been farmed.

Next door at the Amfora, you can sit on the terrace with a plate of grilled sardines and a glass of wine, observing the Dolac in action. Traders from Zagorje and Dalmatia have cabbages, *blitva* and other local vegetables while little bundles of mixed veg (*grinzaig*) are ideal for soups. A hike of 1kn in the price of this culinary essential is as fair an indication of the local economy as any interest rate increase by the Bank of England.

## Hrvatske divote

*Tkalčićeva 80 (01 481 1013).* **Open** 10am-8pm Mon-Sat; noon-8pm Sun. **Map** p45 E1 ❷ **Food & drink**
The name translates as 'Croatian Splendour' and it's a pretty fair description of what you get. Pretty much every branch of authentic Croatian deli produce is in here somewhere. Alongside regulars such as wine, olive oil and truffles, you'll also find pumpkin seed oil, natural bottled fruit juices, speciality rakija (including rarely seen flavours such as myrtle), homemade tagliatelle-style pasta flavoured with nettles, hemp tea, salami made from Istrian *boškarin* cattle – the list is endless. They also sell freshly made *fritule* (tasty deep-fried dough balls sprinkled with icing sugar) from a stall outside.

## ★ Take Me Home

*Tomićeva 4 (01 790 7600, www.takehomehome.hr)* **Open** 10am-8pm Mon-Fri; 10am-3pm Sat. **Map** p44 D2 ❸ **Design accessories**
The aim of this exemplary little shop, near the lower station of the funicular, is to stock quality products made by Croatian designers that also work as souvenirs – in the sense that they're small enough to fit in luggage and might also be useful once you get home. There's a lot to consider here, from Ana Horvat's eccentric but loveable animal soft toys to Sexy-Plexy's wear-with-care coloured shard necklaces. Playful gift ideas include Žvig's one-shot rakija mugs carved from walnut wood (they only stay upright when empty) and Hidden Garden pendants with real herbs inside. For those prepared to splash out on something for the home, Lidia Bosevski's ceramics convey arty elegance while Filip Gordon Frank's Mini Me desk lamp is already something of a Croatian design icon. More than 60 domestic designers are represented in this one store.

## Vešmašina

*Opatovina 45 (01 390 7000, vesmasina.hr).* **Open** 10am-8pm Mon-Fri; 9am-3pm Sun. **Map** p45 E2 ❹ **Fashion & accessories**
If you're looking for unique, non-high-street fashions then Vešmašina or 'Washing Machine' is a real find: a tiny oblong of a shop packed with groovy, alternative-but-glam tops, shoes, hats and accessories that you don't find anywhere else. As well as summery clothes by the LA-based, retro-inspired label Wildfox, Vešmašina stocks brightly coloured rubber purses by P&G, wonderfully eccentric but chic sunglasses, and neat souvenirs (mugs, notebooks, shopping bags) by local duo Safari Sisters.

## Nightlife

### ★ Booze and Blues

*Tkalčićeva 84 (01 483 7765, www.booze-and-blues.com).* **Open** varies. **Map** p45 E1.
Right at the top of the Tkalčićeva strip, this new venue – launched in 2014 – looks exactly how a music bar should, with a small stage at one end of a dark but imaginatively lit space and all kinds of musical memorabilia peppering from the walls. Lamps hidden inside bass drums hang above a long bar stocked with the kind of things that any self-respecting rock-and-roller would want to see – with whiskeys, rakijas and boutique beers (from Istrian brewery San Servolo) lining the shelves. Live music, from Wednesday through to Saturday, features funk, rock covers, and plenty of blues. *Photos p52.*

### Gjuro II

*Medveščak 2 (no phone, www.facebook.com/dubgjuro2).* **Open** 11pm-4am Fri, Sat, also according to event. **Admission** varies, free on Tue. **No credit cards.** **Map** p45 E1.
There's something welcomingly lived-in about the rather worn and tatty Gjuro II (there is no Gjuro I, just so you know), a cult Zagreb location that somehow succeeds in staying popular from one generation to the next. The narrow passageways on either side of the oblong bar ensure that you'll bump and squeeze your way past fellow patrons on your way to the dancefloor. The weekly schedule is an increasingly improvised affair, with DJs offering widely different styles of music on different weekends – checking the club's Facebook page should help. Prices (bottled Beck's, Stella and Corona) are reasonable.

### Jabuka

*Jabukovac 28 (01 24 41 944, www.facebook.com/GKJabuka).* **Open** 11pm-5am Fri, Sat. **No credit cards.**
Everyone in Zagreb knows 'The Apple', where a generation danced and found romance 20 years ago. This Tuškanac club, set in one of the nicest neighbourhoods in town, has a worn-in feel and still provides the rocking sounds of the 1980s in its modest dance room, with multicoloured spotlights. DJs mix R&B and soul with New Wave, those eighties tunes and other retro genres as a mixed age crowd jiggle and writhe; live bands play occasionally. It's a beautiful 20-minute walk north from the city centre, or a quick taxi ride.

## Hotels

### Fulir Hostel

*Radićeva 3A (01 483 0882, www.fulirhostel.com).* **€. Map** p44 D2.
Every place has a story. Fulir, on the north-west corner of the main square, once housed the servants of the fellow sitting nearby in bronze, on horseback, who gives the square its name: Jelačić. Below the hostel, the famed Croatian leader kept his horses. Today, the alley the hostel occupies (it shares it with a solid locals' bar, Pivnica Pinta, *see p49*) still feels as if a group of soldiers might ride up any moment in need of stew and ale. Inside the hostel, there's everything you need but nothing more. It's a small and intimate

**Booze and Blues**. *See p51.*

16-bed place, with a relaxing common room, fully-equipped kitchen, Wi-Fi and washing machines. The owners make the difference: Davor and Leo have a wealth of local knowledge and will likely go out with your group to make sure you have the best Zagreb experience possible. No curfew.

### Hotel AS
*Zelengaj 2A (01 460 9111, www.hotel-as.hr).* €€.
It's something of a mystery why this hotel, which opened in 1999, gets so readily ignored within local hotel circles. Set in Zelengaj Park, it has 22 spacious rooms – 19 rooms, two junior suites and a business suite – with overstuffed furniture, bathrooms with double sinks, reproduction Impressionist paintings and views of that leafy park; it feels like a fancy mountainside retreat. The architecture is a wave of green glass, a cross between feng shui and tree-hugger retro. Also on the property is the longstanding and chichi Restaurant AS, renowned for its seafood. To get to the centre of town from the AS, take the footpath over the hills and then trek through the woods for ten minutes. Seriously.

### Panorama Hotel Zagreb
*Trg Krešimira Cosića 9 (01 365 8333, www. starwoodhotels.com/fourpoints/zagreb).* €€.
The phrase you hear thrown around with regard to this property is 'a good bang for the buck'. The renamed Panorama Hotel Zagreb is located next to the Dom Športova arena on the western edge of the city centre – five stops on the number 9 tram line from the train station – and thus a favourite for those travelling to Zagreb for sporting events and various midsized venue concerts. The 279 straightforward and ample rooms are internet-ready and equipped with everything you would expect: tea- and coffee-maker, safe and satellite TV. The part you might not expect: how helpful and nice the staff are. Sweeping views from the upper storeys means the hotel lives up to its name.

### ★ President Pantovčak
*Pantovčak 52 (01 488 1480, www.president-zagreb. com).* €€. Map p44 A2.
The President, which opened in 2009, is a beautiful boutique hotel built specifically for its surrounding community: the ritzy businessmen and embassies in the vicinity of this posh street, a ten-minute walk uphill from the outdoor market and weekend antique stalls of Britanski trg. Designed by the owner-architect, the son of an art critic, the interior is a combination of old and new. The walls and floors are teak, the furniture is designer-chic, Persian throw rugs and centuries-old trunks and tables are scattered artfully about. The in-room paintings and sculptures come from the owner's collection. The rooms themselves are variously equipped with two-person hot tubs, LCD TVs, Wi-Fi, fine fabrics and floor-to-ceiling windows overlooking the terraces and wooded park. Gazing

from the lobby, across the café, and through those huge windows, it feels as if you're in a tree house with an infinity view of the forest. The restaurant has retractable and sliding windows so that the forest-side wall disappears for morning coffee, or evening summer breezes. It's also well stocked with caviar, champagne and fine cheeses. A new Royal Suite with granite flooring, fireplace and terraces completes this fine picture.

### Studio Kairos
*Vlaška 92 (01 464 0680, www.studio-kairos.com).* €. No credit cards. Map p45 H2.
There is a chronic shortage of B&Bs in Croatia, and the small and welcoming Kairos comes as something of a breath of fresh air. Situated a 15-minute walk from the main square, it's an intimate and friendly place with four small rooms – one of which can serve as a triple, although most are intended for single or double occupancy. Each is decorated according to some Zagreb theme: the Writers' Room evokes memories of local scribblers such as Matoš and Krleža; Granny's Room teases guests with images of fresh veg and home-cooked food. There's a bright breakfast room, and extras such as laundry and bike hire can be arranged. Despite being something of a new kid on the block Kairos is already getting good word-of-mouth, so it's best to book ahead to be sure of nabbing one of the rooms.

EXPLORE

**EXPLORE**

## ★ Taban Hostel

*Tkalčićeva 82 (01 553 3527, www.tabanzagreb. com).* **Map** p45 E1.

Taban is a sprightly hostel opened in 2012, renovated in 2014, and firmly aimed at those who want comfort and cleanliness slap in the middle of Zagreb's principal bar-hopping zone. The hostel itself has a fully stocked ground-floor bar, open to all-comers during the day. Accommodation is on the slick side for a backpacking joint, with high-ceilinged six-bed dorms sharing space with spick-and-span singles and doubles, some with their own bathroom. Breakfast isn't provided, but there are plenty of bakeries and restaurants down the street. Laundry services cost a few kuna extra; Wi-Fi is free.

## LOWER TOWN

The **Lower Town** begins at Jelačić. A crisscross of streets starts with a pedestrianised zone around **Preradovićeva flower market**, by the new bar quarter of **Gajeva**, **Preradovićeva** and **Margaretska**. Stern, grey Habsburg façades run down to the train station, some with shopfronts that have remained virtually unchanged since the 1960s. Parallel to them are two neatly planned rectangles of green public space stretching north-south as far as the train station, bookended by the **Botanical Gardens**.

This is the so-called **Green Horseshoe**, an attempt by 19th-century urban designer Milan Lenuci to create a city in the Austrian mode.

Each park is parcelled up into three parts, centrepieced by grandiose landmark buildings of prominent institutions: the **Academy of Arts and Sciences**; the **National Theatre**, and the **Mimara Museum** alongside. **Zrinjevac**, the northernmost section, features tree-lined paths, a gazebo and a fountain designed by Herman Bollé, responsible for many of Zagreb's major architectural works, including the cathedral. Linked to Jelačić by Masarykova, **Trg Maršala Tita** is notable not only for the neo-Baroque **Croatian National Theatre** but also because the square has kept its name, Tito. In front of the theatre stands one of the most famous works by sculptor Ivan Meštrović, **The Well of Life**.

The Lower Town ends at the railtracks and another fin-de-siècle facade, the neo-classical train station, **Glavni kolodvor**. A major stop on the Orient Express, it echoes another era, when arrival by train was the norm. Next to it was built one of Europe's great railway hotels, the **Esplanade Zagreb**, surrounded by a pedestrianised square of fountains and an underground shopping mall. The main railway lines still run to **Vienna** and **Budapest** – the domestic network is extremely limited.

# Sights & Museums

## Archaeological Museum

*Zrinjevac 19 (01 487 3101, www.amz.hr).* **Open** 10am-6pm Tue, Wed, Fri, Sat; 10am-8pm Thur; 10am-1pm Sun. **Admission** 20kn; 10kn reductions. **Map** p45 E3 ㉜

Established in 1846, the Archaeological Museum's extensive and well labelled collection covers three floors, beginning with the Early Stone Age. The section on ancient Egypt includes sarcophagi, statues and jewellery: the Zagreb Mummy (4th century BC), wrapped in a shroud bearing rare Etruscan texts, is the museum's coup de grâce and shouldn't be missed. Other highlights include the Vučedol Dove, a 4,000-year-old ceramic vessel found near Vukovar and a symbol of peace in recent times; Greek and Roman artefacts; and coins through the ages. There are also temporary exhibitions.

## Art Pavilion

*Trg kralja Tomislava 22 (01 48 41 070, www. umjetnicki-paviljon.hr).* **Open** 11am-8pm Tue-Thur; 11am-9pm Fri; 11am-8pm Sat, Sun. **Admission** 40kn; 25kn reductions. **No credit cards. Map** p45 E5 ㉝

Created for the Millennial exhibition in Budapest in 1896, this impressive, iron-framed building was then shipped back to Zagreb, where it centrepieces Tomislav square facing the train station. It still hosts major events and exhibitions.

## FREE Botanical Gardens

*Marulićev trg 9a (01 48 98 060, hirc.botanic.hr/ vrt).* **Open** *Apr-Sept* 9am-2.30pm Mon, Tue; 9am-dusk Wed-Sun. **Admission** free. **Map** p44 D5 ㉞

These lovely gardens, founded in 1889, contain giant trees, lilypad-covered ponds, an English-style arboretum, symmetrical French-inspired flower beds and ten glasshouses, although the latter are closed to the public. Around 10,000 plant species are on display, with the majority coming from Croatia, although some originate as far away as Asia. It's a shaded spot in summer, with plenty of benches.

---

## IN THE KNOW THE COURTYARDS

A huge success when introduced in 2014, The Courtyards (Dvorišta) is a ten-day-long initiative to bring to life the forgotten courtyards of Zagreb's Upper Town. Food, wine, music and animated chatter fill these neglected spaces, encouraged by live-music acts with a specific ambience – jazz, classics, chill-out – as well as a DJ spinning vinyl-only retro tunes. Quality Croatian wine and nibbles are laid on at reasonable prices, and entrance is free. See www.dvorista.in.

---

## Croatian Association of Artists

*Trg Žrtava fašizma (01 46 11 818, www.hdlu.hr).* **Open** 11am-7pm Wed-Fri; 10am-6pm Sat, Sun. **Admission** 20kn; 10kn reductions. **No credit cards. Map** p45 G3/4 ㉟

This Ivan Meštrović-designed 1930s masterpiece is among Zagreb's most striking sights. Classical columns support a white circular structure made of stone from Brač. In 1941, to attract Muslims to the Fascist regime, the building became a mosque. The three minarets were demolished in 1949. Since 2003 it has housed the Croatian Association of Artists (HDLU), serving as its main exhibition space. The circular walls contain three galleries, which span two floors and provide an outstanding venue for a dynamic programme of contemporary exhibitions and events organised by the association. The central hall has natural lighting thanks to its cupola.

## Ethnographic Museum

*Trg Ivana Mažuranića 14 (01 48 26 220, www.emz.hr).* **Open** 10am-6pm Tue-Thur; 10am-1pm Fri-Sun. **Admission** 15kn; 10kn reductions. **No credit cards. Map** p44 C4 ㊱

Ageing exhibition halls and bad lighting shouldn't put you off the idea of visiting this absorbing collection, which begins with a ground-floor display of items brought home by Croatian explorers, including ritual masks from the Congo, Indian textiles, tree bark paintings from Australia, and Chinese ceremonial dresses. Upstairs is an extensive display of Croatian folk costumes covering all regions of the country, together with domestic artefacts and agricultural implements. Colourful, well-staged temporary exhibitions provide additional reason to visit.

## ★ Galerija Nova

*Teslina 7 (01 487 2582, www.whw.hr).* **Open** noon-8pm Tue-Fri; 11am-2pm Sat. **No credit cards. Map** p44 D3 ㊲

The exhibitions and other events here put the gallery front and centre of Zagreb's cultural scene, and you can find out what's happening via its own newspaper, available free at the premises. It's not the biggest venue but the vision of the curatorial team is admirable. In their own terms, this not-for-profit venture was set up as a 'platform for socially engaged models of cultural production and reflection of social reality'. Prepare to be challenged.

## Mimara Museum

*Rooseveltov trg 5 (01 48 28 100, www.mimara.hr).* **Open** *July-Sept* 10am-7pm Tue-Fri; 10am-5pm Sat; 10am-2pm Sun. *Oct-June* 10am-5pm Tue, Wed, Fri, Sat; 10am-7pm Thur; 10am-2pm Sun. **Admission** 40kn; 30kn reductions. **No credit cards. Map** p44 B4 ㊳

When it comes to historical art collections, the Mimara is certainly Zagreb's biggest in terms of quantity. Donated to the city by wealthy and shady patron Ante Topić Mimara, the collection includes

**EXPLORE**

paintings, statues and archaeological finds, organised chronologically and thematically but with little by way of English explanation. Highlights on the ground floor include oriental carpets, south-east Asian sculpture and Chinese porcelain, while the picture galleries upstairs display works from the Gothic period onwards, with artists like Velázquez, Rubens, Rembrandt and Manet. It's also an important venue for art and archaeology exhibitions. *Photo p56.*

## Moderna Galerija
*Hebrangova 1 (01 604 1040, www.modernagalerija.hr).* **Open** 11am-7pm Tue-Fri, 10am-1pm Sat, Sun. **Admission** 40kn; 20kn reductions. **Map** p45 E4 ❸

Housed in the impressively renovated Vraniczany Palace on Zrinjevac, the Modern Gallery is home to the national collection of 19th- and 20th-century art. It kicks off in spectacular fashion with huge canvases by late 19th-century painters Vlaho Bukovac and Celestin Medović dominating the sublimely proportioned hexagonal entrance hall. From here the collection works its way chronologically through the history of Croatian painting, taking in Ljubo Babić's entrancing 1920s landscapes and Edo Murtić's jazzy exercises in 1950s abstraction. Several contemporary artists are featured here too – sufficient to whet your appetite before hopping over the river to the Museum of Contemporary Art to see some more. The Moderna Galerija's most innovative feature is the tactile gallery, a room containing versions of famous paintings in relief form, with Braille captions, for unsighted visitors to explore.

## Museum of Arts & Crafts
*Trg maršala Tita 3 (01 48 82 111, www.muo.hr).* **Open** 10am-7pm Tue-Sat; 10am-2pm Sun. **Admission** 30kn; 20kn reductions. **No credit cards. Map** p44 C4 ❹

This grand Hermann Bollé-designed palace, founded in 1880, was originally based on 'a collection of samples for master craftsmen and artists who need to re-improve production of items of everyday use'. It has now grown to become the country's premier collection of applied art, with a wide-ranging gaggle of works from Baroque altar pieces to Biedermeier furniture, domestic ceramics, clocks and contemporary poster design. A side room full of synagogue silverware and ritual candlesticks recalls the rich heritage of Zagreb's pre-World War II Jewish community. On the top floor, a collection of 19th and 20th century ball gowns and evening dresses provides glamour.

## ★ Strossmayer's Gallery of Old Masters
*Trg NŠ Zrinskog 11 (01 48 95 117, www.mdc.hr/strossmayer).* **Open** 10am-7pm Tue; 10am-4pm Wed-Fri; 10am-1pm Sat, Sun. **Admission** 30kn; 10kn reductions. **No credit cards. Map** p45 E4 ❹

Built in 1884 to accommodate Bishop Strossmayer's European masterpieces, this neo-Renaissance palace showcases works spanning the 14th to 19th centuries. Of the 4,000 items in the permanent collection, only 400 are displayed at one time, in ten rooms on the second floor. Italians, including Tintoretto, feature in the first six, followed by Flemish, Dutch and German painters (Albrect Dürer among them). French and Spanish artists, with Delacroix and El Greco foremost, complete the collection.

## Technical Museum
*Savska 18 (01 48 44 050, tehnicki-muzej.hr).* **Open** 9am-5pm Tue-Fri; 9am-1pm Sat, Sun. **Admission** *Permanent collection, Planetarium & Tesla* 15kn each. **No credit cards. Map** p44 B5 ❹

A vast space is needed for these aircraft, vintage cars, an 80-year-old snowmobile, a World War II mini-submarine, 19th-century fire engines and a 1912 Dubrovnik tram. There's also a small planetarium, flanked by a life-size model of an unmanned Soviet moon rover, and a similarly true-to-life copy of the American Mercury programme space capsules of the early 1960s. The section dedicated to Nikola Tesla illustrates just how advanced this turn-of-the-century pioneer of electricity generation and radio transmission actually was. Daily demonstrations in his lab involve a short lecture during which some of his inventions are put through their paces.

# Restaurants

## ★ 5/4
*Dukljaninova 1 (01 461 6654, petacetvrtina.com/en).* **Open** noon-3pm, 7-11pm Mon-Sat. €€€. **Map** p45 G3 ❹ **Mediterranean**

The venture established by Dino Galvagno (the power behind the highly praised Prasac), 5/4, or 'The Fifth Quarter', opened in 2013 and established itself almost immediately as Zagreb's latest must-visit culinary sensation. It's certainly a unique place to dine: with twigs and leaves stuck to the wall like a cross between an art installation and a forest hut. The menu changes daily and basically represents what the chef has found at the market and what he feels like cooking. Expect an individually crafted selection of Euro-Med dishes, with Adriatic fish and at least one mainstream meat dish always featured. The smaller dishes and starters are delights in themselves, and it pays to order several if you want to experience the breadth of 5/4's cuisine.

## Bistro Bardot
*Ilica 73 (no phone).* **Open** 10am-midnight Tue-Fri; noon-midnight Sat; 9.30am-4pm Sun. €€. **Map** p44 B3 ❹ **French**

French-owned and with a French-themed menu, Bardot is a welcoming place in which to sample classic European cuisine without dipping too deeply into your wallet. The changing menu, chalked up every day, usually features a balance of classic lamb, poultry, steak, and, er, horse dishes that you might not find elsewhere in Zagreb. House pâté and

**Mimara Museum**. *See p54.*

French cheese platters feature among the starters, and there's a respectable choice of French wines by the glass. The basement location provides a moody, atmospherically lit and slightly bohemian ambience – one wall is decorated with murals by street artist Oko. There's live jazz or blues at the weekends.

### Bistro Fotić

*Gajeva 25 (099 578 8026, www.bistrofotic.com/ index_eng.html).* **Open** 8am-11pm Mon-Sat. €. **Map** p45 E4 ⑮ **Croatian**
Housed in an extension of the Foto Club Zagreb café, this imaginative new leap into Zagreb's growing bistro culture goes for the keep-things-simple approach, with a small menu of five or six mains (at least one risotto, at least one stew, at least one grilled meat dish), all of which are prepared and presented with a bit of style. Fotić offers a slightly better choice of desserts than some other bistros. There's a small street-side terrace; the bright front dining room, with theatrical birdcages and huge butterflies hanging from the ceiling, is your dose of cuteness.

### Bistro Karlo

*Gundulićeva 16 (01 483 3175, hr-hr.facebook.com/ pages/Bistro-Karlo/132081496871018).* **Open** 11am-11pm Mon-Sat. €€€. **Map** p44 D3 ⑯ **Croatian**

More a classy restaurant than a bistro, Karlo brings a touch of modern European culinary experimentation to central Zagreb's standard repertoire of grilled meats and Adriatic fish. The menu is small and subject to daily changes; the chef will come to your table and tell you what's fresh. Lamb brain panna cotta is the most 'out there' of the regular starters, although delicate seafood risottos will calm the nerves of those with less adventurous stomachs. There's a handful of mains, with classic steak, lamb and fish dishes well represented, each accompanied by innovative garnishes. The portions are small and the prices are high, but it's usually worth it. The bright interior is relaxing and cheery, although some details – spangly chandeliers, overly ornate picture frames – err on the kitsch side.

### Bistroteka

*Teslina 14 (01 483 7711).* **Open** 8.30am-midnight daily. €€. **Map** p44 D3 ⑰ **International**
Opened in 2014 and already a leading light in Zagreb's ongoing bistro revolution, Bistroteka strikes the right balance between snack-nibbling informality and slap-up, sit-down dining. The menu, which displays a playful interest in anything from Croatia to the wider Med and the Far East, ranges from thoughtfully compiled ciabatta sandwiches to major meat-and-two-veg meals. The menu changes

### Ćušpajz

*Gajeva 9 (01 48 75 045, www.cuspajz.hr).* **Open** 11.30am-6pm Mon; 11am-6pm Tue-Fri; 11.30am-5pm Sat. **No credit cards. €. Map** p45 E3 ⑲ **Soup**

An instant hit when it first opened in 2011, this venue engendered a soup revolution that shows no signs of letting up. The idea behind Ćušpajz ('Broth') is certainly simple – the changing menu consists of three soups a day (at least one vegetarian). Served in reasonably big bowls, each is garnished with a dainty salad on a stick, a dash of sour cream and a sprinkle of pumpkin seeds; a hunk of good bread comes on the side. It's invariably delicious. It's the brainchild of Leonarda Boban, wife of Croatian football legend Zvonimir Boban. No WAGs here though.

### Gallo

*Hebrangova 34 (01 48 14 014, www.gallo.hr).* **Open** 11.30am-midnight daily. **€€. Map** p44 D4 ⑳ **Mediterranean**

Posh but relaxed, Gallo offers seasonal and organic Med cuisine in a quiet courtyard set apart from the busy traffic of Hebrangova. Outside is a herb garden; sheets of pasta hang in the classic interior. It's not cheap, but in no way extortionate. Truffles are sprinkled wherever possible and the risotto mare i monte with porcini prompts a return visit. The wine list has some 70 Croatian and global varieties.

### Gostionica Tip-Top

*Gundulićeva 18 (01 48 30 349).* **Open** 7am-midnight Mon-Sat. **€€. Map** p44 D3 ⑤ **Croatian seafood**

Locals know this age-old eaterie as Blato as it's run by restaurateurs from Korčula (a small Adriatic island with a little town called Blato). Little has changed here since Tin Ujević and his literary gang were regulars in the 1940s – their pictures and an outline of Tin's iconic hat provide decoration. The front bar has since been converted into restaurant space but the back dining room still provides intimacy. There are inexpensive specials every day, and a seafood-dominated menu that features red mullet, sole or sea bass. Korčula varieties feature on the wine list.

### Konoba Čiho

*Pavla Hatza 15 (01 481 7060).* **Open** 10am-midnight Mon-Sat; noon-midnight Sun. **€€. Map** p45 F4 ⑳ **Dalmatian**

Long considered a solid choice for Dalmatian seafood, this homely and popular venue consists of a street-level bar-restaurant featuring bare brickwork, avocado hues and a mezzanine mounted on metal pillars. The downstairs dining room couldn't be more different, with maritime trinkets and loud wall coverings bringing to mind the parlour of a 19th-century sea captain. Adriatic fish either grilled or baked weighs in at around 360kn/kg; for a repast that's lighter on both stomach and wallet there's a good choice of quality risottos and seafood pastas in the 60kn-80kn bracket.

according to what's fresh and seasonal; daily specials are chalked up on a board. The in-the-know wine list offers a good mixture of boutique and mainstream production from all over Croatia. Bistroteka is a pleasant place to sit and contemplate the good things in life, with white-painted brick ceiling, kooky light fittings and unobtrusive background pop.

### ★ Carpaccio

*Teslina 14 (01 482 2331, www.ristorante carpaccio.hr).* **Open** 11am-midnight Mon-Sat. **€€. Map** p44 D3 ⑱ **Italian**

Opened in 2010 by former staff of the legendary Okrugljak (*see p47*), Carpaccio delivers stylish Italian-themed dining in a wonderfully convenient location. For starters, there's a generous carpaccio selection (marinated Adriatic fish or salmon are among the most succulent choices). There are plenty of vegetarian options in with the standard risotto and pasta dishes, and substantial steaks and veal cutlets among the meaty mains. It's worth leaving room for dessert – the house semifreddo and tiramisu are difficult to choose between. Chic black furnishings, reproduction Art Nouveau posters and a soundtrack of Italian pop provide the backdrop. To complete the fine picture, there is a lengthy list of quality Croatian and Italian wines, a reasonable number available by the glass.

**EXPLORE**

## Korčula

*Teslina 17 (01 48 72 159, www.restoran-korcula. hr).* **Open** 10.30am-11pm Mon-Sat. **€€. Map** p44 D3 ⑤ **Seafood**

Korčula, named after an island off the Dalmatian coast, is as traditional as it gets. This fish restaurant on the corner of Teslina and Preradovićeva was here long before the trendy bars set up around it. The kitchen turns out high-quality versions of seafood standards, tuna fillets or grilled squid with *blitva*, as well as a few specialities worth trying (in particular a succulent baked octopus with potatoes). There are scallops, breaded frogs' legs and grouper or John Dory priced by the kilo. The black risotto (*crni rižot*) is as good as you'll get anywhere in town. Decent, well priced bottles of Dingač and Pošip adorn an excellent wine selection that features dozens of reds and whites of similarly Dalmatian provenance.

## ★ Luna Rossa

*Preradovićeva 12 (01 485 4780, www.luna rossa.hr).* **Open** 8am-midnight Mon-Wed; 8am-2am Thur-Sat; noon-5pm Sun. **€€. Map** p44 D3 ⑤ **Istrian**

This Istrian-themed trattoria mixes traditional home-style cooking with an unashamedly contemporary interior, striking a nice balance between minimal modern greys and folksy textures like pale wood and rope. The mainstay of the menu is the in-house pasta and *njoki* (gnocchi) served with a variety of delicious sauces, ranging from white wine and mushroom to Istrian truffle. Also well worth recommending are the seafood risottos, T-bone steaks and *ombolo*-style pork chops. It also functions as a wine bar (with stools at the counter and outside on the street), serving the best in Istrian boutique production; check out the chalked-up recommendations on the blackboard for affordable options by the glass.

## Mašklin i lata

*Hebrangova 11A (01 48 18 273).* **Open** 9am-11pm Mon-Sat. **€€. Map** p45 E4 ⑤ **Croatian**

Beneath the Old Pharmacy pub and named after farming tools, Mašklin i Lata brings a bit of the sea to the heart of the city. It's got the traditional feel just right. Most of the offerings have a fish or seafood base – lobster, cod, monkfish, squid, prawns, octopus – all combined with homemade pasta, gnocchi, risotto, wild asparagus, Istrian truffles or turned into great stews. Sample the *brodet* or *gregada* (Croatian fish stews) or a hulking platter of mixed fish priced by the kilo with *blitva* (the traditional accompaniment of local Swiss chard and potatoes).

## Nishta

*Masarykova 11 (01 889 7444, www.nishta restaurant.com/zagreb).* **Open** noon-11pm Tue-Sun. **€. Map** p45 D3 ⑤ **Vegan**

Already something of a Dubrovnik institution, classy vegan restaurant Nishta transplanted its winning formula to Zagreb in 2014. Occupying a light-filled, first-floor room in an off-street courtyard, it sticks resolutely to its mission, although the menu is so varied and flavoursome that non-vegans won't feel as if their dining choices have been limited; subtle use of Indian, Asian and Mexican spices enliven the main courses. There's a salad bar with pulses and grains, and the healthy message even extends to the alcohol, which features organic wines from eastern Croatia and small-brewery beer from San Servolo in Istria.

## Oxbo Urban Bar & Grill

*DoubleTree by Hilton, Vukovara 269A (01 600 1914, www.oxbogrill.com).* **Open** 7am-11pm daily. **€€€. Map** p45 H6 ⑤ **Steakhouse/Croatian**

Far from just a hotel restaurant, the Oxbo at DoubleTree by Hilton (*see p64*) is an increasingly important dining and socialising hub for the business and residential community grouped around the fast-developing Radnička cesta strip. Oxbo's chief attribute is its Angus steaks, served in a variety of sizes; all the beef is imported from the US. There's also lots of quality Adriatic fare; you can start with *pršut* (Croatian prosciutto) and continue with fillet of sea bass if you want to stick to tradition. To attract the non-business crowd, there's live music and half-price steaks on Saturdays.

## Pauza

*Preradovićeva 34 (01 48 54 598, www.restaurant-pauza.com).* **Open** 11am-9pm Mon-Fri; noon-5pm Sat. **€€. Map** p44 D4 ⑤ **Contemporary**

Actors, creatives and thirtysomethings come here for homemade food with an imaginative, Adriatic-Asian take on culinary fusion. The interior aims for chic modernity without going 'totally lounge bar', while the background music is cool, jazzy but sufficiently unobtrusive to allow for conversation. The menu changes with the season. Pauza's wok-fried dishes mix Med seafood with eastern flavours although there are plenty of traditional Croatian treatments of meat and fish for those who want something straightforward. There's a terrace; dishes of the day, chalked up on the inside wall, are excellent value; wines by the glass and draught beer are equally affordable.

## Ribice i Tri Točkice

*Preradovićeva 7/1 (01 563 5479, www.ribice itritockice.hr).* **Open** noon-11pm daily. **€€. Map** p44 D3 ⑤ **Seafood**

Offering simple and affordable seafood for people who prefer their restaurants to be fun rather than formal, Ribice bases its menu on the less showy dishes that form the backbone of Dalmatian home cooking. On offer are many treatments that have disappeared from fancier restaurant menus (notably anchovies, bonito and hake), and fish is priced by the fillet rather than weight. Daily specials chalked up on a blackboard outside the entrance take account of what's fresh. The jolly interior features smart

EXPLORE

wooden tables, chairs painted in pastel blue and turquoise hues, and fishy murals by Vojo Radoičić, the Rijeka-based artist famous for his colourful seaside scenes. Waiters in Dalmatian red sashes, and Adriatic folk-pop background music, drive home the maritime theme. It's so popular it lately expanded.

### ★ Zinfandel's
*Esplanade Zagreb, Mihanovićeva 1 (01 456 6666, www.esplanade.hr).* Open 6am-11pm Mon-Sat; 6.30am-11pm Sun. €€€. Map p45 E5 ⑳ International
Zinfandel's is an outstanding spot that transfers the elegance of art deco hotel, the Esplanade Zagreb (*see p65*), built for the Orient Express back in 1925, to the dining room. Beneath the chandeliers, a pianist strokes the keys for a room overlooking the oleander terrace. Dishes include duck, a daily selection of fresh fish, pan-roasted veal with foie gras, or wild boar with a chestnut, truffle and pumpkin mousseline – the menu changes to reflect the season. The Sunday brunch buffet has the best Croatian cheeses and sausage. Don't overlook in-house Le Bistro either, French in style but with standout local *štrukli*.

## Cafés & Bars

### 22,000 milja pod morem
*Frankopanska 22 (01 481 7007, www.22000 milja.com).* Open 7am-2am Mon-Wed; 7am-2am Thur-Sat. No credit cards. Map p44 C3 ㉛
An unexpected find in an unpromising courtyard, '22,000 Leagues Under the Sea' is very much a Zagreb one-off, decked out in wood panelling, metal rivets and with several clusters of dials that look like pressure gauges you might find in a submarine. It's a wonderful piece of steampunk design, and is very popular with young locals – the kind of place that might be full on a Tuesday in February when all the other bars in the neighbourhood are empty. It's also one of the few central pubs that serves bottles of San Servolo beer, the malty boutique brew from Istria.

### ★ Bacchus Jazz Bar
*Trg kralja Tomislava 16 (098 322 804, hr-hr.facebook.com/bacchusjazzbar).* Open 11am-midnight Mon-Fri; noon.midnight Sat. No credit cards. Map p45 E5 ㉜
Just off the first square as you walk up from the station, the Bacchus Jazz Bar is an ideal place to meet friends, listen to jazz and either have a civilised party evening or get revved up for what's to come. The bar exudes a homely Dalmatian feel: there's a fig tree next to the terrace, which is tucked into a passage off the street. Inside you'll find a hodgepodge of wooden furniture, a 1960s-era television and telephone, and wood floors under a brick ceiling. It's almost always busy, so tables will be at a premium. Wines, mainly Dalmatian, have chosen to suit the mood. There are cocktails too, but few pay them much attention. There's live jazz on Fridays.

### ★ Beertija
*Pavla Hatza 16 (01 563 5482, www. facebook. com/thebeertija).* Open 8am-midnight Mon-Wed; 8am-1amThur; 8am-4am Fri, Sat; 10am-midnight Sun. Map p45 F4 ㉝
Opened in autumn 2012, the Beertija quickly became one of the winning locations of the outdoor drinking season. While the terrace sits behind trees and shrubs protected from the busy road, the main body of the bar is in a neighbouring basement. Decked out in a mixture of red-brick and grey, it's pretty postindustrial – there's a glass-wall smoking tank in one corner for days when it's too cold or wet to light up outside. As the name suggests (Beertija is a play on words based on the term *birtija*, a kind of Balkan pub), the accent is on amber liquids, with a simply mind-boggling choice of local and imported ales. This is probably the only place in town where both Newcastle Brown and cult Montenegrin Nikšićko pivo crop up on the same menu, alongside all manner of heady dark liquids dreamt up by crafty Belgian monks. There's also a list of bar snacks that run from garlic bread to smoked pork hock, and a rock/alternative soundtrack that matches the venue perfectly.
▶ *Sharing the same courtyard, Klub (01 56 35 482, subkulturnicentar.comhr) has small-scale gigs and club nights.*

### Bikers Beer Factory
*Savska cesta 150 (099 848 5663).* Open 8am-midnight Mon-Thur; 8am-2am Fri, Sat; 10am-midnight Sun. No credit cards. Map p44 B6 ㉞
Providing another great reason to visit the nether regions of Savska cesta (Vintage Industrial Bar is one other; *see p63*), Bikers is by no means a niche bar for a niche public. Biking provides the design theme and indeed there's a motorbike repair shop at the same address, but the general atmosphere is one of easygoing, alternative lifestyles plus rock'n'roll. The exposed brick interior contains a few postindustrial touches; there's a large inner courtyard beer garden and live rock/blues a couple of times a week. As far as the drink is concerned; there's Erdinger on tap, a good choice of bottled beers and Perković rakija on the spirits menu.

### Chocolat 041
*Masarykova 25 (01 485 5382, www.facebook.com/ Chocolat.041).* Open 8am-midnight Mon-Wed; Sun; 8am-2am Thur-Sat. No credit cards. Map p44 C4 ㉟
Opened in late 2013, Chocolat 041 was quickly enthroned as the most talked-about coffee, cake and ice-cream place in town. The fact that it is owned by former Croatian international footballer Zvonimir Boban is only part of the reason; the ice-cream is superb, and the range of irresistible cakes – all of which are based on chocolate in some way or another – almost guarantees repeat visits. The decor, too, is a talking point: comic strips and album covers recall

EXPLORE

Cogito Coffee.

'You are now entering Evolution Area' says the sign on the door, which leads through to a coolly minimal white space with a handful of tables grouped around the bar. For several years now Eli's has been Zagreb's leading venue for quality coffee, leading a brewing revolution that is slowly spreading to the city's other bars. It is also one of the few cafe-bars that is completely non-smoking, ensuring that you can actually taste and smell whatever it is you're drinking. A foxy young professional clientele gathers here to gas, goss and guzzle coffee from 100% arabica beans selected and roasted by the café owner Nik Orosi, the country's first speciality coffee roaster.

### Hemingway Lounge Bar
*Trg maršala Tita (no phone, www.hemingway.hr).* **Open** 7am-1am Mon-Thur, Sun; 7am-4am Fri, Sat. **Map** p44 C4 ⑲
Hemingway Lounge Bar is part of a chain of upmarket cocktail bars with two branches in Zagreb. This one is located opposite the National Theatre. It has a gilded feel, with ornate trimmings and chandeliers. There are the prerequisite photos of Ernest, of course – in pastel relief. Cocktails with fruit are among the establishment's specialties: the mojito, of course; raspberry martinis, and the Amaretto sour – with fresh oranges and lemons – is a showstopper. If the weather is nice, grab a pavement table among the pretty set dressed in all black and posing over sandwiches, healthy juices and *macchiatos* by day, and classic drinks like mai tais and Long Island iced teas at night to accompany DJs spinning house.
▶ *The classy, more dance-club-esque venue at Tuškanac 1, behind the Tuškanac Cinema, is open noon-5am Monday to Saturday.*

Zagreb pop culture of the 1980s, and a relief on one wall spells out the name Zvečka – a tribute to the new wave-scene café that once stood next door at no.23. The partially glass ceiling means that people seated down below can look up the chair legs of the first-floor lounge – so think about wearing long trousers if you're heading upstairs.

### ★ Cogito Coffee
*Varšavska 11 (no phone, cogitocoffee.com).* **Open** 7.30am-7pm Mon-Fri; 9am-7pm Sat. **Map** p44 C3 ⑯
Flagship city-centre bar of the Cogito bean-roasting outfit, this recently opened clinic for unrepentant caffeine-a-holics is just off the main street, at the start of the mysterious, half-hidden passageway that leads from Varšavska through to Masarykova. Minimally decorated, save for some salvaged furniture and a few pictures, it serves a hard-to-beat brew, plus leaf teas, some freshly-squeezed juices, and that's about it – although you will find muffins and cookies provided by the Piknik bakery and sandwich bar.

### Dobar Zvuk
*Gajeva 18 (no phone).* **Open** 8am-midnight Mon-Thur; 8am-1am Fri; 9am-1am Sat; 10am-midnight Sun. **No credit cards. Map** p45 E3/4 ⑰
Suitably set in an old hi-fi store, this superior music bar is a lively and popular rendezvous for younger, spiky-haired locals and older rockers. Pub-like in style – old Guinness ads, bare brickwork, pictures of Zappa, the Doors, Costello – 'Good Sound' might be guitar-driven but lacks the macho male overtones of other music bars in town.

### Eli's Caffè
*Ilica 63 (091 455 5608, www.eliscaffe.com).* **Open** 8am-7pm Mon-Fri; 8am-4pm Sat; 9am-2pm Sun. **No credit cards. Map** p44 B3 ⑱

### Kolaž
*Amruševa 11 (099 461 3112).* **Open** 2pm-2am Mon-Fri; 6pm-2am Sat, Sun. **No credit cards. Map** p45 E3 ⑳
This small, red-brick basement bar is decked out in wry, kitsch-but-cool details, with a veritable solar system of tiny mirrorballs hovering above the bar, and a seating area that – illuminated by tiny pinpricks of light emerging from bronzey-yellow panels – looks like the inside of a huge honeycomb. During the day Kolaž serves coffee to local office workers and lawyers, while by night it fills up with a sophisticated bohemian set with an easy-going straight-gay-whatever sense of social orientation. The music ventures into similar areas of ambiguity, ranging from PJ Harvey to La Roux with all kinds of indie-rock, synthi-pop, electro-disco and exotica thrown into the mix. Rare Marinsko is among the beers, while the handsome array of spirits includes some fine local liquors. On weekend nights it can be a rather tight squeeze.

### Limb
*Plitvička 16 (01 61 71 683).* **Open** 8am-2am Mon-Sat. **No credit cards. Map** p44 C6 ㉑

Underground, understated and right by the KSET club (see p63), Limb is comprised of two tiny colourful rooms and the glass-enclosed terrace with a tree in the middle. A slightly older, artistic crowd hangs out here – reflecting more than a decade of established patrons. Limb is a good spot for DJed, funky, club beats at weekends.

### Maraschino

*Margaretska 1 (099 866 5294, www.facebook.com/ maraschino.zg)*. **Open** 8am-1am Mon-Thur; 8am-4am Fri, Sat; 10.30am-1am Sun. **No credit cards. Map** p44 D3 ⑫
Named after the cherry liqueur from Zadar, Maraska, this three-floor spot in trendy-bar central is packed to the rafters in the evenings, but a low-key place to try a few local tipples by day. The glitzy interior features spangly chandeliers and light sculptures made from Martini glasses, and the place serves Maraska-infused coffee or hot chocolate, long drinks, and Malvazija and Babić wines. There are DJs at weekends, when punters spill out on to the pedestrianised street outside.

### Sedmica

*Kačićeva 7a (01 48 46 689, caffebar-sedmica.com)*. **Open** 8am-1am Mon-Thur; 8am-2am Fri, Sat; 5pm-1am Sun. **No credit cards. Map** p44 B3 ⑬
Cult bar Sedmica does little to advertise its presence on the street – the clue is a small sign above a residential doorway. It's the meeting place of people from the creative arts: a rendezvous spot before a private view at a trendy gallery or for an impromptu cast party. You enter through a corridor lined with concert and exhibition posters. Inside, a small room contains a crowded bar counter upon which stand taps of Fischer's and Erdinger. Long, thin marble tables provide a place to sit; otherwise you can join the boho crew on the wrought-iron mezzanine behind.

### Vinyl

*Bogovićeva 3 (091 323 4016)*. **Open** 8am-2am Mon-Thur; 8am-4am Fri, Sat; 9am-midnight Sun. **Map** p44 D3 ⑭
Occupying one of the best pitches in central Zagreb, right in the middle of the pedestrianised strip opposite the Grounded Sun sculpture, Vinyl is a bit like a rambling apartment, with five separate rooms on the main floor and a live music and events room downstairs. Each is decorated in a slightly different style. The drinks menu is big on whiskies; among the bottled beers, look out for Rock and Roll, an extremely palatable red variety from Daruvar in eastern Croatia. The previous tenant of this roomy property was a Japanese restaurant, which helps to explain the samurai-fixated graphic art on the walls of the bar. The schedule includes live music on Wednesdays, literary readings on Thursdays, vinyl-only DJs at weekends, and – perhaps uniquely for a Zagreb café – the 'Flying Bookshop' second-hand book exchange on Monday evenings.

## Shops

### Brokula&Ž

*Teslina 9 (01 640 6830, www.brokulaz.com)*. **Open** 10am-7pm Mon-Fri; 10am-2pm Sat. **Map** p44 D3 ⑮ **Fashion**
Not satisfied with being the most boundary-bending advertising agency in the country, Bruketa & Žinić decided to launch their own line of clothes, and opened this small but sharp boutique to sell them in. Going under the name of Brokula&Ž, the range includes both his and hers T-shirts, and underwear in several classic shapes, all made from an eco-friendly blend of organically grown cotton and Promodal cellulose fibres. Brokula means broccoli in Croatian, which is why a friendly green blob adorns many of these items.

### ★ Croatian Design Superstore

*Martićeva 4 (01 580 6565, croatiandesign superstore.com)*. **Open** 9am-9pm daily. **Map** p45 F3 ⑯ **Homewares**
Arguably the most talked-about opening of spring 2015, this long-awaited design store is pretty much everything the title suggests: a showroom-style display of the best contemporary Croatian-designed products. Stock ranges from the inexpensive and portable, such as owl-shaped wooden coasters by Gloopy, to more pricey and unwieldy items of furniture like Fluffy-Hairy by Numen/For Use: a sofa so unusual that it will redefine your entire flat. In between, there are plenty of T-shirts, children's toys and even designer olive oils. Pretty much everything here is imaginative, practical and well made, making it the perfect place for quirky but quality souvenirs.

### ELFS

*Amruševa 4 (01 481 2847, www.elfs.hr)*. **Open** 9am-8pm Mon-Sat. **Map** p45 E3 ⑰ **Fashion**
This is the main city-centre outlet for a deservedly successful local fashion label launched by young Zagreb design duo Ivan Tandarić and Aleksandar Šekuljica. Incorporating an ironic take on today's bling culture, ELFS plays with elements of kitsch without going too far over the top, producing clothes that are fun, sexy and wearable. As well as frocks, bags and tights for the gals, the shop stocks hooded tops for the guys, and babygrows for infant followers of fashion.

### I-GLE

*Dežmanova 4 (01 48 46 508, www.i-gle.com)*. **Open** 10am-2pm, 4-8pm Mon-Fri; 10am-2pm Sat. **Map** p44 C3 ⑱ **Fashion**
The flagship store of local designers Martina Vrdoljak Ranilović and Nataša Mihaljčišin offers striking designs for women and custom ones for men. Their fashions combine relaxed functionality and elegance with evocative colour combinations. The I-GLE label enjoys cult status in Zagreb, where

**EXPLORE**

## IN THE KNOW ADVENT ZAGREB

Zagreb once hosted a traditional but tired pre-Christmas offering of souvenir stalls, mulled wine and sausage stands on the main pedestrian strip. The addition of *rakija* bars, speciality street food, outdoor music stages and a constellation of twinkly lights has recently taken it into another dimension. **Advent Zagreb** (www.advent zagreb.com) is no longer limited to the main square, but has spread to a scattering of nearby piazzas and parks, and the whole thing runs from late November until the first few days of the New Year. On Zrinjevac, stately trees are dressed with spirals of white lights while rows of small white houses sell hand-made crafts, speciality *rakijas* and boutique Croatian wines – including some seasonally appropriate sparkly ones.

the pair have made clothes for several theatre productions, and have gained a foothold at designer stores in the UK and Hong Kong.

### – Love, Ana
*Dežmanova 4 (01 580 1676, www.anatevsic.com).* **Open** 9am-5pm Mon-Fri; 11am-2pm Sat. **No credit cards**. **Map** p44 C3 ⑦ **Accessories**
Designer Ana Tevsić started her own '– Love, Ana' label, a line of quirky interior furnishings and accessories, in defiance of the current market crisis. This is her own sleek shop/studio; she sells a variety of her own designs – including her famous 'Chew On This' wall-hanger in the shape of a pair of red lips – and also stocks products from other promising designers, along with a variety of multilingual magazines. An interesting place to pick up something both useful and original.

### Karma Record Store
*Podgorska 3 (01 363 3685, www.karmavinil.com).* **Open** 9am-8pm Mon-Fri; 10am-3pm Sat. **Map** p44 B6 ⑳ **Books & music**
A bright conservatory full of cacti provides a rather welcoming environment in which to browse one of Zagreb's biggest and best-arranged collections of collectable vinyl, with sections devoted to just about every genre imaginable. Sideboard drawers are packed with seven-inch singles, and there's a growing collection of second-hand films on DVD. Karma also have a huge collection of vintage film posters, and piles of pop-culture magazines.

### Maria
*Masarykova 8 (01 481 1011, www.mariastore.hr).* **Open** 10am-8pm Mon-Fri; 10am-5pm Sat. **Map** p44 D3 ㉛ **Fashion**

Arguably Croatia's leading luxury boutique, Maria was launched in Dubrovnik and opened up in Zagreb in 2010. On sale are the latest collections by top international names across the spectrum of prêt-à-porter collections, including Stella McCartney, Saint Laurent and Alexander Wang. The recently introduced creations of Céline, Chloé and Givenchy fill the window display of the gallery-like, all-white premises. It's not just fancy frocks: ultra-glamorous (and expensive) shoes, bags and belts are here too.

### Natura Croatica
*Predoravićeva 8 (01 48 55 076, www.natura croatica.com).* **Open** 9am-9pm Mon-Fri; 10am-4pm Sat. **Map** p44 D3 ㉜ **Food & drink**
Natura Croatica specialises in local olive oils, jams, soaps, pâtés, vinegars, fruit brandies, liqueurs, sweets, honeys and truffle-based preserves. This is the most central branch of a mini-chain.
**Other locations** throughout the city.

### Što čitaš/Sapunoteka
*Gundulićeva 11 (no phone, www.stocitas.org).* **Open** 10am-8pm Mon-Fri; 10am-2pm Sat. **Map** p44 D3 ㉝ **Soap/books & music**
Hidden away in an off-street courtyard, this is a most unusual and unexpected combination of anarchist bookshop and hand-made soap boutique. Let's begin with the soap, which is made from olive oil and Adriatic herbs by Šibenik-based firm Sapunoteka. It can be bought in big slices priced by weight, or in nicely packaged 100-gram bricks. There's a big choice – particularly recommended are Three Colours White (3 boje bijelo; with aniseed), Not Everything is as Grey as You Think (Nije sve tako sivo; with fennel and lemon) or the excitingly grainy Little Witch (Mala Vještica; poppy seed, clay and lavender). On sale in the anarchist half of the shop are T-shirts with subversive slogans, vinyl singles by anarcho-punk bands, and rabble-rousing books.

## Nightlife

### AKC Medika
*Pierottijeva 11 (no phone, www.pierottijeva11. org).* **Open** According to event. **No credit cards**. **Map** p44 B5.
Still going strong despite the municipal authorities' threat to dramatically raise the rent, this shrine to all things alternative grew out of Zagreb's anarchist movement and is still run as a non-profit-making collective. A courtyard decorated by some of Zagreb's best street artists has a café-bar on one side, a concert venue-cum-club on the other. Events range from anarcho-punk gigs to dub reggae DJs and cutting-edge dance music, with all kinds of other styles thrown in for good measure. Visual arts association Otomptom throw impromptu film evenings with animation and shorts. Popular with a broad spectrum of club-hungry youth, Medika is much more than just a focus for Zagreb's grungy underground culture.

## Boogaloo

*Vukovarska 68 (01 63 13 021, www.facebook.com/ pages/Boogaloo-Zagreb/71567668873).* **Open** varies; usually 8pm-4am. **No credit cards.**

Just 15 minutes' walk south of the train station, this club and live-music venue is housed in a former cinema and cultural centre where Laibach and Einstürzende Neubauten played seminal shows in the mid 1980s. Spacious, with a capacity of 1,500, the varied schedule includes retro parties, house or techno DJs, and international metal acts.

## ★ KSET

*Unska 3 (01 61 29 758, www.kset.org).* **Open** 8pm-midnight Mon-Thur; 8pm-3am Fri, Sat. **No credit cards. Map** p44 C6.

KSET is an excellent, adventurous venue for live music and DJs, with events three or four nights a week. Well worth the hassle of finding, it has actively promoted new bands for decades, an oasis for underground, post-rock, Americana, avant-jazz, punk, rap, ethno and other stylistically diverse artists. With a 400-person capacity, this intimate and friendly space is ideal for catching a band on the cusp of the big time. Drinks are limited to beer, wine and fruit juices, but prices are rock-bottom.

## Pepermint

*Ilica 24 (091 393 9938, www. pepermint-zagreb. com).* **Open** 10pm-6am daily. **No credit cards. Map** p44 D3.

Opening its doors in 2010, Pepermint has been a welcome addition to the growing number of nightspots within staggering distance of the main square. Aimed at the laid-back clubber who wants neither snooty VIP values, nor grungy student surroundings, Pepermint is where to dance, flirt, or simply shout in your mate's ear while watching the action unfold. Minimalist white surfaces and greeny-blue lighting underline the cool minty theme. Expect a mash-up on Wednesdays and Thursdays, and funk on Fridays and Saturdays, when there may be queues at the door and a tight squeeze at the bar. Entry is free till 11pm at weekends, 10pm on Wednesdays and Thursdays, after which there's usually a moderate cover charge.

## Shamballa

*Savska 30 (099 721 7777, www.shamballa.hr).* **Open** 11pm-6pm Sat. **No credit cards. Map** p44 B6.

Multicoloured tiles, lamps, oriental archways and pillars give this relatively new and spacious venue an exotic feel; the rentable VIP lounge tries to posh up the atmosphere. It all feels a little gratuitous but there's no denying the big dance floor and the swirling light show. With Croatian pop and commercial dance music, it's aimed at the younger end of the spectrum – the barkeeps serve Corona, Harp, Croatian wines, and cocktails. You'll find Shamballa beside the Cibona tower, inside the mini shopping mall. The cover charge changes depending on the DJ.

## Sirup

*Koturaška ulica 1 (091 945 0037, sirupclub.com).* **Open** 10pm-4am Thur; 11pm-6am Fri, Sat. **No credit cards. Map** p45 E5.

Sirup is the brainchild of Sergej Lugović, who has 20 years' experience as a clubber, DJ and owner in London, Moscow and Zagreb. The DJs here, domestic and international, attract a healthy mixture of scenesters who know their dance genres, as well as party animals pure and simple. Burlesque nights and live music occasionally squeak their way onto the schedule. Cover charges vary but won't break the bank.

## ★ Tvornica kulture

*Ljudevita Posavskog 1 (01 457 8389, www. tvornicakulture.com).* **Open** *Café* 7am-11pm Mon-Sat. *Club* 11pm-4am Mon-Sat. **No credit cards. Map** p45 H4.

Following a thorough refit in 2011, Tvornica kulture ('The Culture Factory') has lost no time in re-establishing itself as Zagreb's leading medium-sized venue for live rock and pop. The fashionably black, 1,800-capacity main hall (Veliki pogon, or 'Large Workshop') has now been augmented by the addition of a much more intimate Mali pogon ('Small Hall'), which hosts gigs by local bands and disc-spinning after-parties. Mali pogon also works as a café by day. Concerts take place several times a week, with club nights featuring DJs and visuals at weekends. Ticket prices vary depending on who's playing.

## Vintage Industrial Bar

*Savska cesta 160 (01 619 1715, www.vintage industrial-bar.com).* **Open** 10am-2am Mon-Thur; 10am-5am Fri, Sat; 10am-1am Sun. **No credit cards.**

This capacious new music bar occupying a former button factory opened its doors to a deserved media fanfare in 2012. The interior preserves the concrete, exposed brick and metal girders of the original building, but clever lighting and comfortable seating ensures that this is far from being a minimalist, post-industrial experience. The long (indeed, extraordinarily long) bar serves beers from the Ožujsko stable, Leffe in bottles, Erdinger on draught and a full range of Perković rakija. With regular gigs and DJ events in the adjoining hall, it's territory for a proper rock-and-roll night out.

## Hotels

## Arcotel Allegra

*Branimirova 29 (01 46 96 000, www.arcotelhotels. com).* **€€. Map** p45 F5.

Owned by an Austrian chain, this was Zagreb's first designer hotel when it opened in 2003. The marble-clad lobby, with an aquarium and colourful fish, gives access to Joe's Bar and the Mediterranean-themed Radicchio restaurant. The 151 uncluttered rooms come with good soundproofing, pine furniture, funky fabrics with portraits of celebrities

**EXPLORE**

(Kafka, Kahlo and Picasso), and DVD players. Look out for the world map, with a red dot marking Zagreb, on the blue carpets in hallways and rooms. The top floor has a sauna, gym, and good views. It's worth asking about weekend rates, while the hotel is convenient for the city centre, train station and bus station (and therefore the airport).

### Best Western Hotel Astoria

*Petrinjska 71 (01 48 08 900, www.hotelastoria.hr).* €€. **Map** p45 E/F4.

Built in 1932, this hotel sits between the station and the main square. After a thorough makeover, Best Western unveiled it in 2005 as one of its 45 premier properties. The lobby has wood panelling, plush red armchairs and marble floors; it leads to red-carpeted hallways lined by replicas of Croatian masterpieces. Accommodation ranges from smallish twins and queens to more spacious executives, and suites with window-paned sliding doors. The decor leans on a palette of beiges, yellows and creams – and contemporary paintings. There's Wi-Fi too.

### Boutique Hotel No.9

*Avenija Marina Držića 9 (01 562 5040, www.hotel9.hr).* €€.

The exterior of this new hotel at the bus station end of town provides little inkling of what's inside, which is a bit like the hollowed-out interior of a giant wedding cake. The reception and first floor are almost totally white, furniture included, save for the black and white photographs in the rooms. The second 'silver' floor has yet more white, although the chairs and couches are upholstered in silver. The third and final 'gold' floor, done out in black and gold, is the kitschest of the lot, but undeniably sexy. It's by no means overpowering, however, and the excellent buffet, served in the third-floor breakfast room, speaks eloquently of a focus on quality comforts.

### ★ DoubleTree by Hilton

*Ulica grada Vukovara 269A (01 600 1900, www.doubletree.hilton.com/zagreb).* €€.

Rising serenely above Radnička cesta, Zagreb's developing commercial and financial district, the sleek bronze block of the DoubleTree brings a new dimension of contemporary design and comfort to the city's upper-bracket accommodation. All rooms feature a svelte mixture of charcoal, chocolate and ochre; big windows provide plenty of light and a sense of outside bustle. Desk and luggage space is ample, even in the smaller 'standard' doubles. Wi-Fi, and media hubs for playing your gadgets through the hotel TVs and speakers, are standard throughout. Importantly, every room has a bathtub. Another major plus is the top-floor gym and spa centre, with a small pool on one level and a large exercise area just above, plus big wall-to-ceiling windows offering a breathtaking panorama of the city as you pedal or pump. Down on the ground floor are the hotel bar and the Oxbo restaurant (*see p58*).

EXPLORE

Hotel Dubrovnik.

## ★ Esplanade Zagreb

*Mihanovićeva 1 (01 456 6666, www.esplanade.hr).*
**€€€. Map** p45 E5.

Since it opened in 1925 to cater to the wealthy and famous travellers on the Orient Express, the beautiful and opulent Esplanade has accommodated a parade of notable figures including Alfred Hitchcock, Elizabeth Taylor, Orson Welles, Vivien Leigh, Francis Ford Coppola, Queen Elizabeth II, King Alfonso XIII and Louis Armstrong. Fabulous luxury and top-notch service are the name of the game at this Art Nouveau gem beside the train station. After a complete refurbishment, it reopened in 2004. The lobby is a veneered wonder; clocks display the time in six world cities. Stylish guest rooms range in size and configuration, but all come with perks such as heated floors, goose down bedding, mist-free mirrors and fancy toiletries in the marble bathrooms. The chef at Zinfandel's restaurant (see p59) conjures up modern Med cuisine and Croatian traditional dishes, while Le Bistro does the best *štrukli* in town. Relaxation packages are popular: hot stone and chocolate massages in the treatment and sauna rooms for example. There are also deluxe options like a 'bath butler', who'll draw the perfect, bubbled tub. Even the pooch gets in on the act – visiting dogs get a bone, welcome letter and a bed.

## Hotel Antunović

*Zagrebačka avenija 100A (01 20 41 121, www. hotelantunovic.com).* **€€. Map** p44 A5.

The L-shaped business hotel has made a big splash since it opened in 2006 thanks, in part, to its business district location and the top-floor panoramic Vertigo bar. Rooms come with warm colours and smart modern bathrooms while there is a spa with three saunas, pool, whirlpool, facial and body treatments. There's also a restaurant specialising in traditional and Med-style dishes, a self-service restaurant, lobby bar, and conference facilities.

## Hotel Central

*Branimirova 3 (01 48 41 122, www.hotel-central. hr).* **€€. Map** p45 E5.

Just opposite the train station, Central is still the most convenient and cheapest of the decent places to stay if you're coming in by rail. The nondescript five-storey building features a pokey lobby and 76 smallish but clean rooms with en-suite bathrooms (some with showers, some with tubs) and an abundance of unnecessary furniture. For a quieter night, ask for a courtyard-facing room – or sacrifice silence for a room with a view of the station.

## Hotel Dubrovnik

*Gajeva 1 (01 48 63 500/501, www.hotel-dubrovnik. hr).* **€€. Map** p45 E3.

On a corner of the main square, the Dubrovnik is a Zagreb classic. The complex comprises two buildings: the older is a six-storey number from 1929 and has a beautifully spruced-up facade; the younger is a seven-storey, 1980s glass extravaganza. Inside the pair, 258 rooms and eight suites come in different shapes and sizes, but all boast unfussy decor with Old World flair, dark wood and modern trimmings such as Wi-Fi. Rooms in the newer part look onto Gajeva and its cafés; rooms in the older section offer fantastic views of the main square.

## Hotel Palace

*Trg JJ Strossmayera 10 (01 48 99 600, www.palace.hr).* **€€. Map** p45 E4.

This grand and recently renovated Secessionist mansion, the Schlessinger Palace, houses Zagreb's first hotel, opened in 1907. More than a century later, it's still one of the city's most elegant. All 120 rooms – and three suites – are a mix of Art Nouveau decor and contemporary amenities: sturdy dark wood furniture, huge windows, original paintings and spacious bathrooms with tubs. For minimum noise and the best views of Sljeme, book a courtyard-facing room. The ground floor café is decorated with fantastic Habsburg-era frescoes and serves up excellent cheese *štrukli*.

## Sheraton Zagreb Hotel

*Kneza Borne 2 (01 455 3535, www.hotel-sheratonzagreb.com).* **€€. Map** p45 F4.

A true luxury hotel on any scale, the Sheraton has 306 rooms, all with marble bathrooms, well-lit and expansive living spaces, handsome wooden nightstands and desks, and high-speed internet. All in all, it's like a polished version of home – with a turndown service. The lobby flows from the café bar across to the restaurant under cascading glass chandeliers and leather armchairs. There are 17 conferences-rooms, a gym, spa and indoor pool. When you factor in location, service and pampering, it's good value. Even then, weekend specials bring prices down.

## ★ Westin Zagreb

*Kršnjavoga 1 (01 489 2000, hotelwestinzagreb. com).* **€€. Map** p44 C5.

Something of a landmark since it first opened in the 1970s, under the Intercontinental banner, this cool slab has frequently been the top choice for high-end visitors: the Rolling Stones, Sophia Loren and Nick Cave have all graced its halls. In 2005, a €10 million renovation gave the hotel its contemporary feel and current facilities (378 rooms, 13 conference spaces). The rooms come equipped with fog-proof mirrors and marble-effect bathrooms, while the north-facing accommodation has grand views of the Old Town and Sljeme mountain. The 'Heavenly Bed' philosophy prioritises a good night's sleep with deluxe mattresses, pillows and high thread counts. The sparkling, jet-set fitness and beauty centre contains Turkish and Finnish saunas, cutting-edge Nautilus equipment, and offers massage treatments, pedicures, manicures and facials. The 17-metre pool is surrounded by wooden lounge chairs and is bathed in an ethereal blue light.

**EXPLORE**

Mirogoj.

## FURTHER AFIELD

Across the Sava river spread the suburbs of **Novi Zagreb**, Socialist-era housing blocks without the charm of the city's Habsburg hub. Traffic whizzes down multi-laned boulevards, like **Vukovarska**, where Orson Welles filmed his version of Kafka's *The Trial* in 1962. With downtown gridlocked almost all day, city authorities are encouraging businesses to set up here and residents to relocate, most notably with the long-awaited opening of the **Museum of Contemporary Art**. Along with the **National Library** and the prestigious **Lisinski Concert Hall** on this side of the river, a multiplex cinema is soon expected.

Elsewhere, three main attractions are accessible on public transport from the city centre. **Jarun** is a recreational lake by the Sava, on tram route number 17, south-west of Jelačić. Built for the World Student Games in 1987, it's a haven for cyclists and rowers. It also houses several nightclubs, including the landmark **Aquarius** (*see p68*). Another easy tram hop is to **Maksimir**, the city's main park, with public gardens, the zoo and, across the main road, the national football stadium, home of **Dinamo Zagreb** (gnkdinamo.hr). North-east of the city, the beautiful tree-lined cemetery of **Mirogoj** (open dawn-sunset daily), designed by Herman Bollé, is filled with ivy-strewn cupolas and pavilions. The motley gravestones include five-pointed stars, Cyrillic inscriptions, Stars of David and Islamic crescent moons, illustrating Croatia's ethnic tapestry. Works by renowned Croatian sculptors line the neo-Renaissance arcades. From the cathedral, take bus no.106.

### Maksimir Park & Zoo

*Maksimirski perivoj (01 23 02 198, www.zoo.hr)*. **Open Park** 24hrs daily. **Zoo** *May-Aug* 9am-8pm daily; *Apr, Sept* 9am-7pm daily; *Mar, Oct* 9am-6pm daily; *Jan, Feb, Nov, Dec* 9am-4pm daily. **Admission** *Park* free. *Zoo* 30kn; 20kn reductions. **No credit cards.**

A ten-minute tram ride east of the centre, 18 hectares (45 acres) of green were opened to the public in 1794, with what was termed English landscaping of woods, meadows and lakes. At the far eastern end is the zoo with a modest collection of creatures and daily feeding times for seals, sea lions and otters. Opposite stands Croatia's main football stadium and home of Dinamo Zagreb, also called the Maksimir.

### FREE ★ Mirogoj

*Mirogoj 10 (01 469 6700, www.gradskagroblja.hr)*. **Open** *Apr-Sept* 6am-8pm daily. *Oct-Mar* 7.30am-6pm daily. **Admission** free. **No credit cards.**

It's a pity more don't make it to this attractive cemetery as Mirogoj is widely regarded as one of the city's architectural gems. Behind a series of green, onion-shaped cupolas, capping ivy-covered brick

walls, are tiled arcades, monuments to Croatia's most prominent citizens and the final resting place of 300,000 souls of various religious backgrounds. Stejepan Radić, who was shot in the Yugoslav parliament in 1928, is buried here. So are Croatian literary giants Petar Preradović and Tin Ujević. Designed by Hermann Bollé of Cathedral fame, Mirogoj opened in 1876. As the rolling landscape continues to gain residents, it also gathers more museum-worthy sculptures, headstones and memorials; renowned 20th-century Croatian sculptors Ivan Meštrović and Ivan Rendić are responsible for some of them. Of special note is the modern, black marble monument for Franjo Tudjman, worthy of an independent nation's first president. The grave of basketball legend Dražen Petrović, who died in a car accident at 28, is one of the most visited. Mirogoj scintillates on All Souls' Day (November 1) when Croatian families equipped with thousands of flickering candles visit loved ones who have passed – a moving experience.

### ★ Museum of Contemporary Art
*Avenija Dubrovnik 17 (01 605 2 700, www.msu. hr).* **Open** 11am-6pm Tue-Fri, Sun; 11am-8pm Sat. **Admission** 30kn; 15kn reductions.
Costing some €60 million and covering 14,500 square metres, the MCA (MSU in Croatian) is the most significant museum to open in Zagreb for more than a century. Its collection includes some pieces from the 1920s and others gathered since 1954 when Zagreb's

original MCA, in Upper Town, was founded. Of particular note are Carsten Höller's slides, similar to the *Test Site* installation he built for Tate Modern's Turbine Hall in 2006 but custom-made and site-specific for Zagreb – pieces of art patrons can ride to the parking lot. Croatia's outstanding 1950s generation of abstract-geometric artists (Ivan Picelj, Aleksandar Srnec, Vjenceslav Richter, Vlado Kristl) play a starring role, alongside photographs and films documenting the more outlandish antics of legendary performance artists like Tom Gotovac and Vlasta Delimir. The new-media and computer art works produced by the Zagreb-based New Tendencies movement in the late 1960s and early 1970s show just how ahead of its time much of Croatian art really was. *Photos p68.*

## Cafés & Bars

### Spunk
*Hrvatske bratske zajednice (01 61 51 528).* **Open** 7am-1am Mon-Fri; noon-4am Sat; 6pm-1am Sun.
This leading music bar and student hangout has expanded into the next-door room. Located under the gleaming, glass and steel National University Library (NSK), it's a coffee bar for students during the day, and an alternative music bar serving discerning bohos by night. The interior features comic book murals by Igor Hofbauer and twinkling ceiling panels that look like the sky at night. Indie and cover bands occasionally squeeze into the corner.

EXPLORE

## Nightlife

### Aquarius
*Aleja Matije Ljubeka (01 36 40 231, www. aquarius.hr).* **Open** *Café* 9am-9pm daily. *Club* 10pm-6am daily. **No credit cards**.
The one club on the Jarun lakeside to operate 12 months a year, Aquarius covers two floors, has a capacity of 2,000, and has been open since 1992 but it's still ahead of the field. This is thanks to its commitment to mixing danceable beats and innovative DJ styles, augmented by regular live acts. Big-name DJs help achieve the former; international rock and world music combos dominate the latter. The two floors, Aquarius 1 and 2, offer different sounds but do occasionally come together. Friday might feature anything from Goa Trance to R&B while Saturday usually sees an eclectic journey through cutting-edge house and electro (presided over by chief resident DJ Martyn Negro). Entrance fees vary depending on the DJ – check website for details.

### Gallery
*Matije Ljubeka (099 444 2444, www.gallery.hr).* **Open** *late Mar-Oct* 11pm-6am Fri, Sat.
One of the snazziest clubs by Lake Jarun – or indeed in Zagreb – Gallery has hosted DJs such as Ian Pooley, David Guetta and Martin Solveig. The interior is funky-chic and filled with chandeliers and candelabras. Doormen keep a tight control on numbers and enforce a dress code (no trainers or jogging suits, please). Once you pass the face test, you get to rub shoulders with local bling, actors, sports stars and the odd random hipster. Fridays are devoted to hip hop and R&B, Saturdays are for house.

### ★ Močvara
*Trnjanski nasip (01 61 59 667, www.mochvara.hr).* **Open** 8pm-1am Mon-Thur, Sun; 8pm-4am Fri, Sat. **No credit cards**.
This legendary venue has hosted innumerable international names (the Buzzcocks, Jonathan Richman, Mogwai) alongside virtually anybody that matters on the domestic musical scene. It's where young alternatives gather for underground fun and a wide variety of live acts. Set on the banks of the Sava, it holds about 600 people in an abandoned factory imaginatively muralled by graphic artist Igor Hofbauer. The programme ranges from live punk, metal, world and ethno music to retro DJ nights, Goth parties, alternative theatre and mind-bending, one-night art exhibitions. Močvara means 'The Swamp'.
▶ *In the same factory complex, Pogon Jedinstvo (01 46 82 463, www.upogoni.org) has a larger concert hall for alt-rock acts.*

## OUTSIDE ZAGREB

The forested slopes of Mount Medvednica beckon nature lovers for a hike, or a cable car ride above the trees to the highest peak of Sljeme. More than half of **Medvednica** ('Bear Mountain'), is covered in trees – forests of beech, oak, fir and maple –with extensive flora that includes 14 endemic and 93 endangered plant species. In spring and autumn, the area is at its most beautiful with colourful flowers, from saffron to dog-tooth violets, and clear crisp horizons.

**Sljeme** (www.sljeme.hr) offers stellar vistas of Zagreb and the Zagorje countryside. This is where four-time Olympic champion Janica Kostelić learned to ski. Thanks to her success, Sljeme has been developed into a ski centre of international standard. It can be reached by one of the many well-marked paths leading up from the foothills of Medvednica. At time of writing, the cable car from **Gračanski Bliznec** was still under repair.

## GETTING THERE & AROUND

Zagreb's **Pleso airport** is 17km (ten miles) southeast of the city centre. **Airport buses** (30mins journey time, 30kn) run to Zagreb bus station every half hour from 7am-8pm daily, then after each flight arrival. From the bus station to the airport, buses run every half hour, 4.30-9am

Mon-Fri (from 4am Sat, Sun), at 10am, 11am, then every half hour until 8pm. A taxi should cost around 250kn.

Zagreb's main **train station**, Glavni kolodvor, is at the southern fringe of the Lower Town, connected by trams numbers 6 and 13 with the main square of Jelačić, 15 minutes' walk away. **Bus** services from the airport arrive at the station on Avenija Marina Držića (on the no.6 and no.2 tram lines). Website www.akz.hr gives details of the many inter-city bus routes; in Croatia buses are far more frequent than trains.

Zagreb itself runs by **tram**. Some 16 routes cross the city, most passing through the main square of Jelačić. The ticket system operated by local transport authority ZET (www.zet.hr) consists of pre-paid charge cards (30kn) and traditional paper tickets (10kn). Both are available from newsstands; you simply add the amount you're likely to need to the charge card, for which individual journeys are much cheaper. Bleep the charge card, or stamp the paper ticket, when you board. Your journey is then valid for 90 minutes if travelling in one direction. A day ticket is 30kn, a three-day pass 70kn, a seven-day 150kn. There is also a four-line network of night trams (15kn per journey). Tariffs and network maps can be found on the ZET website. City buses serve outlying areas. Ticket tariffs are the same.

**Taxis** can be found at railway stations and around Trg bana Josipa Jelačića. Radio Taksi Zagreb (1717, 1777, www.radio-taksi-zagreb.hr) charges a 10kn starting fee, 6kn/km in transit, and waiting time of 40kn/hr.

## RESOURCES

**Hospital** *Šalata 2 (94)*.

**Internet** *Sublink Internet Centar, Teslina 12 (01 48 19 993, www.sublink.hr)*. **Open** 9am-10pm Mon-Sat; 3-10pm Sun.

**Police** *Petrinjska 30 (92)*.

**Post office** *Branimirova 4 (01 48 40 340)*. **Open** 24hrs Mon-Sat; 1pm-midnight Sun.

**Tourist information** *Zagreb tourist office, Trg bana Jelačića 11 (01 48 14 051, www.zagreb-touristinfo.hr)*. **Open** *Summer* 8.30am-9pm Mon-Fri; 9am-6pm. *Winter* 8.30am-8pm Mon-Fri; 9am-6pm Sun. **Map** p45 E3.

**Museum of Contemporary Art.**
*See p67.*

EXPLORE

# Istria

EXPLORE

Istria feels separate from the rest of Croatia. Christened 'Terra Magica' by the Romans, this small, triangular peninsula was part of Italy until after World War II. Istria has its own, celebrated gastronomy, wines and olive oils. Nothing is ever too far away, and interior is every bit as beautiful as the coast. Remnants of Istria's Roman, Byzantine and Habsburg past can be found in its churches, sites and museums. You can spend the day at the coastal resorts of Rovinj, Poreč or Novigrad and dine luxuriously in the main town of Pula, home to some excellent restaurants. North-east, towards the Slovenian border, is a small hub of quality Istrian restaurants and spa retreats. Inland is dotted with timeless hilltop villages like Grožnjan, Motovun or Hum, and restaurants that Italians cross the border to savour. On the wilder, less-developed east coast, Rabac has seen a number of recent, family-friendly or boutique hotel openings. Oddities such as Tito's surreal island menagerie of Brijuni make a longer stay in Istria a varied and attractive proposition.

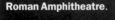

Roman Amphitheatre.

## Don't Miss

**1** **Roman Amphitheatre** One of the Empire's biggest, now used for the Pula Film Festival (p72).

**2** **Euphrasian Basilica** The wonders of Byzantine art in Poreč (p86).

**3** **Batana House** Maritime history at Rovinj (p81).

**4** **Gallerion Naval Museum** In Novigrad, learn how the Habsburgs ruled the Adriatic (p91).

**5** **Motovun** Top views from medieval walls (p95).

# Pula

Pula is as urban as Istria gets. It is indisputably the region's commercial centre, and is home to almost half its population. For shopping, culture or arrival by air, Pula is the place. The city's growing status as a happening focus of the arts has been enhanced thanks to two recently opened exhibition spaces: the spectacularly renovated former church of **Sveta Srca**; and the ramshackle but promising **Museum of Contemporary Art of Istria**. The **Pula Film Festival** in July continues to be the biggest show in town, although the city has been catapulted into the music festival premier league with the recent appearance of two major four-day events: **Outlook** in late August (big names in dubstep and reggae) and **Dimensions** in September (the same but with some more cutting-edge DJs).

What the town lacks in terms of attractive waterfront it more than makes up for in terms of antiquities. The original **Roman Forum** remains the major meeting point with cafés offering outdoor tables. Pula's impressive **Roman amphitheatre**, or Arena, hosts events all summer (both the Pula Film Festival and a season of mainstream concerts). The city's sprawling waterfront includes a port handling close to one million tons of cargo every year, a marina for yachters, a forested stretch of beach with a promenade and, outside the centre, resorts, built in the 1960s and 1970s in **Verudela** and neighbouring **Medulin**.

### INTRODUCING PULA

Pula became a Roman colony a century after they first arrived in 177 BC. It produced wine and olive oil, and by the time of Augustus from 63 BC, 'Pietas Iulia' was a thriving urban centre with a forum, temples and city walls. Between Augustus and the Austrians, Pula diminished to a minor port of a few hundred citizens. The Habsburgs made 'Pola' their naval hub and centre for shipbuilding at the end of the 19th century. After passing into Italian hands, Pula was heavily bombed by the Allies in World War II, then reindustrialised under Tito. Package tourism came in the 1970s. Main hub of an economically booming region, Pula is a rare thing: a coastal town where life goes on in winter.

The must-see attraction is, of course, Pula's **amphitheatre** (Flavijevska, 052 219 028; open summer 8am-7pm daily, winter 9am-5pm daily; 20kn). A short walk north of the city centre, its outer walls are remarkably preserved, and a wonderful backdrop for concerts staged here. Inside in some places is a bit of a mess of green plastic seating and clumps of stone; the view at the top of the sloping interior is a disappointing one of the harbour and crane after crane. But you do get a sense of the gladiatorial contests held

here until AD 400, particularly when you go down to the corridors on the sea-facing side where the lions were kept. Through a long tunnel lined with Roman masonry, you'll now find displays about olive oil production and a detailed map of Via Flavia, which connected Pula with Trieste.

The second of the Roman attractions stands at the south-east entrance to the town centre. The **Arch of the Sergians**, or **Golden Gate**, was built in 30 BC. Its most notable aspects are the reliefs of grapes and winged victories on the inner façade. Passing through the arch and past the statue of James Joyce, marking where the author taught in 1904-05, you walk down the Roman-era high street, Sergijevaca. It leads to the heart of Pula, the Roman Forum, **Temple of Augustus** and nearby mosaic. The Forum, still the main square, is today lined with cafés, the town hall, tourist office and, lining the far side, the six classical Corinthian columns of the Temple of Augustus. Inside is a modest collection of Roman finds (052 218 689; open summer only 9am-3pm daily; 10kn). The floor mosaic, hidden away behind a car park, dates to the second century AD and has geometric motifs plus a depiction of the Punishment of Dirce from *Antiope* by Euripides.

Uphill from the Forum is the **Kaštel** (fortress), built by the Venetians in the 17th century and now housing the **Istrian Historical Museum** (Gradinski uspon 6, 052 211 566; open summer 8am-8pm daily, winter 9am-5pm daily; 20kn). Back downhill towards the amphitheatre is the worthwhile **Archaeological Museum of Istria**. Anything else of interest lies south of the city centre, on or off the main Veruda road leading to the hotel hub and best beaches of Verudela. Halfway to the two nearest beaches, at Stoja and Valsaline, is the ornate, verdant **Naval Cemetery**, built by the Habsburgs, the perfect spot for a stroll on a hot summer's afternoon. Nearer town, on Gajeva, parallel to the sea and the main road of Arsenalska, stands another military remnant, the **Društveni Centar Rojc** (rojcnet.pula.org), a former barracks. This has been transformed into a centre for alternative organisations and artists' studios, with sporadic exhibitions, DJ nights and live concerts.

## Sights & Museums

### Archaeological Museum of Istria

*Carrarina 3 (052 351 300, www.ami-pula.hr).*
**Open** *Summer* 9am-8pm Mon-Sat; 10am-3pm Sun. *Winter* 9am-3pm Mon-Fri. **Admission** 40kn; 20kn reductions; free under-5s. **No credit cards. Map** p75 B4 ❶
Local Illyrian and Roman finds are on display here, a three-storey museum with English-language information. You'll find both medieval and Roman jewellery, coins and weapons, also ceramics and fossils from prehistory, plus mosaics and sarcophagi.

EXPLORE

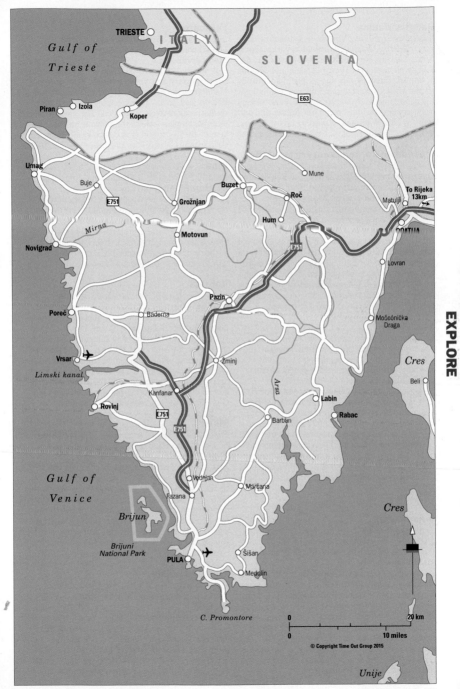

© Copyright Time Out Group 2015

### Galerija Makina

*Kapitolinski trg 1 (no phone, hr-hr.facebook.com/ pages/Galerija-Makina).* **Admission** varies. **Open** 6-9pm Tue-Sun. **No credit cards. Map** p75 A4 ❷
Run by photographer Hassan Abdelghani, Makina is one of Croatia's top spaces for photography shows, with a year-round calendar of exhibitions. Big names frequently feature in the summer season (such as works by film director Ken Russell and portraits by Nick Wall), and on opening nights Makina becomes a meeting point for Istria's cultural cream.

### Museum of Contemporary Art of Istria

*Sv Ivana 1 (052 423 205, www.msu-istre.hr/home).* **Open** *Summer* 11am-2pm, 5-9pm Tue-Sun. *Winter* 11am-7pm Tue-Sun. **Admission** 10kn; free under-7s. **No credit cards. Map** p75 B2 ❸
Very much an embryonic institution, the MSUI doesn't yet have a permanent collection on display but it does mount superb exhibitions by current artists in the cavernous, crumbling halls of an old printing house, midway between the amphitheatre and the Old Town. Be sure to ask about the bizarre, cocoon-like sellotape installation on the building's top floor, designed by Zagreb-based Numen/For Use in September 2010 and left in situ – it's not always open to visitors but can be viewed on request.

### Sveta Srca

*De Villeov uspon 8 (no phone, www.ami-pula.hr/ dislocirane-zbirke/sveta-srca).* **Open** *Summer* 11am-2pm, 5-9pm Tue-Sun. *Winter* 11am-7pm Tue-Sun. **Admission** varies. **No credit cards. Map** p75 B3/4 ❹
Built for the Jesuits in 1908 but used as a warehouse after World War II, the Church of the Sacred Heart was renovated in 2010-11 to become one of Croatia's most spectacular and prestigious exhibition spaces for high-profile, temporary shows. Now run by the Archaeological Museum of Istria, the stunning light-filled interior plays host to a rich menu of special-interest history exhibitions, contemporary art installations and other cultural events.

## Restaurants

### ★ Amfiteatar

*Amfiteatarska (052 375 600, www.hotelamfiteatar. com).* **Open** *Summer* 11am-midnight daily. *Winter* 7am-10pm daily. €€. **Map** p75 B3 ❺
**Mediterranean/Istrian**
With culinary star Deniz Zembo (chef-patron at Le Mandrać in Volosko, *see p118*) overseeing the menu, this venture aims to deliver traditional Med-Istrian cooking at affordable prices, with contemporary panache. The interior is certainly a statement: furniture, tablecloths and napkins all come from the 'any-colour-as-long-as-it's-matt-black' design school. The daily three-course menus are a steal while the à la carte has lots of pasta, risotto and mid-price pork and chicken. Desserts are first class.

### Farabuto

*Sisplac 15 (052 386 074, www.farabuto.hr).* **Open** noon-11pm daily. €€. **Map** p75 A5 ❻
**Mediterranean**
Out in the southern reaches, in a residential street not far from Valkane beach, Farabuto does Mediterranean maritime fare with modern flair. Risotto and pasta dishes employ the best ingredients, imaginatively combined. There's a strong seasonal element – check the daily menus for a true taste of freshly caught seafood and locally gathered delicacies. Equal care goes into desserts.

### Gina

*Stoja 23 (052 387 943).* **Open** noon-11pm daily. €€. **Map** p75 A5 ❼ **Istrian**
Stone walls, polished wood and a fireplace create a cosy space for a family-run restaurant where food and guests get special attention. Along with fish and meat, the Istrian-style menu features seafood-pasta combinations like ravioli stuffed with crab. Pasta and bread are home-made, there's a qualified sommelier and the wine list features about 60 mostly local choices.

### Kantina

*Flanatička 16 (052 214 054).* **Open** 8am-11pm daily. €€. **Map** p75 C5 ❽ **Istrian**
Hidden behind the main market, this lovely terrace restaurant serves Istrian delicacies in a converted Habsburg villa. The decor is contemporary, as is the careful presentation of the food. Truffles feature heavily, either with steak or, more traditionally, with *fuži* (Istrian pasta twists). There are plenty of greens and some 40 types of wine, and the cake selection is outstanding. A small coffee bar serves toasted sandwiches and filled baguettes if you're in a rush.

### Milan

*Stoja 4 (052 300 200, www.milan1967.hr).* **Open** *Summer* 11am-11pm daily. *Winter* 11am-11pm Mon-Sat. €€. **Map** p75 A5 ❾ **Croatian**
Traditionally considered one of the top eateries in town, Milan is set in a modern, family-run hotel by the Naval Cemetery. A display case heaves with riches fresh from the sea, duly listed on a extensive menu – most dishes are reasonably priced considering the quality. Shellfish comes in all types; frogs' legs with polenta is a speciality. For wine, you're spoiled for choice as the cellar has 700 bins, topping out at 1,000kn a bottle. Let the waiter advise.

### Ribarska Koliba

*Verudela 16 (052 222 966, www.ribarskakoliba. com).* **Open** noon-11pm daily. €€. **Map** p75 A5 ❿
**Seafood**
A favourite destination for seafood fans for over 100 years, the 'Fisherman's Hut' was revamped in 2013. It has gone upmarket without losing its reputation for traditional, affordable dishes. Fresh fish and shellfish are the main draws, with tables by one of Pula's main marinas. There's a brand new accommodation

bloc next to the restaurant with well-appointed apartments, most overlooking the yachting berths.

## Vela Nera

*Franja Mošnje 3b, Šišan (052 300 621, www. velanera.hr/en/restaurant-bar).* **Open** 11am-10pm daily. **€€. Seafood-Istrian**

One of the legendary names of Pula gastronomy, the Černul family's Vela Nera moved from its suburban marina spot to the nearby village of Šišan a couple of years ago. It still aims for the culinary highs, with local seafood and countryside dishes served with aplomb in a smart, renovated farmhouse-style environment. The Černuls are known for mixing traditional classics with imaginative signature dishes of their own – try the risotto with scampi and peaches, or the stewed sea bass with black olives.

## Vodnjanka

*D Vitezića 4 (052 210 655).* **Open** *Summer* noon-10pm Mon-Sat. *Winter* noon-5pm Mon-Sat. **No credit cards. €€.** Map p75 B5 ⑪ **Istrian**

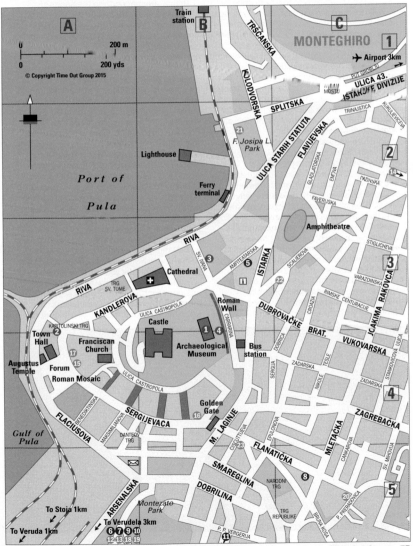

**EXPLORE**

EXPLORE

# TITO'S XANADU

*Brijuni provided a home from home to politicians and tycoons.*

The Brijuni archipelago (www.brijuni.hr) lies off Istria's west coast, a 15-minute boat journey from Fažana, just north of Pula. Most of the 14 islands are off limits to the public. Luckily, there is so much to see on the other two that you're unlikely to feel hard done by.

Veliki Brijuni is the largest and home to most of the treasures. Beautiful and vaguely surreal – English country estate meets Jurassic Park – it consists of well-maintained, green parkland surrounded by the dazzling Adriatic and planted with avenues of prehistoric-looking pines. This is where you'll find a golf course, bird sanctuary, botanical gardens, zoo and safari park, three museums and the main archaeological sites. A map of the islands is posted at its harbour – including details of where to find the dinosaur footprints that dot the shoreline.

Brijuni had to wait until 1893 to be rescued from malaria-infested stupor. It was bought then by Austrian steel magnate Paul Kupelwieser. His dream was to create an English-style country park, and renowned microbiologist Robert Koch was his facilitator. In 1900 Koch was about to begin experiments into the eradication of malaria in Tuscany. The Austrian read about this in the newspapers and contacted Koch, suggesting he carry out his preliminary research on Brijuni. It was a stroke of genius – and an unqualified success. In 1905 Koch was awarded the Nobel Prize for medicine. (He had also succeeded in isolating the cholera and tuberculosis bacteria.) A carved monument erected in his honour stands by the harbour in Veliki Brijuni.

Kupelwieser excavated the archaeological treasures. He built villas, planted trees, landscaped gardens, built the golf course and even established a zoo. He had, in fact, created his own Xanadu, but he died in 1918.

Brijuni later passed into the hands of Mussolini's Italy. After World War II the Brijuni archipelago, along with the rest of Istria, became part of Tito's Yugoslavia. The Yugoslav leader used Brijuni as his base, conducting diplomacy with the Non-Aligned Movement and inviting the world's rich and famous to his idyllic playground. As you step onto Veliki Brijuni's quayside you are following in the footsteps of Haile Selassie, Queen Elizabeth II, JFK, Sophia Loren – anyone who was anyone in the 1960s. You can see them documented in the 'Josip Broz Tito On Brijuni' exhibition housed in the main museum. Another exhibition, 'From The Memory Of An Old Austrian', celebrates the vision and achievements of Kupelwieser.

Tito was regularly presented with exotic animals. As a result, the zoo grew. You can still see many of the beasts, including Indira Gandhi's elephants Sony and Lanka. Those who died were stuffed and placed in Brijuni's Natural History Museum, part of a three-museum complex near the harbour. There's a Tito exhibition next door.

The Brijuni National Park offices are on the quayside at Fažana: you can book excursions, plus yachting, golf and diving expeditions. Independent travellers can hire a bike or electric buggy. Seaside villa lodgings can be arranged via 052 521 367, www.brijuni.hr.

This family-run restaurant is off the main drag, close to the Rojc arts centre. The food is excellent, based on traditional Istrian cuisine with lots of fish and game. The must-try is the house aperitif: three herbal brandies, layered in a single glass, topped off by an ice lid with a hole in the middle.

## Cafés & Bars

### Bass

*Širolina 3 (099 831 9051).* **Open** *Summer* 8am-midnight Mon-Thur; 8am-1am Fri, Sat; 10am-midnight Sun. **No credit cards. Map** 75 A5 ⑫
A great bar set between town and Verudela, Bass has a slew of beers, reasonably priced cocktails, sangria and rakija brandies. On the huge terrace are wooden benches aplenty, plus wicker, teardrop-shaped chairs. Wi-Fi is free; DJs play funky rock on Fridays.

### Bunarina

*Verudela 9 (052 222 978).* **Open** *Summer* 9am-midnight daily. *Winter* 9am- 9pm daily. **No credit cards. Map** p75 A5 ⑬
This local fishermen's bar is sited on the jetty of Bunarina. In high season, tables cover every square inch as customers watch the boats or wait for a ferry to Fratarski island. Food is served in season.

### Caffè Bar Nautika

*Valturska 78 (052 502 125, www.facebook.com/ CaffeBarNautica).* **Open** 6.30am-10pm Mon-Fri; 7am-10pm Sat; 8am-10pm Sun. **No credit cards. Map** p75 C2 ⑭
Locals come to this car-free promenade to check out who's wearing what, and to woo potential partners. Coffee and stronger liquids are served on a terrace under big yellow umbrellas. Inside the bar, above a stone-stacked wall, is a flatscreen TV for football.

### Caffè Diana

*Forum 4 (052 214 779).* **Open** 7am-11pm daily. **No credit cards. Map** p75 A4 ⑮
Opened in 1973, Diana is the classic caffè on the Forum looking directly at the town hall and the Temple of Augustus. The interior has tasteful wood and marble, while the terrace features big white sun umbrellas. Close to the tourist office, it's a good spot to pull out your map and plan the day.

### Caffè Uliks

*Trg Portarata 1 (052 219 158).* **Open** 6.30am-midnight Mon-Fri; 7am-2am Sat; 9am-11pm. **No credit cards. Map** p75 B4 ⑯
The statue outside gives it away. A century ago James Joyce taught here, by the Roman arch. He and his eloper are also honoured with cocktails called a Joyce (Jameson, Martini Bianco and pear liqueur) and a Nora (Baileys, Bacardi and cream). There is bottled Guinness and Kilkenny ale, and Irish coffee too in this altogether rather charming bar.

### Cvajner

*Forum 2 (052 216 502).* **Open** 8am-11pm daily. **No credit cards. Map** p75 A4 ⑰
Or to give it its official title, the Kunstkafe-Cvajner. Either way, it's a splendid bar for the main square of the Roman town centre. Part gallery, part junk shop, the Cvajner is bohemian in appearance but so gratuitously so – non-matching furniture, sculptures and an old carriage are placed around a spacious, high-ceilinged interior. Bottles of Chimay and dark Laško beer complement the standard cocktails, best taken on the Forum terrace.

### ★ E&D

*Verudela 22 (052 213 404, www.eanddlounge. com).* **Open** *Summer* 9am-2am daily. *Winter* 9am-midnight daily. **No credit cards. Map** p75 A5 ⑱
Here you sit in a sculpted hilltop garden, with a small pool and several levels of terrace seating, enjoying fine views of the sea below while sipping cocktails at sunset or coffee in the morning. Above the Lungomare promenade, this stunning café fills up from happy hour onward. In summer, there's a full seafood menu at reasonable prices; DJs spin lounge and dance music on summer evenings. You get here by taxi but it's worth the fare.

### Face

*Širolina 4 (no phone).* **Open** 9am-midnight daily. **No credit cards. Map** p75 A5 ⑲
Long considered one of Pula's best venues for a laid-back evening, with decent and often Latin music, the old Cabahia was gutted by fire in 2009 and has taken a while to get back to its old self. Situated directly opposite Bass (*see above*), the newly named Face looks broadly similar, with a large, almost barn-sized conservatory around a cosy inner sanctum displaying wall hangings made from Brazilian coffee bags. The coffee is indeed a major attraction; there's also a good choice of bottled beers and long drinks.

### P14

*Preradovićeva 14 (052 382 987).* **Open** 7.30am-midnight daily. **No credit cards. Map** p75 C5 ⑳
Jožo Ćurković's alternative haunt at the far end of Flanatička attracts an arty clientele for DJ evenings and one-off literary events. Centrepieced by a snake-shaped bar table, decorated with mushrooms and a lit-up globe, P14 is a spot like no other downtown bar. Dark Laško beer on draught and Istrian spirits flow for visitors and friendly regulars.

### Pietas Julia

*Riva 20 (091 181 1911, www.pietasjulia.com).* **Open** 8am-midnight Mon-Thur, Sun; 8am-4am Fri, Sat. **No credit cards. Map** p75 B2 ㉑
This large, makeshift pavilion – in a stretch of seaside park – serves as pizzeria by day, a bar in the evening, and a clubby DJ bar on Friday and Saturday nights. With two bar areas, a large alcove with sofas,

**EXPLORE**

and plenty of standing and dancing room, it's the most spacious of central Pula's drinking dens. Its location at the amphitheatre end of town means it's also a great place for coffee breaks during the day.

### Rock Caffe

*Scalierova 8 (052 210 975)*. **Open** *Summer* 8am-2am daily. **No credit cards. Map** p175 C3 ㉒ Elvis, Boston, prog and metal classics rock the speakers of this two-decade-old institution, a large two-room bar near the amphitheatre. The interior has dark wood, old posters, music memorabilia and murals featuring subjects like Jim Morrison. A boisterous young, local crowd neck bottled beer, shoot pool, cruise the long bar or roomy booths, and sometimes dance. There is live music three or four nights a week with jazz, blues and rock, mostly from Croatian cover bands; Saturdays offer acoustic sessions. Find it on Facebook by searching for 'Rock Caffe Pula'.

### Scandal Express

*Ciscuttijeva 15 (052 212 106)*. **Open** 8am-2pm, 6pm-2am daily. **No credit cards. Map** p75 B4 ㉓ A tiny, smoky dive where local bohemians meet, this place is near the theatre at the Giardini end of Flanatička. There's no room around the bar at all; regulars hug the corners by the entrance or spill out to the narrow street.

## Nightlife

For mainstream clubbing, arrange for the taxi driver to head north-east of the centre. The best venue there is **Aruba** (Šijanska cesta 1, www.arubaclub-pula.com), with a bar outdoors and crowded two-room disco inside. The **Zen Club** (Dukičeva 1, 052 535 468) is similarly funky if quite mainstream, although admission is free.

Heading south of the centre towards the hotel zone of the Verudela peninsula, the summer-only beach bar and restaurant **Ambrela** (052 215 585, www.arenaturist.com/Hotels/Brioni) invites DJs to thump out house, hip hop and techno while punters enjoy the terrace view over a stony beach. **Club Uljanik** (Dobrilina 2, 098 285 969, www.clubuljanik.hr) in the city centre has been going since the 1960s and still boasts a strong year-round roster of alternative bands and DJ nights, and it opens up a big outdoor terrace in summer. Indie gigs and alternative club nights also take place in the basement of the **Društveni Centar Rojc** arts venue (rojcnet.pula.org), although you should check the schedule before making tracks.

Habsburg-era naval forts count among Pula's most compelling nightlife destinations: **Fort Bourguignon** near Valsaline Bay hosts regular summer DJ events while **Fort Punta Christo**, north along the coast, is the site of the **Outlook** (www.outlookfestival.com), **Dimensions** (www.dimensionsfestival.com) and **Seasplash** (www.seasplash-festival.com) festivals.

## Hotels

### Hostel Pipištrelo

*Flaciusova 6 (052 393 568, www.pipistrelo.com)*. **No credit cards. €. Map** 75 A4. The bright greens and purples of the lobby provide an attention-grabbing introduction to this highly individual 'art hostel', squeezed into a four-storey building on Pula's waterfront. Local designers Noel Mirković, Saša Ergotić, Oleg Morović and Robert Zajc each put their creative energies into the interiors. There's a mix of private doubles and multi-bed dorms, each with a different layout and theme: 'Comic' is a double decorated with pages torn from cartoon books for example, while 'Music' is a seven-bunk dorm with mosaics of album covers. There are only seven rooms and dorms altogether, so book ahead in high season.

### Hotel Amfiteatar

*Amfiteatarska 6 (052 375 600, www. hotelamfiteatar.com)*. **€. Map** p75 B3. The Amfiteatar offers smart, thoughtfully designed rooms in an informal pension-style environment. Only metres away from its Colosseum-like namesake, both the hotel and its highly regarded restaurant succeed in delivering high levels of style and quality at an accessible price. Rooms are reasonably spacious, decked out in slick but soothing shades of grey, green and yellow; bathrooms are modern and in most cases have full-sized tubs as well as showers. Flatscreen TVs and lounge-like furnishings strike a contemporary note. Wi-Fi or cable internet is free.

### Hotel Milan

*Stoja 4 (052 300 200, www.milan1967.hr)*. **€. Map** p75 A5. By the Naval Cemetery, before you get to the Stoja headland, the Milan is best known for its restaurant (*see p74*). Its dozen rooms are clean and comfortable however, and it's within easy reach of the modest beach at Valkane Bay.

### Hotel Omir

*Sergija Dobrića 6 (052 213 944, www.hotel-omir. com)*. **€. Map** p75 B/C4. A handy cheapie in the town centre, this is a socialist era-style guesthouse with old furnishings and light fittings, and a wonderfully weird breakfast room with art and an aquarium. It has 19 quiet rooms and a pizzeria downstairs.

▶ *If you can't get in here, try the ten-room Galija round the corner (Epulanova 3, 052 383 802, www.hotelgalija.hr).*

### Hotel Riviera

*Splitska 1 (052 211 166, www.arenaturist.com/ croatia_hotels/hotel_riviera)*. **€. Map** p75 B2. Classic old Habsburg hotel whose grand façade and marble lobby belie the fact that its 65 rooms are in desperate need of renovation. The hotel is run by the Arenaturist hotel group but the building is owned by the Croatian defence ministry. Neither can decide on refurbishments so, for now, the Riviera remains a charmingly down-at-heel blast from the past.

### Park Plaza Histria Pula

*Verudela 17 (052 590 000, www.parkplaza.com).* €€. Map p75 A5.

Thoroughly renovated in 2010-11, the hotel features double rooms with sea-facing views in the main building, and self-catering apartments arranged nearby. Facilities include a circular outdoor pool, a heated indoor pool – both seawater – a sauna, gym and disco. Some 20 tennis courts and other sports pitches are nearby. It also has a conference centre.

### ★ Valsabbion

*Pješćana uvala IX/26 (052 218 033, www. valsabbion.net).* €€. Map p75 B5

This family-run, upmarket B&B has ten immaculately conceived rooms, half with sea view balconies and all tastefully decorated. Six are doubles, four are suites with varying levels of space and refinement. The buffet breakfast is outstanding, although check to make sure the price is included in the rates when you're staying. There's also a panoramic pool, fitness facilities and various beauty treatments.

## BEACHES & EXCURSIONS

Central Pula has no beaches but there are pleasant spots of coastline nearby. The nearest ones at Stoja and along Lungomare, between Veruda and Valsaline, are adequate, but if you're having to take a city bus (numbers 1 and 4 respectively) to get there, you may as well take the number 2A or 3A out to Verudela, for its nicer shingle beaches and best in town lunches.

If you've come for a beach holiday, leave Pula for Medulin and the windsurfing centre of Premantura, a quick and regular bus journey from Pula, on the numbers 25 and 26 (*see below*).

Beyond Premantura is the beautiful Kamenjak peninsula, at the very southern tip of Istria. Another option is Fratarski island. In summer locals decamp here permanently, spending nights under canvas among the shady pines and commuting to the city by ferry; there are free public showers. Ferries from Bunarina, heaving with sun worshippers for the ten-minute crossing, run every 20 minutes or so at the height of summer. Fares are nominal.

The major excursion from Pula is to the unique Brijuni Islands. To reach them, make for Fažana, eight kilometres north-west of Pula by city bus no.6. A national park (its offices are at Fažana harbour), Brijuni is where President Tito of the former Yugoslavia invited heads of state, who gifted him exotic creatures that still roam here. (*See p76* Tito's Xanadu.)

## GETTING THERE & AROUND

Pula airport (052 530 105, www.airport-pula.com) is six kilometres north-east of the city centre. There is no public transport to town. A taxi should cost about 200kn. In summer there is a regular fast-boat service with Venezia Lines (052 422 896, Italian office +39 041 882 1101, www.venezialines. com) to and from Venice.

The train station is north on Kolodvorska, a ten-minute walk from the centre. A service from Zagreb runs four times a day, journey time about seven hours, partly by bus for the invariable rail repairs along a certain section. There is also a daily service from Ljubljana (four hours).

Pula's main bus station is north-east of the amphitheatre at Trg Istarske Brigade (060 304 090). There are daily international services from Trieste and Venice and a summer one from Milan. There are buses every hour from Zagreb and regular ones from the main towns in Istria (www.pulainfo.hr). Municipal bus firm Pulapromet (www.pulapromet. com) runs services to Vodnjan, Premantura and Medulin as well as ones within town. Buses for nearby Stoja (number 1) and Verudela (numbers 2A and 3A) leave every 20 minutes. Nearly all pick up and drop off on Giardini in the town centre.

There is a taxi office by the Roman wall at Cararina (052 223 228). Otherwise call Cammeo taxi (060 700 700).

## RESOURCES

Hospital *Zagrebačka 30 (052 214 433/376 500, 052 376 000).*

Pharmacy *Giardini 15 (052 222 551).* Open 24hrs daily. Map p75 B4. Ring bell for night service.

Police *Trg republike 2 (052 532 111).*

Post office *Danteov trg 4 (052 215 955, 052 625 200).* Open 7am-8pm Mon-Fri, 7am-2pm Sat. Map p75 A5.

Tourist Information *Forum 3 (052 219 197, www.pulainfo.hr).* Open *Summer* 8am-10pm daily. *Winter* 9am-5pm daily. Map p75 A4. Helpful town centre office in a historic building.

# Medulin Riviera

Pula's playground of Medulin contains the region's solitary sandy beach of Bijeca, surrounded by 70 kilometres (42 miles) of indented coastline just made for watersports. The sleepy fishing village of Premantura is the gateway to Kamenjak, the unspoiled, protected tip of southern Istria. At the base of the Premantura peninsula in Banjole is Batelina.

EXPLORE

## Restaurants & Cafés

### Batelina

*Čimulje 25 (052 573 767).* **Open** 5-11pm Mon-Sat.
**€€. No credit cards.**

Run by the friendly and welcoming Skoko family,
who catch, cook and serve the food, Batelina focuses
on that day's catch. Starters are a particular highlight and might include dishes like grilled scallops,
steamed crab meat in its shell, seared tuna or delicious anchovies and olives – all served with crusty
home-made bread and local olive oils. Mains centre
on impeccably grilled fish, after it has been brought
to table for you to select. There are also home-made
pasta dishes, an excellent wine list, fabulous desserts (chocolate and chilli cake maybe) and a clutch
of local spirits like *biska*, deceptively strong but tem-
pered by a touch of honey. This is one of Istria's most
memorable dining experiences.

# Rovinj

**Rovinj** is Istria's showpiece, its answer to
Dalmatia's Dubrovnik, with far fewer crowds
and a more realistic view of itself. It maintains a
meticulously cared-for old quarter and extensive
tourist amenities without feeling fake or
overdone. The natural setting is stunning: a
harbour nicknamed 'the cradle of the sea' by
ancient mariners because the archipelago of
islands, stretching from here to **Vrsar**, ensured
calm, untroubled waters. The man-made
structures in the Old Town are also attractive:
tightly clustered houses, painted in cheery
Venetian reds and Habsburg pastels, connected
by cobbled streets barely wider than a footpath.

## INTRODUCING ROVINJ

Rovinj has been settled since at least the seventh
century, when it was an island centred around a
low, cone-shaped hill sticking out of the sea. The
populace overflowed to the mainland, and the
construction of a causeway in 1763 turned the
island into a peninsula. The hill still defines the
shape of the mostly car-free Old Town, and an easy
stroll up the spiralling road to the top affords views
of surreal beauty. Rather than overdevelop, Rovinj
has sought to retain its old charm, for which tourists
pay a premium. This is one of Croatia's nicer, and
pricier, resort towns. Before World War II, it was
an Italian resort, and the large Italian community,
which includes many restaurateurs, encourage
an emphasis on fine dining and good living.

Some of the best panoramic views are from
the **Cathedral of St Euphemia** (10am-2pm,
3-6pm daily), which caps the hilltop. This Baroque
structure was built in 1736 to house the remains
of Euphemia, a virgin martyr, who was fed to the
lions by Diocletian around AD 304. Legend says
her massive stone coffin disappeared from
Constantinople and miraculously floated ashore
in Rovinj, providing a fishing town with a catch
from heaven and a patron saint. The tomb and
relics can be seen inside the cathedral.

Other sights worth spotting in town are
the open-air **market** and the **City Heritage
Museum** (Trg maršala Tita 11, 052 816 720,

Rovinj.

EXPLORE

www.muzej-rovinj.com; open summer 9am-2pm, 7-10pm Tue-Sun, winter 9am-1pm Tue-Sat; 15kn), next to the **Balbi Arch**, the original town gate. The museum has some historical exhibits as well as contemporary art. Rovinj has a reputation as a home for artists, and galleries. **Grisia**, a stone-paved thoroughfare leading up to the cathedral, is packed with galleries and ateliers, selling crafts, kitsch and amateur seascapes. In summer, most spill on to the pavement. For the second Sunday in August anyone can exhibit here as part of the **Grisia Festival** with hundreds of artists, amateur and professional.

## Sights & Museums

### Batana House

*Obala P Budičina 2 (052 812 593, www.batana. org)*. **Open** *June-Sept* 10am-2pm, 7-11pm daily. *Oct-Dec, Mar-May* 10am-1pm, 4-6pm Tue-Sun. *Jan, Feb* by appointment only. **Admission** 10kn, · 5kn reductions. **No credit cards.**

Surely the Mediterranean's first multimedia museum dedicated to a fishing boat. The vessel in question is the batana, the traditional, flat-bottomed wooden boat of the Rovinj region. Still very much in use, the batana is a living symbol of Rovinj culture. The museum uses film, music and interactive exhibits, providing a taste of the local lifestyle with guides in traditional costume, and creative workshops where you can make fishing nets or demijohns.

### Rovinj Aquarium

*Giordano Paliaga 5 (052 804 712, www.cim.irb.hr)*. **Open** *Apr-Nov* 9am-9pm daily. **Admission** 20kn. Opened in 1891 as an adjunct to the aquarium in Berlin, this modest venue contains creatures you may later find on your plate.

## Restaurants

### ★ Blu

*Val de Lesso 9 (052 811 265, www.blu.hr)*. **Open** *Summer* noon-10pm daily. **€€€**. **Croatian** Blu has a great waterside location, best enjoyed over a leisurely lunch. Peruse the menu over a glass of Malvazija and home-made thin pizza-style bread with rosemary, sea salt and local, award-winning olive oil. Dishes are seafood-based and range from Novigrad oysters in tempura – or scampi and black truffle risotto – to gilt-head bream baked in a salt crust; a table of four could share a simple roast fish with potatoes, while the dark chocolate soufflé is scrumptious. Prices are less than you'd imagine, considering the quality and the view. In the evening, dinner is a little more formal, set around an old Roman garden. *Photos p82-83.*

### Calisona

*Trg na mostu 4 (052 815 313)*. **Open** *Feb-Dec* 11am-midnight daily. **€€**. **Istrian**

Just beyond the Balbi Arch is a small square where a large awning covers a terrace, diners tucking into sophisticated seafood. Along with Istrian standards (fettuccine with truffles, lobster with tagliatelle, or succulent grilled fish), there are creative offerings such as squid stuffed with scampi, and sole in Chardonnay. The alternatives for red meat carnivores would include steak and the grill for two (cutlets, patties and home-made sausage).

### Giannino

*Augusto Ferri 38 (052 813 402)*. **Open** *Mar-Oct* 11am-3pm, 6-11pm Tue-Sun. **€€**. **Italian** This popular restaurant by the Old Town draws repeat customers with its Italian cuisine. The menu is dominated by fresh catches from Rovinj's fishermen, but the sauces – and pasta – have an Italian influence. The synergy comes with great dishes like noodles mare monti, or rigatoni with lobster.

### ★ Kantinon

*Obala A Rismondo (052 816 075, www.maistra. com)*. **Open** noon-11pm daily. **€€€**. **Istrian** The reopening of the much-changed harbour front favourite raised expectations sky-high in summer 2013, not least because the chief menu consultant was Tom Gretić (head chef at the haute cuisine Wine Vault just round the bay). The new Kantinon offers high-quality, fairly priced Istrian cuisine with the best fresh ingredients. The menu revolves around local seafood, fresh pasta (*pljukanci* perhaps, hand-rolled twizzles) and new takes on old-fashioned country recipes such as seafood stews with barley, or fish fillets topped with Istrian sausage. Kantinon also works perfectly as a Croatian wine and tapas bar, with an expertly chosen wine list, many available by the glass.

### Konoba Lampo

*Sv Križa 22 (052 811 186, lampo-rovinj.com)*. **Open** *Mar-Dec* 11am-midnight daily. **€€**. **Croatian** Disregard the photos of the food and the sign saying 'Fish-Meat'. The place is touristy, no doubt, but the choices are good, the prices reasonable and you simply can't beat the view. On a steep little two-tiered overhang, with bamboo and canvas sunshades, you'll eat mussels, shrimp, salads and pasta while staring down at the water and away from the more touristy spots along the harbour.

### ★ L at Hotel Lone

*Hotel Lone, Luje Adamovića 31 (052 632 000)*. **Open** *Mid Feb-Dec* noon-3pm, 6pm-11pm daily. **€€€**. **Istrian-International** Rovinj's headline-grabbing Hotel Lone (*see p85*) also has a destination restaurant, offering a typically modern-day Istrian mixture of fresh local ingredients and wide-ranging culinary influences. The accent is on seafood but dishes from the Croatian countryside also feature; head chef Teo Ivanišević

**EXPLORE**

is not afraid to throw in the odd Asian-Adriatic curveball. Pretty much everything is awfully good and beautifully presented; terrace tables sit among shrubs and potted trees, looking towards Lone Bay.

### Male Madlene

*Svetog Križa 28 (no phone).* **Open** *June-Sept* 11am-2pm, 6-11pm daily. **No credit cards. €.** Croatian
Male Madlene is the brainchild of retired art historian Ana Balzareno, who decided to capitalise on her lifelong enthusiasm for fine food by opening a restaurant in her living room. The menu is based around a number of bite-sized dishes, ideal for haute cuisine snacking. If you want a full meal, order more and watch the bill mount.

### Mali Raj

*Trevisol 48 (052 816 242).* **Open** *May-Oct* 10am-3pm, 6pm-midnight daily. **€€. Croatian**
Another decent local that gets overlooked thanks to the mediocre eateries by the harbour, Mali Raj is below the cathedral but strangely off the tourist conveyer belt. Owned by the Lesdedaj family, the bistro does the basics: seafood spaghetti, tagliatelle with truffles, and black risotto. You dine on a grapevine-covered terrace.

### ★ Monte

*Montalbano 75 (052 830 203, www.monte.hr).* **Open** *Apr-mid Oct* noon-2.30pm, 6.30-10.30pm daily. **€€. Istrian**
Like an apparition just below the Cathedral of St Euphemia, Monte offers fine dining with an informal, funky feel – fusion with Istria at its heart. Ingredients from Rovinj market are given new life

thanks to owners Tjitske and Danijel Djekić who recommend the five- or seven-course tasting menus, with an array of delicate dishes and wines to suit each. Otherwise, standout mains include baked fish for two, or grillade of the day's fresh catch.

### Puntulina

*Sv Križa 38 (no phone, videooglasi.com/restorani/ puntulina).* **Open** noon-3pm, 6pm-midnight daily. **€€. Italian-Istrian**
A friendly place perched above the sea, this spot adds a gourmet Italian touch to local cuisine. The fish fillet Puntulina (with a delicately spiced tomato sauce), scallops in brandy, or squid in polenta provide exciting ways to enjoy fresh seafood. So does the gilt-head bream in an olive crust. Dine by the window; afterwards go down to the cocktail bar, with a stunning secluded terrace on the sea.

### Trattoria Dream

*Joakima Rakovca 18 (052 830 613, www.dream. hr).* **Open** *Feb-Dec* 11.30am-midnight daily. **€€€. Croatian**
On a bustling Old Town side street, just in from the harbour, this place tries hard, and mostly succeeds. The food is good, service friendly, but prices are not cheap, especially wine. The pretty interior, with fireplace and skylight, has charming furniture. There is an impressive variety of seafood, including salted sea bass, salmon, tuna and frogfish, all cooked with care.

### Trattoria Al Gastaldo

*Iza Kasarne 14 (052 814 109).* **Open** *Mar-early Nov* 11am-3pm, 6pm-midnight daily. **No credit cards. €€€. Croatian**

EXPLORE

**Blu**. See p81.

Top-quality seafood is served amid a cosy clutter of antiques and paintings, around an Istrian-style fireplace used for cooking. This family-run restaurant – located on a quiet corner – is not the cheapest place to eat, but it's perfect for that special holiday meal. Fresh shellfish, sole and lobster are dressed in superior sauces. Specialities include meat dishes baked in a clay oven. In summer, you can dine on the terrace.

### Veli Jože
*Sv Križa 1 (052 816 337).* **Open** 11am-midnight daily. €€€. **Istrian**
Istrian-style dishes flavour the menu of this quaint spot near the harbour with a high-ceilinged interior crammed with antiques and seagoing kitsch. There is seating for 50 on a pavement terrace. Specialities include shellfish lasagne, crab with truffles, cod in white wine, and baked lamb with potatoes. Prices are quite steep but you're getting quality fare.

### Wine Vault
*Hotel Monte Mulini, A Smareglije 2 (052 636 017, www.winevault.com.hr).* **Open** 7pm-midnight daily. €€€. **Mediterranean**
Located on the bottom, sea-facing level of the Hotel Monte Mulini, the Wine Vault has quickly built a reputation as one of the best places in Istria to sample modern Mediterranean cuisine. Under executive chef Radovan Blagić, the accent is on the maritime elements of French cooking, with shellfish, lobster, sea bass, turbot and cod taking pride of place on an inventive menu that is never afraid to juxtapose: you might find swordfish marinated in orange juice for example, served with stilton, sautéed scampi with brown sugar and coffee essence. The wine list runs to over 500 varieties, overseen by sommelier Filip Savić.

## Cafés & Bars

### Art Public Bar
*Carrera 88A (091 519 1340, www.artpublicbar.com).* **Open** 11am-midnight daily. **No credit cards**.
There's a sign reading 'Irish Pub' over the arched alleyway that leads to this nugget of a bar, although everyone in Rovinj knows it as 'Art'. A good place for a quiet drink on weekdays, when it fills up with customers from across the age spectrum, and rowdy in a good-natured way come the weekends, it's the kind of place that's popular with locals all year round, paying little heed to the seasonal ebb and flow of the tourist trade. The recipe is very simple: Guinness and Kilkenny on draught, Irish whiskeys lined up behind the bar, live (usually acoustic) music on Thursdays, DJ parties on Saturdays.

### Caffè Bar XL
*Sv Križa (no phone).* **Open** *Summer* 10am-2am daily. **No credit cards**.
The one spot in Rovinj you should seek out for a drink, coffee or otherwise, it's all about location. Sitting by the cathedral, atop the Old Town, XL has fine views of the sea and sunset. It serves Favorit beer on tap, house wines, cocktails and fruit juices like mango or guava.

### Caffè Cinema
*Trg Brodogradilišta 16 (no phone).* **Open** 7am-midnight Mon-Fri, Sun; 7am-1am Sat. **No credit cards**.
A fashionable terrace adds a touch of class to this busy corner of the harbour and draws a sizeable, mixed crowd. The spacious, dramatic black and white interior is dedicated to great films, with stills from old classics and a life-sized Alfred Hitchcock doing his cameo in the bathroom mirror. Behind the long bar is an oversized clock and, usually, a smiling face serving drinks. Music, ranging from pop to electronic to hip hop, cranks up the BPMs. A fun spot.

### Piassa Granda
*Veli trg 1 (052 811 374).* **Open** *Summer* 10am-1am daily. *Winter* 10am-11pm daily.
Set in Veli trg, the main square when Rovinj was an island, Helena Trošt's Piassa Granda is a wine bar, shop and café with the interior of a serious wine haunt. Under wooden beams with ceiling fans, her shelves are filled with 150 labels, 130 of them Istrian. All can be sampled on site, most by the glass, or bought to take home. Clai, Poletti and other top varieties can be found; around a fifth are offered by the bottle. The small menu has local cheeses, bruschetta and crostini – truffle biscuits, truffle rakija and top-end olive oil are also sold, plus beers like Chimay Blue and Rochefort 8.

**EXPLORE**

### Valentino
*Sv Križa 28 (052 830 683, www.valentino-rovinj. com).* **Open** *Summer* 6pm-2am daily. *Winter* noon-midnight daily. **No credit cards.**
Grab a hold of the rope railing and walk gingerly down the marble steps just off Sv Križa into this pricey cocktail bar, set at the end of the harbour. It has fab seating on a terrace a few feet over the sea. Step off the street, lose the crowds and commune with nature, your cocktail and your companion.

### Viecia Batana
*Trg maršala Tita (091 539 9172).* **Open** 7am-1am daily. **No credit cards.**
Popular with locals for morning coffee, or an early evening drink, this bar has a terrace with a sunny southern exposure facing the busy harbourside square by the Hotel Adriatic. Although the neighbouring bars share the view, they're never quite as full. Your coffee may take a minute longer, but it will arrive with a smile.

## Shops & Services

For fashion, Rovinj-born Mauro Massarotto's **Sheriff & Cherry** (www.sheriffandcherry.com) is by far the funkiest in Istria. The **Startas** range of sneakers designed by Massarotto himself for the Borovo shoe company, plus sunglasses, dresses, T-shirts, bags and brooches designed by leading Croatian talents, are all available through the website – unfortunately Mauro no longer has an outlet in town.
A **Prostor** concept store (2-8pm Mon-Sat, 9am-3pm Sun) has opened at the Hotel Lone (*see below*), offering fashion, accessories and art by local creatives under one roof. For food, Rovinj **market** on Trg Valdibora is open from 7am daily.

### Atelier Devescovi
*Grisia 13 (052 815 919).* **Open** *Summer* 10am-10pm daily. **No credit cards. Gallery**
Set in a lovely, late Renaissance palace from the 17th century, this is where artist Dean Devescovi sells paintings with jazzy influences, a standout among Rovinj's numerous galleries.

### Atelier Sottomuro
*Vrata pod Zidom 2 (091 732 9164, www.atelier sottomuro.com).* **Open** *Summer* 10.30am-10pm daily. **No credit cards. Gallery**
In this super little gallery, UK-raised Jan Ejsymontt purveys her acrylic paintings and jewellery.

### Atelijer Galerija Brek
*Fontica 2 (no phone, www.djuvedj.com).* **Open** Varies. **No credit cards. Accessories**
Quirky accessories and *objets d'art*, including earrings and brooches made from reclaimed and recycled electronic equipment.

## Hotels

### ★ Adriatic
*Trg maršala Tita 5 (052 800 250, www.maistra. com/Adriatic_Rovinj).* **€€€.**
The grand old lady of the Rovinj accommodation scene has been treated to a thorough makeover and relaunched as a boutique hotel, complete with designer interiors, contemporary art and chic social areas – including a French-flavoured restaurant and popular terrace café. It hasn't lost any of its charm and now looks every inch the upscale accommodation choice. Suave rooms are bright and airy, with tea- and coffee-making facilities among the extras.

### ★ Amarin
*Monsena (052 800 250, www.maistra.com/ Amarin_Rovinj).* **€€.**
Six kilometres north of Rovinj, the Amarin resort comprises an attractive cluster of two-person to six-person apartments on a green slope overlooking the sea. Two-thirds are renovated units originally built in the 1970s; the other third is completely new, designed by 3LHD, the Zagreb-based architecture practice responsible for the nearby Hotel Lone. A contemporary Croatian theme runs throughout the resort; graphic art inside the rooms is courtesy of street artist Oko. Famous for drawing phantasmagorical creatures with the heads of animals, Oko was inspired by the local Istrian fauna to create the playful images that adorn the apartments. Amarin also offers a campsite, two pools, tennis courts, entertainment for kids, restaurants and bars.

### Casa Garzotto
*Garzotto 8 (052 811 884, www.casa-garzotto.com).* **€€.**
This beautifully restored four-unit boutique hotel of studio apartments sits in the heart of the Old Town. With its old window shutters and classic furniture from the turn of the last century, Casa Garzotto is already winning repeat custom – two of the apartments have a roaring fire in winter. Breakfast consists of a varied selection of buffet treats in the ground floor tavern bar.

### Istra
*Sv Andrija (052 802 500, www.maistra.hr/Istra_ Rovinj).* **Open** mid Apr-mid Oct. **€€€.**
Many high-end hotels in Croatia now have spa facilities but none occupies a whole island. St Andrew's (referred to as Crveni otok, or Red Island) houses this complex of 376 rooms (plus 50 at the nearby Park Hotel), four restaurants, three bars and three pools. A beach is within 50 metres, while activities include yachting, windsurfing and football on a real pitch. As for the spa, there's relaxation and recharge massages, whirlpools indoor and out, Turkish and Finnish saunas and Kneipp baths. All is set amid lush greenery, the interior imbued with relaxing scents and colours.

**Hotel Istra.**

### ★ Lone
*Luje Adamovića 31 (052 632 000, www.lonehotel. com).* **Open** Mid Feb-Dec. €€€.
The kind of establishment that will be gracing the architecture textbooks in 50 years' time, Hotel Lone is also a fine place to stay, offering the kind of smooth interior design that soothes and relaxes rather than just draws attention to its colour scheme. The amorphous-looking, Y-shaped Lone was designed by Zagreb architects 3LHD to suit an awkward, forested hillside site. Filled with contemporary art, it's very much a showcase for the Croatian creative industries, with sculptor Ivana Franke's wiry installation hovering above a multi-storey lobby linked by sweeping spiral staircase. Rooms feature solid oak desks, swanky furniture and cheeky glass partitions where the bathroom walls should be; 'Jazz' rooms have hot tub-style dipping-pools right on the balcony. There is a fully equipped spa, and at least one of the three restaurants, (**L at Hotel Lone**, *see p81*) has a serious gourmet reputation. Decked out in heavy textiles, the bottom-floor nightclub looks like something from a David Lynch movie.

### Monte Mulini
*A Smareglia 2 (052 636 000, www.montemulini hotel.com).* **Open** Late Mar Dec. €€€.
Rovinj's big hitter until Hotel Lone opened its doors, Monte Mulini has luxury facilities to match its fabulous setting. All of the 99 rooms are fitted with contemporary carpets, bespoke furniture, hot-tub bathrooms and balconies overlooking a small open-air pool. The hotel brushes up to a rocky beach with natural shade from nearby greenery, while a string of cove-like beaches run along one bay to the south. Sports facilities include tennis courts, a basketball court and bowling alley. A spa area and an indoor pool are shared with the Lone next door. Med fusion dishes feature at the Mediterraneo and Wine Vault (*see p83*) restaurants, both overseen by award-winning chef Radovan Blagić.

### Park
*I M Ronjgova 11 (052 808 000, www.maistra.com/Park_Rovinj).* €€.
A relatively functional, three-storey slab of concrete, the Park offers perfectly respectable en-suite rooms, sweeping social areas, and – its main advantage over competitors – superb views of Rovinj's Old Town on the opposite side of the bay. Free Wi-Fi too.

### Vila Lili
*A Mohorovičića 16 (052 840 940, www.hotel-vilalili.hr).* €.
This small hotel (17 rooms and three suites) is in a residential quarter near the sea, and has a sauna, day bar and mansard roof fitted with two decent telescopes for stargazing. Breakfast includes home-made jams and marmalades, and there are supplementary rates for dinner. Pets welcome.

**EXPLORE**

### Villa Valdibora
*Silvana Chiurco 8 (052 845 040, www.valdibora. com). €€.*
Right in the Old Town and close to the sea, this recently renovated 18th-century townhouse of four studio apartments offers tasteful lodging, a great location and extra services – laundry, laptop rental and cycle hire included. The friendly staff are keen to point out the other sporting activities close to hand: tennis, mini golf and kayaking (all paid extras). There are boat excursions too. A cot can be provided on request, while there is a children's pool and playground close by.

## BEACHES & EXCURSIONS

Popular with locals is the small swimming area, consisting of rocks and concreted platforms, on the south side of the Old Town's peninsula. For the pine-forested beaches at the edge of town, you'll need sandals to wade on the jagged shore, but the lack of sand means the sea is incredibly clear, great for snorkelling or diving. The walk along the water is a little more than a kilometre from town: head past the Hotel Park, to the area of Monte Mulini and the succession of pebbly coves that forms the south side of Lone Bay. The bay culminates in the wooded peninsula of **Zlatni Rt** (Golden Cape), beyond which lie quiet stretches where you can find your own private boulder to bask on.

About three kilometres south of town there are two nudist beaches, **Polari Bay** and the adjacent **Cape Eve**. The 13 small islands here have thick forests surrounded by rocky beach.

The most popular excursions are to nearby **Sv Katarina Island** and dazzling **Crveni** ('Red') **Island** (consisting of two islets, Sveti Andrija and Maškin, joined by a causeway). Both are a short hop by regular taxi boat over from the main harbour. Local travel agencies offer trips to the **Limski kanal**, a spectacular fjord of green waters (*see above*, **In The Know**).

## GETTING THERE & AROUND

There are regular bus services from Zagreb and Pula, site of the nearest airport. The **bus** station is at Trg na Lokvi, a short walk east of the Old Town. For a **taxi**, call 098 224 905 or 098 694 859. There is a regular fast **boat** service from Venice with Venezia Lines (052 422 896, Italian office +39 041 882 1101, www.venezialines.com).

## RESOURCES

**Internet** *A-Mar, Karera 26 (052 841 211).* **Open** *Summer* 9am-11pm daily. *Winter* 9am-5pm Mon-Fri.

**Tourist information** *Obala Pina Budićina 12 (052 811 566, www.tzgrovinj.hr).*

---

## IN THE KNOW LIMSKI KANAL

The dramatic natural phenomenon of the Limski kanal creates a narrow ten-kilometre sliver of green sea banked by densely forested cliffs. Its likeness to the Norwegian fjords brought Hollywood star Richard Widmark here in 1963 to film Viking drama *The Long Ships*. The finest restaurant, with uninterrupted views of Limski's calm waters, is **Viking** (052 448 223), its nearest competitor is **Fjord** (052 448 222); both offer oysters as a local speciality.

**Open** *Mid June-mid Sept* 8am-9pm daily. *Mid Sept-mid June* 8am-3pm Mon-Sat. Provides free maps and English-language brochures by the bucketload.

# Poreč

**Poreč** is something of a cross between Pula and Rovinj, although neither as street-smart nor as bohemian. It can be hard at first to recognise its true value. Hoards of visitors fill the treasured sixth-century Euphrasian Basilica, the ancient square built by Romans and the scores of restaurants, cafés and package hotels.

### INTRODUCING POREČ
One of the most important historic sights in the whole of Croatia, the **Euphrasian Basilica & Bishop's Palace** (Sv Eleuterija, 052 431 635; open Mar, Apr, Oct 9.30am-6pm, May, June, Sept 9.30am-8pm, July, Aug 9.30am-10pm, all Mon-Sat; admission church 30kn, belfry 10kn, museum 10kn) was built in the sixth century by Bishop Euphrasius, and constitutes a rare example of Byzantine art.

Restaurant staff attempt to pull you in for a meal in the pedestrianised **Old Town**, and tacky souvenir shops cram the 2,000-year-old stone-paved thoroughfare of **Decumanus**. But if you can see past the crowds, or through them perhaps, you can take in a lot of history. Decumanus, the square **Trg Marafor**, and the ruins of the temples of **Neptune** and **Mars**, are evidence of the Roman occupation. The harbour contains reminders of Venetian dominance which ran until the 18th century, then Poreč was ruled by Napoleon, later still by the Habsburgs. The Venetians built a wall that stretched from the harbourside **Round Tower**, now hosting a bar, to the **Pentagonal Tower**, which is now a restaurant.

The resort hotels are outside town, on a green strip where pine forests run up to the beach, **Plava Laguna** and **Zelena Laguna**, linked by an open-air tourist train.

# Restaurants

### La Cioccolata
*Obala maršala Tita 13 (052 434 276).* **Open**
8am-2am daily. €€€. **Italian-International**
This posh restaurant and lounge bar spill onto the
waterfront promenade, with a large terrace stretched
out under a white tent. The indoor dining room has
its own terrace where waiters serve gnocchi with
truffles, steaks, and grilled fish; the adjoining lounge
bar offers low wicker chairs, 40kn cocktails, draught
Bavaria and local wines.

### Dvi Murve
*Grožnjanska 17 (052 434 115, www.dvimurve.hr).*
**Open** *Summer* noon-midnight daily. *Winter* noon-
11pm Mon, Wed-Sun. Closed 7 Jan-7 Feb.
€€. **Istrian**
Outside the more touristy part of town is this popular konoba (tavern) with a large, pleasantly shaded
terrace with a busy grill in one corner. Indoors it's all
warm earthy tones, wood beams and wooden panels.
They cook up fine seafood, including standards and
local specialities (sea bass baked in salt, lobster in
spaghetti). This is a good place to stray away from
standards though and opt for traditional Istrian
dishes like stew with dried lamb, goulash and noodles, wild game, or a plate of grilled meats.

### Peterokutna kula
*Decumanus 1 (052 451 378, www.kula-porec.com.
hr).* **Open** noon-midnight daily. **No credit cards.**
€€. **Istrian**
In a pentagonal tower built in 1447, near the entry-
way to the Old Town, this restaurant offers indoor
and outdoor seating in nicely restored spaces. As a
170-seater, it's touristy, but the cuisine is designed to
show off the best of Istria, with truffles appearing in
several dishes, including the steak.

### Sveti Nikola
*Obala maršala Tita 23 (052 423 018, www.
svnikola.com).* **Open** 11am-1am daily. €€€. **Istrian**
A winning combination of location, superb cuisine
and elegant ambience has helped Sveti Nikola build
a reputation as one of the top tables in Poreč. The
terrace is on the harbour, the meticulously designed
interior has great sea views and the food features
creative interpretations of Istrian classics. The
seafood carpaccio appetiser is an unusual mix of
scampi, frogfish and octopus; meat carpaccio comes
with truffle, parmesan and rocket. Mains include
fish fillet with asparagus and black truffles.

### Ulixes
*Decumanus 2 (no phone).* **Open** *Apr-Oct* noon-
midnight daily. €€. **Istrian**
Step off crowded Decumanus, down a few steps, and
into a cool, cavernous old stone room, charmingly
cluttered with antiques and old shipping parapher-
nalia. The garden behind, in a secluded courtyard,

is equally attractive. Seafood includes calamari,
octopus salad and fresh fish, also less common varieties like ray and sole. Truffles appear in pasta or as
part of various starters (sheeps' cheese or carpaccio
dishes). Look out for the daily specials.

# Cafés & Bars

### Café del Mar
*Obala maršala Tita 24 (052 858 800, cafedelmar.
hr).* **Open** 7am-midnight daily. **No credit cards.**
This glass-fronted café-bar sits on a jutting spur of
harbour front adjacent to the Palazzo Hotel, offering
good strong coffee and a cabinet full of cakes and
pastries. With tables set out on the stone jetty near
the hydrofoil dock, it's a suntrap in the daytime and
the place to watch crimson-hued skies in the evenings, when DJs set up their decks and the whole
place assumes an animated cocktail bar feel.

### Comitium Cocktail Bar
*Trg Marafor 15 (no phone).* **Open** *Easter-Oct* 6pm-
3am Mon-Sat; 5pm-2am Sun. **No credit cards.**
A garish, oversized cocktail sign alerts passing tourists to a beautiful garden bar amid the Roman ruins of
Marafor. Cocktails, Bavaria on tap and a classy, polished wood and marble interior complete the scene.

### ★ Epoca
*Obala maršala Tita 24 (098 276 167, www.epoca.
hr).* **Open** 8am-2am daily. **No credit cards.**
Good music, friendly staff and a sociable buzz set
this place apart from the other harbourside bars.
Near the tip of the peninsula that holds the Old
Town, at the start of the busy strip of cafés and
restaurants, Epoca offers a spacious interior with
circular wooden bar and sea views, wicker chairs
and wooden tables outside. Bruschetta and other
light bites are on offer, as are granita, frappés and
home-made ice-cream. Dancing might break out in
the evening, though the crowd will be mostly fellow
travellers rather than locals. Good cocktails.

### Mozart Caffè
*Rade Končara 1B (no phone).* **Open** 6am-2am daily.
**No credit cards.**
This terrace and bar really shouldn't be the busiest
location in town. Not only is it set behind the bus
station and Hotel Poreč, separated from the marina
by a small park, they play dubious Italian pop on
the stereo and the fashion channel on the TV. But it's
strangely popular and always packed with a loud
young crowd that includes many locals and thus
offers respite from the tourist hordes.

### Parentino Wine Bar
*Obala maršala Tita 24 (052 400 800).* **Open**
8am-midnight daily. **No credit cards.**
Below the Valamar Hotel Riviera, this is a slick little
wine bar with a terrace facing the yacht end of the
town marina. For holiday sailors, it serves croissants

**EXPLORE**

and coffee in the morning, Stella and Slovene Union beers by day, champagne and wines after dark. Inside, the decor is marble, glass and leather.

### Yesterday

*Park Olge Ban 2 (no phone).* **Open** *Summer* 7am-1am daily. *Winter* 7am-11pm daily. **No credit cards.**
This Beatles theme bar is run by the son of an Oldham-born fan who gave Paul McCartney a loveheart necklace backstage in 1965. Two years later, Jackie Carnihan met a hotel receptionist while on holiday here, got married and had two children. Macca couldn't have written it better. Unplugged local acts play on Fridays. There are two terraces that come into their own during summer.

## Nightlife

Thanks to a quality nightclub, **Byblos**, Poreč is bringing locals here rather than catering to mainstream tourists. The same team also runs the **Paradiso Beach Bar** (www.paradisobeach.hr), for pre-club or after-parties (open 8am-8pm). Elsewhere, discos can feel part of a package tour. You'll be mingling with fellow tourists and some nights you may not find a crowd unless you bring your own. Mainstream spots include **Saint & Sinner** (www.saint-sinner.net), on Maršala Tita, **Villa Club** (www.villa-club.net) on Rade Končara and the long-established **Plava Club** (www. clubplava.com) at Plava Laguna, with risqué shows for boys and girls.

### ★ Byblos

*Zelena Laguna (052 635 281, www.byblos.hr)* **Open** *June-Sept* 11pm-6am Wed-Sat. **No credit cards.**
The quality sound system, cocktails and DJ roster (David Guetta, Deep Dish and Roger Sanchez, for example) define Istria's best club. Mario Lucchi designed the huge interior, mainly black and white, and there's a beach lounge bar too. Ladies' night is Thursdays, international DJs Fridays.

## Hotels

### Delfin

*Zelena Laguna (052 414 000, www.plavalaguna. hr).* **Open** Mid Apr-mid Oct. **€.**
This low-frills resort hotel offers a decent budget option for families. The huge complex of the Delfin has no less than 800 rooms set on a hilltop in a pretty pine-forested peninsula. The rooms are small and plain, but reasonably cool in the tree-shaded building despite the lack of air-conditioning. Pebbled and less crowded rocky beaches nearby are quite separate from the rest of Zelena Laguna. There's a sports centre next door plus an outdoor pool with saltwater.

### Filipini

*Filipini (052 463 200, www.hotel-filipini.hr).* **€.**
In the village of Filipini, five kilometres outside Poreč, this little farmhouse-cum-boutique hotel in the woods is a great and reasonably priced find.

Palazzo.

The eight units have cathedral ceilings, and are filled with antique furniture atop wooden plank floors. The best attraction is the slow-food restaurant. Room rates vary – phone ahead to book a unit or, indeed, a table.

### Flores

*Rade Končara 4 (052 408 800, www.hostin.hr/ hotel-flores-porec-46).* **Open** Mid Mar-Oct. €€.
The Hostin chain only has one hotel in Poreč, and it offers competitive luxury at decent prices. The modern but attractive resort complex, surrounded by pines, is next to the marina beside a strip of seaside greenery that holds all the resorts. Amenities include a swimming pool, sauna, whirlpool, steam room, gym and nearby pebble beach. Diving, boat and bicycle rentals are not far away.

### Palazzo

*Obala maršala Tita 24 (052 858 800, www.hotel-palazzo.hr).* **Open** Mid Mar-mid Jan. €€.
Once called the Riviera, this reconstructed hotel, comprising 19th-century core and modern annexes, reopened in 2009. Right on the water, off the main seaside promenade, it now has 70 rooms and four apartments. Bedrooms have high ceilings, big beds, wood floors and tasteful wooden furniture. The spa (with Turkish and Finnish saunas) and pool are major attractions. There's a restaurant, excursion booking and yacht rental – the back of the hotel opens on to a marina.

### Poreč

*Rade Končara 1 (052 451 811, www.hotelporec. com).* €.
This blocky concrete building is close to the bus station and to a small park by the marina. The 54 comfortable, air-conditioned rooms all have balconies, though views are pretty bland. Staff can organise diving, jet skis, tennis, water-skiing and golf lessons.

### ★ Valamar Club Tamaris

*Lanterna 6, Tar (052 401 000, www.valamar.com).* **Open** Apr-Oct. €€.
Set by the fine beaches of the Lanterna peninsula just outside Poreč, the Tamaris provides the ideal active family retreat. Three outdoor pools, free babysitting for under-fours, free cycle hire, sports courts, tennis, children's entertainment, a mini-disco and mini cinema are all on-site, with sailing and diving schools nearby. Rooms – more than 300 of them – have balconies, and there are four-person family suites. Look out for attractive half- and full-board rates.

### Valamar Diamant Hotel

*Brulo 1 (052 400 000, www.valamar.com).* €€.
A beachside hotel for grown-ups and children, the Diamant combines business (conference and congress rooms) with pleasure (gym and spa treatments) a short drive from Poreč there's parking for €3. Kids have separate pools indoor and out, and are provided with entertainment all summer. While the apartments (Valamar Diamant Residence) are closed Nov-Mar, the main hotel runs year-round.

**EXPLORE**

### Valamar Riviera Hotel & Valamar Villa Parentino

*Obala maršala Tita 15 (052 400 800, www.valamar.com).* **Open** Apr-Oct. €€.
This luxury seafront establishment is now Valamar's flagship hotel among its cluster in Poreč. As well as top lodging (a beauty centre, panoramic lobby bar, wine bar, Spinnaker restaurant) the highlight here is entertainment, with evening music on the terrace and regular jazz concerts arranged in the Old Town.

## BEACHES & EXCURSIONS

Either side of town walkways follow the coast, past rocky or pebbly beaches. The stroll south, towards **Plava Laguna** and **Zelena Laguna**, can be the most rewarding. You can also take the **tourist train** from Trg Slobode and get driven down the six-kilometre walkway to Zelena Laguna, to join the masses. For more privacy, take a **taxi boat** (every 30mins, 7am-11pm daily, 12kn) over to **Sv Nikola** from the harbour. You'll find pine-shaded, paved and pebble beaches; the most notable is the circular one of **Oliva** near the Fortuna Island Hotel.

Halfway to Višnjan, the **Baredine Cave** (www.baredine.com) has been open to the public since 1995. Tours are organised from Poreč. Your 40-minute guide will take you through five chambers, culminating in lakes 60m below ground.

**Venezia Lines** (Trg Matije Gupca 11, 052 422 896, Italian office: +39 041 882 1101, www.venezialines.com) runs day trips to **Venice**, stopping at **Pula**, **Rovinj** and **Rabac**. Tickets (€72) include a one-hour guided tour of the city; the journey time is just over two hours each way, with a five hour stay.

## GETTING THERE & AROUND

The nearest **airports** are in Pula and Trieste, Italy. Half a dozen services a day run to Poreč bus station (Rade Končara 1, 052 432 153) from main towns in Istria, and from Zagreb. Don't forget that the local resort hotels are connected by a little **tourist train** in high season. There is a **taxi** stand at the bus station or call 098 434 261 mobile (www.taxiporec.com) or 098 255 245 mobile (www.porec-taxi.com).

## RESOURCES

**Travel agency** *Atlas, Eufrazijeva 63 (052 434 933, www.atlas-croatia.com).* **Open** *Summer* 10am-9pm daily.
The best people in town to book private rooms, plus excursions and rentals.

**Poreč Tourist Office** *Zagrebačka 9 (052 451 293, www.to-porec.com).* **Open** 8am-10pm daily.
Provides all standard information and can help with accommodation details.

**Baredine Cave.**

# Novigrad

Located north towards Italy, its compact centre attracting day trippers from over the border, **Novigrad** can seem like a humble resort town by Istrian standards. It's neither as posh as Rovinj nor as packed as Poreč, but that's precisely why this can be a charming location for a relaxing time by the sea. The emphasis here is on quality, from the recently renovated **Hotel Maestral** and luxurious **Hotel Nautica**, to the deservedly reputable restaurants including the excellent **Damir i Ornella**. Instead of being crammed with tourist businesses, the seaward tip of Novigrad's Old Town peninsula has a shaded park and a waterside walkway. Still, for a community of fewer than 4,000 people, Novigrad finds room for a surprising number of decent bars, hotels and restaurants. The more modern part of town stretches less than 1 kilometre east, to the bus station and a small hotel complex.

The Old Town curls itself snugly around the harbour, offering fine food, good bar crawls and the **Museum Lapidarium**, specifically built to house Romanesque remains. The Old Town is also connected with the marina via the pleasant seaside promenade of **Rivarella**.

Novigrad was called Cittanova by the Venetians who graced the town with most of its elegant

Located in a Baroque building commissioned by the local Rigo nobility in the late 18th century, this complex was restored in 1994. Now one of Istria's most important independent galleries, it has a fast-moving programme of challenging, contemporary exhibitions throughout the year.

### Istralandia
*E751 road, Nova Vas exit (052 866 900, www. istralandia.hr).* **Open** *June-mid Sept* 10am-7pm daily. **Admission** 150kn, 120kn reductions, children under 1 metre tall free.
Midway between Brtonigla and Novigrad, right beside the Nova Vas exit of the E751, this fun outdoor pool complex opened in 2014 and has already become a hit with vacationing families. It's pretty much everything you would expect a modern aquapark to be: spiralling water slides, wave pool, beach volley-ball and a children's pool with castle. It gets busy on summer weekends, when there may be queues.

### ★ Museum Lapidarium
*Veliki trg 8A (052 726 582, www.muzej-lapidarium.hr).* **Open** *June-Sept* 10am-1pm, 6-10pm Tue-Sun. *Oct-May* 10am-1pm, 5-8pm Tue-Sun. **Admission** 10kn, under-14s free. **No credit cards.**
Istria's first purpose-built museum is a first-class example of how to site modern glass cube architecture within the context of an old town. Designed by award-winning architectural duo Rendič and Turato, the Lapidarium was built to house Novigrad's small but impressive collection of archaeological remains – mostly Romanesque stonework from medieval Istrian churches, although there is the odd Roman-era piece here as well. The Romanesque pieces feature delicately carved inter-twining patterns, familiar Christian symbols and an array of animals and mythical beasts.

### Višnjan Observatory
*Istarska 5, Višnjan (052 449 212, www.astro.hr).* **Open** By appointment. **Admission** donations welcome. **No credit cards.**
A 15-minute drive from Novigrad, and famous for discovering more than 1,400 minor planets over the last decade, Višnjan is one of the world's most prolific astronomical discovery sites. In 2009 the Višnjan team opened a brand new observatory in the nearby village of Tican, housing a one-metre telescope. The observatory is also actively involved in educational projects, organising workshops and seminars.

## Restaurants

### ★ Damir i Ornella
*Zidine 5 (052 758 134, www.damirornella.com).* **Open** *Mar-Sept* noon-3pm, 6.30-11.30pm Tue-Sun. **No credit cards.** €€€. Istrian
Acknowledged as one of the best places on the coast, this 22-seat diner is worth booking ahead for.

historical sights. The Venetian-style campanile beside **St Pelagius**, a Baroque 18th-century church built on the foundations of a medieval basilica, rises over the modest network of streets. In the main square, Veliki trg, and the main street of Velika ulica, stands a landmark loggia, containing the town hall. North of town at **Karpinjan**, near the new marina, is the **Rigo Palace**, built in 1760. As well as new exhibitions, it has a permanent display of historic items.

## Sights & Museums

### Gallerion Naval Museum
*Mlinska 1 (098 254 279).* **Open** *Apr, May* 9am-noon, 4-7pm daily. *June-Jan* 10am-noon, 7-10pm daily. **Admission** 30kn, 20kn reductions. **No credit cards.**
Around the corner from the city harbour, Gallerion is dedicated to the Austro-Hungarian presence in the Adriatic 1815-1918, from a non-Croatian point of view. The two-storey display is filled with explanations of battles, model ships, uniforms and weapons. The well-crafted exhibits outline the area's nautical tradition, in as objective a way as a coastal town can. The curator is a maritime expert, and adroit linguist.

### Gallery Rigo
*Velika ulica 5 (052 726 582, www.galerija-rigo.hr).* **Open** varies. **No credit cards.**

**EXPLORE**

Signposted on Velika ulica, it's set in a narrow side-street near the seafront. Inside, a bare-brick interior is a comfortable setting for fish and shrimp specialities; most of what they serve is raw. Damir and his daughter, the sommelier, run the floor. Ornella runs the kitchen. Desserts include kiwi flan.

## Konoba Čok
*Sv Antuna 2 (052 757 643).* **Open** *Summer* noon-3pm, 6-11pm daily. *Winter* noon-3pm, 6-11pm Mon, Tue, Thur-Sun. **€€. Seafood-Istrian**
While his son Viljam runs the kitchen, Sergio takes care of guests and the wide range of Istrian wines on offer. This simple, well run and highly regarded seafood eaterie is indeed a welcome treat, with fresh sea bream, sea perch, sole, lobster and all kinds of shellfish, including oysters. Truffles decorate the steak and pasta starters, while meals are generally bookended by complimentary fruit brandy.

## Mandrač
*Mandrač 6 (no phone).* **Open** 10am-11pm daily. **€€. Istrian**
The walls of Mandrač's backroom are covered in gastronomic awards and even though there are seats for 200-plus diners, it's best to reserve in summer. Fresh fish and grilled meats are well presented on warmed plates, garnished according to the friendly advice offered by the waiter. Despite the high standards, prices are reasonable.

## Marina
*Sv Antona 38 (no phone).* **Open** noon-3pm, 6.30-11pm daily. **€€. Seafood**
In a case of double nominative determinism this restaurant is at the Novigrad Marina and run by a bright, culinary hope called Marina (along with her partner, Davor). As well as fresh fish, the couple put local greens to excellent use. Quality desserts too.

## Navigare
*Sv Antona 15 (052 600 400, www.nauticahotels. com).* **Open** 7am-midnight daily. **€€€. Istrian**
The flagship restaurant of the waterfront Hotel Nautica (*see p93*) offers top-notch Mediterranean cuisine, prepared in an open kitchen, for guests and non-guests alike. The à la carte changes with the seasons, with local ham, asparagus and truffles a key feature – according to availability.

## ★ Pepenero
*Porporela (052 757 706, www.pepenero.hr).* **Open** 6.30-11pm daily. **€€€. Mediterranean**
The town's heavy hitter, this spot has been given gourmet appeal by renowned TV chef Marin Rendić. Inventive mains include fish fillets in pea, beetroot and pear sauce; home-made ravioli stuffed with sea bass in a black truffle sauce; and poached sea bass with fried seaweed. It's also worth splashing out on the tasting menu, each course served with a glass of the appropriate tipple. The wine list is extensive,

with the best of Istria as well as a wide-ranging global selection. Reservation essential.
▶ *The same team are behind the new Pepebianco pizzeria (see Pepenero website).*

## Restaurant Sidro
*Mandrač 5 (no phone).* **Open** *Summer* 11am-11pm daily. *Winter* 11am-11pm Mon, Tue, Thur-Sun. **€€. Seafood**
In its third generation, this family-run classic, with nautical interior and terrace, has been around since the start of modern Istrian tourism. Sidro ('Anchor') only uses fish from the immediate, shallower waters, so it's heavy on shellfish and sole. It sits on the fishermen's marina and locals show up to eat; for the best shellfish, come in November. The fish platter is a solid tip (white fish, squid, grilled scampi, potatoes and spinach), also the lobster with spaghetti.

## Taverna Sergio
*Šaini 2A (052 757 714, www.hotelmakin.hr/index. php/restoran).* **Open** *Summer* noon-11pm Tue-Sun. *Winter* 11am-3pm, 6-11pm Tue-Sun. **€€. Istrian**
A family business for two decades, this was opened by ex-footballer Sergio Makin. Lobster with tagliatelle, risotto with scampi and asparagus, *fuži* pasta with truffles and manestra soup are house specialities. Oysters and quality white fish are also served. The garden terrace is secluded from the street by thick shrubs, palms and vines. An accordion is provided for guests, as is a list of top Croatian wines. Rooms are let upstairs – note the pool and sauna.

# Cafés & Bars

## City Garden
*Gradska vrata 15 (no phone).* **Open** 8am-midnight Mon-Thur; 8am-1am Fri, Sat. **No credit cards.**
A young, professional crowd hangs out in this swish café in the heart of Novigrad. With art on the walls, a decent choice of whiskies, Istrian bitters, Guinness and Kilkenny by the bottle, it's a cut above most.

## Cocktail Bar Code
*Gradska vrata 20A (no phone).* **Open** 8am-midnight Mon-Thur, Sun; 8am-2am Fri, Sat. **No credit cards.**
This slick, urban, monochrome cocktail lounge seems incongruous among the more low-key cafés of Novigrad, but it works. House music blares from the speakers while muted hip-hop videos flash on a wide screen. The bartender is ready to give a showy shake to 23 basic cocktails, served in pretty generous portions. DJs on Saturdays.

## ★ Vitriol
*Ribarnička 6 (052 758 270, www.vitriolcaffebar. com).* **Open** *Summer* noon-10pm daily. *Winter* noon-5pm daily.
The best bar in Novigrad. Its terrace lapped by the sea, overlooking the setting sun, the Vitriol is trendy

enough to appeal to weekending Italians without losing its young, lively and local character. As a day-time spot for coffee, own-recipe cakes and fruit tarts, this establishment is as good as you'll get. Evening cocktail concoctions have a distinct Italian flavour (Negroni, Garibaldi) but include a zingy Novigrad Beach (gin, Campari and orange juice). Local wines are chalked up on a board outside, beers include Kriek and Kilkenny.

## Hotels

### ★ Cittar

*Prolaz Venecija 1 (052 757 737, www.cittar.hr).* **Open** Apr-Dec. €€.

Its exterior built into a section of Venetian wall in the centre, the Cittar is one of the best deals in Istria. Run by a friendly team under Katjuša Cittar, it has 14 rooms with varnished floors, big beds and bathtubs. A breakfast of warm croissants, meats and cheeses is taken in the sunny conservatory. Half-board is offered in summer, when you should book well ahead.

▶ *The nearby Villa Cittar (052 758 780) has a dozen stylish rooms and is open all year.*

### KOLO

*Krsin 37 (052 758 658, www.kolo-pansion.hr).* €.

Just off a main road, but surrounded by an oak wood and cornfields, this guesthouse and restaurant contains nine comfortable rooms in a relaxed environment. It also has a swimming pool and car park.

### Maestral

*Tere (052 858 630, www.laguna-novigrad.hr).* €€.

Presiding over well-kept gardens a short walk along the shore from central Novigrad, the 1970s-era Maestral has been given a new lease of life following extensive renovations in 2011. Rooms are decked out in neutral grey-blue or camel-brown, while the reception area, lobby bar and sea-facing terrace have the expansive sweep of a big resort hotel. The emphasis is very much on wellbeing: there's a state-of-the-art spa and beauty centre, indoor pool, a huge gym, and several rows of tennis courts on the doorstep. With facilities like these, it's no surprise the Maestral remains popular out of season; it's often used by sports teams as a training camp.

### Makin

*Šaini 2A (052 757 714, www.hotelmakin.hr).* €.

In a residential area 2km north of the centre, the Makin has 14 simple rooms and is run, like the adjacent Taverna Sergio (*see p92*), by the Makin family. There's a pleasant terrace, garden, a pool and sauna.

### ★ Nautica

*Sv Antona 15 (052 600 400, www.nauticahotels. com).* €€.

Opened in 2006 by Novigrad's well-equipped yachting marina, the Nautica combines maritime flavour with contemporary comforts. The bespoke,

dark wood, leather and brass furniture is styled after a ship's fittings – it even extends to the ship's-wheel bedheads. With a restaurant, large lounge bar, indoor pool and spa, it's a welcome addition to Istria's rapidly improving hotel stock. For those on sailing holidays, the facilities could not be better.

### Torci 18

*Torci 34 (052 757 799, www.torci18.hr).* **Open** Apr-Oct. €. **No credit cards.**

Djurdja and Lino Beletić run this sturdy pension and restaurant in the centre of town with a dozen clean, comfortable rooms, some overlooking a courtyard. Their homely dining area is a destination in its own right, offering a fine spread of local specialities at knockdown prices to guests and non-guests alike.

## GETTING THERE & AROUND

There are four **buses** a day to Novigrad from Pula and Zagreb plus an extra service in season. It might be quicker and more convenient to get to Poreč and change for a more regular service between the two towns 18km (11 miles) apart, or take a taxi. The bus station is a ten-minute walk outside town, near the tourist hotels. The centre of Novigrad and its seafront are an easy, pleasant five-minute walk apart. If you do need a **taxi**, call 098 806 124.

## RESOURCES

**Tourist information** *Mandrač 29A (052 757 075, www.novigrad-cittanova.hr).* **Open** *Summer* 8am-8pm daily. *Winter* 9am-3pm Mon-Fri.
Friendly office full of brochures, near the marina.

# North-west Istria

Away from the tourist-swamped resorts of Poreč and Rovinj, **north-west Istria**, towards the Slovenian border, has a wealth of experiences to offer. Age-old villages sit atop panoramic hilltops, surrounded by picturesque forests rich in truffles (*see p98* **Sniffing For Gold**). Prime producers of wine, olive oil and the regional speciality of *pršut* ham supply some of the finest restaurants in all Croatia. Some of these renowned eateries, which attract diners from Italy, also have top-notch hotels attached, providing the discerning visitor with all the ingredients for a perfect luxury stay.

Take, for example, **Brtonigla**, a classic overachiever, a well preserved village and a renowned gastro-enclave. Here the **San Rocco** is a classic case in point, destination dining coupled with high-end hospitality, spa treatments and outdoor pools in rustic surroundings. A short drive away, **Buje** is home to Venetian palaces, medieval architecture and one of the best restaurants in Istria, the **Konoba Morgan**.

The main town of **Umag** is the tennis capital of Croatia. The **Stella Maris** tennis centre, the best in the country, hosts the Croatia Open, part of the pro tennis circuit, every summer. **Istraturist** (www.istraturist.com) has several tennis hotels in Umag, with access to top facilities; people come for lessons, or just to play. The leader is the **Melià Coral** (Katoro, 052 701 000, www. istraturist.com). The main tennis centre is located along a green stretch of seaside north of town. There are tree-shaded beaches on this strip, as well as most of the tennis hotels, additional courts and other resort accommodation.

Apart from tennis and the beach, there are two better-preserved Old Town streets dedicated to the tourist trade. **Obala Sv Pelegrina** is a seaside walkway and row of restaurants, where waiters stand out front, inviting passersby to step inside. The parallel street, **Riječka**, is lined with rear entries to the restaurants and souvenir shops. There's a beach downtown too, albeit with a somewhat prosaic view.

Right up by the Slovenian border, the pretty, unspoiled fishing village of **Savudrija** is where Croatians relax away from the busier resorts on Istria's west coast. Its history reflects the frontier location. For much of the last millennium it was part of the municipality of Piran, which is now in Slovenia. After a brief period of post-war autonomy, Savudrija – Salvore in Italian – became part of Tito's Yugoslavia in 1954. By then most of the Italians who had formed the majority local population had fled. Today most inhabitants are Croatian but road signs remain bilingual.

The main landmark here is the **Savudrija Lighthouse**, built in 1818 at the behest of Habsburg Emperor Franz I, whose inscription still runs around its base. It stands 36 metres (118 feet) high, the most north-westerly point in Croatia (*see p99* **In The Know**). By the harbour stands the community's other main attraction, the twin-aisled **Parish Church**, dating back to the 11th century. Rebuilt around the same time as the inauguration of the Savudrija Lighthouse, the Parish Church contains part of a Tintoretto mural linked to a Venetian sea battle that took place here in 1177.

## Restaurants

### Badi
*Umaška 12, Lovrečica (052 756 293).*
**Open** noon-11pm Tue-Sun. €€. **Seafood**
A renowned establishment in a village just south of Umag, Badi is good for pretty much everything seafood-related. It's set back from the water but the leafy garden terrace more than compensates. Mediterranean cuisine is given an imaginative twist with some raw fish starters, and mains that include traditional seafood alongside specialities (sea bass in bread pastry crust perhaps). The wine list has the best of Istria's boutique wineries.

### ★ Konoba Astarea
*Ronkova 9, Brtonigla (052 774 384, www.konoba-astarea-brtonigla.com).* **Open** 11am-midnight daily. €€. **Istrian**
Astarea's interior is as cosy as a living room, with old photos, a piano and open fire where most of the cooking is done, giving your meal a great smoky taste. The menu is fish-centric, varying according to the day's catch, though likely to include sea bass, conger eel and sole; there are meat alternatives too. Amiable owner Anton talks you through the day's menu. This is traditional food done well: fish soup, scampi buzara, grilled scallops or whole fish cooked under the coals, *ispod peke* style. Booking is recommended.

### Konoba da Lorenzo
*Šetalište V Gortana 74, Umag (091 175 1098).*
**Open** noon-midnight Mon, Tue, Thur-Sun. €€.
**Seafood**
A real find on a stretch of the Riva that is largely taken up with samey, touristy restaurants, the small and congenial Konoba da Lorenzo cooks local seafood with real flair and passion. Grilled and baked fish make up most of the menu; own-recipe ravioli with delectable fish or asparagus stuffing can be sublime. The wine list is very Istrian, and there are plenty of quality but affordable whites to go with the seafood.

### ★ Konoba Morgan
*Bracanija 1, Buje (052 774 520, www.konoba-morgan.eu).* **Open** *Mid Oct-mid Sep*t noon-10pm Mon, Wed-Sun. €€. **Istrian**
This is one of the best, if not the best, countryside restaurants. It's not well signposted – to reach it, take the main road out of Buje, then a track on the left-hand side a kilometre before Brtonigla. Owner Marko Morgan produces simple dishes based on authentic recipes. Italians love it, travelling regularly to eat here, enjoying the large covered terrace with a view of the vines. Marko lets locally sourced ingredients and attention to detail take centre stage. The business involves the whole family: Morgan senior hunts for game, his mother and sister work in the kitchen. There's no fixed menu; Morgan relays to customers what is available that day and invites them to take an aperitif. Time-tested specialities are based on the season – home-made polenta with game perhaps, or slow-cooked and marinated *boškarin* ox.

### Konoba Nono
*Umaška 35, Petrovlja (052 740 160, konoba-nono. com).* **Open** 11am-11pm Tue-Sun. €€. **Istrian**
Just off the main road to Buje, this family business is an ideal place to tuck in to the rural Istrian repertoire of home-made pasta, meats baked under a hot metal lid (including goat), and goulash made from *boškarin*, the local horned cattle. The modern dining rooms are hung with rustic implements and old musical instruments – the owners' neighbouring farm completes the picture. The wine list runs from unpretentious house white to the best of local small winery production.

## ★ San Rocco

*Srednja ulica 2, Brtonigla (052 725 000,*
*www.san-rocco.hr).* **Open** 12.30-10pm daily.
€€€. **Modern European**
This is luxury. Enjoy a swim and a massage, then tuck
into truffle-flavoured dishes prepared with San Rocco's
own olive oil. Meanwhile proximity to the sea means
that the fish is really fresh. Accompanying wines will
be well chosen, comprising a selection of some 200
labels, living up to Brtonigla's gastro-hub reputation.
▶ *The restaurant is part of the equally excellent*
*San Rocco Hotel (see right).*

## Stari Podrum

*Most 52, Merišće, Momjan (052 779 152, www.*
*staripodrum.info).* **Open** noon-1pm Mon, Tue,
Thur-Sun. €€. **Istrian**
One of those places that's highly regarded by locals
and worth driving a few extra kilometres to find, Stari
Podrim is in an old distillery in Momjan, a wine-producing village in Istria's far north-western corner. The
food is as off-the-beaten-track as the location, with
an informal follow-the-staff-suggestions menu that
changes seasonally according to what's fresh. Expect
good home cooking with home-made pasta, soups and
stews garnished with truffles, asparagus and other
regional riches. Be sure to stay for the seasonal fruit
desserts, washed down with the local Muscat.

## Villa Rosetta

*Crvena Uvala 31, Zambratija (052 725 710,*
*www.villarosetta.hr).* **Open** noon-11pm daily.
€€. **Mediterranean**
Within the hotel of the same name (*see right*), this
is a must-stop for gourmets. The ground floor restaurant has a fine dining vibe, and a wicker-laden
terrace that looks on to a field rolling down to a private hotel beach. The family has been in the business
since 1938 and has a few recipes up their sleeve. The
mainly Med menu includes shrimp carpaccio, home-
made pastas with lobster, and fish stew.

## Hotels

## ★ Kempinski Hotel Adriatic

*Alberi 300A, Savudrija (052 707 000, www.*
*kempinski-adriatic.com).* **Open** May-Oct. €€€.
The big hitter in the area, with top-drawer dining com-
plementing the Carolea spa and 18-hole golf course,
the Kempinski ia an all-in-one, luxury resort. Each of
the 186 rooms and suites is sleek, with fashionable,
contemporary furniture and flatscreen TV. Big beds
look out to seaside terraces, where patio tables and
chairs await teatime. Outside you'll also find four
tennis courts, three pools and two restaurants, Dijana
and Slice, serving seafood and Istrian specialities.

## Mulino

*Škrile 75A, Buje (052 725 300, www.mulino.hr).* €€.
Located north and west of Buje close to the
Slovenian border, Mulino is a high-end casino, hotel

and restaurant, well situated to enjoy all of Istria's
delights – if you can pry yourself away from the slot
machine or whirlpool. The hotel is within shouting
distance of the coast, ten kilometres from Umag, and
near a number of wineries, olive oil producers and
fine restaurants. When the day is over you can take a
dip in the pool with a cocktail.

## San Rocco

*Srednja ulica 2, Brtonigla (052 725 000,*
*www.san-rocco.hr).* €€.
For lodging, you'd be hard pressed to do better: the
San Rocco has won the Best Small Hotel in Croatia
award four years running. Twelve beautifully furnished rooms are ranged around two pools, a wine
shop, a wine cellar, a spa centre (with massage treatments) and a standout restaurant. Rooms are man-
or-style rustic with exposed wooden ceiling beams
and spacious floor plans. Some have sea views, others a vista of picturesque Brtonigla.

## Villa Rosetta

*Crvena Uvala 31, Zambratija (052 725 710,*
*www.villarosetta.hr).* €€.
Just 50m from the sea, the renowned Villa Rosetta is
best known for its restaurant (*see left*). It also has 23
spacious, sea view rooms and an apartment. Rooms
have parquet flooring and a balcony overlooking a
private beach complemented by its own cocktail bar.
There is also a spa, saunas, and massage treatments.
It's on the Savudrija Riviera, 4km from Umag.

# Motovun

**Motovun** – Montona to the Romans – is one of
the most beautiful and best preserved of Istria's
medieval hilltop settlements. These days it's best
known for its film festival, which transforms this
otherwise sleepy town into a cultural and party
hub for one week every summer. It's on the summit
of a 277-metre (910-foot) hill in the middle of the
Mirna Valley, surrounded by truffle-rich forest.

When the prehistoric settlement was founded,
it would have been surrounded by water. The
estuary stretched right up to the 'Gates of Buzet'
at the head of the valley. It was down this inlet
that Jason and his Argonauts are supposed to
have fled after capturing the Golden Fleece.

From its strategic position, Motovun
controlled the merchant routes across the
valley floor on the way to the coast. Although
depopulated after the Italian exodus in 1945,
a new wave of inhabitants, including artists
and writers, set up home here. The result is the
**Motovun Film Festival**, started in 1999.

**INTRODUCING MOTOVUN**
Motovun's two sets of fortified walls divide the
town into three sections – the higher you climb,
the older it gets. In the summer non-residents are

**EXPLORE**

banned from driving the town's narrow cobbled streets but there's a car park at the bottom of the hill. As you wend your way upwards, past rather dilapidated, 16th- and 17th-century Venetian-style houses, you pass several shops, offering wine, truffles and grappa.

As the road levels it passes through the main city gate dating from the 15th century. Its walls are hung with Roman tombstones taken from the cemetery of **Karojba**, a village five kilometres away on the road to Pazin. Within the gate is a museum of antique weaponry – the entrance is on the far side of the gate. Also here is the town's art gallery. Next door is a café, the **Montona Gallery**, with a terrace. The view should be stunning but just in case, a telescope is provided. There's also a rare cashpoint machine.

A few steps further, facing the town loggia, is the 13th-century gate into the original heart of Motovun. This walkway is particularly steep and slippery – use the handrail. The entrance houses a lovely restaurant, **Pod Voltom**, which in summertime uses the loggia. From the archway you walk on to the main square. Dominated by a magnificent 13th-century belltower, the piazza is sited over a huge cisterna, or water collection pit, which used to supply the town. You can still see the 14th-century well. Next to the tower is the baroque **Church of St Stephen** and, opposite, a Renaissance palace citadel, housing the local cinema. The piazza also houses Motovun's main hotel, the Kaštel. It's at this point that all the climbing pays off. Stroll along the original 13th-century walls and a stunning 360-degree panorama reveals the whole of inland Istria.

## Restaurants

### Konoba Dolina
*Gradinje 59/1, Livade (052 664 091).* **Open** noon-10pm Mon, Wed-Sun. **No credit cards. €.** Istrian
A short drive from Motovun (head into Livade and take a right at the roundabout), the Dolina is a perfect example of fantastic, local food. It's slightly off the beaten track, not touristy or flash – and all the better for it. It's also incredibly good value. The secret is the quality of the produce: huge plates of porcini (in autumn) served with olive oil; heavenly *fuži* with truffles, with cream sauce or not; or squid with chips, cabbage salad and beans. It gets busy with locals, repeat guests and voluble Italian ladies from a nearby spa.

### ★ Konoba Dorjana
*Livade 4A, Livade (052 664 093).* **Open** 11am-10pm Mon, Tue, Thur-Sun. **€€.** Istrian
This is a great little spot. Across the turnabout from the better-known **Zigante** (*see right*), it has a perfectly homely dining room with something of a French feel – dainty wallpaper, wooden ceiling, black and white photographs, and a bar made of stone. Run by Dorijana Basanese and family, it serves

traditional food with unique touches. Examples include turkey stuffed with truffles, seasonal asparagus soup, and snails with polenta.

### Konoba Mondo
*Barbacan 1 (052 681 791).* **Open** *Summer* noon-3.30pm, 6-10pm daily. *Winter* noon-3.30pm, 6-10pm Mon, Wed-Sun. **No credit cards. €€.** Istrian
Mondo divides opinion. Praise by the *New York Times* led to a local media frenzy, driven partly by a translation that alleged it was 'one of the world's best small restaurants'. Soon after, it was slated by a Croatian critic. In reality, it's an acceptable, friendly konoba with a pleasant terrace in summer.

### Pod Voltom
*Trg Josefa Ressela 6 (052 681 923).* **Open** *Summer* noon-11pm daily. *Winter* noon-11pm Mon, Tue, Thur-Sun. Closed Jan. **€€.** Istrian
'Under the Arch', by the old city gate, serves a selection of honest, regional fare, including truffles, and can always be relied upon to have a fire blazing in winter, terrace seating in summer. Pod Voltom serves some of the best meat in Istria with dishes that have made many visitors sigh with contentment.

### Zigante
*Livade 7 (052 664 302, www.zigantetartufi.com).* **Open** *Summer* noon-11pm daily. *Winter* 11am-10pm daily. **€€€.** Istrian
A short drive from Motovun, this renowned and formal restaurant is the base for an entire industry centred around a world-record event. In 1999, Giancarlo Zigante, and Diana the dog, discovered the biggest white truffle in history, weighing 1.31kg (2.89lbs). Fame spread, the restaurant opened in 2002 and extended three years later. Zigante also runs numerous truffle factories and shops. And the restaurant? Set in a beautiful house with outdoor seating, it offers expensive, impressive dishes (some truffle-free) to an exclusive clientele. *See p98* **Sniffing For Gold**.

## Cafés & Bars

### Caffè Bar Montana Gallery
*Trg Josefa Ressela 2 (052 681 754).* **Open** 8.30am-midnight daily.
Run by couple Claudio and Lela, this hilltop café has stunning views of the Mirna valley. Tables are lined up on the terrace, ideal for sunset, and there are chairs inside for long winter nights. As one of only a few bars around here, it attracts lively, local regulars.

## Shops & Services

Motovun has several small, independent boutiques mostly specialising in a million ways to sell a truffle: black and white, whole or in a paste, in cheese or spirits, complemented by local wines or olive oils. Other local shops sell jewellery and souvenirs. Most are cash-only but there is an ATM at the top of the hill, near the post office. At Borgo 33, Livio Lanča's **Etnobutiga Ča** offers top wine labels, tasteful jewellery, lavender products and liqueurs.

### Benčić Truffles
*Gradiziol 10 (052 681 725, www.bencic-tartufi.com/index.php).* **Open** 8am-8pm daily. **Food & drink** *See p98* **Sniffing For Gold.**

## Hotels

### ★ The Hilltop Retreat
*Angelo Garbizza 5 (+44 7949 777 140, www.motovunvilla.com).* **No credit cards.** **€€.**
Beautifully restored over the last five years by a London-based photographer, this four-storey, 18th-century home is ideal for groups of up to six. The accommodation is fabulous and complemented by two terraces, and a mature herb and fruit garden overlooking the truffle-packed forest below. The traditional character is wedded to modern technology (flatscreen TV, cable, Wi-Fi, range cooker, dishwasher) while a cot and baby-feeding chair are provided. There is parking is close by.

### ★ Kaštel
*Trg Andrea Antico 7 (052 681 607, 052 681 750, www.hotel-kastel-motovun.hr).* **€.**
The only hotel in town opened a spa in 2008 – at that point, the attractive Kaštel moved up from being 'homely' to one of the best mid-priced, stay-and-relax deals in Istria. The spa centre offers a covered hydro-massage pool, saunas, views of the verdant landscape and a lovely garden. Some of the 34 well-appointed rooms have balconies with views; half-board is available. The restaurant is a destination in its own right, with quality Istrian cuisine.

### Villa Angelica
*Palazzo Angelica, Matka Laginje, Oprtalj (052 758 700, www.solea.hr).* **€€€.** **No credit cards.**
The 19th-century Villa Angelica, renovated in 2008, sits on the edge of Oprtalj. A six-bedroom establishment, it has a pool, spa with saunas and a view over the valley, maid service and more terraces than you could possibly need. There's even the option of a private chef and masseuse. A wine cellar and culinary workshops provide added attractions.

## GETTING THERE & AROUND

The infrequent **bus** from the transport hub of Pazin takes 45mins to get to Motovun. The twice-daily Pula-Buzet line also drops off at Motovun, as does the Zagreb-Buzet bus.

## RESOURCES

**Tourist information** *Trg Andrea Antico 1 (052 681 758).*

Motovun

# SNIFFING FOR GOLD
## *Istria's truffle-hunting industry.*

One of the world's most expensive gastronomic delicacies, truffles are big business in Istria. From late summer through to the end of January, you can spot ancient Renault 4s, many without number plates, parked at the edges of the Motovun Forest. They are the vehicle of choice for truffle hunters, who roam between the dense trees – often with three or four dogs in tow – in their secretive search.

The Motovun Forest is the largest and best known hunting ground in Istria. The river Mirna flows through its centre; it regularly used to flood the forest providing essential minerals that promoted truffle growth. Unfortunately, a combination of over-hunting, poor practice and the lack of annual flooding are taking their toll. It's much harder to find truffles than it used to be and their size is decreasing. There are now moves to redirect the river back along its original course to protect the forest's unique and precious commodity.

Most hunters stick to their personal routes, usually a closely guarded secret. Truffles grow chiefly among the roots of oak trees – dogs are trained to locate the truffles and dig them up without snaffling them in the process. Training a truffle hound is a long and arduous process and a good dog is worth a great deal. A few, unscrupulous hunters have been known to lay poison in the forests to nobble the competition – it's a cut-throat business. But then, with white truffles fetching between €2,000 and €3,000 per kilo, depending on their size, stakes are high.

Six species of black truffles and four white are currently found in Istria. White truffles are the most highly prized thanks to their pungency whilst the milder, black truffle is considerably cheaper. Often likened to the smell of old socks, the taste of truffles is, thankfully, very different. In the kitchen, they function best against bland foods (pasta, rice or scrambled eggs for example); a particular local favourite is *biftek s tartufima*, truffle-smothered beefsteak.

Motovun region, and Livade in particular, is the centre of the truffle trade. The renowned Zigante restaurant (*see p96*) is the base for an entire industry centred around a discovery dating to 1999 when Giancarlo Zigante, and his dog Diana, found the biggest white truffle in history, weighing 1.31kg. Celebrity brought opportunity, the restaurant opened in 2002 then extended three years later. Zigante also runs truffle factories and shops. And the restaurant? In a beautiful house with outdoor seating, it offers very expensive if impressive dishes, some even truffle-free.

Meanwhile in Motovun, Benčić Truffles (*see p97*) is a family-run establishment offering a huge range of truffle products, from salt to rakija and pasta. They also offer recipes in various languages, while a video shows the process of gathering, harvesting and cooking this elusive delicacy.

# Grožnjan

**Grožnjan** is one of Istria's prettiest medieval hilltop towns, 228 metres (748 feet) above sea level, with spectacular views: the Adriatic to the west and the dramatic landscape of the Mirna Valley to the east. Istria is rich with these ancient, Italianate settlements. What sets Grožnjan apart is that it feels loved, alive and cared for. With two dozen galleries and plenty of studios, it's a thriving art hub.

After World War II, this part of Istria was assigned to Tito's Yugoslavia. Many emigrated to Italy. In Grožnjan only 20 souls remained. Gradually, visiting artists began using the empty buildings as studios and by 1965 it was formally declared a 'Town of Artists'. Street signs are hand-painted ceramics, rather than state-manufactured enamel; the colours of the shutters are subtle but just right; there are stone seats for enjoying the view; and everywhere you look, there's a gallery. There's a perfect little town square and outside the town loggia on balmy, summer evenings are recitals by operatic tenors or jazzers, performing as part of the **Grožnjan Musical Summer**.

## Sights & Museums

### Fonticus City Gallery
*Trg Lože 3 (052 776 131, www.gallery-fonticus-groznjan.net).* **Open** varies. **No credit cards**. The main public gallery in Grožnjan.

## Restaurants, Cafés & Bars

### Bastia
*Svibnja 1 (052 776 370).* **Open** *Summer*
8am-midnight daily. *Winter* 11am-9pm daily.
**€€**.**Istrian**
Under the church tower, this large, imposing and
traditional restaurant is the main place to eat in
town. Fabulous, authentic local dishes include the
likes of home-made sausage, rumpsteak with truffles and twisted pasta ties *(fuži)* with wild game.
There's a little bar with a piano in the back, and a
few rooms to rent.

### Kaya Energy Bar
*Vincent iz Kastava 2 (052 776 051).* **Open**
*Summer* 9am-midnight daily. *Winter* 9am-10pm
Sat, Sun.
This exceptionally lovely café-bar-gallery was
opened by designer Suzana Colarić, known for her
work on the interiors of hotels and larger projects.
Low tables, wicker chairs and comfortable couches
make up the stone-walled and wood-beamed interior, scattered with art and objects by Colarić or
other local designers – but it never feels cluttered.
There is an emphasis on recycled and natural
materials; as you enter, there's a lamp made from
silkworm cocoons, and table bases made from
driftwood. Though pricey by Croatian standards,
coffee is complemented by delicious cakes and
other snacks (including superb bread), mostly local
or organic. Chilled music helps to set the laidback,
indulgent mood.

## Hotels

### Pintur
*M Gorjana 9 (052 776 397).* **€**.
A modest guesthouse and konoba on the town
square, with four rooms. The restaurant (closed
Nov-Mar) has tables on a raised terrace, in the
shade of an old tree, where you can sip a coffee,
enjoy spaghetti with mushrooms, or home-made
gnocchi with goulash.

## Shops

### MM Gallery
*Postolarska (no phone, www.facebook.com/
GalerijaMM).* **Open** *Summer* 10am-10pm daily.
**No credit cards. Crafts & jewellery**
The MM is a rather lovely little gallery selling jewel-
lery and decorative ceramics: ideal for picking up a
souvenir or two to take home.

### Pharos
*Umberto Gorjana 8 (no phone).* **Open** *Easter-Sept*
10am-8pm daily. **No credit cards. Antiques, art
& souvenirs**
Specialises in local antique furniture, souvenirs and
landscape paintings.

## IN THE KNOW LIGHT MY STAY

Sleeping in one of Croatia's lighthouses
is by far the country's most unique
accommodation option. Off limits until
2000, these peaceful marine outposts now
give tourists a chance to play lighthouse
keeper, watching ships glide by late at night
as they act out Robinson Crusoe fantasies
on one of the uninhabited islands. Of 48
lighthouses scattered along the coast,
11 are available for rent, featuring 20
apartments in total. Savudrija lighthouse
(see p94) is the oldest and northernmost
on the mainland. Of seven island hideaways,
the most isolated is Palagruža on the
remote, eponymous islet between the
coasts of Italy and Croatia, a three-hour
boat ride away from Korčula (see p254).
Lodgings vary in size, sleeping from two
to eight people. The most popular are the
seven permanently staffed lighthouses,
where lighthouse keepers can arrange
food delivery and organise excursions. For
details, see www.lighthouses-croatia.com.

## GETTING THERE & AROUND

There is no public transport to Grožnjan. Your only
option is to take the Buzet-Buje **bus** and ask the
driver to drop you off at Bijele Zemlje, and walk the
3km uphill from there. Usually locals will pick you
up when you're coming up or down the hill.

## RESOURCES

**Tourist information** *Umberta Gorjana 3 (052 776
349, www.groznjan-grisignana.hr).*

# Hum

Enclosed by thick, medieval walls, **Hum** is billed
as the smallest town in the world. To qualify as a
bona fide town, a settlement must have a school,
church, post office, town hall and pub. Squeeze in
a dozen houses and that's Hum. Traditionally it's
been home to just two families, while the priest is
also the publican – but things are changing.

As you wander round the single, circular street,
be careful not to trip over any building rubble.
People have cottoned on to Hum's charm and
slowly the town is coming to life. As you pass
through Hum's massive, metal doors you enter a
cave-like antechamber hewn out of the rock. Above
is the town hall. On the walls are stone tablets
inscribed in ancient Glagolitic, a Slavic script for
which Hum is famous. Ahead is the main square;
to the left is the ludicrously large **Church of the**

Exalted and Blessed Virgin Mary with its magnificent crenellated belltower. The consecration chapel of **Sv Jeronima** in the graveyard houses 12th-century frescoes covered with Glagolitic graffiti. Left is a Lilliputian house with a picturesque loggia. A small gallery signed 'Imela' is the source of Hum's second claim to fame: *biska*. This is mistletoe-flavoured grappa, made from the leaves rather than the poisonous berries. It's either bright green or golden brown depending on whether fresh or dried leaves have been used.

Further up the street is the **Hum Museum** (052 662 596, open summer 11am-5pm daily), which is really a souvenir shop but with a small collection of old Istrian furniture and artefacts. You can also buy Glagolitic alphabet charts here.

Finish the circuit of the town, step out of the main gate and into Hum's single restaurant, only open at weekends. The **Konoba Hum** (052 660 005, 11am-11pm Sat, Sun) has a covered terrace with a beautiful view down into the valley – this is the perfect setting to share a *bukaleta* (drinking jug) of traditional *supa*. Clearly invented by a peasant with no food in the house, this speciality consists of red wine topped off with warm, toasted bread liberally sprinkled with olive oil.

## GETTING THERE & AROUND

Hum is 5km from the main Buzet-Lupoglav road. There is no public transport but coach tours can be booked in summer from most Istrian tourist offices.

# Labin

The only major town on Istria's wild east coast, **Labin** is something of a law unto itself. Sited on a high peak, three kilometres from the sea, Labin is said to have been founded by Celts in the fourth century. They christened it 'Albona' or 'Alvona' ('Town on a Hill') and this ancient name is still in use. A century later the Romans recorded the presence of unruly pirates. The local **Matija Vlačić** was a leading European religious reformer alongside Martin Luther. In recent history, Labin's miners revolted against Mussolini and declared an independent republic. Labin has always had attitude.

## INTRODUCING LABIN

With a population of 10,000, Labin is an economic centre; the plain beneath the Old Town sprawls with a thriving residential and business community. Technically known as 'Podlabin' ('Under Labin'), this is where Mussolini built two new towns to house local miners. There's a reconstructed shaft at Labin's excellent museum.

As you ascend the steep, cobbled hill up to the Old Town you pass by the beautiful villas for white collar workers. Passing through the first city gate

you enter the main square – still named **Titov trg** – with its brightly painted buildings and Venetian loggia. This is the town's social hub dominated by the landmark **Velo** café, restaurant and nightspot.

Labin has a vibrant arts scene and the majority of talent is home grown, artists preferring to stay here. As you continue uphill, through the second gate, and explore the Old Town you pass galleries, studios and workshops. **Municipal Gradska Galerija Labin** (Ulica 1. maja 5, 052 852 123) provides a programme of contemporary exhibitions, opposite the **Labin Museum** (Ulica 1. svibnja 6, 052 852 477). These and other public spaces are commandeered for the annual **Labin Art Republic** series of arts events in July and August: live shows, exhibitions and ad hoc street entertainment, usually with a theme. Studios open their doors and visitors are given access to a number of private and public collections.

Don't miss the sculpture park, **Mediterranean Sculpture Symposium** (MKS; 052 852 464) in nearby Dubrova. Look out for the large, green glass cube, due to be opened as the visitors' centre. International residencies take place each year. Artists provide contributions to a pathway continuously being added to.

Back to the old town, **Šetalište San Marco** is a terrace on the old city walls providing an unbroken vista over **Kvarner Bay**. Locals claim that the shallowness of the sea here, 80 metres (260 feet), encourages growth of a specific plankton, and thus great seafood. If you carry on walking to the top of the town, the whole of eastern Istria is laid out before you. Within immediate view, sited on a spectacular sea cove three kilometres down the hill, is Labin's counterpart port, **Rabac** (*see p101*).

## Restaurants, Cafés & Bars

### ★ Restaurant Kvarner

*Šetalište San Marco (052 852 336, www. kvarnerlabin.com)*. **Open** 10am-10pm Mon-Sat, 11am-midnight Sun. **€€**. **Istrian**
Here a fabulous view comes with outstanding food, all produced locally. It's also the best-sited restaurant in Labin, the terrace seating on Šetalište San Marco with views of Kvarner Bay. There's a wide-ranging menu, including an Istrian hot plate (small portions of local specialities) but the must-try is *krafi* (pasta shaped like ravioli, sweetened with raisins, rum and sugar and stuffed with four types of local cheese). In summer the restaurant grills fish and meat on the terrace; they also have four rooms in Labin and another four apartments in Rabac.

### Velo

*Titov Trg 12 (052 852 745)*. **Open** *Restaurant* 11am-11pm daily. **Café** *Summer* 7am-2am daily. *Winter* 7am-11pm Mon-Fri, Sun; 7am-midnight Sat. Three venues in one, all of them busy, all year round. In the basement, a comfortable, half-trendy,

half-rustic restaurant boasts terracotta walls, plenty of artwork and a traditional open fire in winter. The food is typical Istrian (no pizzas, despite what the sign says) at reasonable prices. It's no wonder artists fill the place. Above, the café and its terrace throng in summer; the Rock Café nightspot occupies the first floor.
▶ Look out also for the Spider Café Bar opposite, another good late-hours drinking haunt, with DJs in the summer.

## GETTING THERE & AROUND/ RESOURCES

See Rabac (below).

# Rabac

If Labin is strong on culture, **Rabac** provides the summer fun. As you travel down spectacular hairpin bends towards Rabac Bay, the small town comes into view like something from the French Riviera. The steep hillside is crowded with brightly painted houses – nearly all offering vacation apartments – and, at the bottom, is the holiday village of Rabac itself. Seaside gentrification is already under way; the Valamar group sited a hub of hotel-leisure complexes here, with access to a Blue Flag beach. Inland, you can explore nature trails, one leading to the **Tears of St Lucia**, a natural spring that is reputed to heal your eyes if you wash them with the water. You are also close to the ferry terminal at **Brestova**, for access to **Cres** (see p132) and **Lošinj** (see p134).

## Restaurants

### ★ Lino Restaurant
*Obala maršala Tita 59 (052 872 629).*
**Open** noon-11pm daily. €€. Croatian
Suzana and Lino Hrvatin offer an all-round dining experience a notch above Rabac's other harbourside restaurants. Seafood dishes all use garlic and olive oil, such as the memorable linguini with clams, and the spicy lobster for two. Lino, who worked for years in New York, also prepares roasted lamb from Cres, while Suzana supervises front of house. Surrounded by pine trees, and with two terraces overlooking the water, this is not just a great place to eat but just the spot for local wine and watching the sunset.

### Nostromo
*Obala maršala Tita 7 (052 872 601, www.nostromo. hr).* **Open** 11am-11pm daily. €€. Croatian
One of the best restaurants in Rabac, Nostromo has a large, roofed terrace where you can enjoy your meal looking out over Maslinica beach in Rabac Bay. Understandably, the menu majors on fish and seafood specialities – although not exclusively – and there's a reasonable range of local wines. Nostromo also rents out rooms and apartments.

## Hotels

### Hotel Amfora
*Gornji Rabac 26 (no phone, www.hotel-amfora.com).* €.
If you want to be in the thick of things, then the Amfora is Rabac's most central hotel, only 30 metres from the seafront. It has air conditioning, a summer terrace and small swimming pool; half the 52 rooms enjoy a sea view. Open year round, its winter rates are a snip considering the setting, as is half board.

### ★ Top Pick Hotel & Casa Valamar Sanfior
*Rabac seafront (052 465 200, www.valamar.com).* **Open** Mar-Nov. €€.
On Istria's lesser-known, wild east coast, this premium accommodation was opened in 2013. Comprising the hotel and the luxury suites of the Sanfior Casa, this major, family-friendly venture sits surrounded by cool pine woods and beaches overlooking Rabac Bay. Of 242 rooms and suites, all those with a sea view have balconies. Along with its swimming pools, the hotel lays on a summer-long programme of child-focused entertainment, and a range of activities for adults. Its spa centre has several saunas, plus massages and treatments; showers, cabins, deck chairs and sunshades are provided on the adjoining Blue Flag beach.

### Valamar Bellevue Hotel & Residence
*Rabac (052 465 200, www.valamar.com/hoteli-rabac/valamar-bellevue-hotel).* **Open** Apr-Oct. €€.
This renovated hotel, under the Valamar umbrella, is sited on the beach just north of Rabac, connected to town by a little train. It comprises 155 rooms, in separate villas, two pools, one for kids, and plenty of family entertainment. Prices, all half-board, are reasonable.

### ★ Villa Annette
*Rajka 24 (052 884 222, www.villaannette.hr).* €€.
This is a stunningly modern boutique hotel overlooking Rabac Bay. Plenty of well placed artwork decorates the 12 suites, well designed with space and character. There's an infinity pool with views to islands of Cres and Lošinj, and a great slow food restaurant. Considering the quality, the cost is not exorbitant.

## GETTING THERE & AROUND

Don't let the 3km of steep hill between Labin and Rabac put you off – there's a frequent daily **bus service**, running from 6am-10pm every day. A timetable is available from the tourist office. Local **taxi firms** include Jasmin (098 916 1863) and Ivanić (098 226 960).

## RESOURCES

**Labin-Rabac Tourist Information** *A Negri 20 (052 855 560, www.rabac-labin.com).* **Open** 7am-3pm Mon-Fri.

**EXPLORE**

# Kvarner

**N**ature really comes to the fore in Kvarner. The main islands of Krk, Lošinj and Rab have long been developed for tourism, but around them the hilly terrain, the Bura wind, and havens for dolphins contrast with easier, consumer pleasures. Cres, in particular, is relatively untouched. Away from the celebrated DJ scene at Zrće, Pag also feels bare and isolated. Pag doesn't officially belong to Kvarner as this long, arid island is divided administratively between the mainland and Zadar, but it is closely connected with the other islands in the Kvarner Gulf. Easy transport links constitute one of the area's boons – both Krk and Pag have bridges to continental Croatia and most ferry hops in this part of the Adriatic are short and frequent. On the mainland, the two main towns are chalk and cheese. For much of its past, the gritty port of Rijeka didn't belong to Croatia at all, but was Habsburg for centuries, then Italian. Next door, elegant Opatija had its glory days in the late 19th century. Further on, Lovran offers quality seafront dining.

Lungomare.

## Don't Miss

**1 Rijeka Modern & Contemporary Art Museum** Outstanding temporary shows (p106).

**2 Cres island** A largely untouched gem of Adriatic wilderness (p132).

**3 Marine Education Centre** Bottlenose dolphins off Lošinj (p135).

**4 Zrće** Summer party hub on Pag (p138).

**5 Lungomare** Opatija's seafront promenade, lined with hotels (p115).

# Rijeka

Croatia's third-largest city with a population of 150,000, **Rijeka** has a busy port that handles ten million tonnes of cargo and a quarter of a million passengers a year, many heading to nearby resorts. It's a nice place for a city break – you can enjoy its fascinating history, great restaurants and kicking, year-round nightlife. This is not a tourist-oriented city though, which is part of its charm: in Rijeka you'll be dining, drinking and dancing with locals.

### INTRODUCING RIJEKA

Founded by the Romans, and Habsburg from the 15th century, Rijeka fell under Hungarian control in the late 18th. The landlocked Magyars built a new harbour, Baroque landmarks and sundry industries, including the world's first torpedo. Much of the city was destroyed by a devastating earthquake in 1750, so earlier monuments were wiped out; hence the Habsburg look in Rijeka's Old Town.

Fiume, as Rijeka is still known to Hungarians, had no indigenous Magyar population. When their legitimacy was challenged in 1868, the Hungarians switched papers on Emperor Franz Josef at the signing ceremony, and a majority Slav population endured 50 more years of rule from Budapest. As a result of the indignation expressed in the influential local newspaper *Novi List*, displaced Dalmatian intellectuals stirred up a groundswell of opinion that resulted in the Declaration of Fiume in 1905, a call for a united land of South Slavs. It failed but it helped spread the notion of 'Yugoslavia' – one that would come to fruition after World War I.

With the collapse of the Habsburg Empire after the war, the Hungarian governor fled his magnificent palace, and in marched Italian patriot, pilot and poet Gabriele D'Annunzio, with 200 soldiers, to proclaim 'Fiume' as Italian and his own state. Mussolini's men took Rijeka a year later, the Germans in 1943. Rijeka industrialised under Tito, rusted in the 1990s, but developments since – a motorway from Zagreb, the road bridge from the nearest airport on Krk island – are bringing change. Rijeka remains the northern Adriatic's main hub of transport and commerce, and as the centre of social and cultural life, it also possesses a palpable year-round buzz. It has even introduced free, communal, city-centre Wi-Fi.

The main **Korzo** runs parallel to the harbourfront Riva. A few Baroque facades (including the remake of the original medieval City Tower) fade behind modern shops and cafés. A short walk west is the main bus station, backdropped by the bizarre, two-level **Capuchin Church**. Further west is the underused train station. Beyond is Opatija (*see p115*), easily reached by regular bus. East, the Korzo ends at the local bus station (where Opatija services set

off) and the so-called Dead Canal, pretty and pedestrianised. Its nearby continuation, the Rječina, is the division between Rijeka and the former separate areas of Sušak and Trsat. Between the wars, this was the border between Italy and newly founded Yugoslavia.

Spending a few hours on the hilltop around **Trsat Castle** can be pleasant, but if you don't have much time, you can turn left from the canal at Titov trg into Žrtava fašizma to find a handful of mildly diverting tourist attractions. First up is **St Vitus' Church**, topped by a Baroque rotunda, a Venetian-inspired creation from the 17th century. Across the street and a few doors down is the quirky computer museum, **Peek&Poke Museum of Informatics & Technology**. St Vitus' stands at the edge of the Old Town. Just above it rises the stately **Governor's Palace**, commanding a view of the sea. Exhibits belonging to the **History & Maritime Museum** here are overshadowed by Alajos Hauszmann's sumptuous state rooms. Next door, the **City Museum** contains modest exhibitions in a two-floor space. Overlooking these two buildings is the **Natural History Museum** with an aquarium and a botanical garden outside. The street of Frana Supila descends towards Trg republike Hrvatske, which contains the University Library, accommodating Rijeka's renowned **Modern & Contemporary Art Museum**.

The best time to visit is for **carnival** (*see p109* **Rio In Rijeka**), when there is a huge parade on the Sunday preceding Shrove Tuesday.

## Sights & Museums

### City Museum

*Muzejski trg 1/1 (051 336 711, www.muzej-rijeka.hr)*. **Open** 9am-7pm Mon-Fri; 9am-1pm Sat. **Admission** 20kn. **No credit cards**. **Map** p107 C1 ❶

Set in a pavilion alongside the Governor's Palace, and thus alongside the History & Maritime Museum (*see p106*) which makes it a convenient first port of call for any first-time city visitor, the three-floor museum has a modest permanent exhibition but stages a number of fascinating temporary ones. Exhibition subjects tend to concentrate on Rijeka's seafaring past.

### Governor's Palace

*Muzejski trg 1 (no phone)*. **Open** varies. **No credit cards. Map** p107 D1 ❷

Built in the 1890s by Hungarian architect Alajos Hauszmann, also responsible for the most famous and ornate coffeehouse in Budapest, the Governor's Palace was where Italian poet and self-styled leader of Rijeka, Gabriele D'Annunzio, seized power in the immediate aftermath of World War I. Hauszmann's huge, sumptuous state rooms now house the History & Maritime Museum (*see p106*); the Rijeka City Museum (*see above*) is in a pavilion alongside.

## History & Maritime Museum

*Muzejski trg 1 (051 55 36 67, www.ppmhp.hr).*
Open 9am-4pm Mon; 9am-8pm Tue-Fri, 9am-1pm,
4pm-8pm Sat; 4pm-8pm Sun. **Admission** 15kn;
10kn reductions. **No credit cards. Map** p107 D1 ❸
Somewhat overshadowed by Alajos Hauszmann's
grandiose Governor's Palace in which it is housed,
this old-school museum contains a modest collection
of period costumes, coins, instruments, weaponry.
Replica ships reflect Rijeka's proud tradition.

## ★ Modern & Contemporary Art Museum

*Dolac 1/II (051 334 280, www.mmsu.hr).* **Open**
*May-Sept* 10am-1pm, 6-9pm Tue-Fri; 10am-1pm
Sat. *Oct-Apr* 10am-1pm, 5-8pm Tue-Fri; 10am-1pm
Sat. **Admission** 10kn. *Temporary exhibitions*
varies. **No credit cards. Map** p107 C2 ❹
Founded in 1948, Rijeka's Museum of Modern and
Contemporary Art (Muzej modern i suvremene
umjetnosti or MMSU) has long enjoyed a reputation for holding some of the most exciting contemporary art exhibitions in the country. It is also the
host of the Biennial of the Quadrilateral, a show
featuring contemporary artists from Croatia, Italy,
Slovenia and Hungary – a quartet of countries that
has had a profound effect on the history of Rijeka.

Works from the museum's large permanent
collection are rarely seen, except during temporary themed exhibitions, as the museum's current
home, in the same building as the Rijeka municipal
library, is too limited. The MMSU is still waiting
for a new home in the Rikard Benčić palace which
was built to serve as the headquarters of a sugar
refinery in 1752 and is currently awaiting a long-
discussed restoration. The completion date lies some
way in the future, although the project will help to con-
firm the MMSU's growing stature as a major player
in the central European art scene. Over the past few
years the MMSU has been run by a string of directors
who have also been big-hitting curators, a trend that
continued with the arrival of Slaven Tolj, former head
of the Lazareti Art Workshop in Dubrovnik, in 2012.

## Natural History Museum

*Lorenzov prolaz 1 (051 553 669, www.prirodo*
*slovni.com/eng).* **Open** 9am-8pm Mon-Sat;
9am-3pm Sun. **Admission** 10kn; 5kn reductions.
**No credit cards. Map** p107 D1 ❺
Behind the Governor's Palace it overlooks, the
museum established its large collection of speci-
mens from the Kvarner Bay, Gorski kotar and Istria,
thanks to private collectors from the mid 19th century
onwards. Key displays include one of sharks and
rays, and a geological history of the Adriatic Sea.

## ★ Peek&Poke Museum of Informatics & Technology

*Ivana Grohovca 2 (091 780 5709, www.peek*
*poke.hr.)* **Open** 11am-5pm Mon-Fri; 11am-4pm
Sat. **Admission** 20kn. **No credit cards.**
**Map** p107 E1 ❻

This quirky attraction contains more than 2,000
examples of vintage computer technology: calcula-
tors, games consoles and oversized terminals from
two decades ago and older. Of particular note are
the Nintendo Game Boy and the Sinclair C5. Opened
in 2007, Peek&Poke is one of the few collections of
its kind in Europe, with connections to the similarly
themed Bolo Museum in Lausanne, Switzerland.
Opening hours are flexible so phone ahead.

## St Vitus's Church

*Grivica 11 (no phone).* **Open** 9am-noon, 5-7pm
daily. **No credit cards.** Map p107 E2 ❼
Standing at the edge of Rijeka's Old Town, St Vitus's
Church is a Venetian-inspired construction from the
1600s, topped by a Baroque rotunda. Inside, the crucifix was the source of many a medieval legend.

## FREE Trsat Castle

*Petra Zrinskoga, Trsat (no phone).* **Open**
9am-midnight daily. **Admission** Free. **Tours**
15kn. **No credit cards. Map** p107 F1 ❽
Visit this fort for the panoramic view alone, best
enjoyed from the Gradina terrace café beneath the
Nugent mausoleum – the Kvarner Bay spreads out
before you. Irish-born Austro-Hungarian naval
commander Laval Nugent-Westmeath fought
Napoleon and rebuilt the medieval Frankopan fortress to house his family and his art collection – his
hoard of Greek vases can now be seen in Zagreb's
Museum of Archaeology (*see p54*). The mausoleum is worth a look, if only for the bad press it
gives Nugent's daughter, the 'evil and eccentric'
Countess Ana. Down back towards the No.1 bus
terminal, you pass Our Lady of Trsat Church and
the small Franciscan monastery.

# Restaurants

## Bistro La Rose

*Andrije Medulića 8 (051 315 504, www.bistro-*
*la-rose.com).* **Open** 10am-11pm Mon-Sat. €€.
**Map** p107 E2 ❾ **French/Croatian**
A cosy bistro with outdoor seating on one of the
Old-Town's tiny piazzas, La Rose offers a well-executed but affordable blend of French-inspired fare
and Kvarner-Istrian staples. The Gallic side of La
Rose's character is most evident in the quick-lunch
dishes such as onion soup, bouillabaisse and quiche
lorraine. Local inspiration lies behind the truffle-
garnished pastas, seafood risottos, fillets of sea bass,
although everything is served with Mediterranean
bistro flair. The ambience – rose-themed decor and
jazzy music – makes it an ideal spot for a lunchtime
tête-à-tête or an intimate evening meal.

## Konoba Blato

*Titov Trg 8C (051 336 970, konoba-blato.*
*blato1902.hr).* **Open** *Summer* 8am-9pm Mon-Sat.
*Winter* 8am-8pm Mon-Sat. €. **No credit cards.**
**Map** p107 F1 ❿ **Croatian**

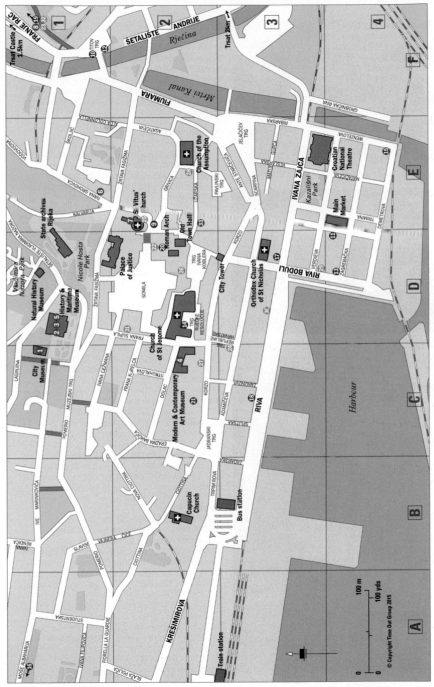

EXPLORE

**Konoba Nebuloza**

In a sturdy wood-and-tile cellar on the pedestrianised square where the two main canals meet, this small, dimly lit eaterie makes home-style seafood and hearty meat dishes in a pleasant family atmosphere. The fish is always fresh and well prepared, as is the octopus salad to accompany it. There are only half-a-dozen tables, busy during work breaks; the tiny bar has a few stools, nearly all occupied by locals.

### Konoba Fiume
*Vatroslava Lisinskog 12B (051 312 108, konobafiume.fullbusiness.com)*. **Open** 6am-6pm Mon-Fri; 6am-3pm Sat. Closed 1st 2 weeks Aug. **€**. **No credit cards**. Map p107 D4 ❹ **Croatian**
Just metres from the main market, near the port and the Korzo, stands the stone-walled, brick-arched, high-ceilinged Fiume, with its daily offering of grilled ray, mackerel, sardines, tuna, squid, goulash and cod stew on Fridays. Simple meals, cooked the local way, are based on the freshest seasonal ingredients from the nearby market. Decent local wines and affordable prices can be expected, as well as a warm welcome from Nena, a big fan of *The Big O*.

### ★ Konoba Nebuloza
*Titov trg 2B (051 374 501, www.konobanebuloza. com)*. **Open** 11am-midnight Mon-Fri; noon-midnight Sat. **€**. **Map** p107 F1 ❷ **Croatian**
A friendly little restaurant next to the Rječina Canal provides perfectly prepared fresh seafood at reasonable prices in a comfortable atmosphere. It serves a lot of the fish that others do, but the menu lets you know whether it has been farmed or caught wild. House special starters include smoked tuna and goulash or lamb stew with local *šurlice* noodles. Meat-eaters get a choice of toppings such as truffle sauce, or rosemary and capers, for their thick, juicy steaks. The amicable waiters not only show you the catch of the day, but tell you what's freshest – even if it's something less expensive, like calamari. The side room has big windows with great views of the canal below.

### Kukuriku
*Trg Lokvina 3, Kastav (051 691 519, www. kukuriku.hr/restoran)*. **Open** noon-midnight daily. **€€€**. **Contemporary Croatian**
This restaurant is the main reason to visit the small town of Kastav, 20 minutes from Rijeka by taxi or No.18 bus – although there is a pretty hilltop old town to stroll through after dinner. You'll get superior seafood prepared by a creative chef, served in several small but tasty courses, and paired with a different wine for each course. This could be the best meal you have in Rijeka, and also one of the most expensive: the waiter will suggest a wonderful set menu, but it's a good idea to check the prices before you dive in. If you're going to splash out on dinner, do it here.

# RIO IN RIJEKA
*Local carnival brings Brazil to Kvarner.*

Croatia's biggest carnival takes place in Rijeka, culminating in a colourful procession of thousands on the Sunday before Shrove Tuesday. The Mardi Gras tradition here dates back centuries, when it was a festival to welcome the coming of spring and to scare off any lurking Turks. Then, as now, masks were elaborate and ugly, and evil spirits were sent packing by local men dressed in animal skins, the *zvončari*, clanging huge cowbells.

Always up for a spot of costumed fun, the Habsburgs revived the concept in the late 19th century, before Rijeka got tangled up in too much political torment for street parties.

Then, in 1982, three masked groups walked down Korzo to the bemusement of onlookers. After that, numbers grew. By 2001 there were around 4,000 taking part in the parades. For the 25th anniversary event in 2007, it was nearer 100,000. No wonder locals call it the 'fifth season', in addition to spring, summer, autumn and winter.

Depending on when Shrove Tuesday falls, the **Queen's Pageant** usually takes place on the third Friday in January, followed by the **Zvončari Parade**, which takes place the next day. By tradition, the bell-ringers clang their instruments and move in steps according to their village of origin. Then, 13 days before Shrove Tuesday, on the Saturday lunchtime, the **Children's Parade** runs through the streets of Rijeka. The big event, however, is the **International Carnival Parade**, which kicks off at noon on the following Sunday. It usually takes the whole afternoon for floats to pass along the main streets. Subsequent celebrations last well into the night, at stalls and tents set up around the canal.

Tour companies like Adriatica (www. adriatica.net) put together packages for visitors attending the carnival. For more information on the carnival itself, see the official website: www.ri-karneval.com.hr.

## Mornar
*Riva Boduli 5A (051 312 222).* **Open** 8am-10pm daily. **No credit cards.** €. **Map** p107 D4 ⓭
**Croatian**
Although newly renovated Mornar is next to the docks and the marine terminal, the views from its L-shaped corner terrace include just a snippet of sea and a whole load of car park. Forget the scenery: hearty meat dishes here satisfy, and the fish comes right off the boats or from the nearby market, which means it's fresher and cheaper than most places in town. Join hungry locals and sailors as you tuck into generous platters of calamari, sardines or superior freshly caught whitefish at amazing prices.

## Municipium
*Trg Riječke rezolucije 5 (051 213 000).* **Open** 10am-11pm Mon-Sat. €€€. **Map** p107 D2 ⓮
**Croatian/International**
Municipium is set in a grand Habsburg-era building, tucked away in a quiet courtyard right in the centre of town. Door staff greet you at the entrance – decorum is all. The menu is vast and fish-oriented, most of it priced in the 300kn/kg range, which is very reasonable considering the quality of service, presentation and the fare itself. Courgettes, wild asparagus and other greens get a look-in and the wine list runs to 150 (mainly Croatian) varieties. Latest developments include a *konoba*-style interior revamp and gluten-free menu choices.

## Na Kantunu
*Wenzelova 4 (051 313 271).* **Open** 8am-midnight Mon-Sat. €€. **Map** p107 E4 ⓯ **Seafood**
This once-tiny seafood bistro expanded into the neighbouring room and kitted itself out with new furniture in 2013; its reputation for serving some of Rijeka's best seafood in a simple setting remains unchanged. Settle at one of the rustic wooden tables in the bright, modern interior and admire the trays of just-caught fish and crustaceans chilling behind the glass. Point at your choice and wait for it to be expertly grilled, perhaps dressed lightly with olive oil and big chunks of sea salt, and then served up as a minimalist masterpiece. The car park terrace gets the sun and gives a view of the docks. You can find fancier, but not much better.

## Pizzeria Ex
*Ulica Miroslava Krleže 11 (051 624 471, www. facebook.com/pizzeria.ex).* **Open** 7am-midnight daily. €. **No credit cards. Map** p107 A1 ⓰
**Pizzeria/Grill**
Seven kilometres from the city centre in a maze of similar-looking streets up the hill, Pizzeria Ex hasn't been found by the tourism industry yet. It's nondescript from the outside, next to a café that often has loud football on TV, but is tastefully decorated inside and has an open smoking area. Prices are suspiciously low; two people can stuff themselves, with dessert, for 120kn or so and the food is excellent.

From *pljeskavica* to pasta to pizza to various meat and fish dishes, everything is good and service is speedy. Great for those on a budget who don't want to resort to fast-food chains.

## Ristorante Spagho
*Ivana Zajca 24 (051 311 122, ristorante-spagho. com).* **Open** 10am-midnight Mon-Sat; noon-midnight Sun. €€. **Map** p107 D3 ⓱ **Croatian/Italian**
This neat little corner restaurant with part rustic, part minimalist interior has a huge list of dependable pizzas in the 45kn range, and an even bigger choice of pastas and gnocchi dishes. The bruschetta menu may sort you out if you are in search of a light bite; otherwise work up your hunger for meaty mains such as steak Florentine.

## ★ Trattoria Riva's
*Riva 12 (051 301 581/hr-hr.facebook.com/trattoria. rivas).* **Open** 9am-11pm Mon-Thur; 9am-midnight Fri, Sat. €€. **Map** p107 C3 ⓲ **Croatian**
Having made his culinary reputation at the upmarket Le Mandrać in Volosko (*see p118*), Deniz Zembo has set out to bring fresh energy to Rijeka's well-established *konoba* culture of good honest cooking at a fair price. Trattoria Riva's is the result, a checked-tablecloth bistro on Rijeka's waterfront boulevard, head chef Bojan Cvetković serving everything from cheap staples like *ćevapčići* and breaded squid to exquisitely grilled fish and steaks. The menu, in fact, is now mainly meat-based, with Serbian favourites such as *Leskovački roštilj*. Pizzas will keep the kids happy and there's free Wi-Fi too.

## Trsatika
*Šetalište J Rakovca 33, Trsat (051 451 716, restaurant-trsatica.com/en).* **Open** 10am-midnight daily. €€. **Map** p107 F1 ⓳ **Croatian/Pizzeria**
Fabulously located up in Trsat, this eaterie, part pizzeria, part grill, offers high-grade versions of renowned standards, with a terrace view to boot. Specialities include roast suckling pig, grilled, roasted or boiled lamb, *šurlice* pasta with goulash from Krk, and roast veal knuckle. A rustic oven in the corner turns out large, cheap pizzas in two sizes; the house Trsatika with ham, mussels, scampi and cheese comes in at under 40kn. If you have a day in Rijeka, it's worth spending a couple of hours here.

## Volta 15
*Pod Voltun 15 (051 330 806).* **Open** 9.30am-10pm Mon-Sat. €€. **No credit cards.** Map p107 D2 ⓴
**Seafood**
Opened in 2011 in a location that's housed restaurants for years, this classic *konoba*, with white stucco walls and exposed masonry and ceiling rafters, serves excellent seafood and good wine in a cosy setting on a hill leading up from the sea in the town centre. The friendly server gives special care to a small dining room with only six tables and a

soundtrack of soft jazz. Coastal Croatian standards such as octopus salad, fish soup, calamari and sea bass are handled expertly – the latter served with the house special sauce of rosemary, lemon and capers. Good local wines accompany, including the house red Plavac Mali and house white Malvasia.

### Zlatna Školjka
*Kružna 12A (051 213 782, www.zlatna-skoljka.hr).* **Open** 11am-midnight Mon-Sat. €€€. **Map** p107 C2 ㉑ **Seafood**
With a good location and a reputation as one of the best places in town, this busy cellar restaurant can charge higher prices than most. Along with the usual seafood offerings, appetisers include fish carpaccio with capers, and marinated salmon. The day's catch is displayed on ice, and includes a wide selection of molluscs. The hefty salads can work as a small meal, followed by a number of cheeses. Snappy service adds to a pleasant atmosphere.
▶ *The same management runs a great pizzeria, the Bracera (Kružna 12), which can be found just down the alleyway.*

## Cafés & Bars

### BAR BAR
*Pod Kaštelom 3 (097 712 9949).* **Open** 10am-midnight daily. **Map** p107 D2 ㉒
Newly opened in 2015 and already something of a fixture on the Old Town drinking circuit, BarBar describes itself as a wine and tapas bar – and, although it's the drink that most people are here for,

there's always a more-than-tempting selection of nibbles ranging from *pršut* and cheese to marinated fish and steak tartare. BarBar has made sensitive use of the ancient building it's housed in, with bare bricks and ancient stonework adding character to the snug interior; the action frequently spills out on to the street on warm weekend nights.

### ★ Beertija & Klub
*Slavka Krautzeka 12 (051 452 183).* **Open** 8am-midnight Mon-Thur, Sun; 8am-4am Fri, Sat. **No credit cards. Map** p107 F1 ㉓
Uphill from the centre in Trsat but well worth seeking out, this Rijeka branch of Zagreb's Beertija bar sticks to the same formula – a superb range of bottled beers from all over the world, and well-chosen weekend DJs. Mingling, Thursday's eclectic-indie night, is one of the best pre-weekend nights out in the city. The next-door Klub (part of the same business but with an entrance fee) has live music four to five nights a week.

### Belgian Beer Café Brasserie
*Trg republike Hrvatske 2 (051 212 148).* **Open** 6am-1am Mon-Thur, Sun; 6am-2am Fri, Sat. **Map** p107 C3 ㉔
There's a real brasserie atmosphere at the BBCB, located so close to the harbour you can see ships passing from the handful of tables outside. Inside is wooden, with Flemish inscriptions on the walls and almost authentic pissoirs. The Belgian dishes are hearty and the selection of compatriot brews have improved of late.

**EXPLORE**

Municipium.

### Celtic Caffè Bard

*Grivica ulica 6B (051 215 235, www.caffebard. com).* **Open** 8am-midnight Mon-Fri; 9am-midnight Sat. **No credit cards. Map** p107 E2 ㉕
On a small square on a hill in Rijeka's Old Town, a Guinness sign announces this quaint old-style wood-and-brass pub with exposed brick. There's Kilkenny beer too, but thankfully it's more than just another faux-Irish joint. The walls are cluttered with interesting local art, and the bar and upstairs gallery are packed with interesting local people, mostly in their twenties and thirties. Music ranges from electronica played by the staff to occasional Irish folk bands.

### ★ CukariKafè

*Trg Jurja Klovića 4 (099 583 8276).* **Open** 7am-midnight Mon-Wed, Sun; 7am-2am Thur, Fri; 10am-2am Sat. **No credit cards. Map** p107 D2 ㉖
A unique corner in a city that is already well supplied with eccentricities, CukariKafè brings all kinds of strange images to mind. It's a bit like drinking in a cross between a modern art gallery, a film set for a children's fairy-tale adventure and a passenger steamer cruising up the River Nile. This multitude of impressions is sparked by an interior that features white walls, white-painted furniture, pale-coloured wooden boards that look like ship's decking, and a deftly chosen mixture of crockery and vintage domestic appliances. Everything about the place exudes character: the list of speciality beers includes not just Duvel and Chimay but several lesser-known Belgian brands as well. And unless you specify otherwise, tea will be served with a dandy slice of fresh orange.

### Filodrammatica Bookshop Cafe

*Korzo 28 (no phone).* **Open** 7am-11pm Mon-Sat. **Map** p107 C2 ㉗
This smart café with a busy terrace has been one of central Rijeka's most popular meeting points since the late 19th century, when the Filodrammatica functioned as a municipal cultural society. Nowadays the caryatid-encrusted Filodrammatica building is shared between the brightly lit VBZ bookshop and this plush cafe at the front, with its sumptuously upholstered benches and the odd chandelier. As well as coffee, cakes and alcoholic drinks, it serves a range of breakfasts and light-lunch sandwiches.

### Kosi Toranj

*Put Vele Crkve 1 (051 336 214).* **Open** 7am-10pm daily. **Map** p107 E2 ㉘
Kosi Toranj has a winning terrace on a small hidden square with an aged leaning tower that gives the establishment its name. The interior is an attractive needle-shaped room, with two long glass walls, big art and low, lounge seating.

### Kuća Istarskog pršuta

*Riva Boduli 3A (no phone).* **Open** 7am-5pm Mon-Thur; 7am-10pm Fri, Sat. **No credit cards. Map** p107 D3 ㉙

A new project from a local food company that also runs a chain of bakeries, the 'House of Istrian Pršut' is basically a delicatessen shop with a handful of stools and tables strewn inside. You can buy Istrian cured hams and other delicacies (truffles, home-made pastas) for home consumption, or, settle down, order a prosciutto sandwich and admire views of Rijeka's Riva through the big floor-to-ceiling windows. It also serves a soup of the day, excellent fresh bread, and a selection of local wines chalked up daily above the counter.

### Laval Caffè

*Riva 8 (051 337 772).* **Open** 7am-midnight Mon-Thur, 7am-2am Fri, Sat; 8am-midnight Sun. **No credit cards. Map** p107 D3 ㉚
Right on the harbour, the Laval's shaded terrace is perfect for checking out a young trendy crowd or gazing out at the tall, silent cranes on the docks as they stand guard over the rippling sea. It gets even busier by night than during the day, but the candlelit tables facing the water lend an almost intimate vibe. Inside there's gallery seating upstairs and primitive-style brown and beige murals. Service is reasonably quick and the drinks prices are competitive.

### River Pub

*Frana Supila 12 (051 213 406).* **Open** 7am-2am Mon-Wed; 10am-4am Thur-Sat; 6pm-2am Sun. **No credit cards. Map** p107 D2 ㉛
Beautifully upholstered furniture sits on an old tiled floor, while a sturdy bar counter has taps of Bass, Caffrey's, Guinness and Kilkenny. The framed photographs from around Istria are a nice touch, old regional maps too, with a few busts of Irish writers. Th pub is set behind a big, wooden door, halfway down from the museums.

### Sabrage

*Petra Zrinskog 2, Trsat (no phone, sabragebar. com).* **Open** 7am-2am daily. **No credit cards. Map** p107 F1 ㉜
Up in Trsat, this lovely spot is well stocked and well staffed. Along with classic cocktails and long drinks, there's a long wine list, a Tinto Reserva hiding among the Zlatni Plavac and Dingač, while Scotch whiskies (a 14-year-old Oban or a ten-year-old Talisker) can be sipped in an elegantly carved wooden interior decorated with portraits of famous locals; nice hot chocolates too. Convenient for a visit to Trsat Castle.

## Shops & Services

### ★ Šta da?!

*Uzarska 17 (no phone, www.happyhobbyshop. blogspot.com).* **Open** 9am-8pm Mon-Fri; 9am-1pm Sat. **Map** p107 E2 ㉝ **Fashion/accessories**
A gold-painted bicycle propped against a gold-painted railing marks the entrance to this fascinating little shop that's simply bursting with creativity. Many of the garments, accessories and household items on display are a tribute to the art

of recycling, with bags made from old sails, pillows fashioned from the leftovers of old tents, and rings made from twisted metal cutlery. Rijeka-based artists are responsible for most items on display. Shop owner Amna Šehović produced the prominent shoulder bags and T-shirts bearing typical Rijeka catchphrases: *Šta da!* ('You Don't Say!') or *Bo!* ('Whatever!'). The shop also sells wool, beads and haberdashery, just in case you're seized with the desire to embark on a hobby project of your own.

## Nightlife

### Boa

*Ante Starčevićeva 8 (091 339 9339).* **Open** 6am-2am Mon-Wed, Sun; 6am-5am Thur-Sat. **Map** p107 E3.

This branch of a successful Malinska club by the same name is a see-and-be-seen scene full of pumping music and pretty people, dressed for success and/ or sex. You are greeted by gorgeous young models in the club's employ, no one on staff is unattractive and none of the drinks are cheap. The decor is mostly white, coloured by fancy lighting. There's lots of posing pre-midnight, but eventually the disco, hip-hop and techno soundtrack gets dancers moving and the crowd mingling. By day it's a slick café.

### Club Nina 2

*Adamicev gat (no phone).* **Open** 9am-4am Mon, Tue; 9am-10pm Wed; 9am-6am Thur, Fri; 4pm-6am Sat. **No credit cards. Map** p107 C3.

This spacious docked boat has been converted into a popular dance spot in the heart of town. Live bands play and DJs spin a range of danceable music, from disco to Latin to electronica, for a mostly young crowd who boogie in a big room with a great bar on the middle floor of the boat. Get out on deck and into the fresh air for conversation and lounging. Three bars keep the drinks flowing.

### Karolina

*Gat Karoline Riječke (091 490 4042, www. facebook.com/KarolinaBarRijeka).* **Open** 7am-2am Mon-Thur, Sun; 7am-6am Fri; 6am-4am Sat. **Map** p107 D3.

A slick, modern glass-enclosed structure, sitting all by itself on a pier in the main harbour, houses an upmarket bar that draws a mix of yuppies, tourists, hipsters and hard-drinking barflies. Its VIP terrace is on the sea; inside is a carefully designed, dimly lit space, with high tables and tall stools in the middle of the bar area, lower chairs with zebra-striped cushions at the ends. The darkness releases inhibitions, and the techno and trance music inspire a good time.

### ★ Phanas Pub

*Ivana Zajca 9 (no phone, www.phanas.hr).* **Open** 7am-1am Mon-Wed; 7am-3am Thur-Sat. **No credit cards. Map** p107 D3.

Down at the harbourfront, this place is best experienced late at night when the two-floor wooden pub with maritime knick-knacks is thick with hormones pinging around the room, to a commercial dance and rock soundtrack. It gets busy late on and difficult to get inside. Guinness, Kilkenny, Stella, wines and cheap cocktails complement the standard Ožujsko beer, but the drinks here are secondary to eye-contact action around the three-deep long bar counter.

### Tunel

*Školjić 12 (091 632 6572, www.facebook.com/tunel. klub).* **Open** 7am-1am Mon-Thur; 7am-2am Fri; 10am-2am Sat; 5pm-2am Sun. **No credit cards. Map** p107 F1.

This tunnel dug into a railway embankment is heaving most nights, especially at weekends when there's usually a band and DJs playing techno and/ or electronica. A vaulted stone ceiling, lasers and a good-looking crowd in their twenties and thirties comprise the decor. Getting to the bar, or just finding a place to stand, can be a challenge. The few tables out front fill up in warmer weather.

## Hotels

### ★ Best Western Hotel Jadran

*Šetalište XIII Divizije 46 (051 216 600, www.jadran-hoteli.hr).* €€. **Map** p107 F3.

Revamped by the Best Western group, Jadran contains 66 nicely fitted rooms in an enviable shoreside location. Set by Rijeka's first stretch of swimmable sea with its own stop on the No.2 bus route, east of town in Pećine, the Jadran ('Adriatic') has been a spot for bathing since it opened in 1914. There's a supplement charged for sea-facing rooms. Half- and full-board deals are available.

### Continental

*Šetalište Andrije Kačića-Miočiča 1 (051 372 008, www.jadran-hoteli.hr/continental).* €. **Map** p107 F2.

Upgraded to a three-star after a renovation in 2008, the central Continental is in a bulky 100-year-old structure overlooking the canal. It's a nice view, though the square below tends to fill with noisy teens when it's not a school night, so a rear window can be better. Reasonably priced, comfortable and convenient. *Photos pp114-115.*

### ★ Grand Hotel Bonavia

*Dolac 4 (051 357 100, 051 357 980, www.bonavia.hr).* €€. **Map** p107 C2.

Rijeka's classiest option, part of the Poreč-based Plava Laguna group and right in the heart of town, this is a modern business hotel with a spa and gym. Sauna cabins and massage and beauty treatments have also been introduced. The 120 rooms are tastefully done out, the in-house Bonavia Classic restaurant is one of the best in town, and the terrace café overlooks the city.

**EXPLORE**

### Neboder

*Strossmayerova 1 (051 373 538, www.jadran-*
*hoteli.hr/neboder/index.php).* €. **Map** p107 F1/2.
If you're looking for a cheapie in town and the
Continental is full, come to the aptly named 14-floor
'Skyscraper' by the flyover. Following renovations a
few years ago it now has an underground car park
and café. The wonderful Socialist-era lobby has,
sadly, been replaced by something more modern –
while the rooms remain adequate.

### Youth Hostel Rijeka

*Šetalište XIII Divizije 23 (051 406 42, www.hfhs.*
*hr).* **No credit cards. Map** p107 F3.
Opened in 2006, the former Villa Kozulić is a modern,
60-bed youth hostel, the first in town. Well sited in
Pećine, east of town by the sea, on the No.2 bus route,
the YHA offers standard dorm beds and three doubles in the attic, all with breakfast included, a snip
for the price and location. Open all year.

## GETTING THERE & AROUND

**Rijeka airport** (051 842 040, www.rijeka-airport.
hr) is on the northern tip of the island of Krk,
near Omišalj, 25km (15.5 miles) south of town.
A **bus** meets arrivals (45mins, 30kn) and runs
to Rijeka's main bus station at Žabica. **Taxis**
should have a set fee of 160kn, but many can
charge at least 300kn.

Rijeka is northern Croatia's biggest transport hub
and biggest port. Jadrolinija **catamarans** serve
Cres and Mali Lošinj, and Rab and Novalja. Tickets
are bought from the Jadrolinija office (051 211 444,
www.jadrolinija.hr, open 7am-6pm Mon-Fri,
8am-2.30pm Sat, noon-3pm Sun) in the new
terminal building on the Riječki lukobran pier,
immediately south of the Riva.

The **bus** station for international and inter-city
buses is just west of the Korzo, on Trg Žabica close
to the city centre. There are hourly buses from
Zagreb (2hrs 30mins) and regular ones from Split
(8hrs 30mins) and Zadar (4hrs 30mins).

The **train** station is further west from the main
bus station, and so slightly further from town.
There are two direct trains a day from Zagreb
(around four hours), and two daily services
from Ljubljana (2hrs 45mins).

You should only need to use the **city bus** network
if you're going to Trsat (No.1) or Pećine (No.2) – the
centre is compact and walkable. Tickets are 15kn
for these zone 1 destinations. The No.32 bus for
Opatija (25mins, 27kn) leaves every 20 minutes
from the suburban station by the canal, passing
the train station.

## RESOURCES

**Hospital** *Krešimirova 42 (051 658 111).*
General hospital near the train station.

**Continental.** *See p113.*

**Pharmacy** *Ljekarna Centar Riva 18 (051 213 101)*. **Open** 24hrs daily except for a few hours on Sun. **Map** p107 B3.

**Post office** *Korzo 13 (051 525 515)*. **Open** 7am-9pm Mon-Fri; 7am-2pm Sat. **Map** p107 D3.

**Tourist information** *Rijeka Tourist Office, Korzo 14 (051 335 882, www.tz-rijeka.hr)*. **Open** *Mid-June-mid-Sept* 8am-8pm Mon-Sat; 9am-2pm Sun. *Mid Sept-mid June* 8am-7.30pm Mon-Fri; 9am-2pm Sat. **Map** p107 D2.
Touch-screen information outside; inside English-speaking staff dish out maps, leaflets and advice.

# Opatija

One of Croatia's first modern-style seaside resorts, **Opatija** was attracting royalty and the well-to-do more than a century ago. They stayed in grand villas and sought to invigorate their health by strolling the **Lungomare**, a stunning seaside walkway that offers some of Croatia's best vistas. The vistas, villas and Lungomare remain, as do the many imposing *fin-de-siède* hotels that enhance Opatija's distinctive Habsburg-era look. This sophisticated destination also boasts a competitive restaurant scene that's made it an important gastronomic hub in Croatia – and a great place to eat out. Opatija is fancier and pricier than many other Croatian resorts, but if you want a luxurious holiday you can find it here.

## INTRODUCING OPATIJA

In the late 19th century, when the Austro-Hungarian Empire reached its apex, the Habsburgs made this town of dazzling vistas and rocky beaches one of the hottest spots in Europe. Opatija was the place where royalty took their holidays and Isadora Duncan took her lovers. Wealthy socialites built Secessionist and neo-classical mansions on the rocks above the sea, or stayed in hotels of imperial elegance. Unlike most Croatian resorts, where a tourism infrastructure was added on to an existing settlement, Opatija was purpose-built for tourists – rich ones.

Before 1844, Opatija was nothing but a fishing village with 35 houses and a church. Higinio von Scarpa then built opulent **Villa Angolina**, named after his wife, and surrounded it with a menagerie, an exotic garden and influential guests. The villa, with its neo-classical interior featuring trompe l'oeil frescoes, now hosts jazz and classical concerts, as well as exhibitions.

The property was bought in the 1880s by the chief of the regional railway board. Soon Opatija was being successfully promoted as an overland getaway destination for a certain class of European, catered for by opulent hotels being built at the same time. An accent on health tourism – spa baths and seaside vigorous walks – kept this clement resort busy year-round. Mahler, Puccini and Chekhov were among the visitors.

This legacy lingers in the stunning architecture, Viennese-style coffeehouses and Central European atmosphere, kept alive by the large number of Austrian tourists. Pricey Opatija has traditionally drawn wealthy, conservative visitors, who prefer seaside strolls to raucous nightlife. But there is a local young contingent, coming from Rijeka and elsewhere along the coast, who keep the late-night bars and the town's disco busy. And the modern-day counterparts of fin-de-siècle spa establishments, in the shape of 'wellness' and boutique hotels, are opening along the riviera, attracting a trend-conscious clientele. Meanwhile, few other Croatian towns can boast the gastronomic quality offered by adventurous young chefs who have made Opatija and neighbouring **Volosko** their base – in this part of Croatia, Opatija rules the roost where contemporary cuisine is concerned.

The resort is deliberately arranged on a steep hill facing the sea, offering fine views of the Bay of Kvarner. Further vistas and several beaches can be found along the 12-kilometre **Lungomare**, the shaded promenade that follows the rocky coast here. Stretches of rocky beach are fronted by towering villas, some abandoned and others

EXPLORE

converted into luxury hotels. Further along stretch the quieter, pebbly shores of **Ičići** and **Lovran**, before **Medveja**, with its own attractive shingle beach.

## Restaurants

### ★ Bevanda
*Zert 8 (051 493 888, www.bevanda.hr).* **Open** noon-midnight daily. €€€.
**Seafood/International**
Bevanda has undergone an extensive and highly impressive recent renovation to add a ten-room hotel and bar to the space occupied by its renowned restaurant. The recent appointment of Andrej Barbieri as chef, previously of Time Out favourite Konoba Tramerka, a few miles down the coast in Volosko, was a good move. Given its proximity to the sea, it's no surprise that Bevanda offers a wide selection of fresh seafood. The menu is innovative, from scampi soup to lobster and cuttlefish risotto, plus sashimi and tartare dishes, as well as traditional salads and steaks. Highly recommended; book early to guarantee a table.

### Bistro Pizzeria Moho
*Obala Frana Supila 8 (099 256 2289, www. facebook.com/p.MOHO).* **Open** 10am-midnight daily. €. **Italian/Croatian**

Pizzas, pastas and salads are served in this bright bistro furnished with rustic oak tables and brightly painted chairs. Culinary riches of the Kvarner region are an important part of the menu, with local goodies like asparagus and truffles making seasonal appearances. The terrace, with its recycled chairs inherited from the Opatija summer theatre, looks out on Volosko harbour's bobbing boats.

### Bistro Yacht Club
*Zert 1 (051 272 345, www.yacht-club-opatija.com).* **Open** 9am-1am daily. €€€. **Seafood**
Non-sailors can be pampered at this superb seafood restaurant on the water at Opatija's marina. The kitchen handles all the basics expertly, while throwing in a superb *bakalar in bianco* (a kind of cod pâté that you spread on hearty light-brown toast); all manner of scampi and shells; and fine white fish either grilled, baked, or cooked in wine. The smart interior, done in cheerful light blue, and the relaxed but deferential waiters, make you feel like you have a 60-footer floating somewhere nearby.

### Cantinetta Sveti Jakov
*Ulica Pava T momašića 1 (051 278 007).* **Open** noon-11pm daily. €€. **Italian/Croatian**
A unique restaurant set beneath the grand arcades, and perhaps one of the Opatija's best kept secrets,

Opatija.

EXPLORE

the Cantinetta Sveti Jakov may be best described as a blend of Italian trattoria and wine bar. It also combines old and new, set in a historic building while providing a modern-day dining experience – casual but upscale, friendly and affordable. The menu is focused on good and simple Mediterranean cuisine, such as grilled fresh daily fish, grilled steak, fish soup and home-made pasta, with a commitment to using local and sustainable produce. This includes high-quality Istrian and Dalmatian prosciutto, a wide selection of cheese and freshly baked bread.

### Gostionica Istranka
*Bože Milanovića 2 (051 271 835, www.istranka. net).* **Open** 10am-11pm daily. €. **Croatian**
A simple *konoba* where the locals go when they want affordable seafood and Istrian specialities. There's not much of a view from the terrace on a hill, attempts to dress up the sparse interior are naff and the atmosphere is pretty informal, with servers chatting to a convivial core of regulars. The food is why you're here. Hearty inland cookery includes venison goulash, minestrone with sausage and corn, and tripe with polenta. All are fresh, filling and affordable – a grilled rump steak goes for only 70kn, most other meats for less. Among the fancier seafood offerings is grilled monkfish in wine sauce (105kn).

### Hotel Miramar Restaurant
*Ive Kaline 11 (051 280 000, www.hotel-miramar. info).* **Open** 12.30-11.30pm daily. €€. **Croatian**
Located at a serene turning point in the promenade, this resort hotel's restaurant serves fine seafood on a sea-view terrace. The kitchen applies Austrian finesse to fresh local ingredients, such as truffles, available with fillet of beef or with *fuži*, pasta twists. Grilled fish and calamari dishes are well prepared, and there's also a daily set menu.

### Johnson
*Majčevo 29B, Mošćenička Draga (051 737 578 www.johnson.hr).* **Open** noon-11pm daily. €€€. **Seafood**
Named after American president Lyndon Johnson (the former owner was a big fan), this restaurant is a pillar of the Opatija Riviera culinary scene, serving freshly caught fish, lobster and shellfish with a haute cuisine sense of style. Pride of place goes to the scampi, caught locally and prepared in a variety of ways. Johnson is undoubtedly one of the best places to enjoy the traditional Kvarner seafood repertoire, although the prices are correspondingly high.

### Konoba Tramerka
*Dr A Mohorovića 15, Volosko (051 701 707).* **Open** 1pm-midnight Tue-Sun. €€. **Seafood**

**EXPLORE**

Just up the steps from Volosko's two great harbourside restaurants, Plavi Podrum and Le Mandrać, this rustic cellar space, with exposed stone and wood beams, a huge tortoise shell and a pretty fireplace, has less panoramic seating than its neighbours but puts a lot of effort into creating equally pleasing seafood dishes. You can read the short, seasonal menu, but it may be more rewarding to let the friendly waiter tell you what's fresh for the day. Watch for fancy salads, like octopus in a brown beer and soy sauce. The fish is superb, as it should be, but the home-made bread and other nice touches are reminders that the kitchen doesn't just use good materials, it also cooks well.

### Laurus

*Nova cesta 12A (051 741 355, www.villakapetanovic.hr).* **Open** noon-11pm daily. **€€€€. Croatian**

It's a lung-busting walk up a steep hill or a 50kn taxi ride, but once you reach the terrace restaurant of the Villa Kapetanović hotel, you can settle in for a gourmet meal with spectacular vistas. Watch postcard sunsets over the bay of Kvarner while the award-winning kitchen prepares treats such as calamari stuffed with scampi, steak with truffles, or lobster that's just been yanked from the fish tank. Knowledgeable and friendly servers are happy to guide you through the menu and the long list of well chosen Croatian wines. This is superb, slightly modernised Croatian cuisine, with creative use of the best local and seasonal ingredients. For the full gourmet experience, there are tasting menus, with four courses for 450kn and seven courses for 700kn. Laurus costs a little more – but it's special.

### ★ Le Mandrać

*Obala Frana Supila 10, Volosko (051 701 357, www.lemandrac.com).* **Open** noon-midnight daily. **€€€. Contemporary Croatian**

This classy spot in the Volosko gastro-enclave employs local ingredients to craft contemporary Croatian and fusion cuisine. Star chef Deniz Zembo uses the freshest ingredients creatively in a modern, tasteful glassed-in terrace, turning the treasures of the Adriatic into delightful, Med-based dishes that remain in touch with their Croatian roots. Three-course set lunches can be a steal. More recently, as Zembo has expanded to other venues, Le M itself has become less inventive and high-end.

### Mali Raj

*Maršala Tita 191, Ičići (051 704 074, www.maliraj.hr).* **Open** 10am-midnight daily. **€€. Croatian/Seafood**

Down the main road, some three kilometres from town, Mali Raj is in the neighbouring village of Ičići – an appetite-building seaside stroll along the Lungomare. Secluded in a cool, woody section of the promenade, on the bottom floor of a tiny pension, Mali Raj provides one of the prettiest terraces

and best meals in a town, full of great food and great views. The service is swift, friendly and professionally unobtrusive. They push the top-quality white fish – the fresh, succulent sea bass is worth the price. Splash out on lobster or scallops here with confidence or get equal pleasure from the satisfactory steaks.

### Plavi Podrum

*Obala Frana Supila 12, Volosko (051 701 223, www.plavipodrum.com).* **Open** noon-midnight daily. **€€€. Contemporary Croatian**

A Volosko destination par excellence. This is the oldest restaurant on the Opatija Riviera, today run by Daniela Kramarić, an award-winning sommelier, with a cellar holding 300 varieties of wine, 60% of them Croatian. The wine also gets used in the food, which centres around fillets of finest fresh fish served in a much more imaginative range of sauces than you find in more traditional Adriatic restaurants. You'll get a full introduction to the Plavi Podrum style by opting for one of the four- or five-course tasting menus (400kn-440kn). Meals come with flavourful black bread, made with cuttlefish ink.

### Restaurant Ariston

*Hotel Villa Ariston, Maršala Tita 179 (051 271 379, www.villa-ariston.hr).* **Open** noon-11pm daily. **€€€. Seafood**

The sumptuous dining room and shaded garden of an old villa converted into a hotel are the settings for superior seafood dinners. These are augmented with fancier dishes, like fillet of brancin stuffed with scampi, monkfish in white wine or tuna in a rosemary-tinged Mediterranean sauce. Deferential waiters also offer a complimentary appetiser of petit fours with fish stuffing. You can sit under your own gazebo or on the upper terrace for a commanding view of the sea.

### Valle Losca

*Andrije Štangera 2, Volosko (095 580 3757).* **Open** 1-10pm Wed-Sun. **€€. Croatian**

The historic fishing village of Volosko at Opatija's northern end probably boasts more outstanding restaurants per square kilometre than anywhere else on this side of the Adriatic. Valle Losca arguably gets less attention than it deserves because it is slightly uphill from Volosko's tiny harbour and doesn't have the same views of bobbing boats from its terrace. A small stone interior with wooden tables provides the setting for perfectly prepared traditional fare including all the Kvarner-Istrian favourites – fresh fish, scampi, home-made pasta and *boškarin*-beef steaks. Given the size of the place and its growing popularity, you'd be wise to reserve.

## Cafés & Bars

### Bevanda Bar

*Zert 8 (051 493 888, www.bevanda.hr).* **Open** 10am-2am daily. **No credit cards.**

EXPLORE

Hotel Bevanda's bar is perfectly located, with a breathtaking view of the islands. Quality snacks and drinks can be followed by the cigar bar if so desired. Prop up the indoor bar for a cocktail or relax waterside to watch the lights of Opatija twinkle on the Adriatic.

### Café Wagner

*Hotel Milenij, Maršala Tita 109 (051 202 071, www.milenijhoteli.hr).* **Open** 7am-midnight daily.
A Viennese-style café invoking Opatija's Habsburg heritage with its creamy cakes, Wagner gets mobbed for mid-afternoon teatime. Superior central European desserts are prepared with seasonal local ingredients. The quality of the espressos and other brews stands up to the cakes, with beans selected from around the globe.

### Caffè Bar Kon-Tiki

*Obala Frana Supila 12, Volosko (051 701 661).* **Open** 8am-midnight Mon-Thur, Sun; 8am-2am Fri, Sat. **No credit cards**.
Right between Volosko's two gourmet restaurants is this seaside terrace spot, ideal for before- or after-dinner drinks. It's busy all day with a good mix of locals and visitors enjoying Croatian beer on tap for 18kn a pint, bottled varieties including Guinness, or one of many shots and cocktails. The gorgeous harbour view and convivial atmosphere are compelling reasons to hang around and watch the sun set over the distant hills.

### Caffè Bar Leonardo

*Maršala Tita 129 (no phone).* **Open** 8am-2am daily. **No credit cards**.
Located as the road slopes east of town, this fine terrace and triangular-shaped bar has a commanding view of the bay and a casual, comfortable feel that encourage you to hang around on the low, well-cushioned chairs. You won't find anything by way of cocktails, but there are decent coffees, and the standard beers, wines and spirits. All in all, it's a fine place to refresh and recuperate in the thick of things.

### Choco Bar

*Maršala Tita 94 (051 603 562, www.kraschocobar.com).* **Open** 8am-midnight daily.
Classic Croatian chocolatiers Kraš have opened this palace of decadence disguised as a café on Opatija's main drag. Along with elaborate sweets, tantalisingly displayed under glass in the glitzy interior, it also serves cakes, mousses, ice-cream and cocktails, all made of chocolate, plus the hot-drink variety. It goes without saying that excellent coffee is also available. The pretty covered terrace, with modern decorative touches, is a nice place to relax and watch the busy boulevard go by.

### Hotel Mozart Piano Bar

*Maršala Tita 138 (051 718 260, www.hotel-mozart.hr).* **Open** 8am-midnight daily.

The café of this five-star hotel on the harbourfront near the centre of town has a stunning interior, with art nouveau-style stained glass, Biedermeier-striped furniture and a piano, where local talents play background music while you have coffee and cake or slam back vodkas and imagine you're a Habsburg. The top-notch service and quality beverages are also available in the hotel's seaside terrace tucked just outside.

### ★ Monokini

*Maršala Tita 96 (no phone, www.facebook.com/monokini.opatija).* **Open** 7am-2am daily. **No credit cards**.
Opatija's leading contemporary bar attracts a younger, more bohemian crowd. Friendly staff give enthusiastic service, even though things can get hectic later on. The bar, on the main road through the heart of town, comes with funky decor with retro 1960s overtones. Monokini also accommodates regularly changing exhibitions by Croatian artists. Music ranges from techno to rock. There's an internet café at the back.

## Nightlife

### Colosseum Beach Bar

*Maršala Tita 129 (095 579 0332/hr-hr.facebook.com/colosseumopatija).* **Open** *Summer* 8pm-4am daily. **No credit cards**.
Visible from the main street through the town centre, this prominent open-air disco-bar has a waterside location (on the concrete lido, not a 'beach' as such) spread with loungey furniture, with a dancefloor and DJ podium. Colosseum is frequently the venue for glitzy parties with hostesses, but the place also attracts a fair cross-section of locals, tourists, young and not-so-young, and drinks prices aren't noticeably higher than in the more mainstream bars around town.

### Hemingway Medveja

*Medveja beach, Lovran (051 272 887, www.hemingway.hr).* **Open** *Summer* 7am-2am daily.
The folks behind the Hemingway in Opatija – and, indeed, Split and Zagreb too – run a disco on the popular pebbly beach of Medveja, just outside Lovran. The tented-over café is good for beachside drinking during the day, but the party begins after dark, when sunbathers have gone.

### Hemingway Opatija

*Zert 2 (051 718 802, www.hemingway.hr).* **Open** *Bar* 7am-4am daily. *Restaurant* 7am-midnight daily.
This slick seaside space of several bars and two small dancefloors is the main local spot to drink and party. After sundown it heaves with fun-seeking holidaymakers looking to mingle over Opatija's best cocktails. Plush, low chairs make it hard to leave the covered terrace, with its view of the marina on one

**EXPLORE**

**Grand Hotel Adriatic.**

side and the open sea on the other. The dancefloors are serviced by DJs and gratuitous go-go dancers. A recently added restaurant serves sandwich-plus-salad brunches during the morning, plus good-quality pasta, steaks and seafood dishes until 2am.

## Hotels

### Agava

*Maršala Tita 89 (051 278 100, www.milenijhoteli. hr).* €€.

This villa, built in 1896, was renovated a century later to make a 76-room hotel in a luxurious setting near the sea and pretty Angolina Park. The rooms are stunning – polished wood floors, period-style furnishings, air-conditioning and internet. Little extras, such as international newspapers delivered to your door, and laundry and room service available from 6am to 10pm, offer that special touch.

### ★ Bevanda

*Zert 8 (051 493 888, www.bevanda.hr).* €€. **No credit cards**.

The new design hotel attached to recommended restaurant Bevanda (*see p116*) is luxurious, to say the least. With only ten rooms, each elegantly furnished and each named after a famous visitor to the Opatija region, the Hotel Bevanda lives up to the good reputation earned by its restaurant. Little touches such as its 'personal sommeliers' – wine-

dispensing machines serving a range of wines and champagnes, day or night – are what make this beachfront hotel such a special place to stay. Local spa treatments or island trips in the hotel's speedboat can be arranged for extra.

### Design Hotel Astoria

*Maršala Tita 174 (051 706 350, www.vi-hotels.com/en/astoria).* €€.

This hotel, originally constructed in 1904, was stylishly renovated a century later. Its slick, modern interior in a classic old building created a splash in Opatija. The lounge bar is a destination in its own right while the 50 rooms – done up in natural tones and striking furnishings – all come equipped with flatscreen satellite TVs, air conditioning and high-speed internet. Room service is another attraction.

### ★ Grand Hotel 4 Opatijska cvijeta

*VC Emina 6 (051 278 007, www. milenijhoteli.hr).* €€.

A villa that once belonged to the noble Eszterházys family has been combined with a fin-de-siècle hotel and renovated to form a campus of four striking, pastel-coloured buildings amid pretty shaded lawns. It stretches uphill from the marina, a boon for the majority of the 248 rooms with balconies. There are also indoor and outdoor pools, a spa, gym and restaurant.

### Grand Hotel Adriatic

*Maršala Tita 200 (051 719 000, www.hotel-adriatic.hr).* €€.

This new spa- and sport-oriented hotel near the seafront also contains a casino and convention centre. Pride of place goes to the top-floor health area: heated seawater pool; Finnish sauna; Turkish bath, plus a dozen massage and bath units. There's a beauty centre too. Outside, the expansive terrace has a view of the Kvarner Bay. The 300-room complex comprises two hotel buildings; guests in the cheaper Adriatic II three-star are also allowed access to the spa and swimming pool. The Adriatic can arrange climbing and hikes around National Parks.

### Milenij

*M Tita 109 (051 202 000, www.milenijhoteli.hr).* €€€.

A newly renovated villa from the late 1800s and an adjacent modern building offer some of Opatija's fanciest and certainly most expensive accommodation – though the Milenij can seem as if it's struggling to deserve its five-star status. The rooms are tastefully decorated and kept in impeccable shape, but they're small. All are air-conditioned, with internet connections and fluffy bathrobes. Luxuries include a pool with a retractable glass roof, 24-hour room service and a spa centre. The hotel's superb Sveti Jakov (*see p116*) restaurant and old-school Café Wagner (*see p119*) serve guests

and non-guests alike, and there is a more contemporary café terrace overlooking the sea.

### Miramar

*Ive Kaline 11 (051 280 000, www.hotel-miramar.info).* €€€.

The 1876 Villa Neptune has been superbly renovated and expanded to include three guest villas, creating a full-service resort hotel with its own rocky beach. Stylish, comfortable and air-conditioned rooms have their own balcony or terrace. There's a spa with a heated pool, whirlpool, saunas, steam room and beauty treatments. Cross the footbridge from the Lungomare for the private fenced-in beach.

### Mozart

*Maršala Tita 138 (051 718 260, www.hotel-mozart.hr).* €€€.

Of all the refitted fin-de-siècle confections on Opatija's shore, perhaps the Mozart is most true to the genre. Behind a striking façade of art-nouveau curves and sea-facing balconies, 26 rooms echo the grandeur of the period. There's enough space for a cosmetic studio and piano bar, and meals can be taken in a pretty courtyard. If you're not bothered about state-of-the-art, but happy to pay for luxury, come here.

### ★ Remisens Premium Hotel Ambasador

*Feliksa Persića 5 (051 710 444, www.remisens.com/en/hotel-ambasador).* €€€.

A masterpiece of 1960s architecture that has been fully renovated, the Ambasador is an impressive spa hotel on ten floors, 180 rooms, a private beach and, best of all, the Five Elements Wellness Centre. Over two floors, this involves saunas, an indoor heated seawater pool, an eight-person whirlpool, a children's pool, massage showers and treatments based on the Five Elements principle. Throw in the Hortenzia summer garden restaurant, the Palma bar and Manhattan cocktail bar, and you have a very tidy year-round operation indeed. Next door, the Remisens Premium Villa Ambasador (same phone number) offers more intimacy but guests may still use the facilities of its sister hotel.

### Remisens Premium Hotel Kvarner Amalia/Villa Amalia

*P Tomašića 1-4 (051 710 444, www.remisens. com/en/hotel-kvarner).* €€€.

Completely revamped by the Remisens group in 2014, the Kvarner was Croatia's first luxury hotel on the Adriatic. Right on the promenade, it remains an imposing imperial presence in the heart of Opatija. Fans of grandeur will love the majestic size of the Crystal Ballroom, the ornate hotel lobby and the splendid seaside terrace beyond it. The rooms themselves are large, furnished in antique style and now have modern conveniences such as air-conditioning. Prices are a little higher for the sea-view rooms, but worth it, as they are usually larger. With restaurant, bar and terrace café, there are plenty of good places to lounge, plus there are massage treatments, a sauna and an indoor pool. The grounds include an outdoor pool surrounded by a patio and steps leading down to the hotel beach. Note that guests at the equally revamped Reminsens Premium Villa Amalia (same phone number) next door can take advantage of the facilities at the hotel. *Photo p124.*

### Villa Ariston

*Maršala Tita 179 (051 271 319, www.villa-ariston. hr).* €€.

A short walk along a beautiful wooded section of the shore-hugging Lungomare takes you to a majestic restored villa with a masterpiece of a garden, a great restaurant and caring service – all at reasonable prices. The tall yellow exterior of the old mansion is striking, and the lobby oozes old-time luxury. The rooms run from comfortable doubles or singles to suites with polished wood floors. In all, there are only 22 rooms, which means you can always find a quiet place in the beautiful green grounds. The villa is affordable because it lacks a spa centre and other such luxuries – but it sure feels grand.

### Villa Beller

*Poljanska cesta 12, Ičići (051 704 687, www.villa-beller.com).* €€.

Seven comfortable apartments set in a villa a short way down the Lungomare from Opatija, near the ACI marina at Ičići. Properties are generally hired for a week or more. All come with a private terrace, internet and air-conditioning, and private parking is a boon for traffic-swamped Opatija. Units accommodate two people comfortably, four easily, and are a short walk from the sea and a sports centre with tennis courts.

### ★ Villa Kapetanović

*Nova cesta 12A, Volosko (051 741 355, www.villa-kapetanovic.hr).* €€.

Built around ten years ago on a hillside above Volosko, and recently refurbished and expanded, this tasteful, modern hotel with 27 rooms has amazing views of Kvarner Bay, an outdoor pool with sundeck, spa facilities, massages and a well-respected restaurant, the Laurus (*see p118*). The family-run business offers personal and helpful service. It's probably more convenient to have a car to stay here, but there are shuttle buses making the steep trip from the hotel down to the centre of town.

## GETTING THERE & AROUND

National services within Croatia are all linked to the transport hub of Rijeka. **Bus** No.32 runs every 20 minutes from Rijeka suburban bus station, by the canal, to Opatija (25mins, 15kn). It also stops at Rijeka train station en route. From Opatija, it leaves for Rijeka from the slight incline by the bus information office.

## RESOURCES

**Cruises & boat hire** *Katarina Line, Obala m Tita 75/I (051 603 400, www.katarina-line.hr).* **Open** 8am-8pm daily.

**Tourist information** *Opatija Tourist Office, Obala m Tita 128 (051 271 310, www.opatija-tourism. hr).* **Open** *Apr-Sept* 8am-9pm Mon-Sat; 3-8pm Sun. *Oct-Mar* 8am-3pm Mon-Fri; 8am-2pm Sat.

# Lovran

Arranged along the foot of sheltering Mount Učka, and set on a rise above the sea that provides some astonishingly beautiful views, Lovran is an ancient settlement with a centuries-old town centre and Habsburg-era villas dotted along a lush, green seaside promenade. The town is smaller and feels more exclusive than Opatija, its neighbour about five kilometres away. But despite this, there's still plenty of life here, taking it easy on the pebbly beaches and or getting busy in the jumping bars, which get packed with a generally younger crowd.

As with other towns along the Lungomare promenade, Lovran's collection of superb restaurants is sufficient reason to visit.

## INTRODUCING LOVRAN

Lovran, with a population of 5,000, wasn't always the small fry in Kvarner. A busy settlement since at least the seventh century, 'Lauriana' was named after its many laurel trees. In the 12th century, the Arab writer and geographer Al-Idrisi said: 'Lovran is a large and progressive city, which has ships always ready, and shipbuilders always employed.' Along with shipbuilding, Lovran traded locally grown cherries, peaches and their well-known sweet chestnuts, called *marrons*, celebrated with their own festival in October.

Lovran was ruled by the counts of Istria until the 15th century, when Austrians took over. It remained under Austrian rule until the Habsburg empire fell apart at the end of World War I. Modern tourism came here in the late 1800s, as the wooden sailing ships that had employed Lovran's builders were being replaced by steam vessels built elsewhere. Following the lead of Opatija, which was becoming known as a destination for holidaymakers seeking a healthy climate, Lovran shifted its economy toward tourism. Many luxury villas went up by the sea, mostly along the main road of **Šetalište maršala Tita** and the **Lungomare** promenade.

Today, many villas have been restored into superior forms of hotel accommodation, offering relative seclusion by the sea, with four-star extras. Even if you don't check in, it's worth checking out the grand exteriors of these old mansions while taking in amazing sea vistas on the shaded Lungomare.

The Old Town of Lovran is perched above the harbour. It's easiest to access through the eastern city gate, **Stubica**, which faces the sea. Inside is a quaint asymmetrical clutter of streets, courtyards and old houses centred around St George's Square (Trg sv Jurja). The square is dominated by **St George's Church**, built in the 12th century and reconstructed in the 15th, when local artists added Gothic frescoes. The church was enlarged in the 17th century; Baroque chapels were added and the bell tower was attached to the rest of the structure. Both the square and the church are named after the town's patron saint, a likeness of whom can be seen slaying a dragon in one of the decorative doorway arches in the old town. With the exception of the **Old Town Tower**, diagonally facing the church, the medieval fortifications are gone, most built over with houses. Left unprotected, the Old Town has been invaded by tourists.

## Restaurants

### Draga di Lovrana

*Lovranska Draga 1 (051 294 166, www. dragadilovrana.hr).* **Open** 1-11pm daily. **€€€**. **French/Croatian**

**Remisens Premium Hotel Ambasador.**
See p121.

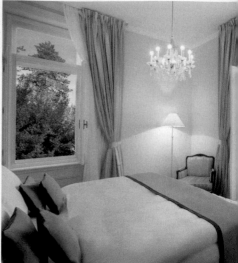

**Remisens Premium Villa Amalia.**
*See p122.*

The perfect mixture of local gastronomy and the classic French approach to quality cuisine is the hallmark of this hotel restaurant on the slopes of Mt Učka, reached by winding road from Lovran. Fresh local ingredients are the order of the day – as you would expect, Adriatic fish and Kvarner scampi are the stars on the menu, but exquisite lamb and duck options ensure that this is one place where you might consider taking the night off from seafood. Desserts are delectable, and the view from the terrace is a bit special.

### Konoba Marun

*Stari Grad 52 (091 788 3993, konoba-marun. jimdo.com).* **Open** noon-1am daily. **€. No credit cards.** Croatian

There's no fish, but plenty of the cuisine from inland Istria in this small indoor tavern-restaurant in the Old Town. Istrian *fuži* pasta is prepared with beef and parmesan or truffles, which are also served in risotto or with steak. Other pastas include small but delicious portions of own-made meat ravioli, served with courgette and camembert or gorgonzola sauce. You'll get equal satisfaction from the meaty mains, the likes of steak, lamb chops and veal. Good meat starters include *pršut* Istrian ham or *kulen*, a spicy salami.

▶ *For seafood close by, try the pricier Lovranska Vrata (Stari Grad 94, 051 291 050), right on St George's Square.*

### Pizza Delfino

*26. Divizije 4 (051 293 293, www.delfino.hr).* **Open** 11am-midnight daily. **€. Pizzeria**

A short walk up from the harbour takes you to a restaurant with a spacious interior containing kitsch murals, a beautiful garden offering glimpses of the sea below and some of the best pizzas in Kvarner. The deservedly popular Delfino lists 16 varieties of pizza, nine of which feature ham. The limited variety isn't a problem as the superb sauce, thick melted cheese and thin hard crusts are all so good. Pastas, lasagnes and grilled meats are also available.

### Restoran Knezgrad

*Trg Slobode 12 (051 291 838).* **Open** 11am-11pm daily. **€€.** Croatian

Slip away from the crowds for good seafood on a terrace facing a pretty little park, at the edge of the Old Town. Along with standard appetisers like *pršut* ham and a delicately seasoned octopus salad, it offers goulash with dumplings and pasta with scampi in cream sauce. There's a good choice of top-quality fish, shellfish and calamari too. Steak, liver and grilled meat round out the rather long menu. Service is friendly and unobtrusive.

### ★ Restoran Najade

*Šetalište maršala Tita 69 (051 291 866).* **Open** 11am-1am daily. **€€. Seafood/Grill**

With superb seafood, a great terrace at sea level (below most of the town) and reasonable prices despite the 7kn-per-diner cover charge, the Najade is a contender for best meal in Lovran. The wide selection of fresh fish includes less common varieties like sole, monkfish and turbot; crustaceans include scallops and lobster, served grilled, or stewed *buzara* style. The mixed fish platter is a great way to get the freshest fish in the place. Meat eaters can get châteaubriand for two or Balkan-style grill. The long wine list includes around 30 whites and 25 reds,

mostly Croatian. The relaxed waiters might even break into song between tables.

## Bars

### Buffet Stubica
*Stari Grad 25-26 (091 586 1429)*. **Open** 7am-10pm daily. **No credit cards.**
In front of the Stubica gate leading to the Old Town, on a terrace with a great view down to the harbour and sea below, locals gather for beery conversation and philosophising. There is food here, too, but the main attraction is affordable alcohol and a chummy crowd, which convenes early, for breakfast beers, and tends to linger through the day.

### ★ Caffè Bar Orange
*Šetalište maršala Tita 57 (098 924 3265)*. **Open** 8am-2am daily. **No credit cards.**
The gorgeous view from the terrace – on a low bluff just above the sea, along the Lungomare – is reason enough to come here. Add in funky decor, friendly local regulars, a sweetly sarcastic barmaid and a soundtrack from rock to R&B, and you have a winning bar. A young crowd filters in and out all day, and by nightfall the place has usually become quite lively – when students are in town there's sometimes a party vibe with DJs and dancing. The interior features pebble paths on the floor, leopard- and zebra-patterned furniture and raised bathroom tiles over the toilet urging customers to 'sit please relax'.

### Caffè Bar Guc
*Šetalište maršala Tita 63 (no phone)*. **Open** 10am-2am daily. **No credit cards.**

Right on the harbour, below the rest of town, an amicable young staff runs a comfortable terrace bar with a good mix of music. Drinks – including 28 types of cocktails – are cheap, and there are DJs and live music; closing time can sometimes be delayed until first light. During the day, the Guc is a gorgeous setting for a quiet cup of coffee.

### Gradska Kavana
*Šetalište maršala Tita 41 (051 294 444)*. **Open** 7am-midnight daily.
On the main street, this Habsburg-era cafe brings a little bit of old Vienna to Lovran. The fancy Baroque-style interior and classy-looking terrace provide a perfect setting for gooey cakes, ice-cream, and good coffee. There are more than 50 cocktails and the speciality is an ice-cream cocktail: your choice from seven flavours, vodka, Triple Sec, grenadine and sugar. There's an à la carte restaurant around the side.

### Lovranski Pub
*Šetalište maršala Tita 41 (051 293 237)*. **Open** 7am-2am daily. **No credit cards.**
With its old-style, dimly lit wood and brick interior, and taps dispensing Guinness and decent beers, Lovranski is done up like a classic pub. But the big back garden, fenced in by greenery and shaded by umbrellas and baby palm trees, is far too idyllic to belong to an ordinary bar. There's even a children's playground in one corner. In the evenings, there's a sizeable crowd of locals and visitors, also DJs or live music. Hopheads may appreciate the beer glass, a tray with 16 foamy glasses. The kitchen opens at noon, serving pizzas and sandwiches.

EXPLORE

► *If the children get bored in the playground, treat them to a cake or ice-cream in the Gradska Kavana upstairs (see p125).*

## Hotels

### Lovran
*Šetalište maršala Tita 19/2 (051 291 222, www.hotel-lovran.hr). €.*
Two renovated villas have been converted into one medium-sized, with 53 moderately-priced rooms, near the centre of Lovran. Those with air-conditioning facing the sea are more expensive. There is a bar, a restaurant and a tavern on the premises, as well as a concrete hotel 'beach', and tennis courts nearby. Could be an affordable way to fit the family into an old villa.

### Pansion Stanger
*Šetalište maršala Tita 128 (051 291 154, www.pansion-stanger.com/uk). €.*
Among the cheaper and simpler local lodging options, this modern pension is located along the sea, about a kilometre from the centre of Lovran towards Medveja and its fine beaches. The 21 rooms are in decent condition; each has a bathroom, a fridge and a balcony. All in all, it's a good base for an affordable seaside getaway.

### Park
*Šetalište maršala Tita 60 (051 706 208, www.hotelparklovran.hr). €€.*
With a commanding position at a bend in the main road, next to the Old Town and above the harbour, the Park is as central as you can get. The pretty old structure was renovated a few years ago. The priciest rooms face the sea; the others face the forest behind the hotel. There is a small indoor pool, a gym and a jacuzzi, and beauty treatments and 'wellness packages' are available.

### Reminsens Hotel Excelsior
*Šetalište maršala Tita 15 (051 710 444, www.remisens.com/en/hotel-excelsior). €€.*
Lovran's biggest hotel is now part of the Opatija-based Reminsens group. It has pools outdoors, indoors and for children, a sauna, 177 rooms and a complimentary deckchair and umbrella for the adjoining beach. A stay here offers the classic resort hotel experience but it's a comfortable choice if you want all your needs seen to in one place.
► *For something cheaper nearby, the Bristol (No.27, 051 291 022) is a sister hotel with the same phone number and website details.*

## BEACHES & EXCURSIONS

There are two good beaches in town. **Kvarner beach** is on a bend in the Lungomare promenade, past the Old Town in the Opatija direction. This is a terraced concrete beach, usually the busier one in town, with simple food and decent drinks available from the snack bar/café. **Plaža Peharovo**, in the other direction, toward Medveja, is right next to the No.32 bus terminus in Lovran, along the main drag of Šetalište maršala Tita. This is a pretty, well-shaded pebbly beach, with its own snack bar, surrounded by tall woods on three sides.

Probably the best beach around is **Medveja**, a large pebbly crescent that's a ten-minute walk south from Lovran on the main drag. All along the Lungomare promenade, there are spots where you can get down to rocky beaches. If you can handle the rocks (bring flip-flops), you can usually find a quiet patch to call your own.

## GETTING THERE & AROUND

**Bus** No.32 runs every 20 minutes from Rijeka suburban bus station, via Opatija. The journey takes half an hour and costs 15kn. Lovran is at the end of the line.

## RESOURCES

**Tourist information** *Lovran Tourist Office, Trg slobode 1 (051 291 740, www.tz-lovran.hr). Open Summer* 9am-9pm daily.

# Krk

As you cross the high-altitude bridge connecting the Rijeka motorway to Krk island, the sea looks huge, but the tall rocky cliffs that swallow the road ahead are even more imposing. By the time you reach Croatia's largest and most populous island, the mainland feels miles away.

A widely varied group of attractive resort towns awaits. Heavily touristed **Krk town** has bustling bars, naff souvenir stands and fancy gift shops, arranged in and around ancient buildings. Near Krk island's southern tip is another busy resort, **Baška**, with a famous Blue Flag sandy beach: at nearly two kilometres, it's one of the longest of its kind on the coast. **Malinska**, with perhaps the island's best concentration of good restaurants, is less hectic, though it does boast a destination late-night club. **Vrbnik** is a quieter place to go for gastronomic delights. **Omišalj**, one of the towns closest to the mainland bridge, is the home of Rijeka's airport.

### INTRODUCING KRK
Krk's tradition of tourism goes back as far as almost anywhere on the coast – they were issuing picture postcards here in 1866. Krk town's walls date to pre-Roman times, and the oldest of the towers in that wall, the square one at Trg Kamplin, was built in 1191. The best-preserved historical site, the three-nave **Cathedral of the**

**Assumption** (Trg sv Kvirina, open 9.30am-1pm, 5-7pm daily), built on the site of an early Christian basilica, dates from the early 1200s, with a bell tower from the 16th to 18th centuries. The **Kaštel**, with a cylindrical tower, is Venetian, as are the three city gates and the rest of the wall. The Old Town's squares and main thoroughfare of JJ Strossmayera, now lined with souvenir shops and fast-food outlets, throng with tourists all summer long.

Nearby is **Punat**, where a beautiful bay shelters a large harbour. In the middle is the islet of **Košljun**, home to a 15th-century Franciscan monastery with a religious treasury. Tourists also pack **Baška** in the south, Krk island's other main spot. Its sandy shore, beach towel to beach towel in high season, begins at the harbour edge. You walk to it via a café-lined promenade – in summer you'll be walking three abreast.

## Sights & Museums

### Baška Aquarium
*Na K Tomislava 2 (051 856 052, www.akvarij-baska.com.hr).* **Open** *June-Sept* 10am-9pm daily. *Apr, May, Oct* 10am-3pm daily. **Admission** 30kn; 20kn reductions; free under 5s. **No credit cards.**
Below ground, near the bus station, the Baška Aquarium comprises some 20 tanks containing more than 100 species of fish, as well as one of the richest collections of shellfish and snails in Croatia.

## Restaurants

### Bistro Trattoria Franica
*Ribarska 39, Baška (051 860 023, www.franica.hr).* **Open** 11am-midnight daily. €€. **Croatian**
The big terrace by the bustling harbour is not the only asset here – Franica offers some of the better food on tourist-swamped Baška. The seafood menu includes two types of fish platter for two, plus scallops, tuna steak and mackerel. It also focuses on old-style recipes from Kvarner and Istria. Local delights, concocted with seasonal ingredients, include a hearty goulash with potatoes Krk-style, and a roasted octopus so rich and filling that, were it not for the taste, we would swear it was beef.

---

**IN THE KNOW CANING IT IN KRK**

The harbour bars of Baška are a good place to try cocktails, in spots such as **Havana** (Palada 11) or **Caffè Bar Sun & Fun** (Palade 4). Krk town has crowded bars along the harbour and around nearby Vela Placa, the entrance to the Old Town. Most bars close around 1am. If you want to keep the party going longer, there's **Jungle** (see p128) in Krk town or the **Boa** (see p113) in Malinska.

---

### Cicibela
*Emila Geistlicha 38, Baška (051 856 013, www.cicibela.hr).* **Open** *Jan-Oct* 10am-midnight daily. €€. **Croatian/Seafood**
Amid the long line of establishments on Baška beach, Cicibela, run by the jolly Bogdesić family, stands out for its cookery. You can opt for lobster or one of many seafood-pasta combinations: squid in its own ink or scampi with spaghetti. Unfortunately there's no outdoor seating but grab a sought-after table by the window for a sea view.

### Frankopan
*Trg Svetog Kvirina, Krk town (051 221 437).* **Open** *Jan-Oct* 10am-11pm daily. €€. **Croatian**
This terrace restaurant under the belltower of the cathedral, in a pretty part of Krk Old Town, serves fine seafood, pizzas and schnitzels to a steady stream of tourists. Appetisers include *pršut*, Pag cheese and Istrian truffles. Stand-out main dish is langoustine lobster. Staff can be overwhelmed in peak season – set aside time, though, and you won't be disappointed.

### Konoba Corsaro
*Obala Hrvatske mornarice 2, Krk town (no phone, www.konoba-corsaro.com).* **Open** 11am-2am daily. €€€. **No credit cards. Croatian**
Of the decent restaurants on Krk town harbour, this is the more spacious, with 120 seats, 90 on the terrace. It also has the more attentive waiters. Along with recommended seafood – catch of the day and the platter for two in particular – Konoba Corsaro offers *šurlice* with goulash, and a rather delicious steak with truffles.
▶ *Nearby Konoba Šime (Antona Mahnića 1, 051 220 042) is similar to Konoba Corsaro, but just a little cheaper.*

### Konoba Nino
*Lina Bolmarčića, Malinska (051 859 011, www.konoba-nino-malinska.hr).* **Open** 7am-11pm daily. €€. **No credit cards. Seafood**
Serious seafood is served in a casual atmosphere at this roofed-over terrace, cluttered with maritime kitsch, in a shady spot a few steps from Malinska's downtown beach. The fish mix, varying according to that day's catch and comprising three varieties with potatoes is a good choice. Prices are reasonable.

### Portić
*Portić 10, Malinska (no phone).* **Open** *Apr-Sept* noon-midnight daily. €€. **No credit cards. Croatian/Seafood**
The appetiser of bread with fish spread plonked down before your order arrives hints that dinner here will be a treat – and it is. Starters such as spa-ghetti with mussels or fish soup swimming with shrimp, stand out. The fish is cooked perfectly, served to your terrace table lapped by the sea. This Malinska place is popular; service can be harried but always courteous.

EXPLORE

### Restoran Galeb

*Emila Geistlicher 38, Baška (no phone).*
**Open** 9am-midnight daily. **€€**. **Croatian**
A classier choice on a promenade full of snack bars, the Galeb offers great fish in a covered terrace overlooking Baška beach. The menu also features steaks and *pljeskavica* but it's the exceptional variety of seafood that's the main attraction. Try the mixed shellfish platter, with scallops, oysters, mussels and clams.

### ★ Rivica

*Ribarska obala 13, Njivica (051 846 101, www.rivica.hr).* **Open** noon-10pm Tue-Sun.
**€€€**. **Croatian/Global**
An 80-year-old family business that has morphed into one of the Kvarner Gulf's best-known gastronomic destinations, the smart, stylish Rivica is one of those places that strikes an almost perfect balance between local cuisine and modern European fine-dining expectations. The menu is Mediterranean- and seafood-based, with plenty of favourites from the local repertoire (shrimp and courgette risotto), Kvarner classics such as *škampi buzara* (scampi in wine sauce), and the odd fusion recipe (a tuna starter with wasabi and soy sauce). And if you just want expertly grilled fresh white fish, then Rivica is one of the best places to dig in.

### Tri Maruna

*Poljica 11, Poljica (098 164 7106).* **Open** noon-10pm daily. **€€**. **No credit cards**. **Croatian**.
This well-hidden gem in Poljica, run by the Mršić family, is set in a 400-year-old stone house renovated by Željko Mršić himself. An accordion might play as you tuck into *šurlice* and goulash or the recommended grilled lamb or pork. Željko can offer local tips aplenty.

## Cafés & Bars

### Casa del Padrone

*Trg Sv. Bernardina, Krk town (099 702 2727).*
**Open** *Apr-Sept* 8am-midnight daily. **No credit cards**.
This harbourside café bustles day and night with a young, party-minded crowd, squeezed into an enclosed terrace overlooking the harbour and a two-floor indoor space. After dark, DJs play mainstream party tunes for summer abandonment.

### Pub Tiffany

*A Stepinca, Krk town (no phone).* **Open** *Apr-Sept* 8am-1am daily. **No credit cards**.
Half-a-dozen large tables, for sharing with strangers, and a stunning terrace enjoy gorgeous sea views atop a stretch of Old Town fortification. This place gets packed after dark, when rock and disco numbers mingle with the animated conversation of the young visitors. It's also popular for coffee during the day.

### Tajana

*JJ Strossmayera, Krk town (no phone).* **Open** *Apr-Sept* 9am-midnight daily. **No credit cards**.
Even with an Old Town setting and over-the-top decor, the Tajana feels like a local. The big, marble-covered bar counter, the pool table and fruit machines create a comfortable environment for regulars and visitors to step off the busy tourist thoroughfare to chat and nod their heads to a nice mix of rock and dance.

## Nightlife

### Club Boa

*Dubašljanska 76, Malinska (091 33 99 339).* **Open** *June-Sept* 11pm-5am daily. **No credit cards**.
A downtown cellar done up in black, with a genuine boa inside a terrarium, draws a young crowd for local DJs and guests playing commercial electronica and techno-based dance music. Opened in 2006, this is Malinska's only club since the Crossroad closed down.

### Cocktail bar Volsonis

*Vela Placa 8, Krk town (051 220 052, www.volsonis.hr).* **Open** 8am-3am daily.
**No credit cards**.
A doorway in the Old Town wall opens to the gorgeous garden terrace of this party hub, also a cavernous two-floor indoor club. It is often the liveliest bar in Krk, with drinkers packing in from early in the evening. The garden has a great bar that serves cocktails until 2am – but go inside for DJs from Italy and Croatia, live music and later drinking.

### Disco Bar Jungle

*Stjepana Radića, Krk town (no phone, www.junglekrk.com).* **Open** *May-Sept* 9pm-5am daily. **No credit cards**.
A summer disco in the heart of Krk Old Town pumps out mainstream pop and disco hits for lighthearted holidaymakers. Guest DJs from around Europe break up the regular beat. The crowd is predominantly young but, because there are few other places around, there is a little more age range than in most Croatian clubs. Open sporadic weekends in winter.

## Hotels

Malinska has developed its tourist infrastructure tastefully. Here, the **Malin** (Kralja Tomislava 23, 051 850 234, www.hotel malin.com, **€€**) and the **Pinia** (Porat, 051 866 333, www.hotel-pinia.hr, **€€€**) are complemented by the **Blue Waves Resort**, the most recent major opening on Krk island, with a spa centre and children's entertainment. The **Adria** (Obala 40, 051 859 131, www.hotel-adria.com.hr, **€**) provides basic lodging at fair prices, by Malinska beach.

Rab. *See p130.*

Rab. *See p130.*

## ★ Atrium Residence Baška
*Emila Geistlicha 38, Baška (051 656 111, www.hotelibaska.hr).* **Open** Apr-Oct. **€€/€€€**.
The most luxurious lodging in Baška. As close as you can get to the water without swimming in it, this quality establishment offers quiet rooms to the rear and luxury ones facing the sea. Most units are fixed up as studio apartments or suites, with kitchenettes and varying degrees of comfort. The best have more than 100sq m (1,100sq ft) of space, in-room saunas and outdoor jacuzzis on spacious private balconies.

## Blue Waves Resort
*Rova 33, Malinska (051 654 002, www.bluewaves.hr.)* **€€**.
A new medium-sized resort hotel offers two outdoor swimming pools, an indoor one, a spa centre and children's activities – all about a half-mile from the centre of Malinska, one of the quieter and more pleasant tourist-oriented settlements on Krk. The 97 rooms have satellite TV, air-conditioning and other standard comforts. The pricier ones come with a balcony or terrace. In late July and August, the minimum stay is five days.

## Hostel Krk
*Dr Dinka Vitezića 32, Krk town (051 220 212, www.hostel-krk.com).* **€**. **No credit cards**.
In a typical tangle of Krk Old Town streets, this clean, comfortable and eminently affordable 60-bed hostel offers five doubles alongside its five dormitory-room options. A summer-only pizzeria is another boon.

## Kanajt
*Kanajt 5, Punat (051 654 340, www.kanajt.hr).* **€€**.
This comfortable, family-run hotel offers 20 rooms within easy reach of Krk town but closer to pretty Punat. Overlooking the marina, the Kanajt was a 16th-century summer retreat for local bishops, and somehow that ecclesiastical calm still reigns. The warm welcome – and warm bathrooms – engender repeat custom.

## ★ Marina
*Obala Hrvatske mornarice 8, Krk town (051 221 128, hotelmarina.hr).* **€€**.
The Hotel Marina has ten luxury units on three floors, in the centre of the action in Krk town. The hotel entrance is at one end of the small harbour but rooms are air conditioned and you can shut out the noise. All accommodation has a sea view; the pricier rooms come with their own balconies. The restaurant is by the hotel entrance, on a seaside terrace, with prices to match.

## Tamaris
*Emila Geistlicher 54B, Baška (051 864 200, www.baska-tamaris.com).* **Open** Apr-Nov. **€**.
Set on Baška beach, this modest three-star provides 15 doubles, 15 apartments and a large terrace. Rooms are standard but shoulder-season rates are fair, particularly half-board at an extra €5.

## GETTING THERE & AROUND

The **airport** by Omišalj on the northern tip of Krk serves Rijeka on the mainland. At present there is no public transport to Krk town, 20km (12 miles) away – a taxi (098 369 730) should cost about 300kn.

Regular **buses** run from Rijeka (1hr 20mins) to Krk town, via Malinska and then down to Baška. A couple a day come from Zagreb.

**Ferries** hop between Valbiska and Merag on Cres (30mins), and Baška and Lopar on Rab (50mins). In high season only, there is a regular service between Crikvenica on the mainland and Šilo on Krk's north-eastern tip (30mins).

## RESOURCES

### Tourist information

**Krk Island Tourist Office** *Trg sv Kvirina 1, Krk town (051 221 359, www.krk.hr).* **Open** 8am-3pm Mon-Fri.

**Krk Town Tourist Office** *Obala Hrvatske mornarice, Krk town (051 220 226, www.tz-krk.hr).* **Open** 9am-9pm daily.

# Rab

Verdant in the south-west, rocky in the north and east and rocking in the middle, Rab has a lot to offer. It's known as both the greenest and busiest island in the Kvarner string. Families like the safely shallow, sandy beach in the northern peninsula of **Lopar**, while nature lovers and naturists hike to the wilder beaches there. **Rab town**, near the centre of the island, is a bustling tourist destination, with an interesting mix of busy bars and a historic Old Town.

The Romans were so smitten with Rab town Emperor Octavian Augustus gave it municipal status in the 1st century BC. The main square is still called Trg Municipium, but the town's well-known skyline of four bell towers (*photo p129*) came after the Romans, in medieval times, and many of its architectural treasures were shaped by that era. Other attractions on the island include the stunning beaches in **Kampor** and **Pudarica**, and sprawling parklands with extensive pine and oak forests in **Kalifront** and **Dundovo**.

## INTRODUCING RAB

Illyrians settled on Rab in 350BC, followed by Greeks and Romans, then the Venetians, before two waves of plague hit in the 15th century. Venice allowed refugees to come in and run local businesses and the island was developed for tourism from the late 19th century, meaning it has a well-established tourist infrastructure of bars and restaurants.

**Rab town** is on a skinny peninsula that sticks out parallel to the mainland, bounded within city walls, distinguished by those four church towers. Three main streets – Upper, Middle and Lower – are interlinked with tiny lanes. The town is also divided into the oldest quarter, **Kaldanac**, at the far south-eastern end, and **Varoš**, with elegant Gothic and Renaissance buildings. The historic core is accessed by focal **Trg sv Kristofera**. The church of **St Mary the Great** (open 10am-1pm, 7.30-10pm daily) has the biggest of Rab's four towers. The church itself, consecrated in 1176, is quite plain with later Renaissance touches. You can climb the campanile for superb views. The oldest belltower is at neighbouring **St Andrew's**, a mix of Renaissance and Baroque styles. Further inland on the hillcrest, the church of **St Justine** contains a modest collection of sacred art, while the fourth tower belongs to the church of **St John**. Not much survives aside from the tower but you can climb it for great views. This hilltop row of churches sits above an Old Town that drops straight down to the sea. Stairs lead down to the water.

Inland from the old walled town, where the peninsula meets the mainland, there is a beautiful park called **Komrčar**, with paths winding around heavily wooded hills and emptying out on to the beaches, which are crowded in high season.

Unlike Rab town, most of **Lopar** is new. Its centre – a school, a church, the post office opposite and a few shops – consists of one street, and addresses are given as one number: no need to name the street. Few come to Lopar for its services – central Europeans (you'll see German, Czech and Hungarian on most menus) still descend in droves for its beaches.

## Restaurants

### Astoria

*Residence Astoria, Dinka Dokule 2, Rab town (051 774 844, www.astoria-rab.com).* **Open** *May-Nov* noon-3pm, 6-11pm daily. **€€€**. **Croatian**
Attached to a small, family-run apartment hotel is this professional restaurant in Rab town. With fine food, considerate service and an upstairs terrace overlooking the main square and harbour, it's one of the best choices in town. Top-quality monkfish and bass lead a dependable line-up of seafood, with steaks and vegetarian dishes too. Snappy table settings add a touch of class.

### Fortuna

*Lopar 533 (051 775 387, www.lopar-rab.com/ restoran_fortuna.html).* **Open** noon-midnight daily. **€€**. **No credit cards**. **Seafood**
Uphill from the beach and across from the Hotel Lopar stretches this beautifully sculpted terrace, where palm trees grow from a tiled floor, providing a sought-after shaded spot for pleasant meals in an attractive, casual atmosphere. Fortuna has the usual seafood offerings, plus mackerel, hake and sole – lobster can be ordered a day in advance. Check the chalkboard for specials, written up in German.

### Gostionica Feral

*Lopar 69 (051 775 288).* **Open** *May-Sept* noon-3pm, 5pm-midnight daily. **€€**. **No credit cards**. **Croatian**
Near Lopar's ferry slip on the main road is a pretty porch/terrace, covered with vines that look as if they've been growing since this place opened as a restaurant in 1971. Though the atmosphere in this family-run establishment is relaxed, food and service are taken seriously. The speciality is lobster, cooked how you like it, top-quality white fish or calamari Feral-style – stuffed with *fruits de mer*, potatoes and local green *blitva*. Book a day ahead for fish stew old-fisherman style or suckling pig on a spit.

### Gostionica Labirint

*Srednja ulica 9, Rab town (051 771 145).* **Open** 11am-3pm, 5.30pm-midnight daily. **€€**. **Seafood**
Distinctive dishes are served in this Old Town spot with a warm, rustic interior and a split-level roof terrace – though the only view is other rooftops. Local

specialities include Rab-style fish soup with good-size chunks of fish, mussels; scampi, potatoes and rice in hearty broth; and 'fish prepared in the manner of a good housewife of Rab', in other words, baked. Look out too for fillet of shark and langouste lobster, grilled or broiled.

## Laguna
*Lopar 544 (051 775 177, www.laguna-lopar.com).* **Open** *Summer* 8am-10pm daily. €€. **No credit cards.** Croatian

Located just steps from the entrance to Lopar's Paradise Beach, this large eaterie with a bright, airy interior and spacious, tree-shaded terrace offers decent seafood and good service in a no-frills atmosphere. The calamari, scampi, sea bass and mussels are all straight from the Adriatic and deftly prepared; the delicate, flaky mackerel, roasted with fresh rosemary, is sublime. Pizzas and meat options keep non-fish fans happy.

## Santa Maria
*Dinka Dokule 6, Rab town (051 724 196).* **Open** 10am-11pm midnight daily. €€€. Croatian

In Rab's Old Town, around the corner from the main square, the Santa Maria creates an impression with its pretty interior of rough stone walls and gorgeous sea views. Little wonder that this was a palace 200 years ago. Lovely outdoor seating also faces the harbour. The food does justice to the setting: excellent scampi and seafood; steaks and stews. It's a little bit pricier than the local competition but reasonable all the same.

## Cafés & Bars

### 1492 Cocktail Bar
*Dinka Dokule, Rab town (051 724 196).* **Open** 6pm-2am daily. **No credit cards.**

The people behind next door's Santa Maria restaurant (*see above*) also run this slick cocktail bar with great service and music ranging from Latin to electronic. There are over 50 cocktails on offer, frozen, champagne-based and sours, with happy hours from 6pm.

### Banova Vila Beach Bar
*Šetalište fra Odorika Badurine, Rab town (098 442 038).* **Open** 9am-2am daily. **No credit cards.**

On the seaside walkway beneath the spot where Komrčar Park meets the Old Town, Banova Vila may not be paradise – but get the right sunset with the right someone, and this little beachside bar will be damn close. A thatched roof and 25 types of reasonably priced cocktails help things along nicely. Everyone, staff included, seems young and good-looking, and you can sip drinks by the sea until 2am.

### Caffè Biser
*Srednja ulica, Rab town (no phone).* **Open** 9am-midnight daily. **No credit cards.**

Beside Trg Sv Kristofor, where Rab's Old Town begins to bustle with bar life, this attractive café has a spacious, shaded terrace, a pleasant interior and a small gem of a courtyard at the back. It's a fine place for a daytime coffee or to kick off an evening's bar crawl. Generous, reasonably priced drinks, snappily served, are an added incentive.

### Escape Lounge Bar
*Obala P Krešimira 4, Rab town (no phone).* **Open** *Summer* 8am-3pm, 5pm-2am daily. **No credit cards.**

It's hard to miss Escapes, the night spot of the Hotel International (*see p132*), slap in the middle of Rab town's harbourside, inside a piece of city wall in the Old Town. As the bars around close, this decent-sized dance space fills with a fun-loving crowd, ready to party to commercial dance tunes. The staff are up for a party too, and the volume of holidaymakers should guarantee an entertaining evening. By day, the terrace comes into its own for relaxed coffees.

### Forum
*Donja ulica 9A, Rab town (098 872 664).* **Open** *Summer* 6pm-2am daily. **No credit cards.**

The boat-shaped cocktail bar in Forum's front terrace, in the heart of Rab's Old Town, lends a slightly naff touristy look to the place, but this is a real bar, the spot where Croatians tend to hang out when they visit Rab. As the night draws on, the action shifts from the terrace to the dark pub-like interior. The music, nodding towards rock by day, drifts to dance tunes by the evening, with DJs playing weekend nights. Not quite a club, but a busy late bar.

▶ *Rab town's main square of Trg Municipium Arba has its fair share of late-opening bars, as well as the San Antonio Club (No.4, 051 724 145, www.sanantonio-club.com), the best centrally located nightspot. It's run by the same people as the Santos Beach Club (see below) at Pudarica beach.*

## Nightlife

### Santos Beach Club
*Pudarica beach (051 724 145, www.sanantonio-club.com).* **Open** *Mid July-early Sept* until late daily. **No credit cards.**

Catch one of the hourly buses from 10pm from Rab town for the ten kilometre trip to Pudarica beach by Barbat, and a decadent outdoor dance experience. Hundreds of punters, plus the occasional go-go dancer, shimmy on the pebble beach to house and disco hits. There are also gigs by local bands. SBC has a thatch-shaded lounge, a beach volleyball court and a small pool for those who show up (and pose) by day. Modelled after the beach clubs on nearby Pag, the Santos may not be original but it can guarantee you a busy party most nights in high season.

**EXPLORE**

## Hotels

### ★ Arbiana Hotel
*Obala P Krešimira 12, Rab town (051 775 900,*
*www.arbianahotel.com). €€.*
Set in an elegant old villa, the Hotel Arbiana, with 28 rooms, provides comfortable lodgings. The building originally opened in 1924 as the Hotel Bristol and was given a complete renovation in 2006. As it's set at the tip of the peninsula that holds Rab's Old Town, it's near everything but away from the busiest part of the harbour. Most rooms have balconies overlooking the harbourside walkway and the sea beyond. All are spacious and decorated with classic, antique-style furniture and expansive, comfy chairs. Also beautifully furnished are the two bars and the notable restaurant, the San Marino.

### Grand Hotel Imperial
*Palit, Rab town (051 724 522, 051 667 788,*
*www.imperialrab.com). €€.*
An imposing five-storey Mediterranean-style building, the Imperial is set inside a seaside park that connects Rab Old Town with its nearest beaches. This was one of Rab's first hotels, built a century ago, but its 134 rooms have been renovated, and now each has air-conditioning and standard four-star fittings. The grounds contain three tennis courts, a goofy golf course and terrace cafés. There is public car parking nearby. Given its convenience, the Imperial works out to be one of the better deals in town.

### Epario
*Lopar 456A (051 777 500, www.epario.net). €.*
This recently constructed, comfortable establishment provides 28 small and functional rooms, all with air-conditioning, a stone's throw from Lopar's popular main beach. There is also an exercise room, a playroom and a modest restaurant – decent, affordable and all located by the sea. Dinners can be included in the price of your stay for an extra €5 a head.

### International
*Obala P Krešimira 4, Rab town (051 602 000,*
*www.hotelrab.com). €€.*
With a modern building tastefully incorporated into the old city wall, this rebranded hotel has the most central location in town – Rab's Old Town action is right on your doorstep. Facilities include a restaurant and two bars, a swimming pool, sauna, jacuzzi and gym; an impressive number of beauty treatments and massages are available. There are close to 140 rooms, with contemporary fittings and air-conditioning.

### Istra
*Markantuna de Dominisa, Rab town*
*(051 724 134, www.hotel-istra.hr). €.*
This old building of 100 rooms, with tiny bathrooms and no air-conditioning, provides a modest budget option in a central location in Rab town. No frills but this pretty structure stays cool on summer evenings and has a terrace café.

## GETTING THERE & AROUND

Regular **ferries** run from litoral Jablanac (30mins) to Rab's southern tip at Mišnjak. A summer one links with Baška on Krk. **Buses** from Mišnjak go via Rab town to Lopar.

In summer a daily **catamaran** runs from Rijeka (2hrs), then to Novalja on Pag (50mins). Three daily **buses** run from Rijeka to Rab town (3hrs 30mins), two from Zagreb (6hrs).

## RESOURCES

**Tourist information** *Rab Tourist Office Trg Municipium Arba 8, Rab town (051 771 111, www.tzg-rab.hr).* **Open** *Summer* 8am-10pm daily. *Winter* 10am-2am Mon-Sat.

# Cres

One of the largest but least developed of Croatia's islands, the relatively untouched gem of **Cres** contains 400 square kilometres (155 square miles) of rugged wilderness, an estimated 80 breeding pairs of the rare griffon vultures and only 3,000 full-time human residents. There are a couple of resort settlements, but not much else in the way of luxury vacations. For more sophistication, take a room in ancient **Cres town**; for wilderness, get a campsite in the hills. Either way, you can expect a simpler and quieter time than at many of Kvarner's other resorts.

## INTRODUCING CRES

Cres is long enough to have two very distinct landscapes: verdant in the north, known as Tramuntana, but barren to the south. The north contains the two settlements of **Beli** and the commercial centre of Cres town. There, fishing boats bob in the café-lined harbour, behind which serpentine, car-free streets weave between attractively austere buildings with fading pastel frontages.

Cres town dates back at least a couple of millennia, and the island itself has been inhabited since the Palaeolithic era. Romans and Byzantines successfully ruled it until the advent of the first independent Croatians around AD 822. The Venetians then took over the island for 400 years, beginning around the tenth century, and it was they who are responsible for the older remaining landmarks in Cres town. Of particular note is the church of **Our Lady of Snow**, in the heart of town, dating from the 16th century with a bell tower from the 18th.

If you continue west from Cres town harbour, you reach the Lungomare seaside promenade that leads to the town's pebbly beach. In the opposite direction you get to the town marina, and beyond that to a beautiful natural seaside walk along the wide bay that the town sits upon.

The southern part of Cres island has the former regional capital of **Osor**. As a major trading port, 'Apsorus' was the largest Roman settlement on the Croatian Adriatic after Pula. Since then, Osor has been in decline, although its **Archaelogical Museum** (open 10am-noon, 7-9pm daily, 10kn) reveals that medieval Osor was still sizeable.

In between north and south are the ancient villages of **Lubenice** and **Valun**, both with nice beaches; and **Martinščica**, a small tourist development centred around a 10th-century monastery and a good pebbly beach. The 4,000-year-old settlement of Lubenice is home to just 20 ageing souls and some crumbling stone buildings, including a Romanesque chapel used as storage space. On the jagged coast, a series of secluded pebble coves is reached by a steep footpath leading through the underbrush. Nearby Valun is a charming fishing village whose parish church contains the 11th-century Valun Tablet. Its inscription is an early and fascinating example of the ancient local tongue of Glagolitic.

In the middle of the island, the large but shallow freshwater **Lake Vrana** has its surface above sea level, but its bottom below the level of the local sea floor. It supplies both Cres and Lošinj, and is an important bird reserve. **Porozina** at the northern tip is the main point of entry from the little port of Brestova, on the Istria-Kvarner border.

## Restaurants

### ★ Gostionica Bukaleta

*Loznati 9A (051 571 606, www.mali-losinj.com/bukaleta.htm).* **Open** Apr-Sept noon-11pm. **No credit cards. €€. Croatian**

Do the local delicacy justice by heading about five kilometres from Cres town to the hilltop village of Loznati, where a family lovingly raises their own lambs and then serves them fresh. The meat can come spit-roasted, grilled or cooked several other ways. Good fish and shrimp add variety to the menu, and the bread and olive oil are own-made. It's a relaxing spot, with rustic farmhouse decor and lush green surroundings, also welcoming front of house staff, but it's highly popular, so best book ahead.

### Restaurant Santa Lucia

*Lungomare Švetog Mikule 4, Cres town (051 573 222).* **Open** 9am-midnight daily. **€€€. Croatian**

This waterside terrace spot in Cres town is slightly pricier than its competitors, but worth it. Seafood is handled superbly, whether it's lobster cooked to order, octopus baked in a *peka* dish, or simple fish soup adorned with scampi. Truffles show up as an appetiser with cheese, served with *fuži* noodles, or in classic style with steak.

## Cafés & Bars

The island is not known for its late-night scene. However, on the Cres town harbour front, venues like the **Astoria**, **Arsan** and **Burin** stay open until 2am; the **Fortis** and **Morena** are also busy. **Štala** (Turion 3, 051 571 897/098 491 975), just outside the Old Town, is the only nightspot that might be described as a 'commercial disco' – foam parties have been known to happen.

EXPLORE

Cres.

## Hotels

### Kimen

*Melin 1/16 (051 573 305, www. hotel-kimen.com).* **€**.

The no-frills Kimen offers a total of 223 affordable, basic rooms in three buildings on a big wooded campus right alongside Cres town's long beach. The 1970s-style main building has the slightly more expensive, recently renovated rooms, with bathrooms, balconies and air-conditioning. Various sports facilities are located nearby.

### ★ Zlatni Lav

*Martinšćica 18D (051 574 020, www.hotel-zlatni-lav.com).* **€/€€**.

Cres island's nicest hotel, the small Golden Lion is set above the bay of Martinšćica, a tiny seaside village with a fine gravel beach. The hotel has five suites and 25 doubles with air-conditioning and showers. The pricier rooms have their own balconies and sea views. The restaurant, serving seafood, lamb and brick-oven pizza, is handy in this small settlement with limited amenities, and there's also a bar. All in all, nothing too fancy, but all the basic comforts in a secluded seaside paradise setting.

## GETTING THERE & AROUND

Two **ferries** hop to Cres: from Brestova on the Istrian mainland to Porozina; and from Valbiska on Krk to Merag. Both run every hour or so and take around 30mins.

In summer a daily **catamaran** service links with Rijeka (1hr 20mins) and Mali Lošinj, all going into Cres town, some to Martinšćica.

At least five **buses** a day run between Cres town and Mali Lošinj on Lošinj, two linking with Zagreb. Summer weekdays, some six buses run between Cres town and Osor, significantly fewer at weekends and in winter.

Transport to north Cres is scarce but there is a **taxi** rank at Cres town bus station (Zazid 4, 051 571 664, 098 947 5592).

## RESOURCES

**Tourist information** *Cres Tourist Office, Cons 10, Cres town (051 571 535, www.tzg-cres.hr).* **Open** *Summer* 9am-10pm daily.

# Lošinj

The rocky seabed around Lošinj means there's no sand to cloud the water, and you can see straight down for a long way. Thanks to this seabed, the currents and conservation, the water around the island is some of the cleanest in the Adriatic, which is why this area is a magnet for dolphins; you may see the beautiful creatures chasing the ferry boat that brings you to this island. The clean water is also an attraction for spearfishers, who hold regular tournaments here, as well as ordinary holidaymakers, who enjoy swimming in the clear waters. Back on shore, the attractions of Lošinj include beautiful nature as well as resort settlements full of good bars and restaurants.

## INTRODUCING LOŠINJ

Cres and Lošinj used to be one island until the ancient Liburni tribe dug a canal at Osor. The healthy effects of its sea breezes, clean water and 2,600 hours of annual sunshine earned Lošinj an official designation as a health resort in 1892. Habsburg royalty followed and now tourism is the island's main industry.

Activity centres around two towns with misleading labels. **Mali Lošinj**, 'Small Lošinj', is the bigger settlement, about four kilometres from quaint little **Veli Lošinj**, 'Great Lošinj'.

Mali Lošinj, the largest island town in the Adriatic, with a population of 7,000, is set around a long, wide harbour, lined with Habsburg-era facades. Strolling from one end of the harbour to the other takes 20 minutes – it's a nice waterside lined with great restaurants and bars. Trg Republike Hrvatske is the big square. Pop into the **Art Collections** (Vladimira Gortana 35, 051 231 173, open summer 10am-1pm, 7-10pm daily, winter 10am-noon, 7-9pm daily) for modern Croatian pieces as well as Italian art works from the 17th and 18th centuries.

There are good beaches near Mali Lošinj, including the popular rocky and pebbly stretches in wooded Čikat, just on the other side of a hill from the harbour.

Neighbouring Veli Lošinj is centred around a small harbour surrounded by steep hills. On one rise, right on the harbour, is the boxy pink church of **St Anthony**, which contains seven Baroque altars and works by Italian masters. The sinners hang out down below, in a bustling clutch of good bars and restaurants. On another hill above the harbour is a crenulated **Venetian tower**, built as a fortification in 1455 and used for exhibitions. Walk along a ridge above the beach for the other harbour, tiny **Rovenska**: three restaurants and a pebbly beach.

The **Marine Education Centre** in Veli Lošinj promotes conservation with a special focus on the nearby bottlenose dolphin colony.

## Sights & Museums

### Marine Education Centre
*Kaštel 24 (051 604 666, www.blue-world.org).* **Open** *July, Aug* 10am-9pm daily. *June, Sept* 10am-6pm daily. *Nov-May* 10am-2pm Mon-Fri. **Admission** 15kn; 10kn reductions; free under-6s. **No credit cards**.
Run by the Blue World/Plavi Svijet Institute, the Marine Education Centre promotes conservation issues throughout the Croatian Adriatic, with particular reference to the bottlenose dolphin colony off the Lošinj coast. An attractive display introduces the

world of the dolphin and the importance of protecting it. Visitors are shown a short film (with English subtitles), dioramas and computer graphics. An 'acoustic room' demonstrates how dolphins communicate, and also how easily they can be disturbed by the rumble of boat engines. The MEC does not recommend dolphin trips (the whole point of the operation is to protect the dolphins as wild creatures, not disturb them or tame them), but it does have an important role in educating local boat captains how to respect dolphins when out on the water. Visitors who want to get involved in dolphin conservation can become a godfather or godmother to a dolphin for one year (from 200kn).

The MEC is also becoming more and more involved in the conservation of sea turtles, who inhabit the sandy shallows of the Kvarner Gulf. July 2013 saw the opening of a sea-turtle rescue centre on the Čikat peninsula, right between the Aurora and Vespera hotels. Here, sick turtles will be kept in tanks until they're healthy enough to be set free. (Previously, poorly turtles had to be sent all the way to Pula on the Istrian mainland).

EU funding should enable the Centre to expand its activities and move to much bigger, purpose-built premises in Mali Lošinj harbour some time after 2015.

## Restaurants

### ★ Bora Bar Trattoria/Tartufferia
*Rovenska 3, Veli Lošinj (051 867 544, www. borabar.net).* **Open** *Apr-Oct* 10am-11pm daily. **€€. Croatian**

Lošinj.

This charming spot is run by chef Marco Sasso. Born in Pisa, Sasso was a truffle dealer in the United States before coming to Croatia. He gets the fungus fresh from Istria and uses it in starters, such as tuna carpaccio with marinated celery roots. Other ingredients come fresh from the sea on which the terrace is perched. Desserts include own-made panna cotta or chocolate mousse.

### ★ Gostionica Marina
*Obala maršala Tita 38, Veli Lošinj (051 236 178, www.gostionica-marina.hr/en).* **Open** *Apr-Oct* 9am-midnight daily. €€. **No credit cards.**

**Seafood**
White tablecloths, attentive service and wonderful food make this place feel more upmarket than other fish-oriented restaurants in Veli Losinj's main harbour, but the prices here are competitive. Fresh bruschetta, made of chopped tomatoes and garlic with thick, flame-broiled toast, is slapped on the table as soon as you sit down. The servers are familiar with the bottles on the long list of Croatian wines. You can see fish delivered here by boat in the morning, and come lunchtime have that fresh catch, or steak or lamb, cooked over a wooden flame on the terrace, which is at the bend in the harbour and has great views of both the town and the sea.

### Konoba Ribarska Koliba
*Obala maršala Tita, Veli Lošinj (051 236 235).* **Open** *Apr-Oct* 9am-midnight daily. €€. **Seafood**
One of the fancier spots on Veli Lošinj's little harbour, the Koliba has offerings like a tasty shark steak with a delicately garlicky sauce, a *brodetto* tomato-based fish stew, and baked fish. Calamari can be fried, grilled or stuffed with seafood, and lobster comes grilled or with spaghetti. Along with the usual steaks, meats also include lamb on a spit.

### Konoba-Pizzeria Bukaleta
*Trg žrtava fašizma 7, Mali Lošinj (051 231 777, losinjcroatia.eu/konoba-pizzeria-bukaleta).* **Open** 10am-11pm daily. €. **Pizzeria**
The hulking oven here turns out the kind of pizzas that would pass muster in Italy: a perfectly molten mix of cheese and sauce atop a thin, crispy crust. Despite the casual rustic feel, attention is paid to detail. Each table gets a Peugeot pepper grinder, the pizza comes with a sharp, heavy stainless steel knife, the servers are fast, and care has been taken with the food.

### Lošinjsko Jidro
*Sv Marije 11, Mali Lošinj (051 233 424).* **Open** *Feb-Dec* 9am-11pm daily. €€. **Seafood**
Just a few hundred metres uphill from the tip of the harbour awaits cuisine that you'd happily walk much further for. The sheltered terrace has no spectacular vistas: the most interesting sight is the wood-fired grill, and the fresh fish sizzling on it. There's a big kitchen inside too, ready with a range

of seafood, including scallops, sea snails and other lovely shell-dwellers. The place is famous for its *brodet*, a stew with a thick tomato sauce and a wealth of fish and seafood. Charming servers make you feel at home. It's easy to see why this place is a favourite among locals.

## Cafés & Bars

Mali Lošinj harbour is lined with cafes and bars that stay open late in summer. **Catacomba** (Del Conte Giovanni 1), just behind the harbour in an alley, has frequent live music.

In Veli Lošinj, the harbourside **Caffè Bar Saturn** (Obala maršala Tita 1) has a fun mixed crowd and usually fills up first.

At Rovenska, beachside boozer and snack bar **Beach Bar Rovenska** (051 236 256) has a popular late party scene. Things also go on late at the nearby **Timi Beach**, which draws a crowd of student-aged partiers.

## Hotels

### Apoksiomen
*Riva Lošinjskih kapetana 1, Mali Lošinj (051 520 820, www.apoksiomen.com).* **Open** Apr-Oct. €€.
This boutique hotel nicely located near the harbour has 24 tasteful and unusual rooms, decorated with original paintings by name Croatian artists. All rooms are air-conditioned; most have harbour views. The à la carte restaurant has a waterside terrace; you can have the food sent up.

### ★ Family Hotel Vespera
*Sunčana uvala (051 667 300, www.losinj-hotels. com).* **Open** May-mid Oct. €€.
The Vespera has been earmarked by the Lošinj Hotels group to serve as the main family hotel on the island, and boasts pretty much everything that parents travelling with children might need, with playrooms, sports facilities, crèches for the smallest, and supervised activities and entertainment for older kids. They even have a stock of prams and pushchairs so you don't have to pack your own. The Vespera shares the outdoor pool complex of the next-door Aurora. Immediately below the hotel is Borik, one of the Adriatic's finest rock-slab beaches, which catches the sun until quite late in the evening. For parents making use of the Vespera's baby-sitting service, the Borik Mediterranean bar, right on the beach, with pillows spread across the rocks, is a great place to watch the sunset.

### Mare Mare Suites
*Riva Lošinjskih kapetana 36, Mali Lošinj (051 232 010, www.mare-mare.com).* €€.
Near Mali Lošinj harbour, this boutique property with 24 beds is chic but friendly. Rooms and suites are done up cheerfully, while the rooftop terrace has gorgeous views, a jacuzzi and a champagne bar – sip,

soak and gawp away. There's a spa and cocktail bar too. The hotel can also lay on tours of the island, plus bike and kayak rental.

### Pansion Saturn
*Obala maršala Tita 1, Veli Lošinj (051 236 102, www.losinj-hotels.eu).* €.
Central, cheap and cheerful, with a youngish clientele, Pension Saturn is housed in a renovated red building on Veli Lošinj harbour. There are nine simple, tasteful rooms, four of them air-conditioned. The bar is recommended.

### ★ Vitality Hotel Punta
*Šestavine (051 661 111, vitality.losinj-hotels.com/ hr).* **Open** Mid Mar-mid Oct. €€.
Reopened in 2012 after thorough renovation, the Punta offers a choice between self-catering apartments in the shoreside building, or smart well-equipped doubles in the terraced building just behind it. It's one of the best places in the Kvarner Gulf to enjoy an invigorating spa break: as well as an indoor pool, the Punta's wellness area includes the Iuvena massage centre and a studio devoted to PBS body technique – a blend of pilates, yoga and aquagym exercises pioneered by Zagreb-based fitness innovator Ana-Marija Jagodić Rukavina. The PBS studio also offers the chance to experience gravitronics – a yoga-based exercise that involves swinging in slings suspended from the ceiling. The Laurus aromatherapy centre offers essential oils based on the plants and herbs that grow naturally on the island. You can sign up for essential-oil treatments and participate in oil-making workshops. If all you want is sea and sunshine, the Punta has got a rocky-slab beach right in front of it. *Photo p139.*

### Wellness Hotel Aurora
*Sunčana uvala (051 667 200, www.losinj-hotels. com).* €€.
This modern, luxury resort hotel stretches across a wooded headland overlooking Sunčana uvala or 'Sunny Bay', one of the main beach areas of the Čikat Peninsula just west of Mali Lošinj town. There's a large and well-appointed Laurus spa centre featuring indoor pools fed with seawater, a range of saunas, Turkish and Roman baths, an indoor massage area and an outdoor terrace where you can enjoy massages with a sea view. The oils and skincare products are made in Laurus's own laboratories using Lošinj-gathered plants and herbs. There's a profusion of tennis courts and sports grounds in the woods behind the hotel. As well as the choice of shingle and rock-slab beaches immediately below the hotel, there's a terraced outdoor pool complex (including kids' paddling area) to one side.

## BEACHES & EXCURSIONS

The nicest beaches near Mali Lošinj, with either rocky or pebbly surfaces, are to the west and

---

### IN THE KNOW UPSCALE LOŠINJ

Local tourism concern **Lošinj Hotels & Villas** (www.losinj-hotels.com) has big plans for the island, accentuating the sport and spa aspects of local tourism and updating all of its hotels to four-star standard (the Aurora, Punta and Vespera have already been done). The 1960s-era Helios will be rebuilt as a state-of-the-art thalassotherapy centre, while the currently modest Alhambra, a fine Habsburg-era villa, will ultimately be transformed into a small and intimate five-star. In addition, Mali Lošinj also has two good boutique hotels, the Apoksiomen and Mare Mare.

---

north of town, in the wooded bays of **Čikat** and **Sunčana Uvala**, an area with several resort hotels that can be reached on foot from Mali Lošinj or via special hotel buses.

In Veli Lošinj, **Timi** beach near the old cemetery and **Rovenska** beach in Rovenska harbour provide pebbly and concrete surfaces, plus snack bars. Follow the coastal path from Rovenska and you pass more secluded rocky beaches. If you continue along this shore for close to three kilometres however, you'll reach quiet **Javorna**, a small but beautiful crescent of pebbles, backed by fragrant woodland.

## GETTING THERE & AROUND

In summer, a daily **catamaran** runs from Rijeka to Mali Lošinj (2hr 50mins). Several **buses** a day link Cres town and Mali Lošinj; two link with Zagreb. From mid June to September, a **car ferry** runs twice weekly to Mali Lošinj from Zadar and Pula.

## RESOURCES

**Tourist information** *Lošinj Tourist Office, Riva Lošinjskih kapetana 29, Mali Lošinj (051 231 884, visitlosinj.hr).* **Open** *Summer* 8am-8pm daily. *Winter* 8am-5pm Mon-Fri; 8am-1pm Sat.

# Pag

Approaching Pag on the regular 20-minute ferry hop from the mainland, you may be forgiven for thinking that you've landed on the moon. The east coast of the island is a bleak, forbidding landscape of stark white and barren limestone karst against the relentless blue expanse of sea and sky – everything blown bare by the Bura wind. When it's hot, it's baking, especially in August. The upside is the excellent food produced here under such harsh conditions: outstanding lamb and the famous cheese called *paški sir*.

## INTRODUCING PAG

Pag is thin and 64 kilometres (40 miles) long, made up of two parallel mountain ranges. Settlements are mainly sleepy fishing villages, with two towns of any size, **Novalja** and **Pag town**. Novalja is a resort town that's become party central. **Zrće beach**, a short bus ride away, is the biggest club hub in Croatia.

By contrast, the administrative and commercial centre of Pag town exudes cultural heritage. Narrow, fortified medieval streets weave beneath a 15th-century Gothic cathedral and the sun beats hard off the white stone pavement as local ladies painstakingly stitch Pag lace in doorways.

The flavours on the Pag dinner table are influenced by its arid, saline environment. Inhabited by more sheep than humans, Pag has lamb that is flavoured with the aromatic herbs that browsing sheep consume – as is the trademark Pag cheese. Fish tastes different too, a result of the particularly salty waters. What with the local *žutica* dry white wine and the stiff digestif of *travarica* herb brandy, the Pag culinary experience is especially attractive to foodies.

## Restaurants

### Boškinac
*Novalja Škopljanksa 20 (053 663 500, www. boskinac.com).* **Open** noon-midnight daily. €€. **Croatian**
Hands down the nicest place to wine and dine on Pag, with a superb hotel attached (*see right*). Home-grown cuisine is to the fore, the seasonal ingredients of Pag – in particular fish and lamb – combined with herbs and contemporary creativity – and a huge selection of local wines. Staff follow the lead of owners Mirela and Boris Šuljić, the epitome of hospitality.

### Konoba Bile
*Jurja Dalmatinca 35, Pag town (023 611 127).* **Open** 11.30am-11pm daily. €. **No credit cards. Croatian**
This atmospheric little stone-walled cellar is the place to go to try the local wines, hams and cheeses, served with a smile but with little fuss. The chatty regulars seem to enjoy the informal grazing as much as you will. Close to the church, this is an ideal spot for a late, light lunch after a morning spent at the beach.

### Na Tale
*Stjepana Radića 4, Pag town (023 611 194, www. ljubica.hr).* **Open** noon-11pm daily. €€€. **Croatian**

This fine establishment is commonly acknowledged to be the top table in Pag town. Overlooking the bay at the edge of the seafront, at Na Tale the food certainly matches the wonderful location. The seafood in particular is another attraction, the fresh white meat of the catch of the day brought out by superb sauces. Octopus lasagne and Pag lamb are other specialities, best enjoyed away from the burning sun in the shaded courtyard.

## Bars & Nightlife

In Novalja, pre-club bars dot Trg Loža, before the action shifts to **Zrće**, and the landmark clubs **Kalypso** (kalypso-zrce.com), **Papaya** (papa-ya.com.hr) and **Aquarius** (www. aquarius.hr), all open-air and stretched out on the white, pebbly beach. Most are near 24-hour operations, with sports and poolside drinking by day.

### Vanga
*Stara Riva (no phone, www.facebook.com/ dub.vanga).* **Open** May-Sept 3pm-4am daily. **No credit cards.**
This popular place is the main nightspot in Pag town with foam parties, mainstream DJing and occasional karaoke. Take it or leave it. Named after a boat, Vanga also runs occasionally on winter weekends – check its Facebook page for details.

## Hotels

### ★ Boškinac
*Novalja Škopljanksa 20 (053 663 500, www.boskinac.com).* €€.
By a field near Novalja, this hotel and restaurant is the nicest place to dine and lodge on Pag island. Set in bucolic surroundings, on grounds containing their own vineyards, owners Mirela and Boris put classic Croatian flavours, modern design and top service to the fore. Dishes in the restaurant (*see left*) – which, with its cascading stone terraces, and an informal *konoba* filled with hanging hams below, is worth visiting in its own right – showcase traditional flavours and home-grown produce. The dozen rooms and suites, each named after local flora, are individually decorated in soft Mediterranean colours, with expansive views of the surrounding pine woods, olive groves and vineyards. Boškinac also lays on special gastronomic and wine weekends, horse-riding and a range of other activities.

### Plaža
*Marka Marulića 14, Pag town (023 600 855,).* **Open** Mid June-mid Sept. €€.
This relatively modern four-star provides views across the bay to the Old Town, as well as 23 well appointed doubles and six apartments. All have access to the pool, gym, sauna and spa – and there is a cocktail bar and restaurant on-site too.

EXPLORE

Vitality Hotel Punta. *See p137.*

### Tony

*Dubrovačka 39, Pag town (023 611 370, www.hotel-tony.com).* **Open** June-Sept. €€.
Twenty spacious rooms just north-east of Pag Old Town offer relaxation and a bit of beach nearby. There's no need even to go into Pag if you're feeling lazy – the Tony has its own restaurant, and the half-board rates are more than reasonable. You will have to book early though, as this is a popular getaway and only open for four months of the year. Staff are happy to help with boat hire and Wi-Fi is also provided on every balcony so you can web-surf while admiring the view.

### ★ Luna Hotel

*Jakišnica, Lun (053 654 700, lunaislandhotel.com).* **Open** Mid Mar-Sept. €€.
The swishest hotel on Pag is a 20-minute drive from Novalja, and is a much needed quality option with two pools (including one for children), a spa centre, lounge bar and restaurant. It is also right on the water, on the northern tip of the island, and a short drive from the ferry port of Žigljen with its regular connection to the mainland. Most of the 93 rooms, divided into three categories, face the sea. All have internet access. Standard rooms out of high season are a bargain considering the facilities on offer.

## GETTING THERE & AROUND

The easiest hop to Pag is the hourly **ferry** from Prizna on the mainland to Žigljen (20mins) on Pag's north-eastern tip, 5km north of Novalja.
Twice daily **buses** between Rijeka and Zadar call at both Novalja and Pag town, the only public transport link (30mins) between the two. There's a **taxi** stand (098 282 872 mobile) at the ferry port in Novalja.
In summer a daily Jadrolinija **catamaran** runs in the morning from Novalja to Rijeka (2hrs 30mins), turning round at Rijeka in the afternoon. It also passes by Rab town, so it's possible to hop from Rab town to Novalja (50 mins) in the afternoon, and go from Novalja to Rab in the morning.
Pag town is an hour from Zadar, three hours from Rijeka and five hours from Zagreb – there are five **buses** a day from the capital.

## RESOURCES

### Tourist information

**Pag Town Tourist Office** *Od Špitale 2 (023 611 286, www.tzgpag.hr).* **Open** *Summer* 8am-8pm daily. *Winter* 9am-noon Mon-Fri.

**Novalja Tourist Office** *Trg Brišćić 1 (053 663 238, www.visitnovalja.hr).* **Open** *Summer* 9am-6pm daily.

**EXPLORE**

# Zadar & Northern Dalmatia

EXPLORE

**Z**adar and Šibenik in northern Dalmatia are far from famous given the historic lack of international transport links. Yet they offer history, natural beauty and, in Zadar's case, entertainment. Šibenik is still isolated as far as planes, trains or boats are concerned but Zadar is now firmly on the map thanks to the success of Brit-run bar and DJ terrace the Garden and its annual music festival. The Zadar archipelago and the islands of the Kornati National Park are reason enough to visit the region; the cathedral city of Šibenik is the gateway to another great natural attraction, Krka National Park. Primošten and Tribunj offer tranquillity in contrast to the tourist towns of Vodice and Biograd.

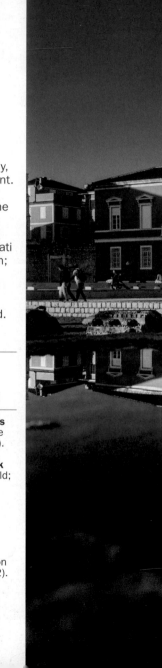

Sea Organ.

## Don't Miss

**1 Cathedral of St James**
A Gothic-Renaissance wonder in Šibenik (p161).

**2 Kornati National Park**
A stunning island world; get there by boat (p168).

**3 The Garden**
Zadar's panoramic, landmark bar (p149).

**4 Sea Organ**
Musical installation on the Zadar seafront (p142).

**5 Krka National Park**
Crystal pools and a famous waterfall (p167).

# Zadar

There seems to be no stopping Zadar, the main city of northern Dalmatia. This once-Italianate seaside town has in the last few years attracted some of Croatia's most visionary initiatives: the Garden club and its various festival offshoots; landmark public installations such as the Sea Organ and Greeting to the Sun; and the Arsenal, an arts centre in a beautifully restored Venetian armoury.

Just out of town at Petrčane, Falkensteiner's huge Punta Skala Resort, centred around five-star spa hotel Iadera, has helped to propel Zadar's tourist profile into the international luxury league. In Zadar itself, the excellent Museum of Ancient Glass has bolstered the city's sightseeing potential. Once the city authorities decide what to do with the notoriously derelict Hotel Zagreb (a promenade-hugging building once patronised by Alfred Hitchcock and other celebs), the city's transformation will be complete.

## INTRODUCING ZADAR

Stuck out on a peninsula halfway between Split and Rijeka, Zadar was isolated from the mainland for significant chunks of the 20th century. Italian between the wars (when it was called Zara), it suffered heavy Allied bombing in World War II, then became part of Tito's Yugoslavia until 1991. Under serious threat by Serbian forces during the 1991-95 war, the city was cut off from Zagreb completely for 14 months.

Zadar's isolation has given it a distinctive local culture. It is perhaps most identified with the cherry liqueur maraschino – you'll see the sign of the local producer, Maraska, all over town. It is also known for its sunsets, which drew Alfred Hitchcock here for one memorable evening in 1964. Hitch's portrait can still be seen around town and he provided inspiration for Nikola Bašić's art installation *Greeting to the Sun*. The setting could not have been scripted better – although, sadly, Hitchcock never did make a film here.

Everything takes place on a tongue of land some 600 metres (1,970ft) long and 300 metres (980ft) wide, encircled by the Venetian fortifications, with scenic quays below and the sea beyond. Cars are only allowed as far as the quays; locals scurry about their business by foot in the narrow downtown streets. To reach the mainland, pedestrians have to walk as far as the narrow section of channel at Foša, halfway to the bus and train stations away to the east; cross the busy footbridge enclosing the border of the marina of Jazine; or, as people have been doing for centuries, throw a few coins into the ferryman's open sack to take them over the water.

The most central point of entry is by boat, with three ferry points dotted on the north embankment, in addition to the new ferry terminal on the south embankment.

The Romans built Iadera, the peninsula, with a regulated street pattern, four gates and a forum – much of which are still visible today. Part of the old Roman Forum forms the main square Zeleni trg; sundry sections of stone pillar peter out towards the south quay of Obala kralja Petra Krešimira IV. On and adjacent to Zeleni trg are Zadar's four main sights: **St Donat's Church**, the **Cathedral**, the **Archaelogical Museum** and **St Mary's Church & Treasury**. Distinctive St Donat's and the Byzantine treats of the Treasury are the absolute 'don't miss' sights. Alongside the Forum runs the spinal street of Široka, usually called Kalelarga, linking the new cultural hub of Three Wells (Trg tri bunara) to historic Five Wells (Trg pet bunara) at each end of the city centre.

The south embankment was once the chic side of town, with a pier for fast passenger ships and four-storey buildings in the classic Habsburg mould. Much was built with Maraska money, the local manufacturer having grown rich from liqueur sales. The Hotel Bristol and its namesake coffeehouse were landmarks, even after the Italians moved in and renamed them Excelsior. The quay was almost completely destroyed by Allied bombing; all that remained was the hotel, renamed the Zagreb and still the subject of a long-running saga to renovate it.

The unusual **Sea Organ**, inaugurated in 2005, was designed by architect Nikola Bašić and built in nearby Murter. Thirty-five organ pipes emit unworldly tones through holes bored into the quayside's smooth paving stones, the size and velocity of the waves determining the sounds that are made. Come here after dark and you'll also be greeted by a stunning light show from the adjacent **Greeting to the Sun**. Created by the same designer, it consists of 300 multi-layered glass plates arranged in a circle. Beneath the glass are solar modules that light up at sunset to simulate our solar system, while a metal ring around the edge is inscribed with details from a medieval calendar originating from Zadar but now kept in Oxford. Regardless of the technology responsible, kids love the results, their ears to the ground listening to the sounds or chasing the lights around the solar system. These public art initiatives were the first stage in the renovation of this part of the waterfront.

Further along, you find the three ferry terminals including a new pier for cruise ships; one of Croatia's biggest and best morning markets; and the Port Gate, one of two Renaissance-era stone entrances to town that carry the carved Lion of Venice.

The eastern end of the Old Town is centred on Narodni trg, surrounded by the **Guard House** and **City Loggia**, both original Renaissance structures built by the Venetians. The former is now rediscovering its role as the Ethnographic

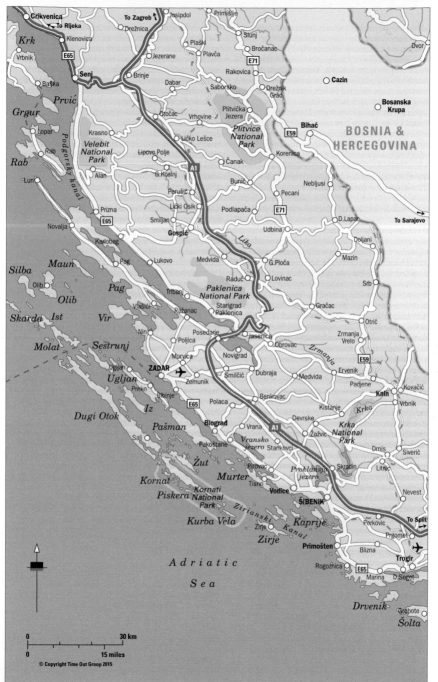

EXPLORE

Museum, the exhibits slowly returning after wartime storage; the latter is an art gallery. Nearby is **St Simeon's Church** (Trg Petra Zoranića 7, 023 211 705, open summer 8.30am-noon, 5-7pm daily, winter 8.30am-noon daily), named after Zadar's patron saint. It houses the ornate Silver Casket of St Simeon, commissioned by Elizabeth of Hungary in 1377.

Nearby, around Five Wells, is the Venetian **Land Gate,** the narrow channel of Foša and the little warrens of the old Varoš quarter, including curving, bar-lined Stomorica, the nightlife hub, which fills with revellers in summer. Head towards the footbridge along the outer road, on top of the wall, and you will find the **Zadar Museum of Ancient Glass.**

## Sights & Museums

### Archaeological Museum
*Trg opatice Čike 1 (023 250 513, www.amzd.hr).* **Open** *July, Aug* 9am-10pm daily. **Admission** 30kn. **No credit cards. Map** p145 C2 ❶
Founded in 1832 but now housed in a modern building by the Forum, this museum is arranged over three floors. At the top is a prehistoric section of ceramics and weaponry; below is a Roman and Liburnian floor, including a model of how the Forum would have looked. The Middle Ages are covered on the ground floor, with beautifully carved stone panels and bizarre local gravestones. A new collection of Roman antiques arrived in 2014 to form part of the permanent display.

### St Donat's Church
*Trg Rimskog Foruma (023 316 166, www.amzd. hr).* **Open** *June-Sept* 9am-9pm daily. *Apr, May, Oct* 9am-5pm daily. **Admission** 20kn. **No credit cards. Map** p145 B3 ❷
This Byzantine rotunda with its unusual cylindrical shape is an emblem of Zadar, although it's no longer a place of worship. Built at the beginning of the ninth century, in the pre-Romanesque period, it has a simple, high-ceilinged interior with exceptional acoustics – ideal for the set-piece concerts and events such as the St Donat Musical Evenings (every July) for which the church is used today. The building is open daily for visitors in summer; off-season sightseeing access is highly unpredictable.

### ★ St Mary's Church & Treasury
*Trg opatice Čike 1 (023 250 496).* **Open** *Church* 8am-noon 5-8pm daily. **Treasury** 10am-1pm, 6-8pm Mon-Sat; 10am-1pm Sun. **Admission** 20kn. **No credit cards. Map** p145 C3 ❸
The jewel in Zadar's crown is this Benedictine convent's church, a 16th-century remake of an early Romanesque building dating from 1066. The bell tower, restored after Allied bombing damage during World War II, also dates from this early period. The nuns are responsible for the care of the stunning Treasury next door, known as the Gold and Silver

of Zadar (Zlato i Srebro Zadra). Set over two floors, the Treasury houses the city's finest ecclesiastical artefacts, including delicately crafted examples of Byzantine ornamentation and Venetian religious art from the 16th century. There are sumptuous gold and silver reliquaries (containing saints' limbs), icons and crucifixes, and everything is beautifully presented and illuminated.

### Zadar Cathedral
*Trg Sv Stošije (023 251 708).* **Open** *Cathedral* Summer 8am-6pm daily. Winter 8am-noon daily. *Campanile* Summer 8am-10pm daily. **Admission** *Cathedral* free. *Campanile* 10kn. **No credit cards. Map** p145 B2/3 ❹
The Cathedral of St Anastasia (Katedrala Sv Stošije), beside St Donat's, is the largest cathedral in the whole of Dalmatia and was built in late Romanesque style during the 12th and 13th centuries. Decorative friezes and delicate stonework depict birds, animals and religious figures, although many visitors enter just to be able to climb the campanile (bell tower) for the fabulous view of Zadar. Partially built in the second half of the 15th century, the tower was completed in 1894 to the design of English architect TG Jackson.

### ★ Zadar Museum of Ancient Glass
*Poljana Zemaljskog odbora 1 (023 363 831, www.mas-zadar.hr).* **Open** *Summer* 9am-9pm daily. *Winter* 9am-4pm Mon-Sat. **Admission** 30kn. **No credit cards. Map** p145 D2 ❺
Opened in 2009 and housed in the renovated 19th-century Cosmacendi Palace, east of the footbridge to the mainland, this is one of the best holdings of ancient glassware outside Italy. The extensive collection contains every glass object imaginable, all of which have been retrieved from rich archaeological sites in Croatia (mostly from around Zadar), many of which have still to be fully excavated. Part of the display is given over to the history of the building including its conversion to a museum – but the focus is, of course, on the glass. Apart from the historical interest of the pieces that span the first to fifth centuries, this is also an absorbingly educational experience where you can learn how glass was made, watch glassblowing displays and have a go at doing the same yourself.

## Restaurants

### Atrij
*Ulica Jurja Barakovića 6 (023 316 424, www. atrijzadar.com).* **Open** 8am-1am daily. **No credit cards.** €€. **Map** p145 D2 ❻ **Dalmatian**
A stone's throw from the main street of Kalelarga, Dalmatian *MasterChef* judge Mate Janković serves fresh local ingredients in delicious small dishes. The wine selection is impressive too, and can be ordered by the glass. Decorated tastefully in a modern style that respects the building's age, the restaurant also

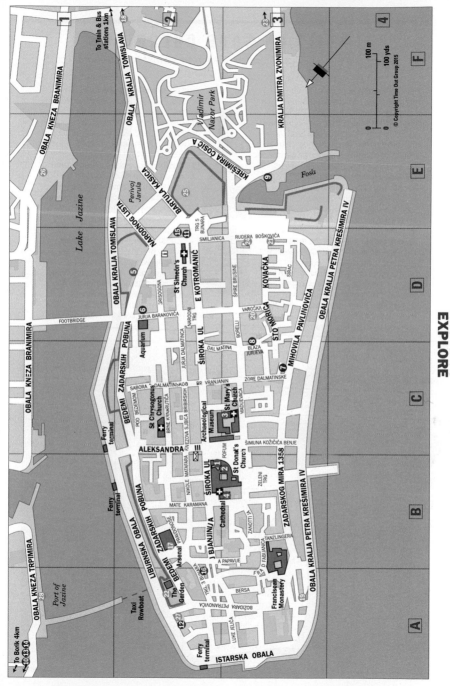

EXPLORE

**EXPLORE**

# BUILT ON SOUR CHERRIES
*Zadar is the birthplace of one of the world's most famous liqueurs.*

The Dalmatian sour cherry, marasca, probably originated from around the Caspian Sea and Anatolia. Thriving in the northern Dalmatian soil at heights of 200m (656ft) above sea level, and nurtured by the Mediterranean climate, marasca cherries are richer, sweeter and fleshier than any other – high in fruit content and full of minerals. They are the key ingredient of the fruity, aromatic maraschino liqueur.

The recipe for maraschino was created in the 16th century in the Dominican monastery of Zadar and named *rosolj*, derived from the Latin *ros solis*, or 'sunny dew'. Commercial distillation started in the 17th century and developed in the 18th. Maraschino became the *plus ultra* of chic drinks. George IV and Queen Victoria sent warships to bring back their favourite tipple while it was also enjoyed by Napoleon, French kings, Russian

tsars and other top bananas. As capital of Dalmatia, Zara (as Zadar was then known) received foreign dignitaries such as Girolamo Luxardo, consular representative of the King of Sardinia. His wife perfected the liqueur at home and, in 1821, Girolamo established the first Luxardo distillery. The business operated in Zadar until bombed by the Allies in World War II, then a Luxardo family survivor fled to Italy with a cherry sapling and started all over again; the firm is now based just outside Padua but still makes the liqueur.

Zadar retains a cherry liqueur industry however. The Maraska company was founded in the immediate post-war years, and makes great play of its local heritage. But Luxardo Maraschino or Maraska Maraschino? Which should you use in your Papa Doble cocktail? Only a taste test will let you figure that one out…

has a small terrace that's shaped like a wooden boat in two halves. After nightfall, Atrij becomes an intimate jazz bar with the occasional soul performance.

## Bruschetta

*Mihovila Pavlinovića 12 (023 312 915, www.bruschetta.hr).* **Open** 11am-11pm daily. €. **Map** p145 C3 **7** **Italian/Dalmatian**
A relatively recent addition to the Old Town restaurant scene, Bruschetta offers brisk, informal but good-quality dining in a crisply furnished, glass-fronted space. It's hugely popular with local lunchers eating their way through the pizza and pasta section of the menu, although there's a good deal of traditional Dalmatian seafood on offer too. The off-season *marende* (set lunches) are a real treat at 55kn-60kn.

## Dva Ribara

*Blaža Jurjeva 1 (023 213 445, www.2ribara.com).* **Open** 10am-11pm Mon-Sat; 11am-10pm Sun. €€. **Map** p145 C/D3 **8** **Dalmatian**
A restyled minimalist interior, with a glass-encased, stainless-steel kitchen and wood-fired pizza oven, provides modernity and increased capacity for Dva Ribara. The location is firmly downtown, adjacent to the bar quarter of Stomorica. The new, wider-ranging menu includes pretty much everything in the traditional Dalmatian cookbook and maintains consistently high standards, although it's the good-value pizzas that draw most of the local trade.

## Foša

*Kralja Dimitra Zvonimira 2 (023 314 421, www.fosa.hr).* **Open** noon-11pm daily. €€€. **Map** p145 E3 **9** **Seafood/Dalmatian**
This well-established fish restaurant stands just outside the city walls in a recently renovated stone building at Foša harbour. While the interior is all clean lines, natural woods and pale colours, the outdoor terrace offers an altogether traditional (and rather delightful) panorama of moored boats and distant islands. All the standard white fish and shellfish are served, either with traditional local green *blitva* and potatoes, or as part of a seafood risotto or pasta dish. There's also a range of carpaccio dishes, including raw monkfish on a bed of rocket. Other options include stewed lobster with polenta, cuttlefish *brodet* and grilled pork with lentils. Prices are a notch above average, unless you opt for one of the four-course set menus, which deliver bruschetta, salad, fish and a dessert for a reasonable 235kn.

## Konoba Rafaelo

*Obala kneza Trpimira 50 (023 335 349).* **Open** noon-midnight daily. **No credit cards.** €€. **Map** p145 A1 **10** **Dalmatian**
A local favourite overlooking the marina, Konoba Rafaelo is a good, old Dalmatian affair: seafood, grilled meats delivered in generous portions and local wines. Book ahead in high season – the decent food and fair prices mean it's often full.

## Konoba Skoblar

*Trg Petra Zoranića 4 (023 213 236).* **Open** *Summer* 8am-midnight daily. *Winter* 8am-4pm daily. €€. **Map** p145 D2 **11** **Dalmatian**
This traditional tavern located between St Simeon's Church and Five Wells is named after the old football player who owned the place before passing it on to his cousin. It fills at *marenda* time around elevenish, with locals snacking on salted anchovies or octopus salad while mulling over the fate of the popular city basketball team. Skoblar does full lunches and dinners too, and in summer the meat offerings are reduced to leave kitchen space for plenty of fish and shellfish dishes – there are at least three kinds of shellfish in the black risotto. Sweet desserts are the house speciality; try the kalelarga cheesecake or Sv Stošija, a cherry cake made with maraschino.

## ★ Kornat

*Liburnska obala 6 (023 254 501, www.restaurant-kornat.com).* **Open** noon-midnight daily. €€€. **Map** p145 A2 **12** **Dalmatian**
Located by the ferry port adjacent to the Q bar, the Kornat is classy enough to have a cloakroom, refined enough to have a superb selection of Croatian wines but relaxed enough to avoid giving a stuffy, formal dining experience. The wine bottles are on display around a bright, modern interior, its 20 tables ably manned by equally bright, English-fluent staff. Although prices are much as elsewhere, ingredients are not: truffles are used in a sauce for the standout monkfish, dried porcini flavour the steak. Specialities include black risotto, anglerfish, and chocolate cake. The set lunches (choose between a meat or fish main) are a steal at 60kn – but not offered in high season. The main menu changes every four months. A renovated terrace opened for 2015.

## Lungo Mare

*Obala kneza Trpimira 23 (023 331 533, www.lungo-mare.com).* **Open** 10am-midnight daily. €€. **Map** p145 A1 **13** **Dalmatian**
The loveliest restaurant terrace in Zadar overlooks the sunset on Maestral Bay, a 15-minute walk from town. Inside is a wonderfully cosy café-restaurant, the decor more modern than the traditional, neat waitstaff would suggest. Lungo Mare is appreciated equally for its seafood and meat dishes, such as the house fish platter or pork fillet, stuffed with scampi, cheese or pršut and mushrooms. Prices represent excellent value, while the wine list runs into three figures and includes a few French and Italian names among the classic Croatian ones. Don't leave without trying the house cheesecake.

## Niko

*Obala kneza Domagoja 9 (023 337 888, www.hotel-niko.hr).* **Open** noon-midnight daily. €€. **Map** p145 A1 **14** **Dalmatian**
One of the first restaurants to be privatised in the former Yugoslavia, back in 1963, Niko is not that

**EXPLORE**

EXPLORE

pretty from the outside, but houses one of the most popular kitchens in Zadar. Near Marina Borik on Puntamika's southernmost headland, Niko has both a small hotel and restaurant with an extensive winer choice. Fresh fish arrives daily and is cooked with choice olive oil over a wood-fire grill. Regulars favour green tagliatelle with scampi, and tiramisu. The terrace looks out towards the Puntamika yacht marina.

### Pet Bunara
*Ulica Stratico/Trg pet bunara (023 224 010, www. petbunara.hr).* **Open** 11am-11pm daily. **€€€. Map** p145 D2 ⑮ **Dalmatian**
Increasingly a local favourite when it comes to traditional Adriatic fare with a contemporary twist, Pet Bunara has a reputation for digging out old recipes and giving them a new lease of life. Typical starters include orzotto (similar to risotto but made with barley), house ravioli with scampi and figs, and black squid stew with chickpeas. Signature mains include steak with figs, or fish fillets with orange and chickpea purée. They also do some of the best pizza in the city. Excellent desserts make full use of Dalmatian ingredients such as carob, quince and fig.

### Pizzeria Tri Bunara
*Trg tri Bunari (023 250 390).* **Open** *Summer* 7am-11pm daily. *Winter* 7am-10pm daily. **No credit cards. €€.** Map p145 A2 ⑯ **Pizzeria**
A solid, unpretentious and good-value pizzeria, with a simple terrace, hidden off the main thoroughfares

near the Hotel Bastion. Said to be the oldest pizzeria in Zadar, it is one of the few places in the Old Town in which to get a proper pizza.

## Bars & Nightlife

### Arsenal Zadar
*Trg tri Bunara 1 (023 253 821, www.arsenal zadar.com).* **Open** *June-Aug* 9am-2am daily. **Map** p145 B2 ⑰
Set in an expansive renovated 18th-century warehouse, Arsenal Zadar is unique in Croatia, in terms of size, ambience and the sheer variety of events and attractions. The spacious stage hosts world music, *klapa* choral-singing, name DJs and local bands. The sound is superb, thanks to installation by the Garden crew. Tables between stage and bar allow for lounging, sipping and snacking. In high season, Arsenal Zadar is a local exhibition centre by day, with interactive displays of local history and regional produce on sale; after dark, it opens on a by-event basis.

### Back-Door Bar
*Polačišće ulica 9 (023 779 042).* **Open** 7am-midnight Mon-Sat; 4pm-midnight Sun. **No credit cards. Map** p145 F1 ⑱
The Back-Door Bar is a tiny, intimate spot with just enough space for a few people to enjoy the cosy atmosphere. With a 1920s feel and red-brick walls, it's notably warm and inviting. Back-Door offers a selection of home-made *rakijas*, beers, cocktails

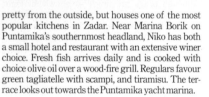

Garden.

**EXPLORE**

and local island wines. Music tends to be jazz, bossa nova, soul, downtempo, lounge or blues; the staff are friendly and polite. Seats can be reserved.

### Café Brazil
*Prilaz hrvatske Čitaonice 1 (091 208 5561).* **Open** 8am-1am daily. **No credit cards. Map** p145 A3 ⑲
Tucked in from the newly landscaped embankment close to the Sea Organ, this handy little café offers sea views from its gravel terrace, an ice-cream stall outside in summer and long drinks (from 15kn) that include a Bruce Lee, a 007 James Bond and a Café del Mar. Bottled Leffe and Hoegaarden, and morning coffees, are served from the sunken bar inside.

### Djina
*Varoška 2 (091 324 7555).* **Open** 7am-midnight daily. **No credit cards. Map** p145 D3 ⑳
A great little gallery bar off the main square, done out with bizarre egg-shaped heads designed by Silvijana Dražković. A trendy crowd gathers by day to drink any number of fruit teas, the electronic musical backdrop increasing as the night wears on. There's a couple of chairs on the busy street outside.

### Factory Bar
*Poljana Pavla Pavlovića (097 730 2662).* **Open** *Summer* 8am-1.30am daily. *Winter* 8am-11pm daily. **No credit cards. Map** p145 D3 ㉑
A bare brick interior plastered with pictures of New York City combines with a constant barrage

of techno beats to make this one of the most popular places in the centre for a Friday-night meet-up. Factory is just round the corner from the University, and gets its fair share of coffee-break trade during daylight hours.

### ★ Garden
*Liburnska obala 6 (023 364 320, www.watchthe gardengrow.eu).* **Open** *Late May-late Sept* 10am-1am daily. **No credit cards. Map** p145 A2 ㉒
This superbly located outdoor lounge bar features quality live music and name DJs all summer, as weather permits. The focus is a vast panoramic terrace with private cabanas and low, comfortable white sofas amid established trees, and great views. By day, locals and tourists relax, play board games, read the papers and watch passing ships. By night, there's a full musical agenda, piped through a state-of-the-art sound system.

Well-chosen local wines and well-priced cocktails oil the wheels of happiness – Croatian and Belgian beers are equally good value too, considering the quality of venue and musical backdrop. The Garden is one of the most important things to have happened to Zadar in recent years, and the UK team behind it – UB40 drummer James Brown and music producer Nick Colgan – have not rested on their laurels. From this has grown a major music festival of the same name, club Barbarella's (which is near the festival site) and several other projects that are currently in the pipeline.

**EXPLORE**

### Hitch Bar

*Kolovare (091 796 3860).* **Open** *Summer* 7am-5am daily. *Winter* 8am-2am daily. **No credit cards.** **Map** p145 F3 ㉓

Right by the water's edge on Kolovare beach is this spacious café-cum-club with a cool white design theme, lots of comfy sofa seating and two well-stocked bars. Live bands, resident DJs and guest disc-spinners raise the temperature at weekends, when this is a major destination for club-hungry locals – the fun spills out on to the neighbouring shoreline in summer.

### Illy Bar

*Ulica Ruđera Boškovića 4 (no phone, https://hr-hr. facebook.com/IllyZd).* **Open** 7am-9pm Mon-Sat; 7am-2.30pm Sun. **No credit cards. Map** p145 D3 ㉔

If, like many Croats, you need decent coffee to get things going, this place should set you up: Illy-brand java served by trained baristas. The summer terrace has a natural birdsong backing track to help ease you into the day.

### Ledana Bar

*Perivoj kraljice Jelene Madijevke (098 630 760, www.ledana.hr).* **Open** 8am-4am daily. **No credit cards. Map** p145 E2 ㉕

Ledana (Icehouse) is named after the building's original use; ice was brought down from the Velebit mountains and stored here, to be distributed to city cafés. Located in the beautiful gardens of Queen Jelena

Madijevka, the first formal public park in Croatia, it hosts many events, parties and performances.

### Maraschino

*Obala kneza Branimira 6A (023 224 093).* **Open** *Summer* 7am-5am daily. *Winter* 8am-11pm daily. **No credit cards. Map** p145 E1 ㉖

Just outside the Old Town across the footbridge, Maraschino is a huge café-bar on the northern side of the Jazine that boasts a vivacious 1970s' themed interior and an impressive stretch of terrace out front. The place attracts a frisky local crowd on summer nights, with DJs and live bands appearing regularly throughout the year. Maraschino's cocktail menu is probably the longest in Zadar, and none of the concoctions are prohibitively expensive.

### ★ Q Bar

*Liburnska obala 6 (099 851 2029, www.facebook. com/qbar.zadar.5).* **Open** 7am-3am Mon-Wed; 7am-4am Thur-Sat; 10am-midnight Sun. **No credit cards. Map** p145 ㉗

The enigmatically named Q (formerly the Maya Pub) remains a key way-station on the city's nocturnal itinerary for hedonists. It's a big and relatively sparse space but decorated in strong colours, consequently perfect for DJ-driven club nights, or occasional rock or pop gigs. Thursday's Trash Electro Party is a particularly popular date on the local party calendar. The quayside terrace is a good place for a quiet daytime pint.

**Art Hotel Kalelarga.**

### Vinyl Bar

*Obala kneze Trpimira 4 (099 670 0490).* **Open**
7am-1.30am daily. **No credit cards. Map** p145 A1 ㉓
Bang on the coastline, Vinyl Bar is so pet-friendly a
recent terrace expansion happened for the benefit of
our furry friends. It's a lovely spot to enjoy the sunrise and sunset, as Hitchcock did when he visited in
1964. Indoors, the venue's name becomes apparent:
scores of LPs decorate the floors, walls and tables.
Local or international DJs play underground house,
electro, funk, jazz, R&B and soul every weekend.

## Hotels

### Aparthotel Lekavski

*Draznikova 15, Zaton (023 265 888,
www.lekavski.de).* **No credit cards. €.**
In the picturesque Dalmatian village of Zaton,
between Nin and Zadar, the Aparthotel Lekavski is a
cosy, modern family affair. Offering a range of amenities including a lovely café-bar terrace and swimming pool, it also organises entertainment. Cocktail
parties, candlelit dinners and dancing feature, as do
excursions (extra cost) to the nearby national parks.

### ★ Art Hotel Kalelarga

*Majke Margarite 3 (023 233 000, www.arthotel-
kalelarga.com).* **€€. Map** p145 D2.
Opened in 2012, this ten-room boutique hotel occupies the laboriously renovated interior of an old stone
house on Široka ulica – the main street popularly

known as Kalelarga. Rooms feature exposed stonework, natural wood floors and furnishings, and a
palette of soothing ochres and pastels. Moody lighting and smart modern bathrooms provide an aura
of cosy luxuriance. The chic top-floor apartment is
snug under attic windows. Breakfast offers a broad
choice of cold treats and the hotel's café-restaurant
is already hugely popular on account of its superb
range of own-made cakes and sweets.

### Bastion

*Bedemi zadarskih Pobuna 13 (023 494 950, www.
hotel-bastion.hr).* **€€. Map** p145 A2.
Zadar's prime city-centre hotel is historic and stylish with all the contemporary trappings. Opened in
2008 and a Relais & Châteaux member since 2013,
Bastion blends vintage and contemporary with flair,
thanks to Slovene architect Jani Vosel. It's a boutique
operation, with 23 rooms and five apartments, a
video conference room, restaurant, bar, two terraces
(one of them atop the restored stone battlements)
and a beautiful, atmospheric spa. Original stone
is featured throughout, including the spa, where
the edge of the stone floor marks the boundary of
the 13th-century fortress Kaštel on which the hotel
is built. Inside and out you'll find the original cannonballs used to defend it. The 60-cover restaurant
focuses on Mediterranean-style 'slow food' – the
owner has a fish shop in the market, so it ought to
be good. There's plenty of parking but it does cost
extra. Thoughtfully, the windows are well soundproofed for when Zadar gets going at night.

### ★ Boutique Hostel Forum

*Široka 20 (023 250 705, www.hostelforumzadar.
com).* **€. Map** p145 B2.
Smack in the middle of Zadar's pedestrianised centre, and steps away from the Roman Forum from
which it gets its name, this is one of the most talked
about of Croatia's new-generation hostels. With an
interior by designer Damir Gamulin Gamba (also
responsible for the Goli & Bosi hostel in Split), it
features clean surfaces, bold stripes and pictograms
that seem more suited to an international space station than the centre of an ancient Mediterranean
town. Dorm beds have a self-contained, almost
cubicle-like appearance that lends a little more privacy than usual; the small but cute private doubles
are up to hotel standard. Breakfast is included in the
price of a double; for dorm guests, it's an extra. The
kitchen is handy for making tea, coffee or snacks,
there's a common room, and great terrace views.

### Falkensteiner Punta Skala Resort:
### Hotel Diadora & Hotel & Spa Iadera

*Petrčane (Punta Skala 023 555 600, Diadora 023
555 911, Iadera 023 500 601, www.falkensteiner.
com).* Hotel Diadora **€€**. Hotel & Spa Iadera **€€€**.
**Map** p145 A1.
Opened in stages and completed in 2012, this
self-contained complex just outside Petrčane, 12km

**EXPLORE**

(7.5 miles) west of Zadar, has quickly established itself as northern Dalmatia's leading resort for family holidays and pamper-breaks. Centrepiece is the Spa Iadera, a sleek, wishbone-shaped building that houses the largest spa centre in Croatia. There's a choice of indoor and outdoor pools, saunas and Turkish hammams, and a full menu of massage and beauty treatments. Spacious rooms display a bold use of colour, and social areas are really quite groovy thanks, in large part, to the modernist instincts of Italian architect Matteo Thun. The Diadora is designed to be the last word in family holidays. Its 250 family-suite apartments, most with sea views, each accommodate two adults and two kids, there is entertainment at Falky Land (supervised swimming pools, pirate ship and petting zoo), a full programme of sports and games, as well as crèche facilities for toddlers and mini-discos for young teens. The resort is surrounded by grassy lawns and only a few minutes' walk from the seafront, where you have a choice between natural rock-slab beaches and shallow coves carpeted with sand. Petrčane village is a short walk along the waterside path.

### Hotel Club Funimation Borik
*Majstora Radovana 7 (023 206 100, 023 555 600, www.falkensteiner.com/hr/hotel/borik). Adriana* €€€. Borik €€.
The big attraction of this family hotel – apart from its year-round availability – is the Acquapura spa complex. This has four areas: a spa with thalasso seawater treatments; a steam and dry sauna; indoor and heated outdoor pools, plus one for kids; and a gym. The thalasso area contains 16 treatment rooms alone. All summer, the Funimation puts on kids' events, and child-minding facilities allow grown-ups to spend at least part of the day doing their own thing. Also included in the price are windsurfing, tennis and volleyball – plus three daily buffet meals. You will, however, have to pay extra for courses in diving and sailing. Club Funimation includes the formerly separate Hotel Adriana (023 206 300). This refurbished part of the resort, with swimming pool area and easy sea access, is ideal for quieter couples.

### Kolovare
*Bože Perišića 14 (023 203 200, www.hotel-kolovare.com).* €€. Map p145 F2.
A modernist classic from the socialist era, the upgraded Kolovare stands on the edge of the city centre towards the bus station. It is surprisingly large, with 203 plain rooms, a third of them singles for the passing domestic business crowd. A stone's throw from the pebbly Kolovare beach, it also has an outdoor swimming pool and a gym.

### Venera
*Šime Ljubića 4A (023 214 098).* No credit cards. €. Map p145 D3.
A modest cheapie in a narrow side street of the downtown bar quarter of Stomorica – so convenient

for a bar hop. A dozen small rooms above a travel agents have been renovated to incorporate a little shower and twin beds for simple, clean comfort. Singles pay the double-room rate in high season. It's also referred to as the Jović Guesthouse.

### Villa Hrešć
*Obala kneza Trpimira 28 (023 337 570, www.villa-hresc.hr).* €€. Map p145 A1.
Overlooking Maestral Bay a ten-minute walk from town, this is by far the best mid-range option for comfort in Zadar. The suites are suitable for two to four guests, six at a push for a nominal extra fee. More like condominiums, they consist of a living room, kitchenette, dining room, bedroom and a modern bathroom with a marble washbasin – all capacious, all immaculately furnished and all overlooking the sea. The bigger ones have a terrace; the largest one has a terrace the size of half a football pitch. The view is stunning, same the line of vision from the outdoor pool with its fierce water jet in the corner. There's a decent terrace restaurant here too, where non-guests can also tuck into good Med fare.

## BEACHES & EXCURSIONS

Family-friendly beaches line the seafront complex of **Borik**, which caters for package tourists and is ten minutes from town on bus no.5 or no.8. For real beach relaxation, take a catamaran or boat from Zadar to the relatively unspoilt archipelago nearby. An island hop might require an overnight stay, but the reward is a sandy sea-floor and dramatic scenery. Most routes are run by Jadrolinija and take about 90 minutes. The exception is the hydrofoil service to Premuda, Silba and Olib run by Mia Tours (www.miatours.hr): leaving daily from Zadar, it takes two hours and costs 30kn (50kn in high season).

The most accessible island from Zadar is **Ugljan** (*see p153*), with hourly Jadrolinija ferries to the largest village, Preko (20 minutes), which has a relatively new marina (www.marinapreko.com). Another new marina, Olive Island at Sutomišćica, has also helped increase tourist traffic. Pick a quiet weekday to swim around here. The largest of the islands is **Dugi otok**, 'Long Island' – 50 kilometres (31 miles) long in fact. Its intricate, indented coastline hides any number of coves and beaches, many only accessible by boat. The lovely nature park of Telašćica Bay, with its verdant cliffs and saltwater lake, is within relatively easy reach of the main port of Sali (served daily by Jadrolinija ferries). This southern tip of the island intertwines with the northern end of **Kornati National Park** (*see p168* **Island Life**), with whom it compares for natural beauty. The northern tip of Dugi otok is best accessed via catamaran from Zadar to Božava. The attraction here is the white sandy beach of Saharun, just south of the village of Veli Rat, and the sandy beach of Pantera Bay.

EXPLORE

A trip to **Nin** (www.nin.hr), 45 minutes from Zadar by bus, gives you the option of a morning in old churches and an afternoon at the sandy beach 15 minutes' walk north of town. Nin is a historic, fortified town on a small island in a lagoon. An old Roman settlement, it was home to the first Croatian kings, as its excellent Archaeological Museum (023 250 516, open June-Aug 8am-10pm daily, May, Sept 9am-noon, 5-8pm daily, Oct-Apr 8am-2pm daily, 15kn) illustrates. The tiny Church of the Holy Cross is Croatia's oldest.

## GETTING THERE & AROUND

Zadar airport (www.zadar-airport.hr) is 8km south-east of town at Zemunik Donji. Liburnija buses meet domestic arrivals and run to the bus station before terminating at the northern ferry quay by the Old Town (25kn, one journey 5mins). Buses are scheduled to set off from the same points 60-80 mins before each Croatia Airlines departure – other passengers should take the nearest service to their flight, or a taxi (220kn). Ferries serving Rijeka, Dubrovnik and the islands in the Zadar archipelago dock at the same northern quay.

There are buses almost hourly to Zadar from Zagreb (3.5hrs), Rijeka (4.5hrs) and Split (3.5hrs). A modest train service links with Knin (2.5hrs) and the intercity line between Zagreb and Split. Zadar bus and train stations are next to each other 1.5km east of the Old Town centre, a 15min walk.

Bus nos.2 and 4 go to the ferry ports, bus nos.5 and 8 to Puntamika and Borik. Tickets are 8kn (valid for a single journey) when bought from the driver; 13kn (valid for two journeys) from a kiosk. For a taxi, call 023 251 400, 023 494 494 (www.lulic.hr/taxi) or 098 922 2932 mobile (www.taxi-zadar.com).

## RESOURCES

**Hospital** *Bože Peričića 5 (023 505 505).*
Out by the Hotel Kolovare, towards the bus station.

**Internet** *Lanarchy Varoska 3 (023 311 265, http://lanarchy.net).* **Open** 9am-midnight daily. **Map** p145 D3.

**Pharmacy** *Ljekarna Centar, Jurja Barakovića 2 (023 302 931, 023 302 920).* **Open** 7am-8pm Mon-Fri; 7.30am-1.30pm Sat. **Map** p145 D2.

**Police station** *Zore Dalmatinska 1 (023 345 141).* **Map** p145 C3.
For emergencies, dial 112.

**Tourist information** *Zadar Tourist Office, Ilije Smiljanića 5 (023 212 222, www.zadar.travel).* **Open** *Summer* 8am-midnight daily. *Winter* 8am-8pm Mon-Fri; 9am-1pm Sat, Sun. **Map** p145 D2. English-speaking office by Pet bunara.

# Ugljan

The most accessible island from Zadar is Ugljan (pronounced 'oog-lee-an'), with hourly boats taking 20 minutes to the largest village of Preko – it's so close that it feels like part of the city. This 52-kilometre (32-mile) long, green island is separated from the mainland by the narrow Zadar channel and connected by bridge to its less populated neighbour, Pašman.

Ugljan takes its name from the Croatian word *ulje*, 'olive' – the island is covered with more than 200,000 olive trees. The crop has been harvested here for more than 2,000 years and, along with fishing, remains central to the local economy and culture. The olive trees are also responsible for Ugljan's unique position as a private island. Each local family owns one of the hundreds of orchards that cover the largely unpopulated western slopes. With so many small, private plots, land purchase is rendered all but impossible.

Two new marinas may, however, go some way towards changing the lie of the land. The **Olive Island Marina** (023 335 809, www.oliveisland marina.com) at Sutomišćica has been given permission to develop a resort area there; and **Preko Marina** (023 286 169, www.marinapreko. com), which opened in 2008 close to the ferry port, has a user-friendly system for booking into berths and an environmentally friendly approach to dealing with nautical waste.

A network of paths for hikers and bikers covers large areas of Ugljan, and campers will be well served with several large sites situated on the flatter, northern part of the island. Currently lacking chic hotels, swanky bars or cool nightlife, it often passes under the radar when people talk about Croatian islands. People don't come here to be seen or because it's fashionable. Life goes on at a slow pace with little fuss and the friendly locals expect visitors to take it or leave it. Tourists and Zadar residents come to enjoy the simple things in life in an unhurried, uncontrived way, on an island with a distinctive Mediterranean feel.

Two buses are synchronised with the arrival of the inbound ferry from Zadar and fork both north and south on the one main road that connects the villages spaced along the populated eastern side. Exploring the island by bike or on foot is made simple by the excellent network of clearly marked routes – pick up a map from the tourist offices in Preko, Kali or Kukljica. Drivers should be wary, however, as the tracks are narrow. If you're wondering about slogging along a hiking trail in the daytime heat, it's worth knowing that remote and barely visited swimming spots are usually the reward for carrying on. A hike to **Mount St Michael** is recommended, especially if you can arrive before sunset. A moderate 265 metres (870 feet), the summit is occupied by the remains of a 13th-century Venetian fort and a communications

**EXPLORE**

centre. The 360-degree views of Ugljan and the surrounding islands are extraordinary.

**Preko** town is a brisk walk from the port and makes a good base for exploring. You can hire bikes from the tourist office (023 286 108, www. ugljan-pasman.com) and mopeds from private companies. It has a good swimming beach, although a better swimming spot can be found on the tiny island of **Galevac**. A few metres offshore, accessible by taxi boat, this lovely island is home to a 15th-century Franciscan monastery.

Pretty **Kali**, a short drive from Preko, has a couple of spots to eat and drink. **Kukljica**, further south, offers a market, good fish restaurants and boat trips to Kornati (*see p168* **Island Life**). The holiday village of Zelena gives Kukljica a resort atmosphere.

## Restaurants & Hotels

In Preko, waterfront **Ivo** (Mul 3, 023 286 390, closed Jan, Feb) is the biggest restaurant, serving an excellent fish stew. To the north, Ugljan village consists of nine hamlets. Fishermen sing over end-of-day drinks by the harbour. The **Ritam** beach bar on the south side of the harbour has waterside seating and stays open late.

There are few hotels on the island. The four-star **Villa Eden** (Jaz 18, 098 165 2165, www.eden. hr) has apartments overlooking a sandy beach, while the **Hotel Ugljan** (023 288 004, www.hotel-ugljan.hr) is standard but reliable. The best choice would be the three-star **Villa Stari Dvor** (023 288 688, www.staridvor.hr) in Batalaža outside the town of Ugljan, with a rooftop pool and decent restaurant serving local cuisine.

# Murter

You won't find many gems of Dalmatian medieval architecture on Murter, but it does offer a gentle landscape, a web of tempting paths leading to secluded bays and beaches, and breathtaking views of Kornati. It is also easily accessible, and has picturesque villages that quietly carry on with their own business away from the commercial imperative of the tourist trade.

In many ways, it's a family- and activity-oriented island, and is one of the main centres on the Adriatic for sailing, diving and big game fishing – as well as the more usual pastime of simply lying on the beach and catching some sun. Murter is ideally placed for exploring the countless islands of Central Dalmatia, and is the closest departure point for the wonderful Kornati National Park. The island can also serve as a base for exploring the well-preserved medieval cities of Šibenik and Zadar, as well as the other splendid national parks of Krka (*see p167* **Watery Wonders**) and Velebit.

Villa Stari Dvor.

EXPLORE

Traditionally, the villages on the island have quite distinct local identities, with Jezera known as the main fishing village, Betina as the place where traditional shipbuilding still goes on, and Murter as the home of the slightly aristocratic owners of the uninhabited islands of Kornati. All the towns and villages on the island are linked by one road, and easily reached by frequent bus services, interrupted twice a day for half an hour at 9am and 5pm, when the bridge at Tisno is raised to allow sailing boats to pass.

The town of **Murter** is the biggest settlement on the island, famous for its sandy beach (Slanica) and buzzing restaurants and cafés. A short walk uphill from the crowded centre takes you to the Ghetto, with its maze of steep side streets and traditional architecture.

**Betina** is a very attractive stone town set on a hill, with a circular street layout that offers an enjoyable walk up to the village church. If you're lucky, the priest will let you scramble up the church tower for an amazing view of the island. The craftsmen of Betina still practise the ancient art of boatbuilding, making the island's distinctive *gajeta* fishing boats with their lucky painted eyes. The centre of Betina, with its square full of cafés, is a good place to watch local teams play waterpolo in the sea of the old port as older residents concentrate on a game of bowls.

**Jezera** is the island's best kept secret, missed by many of the tourists who rush on to Murter and Betina. This village is where most of the island's fishermen reside, as its bay provides the nearest safe harbour to the open sea. Around sunset, fishermen head back to harbour. Although it's tempting to join the crowd jostling by the boats to buy fresh fish, a more reliable option is to get up early and head to the market behind the tourist office. The municipal beach here is a simple concrete and pebble affair, but there's a little beach bar and a fabulous view of the islands. Continue walking along the beach to find your own peaceful spot under the shade of an olive tree – then watch as the fishing boats and yachts come in and out of Jezera harbour. There is also a waterslide and rentable paddle boats.

You don't need more than a mountain bike to reach any number of secluded beaches and bays around the island. A favourite is **Koromašna Bay**, signposted from Jezera, which has a small half-island with an unbeatable sea view. **Slanica** is a fair walk from Murter town, but it's one of the very best beaches on the island, and much better than the downtown alternative. It has an amazingly turquoise sea, its shallowness ideal for games of frisbee and general fooling about in the water. It can get very crowded in midsummer, with noisy cafés and pizzerias, so make sure to get there early. Alternatively, walk through the campsite to the next bay, which has similar characteristics but is virtually undiscovered.

## Restaurants

### Konoba Kandela

*Obala Sv Ivana, Jezera (022 438 627).* **Open** *Mid Apr-mid Oct* 5-11pm daily. **€€**. **Dalmatian**
This restaurant is on the posher end of the scale and has a lot of regular guests, so in season it tends to fill up fast – booking is advisable. They serve all the classic Dalmatian specialities, with excellent scampi *buzara* and a tasty vegetable risotto as a side dish to grilled fish or meat.

### ★ Tic Tac

*Hrokešina 5, Murter (022 435 230, 098 864 619 mobile, www.tictac-murter.com).* **Open** *Apr-Sept* noon-11pm daily. **€€€**. **Dalmatian**
Opened as a café by the son of a lighthouse keeper in 1971, this is one of the most famous restaurants on the Adriatic – it can be hard to find a table in high season. Tic Tac is tucked down an alleyway that leads straight to the sea, with tables all the way along. The restaurant became famous for offering sushi as an alternative to traditional Dalmatian fare. The *brodetto* with monkfish and the imaginative starters are highly recommended, although not every dish seems to work as well as these.

### Zameo ih vjetar

*Hrvatskih Vladara 5, Murter (022 435 475).* **Open** *Apr-Nov* noon-2pm, 5pm-midnight daily. **€€**. **Dalmatian**
At this elegantly designed modern restaurant, it's hard to resist the *bubizza* or 'sister of the pizza,' topped with roasted veg like courgette or artichoke. This is also a good place to try a range of unusual starters and mains, from baked octopus to chickpea salad. The restaurant belongs to the family of the architect Bašić, famous for creating the Sea Organ in Zadar, so keep your eyes peeled for interesting detail.

## Bars & Nightlife

### Gallileo

*Obala Sv Ivana 32, Jezera (no phone).* **Open** *Summer* 10am-2am daily. **No credit cards**.
Usually the noisiest bar on the harbour, this blue neon spot is a hit with young fishermen and the summer party crowd. On a big night, locals go for cheap brandy chasers, or just don't bother with beer at all. The trail from here leads up to the Zenit nightclub at the car wash. From there, it can only go downhill.

### Tony

*Obala Sv Ivana, Jezera (no phone).* **Open** *Apr-Sept* 8am-1am daily. **No credit cards**.
If you happen to be here when the sport fishermen come back, you may see a large tuna strung up. If you're interested in catching one yourself, ask at the bar as Tony runs most of the boats moored at the jetty. Otherwise, just turn up for drinks at the closest café to the beach.

**EXPLORE**

## Hotels

### Borovnik

*Trg dr Sime Vlasica 3, Tisno (022 439 700, www. hotel-borovnik.com).* **No credit cards. €€.**
Overlooking the bridge to Murter island in Tisno, this hotel has been renovated lately. With a restaurant and small outdoor pool, it's popular with larger groups.

### Camp Slanica

*Podvršak, Slanica Bay (022 434 580).* **Open** Mid May-Oct. **No credit cards. €.**
Set in a pine forest, Camp Slanica is near Slanica beach, which is less crowded than Lučica beach and the half-island of Školjić. The campsite has two restaurants, a supermarket and tennis courts.

### Colentum

*Butina 2, Slanica Bay (022 431 100, www.hotel-colentum.com).* **No credit cards. €.**
This 200-bed hotel in Slanica Bay is in an excellent location if your priority is to be first on the beach in the morning. For Murter town, it's a bit of a trek.

### Jezera Village Holiday Resort

*Jezera Lovišća (022 439 600, www.jezeravillage. com).* **€.**
This is the biggest campsite and apartment village on the island, a short walk from Tisno and Jezera. Set in its own bay, it has tennis courts, a diving centre, restaurant and shop. Aqua aerobics are announced at regular intervals. It's at the start of a pleasant bike-friendly walk on the old road to Betina.

### Kosirina

*Put Kosirine, Betina (022 435 268).* **No credit cards. €.**
Probably the most beautiful campsite here, in a spot where no one passes without stopping for stunning views of the Kornati archipelago, clearest when the Bura blows. There are unspoilt inlets and rocky outcrops easily reached on foot. Facilities are basic.
▶ *The same management run the nearby Plitka Vala site (same phone), close to Betina.*

## GETTING THERE & AROUND

Buses go to Murter town from Šibenik (journey 1hr) and Vodice (30mins) about every 2hrs. There are two daily buses from Zadar (2hrs). The bus serving the main road along the island is frequent, fares are low.

## RESOURCES

**Tourist information** *Murter Tourist Office, Trg Rudina (022 434 995, www.tzo-murter.hr).* **Open** *July, Aug* 8am-10pm daily. *Sept-June* 8am-noon Mon-Fri.

# Biograd

Biograd na moru (Biograd-on-Sea), the biggest town between Zadar and Šibenik, is a lively seaside tourist spot and an excellent base from which to embark on a family holiday. It was the coronation site for Hungarian kings in medieval times, but was demolished by the Venetians in 1125, and again in 1646, in the retreat from the Turks. What little remains of its once royal heritage includes the **Church of St Anastasia**, built in the remains of the royal cathedral in 1761; the early Romanesque **Church of St Anthony**, reconstructed and used for art exhibitions in summer, and the 11th-century ruins of **St John the Evangelist's Basilica**.

Biograd's location is its major asset – it's a good place from which to explore the nearby Kornati Islands. Pašman, joined to Ugljan by a road bridge, is a 15-minute ferry trip; Zadar and Šibenik are either side, and Vransko Jezero, Croatia's largest lake, is next door. Krka National Park (*see 167* **Watery Wonders**) is a half-hour drive away and, with the mountains stepping back from the coast for a distance, this is also good cycling country.

Set on a small peninsula, the centre of town is packed with bars and restaurants. Another clutch of bars is crammed into the street at the head of the peninsula, by the ferry terminal, where you'll find the small **Regional Museum** (Krešimirova obala 22, 023 383 721) featuring treasures from a 16th-century Venetian galley that sank off the islet of Gnalić, in the Pašman Canal.

Head along the car-free seafront promenade past the Ilirija hotels and you come to the Olympic pool area and Dražica beach. Further on, past the extensive tennis centre, you'll arrive at Soline's sandy beach with bars galore. Walk away from the peninsula in the other direction, past Marina Kornati, and you'll find another long beach, a couple of campsites, more bars and restaurants.

## Restaurants & Bars

A handful of venues are open all year, including the **Marina Kornati Restaurant** (Šetalište kneza Branimira 1, 023 384 505, www. marinakornati.com) offering anything from full-blown formal dining to a quick snack; **Konoba Barba** (Frankopanska 2, 023 383 087, www. konoba-barba.com.hr), a characterful, good-value locals' haunt that majors on fish, especially sardines; and **Casa Vecchia** (Kralja Kolomana 30, 023 383 220), a service-oriented pizzeria in a converted stone house with a delightful walled terrace. **Konoba Bazilika** (ulica Sv Ivana 5, 091 152 0149, www.konoba-bazilika.com, open

**EXPLORE**

**Biograd**.

mid Apr-mid Oct 5pm-midnight daily), tucked away by the Basilica ruins, has an innovative menu that includes vegetarian dishes, salt cod pâté, main-meal salads and aromatic fig pancakes. **Konoba Cotonum** (Josipa bana Jelačića 2, 091 520 6338) is newly refurbished with a Roman theme and lovely courtyard.

Summer highlights include the **Lavender Bed Bar** (Ilirija Resort, Tina Ujevića, www. facebook.com/lavenderbar), where you can sip your cocktail from the comfort of a lilac-coloured bed surrounded by greenery and sea views. **Pocco Locco** (put Solina, 098 194 0203, www. facebook.com/poccolocobiograd) is the beach bar for partying Caribbean style – many of its cocktails are sold by the metre.

## Hotels

Biograd's hotels are mostly of the package holiday style, but the three hotels in the **Ilirija Group** (Tina Ujevića 7, 023 383 165, www. ilirijabiograd.com), Kornati, Ilirija and Adriatic, deliver contemporary facilities; the Ilirija also has a useful top-floor spa.

The town also has two family-run hotels: the **Palma** (Vlaha Bukovca 3, 023 384 463, www. hotelpalma.com.hr) and **Villa Mai Mare** (Marka Marulića 1, 023 38 43 58, www.maimare.hr). Both are a five-minute walk from the beach and offer good value modern comforts.

## GETTING THERE & AROUND

The bus station (023 383 022) in the centre of the peninsula has regular services from Zadar and Šibenik. Ferries to Tkon on Pašman run at least hourly in the summer. Rent a boat from the small marina outside the Ilirija Group hotels to explore around 150 islands and islets within a 2hr reach.

## RESOURCES

**Tourist information** *Biograd Tourist Office, Trg hrvatskih velikana 2 (023 383 123, www. tzg-biograd.hr).* **Open** *Summer* 8am-9pm Mon-Fri. *Winter* 8am-3pm Mon-Fri.

# Tribunj

Tribunj used to be a quiet fishing village with a great big unfinished concrete building and several fishing boats. The building is now part of an extremely smart marina filled with posh yachts; the fishing boats remain outside. Yet for those in the know, Tribunj is a gem of a destination. The Old Town is on a tiny oval island, connected to the mainland by a small stone bridge. Most of the north-east side of the island faces the marina; on the south-west side are bars, cafés and municipal boat moorings. Beside the bridge are the tourist office (summer 8am-1pm,

**Tribunj.**

5-9pm Mon-Sat, 8am-noon Sun) and the post office. Restaurants are scattered all around the area, both on and off the island.

As if that's not enough, the more cosmopolitan tourist town of Vodice (*see right*) is a lovely 40-minute walk away, linked by a blue-flag beach; the tranquil area of Sovlje, with its secluded beach, is also nearby.

## Restaurants & Hotels

In the Old Town, **Konoba Šimun** (Ribarska, 091 523 6004, closed Oct-mid Apr) is lovely inside and out, though perhaps verging on the snooty. Expect to pay 500kn per kilo of lobster sailor-style and 60kn for mussels *buzara*. Nearby **Konoba Bepo** (091 524 0746, www.konoba-bepo.com) on the same street is more reasonably priced and also offers two apartments.

**Plavi Val** (022 446 644, 098 337 154, www.plavi-val.com) contains seven apartments, while the stylish **Movie Resort Apart Hotel** (Jurjevgradska 49, 022 446 755, 099 434 6950, www.the-movie-resort.biz) has its own pebble beach, pool, children's pool and 300-seat restaurant with terrace.

On the same marina road, nearby **Villa Diana** (Jurjevgradska 6, 022 446 023, www.hrv. villadianacroatia.net) is a recently refurbished, 15-room hotel/pension with a great location near Bristak beach.

# Vodice

Vodice, 11 kilometres west of Šibenik, is a lively and established tourist centre. The town derived its name from the abundance of freshwater wells in the area and exported drinking water up to the end of the 19th century.

Architecturally, there's not a lot to show for the Turkish and Venetian days, with the stones from the city's defensive walls and towers used to build houses. However, the **Coric Tower**, built from Brač stone by a rich Šibenik family, dates from 1646, the tiny Gothic church of **St Cross**, built in 1402, is used for summer exhibitions, while the parish church of **St Cross** (1746-49) is the work of Šibenik Baroque builder Ivan Skok. The **Aquarium** (obala Matice Hrvatska 33, 098 214 634, admission 20kn) is by the main square.

West of town is the Punta peninsula with the tall Hotel Punta and a number of concrete-piered beaches. There are more beaches along the four-kilometre coastal path to Tribunj (*see p158*), with its beach bars and ice-cream shops.

## Restaurants

There's no shortage of choice in Vodice. **Arausa** (Trg Dr Franje Tuđmana 17, 022 443 152, open Apr-Sept) is a traditional Dalmatian restaurant with an expansive sea-facing terrace, plenty of atmosphere and a wide menu choice. **Konoba Rustika** (Kamila Pamukovića 5, 099 807 2213, www.konoba-rustika.com) provides reasonably priced Dalmatian food in traditional surroundings. Quietly chic **Pizzeria Spalato** (Obala V Nazora 14, 022 441 414), on the seafront, is good value and serves more than pizzas. **Santa Maria** (Kamila Pamukovića 9, 022 443 319, www. santamaria-vodice.com), the oldest restaurant in town, is known for its quirky interior.

## Bars & Nightlife

Located by the war memorial, **Café Dalmatino** (Obala V Nazora 18, 022 440 240) is a great bar for all weathers; watch the ferries go by or lounge on the sofas. **Caffè Bar Lanterna** (Obala V Nazora 13, 022 443 230) serves prize-winning home-made ices and a selection of cakes either outside or in a bright, bold interior. **Makina** (Ive Juričev Cote 20, 022 440 015) comprises a smart traditional indoor *konoba*, an expansive restaurant terrace and, nearer the sea, an outdoor bar and disco mecca for youngsters in summer. It also rents out seven rooms.

Commonly acknowledged to be one of the best nightclubs in Croatia, **Hacienda** (Magistrala, 099 333 3005, www.facebook.com/hacienda.hr, open summer only) is the closest Croatia gets to a superclub. A powerful laser

**EXPLORE**

beams out for 50 kilometres (31 miles), pointing to the spot where 2,000 clubbers come together from Split to Zadar on several dancefloors. DJs here have included David Guetta, Martin Solveig and Ian Pooley.

If you head on to the Magistrala back into Vodice, at the marina you'll find one of the most promoted clubs on the coast: **Exit** (Obala JI Cota, open summer only). Quite small, with a two-floor interior, it's commercial but fun. A broad terrace overlooks the bobbing boats, the music is pretty standard and there's a pizza kitchen if you get hungry. **Opium** (091 762 2105) is also at the marina – look it up on Facebook. The **Hookah Bar** (Ljudevita Gaja 2, 091 557 4237, open summer only, also see Facebook), in front of Hotel Punta, is a luxurious oriental-styled lounge bar with resident DJ and guests; a second bar in the same style is in the grounds of Hotel Olympia. The **Caffè Bar Virada** (Obala V Nazora 19, 098 792 434, www.facebook.com/virada.bar) has DJs and live bands all year (weekends only in winter).

## Hotels

Most accommodation is in the form of large, package-type hotels or apartments in the resort area just east of town. **Hotel Imperial** (Ulica Vatroslava Lisinskog 2, 022 454 454, www. rivijera.hr) is probably the biggest and most

expensive of the three-star resort hotels. **Hotel Olympia** (Ljudevita Gaja 6, 022 452 493, www.olympiavodice.hr, open mid Mar-Nov) earned a fourth star with improvements inside and out, including entertainment for children. **Hotel Orion** (Stablinac 2, 022 440 652, www.orion-vodice.com) is a good value three-star on the main road. **Hotel Punta** (Grgura Ninskog 1, 022 451 484, www. hotelivodice.hr) is a modern, smart operation close to town with its own pine woods and beach. Most rooms have uninterrupted sea views and the spa facilities include indoor and outdoor pools, a VIP room for couples and a medical centre offering dental treatment and cosmetic surgery.

## GETTING THERE & AROUND

A bus to Vodice takes 90mins from Split, 1hr from Zadar and 15mins from Šibenik. Buses run at least once an hour. Vodice bus station is behind the marina buildings, east of the town centre. Many local tour agencies will arrange transfers by mini-bus to Zadar or Split airports.

## RESOURCES

**Tourist information** *Vodice Tourist Office, Obala V Nazora (022 443 888, www.vodice.hr).* **Open** *Summer* 8am-10pm Mon-Sat; 9am-5pm Sun. *Winter* 8am-3pm Mon-Fri.

Vodice.

# Šibenik

After a long period of playing second fiddle to more glamorous neighbours Split and Zadar, Šibenik is swiftly turning into Dalmatia's surprise package. Like Zadar, Šibenik suffered a hammering in the 1991-95 war and is still recovering but change is evident. The industrial suburbs, a reminder of its past and significance as a port, camouflage a delightful Old Town.

Alleyways and stone steps threaten to lead nowhere but are full of surprises; historic churches and atmospheric squares are tucked around almost every corner, and the golden globe atop the unmissable Cathedral of St James pops up in the distance when least expected.

The busy seafront Riva, with bars and restaurants, thrives in summer, overlooked by the ancient network of crumbling fortresses atop the city, guarding the entrance to the Krka estuary that leads to the town from the sea. Šibenik is also a good base from which to explore the Krka National Park (*see p167* **Watery Wonders**), **Etnoland** discovery park, Dubrava Sokolarski Center for Falconry, and nightspots in Vodice and Primošten.

First mentioned in 1066 by King Petar Krešimir IV, Šibenik is one of few coastal towns with a Croatian rather than Greco-Roman heritage. However, it was the long period of Venetian rule (1412-1797) that left the deepest imprint, and most buildings in the centre, including the **Cathedral of St James**, date from this era.

Across the square from the Cathedral, the restored **Bunari**, a medieval water cistern, was initially redeveloped as a private museum; its future is currently uncertain. Down an alley by the Cathedral in what was the Duke's Palace is the refurbished **City Museum** (Gradska vrata 3, 022 213 880, www.muzej-sibenik.hr), covering the history of Šibenik from prehistoric times to now. Much of the permanent collection is in storage, although there are regular temporary exhibitions.

South of the Cathedral and main square, the 15th-century Gothic St Barbara's church hosts the **Museum of Sacred Art** (Kralja Tomislava 19, open June-Sept 10am-12.30pm, 5-7pm daily, 10kn). It's a modest collection spanning the 14th to 17th centuries, with religious paintings, polyptychs, ancient manuscripts and engravings.

After three further churches on Zagrebačka, the steeply stepped street emerges at **St Mihovil's Fortress** (open dawn-sunset daily, 10kn). Built during Venetian rule as a defence against the Ottomans, this now decrepit structure rises on the site of an earlier stronghold. Nothing impresses so much as the rooftop and the view across the estuary to the surrounding islands.

## Sights & Museums

### ★ Cathedral of St James
*Trg Republike Hrvatske (098 172 5224).* **Open** *Apr-Oct* 8.30am-8pm daily. *Nov-Mar* 8.30am-noon daily.
Gothic and Renaissance fuse beautifully in this monumental three-aisled basilica. Delayed by plague and fire, it took over 100 years to build, with the work overseen by a series of architects, most notably Zadar-born Juraj Dalmatinac and his successor Nikola Firentinac. It was eventually consecrated in 1555. An Ivan Meštrović statue of Dalmatinac stands outside the entrance.

Inside, features of note include the octagonal cupola, the stunningly ornamented baptistry with a vaulted ceiling displaying angels and cherubs, and an external wall frieze that manages to span all three apses. This features 74 sculpted stone faces of prominent Šibenik citizens, allegedly those who refused to contribute funds. During the 1991-95 war, the unique vaulted roof of interlocking stone slabs was badly damaged and it took a team of international experts to rebuild it – their efforts constitute your reward if you take the time to look.

### Etnoland
*Oštarija 9, Pakovo Selo, Drniš (099 220 0200, www.dalmati.com).* **Open** *Easter-Oct* By appointment only. **Admission** Varies, see website. **No credit cards.**
This ambitious theme park illustrating the traditional Dalmatian way of life is a short drive from Šibenik, in the village of Pakovo Selo, on the road to Drniš. Unassuming on the outside, the walled complex contains an ensemble of green-shuttered stone houses, each filled with the kind of rustic furnishings that would have been in domestic use a century or so ago. Local activities such as *pršut*-making and *rakija*-distilling form an important part of the display, and Dalmatian folk songs are performed on summer weekends.

Etnoland can only be visited by pre-booked tour, which lasts 75 minutes or three and a half hours (the latter includes lunch). Individual visitors should enquire in advance about the possibility of joining a tour, or negotiate a price based on numbers in party and desired length of stay.

### Medieval Mediterranean Garden of St Lawrence's Monastery
*Strme Stube 1 (022 212 515, 098 341 198).* **Open** *Apr-mid Nov* 9am-midnight daily. **Admission** 10kn. **No credit cards.**
Opened in 2007, fully restored after a century of neglect, the garden of the St Lawrence monastery complex is the only one of its kind in Croatia and also surprisingly rare in Europe. The restoration was completed by award-winning landscape architect Dragutin Kiš and follows pathways designed in a cross, with areas filled with sweet-smelling

**EXPLORE**

**EXPLORE**

medicinal plants and herbs. Tourist events (run by the Cromovens tourist agency on the main square of Trg Republike Hrvatske 4, 022 212 515) include the torch-lit Medieval Evening in Dalmatia, with a traditional three-course meal served by staff in medieval costume to the sounds of Dalmatian music. There's also a café and restaurant.

## Restaurants

### Barun

*Podsolarsko 66 (022 350 666).* **Open** *Summer* 11am-11pm daily. €€. **International**
Some four kilometres out of town, on the road to the Solaris hotel resort, family-run Barun has long been a favourite with locals out to impress their new date/in-laws/business associates. Located in a large modern house that is also a hotel, the first-floor dining room has a fantastic view over cultivated fields and offshore islands. The interior is as classy as the view – antique chairs, smart tablecloths and plenty of greenery. In business for three decades, Barun has a menu best described as upmarket traditional, with Italian and French influences well to the fore. A popular choice is steak: châteaubriand for two or biftek café de paris. Eight apartments are for rent too (500kn-900kn per person).

### ★ Gradska Vijećnica

*Trg Republike Hrvatske 3 (022 213 605).* **Open** 9am-midnight daily. €€. **Dalmatian**
Set in the former Venetian town hall, from which it takes its name, the GV makes use of its nine arches and splendid terrace view of the Cathedral to provide a superb setting for sampling top local cuisine at prices just above average. In winter, dine inside a small restaurant with a big mirror and crisp white tablecloths – the sort of place you'd take your parents. Look out for the chalked-up daily menu of late morning to lunchtime specials.

### No.4/Četvorka

*Trg Dinka Zavorovića 4 (092 294 0964).* **Open** noon-11pm Mon-Thur, Sun; noon-1am Fri, Sat. **No credit cards**. €€. **Dalmatian**
A younger clientele munches on pepper, cheese or truffle steaks, or one of the gnocchi or lasagne dishes. In the morning, it's a café; at night, a cocktail bar. The terrace is a pleasant and shady place, embellished by a mural of a braying donkey, and there are two cosy bars up a steep flight of stone stairs. On the second floor is an intimate, wooden-roofed balcony with four tables and views of the square and its Gothic-Renaissance church. Look it up on Facebook.

### ★ Pelegrini

*Jurja Dalmatinca 1 (022 213 701, www.pelegrini. hr).* **Open** noon-midnight daily. €€€.
**Contemporary Dalmatian**
Hands down the nicest place to eat in Šibenik, Pelegrini is run by owner and chef Rudi Štefan, who

turns out excellent dishes with an inventive twist. Top-notch prosciutto and local cheeses are the obvious choices when it comes to starters. Mains include slow-stewed calf cheeks, and baked fish in lemon sauce. There are also home-made pasta dishes and a daily changing risotto. The interior has rough stone walls, dark wood and an open kitchen. Outside, the view could hardly be bettered, with tables on the stone steps overlooking the cathedral and a lovely terrace on the roof of the Bunari (the medieval water cistern building, complete with carved well-heads). Service is polite and attentive, and prices reasonable.

### Peškarija

*Obala palih Omladinaca (no phone).* **Open** 11am-11pm daily. €€. **Dalmatian**
Walk through an atmospheric stone passageway and up some steps to reach a terrace wedged against the hillside of the Old Town, with a couple of tables and benches set in greenery. To look at the water instead of the pink decor inside, sit in the glass-enclosed loggia in the back. Quality fish and meat options include standards as well as more offbeat dishes such as fried shark, Dalmatian frogs' legs and Mexican paella with chicken, veal and vegetables. Save space for the baked ice-cream in breadcrumbs. They have a Facebook page.

### Tinel

*Trg pučkih Kapetana 1 (no phone).* **Open** *Summer* noon-3pm, 6.30-11pm Mon-Sat. €€. **Dalmatian**
Sample well-prepared regional mainstays at this stylish spot on a small square facing St Chrysogonus' Church, the town's oldest. On a hot day, book a table

Šibenik.

on the tree-shaded stone terrace. The narrow town-house has an elegant but crammed two-floor interior with seashell-themed paintings. Specialities include *pašticada* (beef with plums in a wine-and-vinegar sauce, served with gnocchi) and rayfish fillet with rocket, courgettes and tomato sauce. Dried figs in wine are the best dessert choice. Check out their Facebook page.

### Torcida
*Donje polje 42 (022 565 748, www.restoran-torcida.hr)*. **Open** 8am-midnight daily. €€. **Dalmatian**
The back road from Šibenik to Split reveals a number of fine restaurants. Arguably the best, packed with locals, is Torcida, located about 12 km outside Šibenik (click on *kako do nas* on the website for a map). The speciality is meat roasted on the spit – suckling pig or local lamb – but you can also get excellent *peka* (slow-cooked chicken) or octopus, and grilled meats. Try the mellow house red and finish with pancakes or cakes. The vast terrace overlooks rolling fields. All very good value with plenty of ambience and easy parking – but it's not for those in a hurry.

### Uzorita
*Bana Jelačića 58, Šubićevac (022 213 660, www.uzorita.com)*. **Open** *Summer* noon-11pm Mon-Thur; noon-1am Fri-Sun. *Winter* noon-11pm Mon, Wed, Thur; noon-1am Fri-Sun. €€. **Dalmatian**
A local favourite in Šubićevac, a 20-minute walk from the Old Town, Uzorita has been dishing out top Dalmatian food since 1898. The patio has a lovely open hearth and vine-covered seating, while the glass-enclosed interior features exposed stone walls and an old-fashioned fireplace. The menu covers just about everything in the Dalmatian culinary repertoire, although the real star is the seafood: try the stuffed squid.

### ★ Zlatna Ribica
*Krapanjskih Spužvara 46, Brodarica (022 350 695, www.zlatna-ribica.hr)*. **Open** 11am-11pm daily. €€€. **Dalmatian**
Well worth the eight-kilometre taxi ride from Šibenik, this gourmet institution still offers consistently excellent seafood. The covered terrace has a scenic view to the island of Krapanj, while the interior comes with floral decor. The meal starts with bread and home-made fish pâté, followed by your pick of fish from the big platter at the entrance. If in doubt, order the excellent gilthead sea bream or sea bass with *blitva* or the fish platter for two. The same family runs a small simple hotel behind the restaurant – the half- or full-board here is one of the best gastronomic deals in the Adriatic.

## Bars & Nightlife

### Giro Espresso
*Zagrebačka 2 (022 310 166, www.giroespresso.com)*. **Open** *Summer* 7am-1am Mon-Thur, Sun; 7am-2am Fri, Sat. *Winter* 7am-10pm Mon-Thur; 7am-2am Fri, Sat. **No credit cards.**
Occupying a key position on one of the Old Town's main thoroughfares, this café offers great coffee in a sleek interior. There's also a handful of outdoor tables opposite the grey portals of Šibenik's Orthodox church.

Vino & Ino.

### ★ Godimento

*Bana Jelačića 3 (no phone, hr-hr.facebook.com/ pages/Caffe-bar-Godimento/209726552387641).* **Open** 7am-11pm Mon-Sat; 7am-10pm Sun. **No credit cards**.

Set beside the Šubićevac tennis courts (and well worth a visit if you've just dined at the nearby Uzorita restaurant), Godimento bridges the gap between snug local café and energetic weekend DJ-bar better than anywhere else in town. Curving white walls, discreet neon lighting and zebra-print upholstery give the place an upmarket clubby feel, but friendly informality helps to bring out the fun-loving rather than the fancy. Expect an r'n'b to house music policy, reasonably priced bottled beers and a choice of Croatian *rakijas*.

### Moderato Cantabile

*Stjepana Radića 1 (022 213 647).* **Open** 7am-11pm Mon-Sat; 7am-10pm Sun. **No credit cards**.

Despite being subjected to a decidedly chintzy makeover by new management, Moderato Cantabile (still known to many locals by its previous name of Europa) remains the most popular of Šibenik's daytime venues for a coffee- and cake-assisted rendezvous. The sizeable tree-shaded terrace fills up fast in spring and summer; the secluded smoking section to the back of the bar comes into its own in winter.

### ★ Vino & Ino

*Fausta Vrančića 1 (091 250 6022).* **Open** 9am-1am daily.

Exactly what central Šibenik needed, this chic but convivial wine bar and design shop provides a great selection of Croatian wines with a particularly strong showing from local boutique wineries – notably, Bibich from the hills above Skradin just inland. It's also a great place to sample herb-infused *rakijas* and other indigenous spirits. While you're sipping, peruse the range of accessories by Croatian designers. The location is ideal: in the heart of old Šibenik but not too close to the tripper-thronged cathedral.

## Hotels

### Jadran

*Obala dr Franje Tudjmana 52 (022 242 000, www.rivijera.hr/Home/Jadran.html).* **€€**.

Aching for renovation, the Jadran occupies a four-floor building on the waterfront. After negotiating the lobby, you'll find the small rooms have equally miniature tubs in the ensuite bathrooms, but no balconies. Request a sea-facing room – it costs the same as the others. Nice views from the terrace café, at least.

### Konoba B&B

*Andrije Kačića 8 (091 601 9789, www.bbdalmatia. com).* **No credit cards**. **€**.

A friendly Dutch-run B&B, offering a studio and two apartments in two beautifully restored old stone houses in the Old Town. The apartments come with kitchen facilities and are ideal for families or groups. Breakfast costs an extra €6.50 per person.

### Panorama

*Šibenski most (022 213 398, www.hotel-panorama. hr).* €.

Fab views of the Krka estuary are the main draw of this 1970s concrete-and-glass cube by the Šibenik Bridge, four kilometres west of town. An extra floor was added in 2011, but the hotel retains its intimate, medium-size feel. A marble-floored lobby with a vaguely nautical theme leads to a series of blue-carpeted rooms. These ensuite units are a little on the dark side but all come with air-conditioning, balconies and cherry-wood furniture. For panoramas, pick one of the south-facing rooms (and try to be up to watch the sunrise from your balcony) or dine modestly in the terrace café-restaurant. Entertainment is provided by a gym, a mini football pitch and bungee jumping from the bridge. Regular local buses (to Zaton) ply this route and inter-city buses will drop off here, though not pick up.

## GETTING THERE & AROUND

Šibenik is 2hrs from Split and 1.5hrs from Zadar by hourly bus. Knin is 80mins away, linking with the intercity train between Zagreb and Split. The bus station is near the ferry terminal at Obala Hrvatske Mornarice, just south of the town centre. There are currently no mainline ferry services into Šibenik, only services to the nearby islands.

## RESOURCES

**Tourist information** *Šibenik Tourist Office, Obala Dr Franje Tudjmana 5 (022 214 411, www.sibenik-tourism.hr).* **Open** *July, Aug* 8am-10pm daily. *May, June, Sept, Oct* 8am-8pm daily. *Nov-Apr* 8am-3pm Mon-Fri.

# Zlarin & Privić

A short ferry hop from Šibenik are the lovely islands of Zlarin and Prvić. A landscape of olive groves and vineyards is dotted with typical Dalmatian fishing villages and fringed with quiet pebble and rock beaches. A couple of restaurants, hotels – including a stunner, the Maestral – and an occasional apartment rental reveal recent signs of tourist development.

Zlarin is 30 minutes by ferry, its sleepy bay village featuring a 15th-century church, a single hotel-restaurant, the **Koralj** (Zlarinska obala 17, 091 354 7684, www.facebook.com/zlarinkoralj), and shops selling coral, the ancient local trade all but fading out. A further 15-minute boat ride takes you to Prvić Luka, the main village on the island of Prvić. Here, you'll find one of the most

stylish hotels on any Adriatic island, the **Hotel Maestral** (022 448 300, www.hotelmaestral.com), a 19th-century schoolhouse on the main square, where 12 air-conditioned, mostly sea-facing rooms combine sleek contemporary decor with typical local elements such as exposed stone walls and green wooden shutters. The house restaurant, Val, serves excellent Med fare on a waterfront terrace. From here, a scenic path leads north-west to the picture-perfect village of Šepurine. Were it not for the classy **Ribarski Dvor** restaurant, it would feel frozen in time.

In high season, there are five ferries running between Šibenik and the islands from Monday to Saturday, and two on Sunday. Off-season, boats are less frequent.

# Primošten

Primošten, 28km (17 miles) south-east of Šibenik, is a languid little seaside town. Despite its lack of tourist attractions – or tourists, come to that – this half-island is a decent spot for a couple of days' unwinding. Fragrant pines back its pretty beaches, hilltop restaurants offer fresh seafood and stunning views, and seafront cafés fill with locals. Younger visitors don't come for any of this: they come to Primošten for the **Aurora**, one of the best clubs (and certainly the best located) in Croatia, and similar nightspots within an easy drive.

Primošten's car-free core is set on a small picturesque island linked to the mainland by a short causeway. Winding alleys lined with green-shuttered stone houses lead uphill to the **Church of St George** (1485). From the small cemetery, stellar sunset views stretch to the open sea and the seven islets that front the coastline. A promenade around the Old Town features a mix of nicely restored stone mansions and their modern concrete counterparts.

North of here, the Raduća peninsula contains pine forests, pebbly beaches and Primošten's main hotel, the **Zora**. Raduća and the Old Town are linked by the Mala Raduća cove. Beyond, a hinterland contains rolling vineyards and 30 or so hamlets. The most famous and most visited of them is the village of Primošten Burnji, where locals make red Babić wine.

## Restaurants

### Konoba Papec

*Splitska 9 (no phone, hr-hr.facebook.com/konoba. papec).* **Open** *Summer* 7pm-midnight daily. **No credit cards.** €€. Dalmatian

Don't miss the pre-dinner samples of local specialities at this rustic tavern in one of Primošten's oldest and most photographed townhouses. The small, dark interior with thick stone walls is decorated with traditional costumes and wine-making equipment.

EXPLORE

Outside, wooden benches and wine-barrel tables provide lovely seafront seating. The friendly owner, born in the house, brings out reasonably priced bite-size portions of goats' cheese soaked in olive oil, prosciutto and olives, paired with a glass of Babić wine or a shot of *rakija*, all own-made in the local villages.

### Konoba Torkul

*Crnica 1 (022 570 670, 098 337 515, www.konobatorkul.com). Open Apr-Oct 10am-midnight daily.* **€€. Dalmatian**

A great location, this. Pick a table by the beach for great sunsets over the bay between the Old Town and the Raduća peninsula or sit in the shady green terrace on the other side of the building, near the tiny church. All the standard Dalmatian fish and steak dishes are offered, plus a budget meal of the day.

### Restaurant Kamenar

*Trg biskupa J Arnerića 5 (022 570 889, www.restaurant-kamenar.com). Open Easter-Dec 9am-1am daily.* **€€€. Dalmatian**

Mulberry and acacia trees shade the terrace of this pair of renovated stone houses facing the Old Town gates. The pricey menu runs the full gamut of seafood mainstays. Just name your fish – sea bass, grouper, john dory, bream – and it will come to you fresh and delicious. House specialities include steak in scampi sauce and anglerfish with lemon. Of the two dining rooms, pick the one in the back with family bric-a-brac: black and white snapshots, an old radio and aerial photos of Primošten from the 1960s.

▶ *There are some excellent rooms to stay in here; see p169.*

### ★ Restoran Panorama

*Ribarska 26 (022 570 011, 091 253 9071, www.panorama-primosten.hr). Open Summer noon-2pm, 6pm-midnight daily.* **No credit cards. €€. Dalmatian**

Gorgeous sea vistas complement a well-executed repertoire of Adriatic seafood at this addition to Primošten's terrace dining scene. Right below the church, it's often less crowded than its hilltop neighbours, and better for a romantic sunset meal. Forget the tiny, nondescript interior and grab a white wooden bench outside, by a small swimming pool. The monkfish fillet is nicely prepared and the mixed fish platter for two great value. Recommended.

▶ *If all the outdoor seating is taken, walk around the island until you see the signs for Babilon (Težačka 15, 022 570 0940) and Galeb (Težačka 19), both summer-only restaurants atop a long set of steps with great views.*

## Nightlife

### ★ Aurora

*Magistrala (098 920 1964, www.auroraclub.hr). Open June-Sept 8pm-4am daily.* **No credit cards.**

Set two kilometres south of town, Aurora was opened just as war was breaking out in May 1991. It has spanned many trends in dance music and hosted almost every known domestic DJ, plus international names. The first floor, containing a cocktail bar, steakhouse, pizzeria and pool tables, is open during the day. After 11pm, the second level swings into action: three dancefloors, an open-air palm-fringed area, six bars, pool and a chill-out lounge zone, all open till 4am. Expect foam parties, retro nights, r'n'b and hip hop, and a crowd of anything up to 3,500.

### Legends Pub

*Don Ive Šarića 1 (no phone, www.thelegendspub.com). Open Summer 7am-4am daily. Winter midnight-4am daily.* **No credit cards.**

Just outside the town centre, Legends is housed in a large old building, revamped to an Irish theme. It appeals to older locals and mainstream expats with a musical agenda of *klapa* and vintage hits.

### Marina Frapa

*Uvala Soline, Rogoznica (www.marinafrapa.hr). Open May-mid Sept 11pm-4am daily.* **No credit cards.**

Marina Frapa is Croatia's classiest marina, with quality apartments and entertainment in a big complex within easy walking distance of Rogoznica, a short drive from Primošten. Its late-opening bar, the Captain's Club, offers cocktails on a sea-facing terrace. Directly under the pool, the glass-ceilinged Admiral is a mainstream disco with pop bands and holiday entertainment. *Photo p169.*

## Hotels

### Apartmani Jerko

*Crnica 1 (022 570 380, 098 322 095 mobile, www.apartmani-jerko.hr).* **€.**

The year-round Jerko is run by an enterprising and charming young couple who have lovingly restored this family house in arguably the best location in town. The four identical apartments, set on the first floor, are individually accessed from the external stairs, overlooking the terraced restaurant area. Each air-conditioned unit has a double bedroom, a lounge with a sofa-bed, a shower/toilet, kitchen area and a dining room looking out over the sea. Sadly, no balconies but the beach is just in front of you.

### Apartmani Silvija

*Rupe 24 (099 213 5237, www.hotelsilvija.com). Open May-Oct.* **€.**

For unobstructed sea and Old Town views, book one of the 11 well-equipped suites inside this white modern structure, which is just a ten-minute walk uphill from the busy main road. Don't expect villa-like luxury, but you can count on balconies, kitchenettes, separate bedrooms and air-conditioning in most of the units. The floor plans do differ – some bathrooms

# WATERY WONDERS

*Dramatic Krka National Park offers pools, cascades and waterfalls.*

Niagara is the nearest comparison you could possibly make. The 800m (2,625ft) wide waterfall of Skradinski buk, the picture-postcard main draw of the Krka National Park (www.np-krka.hr), leaves onlookers in awe with its 17-step series of cascades. Its surrounded by boardwalks for easy access, and holidaymakers can take a dip in the clear pools beneath the falls. But this is only one of many attractions in this most versatile and surprising of Croatia's eight national parks.

Located by the beautiful town of Skradin, near Šibenik in central Dalmatia, the park is named after the 75-kilometre (47-mile) long Krka river it practically encompasses. Krka, like Plitvice Lakes National Park, is awash in the marvel and miracle of travertine. Where the two differ is the degree of interaction with nature. Where Plitvice has sheer wow power, Krka offers close-up interaction with the natural world.

To find out, take the four-hour boat tour to Roški slap cascades. Some 222 bird species, 19 different reptiles, 18 species of bat and 860 plant types, and rushing tributaries leading to the Krka estuary and the Adriatic, give Krka its flavour. En route, you can visit the park's strange treasure: Visovac. This man-made islet is home to a working Franciscan monastery where trainees spend a year enjoying occasional games of basketball and greeting tourists with enthusiastic waves.

As you arrive back on land – while swans glide past local fishermen in threadbare sweaters and rubber waders – you realise that Krka isn't just one thing but many at once. It's a river, a gorge, a monastery, a collection of villages and a source of food. Visitors can also drop in on the stone houses of an 'ethno-village' with its mills, traditional weaving looms (still in use) and the not-so-traditional souvenir shop.

Beside the visitor centre at the park's main entrance in Skradin is the three-star **Hotel Vrata Krke** (022 778 092, vrata-krke.hr), with 50 rooms and its own restaurant and bar. Speak to reception to arrange trips to Krka.

**EXPLORE**

# ISLAND LIFE

*An archipelago of 140 islands accessible only by boat.*

The **Kornati National Park** (www.np-kornati. hr) has qualities that make it unique. It consists of 140 islands and islets in an area only 35 kilometres (22 miles) long and 14 kilometres (nine miles) wide. Between the long, thin island of Kornat, which faces the mainland, and the chain of islands on the other side, there is a stretch of water naturally protected from the open sea, with dozens of safe bays. Once you pass through one of the two narrow entrances to the north and south, you leave the worst of the waves behind, and enter a strange, otherworldly environment, with barren-looking, treeless hills.

The islands within the national park seem deserted. You might sight the occasional sheep, or a small votive chapel, built by a grateful sailor saved from a storm by the natural barrier of the islands; otherwise, there's little sign of habitation. It's a very meditative and minimal landscape, unlike any other island chain in the Adriatic. When you enter Kornati, you know you've arrived somewhere completely different.

Whether you have your own yacht, or come on one of the many tour boats, you will also get to experience the outer side of the archipelago. The contrast between the calm inner space of Kornati and the wild world of the open sea is unmistakable, not least in the geomorphology of the exposed rocks. Sheer cliffs offer spectacular scenes and dramatic sounds, from crashing waves to the echo of the human voice. The seaward side of the island of Mana is the most impressive; boats can come right up close to the 100m (328ft) cliffs that stretch for 1.5km. If the sea is not too rough, the outer edge of Kornati is a great place to swim and snorkel, with much marine life just below the surface of the rocky shoreline.

A few centuries ago, the islands were reputedly covered with oak trees – now even most of the soil has gone, leaving a thorny, stony environment, where the largest surviving fauna are frogs, lizards, snakes and birds. The wildest part of the park is in the far south, where a 500m (1,640ft) exclusion zone has been declared around the islet of Purara, to allow the development of natural life. One hopeful sign is a colony of dolphins that lives between Kornati and the mainland and manages to co-exist with the fishermen, thrilling lucky visitors who get a leaping dolphin escort across the straits.

Although signposts at the motorway exit for Murter suggest it's an easy journey from there to Kornati, visiting the national park is more complicated in practice. There is no ferry or public transport, and no way to get around the islands without a boat. There are also very few accommodation options in Kornati; most overnight visitors stay on their own yachts. If you have an international captain's licence, then you can rent your own sea-borne transport – otherwise, the only way to reach the park is on a tour. The best are those offered by the fishermen of Murter. Tourist boats also leave from Vodice, Pirovac and Šibenik. Visitors pay a day fee: 40kn for excursion tourists, 80kn for yachtsmen and guests. Recreational fishing permits are 150kn per day.

If you have your own boat, the ideal place to enter Kornati is through the straits of Opat, between the south side of Kornat and Smokvica. Park rangers on speedboats will sell you an entrance ticket. There are reception centres on the islands of Ravni Žakan and in the village of Vruje. Overnight mooring is possible in a dozen bays in the park, mostly at floating moorings marked by red buoys. Among the best bays for overnighting are Lavsa, Levrnaka and Ravni Žakan. There is also a summer-only marina on the island of Piškera.

The nearest departure points for an excursion to Kornati are on the island of Murter (*see p154*). If you take a stroll along the harbours of Jezera or Murter town, you'll see several boats offering day trips to Kornati. All are similar, including entry to the national park, a journey around the most impressive natural sights, the chance to swim, and a fish barbecue washed down with a couple of glasses of the local red. Most of the vessels are converted fishing boats, and many convert back during the winter months, when the surly tourist guides return – perhaps gratefully – to their true profession.

are on the small side – but the decor is standard 1970s chintz. A cleaning fee is slapped on to the bill at the end.

### Hotel Zora

*Raduća (022 570 048, www.hotelzora-adriatiq. com). Open Apr-Oct. €.*
Now part of the Adriatiq group, this complex of nine interlinked low-rise buildings, set in pine forest, has modern decorative touches. Marble floors, stylish armchairs and shiny columns dress the lobby. The café-bar offers a lovely sea-facing terrace, while rooms, though small, come with balconies, pine floors and colourful wall prints; most have superb views. The glass-domed seaside heated pool area has underground treatment rooms and a roof that opens when the sun's out or stays closed if you want to swim beneath the stars. The herbal garden is a nice touch too while there's entertainment for kids as well as sports and excursions.

### ★ Kamenar

*Trg Biskupa J Arnerića 5 (022 570 889, www. restaurant-kamenar.com). Open Mar-Nov. No credit cards. €.*
This is the most old-world charm you can get for your money in Primošten, in a 150-year-old stone building at the entrance to the Old Town. Above the family-run restaurant of the same name (*see p166*)

are seven small but pleasant rooms with pinewood floors. The communal balcony has lovely views of the surrounding rooftops, and it's all very intimate and informal. Prices include a modest breakfast at the restaurant.

### Villa Koša

*Bana Jelačića 4 (022 570 365, 098 211 704 mobile, www.villa-kosa.htnet.hr). No credit cards. €.*
A ten-minute walk east of the Old Town, this pair of garish pink-yellow buildings has a string of modern suites inside and a pebble beach just in front. Units vary in size and layout – some have kitchens and separate living room areas – but all come with natural light, a balcony or loggia. Great views of the Old Town too.

## GETTING THERE & AROUND

Primošten is an easy hop from near northern neighbour Šibenik. Buses leave every couple of hours and take 25mins. Once in Primošten, walking is the only option.

## RESOURCES

**Tourist information** *Primošten Tourist Office, Trg biskupa J Arnerića 2 (022 571 111, www. tz-primosten.hr). Open June-Oct* 8am-10pm daily. *Nov-May* 8am-noon Mon-Fri.

**Marina Frapa**. *See p166.*

**EXPLORE**

# Split &
# Central
# Dalmatia

**E**very summer, thousands flock to Split, the departure point for the key islands of Brač, Hvar and Vis. More are also taking time to explore the city itself, where, behind the terraces of the Riva, a gastronomic revolution has taken place. Meanwhile, a regular traffic of car ferries, catamarans and fast boats glide to the islands: family-friendly Brač with its famous beach of Zlatni Rat; party-centric Hvar, darling of the yachting crowd; and the more remote Vis. Back on the mainland, Trogir and, to a lesser extent, Kaštela fill with seasonal visitors. South of Split, Omiš and Dugi Rat attempt to lure trade from the hotel-lined Makarska Riviera.

Carpe Diem.

## Don't Miss

**1 Diocletian's Palace**
Roman hub where Split sips and shops (p172).

**2 Meštrović Gallery**
Workshop and exhibition space built by Croatia's finest sculptor (p188).

**3 Zlatni Rat** Shifting sands and surfing winds at this famous beach (p206).

**4 Carpe Diem** For Hvar's beautiful people (p220).

**5 Konoba Roki** *Peka* dishes and own-made wines on Vis (p227).

**EXPLORE**

# Split

The days when Split was nothing more than a departure point to nearby Brač, Vis and Hvar are gone. Boasting antiquities aplenty, cool café-bars, highly individual restaurants and a rash of new, quality hotels, Croatia's main ferry port is also the country's most promising all-round city-break destination.

Almost every month, a new eaterie opens, highlighting Split's new-found status as a food destination. Venues such as **Restoran Paradigma**, **Bokeria** and **Kadena** are stand-out examples of this recent phenomenon. Split's growing accommodation stock continues to make the news, too, with the arrival of the Cornaro and Marul and the elegant old Park getting an upgrade.

Despite this progress and property price hikes, Split has not sold its soul to tourism in the way that Dubrovnik has been perceived to have done. Café terraces on the main promenade, the Riva, fill on sunny days with locals happy to chat all day. Equally, the city's prime tourist sight, the former Roman palace behind the Riva, awaits tourists who need pay no admission charge: the grand shell of Roman Emperor **Diocletian's Palace**, a 30,000sq-metre maze, the atmospheric ruin where you will be spending most of your time.

## DIOCLETIAN'S PALACE & AROUND

Some 1,700 years on, the Emperor Diocletian would still recognise his palace – or the shell of it, at least. This vast, rectangular complex fell into disuse in the sixth century, 300 years after its construction as a grand retirement home by the locally born leader of the Imperial Guard. In AD 614 refugees flooded in from nearby Salona (Solin) and locals have been eking out a living in its alcoves and alleyways ever since. Today its two-metre-thick walls hide any number of shops, bars and businesses. Wandering aimlessly around the palace is one of Split's essential experiences. There is no ticket office or protocol – you just stroll in. Four gates guard its main entrances: Golden, Silver, Iron and Bronze. The latter gives access, through the basement of Diocletian's old Central Hall, now filled with souvenir and craft stalls, to the Riva. In 2015, a viewing point was created in the northern wall of the palace, providing a handy panorama of the complex as a whole.

Amid the chaos, added to over the centuries, two landmarks stand out: the courtyard of **Peristil**, a major crossing point, and, beside it, the **Katedrala**. Once the site of Diocletian's mausoleum, and still guarded by a granite sphinx from Ancient Egypt, this octagonal building was converted into a church by the refugees from

Salona. Through the Middle Ages, it was given finely carved doors, an equally beautiful pulpit and eventually a belltower offering a panoramic view of the palace. The climb can be quite dizzying, so only try it if you have a head for heights.

In the north-east corner of the palace, the **Split City Museum** is worth visiting for the 15th-century Gothic building itself rather than sundry paintings and weaponry within. By the time Split was part of the Venetian empire, the population had long since spread outside the palace walls. Split's role as the main access point for trade in fast boats between Venice and the East – thus avoiding the pirate-infested waters further north – helped the local economy prosper. A short period of French rule saw rapid urban development, such as the landscaping of the waterfront embankment below the arches that once enclosed Diocletian's living quarters. The **Riva** (officially Obala hrvatskog narodnog preporoda) is Split's main drag. Its makeover by Zagreb-based architects 3LHD has been grudgingly accepted by the notoriously conservative locals. Recently, renovation of the promenade was extended west towards the fishermen's cove of Matejuška.

The palace is fringed by two prominent statues by Dalmatian sculptor Ivan Meštrović: one of literary scholar Marko Marulić in Trg braće Radić in the south-west corner, the other of medieval bishop Grgur Ninski by the Golden Gate. Opposite stands the **Split Fine Art Gallery**. To the east, the **Silver Gate** was only discovered accidentally after Allied bombs in 1944 shattered a later outer wall. Just beyond, the city's main market runs daily. Beyond that, past the nearby train and bus stations, and harbour opposite, over the railtracks is the city beach and modest leisure complex of **Bačvice**. You can walk from the Roman palace to Bačvice in 15 minutes.

On the western side of the palace, the busy **fish market** is found in a little square alongside Kraj Sv Marije. Adjacent runs **Marmontova**, another Napoleonic introduction, a smart(ish) pedestrianised avenue, Split's main shopping street and location of the French Institute. At the top stands the stern edifice of the Croatian National Theatre.

## Sights & Museums

### Ethnographic Museum

*Iza Vestibula 4 (021 344 161, www.etnografski-muzej-split.hr).* **Open** *June-Sept* 9.30am-7pm Mon-Sat; 10am-1pm Sun. *Oct-May* 9am-4pm Mon-Fri; 9am-1pm Sat. **Admission** 15kn. **No credit cards.** **Map** p177 C2 ❶

Underrated and little visited attraction in the heart of the palace, but well worth the effort of cutting into your holiday time for. This century-old museum focuses on the traditions of the Dalmatian region,

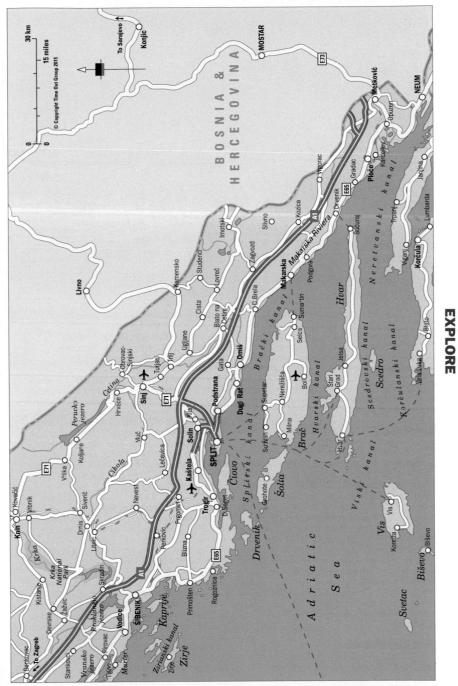

**EXPLORE**

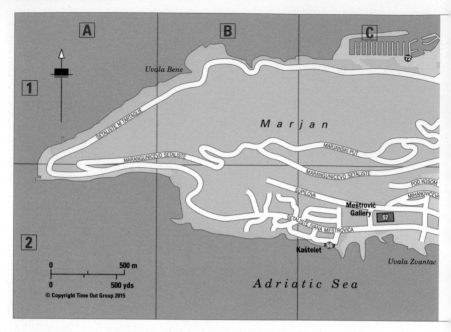

most notably its crafts and trades. Note the delicately carved ceramics and beautifully embroidered costumes in the reconstructed rooms of typical peasant houses. This house itself was the former private residence of the Roman Emperor Diocletian, the main door to his living room still visible. A new attraction is the anteroom at the top of the vestibule, which offers a great view of Split's historic centre.

### Katedrala

*Kraj Sv Duje (021 345 602).* **Open** 8am-7pm Mon-Sat; after mass on Sun. **Admission** *Cathedral, belltower, treasury* each 15kn. *Temple of Jupiter, Crypt* each 10kn. *All* 45kn. **No credit cards. Map** p177 C2 ❷

Once the site of Diocletian's mausoleum, and still guarded by a 3,000-year-old granite sphinx from Egypt, this octagonal building was converted into a church by refugees from Salona. Ironically, the cathedral is dedicated to Sveti Duje, patron saint of Split, a Christian martyr executed by Diocletian. During the Middle Ages, it was given finely carved doors, an equally beautiful pulpit and eventually a belltower offering a panoramic view of the palace. The climb (15kn) can be quite dizzying, so only try it if you have a head for heights. The crypt contains rare ecclesiastical treasures dating back to the eighth century.

### Split City Museum

*Papalić Palace, Papalićeva 1 (021 360 171, www.mgst.net).* **Open** *May-Oct* 9am-4pm Mon, Sat, Sun; 9am-9pm Tue-Fri. *Nov-Apr* 9am-5pm Tue-Fri; 9am-1pm Sat; 10am-1pm Sun. **Admission** 20kn. *Palace wall* 40kn. **No credit cards. Map** p177 C2 ❸

This museum in the heart of the palace is mostly worth visiting for the 15th-century Gothic building itself rather than for the sundry paintings and weaponry contained within. You'll also find photographs, documents, maps and old papers relating to the city, but the permanent collection appeals more to historians rather than offering the general public a rough idea how this fascinating port developed. For an extra fee you can access part of the north wall of the palace for a fine view of Split's historic centre.

### ★ Split Gallery of Fine Arts

*Kralja Tomislava 15 (021 350 110, www.galum. hr).* **Open** *June-Sept* 11am-4pm Mon; 11am-7pm Tue-Fri; 11am-3pm Sat. *Oct-May* 9am-2pm Mon; 9am-5pm Tue-Fri; 9am-1pm Sat. **Admission** 20kn; 10kn reductions. **No credit cards. Map** p177 C1 ❹

The major cultural opening – in fact, reopening – in town for many years, this attractive collection of art from the Adriatic region includes pieces by leading figures from modern times, most notably Vlaho Bukovac, as well as works from as far back as the Renaissance. There is contemporary stuff too – paintings and photographs – to lend the venue kudos. There are temporary exhibitions and the Galerija café on the ground floor.

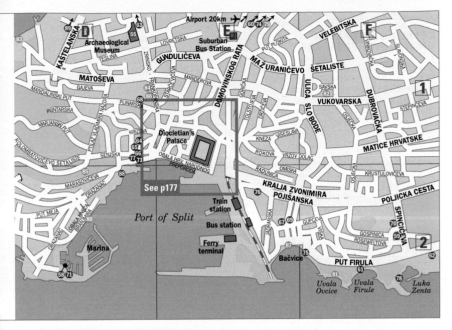

## Restaurants

### ★ Apetit
*Šubićeva 5 (021 332 549, www.apetit-split.hr).*
**Open** 11am-midnight daily. €€. **Map** p177 B2 ❺
**Dalmatian**
This splendid new venture from a Croatian who
has spent many years in Berlin, lies on the western
boundary of Diocletian's Palace, near the Riva,
partly occupying a former nobleman's palace. Green
partitions, stone walls, bright art and simple furnishings make this a great place for an upmarket
lunch. The traditional Dalmatian menu features
house-made elements such as pasta and bread,
includes a veggie corner plus plenty to appeal to
meat and fish lovers. Round off your meal with own-
made chocolate cake.

### ★ Bokeria Kitchen&Wine
*Domaldova 8 (021 355 577, www.facebook.com/
bokeriasplit).* **Open** 8am-1am Mon-Thur, Sun;
8am-2am Fri, Sat. €€. **Map** p177 B2 ❻
**Mediterranean**
The owners of Bokeria, the Bokavšek family,
named their establishment after the famous market
in Barcelona to bring a spirit of diversity to Split.
Judging by the growing popularity of this place
since opening in 2014, that's what they've achieved.
Bokeria is set in a building that once was a hardware
store. It's a big restaurant, compared to most others
in Split, but it's far from cold – the interior design
is supreme in its simplicity. The food is conceived

along the same lines, and also takes its lead from the
venue's full name of Bokeria Kitchen&Wine. What's
on offer here is seasonal, with ingredients supplied
from the local produce and fish markets. If there is
a style to Bokeria's cuisine, then it's Mediterranean,
with dishes running from excellent vegetable concoctions to bruschetta to seafood, all the way up
to steaks and beyond. The wine list has the finest
possible Croatian selection. The owners recently
instigated theme nights, and occasional smooth live
music, mostly jazz.

### ★ Brasserie on 7
*Obala Hrvatskog narodnog preporoda 7 (021 278
233, www.brasserieon7.com).* **Open** 7.30am-1am
daily. €€. **Map** p177 A2 ❼ **International**
Brasserie on 7 is a take on the long-established contemporary Croatian eatery Zinfandel, sharing its
ownership and philosophy. It also enjoys the most
prime spot in the city, slap on the main seaside promenade of the Riva. No wonder, then, that Brasserie on
7 has become one of the leading lights of Split's new
gastronomic scene, with a tidy selection of redefined
local and international dishes. Highlights include a
chilled seafood platter; smoked salmon and octopus
salad with fish; a Black Angus burger with pancetta and Portobello mushrooms; and leg of lamb
with rosemary and yoghurt. Brasserie on 7 has also
become known for its desserts, especially the all-
the-sweets-you-can-eat deal for 29kn. As for drinks,
there's an impressive wine list, plus selected beers
including micro-brewed San Servolo from Istria. As

## IN THE KNOW SPLIT'S UNDISCOVERED ISLAND

Now with a major boutique hotel, the island of Šolta is looking to attract tourists away from Brač and Hvar. It's not only about heliports and heated pools, although the seriously high-end Martinis Marchi (Maslinica, 021 572 768, www.martinis-marchi.com) can provide both. Šolta is a haven of olive groves, vineyards and unspoiled beaches. There's more beach fun at Rogač, which is also the main ferry port for the frequent, cheap services from Split. Affordable lodgings are provided at the Villa Šolta (021 654 540, www.villa-solta.com) on the outskirts of Rogač, where you'll also find a restaurant offering classic Dalmatian cuisine.

this is the Riva, Brasserie on 7 is popular for sipping coffee on a sunny afternoon as the world passes by.

### Chops-Grill Steak&Seafood
*Kamila Tončića 4 (091 317 3001, www.chops-grill. com).* **Open** *Summer* 8am-midnight daily. *Winter* 2-10pm daily. €€. **Map** p177 A1 ❽ **Grill**
Split previously lacked a good steakhouse – so Chops-Grill has fitted right in. Meats range from several variations of rib-eye steak and a gigantic half-kilo T-bone to a Black Angus burger. There's also quality Adriatic seafood such as monkfish and tuna. What also makes Chops-Grill different from the competition is its breakfast selection, obviously created for those who like to start a day with something substantial. This is a pretty big restaurant by Split standards, with a nice position just off the main shopping street, Marmontova.

### Corto Maltese
*Obrov 7 (095 820 9995).* **Open** 8am-midnight daily. €. **Map** p177 B2 ❾ **International**
Taking its name from Hugo Pratt's comic-book character, this is the latest addition to Split's modern affordable eateries. This one is excellently positioned next to the old fish market. As well as the quick and easy-to-cook gnocchi, chicken and meatballs, the menu includes blue fish and a small but handy selection of cold and warm appetisers, some a simple meal in themselves. Corto Maltese is popular among younger tourists, thanks to its prices and its attractive interior, with an open kitchen so you can watch the whole process of your dish being made. See the restaurant's Facebook page for more information.

### Diocletian's Wine House
*Julija Nepota 4 (099 207 6609, www.facebook.com/ DiocletianswinehouseSplit).* **Open** 8am-midnight daily. €€€. **Map** p177 C2 ❿ **Dalmatian**

Until last year, this was one of those restaurants with acceptable but not outstanding food, which relied on its attractive palace location to bring in the tourists. But now, following renovation, Diocletian offers more artisanal and ambitious food and, most notably, the wine list has improved no end; it's now one of the best in town. The place is furnished with photos of old Split, showing different phases in the city's history, and old (or wannabe old) furniture, lending a home-like feel. There is also outdoor seating on the street – said to be the one where the last legal emperor of the Western Roman Empire, Julius Nepos, was killed.

### Galija
*Tončićeva 12 (021 347 932).* **Open** 9am-midnight Mon-Sat; noon-midnight Sun. €. **Map** p177 A1 ⓫ **Pizzeria**
Hulking great pizzas are served at bargain-basement prices at this modest little spot just off Marmontova west of the palace. No surprises in the selection, but that doesn't seem to bother the many local regulars and tourists delighted to find this place off the beaten track. It also serves simple grilled meats.

### Konoba Kod Joze
*Sredmanuška 4 (021 347 397).* **Open** 10am-midnight Mon-Fri; noon-1am Sat, Sun. €. **Map** p177 C1 ⓬ **Dalmatian**
Joze's friendly Tavern is central but slightly off the beaten track – head out of the Golden Gate, over the park and Sredmanuška opposite, up a slight incline. It's been serving up splendid local food at reasonable prices for over 30 years, making it one of Split's most solid and reliable choices. After a tasty starter of Dalmatian ham or one of seven soups, choose your fish from the tray of the day's catch – it will be simply but satisfyingly prepared – or tuck into one of the excellent game dishes as you observe adjacent street life from the terrace, or relax in the homely interior downstairs.

### Konoba Marul
*Trg braće Radića 2 (021 339 068, www.konoba-marul.com/split.html).* **Open** 8am-midnight daily. €€. **Map** p177 B2 ⓭ **Dalmatian**
This local restaurant, perfectly located with a terrace overlooking a prominent square by the palace, has a menu that reflects its traditional bare-stone-and-old-oak interior. Most of the classic Dalmatian dishes are done here, well presented and accompanied by a full range of Croatian wines. The same management also run the nearby ST Riva cocktail bar (*see p183*) on the waterfront.

### Makrovega
*Leština 2 (021 394 440, www.makrovega.hr).* **Open** 9am-9pm Mon-Fri; 9am-5pm Sat. €. **Map** p177 A1 ⓮ **Vegetarian**
Still the only strictly vegetarian restaurant in Split – and still one of the hardest to find. Check the map on the website to find this place, at the far end of a

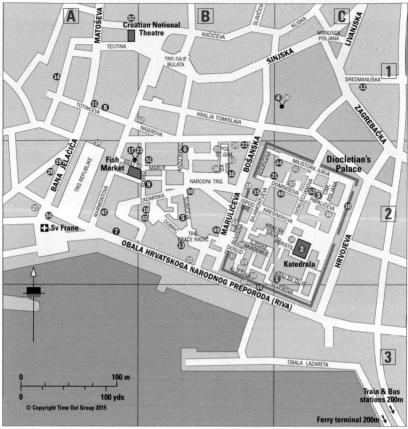

residential courtyard near Marmontova. The interior is sharp, minimalist and a little feng shui. The food is varied and the portions are generous. The changing daily menu comes with or without soup, and in two forms, macrobiotic or vegetarian. It's a dry ship.

### ★ Mazzgoon

*Bajamontijeva 1 (098 987 7780).* **Open** 8am-1am daily. **€€. Map** p177 B2 ⑮ **Dalmatian**
Another small but mighty stronghold of Split's new gastronomy scene is owned by young couple Sara and Toni Vrsalović. It's set right next to the Iron or Western Gate of the Diocletian's Palace. Now, there is this contemporarily designed indoor space, beside a shady and pleasant terrace in the backyard of one of Split's medieval palaces. Mazzgoon is named after the Dalmatian word for mule (*mazga*), known for its never-say-die persistence. The cuisine is a combination of traditional regional dishes and international influences. You'll find excellent Dalmatian *brodetto*, with home-made pasta from Korčula, but there are also shrimp burgers and street-food dishes.

Mazzgoon is a source of new happenings in town: its menu is also a monthly magazine called *Mazzgoon Times*, with news about Split's culinary and clubbing scene. Nice touch.

### ★ NoStress Bistro

*Iza lože 9 (099 498 1888, www.facebook.com/ caffebarnostress).* **Open** 7am-2am Mon-Sat; 8am-2am Sun. **€€.** Map p177 B2 ⑯ **Dalmatian**
There are very few places in Split that can beat the location of NoStress, right at the busiest part of the city's main square. This should be the perfect spot for a tourist trap. However, NoStress is far from that. Since owners Žana and Željko Alfirević hired chef Željko Neven Bremec, NoStress has become one of the most innovative eateries in town, a leader in the new wave of Split's gastronomic scene, experimenting with reinterpretations of Dalmatian culinary traditions. Its cuisine is mostly created from local ingredients, such as dishes made from *boškarin*, a cattle breed raised in the traditional way in Istria, and certified for authenticity. There are also ever-changing seasonal

Restoran Paradigma.

specialities such as wild asparagus in spring or home-made sausages in winter, plus Žana and Željko are also dedicated to reviving some of the nicest elements of Split's urban traditions, with regular events such as open-air dancing to nostalgic tunes of the 1970s and 1980s. If by chance you stumble upon NoStress in the morning, you'll discover that it's also one of the most popular coffee-sipping spots in town.

### Noštromo

*Kraj Sv Marije 10 (091 405 6666, www.restoran-nostromo.hr). Open 10am-midnight daily. €€. No credit cards. Map p177 A2* ⑰ **Dalmatian**
Run by chef-owner Zlatko Marinović, this is one of the best restaurants in Dalmatia, let alone Split. Traditional recipes are given a contemporary twist – look out for the ray-fish stew and batter-fried sea anemone. Amid the artwork, locals treat each other or celebrate birthdays over a fish platter for two, as fresh as you'll find anywhere – it's right next to the fish market.

### Oyster & Sushi Bar Bota

*Morpurgova poljana (021 488 648, www.bota-sare. hr). Open 10am-midnight daily. €€. Map p177 B2* ⑱ **Japanese/Dalmatian**
After the successful Samurai (*see right*) opened across town in 2013, local restaurateurs have discovered the potential of Japanese cuisine. One of those currently riding this wave is the Oyster & Sushi Bar Bota, set in the south-western corner of Morpurgova poljana, sharing it with the terrace of the Goli&Bosi Hostel. Bota is part of a well respected Croatian

chain. Their oysters are a must-try, along with the Dalmatian specialities that complement the wide selection of makis, nigiris, rolls and sashimis.

### ★ Restoran Paradigma

*Ulica Bana Jelačić 3 (021 645 103, www.paradox. hr). Open Summer 7.30am-midnight daily. Winter 11.30am-11pm daily. €€. Map p177 A2* ⑲
**Mediterranean**
This was one of the most eagerly awaited openings of 2014, the latest venture from the team that brought you Wine & Cheese Bar Paradox (*see p193*). Its aim was to provide a combination of modern Mediterranean cuisine and a best-of-Croatia wine list. Occupying a single-storey building opposite the Bellevue Hotel, the restaurant also featured a superb roof terrace. Now a year down the line, Paradigma is a fixture in the upscale bracket of Split's dining scene, with theme nights and guest chefs.

### Samurai

*Bana Josipa Jelačića 1 (021 786 640, sushibarsplit. com). Open noon-11pm Mon-Sat; 5-11pm Sun. €. Map p177 A2* ⑳ **Sushi**
Opened by retired engineer Masahiro Okamoto in 2013, this is pretty much what central Dalmatia was crying out for: a sushi bar that's welcoming, inexpensive and serious about producing quality sushi. Samurai's sushi makes the best use of local ingredients – you can have *pršut* sushi roll as well as more traditional shrimp and salmon varieties. The other Japanese dishes on the menu – beef

given the excellent fare on offer in this informal but excellent snack bar cum bistro. A small box-shaped room with a counter and a kitchen squeezed into one side, a few stools propped against a ledge at the other, Spiza offers fast-ish food, traditional Split style. You can order grilled anchovies, ask what's stewing in one of the pots, or wait while they cook you up a risotto to order – the menu will be chalked up on the wall, and dictated by what was fresh at the market that morning. Locals pop in for a beer or glass of wine, and there's frequently a lively drinking session taking place on and around the bench in the alley outside. Check the restaurant's Facebook page for more information.

### Zlatna Ribica
*Kraj sv Marije 8 (021 348 710).* **Open** 6am-9pm Mon-Fri; 6am-2pm Sat. **€. Map** p177 A2 ㉓
**Dalmatian**
Beside the fish market and the upscale Noštromo, the bar-like Zlatna Ribica is the kind of place where they serve up a plate of grilled squid and a glass of beer for around 50kn. Most things, in fact, come out of the frying pan, but it's honest fare at honest prices. The restaurant's Facebook page has more information.

## Cafés & Bars

### ★ Academia Ghetto Club
*Dosud 10 (021 346 879).* **Open** 9am-midnight Mon-Sat. **No credit cards. Map** p177 B2 ㉔
The most bohemian of the bars in the palace, the AGC comprises a front courtyard, a small bar leading to a muralled main room with a vaguely erotic theme ('Welcome to the House of Love'), and an upstairs gallery, open according to event. Arty locals mingle with tourists happy to hear reliably good music. The bar is at one end of the narrow, stepped Dosud bar run. See the Facebook page for more information.

### Bifora
*Bernardov prilaz/Poljana stare Gimnazije (no phone).* **Open** 7pm-1am Mon-Sat. **No credit cards. Map** p177 B2 ㉕
One of the many Old Town bars you might want to find again, this DJ den is set on an unmapped square just behind Iza Lože and the youngsters sinking cheap cocktails at Gaga. Bifora brings a giggly clientele to a dim space whose mural depicts red-spotted mushrooms and grinning pixies. Alternatively, get yourself a table on the quiet square.

### Caffè Bar Galerija
*Kralja Tomislava 15 (098 939 5418).* **Open** 8am-11pm Mon-Sat; 10am-10pm Sun. **No credit cards. Map** p177 C1 ㉖
In the lobby area of the Split Gallery of Fine Arts, this minimalist cafe is a popular local haunt for morning coffee, largely on account of its south-facing, suntrap outdoor terrace. Velebitsko beer in bottles and a good range of Dalmatian wines may persuade you to linger longer – perhaps the laid-back live music too.

sukiyaki bowl, mixed tempura bowl and several noodle dishes – are ideal light-lunch material.

### ★ Uje Oil Bar
*Dominisova 3 (095 200 8008, www.facebook.com/ UjeOilBar).* **Open** 11am-11pm daily. **€. Map** p177 B/C2 ㉑ **Mediterranean**
Launched by local olive oil retailers and delicatessen specialists Uje, this is much more than the title suggests; it's a quality wine and food bar that offers the best of Mediterranean fare in elegant surroundings. Located on the corner of intersecting alleyways in an (until now) little traversed corner of the palace precinct, Uje is filled with the kind of solid wooden furniture that makes it feel like a welcoming farmhouse kitchen. Shelves packed with jars of preserves bolster the homely feel. The menu changes according to what's in season and includes many of the more old-fashioned things in the traditional Dalmatian repertoire – fish soups, dishes with beans and pulses, and more. You can also dunk your bread in various olive oils – the nearby islands are famous for producing highly individual blends. Uje's wine list is brief but well chosen; the desserts are divine. You'll find Uje's wine bar, tapas spot and spirits bar alongside down the same street – and Uje delicatessens around town.

### Villa Spiza
*Kružićeva 3 (091 152 1249).* **Open** 11am-11pm daily. **€. Map** p177 B2 ㉒ **Dalmatian**
*Spiza* is Dalmatian dialect for 'food' in the sense of 'grub' or 'nosh' – an ironic exercise in understatement

EXPLORE

## Caffè Libar
*Trg Franje Tudjmana 3 (021 349 044).* **Open**
*Summer* 7am-1am daily. *Winter* 7am-midnight
daily. **No credit cards. Map** p177 A2 ㉗
This is a great find just off the Riva, by Sv Frane
church, with a first-floor terrace overlooking street life.
There's also free Wi-Fi, real chips, tapas and snacks
such as buffalo wings and whitebait, plus sport on two
big TV screens on the terrace. Owner Kristijan Kuko
keeps his prices low and his ambitions high.

## Čajoteka Natura
*Bosanska 2 (021 341 024).* **Open** 9am-8pm
Mon-Fri; 9am-2pm Sat. **Map** p177 B2 ㉘
This nice little teashop down a stone alleyway also
has two or three tables outside where customers can
sit under a cool archway and enjoy a cup of their
favourite exotic brew.

## ★ Charlie's Bar
*Kružićeva 5 (021 355 171).* **Open** 5pm-2am daily.
**No credit cards. Map** p177 B2 ㉙
Charlie's is one of the central points of wild summer
pub crawl tours around Split, with groups of youngsters wearing phosphorescent necklaces running
around with only one goal in mind. The bar – in an
atmospheric alley just outside the palace precincts
– is owned by two Australians of Croatian origin,
and is part of the hospitality group that includes
Zinfandel, Brasserie on 7 and a hostel opposite. This
logistic makes it especially popular among backpackers, a Brit-Australian refuge in Split. Charlie's
Facebook page has more information.

## Dioklecijan
*Dosud 9/Alješina (021 346 683).* **Open** 7am-1am
daily. **No credit cards. Map** p177 B2 ㉚
Locals would class this as a restaurant and it serves
food, to be sure. They would also called it the 'Tri
Volte', after the arches overlooking the sea, the main
reason for coming here in the first place. To find it,
mount the steps by the sphinx at Peristil, cut through
the vestibule with the hole in the roof. Past the chairs
outside the Hotel Vestibul Palace on your right will be
a yellow arrow saying 'Grill'. Follow it. You will find
the only bar within the palace overlooking the waterfront from above, an enclosed terrace of tables ideally
located for a sundown beer. Inside is a traditional
*konoba*, with cheap meats and such like, and saggy
regulars getting into some serious drinking. If you're
hungry, call up a doorstep sandwich of cheese and
ham carved from the huge hock behind the bar.

## Figa
*Buvinina 1 (no phone).* **Open** 8am-1am Mon-Thur,
Sun; 8am-2am Fri, Sat. **No credit cards. Map**
p177 B2 ㉛
The legendary Puls 2, for years an essential stop-
off on any nocturnal alcohol-fuelled tour of the
palace, has been reborn as Figa, a café-cum-food
bar in which salads, risottos, sandwiches and daily

specials join the customary roster of coffee, cocktails
and *rakija*. The location itself – set at the bottom of a
stepped street with benches and cushions set out on
the stairs – is enough to ensure that Figa still retains
the old Puls magic. Most of the action remains outside, especially in the evening – although the interior,
mixing ancient stone walls with smart modern furniture, is a calm and comfortable place in which to
confront Figa's new lunchtime-friendly personality.

## Fro
*Obala Hrvatskog narodnog preporoda 11 (021 344
321, www.facebook.com/Freud2013).* **Open**
7am-7pm daily. **Map** p177 B2 ㉜
This is another Split venue that everyone knows
but few could name. Most locals call it simply
'Isprid banke' ('In Front of the Bank'). The name
Fro is derived from the fact that Sigmund Freud
once stayed briefly in the strange-looking house
with mixed Venetian-Moorish style where this café
is based. It's probably the most central spot for
coffee-sipping, socialising and enjoying the eter-
nal sun on the Riva, a place to see and to be seen.
There also seems to be a permanent photo session
by prominent Split snapper and regular guest
Valentino Bilić Prcić.

## Gaga
*Iza Loža 5 (021 348 257).* **Open** 8am-2am daily.
**No credit cards. Map** p177 B2 ㉝
Just behind Narodni trg, Gaga is a permanently busy
cocktail bar filling a tiny old square (check out the
authentically retro barber's signs) with a young,
party atmosphere. Cocktails, the only drink served
from the counter set up outside, are dangerously
cheap. Inside a standard interior, loud mainstream
music keeps beer drinkers from too much conversation. Yes, that is a barber's shop from the 1960s next
door, and yes, it's still in business. There's more information on Gaga's Facebook page.

## Kavana-Restoran Bajamonti
*Trg Republike 1 (021 341 033, www.restoran-
bajamonti.hr/en).* **Open** 7am-midnight daily.
**Map** p177 A2 ㉞
Named after visionary 19th-century mayor Antonio
Bajamonti, founder of the theatre that once stood
on this spot, this suitably grand café at the top of
the arcaded square is furnished with a selection of
cosy sofas and smart upright chairs. So popular is
it among the Saturday-morning caffeine-fuelled gossip brigade that people will gladly queue for a table.
Good coffee and a choice of croissants, pastries
and cakes are the things that keep locals coming in
droves; there's also a first-floor restaurant serving
local seafood and Mediterranean pastas and salads.

## Lvxor
*Kraj sv Ivana 11 (021 341 082, www.lvxor.hr).*
**Open** 8am-midnight daily. **No credit cards.**
**Map** p177 C2 ㉟

EXPLORE

**Marcvs Marvlvs Spalatensis Library Bar.**

The black sphinx sitting on the opposite wall of the Peristil provides the inspiration behind this Egyptian-themed café, although the inner decoration, with its florid ceiling paintings and rich fabrics, leaves no style unturned. Observe the regular passage of people from the comfort of a relaxing sink-in chair. In summer, cushions are set out on the steps outside – providing what is arguably the most evocative coffee-sipping location in the entire palace. In high season, the action moves into the square, with live music and spontaneous dancing. Luxor has recently extended its terrace, offering Dalmatian food on the other side of the square.

### Marcvs Marvlvs Spalatensis Library Bar

*Papalićeva ulica 4 (098 963 7067, www.facebook. com/marvlvs).* **Open** noon-midnight daily. **No credit cards. Map** p177 C2 ㊱

This library/bar is in the heart of the Diocletian Palace, in a house where famous Renaissance writer/philosopher Marko Marulić, the father of Croatian literature, is said to have been born. The building retains many of its 15th-century features, and provides an interesting place to sip a drink and browse a vast collection of books to an easy listening soundtrack. Owner Agustin Sanchez (an Argentinian of Croatian descent) is a poet and artist himself, and has amassed a collection of Marulić works in various languages. Occasional literary evenings see both Croatian and international poetry read to a relaxed audience. This is also a rare non-smoking venue.

### Na Kantunu

*Dominisova 9 (no phone).* **Open** 7am-1am daily. **No credit cards. Map** p177 C2 ㊲

Tiny bar within the palace, with a few tables scattered outside. It's in a major hub of bars on Majstora Jurja on the palace's north side – others in the vicinity include Teak, Kala, Porta, Dante and Whisky Bar – so it's easy to find. Just follow the noise on a busy summer's evening.

### ★ Po Bota

*Šubićeva 2 (095 877 8899).* **Open** 6pm-midnight Mon-Thur, Sun; 8am-2am Fri, Sat. **No credit cards. Map** p177 B2 ㊳

Tiny Po Bota is tucked away to the left of the Milesi Palace on Trg braće Radić. There's just enough room for a couple of tables, fish motifs on a bare-brick wall, a corner of bar counter and a tap of Stare Brno. An in-the-know crowd does the rest. Hard to believe that such a small place can host art exhibitions, but it does – opening nights can be a riot.

### Split Circus

*Dosud 6 (097 782 4327, www.facebook.com/split circus).* **Open** 8am-1am Mon-Thur, Sun; 8am-2am Fri, Sat. **No credit cards. Map** p177 B2 ㊴

A cute spot on the Dosud drinking strip, Split Circus is something of a shrine to *rakija*, with a mind-boggling list that runs to far more than the usual

**EXPLORE**

# THE BEACH BOYS

*Split is the home of the seaside sport of picigin.*

For most visitors, Split's city beach of Bačvice is a modest affair – a half-moon of shingly sand a short walk from the main harbour, a couple of showers, a little greenery and shallow sea that's just right for children. But to locals, Bačvice is Wembley, the home and temple of the city's best-loved sport: picigin.

As much an art form as a sport, picigin is something like volleyball in shallow water, but with a much smaller ball, no net and usually no points. Here it is played according to the classic rules: five players and a bald tennis ball, or *balun*. Traditionally non-competitive, the aim of the game is to keep the ball out of the water for as long as possible. To this end, players bat it between each other with the palm of either hand. The artistry comes in keeping the ball dry. A dazzling leap or dive to keep the *balun* on its journey should score well – if scores are being kept.

Bačvice makes a perfect picigin pitch for two main reasons. Firstly its sandy, gently sloping beach allows for optimum acrobatic performance while minimising the risk of injury. Ideally, for speed and a cushioned fall, the water should be just above the ankles and well below the knees. Just as importantly, the beach is lined with a number of bars and cafés, so that players can strut their stuff to a relaxed and appreciative audience – in other words, females. No more peacock sport was ever invented.

Non-competitive its origins may be but picigin is being taken increasingly seriously by its aficionados. Associations and competitions are growing up around it, not least the New Year's Day's dive-off for die-hards. Off-season, you'll recognise seasoned and serious players by a distinctive limp caused by repeated injuries to their big toe. In summer, any picigin player worth his salt will be wearing the obligatory figure-hugging Speedos.

Other picigin pitches include the beaches at Sunj on Lopud near Dubrovnik; Medulin, on the southern tip of Istria, and Baška on Krk. It is even played inland, on the banks of the Drava river in Osijek, as far as you can get from Bačvice without being in Hungary.

EXPLORE

grappa, plum, herb, honey and pear varieties. If you've never had blueberry, quince or strawberry brandy, this is the place to try it. Wines and beers are also available, but take up a lot less space on the menu. A newly opened branch of Split Circus at Jadranska 1 near Bačvice beach (open 8pm-1am daily) has a bit more space for DJ events and gigs.

### ST Riva
*Obala hrvatskog narodnog 18 (095 907 5166).* **Open** 7am-2am daily. **No credit cards. Map** p177 B2 ⓶⓪
Situated on the south side of the Diocletian Palace, this bar's interior harks back to ancient Split. The intimate balcony offers a great view over the Riva promenade, making it a comfortable and intimate place from which to watch the never-ending stream of locals stroll by in a typically relaxed Dalmatian fashion. See St Riva's Facebook page for more information.

### Teak
*Majstora Jurja 11 (021 362 596).* **Open** 9am-midnight Mon-Thur, Sun; 9am-1am Fri, Sat. **No credit cards. Map** p177 C2 ⓶①
One of several busy venues in the busiest bar hub in the palace, up at its northern edge. Teak gets the nod over its rivals thanks to its convivial courtyard and under stated, wooden interior, making it stand out above the brash and the bland. Drinks prices are reasonable and the background sounds bearable. Recently, Teak has added another, posher smoke-free room.

### ★ To je to SPLIT!
*Ulica Tome Nigera 2 (no phone, www.facebook.com/ tojetocaffe).* **Open** 8am-1am daily. **No credit cards. Map** p177 A/B1 ⓶②
To je to ('That's it!') is somehow not typical among the bars in Split. It's more than just a place to drink and hang out with friends. Its owner, American Tim Bourcier, has turned it into a spot with karaoke, live music, open-mic and pub quiz nights. The place is tiny, with the smallest stage in the city, but this just adds to its casual atmosphere. It's also an excellent place to watch sport – feel free to ask them to change channels if need be. Not surprisingly, To je to boasts a healthy customer base from among Dalmatia's many expats.

### Zinfandel
*Ulica Marka Marulića 2 (021 355 135, www. facebook.com/Zinfandelsplit).* **Open** 8am-1am daily. **Map** p177 B2 ⓶③
Just outside the palace on one of the narrow medieval streets slanting away from Narodni trg, Zinfandel lays down a contemporary gauntlet to all the ancient stonework of Split's Old Town, with matt-black interior, clever lighting and suave design touches. It's primarily a wine bar (with a good selection of Dalmatian tipples by the glass) but you also get a menu of Mediterranean food (dainty portions rather than stomach fillers) and some really quite excellent platters for sharing – cold cuts, cheeses and marinated seafood.

## Shops

### ★ Art Studio Naranča
*Majstora Jurja 5 (021 344 118, www.studio naranca.com).* **Open** 9.30am-11.30pm daily. **Map** p177 C2 ⓶④ **Gallery/accessories**
Pavo Majić founded Art Studio Naranča in 1983, and it moved to this bar-filled alley in the palace in early 1990s. Naranča ('Orange') is a serious gallery specialising in graphic art. Besides selling works by some of Croatia's artists, Naranča also organises exhibitions, and Pavo is a founder of internationally recognised Graphic Biennale. There are souvenirs too, uniquely printed T-shirts, coffee mugs, even grocery bags, as well as jewellery designed by Maja Mijač Majić. There are art books too. If you can carry it home, maybe be even one of the artworks here might also catch your eye.

### bio&bio
*Morpurgova Poljana 2 (021 343 076, www.biobio. hr).* **Open** 8am-9pm Mon-Sat. **No credit cards. Map** p177 B2 ⓶⑤ **Food & drink/health & beauty**
An excellent range of organic foods, natural supplements and organic cosmetics is now available in Split. The place to go for vegetarian, vegan, macrobiotic and other ethical products, with a convenient downtown location.

### Bobis Riva
*Obala hrvatskog narodnog preporoda 20 (www.bobis-svagusa.hr).* **Open** 6am-10pm Mon-Sat; 7am-10pm Sun. **No credit cards. Map** p177 B3 ⓶⑥ **Food & drink**
'With you since 1949' says the website of this venerable and much-loved cake shop on the Riva embankment. Pastries, cream cakes, ice-creams: all can be taken away to enjoy as you stroll down the Riva or eaten in place, and there are coffees and soft drinks to accompany. Branches throughout Dalmatia.

### Crème de la Crème
*Ilićev prolaz 1 (021 355 123, www.facebook.com/ creme.delacreme).* **Open** 7.30am-11pm daily. **Map** p177 A2 ⓶⑦ **Food & drink**
One of the best pâtisseries in town. Joining Paradox Hospitality, which also owns Paradox Wine&Cheese bar and Paradigma restaurant, has improved Crème no end. It already enjoys a great location, on a small square near the lower part of Marmontova. It's in the French style of pâtisserie, with central European influences. Favourite products are the various handmade cakes, the fresh, artisanal desserts and the excellent macaroons. It's also a café, with a wide assortment of drinks, thanks to leading Split barista Nikola Besednik.

### ★ GetGetGet
*Dominisova 16 (021 341 015, www.getgetget. hr).* **Open** 9am-2pm, 5pm-8pm Mon-Fri; 9am-2pm Sat. **No credit cards. Map** p177 C2 ⓶⑧
Accessories

EXPLORE

Set in new premises downtown, this shop sells accessories and *objets d'art* made by independent local designers. There's a lot of highly individual, quirky and attractively priced stuff here, from Lidia Boševski's ceramic cups to Filip Gordon Frank's lamps.

## Judita Gourmet & Wine Shop

*Marulićeva 1 (021 355 147).* **Open** 9am-9pm daily. **Map** p177 B2 ⑲ **Food & drink**
This lovely little boutique specialises in local wines, olive oils and preserves, mainly produced by the Stella Croatica team based on Mljet. The products make good gifts or souvenirs to take home, authentic ones at that, but why not pick up one of their sausages to provide that quality touch to the picnic you're taking down to the beach?

## Kraš

*Narodni trg 6 (021 346 138, www.kras.hr).* **Open** *Summer* 7am-9pm Mon-Fri; 7am-8pm Sat. *Winter* 8am-9pm Mon-Fri; 8am-8pm Sat. **Map** p177 B2 ⑳ **Food & drink**
Approaching its centenary, one of the most famous brands in Croatia was renamed after an anti-fascist hero from World War II, Josip Kraš. The confectionery makers have since branched out from bonbons to produce wafers, tea biscuits, powders, sprinkles and oozing chocolates. Pride of place goes to Kraš Bajaderas, exquisite almond-enriched sweets, all individually wrapped and oriental in flavour. Griottes have sour-cherry centres in dark chocolate coating. There are selection and souvenir boxes too. Ideal gifts, but you may be tempted to dip in.

## Kruščić

*Obrov 6 (099 261 2345, www.facebook.com/ Kruscic.Split).* **Open** 8am-2pm daily. **No credit cards. Map** p177 B2 ㉛ **Food & drink**
There are many bakeries in Split, but this is a special place near the fish market. Kruščić, 'Little Bread', was founded back in the 1980s, but after war broke out founder Anand Štambuk moved to New York. Now he's back, and continuing where he left off. Kruščić is called an artisanal bakery for good reason. Its selection isn't huge, but if you're after bread that hasn't been mass-produced, or a pastry, this is the place to come.

## Luka Ice Cream & Cakes

*Svačićeva 2 (091 908 0678, www.facebook.com/ LukaIceCream).* **Open** 9am-11pm daily. **No credit cards. Map** p177 A1 ㉜ **Food & drink**
Split has many ice-cream parlours, but Luke Ice Cream & Cakes, opened in 2014, has turned the whole scene upside down. Before, most venues offered the routine assortment of flavours, so when Polish expat Luka Klimczak unveiled something completely new, right behind the National Theatre, it became popular almost overnight. The selection of flavours is fairly modest, but it changes on a daily basis, so you never know what you'll find among the dozen or so choices in the fridge. These might be apple pie, panacotta raspberry, blueberry or cheesecake; there might also be mojito, rosemary vanilla, fig or yoghurt with pear. Flavours taste like they're supposed to taste and all ingredients are guaranteed to be natural and fresh – and the same goes for the cakes too. Prices are competitive, and at seven kunas a scoop, you can easily go double.

## Nadalina

*Dioklecijanova 6 (021 212 651, www.nadalina-cokolade.com.hr).* **Open** 8am-8pm Mon-Sat.
**Map** p177 C2 ❸ **Food & drink**
Is chocolate-making the new rock 'n' roll? Well it certainly is as far as Marinko Biškić is concerned. The veteran Split punk rocker is the brains behind Nadalina, a range of unique, Dalmatian-flavoured chocolate bars that have become something of a cult purchase in recent years. Biškić's bars contain 70% cocoa solids and a range of this-could-only-be-Dalmatia flavours such as carob, lavender (far tastier than it sounds), dried fig and prošek dessert wine. The shop on Dioklecijanova also sells truffles and pralines by weight, alongside jars of chocolate spread. One of Nadalina's best-selling items is a piece of chocolate in the form of a seven-inch single (featuring retro Italian hit 'Guarda che Luna'), which can actually be played on a turntable prior to eating.

## ★ La Regina del Formaggio

*Bana Jelačića (091 558 4012, www.reginadel formaggio.com).* **Open** 9am-10pm daily. **No credit cards. Map** p177 A2 ❹ **Food & drink**
Right opposite the pizzeria Galija is this small venue, something between a delicatessen and an exclusive wine and cheese spot, opened in the summer of 2014 by former handball player Dijana Jelaska, who had a significant career in Italy. There she was imbued with a love of Italian food and wines. Pretty much all her products – cheeses, hams, wines, salamis, pastas – come from Italy, the major influence in Split's gastronomic scene. There are also selected smoked hams and cheeses from inland Dalmatia and, of course, the finest Croatian wines. What makes La Regina different is that almost all products are available for tasting before purchase, so it's not unusual to see people sitting in front of the shop, at the barrels that serve as tables, sipping a glass of wine and nibbling at some cheese and ham.

## Hotels

### Adriana

*Obala hrvatskog narodnog preporoda 8 (021 340 000, www.hotel-adriana.com).* €. **Map** p177 B2.
The 14 well-priced rooms above this waterfront restaurant offer a simple, comfortable stay within an easy walk of Split harbour. Some are quite small – choose if you can. Breakfast on the terrace is included in the price.

### ★ Cornaro

*Sinjska 6 (021 644 200, www.cornarohotel.com).* €€€. **Map** p177 B1.
The Cornaro is named after the nearby fortification, built in Venetian times, and its modern interior design creates an interesting mix of styles. A year after opening, this boutique lodging made significant improvements, more than doubling the number of room and suites, and making it an even smarter addition to Split's hotel stock. Now there are 74 rooms, three junior suites and one premium suite. Among the various contemporary in-room features, each has a tablet, allowing guests to order breakfast, check airline schedules and even print boarding passes. There's

**EXPLORE**

GetGetGet.

also a restaurant, wine bar, conference room and spa. With an excellent central location close to the Gallery of Fine Arts and minutes from the Diocletian's Palace, the Cornaro is one of Split's most prominent hotels.

### Dalmatian Villas
*Kralja Zvonimira 8 (021 340 680, www. dalmatinskevile.hr).* €. **Map** p175 E2.
These tastefully refurbished apartments are in traditional stone houses a short walk from the Old Town. Each apartment sleeps from two to eight people, with all the usual facilities. There are also a few double rooms priced by the week – single days are available but expect to pay a premium. The owners also have accommodation on the Dalmatian islands.

### Diocletian Heritage Hotel
*Kraj Svetog Ivana 2 (021 786 500, www. hoteldiocletian.com/en).* €€€. **Map** p177 B2.
The Diocletian is located in the historic centre of Split, surrounded by the walls of the palace of the same name. It's a small boutique hotel, with only 17 rooms – those with balconies have an excellent view of the rooftops and harbour. They are decorated to a kitsch 17th-century theme, with murals and faux-antique furniture. There's a sauna and jacuzzi, a lounge bar with roof terrace, and private parking, hard to find in central Split.

### ★ Goli & Bosi Design Hostel
*Morpurgova poljana 2 (021 510 999, www.gollybossy.com).* €. **Map** p177 A2.
Located in a thoroughly renovated historic building just outside the palace, this bold exercise in

contemporary Croatian design muscled its way into the media limelight almost immediately upon opening a few years ago. The minimalist rooms are spread across several floors, including some nifty split-level doubles and family rooms as well as larger dorms. Out in the corridors, floors are decorated with important dates from Split history and local-dialect references to famous Dalmatians. The building was used as a shopping mall from 2000 to 2010, which helps to explain the elevators and sweeping staircases that link the floors. There's an airy café-bar and restaurant in the open-plan reception area-cum-common room, and an area where films are screened on one of the upper floors. Slick, shiny, clean and good value – although it's very, very yellow.

### Jupiter Luxury Hotel
*Grabovceva Sirina 1 (021 786 500, www.lhjupiter. com).* €€€. **Map** p177 B2.
Opened in June 2012, Hotel Jupiter is situated right behind the Jupiter Temple and the Peristil in the heart of the Diocletian's Palace. It's an excellent location for those wishing to explore the history and culture of Split Old Town, and close to the main promenade and its bars and restaurants. Previously a cheap hostel, the Jupiter is small, aiming for the boutique market. Its 14 rooms are complemented by a lounge bar with roof terrace, sauna, jacuzzi and nearby parking. Wi-Fi throughout.

### Kaštel
*Mihovilova širina 5 (021 343 912, www.kastelsplit.com).* €. **Map** p177 B2.

Hidden away at the end of a narrow alleyway just off Vočni trg, Kastel was built in 1896 as a private home, converted into a hotel in 2005 and refurbished in 2008. Its ten rooms are simple, clean and very good value for small groups of palace-bound partygoers. Another pleasant surprise is that some overlook the Riva seafront – surprising, considering the main building is in a tiny cul-de-sac.

### ★ Marmont Hotel
*Zadarska 13 (021 308 060, www.marmonthotel. com). €€. Map p177 B2.*
Opened in 2009, this swish city-centre property is close to the palace and comprises 21 rooms, a presidential suite and a roof terrace – all in a tastefully refurbished historical house. Original exposed stone, wooden floors and minimalist style characterise the common areas – classy walnut furniture and free Wi-Fi feature in the guestrooms. There's a restaurant, the Marshall, on the ground floor, named in honour of Marshall Marmont, the governor of Dalmatia in Napoleon's day.

### Piazza Luxury Suites
*Kraj Svete Marije 1 (021 553 377, www.piazza-luxurysuites.com). €€€. Map p177 B2.*
A small boutique hotel set on a central city square. Both exterior and interior are like nothing you'll see elsewhere in Split. This art nouveau building, erected in 1906, looks as if it should be in Vienna. The suites themselves are on the first floor, seven luxurious rooms decorated like a stylish 18th-century salon. The rooms are big and comfortable, with all the usual four-star amenities. As you're in the hub of the city, everything and everyone passes by the hotel windows, providing endless opportunities for people-watching.

### Peristil
*Poljana kraljice Jelene 5 (021 329 070, www.hotelperistil.com). €€. Map p177 C2.*
This modern hotel in the palace now has a terrace restaurant, the Tifani, overlooking the Peristil. There are nine simple, comfortable doubles and three singles, all reasonable for the price and location. Rooms are artfully decorated with wooden floors and taffeta curtains, and contain TVs.

### ★ President
*Starčevićeva 1 (021 305 222, www.hotelpresident.hr). €€. Map p177 B1.*
Behind the National Theatre, the President is one of Split's best-kept secrets. Superbly finished in period style, the hotel has 63 rooms of varying size and ten suites, all with jacuzzis and the latest mod cons. It's classy, spacious and centrally located.

### Slavija
*Buvinina 2 (021 323 840, www.hotelslavija.hr). €€. Map p177 B2.*
For years this was the only hotel in the palace. A recent refurbishment has seen all 25 rooms fitted with showers and a TV. Unfortunately, rooms

overlooking the bar-lined alleyway outside will still have nightlife noise drifting up until 1am at least.

### Sobe Simoni
*Zlodrina poljana (021 488 780, www.sobesimoni. com). €. No credit cards. Map p175 E2.*
Tucked away in a quiet street behind the railway station, this small, friendly and convenient place offers some of the best value digs in Split. Ask for a room with air-conditioning.

### Vestibul Palace
*Iza Vestibula 4 (021 329 329, www.vestibulpalace. com). €€€. Map p177 C2.*
Set in a modest little building adjoining the open-roofed vestibule in the palace, this friendly seven-room boutique hotel is certainly swish. Rooms have nice decorative touches, such as natural brick, but the building simply isn't big enough to allow for many additional facilities. There is a restaurant, the Diocles, and tables outside on the square beside the Ethnography Museum. Extra accommodation is available at the Villa Dobrić annexe just a few steps away to the west, a stone medieval building comprising two guestrooms on the first floor, with two junior suites sit above. There are good weekend deals available if you book off-season.

### Villa Dobrić
*Dobrić VII (021 308 000, www.vestibulpalace.com). €€. Map p177 B2.*
The Dobrić, under the same ownership as the Hotel Vestibul Palace, has two guestrooms on the first floor and two junior suites above. The stone walls and the lobby bar (with inside and outside terraces) display style you would expect from the Vestibul stable.

## AWAY FROM THE PALACE

North of the National Theatre, the arterial street of Zrinsko Frankopanska leads to the **Archaeological Museum**. A short climb northwest takes you to the Poljud stadium, home of local football club Hajduk Split and still a modern-architecture masterpiece. The arena also hosts the major DJ festival Ultra Europe in July.

Two further cultural attractions are set within reasonably easy reach. The most rewarding is Ivan Meštrović's own **Meštrović Gallery**, a neoclassical villa built by the sculptor himself in 1931. Down the street, the **Kaštelet** at no.39 (same admission ticket) accommodates his religious carvings. The beach below, also called Kaštelet, is less well known but has a couple of decent bars on it.

Most locals prefer bustling **Bačvice beach** (*see p182* The Beach Boys) to the east, where games of *picigin* keep young locals occupied. Beyond it, the waterfront developments at **Firule** and **Zenta** contain key restaurants, mainstream nightspots and the tennis centre where Wimbledon champion Goran Ivanišević first played.

**EXPLORE**

Meštrović Gallery.

**EXPLORE**

## Sights & Museums

### Archaeological Museum

*Zrinsko-Frankopanska 25 (021 329 340, www.mdc.hr/split-arheoloski).* **Open** *June-Sept* 9am-2pm, 4-8pm Mon-Sat. *Oct-May* 9am-2pm, 4-8pm Mon-Fri; 9am-2pm Sat. **Admission** 15kn. **No credit cards. Map** p175 D1 ⑤⑤
Just north of the National Theatre stands the Archaeological Museum where key historical finds from the nearby Roman capital of Salona are the main draw: mosaics, sarcophagi and such like. The permanent exhibition covers the Greek and Roman periods, as well as pagan and medieval. All in all, a worthy attraction a shortish walk from the city centre.

### Kaštelet

*Šetalište Ivana Meštrovića 39 (021 340 800, www.mestrovic.hr).* **Open** *May-Sept* 9am-7pm Tue-Sun. *Oct-Apr* 9am-4pm Tue-Sat; 10am-3pm Sun. **Admission** combined with Meštrović Gallery 30kn. **No credit cards. Map** p174 C2 ⑤⑥
Standing near the Meštrović Gallery and converted from a 16th-century summer house by the famous sculptor himself, this is where you'll find the most satisfying of all his works, a series of 28 reliefs carved out of wood loosely illustrating the life of Christ. You'll notice touches of folk art, modernism and classicism as you gaze at what represents two decades of labour on the part of this 20th-century master. The building, too, has religious echoes.

### ★ Meštrović Gallery

*Šetalište Ivana Meštrovića 46 (021 340 800, www.mestrovic.hr).* **Open** *May-Sept* 9am-7pm Tue-Sun. *Oct-Apr* 9am-4pm Tue-Sat; 10am-3pm Sun. **Admission** combined with Kaštelet 30kn. **No credit cards. Map** p174 C2 ⑤⑦
Probably the most rewarding of Split's cultural attractions is Ivan Meštrović's own gallery, a neo-classical villa built by the man himself in 1931. Not only does it display the range of work created by Croatia's most renowned sculptor – statues large and small, even portraits, all with classical, folk and modernist influences – but it tells the remarkable story of his life growing up in a country that became Yugoslavia. Visits can be combined with entry to the nearby Kaštelet, which houses his religious works.

## Restaurants

### Adriatic Grašo

*Uvala Baluni (021 398 560, www.adriaticgraso. com).* **Open** noon-midnight daily. €€. **Map** p175 D2 ⑤⑧ **Dalmatian**
Occupying a raised promontory just above the ACI marina, this glass-enclosed pavilion offers superb views of the Adriatic, with outdoor tables stretching along the promontory towards the south. The main, formal part of the restaurant occupies the western

side of the building: here the menu concentrates on classy Dalmatian fish and seafood dishes, prepared with a focus on originality and attention to detail. On the eastern side of the building is the Adriatic Grašo pizzeria – a relaxed and inexpensive place to sample good food and enjoy splendid views. Owner Zoran Grašo is an ex-basketball star and his son Petar is a well-known singer, so it's no surprise that this place is popular with Split society.

### Boban
*Hektorovićeva 49 (021 543 300, 098 208 407, www.restaurant-boban.com).* **Open** noon-midnight daily. €€. **Map** p175 F2 ⑤ **Dalmatian**
Opened in 1973 and praised in Croatia's top food guides, Boban is tucked among residential buildings a short walk up from Firule – the taxi driver will know it. Specialities include house-made gnocchi filled with scampi and prosciutto, *filet mignon* in red wine and truffle sauce, and monkfish fillets wrapped in pancetta and served on rice with a cream sauce. Expect the best local wines.

### ★ Cardo
*Hotel Atrium, Domovinskog rata 49A (021 200 000, www.hotel-atrium.hr/restaurant-cardo.htm).* **Open** noon-midnight daily. €€. **Map** p175 E1 ⑩ **Dalmatian/modern European**
The Hotel Atrium's big ground-floor restaurant has been renamed after one of the main streets in the Diocletian's Palace but remains acknowledged as one of the city's prime culinary destinations. Here the traditional Dalmatian repertoire is jazzed up with an injection of modern European attitude. The kitchen sticks to a handful of top-notch dishes: fish mains are limited to fillets of sea bass served in inventive combinations of sauce and garnish – and there's usually at least one classic game, fowl and steak selection on the menu. Risotto with spinach and asparagus is the perfect choice for a light and delicate lunch, while the house take on Dalmatia's favourite stew (*pašticada*) delivers satisfyingly generous portions of succulent meat. An unusual speciality is a selection of dishes prepared after recipes in the only cookbook that has survived from the Roman era, written by Marcus Gavius Apicius. One such dish is roast lamb 'haedum pasticum', boiled in prune sauce with white wine and sun-dried herbs, seasoned with balsamic vinegar.

### Dvor
*Put Firula 14 (021 571 513).* **Open** 8am-1am daily. €€. **Map** p175 F2 ⑪ **Dalmatian**
Situated just above the coastal path that works its way east from Bačvice Beach, Dvor is a uniquely calming place from which to admire the inviting silhouettes of Šolta and Brač across the water. Sit in the conservatory or venture out on to the terrace shaded by trees. Dvor functions perfectly both as café and restaurant – fish, steak and fowl are fired up on the open grill overlooking the lawn outside, and there's

an excellent choice of Croatian wines by the glass. Its Facebook page has more information.

### Kadena
*Ivana pl Zajca (021 389 400, www.restoran kadena.com).* **Open** 9am-midnight Mon-Thur, Sun; 9am-1am Fri, Sat. €€€. **Map** p175 F2 ⑫ **Dalmatian/Mediterranean**
On a panoramic terrace, Kadena enjoys fabulous views over Zenta Marina towards the distant islands. Various *bruschette* and creative desserts add to a classic Dalmatian menu already given an extra dimension by the imaginative introduction of additional ingredients and sauces. The creative force behind it all is Braco Sanjin, renowned in Croatia for his personal interpretation of Mediterranean seafood. The wine list requires a huge cellar. Ideal for a romantic dinner.

### Kebap & Meze bar İştah
*Put Supavla 1 (021 380 640, www.istah.hr).* **Open** noon-8pm Mon-Thur, Sun; 1-11pm Fri; noon-11pm Sat. €. **No credit cards**. **Map** p175 D1 ⑬ **Turkish**
Non-Croatian cuisine in Split has developed significantly of late. One place at the forefront of this global push is İştah, Split's first Turkish restaurant, owned and operated by Onad Ozyurt and his Split-born wife Tanja, in an office building close to the Poljud stadium. A traditional Turkish menu has a wide range of vegetable and meaty meze dishes, plus kebabs and other mains. Prices are more than friendly and the food even better than these prices might suggest. İştah is also the only venue of any kind in Dalmatia with a halal certificate. It's a dry ship too, but the mint lemonades are just what you might need in the middle of summer.

### Konoba
*Obala pomoraca, Vranjic (095 707 0777).* **Open** *Summer* 4-11pm Tue-Sun. *Winter* 10.30am-5pm Tue-Sun. €. **Dalmatian**
In the age of socialist industrialisation, Vranjic was surrounded by factories and Split's nearby cargo port. They are still there, some of them not working, but this small peninsula between Split and Solin has since regained some of the charm that once earned it the nickname of 'Little Venice'. It's a classic Dalmatian village, with stone-built houses, narrow alleys and a sun-bathed waterfront. Davor Grabovac and his wife Nataša opened a new venue here in 2015, calling it, simply, Konoba (a common term for 'tavern' and also a place where people kept their wine, oil and anything else they produced). The setting is simple, pleasant and intimate, with only ten inside tables, and since 'Graba' is also a fish supplier for the local market and other restaurants, his menu is pure improvisation. Whatever the daily catch, that's what you'll get. Sometimes, it will be just sardines or some other small blue fish, grilled or fried, or their main speciality, a conger 'painted white' – a sort of

**EXPLORE**

brodetto. Prices are reasonable, and there are parking spaces between the restaurant and the sea. The restaurant's Facebook page has more information.

### ★ Konoba Hvaranin
*Ban Mladenova 9 (099 667 5891).* **Open** 11am-midnight daily. **€. Map** p175 D1 🔢 **Dalmatian**
Once a bland café, the Radovani family's Hvaranin is one of the liveliest of Split's traditional venues. With mum and dad in the kitchen and son behind the bar, this is a second home for many journalists and writers, whose books sit on the shelves. Everything is simple, home-made and delicious. Specials include gregada fish stew Hvar-style, and white risotto with mussels. Don't miss the traditional dessert, *rožata* crème caramel. Seating is limited so book ahead. There's more information on the restaurant's Facebook page.

### Konoba Marjan
*Senjska 1 (098 934 6848, www.facebook.com/ KonobaMarjan).* **Open** 11am-11pm daily. **€. Map** p175 D1 🔢 **Dalmatian**
This small, family-run, checked-tablecloth restaurant in the heart of the Varoš quarter is a long-standing local favourite. Pretty much everything in the Adriatic seafood repertoire is here – grilled fresh fish, seafood risottos, scampi and squid. It's also the kind of place where you will find traditional Dalmatian fare like *pašticada*, the trademark local stew made from beef marinated in wine and prunes.

### Konoba Matejuška
*Tomića stine 3 (021 355 152, www.konoba matejuska.hr).* **Open** noon-11pm Tue-Sat; noon-5pm Sun. **€. Map** p175 D1 🔢 **Dalmatian**
Hidden way in an alley just off the main road into the Varoš quarter, this is another excellent family-run *konoba* in an area that's increasingly well known for them, with five or six tables squeezed into a homely dining room slightly below street level. Matejuška very much sticks to the basics: grilled fresh fish priced by weight (they'll show you what they've got and let you choose). The tuna marinated in red wine and herbs makes an excellent two-person starter. Prices are fair and the house wine is good and cheap.

### ma:Toni
*Prilaz braće Kaliterna 6 (021 278 457, www. facebook.com/konobamatoni).* **Open** noon-10pm daily. **€. Map** p175 E2 🔢 **Dalmatian**
The former home to the Enoteca Terra restaurant and wine shop, and then the Tinita tavern, this stone-clad basement of a century-old building behind Bačvice now houses a brand new venture: ma:Toni. 'Matoni' was opened in late 2014 by a couple: Toni Arnerić, the chef, and his girlfriend Tisija Prohić, responsible for front of house. Unlike many other venues with orthodox traditional Dalmatian cuisine, ma:Toni's menu brings non-conventional creations, such as

home-made pasta with beef cheeks, gnocchi with duck breast, bull's tail with mashed carrots and lamb-liver stew. Imaginative vegan-inspired dishes include palako pear: pear in black tea with vegan chocolate and ice-cream. With a location just metres from Bačvice beach, this place has potential in spades, and its dungeon-like setting provides welcome refreshment on hot days, especially when combined with a soundtrack of jazz, funk and bossa nova.

### Le Monde
*Plinarska 6 (021 322 264).* **Open** 10am-11pm daily. **€€. Map** p175 D1 🔢 **Dalmatian**
Le Monde is tucked in an alley behind the National Theatre. With an upstairs dining room and a beautiful courtyard alongside, it's an eminently soothing place in which to tuck into classy Dalmatian dishes. Mainstays are fish fillets in rich sauces and classic cuts of steak and veal. Your attentive waiter will also recommend the special of the day. Le Monde's Facebook page has more information.

### Oštarija U Vidjakovi
*Prilaz braće Kaliterna 8 (021 489 106, ostarijauvidjakovi.com).* **Open** 9am-midnight daily. **€. Map** p175 E2 🔢 **Dalmatian**
Between the port and Bačvice this homely *konoba* offers simple relaxation. Pictures of Split throughout its history hang beside old Hajduk ones. Tasty, well-priced food keeps locals happy: peppers stuffed with mincemeat and rice, *pašticada* stew and fish served in the Dalmatian way with *blitva* greens.

### Pimpinella
*Spinčićeva 2A (021 389 606, www.pimpinella.hr).* **Open** 9am-midnight Mon-Sat. **€. Map** p175 F2 🔢 **Dalmatian**
The unabashedly modest Pimpinella is one of the most popular lunch spots in Split, with a list of inexpensive daily specials chalked-up in the dining room. Although they might not be on offer every day, the kitchen prides itself on its steak or fish prepared on a charcoal grill, its black risotto with shellfish, its gregada fish stew and its octopus or veal *peka* slowly cooked with potatoes under a baking bell. A small front terrace contains a couple of tables handily placed in the shade.

### Pizzeria Skipper
*Uvala Baluni (021 398 437, www.skipper-graso. com).* **Open** 11am-midnight daily. **€. Map** p175 D2 🔢 **Pizzeria/grill**
The self-contained pizza section of the highly regarded Adriatic Grašo restaurant has a reputation in its own right, thanks to the good-quality, thin-crust pizzas turned out by its log-fired oven. Amazing views of downtown Split also help, albeit from the sometimes rather windy terrace. Traditional grilled meats (*ćevapi, pljeskavice*) form part of the menu – fans of Balkan *roštilj* will consider the pilgrimage here worthwhile.

## Re di mare

*Lučica 4 (095 725 5555, www.redimare.com).*
**Open** 8am-1am Mon-Thur; 8am-2am Fri, Sat;
8am-midnight Sun. **€€. Map** p174 C1 **72 Seafood**
Re di mare once was a place where boat owners at the
Spinut sport marina could have a quick lunch. Since
a change of ownership, it has become one of the leading places in Split for seafood, mostly undiscovered
by tourists due to its off-the-beaten-path location.
This marina is not one in regular use by foreign
sailors, but a place where locals keep their boats for
tours around nearby islands. The restaurant terrace
provides a beautiful view across the marina and the
bay of Kaštela, all very different from the summer
hubbub around the Diocletian's Palace. The main
element brought in by the new owners is the selection of fish – they also own a chain of fish stores that
supplies many local restaurants. Yet the food in Re di
mare is rather simple, always reliable, and the grill
chef is a master of his craft. The fish platter for two,
with vegetables on the side, would be a wise choice
here, the daily catch sure to be fresh. Prices are reasonable, in fact lower than in some of the more promoted downtown restaurants of the same category.

## ★ Šperun

*Šperun 3 (021 346 999).* **Open** *Feb-Dec* 9am-11pm
daily. **€. Map** p175 D1 **73 Dalmatian**
This great little Dalmatian bistro is just behind Sv
Frane church near the Riva. In a neat rustic interior, a
table groans with Adriatic goodies – little fish, fresh
vegetables, olive oils and so on. Prices here are completely reasonable – even for a blue fish mixed grill,
grilled tuna with capers or oven-roasted sea bream
with olives – and the portions generous. Marinated
cheese and octopus salad feature among the many
starters – or let the waiter recommend something
from the cheap-and-quick daily specials.

## Stare Grede

*Dominovskog rata 46 (021 485 501, www.
restaurant-konoba-staregrede.com).* **Open**
*Summer* 9am-11pm daily. *Winter* 9am-11pm Mon-
Sat; noon-11pm Sun. **€. Map** p175 E1 **74 Grill**
On the main road heading north from the city centre,
near the Art Hotel, this spot would be easy to miss.
It's enormously popular with the locals on account
of its meaty main courses, with inexpensive roast
meats, meat stews and goulash delivered in generous portions. Grilled squid, fish fillets and brodet
fish stew are the order of the day on Fridays. It gets
busy at weekday lunchtimes and weekend evenings,
so book or be prepared to wait.

## Stellon

*Bačvice (021 489 200).* **Open** 10am-midnight Mon-
Fri; 10am-1am Sat, Sun. **€. Map** p175 F2 **75**
**Pizzeria/Dalmatian**
Named after Luciano Stelli, a founder of local foot-
ball club Hajduk, this fashionable spot is owned by
ex-Hajduk, Barcelona and Cologne midfielder Goran

Vučević. It's a fine place for a drink, to dine out, or
simply to be seen. Overlooking Bačvice, the terrace
is divided between bar and restaurant. Modestly
described as a pizzeria, the latter offers grilled fish (sea
bream, angler), gnocchi with truffles, and so on. Book at
weekends when you're passing by during the day. The
restaurant's Facebook page has more information.

## Toć

*Segvićeva 1 (021 488 409).* **Open** 8am-11pm daily.
**€. Map** p175 E2 **76 Dalmatian**
A five-minute walk from the Riva, this smart but
affordable neighbourhood *konoba* is a good place
for traditional Dalmatian lunches, with squid risottos, simple fish fillets and home-made pasta with
goulash combinations frequently chalked up on a
board outside. Whatever you eat, be sure to include
dessert in your dining plans – the home-made cakes
are in a class of their own. See the Facebook page
for more information.

## Trattoria Tinel

*Tomića stine 1 (021 355 197, www.trattoria-tinel.
com).* **Open** 8am-midnight daily. **€. Map** p175 D1
**77 Dalmatian**
The growing cluster of restaurants at the gateway
to the Varoš quarter is slowly turning the area into
one of Split's prime dining-out strips. Latest addition Tinel is another establishment that endeavours
to deliver quality Dalmatian fare at affordable prices,
with seafood risottos and pastas in the 50kn range,
and the likes of scampi and lobster at the more
expensive end of the menu. The restaurant features a refreshingly neat and colourful interior that
doesn't go in for retro Dalmatian clichés, and a cosy
outdoor terrace at the back.

## Velo Misto

*Šetalište Kalafata 2 (021 388 777, www.velomisto.
hr).* **Open** 10am-midnight Mon-Thur; 10am-1am
Fri, Sat. **€. Map** p175 F2 **78 Pizzeria/Dalmatian**
Overlooking Zenta Marina, this modern restaurant
is as expansive as its menu, yet still has queues on
Saturday nights in winter. The walls display the
work of a keen photographer and outside there's
a bare terrace looking out over the boats. Food
includes good pizzas and great prices, decent grilled
meat, a fish platter for two and a stellar squid stuffed
with *pršut* and sheeps' cheese.

# Cafés & Bars

## Clo Bar

*Domovinskog rata 104B (098 177 0314, www.do.
hr).* **Open** 7am-2am Mon-Thur, Sun; 8am-2am Fri,
Sat. **No credit cards. Map** p175 E1 **79**
Opened by the former manager of Hedonist in 2014,
the Clo Bar is one of the most popular café-club venues to appear of late, with a spacious, well-designed
interior that lends itself perfectly to a relaxing spot
of coffee-sipping during the day, and more raucous

**EXPLORE**

DJ-fuelled fun at night. A good deal of thought and creativity has gone into the furnishings, with cucumber-cool grey and white surfaces setting off straight-backed seats in primary colours. It's a little way out of central Split on the main road to Solin, but is straightforward to reach in a taxi.

### F-Marine
*Obala kneza Branimira (098 939 6214, www. facebook.com/fmarineST).* **Open** 7am-midnight daily. **Map** p175 D2 ⑥
The Riva and Diocletian's Palace are the busiest places in Split. To observe both at the same time, find a spot in F-Marine. It's based at Zapadna obala, the western Riva, a newly remodelled part of the promenade with a view towards the Old Town and the city harbour. It's ideal for both morning coffee and drinks after dark. If it's full, there are two more 'F' venues on the same promenade: F-Maduro and restaurant F-De Mar. They are all part of the chain that also runs the F-Caffe on the Riva and the travel agency F-Tours.

### Kavana Ovčice
*Put Firula 4 (095 817 6171, www.facebook.com/ pages/Kavana-Ovčice/651929101550890).* **Open** 8am-1am daily. **No credit cards. Map** p175 F2 ⑥
The seaside strip of east Split features clear seawater and numerous bars, clubs and restaurants. After recent renovation, Kavana Ovčice is one of the more pleasant options. It's set on a small pebbled beach between the two main ones of Bačvice and Firule. During the day, year-round, it's a great spot for slow coffee sipping. During the swimming season, it changes character because you can enjoy your drinks with your feet dipped in the sea. It comes alive at night; regular weekly live acts, mostly local rock and blues cover bands, churn out a few old favourites. There are also literary readings and other events. Search for 'Beach bar Ovčice' on Facebook for more details.

### Kobaje
*Vukovarska 35A (095 898 9889, www.facebook. com/kobajekobaje).* **Open** 10am-midnight daily. **Map** p175 F1 ⑥
Launched after high season in 2014, Kobaje is off the beaten track. Its owner also runs a wine store near Bačvice, so it was something of a surprise when he decided to have this combination of a pub and a snack-like eatery. That wasn't the only surprise. Kobaje probably has the biggest beer selection in town, with dozens from Belgium, the Czech Republic, Germany and Mexico, among others. To help all those beers go down smoothly, Kobaje (a slang word for 'sausages') has quality grilled meats.

### ProCaffe
*Spinutska ulica 67 (021 384 323).* **Open** 7am-midnight Mon-Sat; 8am-midnight Sun. **Map** p175 D1 ⑥
ProCaffe is in an area called Spinut, close to the Poljud football stadium and Marjan hill. Inside

**Wine & Cheese Bar Paradox.**

it's stylish, maybe even too stylish, with a space recently refurbished as a Baroque tea room. It also has one of the most beautiful terraces in town, with a great view toward Kaštela, a completely different perspective of Split from the one you might see in the Old Town. Next door is another good reason to visit: a great selection of cakes. Search for 'Kavana ProCaffe' on Facebook.

### Treće Poluvrijeme (Kuka)
*Zrinsko-Frankopanska 17 (no phone).* **Open** 6am-midnight Mon-Thur, Sun; 9pm-6am Fri, Sat. **No credit cards. Map** p175 D1 ⑥
If it's past the palace closing time of 1am and you're still thirsty, head to this small bar behind the National Theatre near the old football ground; everyone else does. The 'Third Half' is handy for post-match relaxation while rock, pop and house sounds keep you out of mischief until dawn. Don't be surprised to see burly types covered in mud meeting up for coffee during the day – Treće Poluvrijeme is the main post-training meeting point for members of Split rugby club next door.

### ★ Vidilica
*Prilaz Vladimira Nazora 1 (021 394 925).* **Open** *Mar-Dec* 8am-midnight daily. **No credit cards. Map** p175 D2 ⑥

No terrace offers a better view than this, the whole of Split laid out before you – and islands beyond – from atop Marjan hill. The bar contains blown-up sepia postcards of pre-war Split but most customers try to find an outside table; a stone wall guards the steep drop. To get here, climb the stepped streets of the evocative Varoš quarter.

### Wine & Cheese Bar Paradox
*Poljana Tina Ujevića 2 (021 395 854, www. paradox.hr).* **Open** *Summer* 9am-1am Mon-Fri; 9am-2am Sat, Sun. *Winter* 9am-midnight Mon-Sat; 5pm-midnight Sun. **Map** p175 D1 ⊛
One of the hits of recent years, Paradox offers pretty much what it says in the title – wine by the glass, and platters of Croatian and international cheeses to help it slip down. The interior is quite small; the crowd outside on the pavement creates the buzz.

### ★ Žbirac
*Bačvice (091 883 3710, zbirac.com).* **Open** 7am-1am Mon-Thur, Sun; 7am-2am Fri, Sat. **No credit cards. Map** p175 E2 ⊛
The best of the Bačvice bars, this one is a small detached terrace right on the beach whose popularity is due to a slightly more clued-up clientele than the young locals on the pull in the main Bačvice pavilion. The little touches make it, too – the framed old colour photographs of the same Bačvice view you're gawping at, the comical picture of fat blokes playing football on the menu cover. Once it closes, there are later options just beyond the beach in the pavilion.

## Shops

### Mali dućan-Matejuška
*Trumbićeva obala 7 (www.facebook.com/ maliducanmatejuska).* **Open** 6.30am-midnight Mon-Thur; 6.30am 1am Fri-Sat; 7am-9pm Sun. **No credit cards. Map** p175 D2 ⊛ **Food & drink**
In the last few years, one of the most popular spots in summer – especially for younger locals – is Matejuška, the old fishermen's cove near the Riva. Recently joined by tourists, they sit around and sip beers on the seafront. These drinks come from Mali dućan ('Little Shop'), something more than just a corner shop. This is the best-supplied store in town for beer. Here there are more than 150 varieties from all over the world, with a reasonable pricing policy too.

### Ribarnica Brač
*Ulica 8, Mediteranskih igara 9 (021 380 668).* **Open** 7am-8pm daily. **Map** p175 D1 ⊛ **Food & drink**
Mention Ribarnica ('fish market') in Split, and the first association is with the old one in the city centre. Recently, there is another venue is being mentioned,

and visited. It's the Ribarnica Brač and its main store is close to the Poljud stadium. There are four more in Split and around, the same people run the excellent restaurant Re di mare. Ribarnica Brač has the fresh, daily catch – ideal for anyone who wants to test their cooking skills when on holiday. Under the same roof is a small deli with salads and risottos, seafood pasta, stews, fish sandwiches and plain fried fish. Search for 'Ribarnica Brač' on Facebook.

## Nightlife

### Hedonist

*Put Firule (099 211 0203, hedonist.fullbusiness. com).* **Open** 7am-2am daily. **No credit cards. Map** p175 F2.

Opposite Firule's tennis courts, Hedonist has been a swift hit with affluent young Splićani after a celebrity champagne-and-oysters opening in 2009. The modest exterior hides an interior that is also modest, in size, but full of colourful cushions on benches that face uncomfortable-looking chairs in the shape of question marks. Irrespective, the party soon starts to swing with house and lounge music, while le tout Split floods in. Hedonist shares owners with Egoist, an equally cool café on the same street.

### Hemingway Bar Split

*Osmih Mediteranskih igara 5 (099 211 9993, www.hemingway.hr/split).* **Open** 10am-midnight Mon-Thur, Sun; 8am-4am Fri, Sat.

Upmarket chain Hemingway took over from the long-established Tribu, down by the sea near the Poljud stadium. A large central bar is complemented by an equally large and chic interior, plus an outdoor area. It's a huge space to fill, but this venue packs in trendy young things every night. The brand, established in Zagreb, Opatija and elsewhere, is best known for its quality cocktails. It's pricey by local standards, hence the fashionable crowd and domestic pop stars who show face.

### ★ Imperium

*Gat svetog Duje (www.imperium.hr).* **Open** 8am-1am Mon-Thur, Sun; 8am-5am Fri, Sat. **No credit cards. Map** p175 E2.

Occupying virtually the entire top floor of Split's passenger ferry terminal, Imperium hosts DJ parties at weekends, and live gigs by pop and pop-folk attractions from all over Croatia and the rest of the former Yugoslavia. A polished black stairway leads to a long, rectangular lounge, its lines broken up by partitions perforated with porthole-effect circular openings; swanky modern sofas are strewn with cushions. Imperium offers sweeping views in every direction; ferry passengers can stop off for a pre-boarding coffee.

### Judino drvo

*Kopilica 24 (no phone, www.facebook.com/judino drvo).* **Open** according to programme. **Admission** varies. **No credit cards.**

The same team responsible for the excellent alternative club Minus3 a few years ago came back in 2014 with an even bigger project, Judino drvo ('The Judas Tree'), based in deserted railroad warehouses in the suburb of Kopilica. The interior is post-industrial chic-cum-art installation with similar attention paid to important issues such as the sound system. Judino drvo is hard to find for any outsider, and there is no bus or other public transport that comes here, so the club has hired a taxi service (Krema, 091 230 0300). Gigs usually begin around 11pm, sometimes later, and the line-up might include some of the biggest names in Croatian rock 'n' roll, and from across the former Yugoslavia. Occasionally there are international acts, including DJs. Tickets are usually available at the downtown Goli&Bosi hostel.

### Jungla Club

*Šetalište Ivana Meštrovića (098 745 557, www. facebook.com/JunglaClub).* **Open** 8am-midnight Mon-Wed, Sun; 8am-4am Thur; 8am-6am Fri, Sat. **No credit cards. Map** p175 D2.

At the city end of Ivana Meštrovića, near the ACI Marina, this prominent terrace bar offers relaxation after a day at Kaštelet beach. Families and couples gather over evening drinks on the terrace. After dark, techno and house DJs such as Craig Walsh and Nathan Coles take over.

### Kocka

*Savska (021 540 537, www.kum-split.hr).* **Open** Oct-June according to schedule. **No credit cards. Map** p175 F1.

A legendary performance space in the Youth Cultural Centre basement, Kocka hosted punk, electro, drum 'n' bass or techno in gritty, graffiti-and-concrete surroundings. After a break in activity, the venue was revived in late 2014 with a string of non-mainstream concerts of Croatian and international bands. Admission prices and drinks are cheap, concerts are announced with posters and flyers around the city, or by local listings resources such as infozona.hr.

### Legends Bar

*Bačvice (091 531 0360, www.facebook.com/The LegendsBarSplit).* **Open** 8pm-4am daily. **Admission** varies. **No credit cards. Map** p175 F2.

Legends has been in business for several years, but after turmoil, closures and moves, it finally settled at its best location – at the eastern-most end of the main city beach of Bačvice. Recently, it has become a popular destination for loud and live rock 'n' roll almost on a nightly basis, mostly by Croatian bands. Like everywhere in Split, concerts begin around 11pm or even later. Tickets are usually available on the door.

### O'Hara Music Club

*Uvala Zenta 3 (091 794 1349, www.ohara.hr).* **Open** 9am-6am daily. **Map** p175 F2.

On the Zenta waterfront, O'Hara's has attracted locals and tourists with a wide variety of music, from reggae to Dalmatian folk, since opening in 2004 on a site previously occupied by a brace of cult bars and clubs. It's a popular venue for rock gigs as well as weekend DJ sessions, and you'll frequently see O'Hara posters plastered around town on the eve of big events. Two floors, a summer terrace and outside bar allow plenty of space to dance or relax.

### ★ Obojena Svjetlost
*Šetalište Ivana Meštrovića 35 (021 358 280).* **Open** noon-3am daily. **No credit cards.** **Map** p174 C2.
The wide terrace of this disco-bar is right on Kaštelet beach, on a quieter stretch of seafront below the Meštrović Gallery – look out for the green Zlatorog beer sign on the main road above. Palm trees and wicker chairs create an idyllic tableau; inside, Coloured Light puts on DJs and regular live music, an open-air attraction in summer. It's a handy alternative to Bačvice and fairly central too.

### Octopus Bowling
*Ulica Jurja Dobrile 1 (021 469 070, www.bowling-split.com/hr).* **Open** 8am-1am Mon-Fri; 8am-2am Sat, Sun. **No credit cards.**
Not just regular bowling, but disco bowling. Harking back to old-school TV shows, this is a great idea for an unconventional night out with friends. Local DJs provide the soundtrack, whilst the bar offers a variety of drinks including their speciality Žirafa, a metre-high beer. Very reasonably priced, it also offers party packages: two hours of bowling, a jumbo-sized pizza and a Žirafa for €30.

### Quasimodo
*Gundulićeva 26 (www.facebook.com/quasimodoklub).* **Open** 7pm-2am Mon-Thur, Sun; 9pm-4am Fri, Sat. **No credit cards.** **Map** p175 E1.
Located somewhat improbably on the second floor of an office block, the minimally decorated, moodily lit Quasimodo is Split's leading venue for indie gigs and DJ nights – if leading bands from Croatia or the former Yugoslavia are on tour, then it's probably Quasimodo where they'll play. With spoken-word evenings and pub quizzes also featuring on the programme, it's an important cultural hub as well as an excellent alt-rock drinking den.

### Tropic Club
*Bačvice (099 203 9222, www.tropic.hr).* **Open** May-Oct 10.30am-5am daily. **No credit cards.** **Map** p175 E2.
Occupying a sweeping first-floor terrace jutting out over the Adriatic, the Tropic (still known as the 'Equador' to many) is glitzy enough to be a nightspot, informal enough to be a comfortable café-bar meeting point. By day it's ideal for a post-beach sundowner, by night it's a disco bar, crowds milling, finding floor space to dance near the half-moon of starlit patio.

### Vanilla
*Bazeni Poljud, Poljudsko šetalište (098 831 3050, www.vanilla.hr).* **Open** 8am-10pm Mon-Thur; 8am-5am Fri, Sat.
Adjoining the Hemingway in the sports complex, Vanilla is the kind of place that Croatians call 'fancy': it sells drinks with umbrellas in, and its crowd is over-dressed. As a pre-club bar, Vanilla does a job, although it's really just some wicker furniture overlooking a pool and clubby music.

## Hotels

### ★ 101 Dalmatinac Design Hostel
*114 Brigade 10 (021 585 270, www.101 dalmatian.com).* **€.**
This modern hostel opened in 2014, right on time for July's Ultra Europe DJ festival. Taking its decorative cues from both the region and the dog breed, Dalmatinac has exactly 101 beds, each one of them is named after different island, with basic facts about the relevant island on the wall by that bed. Each room has a shower and toilet, and there are doubles available too. Beds in dorms have adjacent lockers. There are also public spaces with a games room and a TV lounge, plus free Wi-Fi everywhere, 24/7 reception, washing machines, restaurant and bar. The hostel is pretty far from the city centre, but well connected by the public transport – one of six buses can take you downtown in about 15 minutes, the stop only 50m from the hostel door. Even if you decide to walk, it's 30 minutes maximum. For visitors to Ultra Europe, the Poljud is even closer and easy to find from the hostel. *Photos p197.*

### Art Hotel
*Ulica Slobode 41 (021 302 302, www.arthotel.hr).* **€€.** **Map** p175 E1.
In a tastefully renovated factory building and now part of the Best Western group, the Art offers 36 spacious rooms, large beds and modern facilities including a gym. There is also a small spa centre featuring sauna, steam-bath and massage treatments.

### Atrium Hotel
*Domovinskog rata 49A (021 200 000, www.hotel-atrium.hr).* **€€.** **Map** p175 E1.
Located a brisk 20-minute walk north of the Old Town, the sleek Atrium is set almost next door to the not-as-funny-as-it-sounds Joker Centre shopping mall. Behind a dark-glass exterior (look out for the remains of a Roman aqueduct in the lobby gallery), a seven-floor interior contains 124 large rooms and four suites, all done out very elegantly in wood and marble. It's a great place to relax and decompress, with muted and soothing colours on the walls, a few good spots for a quiet drink, and staff who are helpful without straying into over-attentiveness. The spa centre offers superior saunas (infra-red and Finnish), a pool, hot tub and gym, while the ground-floor restaurant is gourmet class.

## Camping Split

*Svetog Lovre 6, 21311 Stobreč-Split (021 325 426, www.campingsplit.com).*
In the last few years Split has seen plenty of hostels open, and even more apartments, but there is only one camping site, recently revamped and reopened in an eastern suburb of Stobreč, on the D8 road from Split to Dubrovnik. In 2014, it was already getting a name among campers: those who sleep in tents, those who prefer caravans and bungalows, and those who have their own campers. The site is excellently located by the sea, in a small forest with its own pebbled beach, and the long sand beach of Stobreč is only metres away. All pitches are neat and well marked, most of them in shade. There is also a playground for kids and a golf driving range, owned by the club across the road. Other sports include snorkeling, windsurfing and waterskiing. The camp has its own pizzeria and a restaurant, there's Wi-Fi and computers with internet connections.

## Consul

*Tršćanska 34 (021 340 130, www.hotel-consul.net).*
€. Map p175 E1.
A handy little hotel, a 15-minute walk north of the palace, with 15 well-facilitated rooms and four suites. Nice big terrace, too, and half- and full-board rates available for reasonable supplements. It's quickly booked out, so phone ahead well in advance.

## ★ Dioklecijan Hotel & Residence

*Kranjčevićeva 45 (021 585 100, www.hotel-dioklecijan.com).* €€. Map p175 F1.
A former luxurious retirement home, the Dioklecijan Hotel & Residence is dedicated to health tourism and all kinds of spa treatments. An outdoor swimming pool sits on top of the hotel offering a truly spectacular view of Split, including Marjan and the harbour. Under the roof are hot tubs and saunas as well as a film screening room, library and restaurant. Rooms are big and comfortable, each with a balcony, most with sea views.

## Divota Apartment Hotel

*Plinarska 75 (021 782 700, www.divota.hr).* €€.
Map p175 D1.
Veli Varoš is a real Mediterranean neighbourhood on the eastern slopes of Marjan hill, looking towards the city centre, whose narrow streets and stone houses have been home to many a tourist apartment in recent years. Here, you're close enough to the action but surrounded by peace and quiet. The luxury lodging complex of Divota comprises several stone-built villas within walking distance of the Diocletian's Palace. Under the Divota umbrella are carefully refurbished old properties, part rustic, part historic-Dalmatian. The one in Radmilovića, for example, is a 110-square-metre, two-floor stone house with a courtyard, with all mod cons. All in all, it's nice to know that respecting tradition still gives the best results.

## Emanuel

*Tolstojeva 20 (021 786 533).* **No credit cards.**
Map p175 E1.
Among Split's growing collection of chic, contemporary, design-conscious hotels is Emanuel, which occupies a stylishly converted ground-floor flat in an attractive pre-World War I apartment block. Counterpointing the minimalist grey floors and matte-brown wall surfaces are furnishings done out in Mediterranean pastel shades of turquoise and terracotta. The bunk beds come in semi-cubicle form to provide an extra bit of privacy, and you get a croissant and coffee for breakfast. Despite being only a short hop away from the Old Town, Emanuel seems to belong to a different world, nestled among leafy residential streets lined with 19th- and 20th-century villas. The hostel's social spaces are relatively small, making it something of a calming bolthole rather than a party palace. There is Wi-Fi throughout and a couple of laptops are at guests' disposal. Search for 'Hostel Emanuel' on Facebook.

## Filomena Spa & Lifestyle Club

*Put Radosevca 39, Znjan (021 472 777, www.filomena.hr).* €€. Map p175 E1.
This luxury spa centre at Znjan, outside Split, also offers a number of well-equipped rooms, mainly for its customers signed up to longer-term spa packages or relaxation treatments. Rooms have king-sized beds and internet access, while the spa offers aromatherapy, day treatments for both ladies and gentlemen, and month-long programmes for those with back or weight problems. There's an outdoor pool too.

## Globo

*Lovretska 18 (021 481 111, www.hotelglobo.com).*
€€. Map p175 E1.
Renovated in 2007, and with substantial investment in continuous refurbishment, this smart, modern hotel is located north of the palace, a 15-minute walk from the Riva. It's geared towards the business community, hence the recently added conference room, and particularly helpful staff.

## Katarina Hotel

*Podi, Dugopolje (021 712 333, www.hotelkatarina.hr).* €€.
Dugopolje seems set to become the new gateway to Split, located by one of Croatia's busiest motorway exits and with plenty of investment in shopping and business centres. A football facility in the nearby sports centre may also create trade. This decent hotel is another attraction. Its seventh-floor spa area provides exotic-sounding massages, an indoor pool with views of Mosor hill, spa baths, a sauna and a gym. The bar stays open until 3am and a large restaurant features Dalmatian specialities, imaginatively prepared.

## ★ Luxe

*Kralja Zvonimira 6 (021 314 444, www. hotelluxesplit.com).* €€. Map p175 E2.

Opened in 2010, this design-oriented establishment is both good to look at and fun to stay in. Local architects Vjeko Ivanišević and Lea Aviani were responsible for the overall design, a sleek slab of grey built on the site of a former factory. The interior is anything but industrial: walls and surfaces are sparkling white, carpets and other fabrics feature strong blues and purples. The rooms themselves all face south towards Split's harbour – those on lower floors won't have much of a view, but those higher up provide an exciting sense of Split's passenger-port bustle. 'Superior' doubles are slightly more spacious than the regular rooms and also boast small balconies. With only 30 rooms, the Luxe preserves an intimate boutique feel, and the location adjacent to both port and palace couldn't be bettered. There's a spa centre in the basement with gym, sauna, and an atmospherically domed lounge with a bubble pool. There is free Wi-Fi throughout, and parking is available in a nearby side street. *Photo p199.*

### Marul
*Ćiril-Metodova 7 (021 566 000, www. hotelmarul.hr).* €€. **Map** p175 E1.
The Hotel Marul is based in a quiet neighbourhood close to the Croatian National Theatre, minutes from the heart of the city. It's brand new, having opened in 2014, but has already gained a reputation as an attractive, family-run and family-oriented boutique venue. The whole building was carefully remodelled from the old houses that once stood here, retaining touches of the traditional architecture. The rooms are spacious and comfortable, and amenities include Wi-Fi and nearby parking, both free. 'Marul' refers to Marko Marulić, the Split-born 15th-century writer and father of Croatian literature. His sculpture created by Ivan Meštrović stands on Voćni trg in the palace.

### ★ Le Méridien Lav
*Grljevačka 2A, Podstrana (021 500 500, 021 500 300, www.lemeridienlavsplit.com).* €€€.
Set 11km (6.5 miles) away at Podstrana, Le Méridien is Split's top-of-the-range crash pad. In these luxurious surroundings you can take a dip in the infinity pool with a view along the sun-drenched coast towards Split, luxuriate in the wine or truffle therapies of the top-notch Diocletian spa, or gaze longingly at the superyachts in the marina from the large terrace. The rooms are spacious and stylish, service standards are high, and there are conference facilities – yet the atmosphere is pleasantly relaxed. The main restaurant, Spalatum Galerija, does superb sea bass, and steak. To follow, there's a fab, sunken champagne bar, as well as an old-style pivnica pub left deliberately unmodernised; a casino and nightclub provide more mischievous entertainment if you feel like staying up. There are shuttle services into town several times a day and regular water taxis from the airport. It also has its own private pebble beach.

**101 Dalmatinac Design Hostel.**
See p195.

EXPLORE

## More
*Šetalište Pape Ivana Pavla II 27, Znjan
(021 462 112, www.hotelmore.hr).* €€.
This friendly little venue out near the seafront at Znjan is a pleasant choice if you just want some beach time with occasional forays into town. All eight rooms have a sea view, half with a verdant terrace to boot, and there's a suite available too. Check the website for special deals for three-, five- and seven-day stays. There are also half-board rates.

## ★ Park
*Hatzeov perivoj 3 (021 406 400, www.hotelpark-split.hr).* €€€. **Map** p175 F2.
As one of the oldest and most revered hotels in Split, the Park underwent a major renovation over the winter of 2014-15. This upgraded the hotel, adding conference facilities, a swimming pool, new terrace and spa – as well as better, bigger and more luxurious rooms and suites. The Bruna restaurant and hotel bar have also been overhauled. The Park enjoys a prime location behind Bačvice beach, Split's most popular.

## President Solin
*Ulica Kralja Petra Krešimira IV 11, Solin
(021 683 300, www.hotelpresident.hr).* €€.
Under the same ownership as its namesake in central Split, this new hotel offers stylish luxury 6km (3.5 miles) away in the suburb of Solin, near the ruined Roman city of Salona. The 96 rooms and apartments cater for all guest combinations and have all the latest comforts and technology. For relaxation there are three pools (mineral, sea- and fresh-water), fitness, beauty and massage centres, and more besides.

## Quasimodo Hostel
*Gundulićeva 26 (095 856 5804, www.facebook.
com/QuasimodoHostelSplit).* **Open** June-Sept.
**Map** p175 E1.
After a successful trial in 2014, this venue – which hosts bands and comedians in winter – becomes a small, cosy and popular hostel in summer. In a former department store, there are a quartet of four-bed dorms, one double room with a private bathroom, another double with shared bathroom. The stage area becomes the communal space for the summer, with a terrace bar, Wi-Fi and TV allowing plenty of opportunity to meet other guests and staff.

## Radisson Blu Hotel
*Put Trstenika 19 (021 303 030, www.radissonblu.
com/resort-split).* €€€.
Refurbished in 2010, the luxurious Radisson Blu Split (formerly the Hotel Split) has 246 stylish modern rooms and suites, six with disabled access, as well as two restaurants, indoor and outdoor swimming pools, sauna and steam bath, gym and spa.

## San Antonio
*Grljevačka 28 (021 336 111, www.hotelsan
antonio.com).* €€.

Some eight kilometres from Split's city centre on Podstrana beach is the Hotel San Antonio, which opened in 2008. Consisting of three main buildings offering different types of room, but all furnished in a neat modern fashion, the hotel also has an indoor swimming pool with a bar, sauna and fitness area. For those who prefer being beside the sea, the outdoor bar is right on the pebble beach and serves a range of beverages including Croatian wines. Luxury rooms have balconies with sea views and indoor jacuzzis; all rooms are quite large and well presented. Wi-Fi throughout.

## Split
*Strožanačka 20 (021 420 420, www.hotel-split.hr).* €.
When it comes to accommodation, the area of east Split, towards Makarska and Dubrovnik, is known mostly for apartment rentals and the luxury Le Méridien Lav (*see p197*). In the last few years, new hotels have opened up here showing that this seaside stretch has potential; Hotel Split is one of them. This venue, between Stobreč and Le Méridien Lav, was set up by the Tomić family, and that's one of its main qualities – it is much more carefully run than chain resort hotels. It's set just above a nice pebbled beach and from the street you couldn't tell that this is actually a seven-storey building – half the floors are almost invisible from that side. From the sea, the hotel looks completely different. All rooms have a sea view, and most of them are identical, except in one detail: the walls in each are painted a different colour, in Mediterranean hues of sage, lavender, and so on. There are also a few rooms designed to make you feel as if you're sleeping on a yacht. There are all the usual amenities, including a spa, a restaurant with a sea-facing terrace and a bar.

## Villa Matejuška
*Tomića stine 3 (021 396 610, www.villamatejuska.
hr).* €. **No credit cards. Map** p175 D1.
This is an excellent little apartment-hotel in the Varoš neighbourhood, with six rooms in a quiet street just behind Sv Frane, less than five minutes' walk from the palace. Rooms have kitchenettes and new bathrooms and some have exposed stone. Breakfast in the reliable *konoba* downstairs is included.

## Villa Varoš
*Miljenka Smoje 1 (021 483 469, www.villavaros.hr).* €.
**Map** p175 D1.
Tucked away in the Varoš neighbourhood near the palace, this is one of the best options for price and comfort. Owned by Joanne, a Croat from New York, the lovely old stone house harbours new, simply furnished but chic rooms, with satellite TV, air con and Wi-Fi. There are three apartments with spacious living areas, including one top-floor apartment with terrace. Breakfast is available in a restaurant round the corner for a modest extra fee, and alley parking is available for €10/day.

## GETTING THERE & AROUND

Split **airport** is 23km (14 miles) north-west of town between Kaštela and Trogir. A Pleso prijevoz **bus**, linked with incoming Croatia Airlines flights, around six or seven times daily (30kn, 30min journey time; www.plesoprijevoz. hr), takes you to Split **bus station**. For your return journey, check times with the Croatia Airlines office on the Riva (Hrvatskog narodnog preporada 9, 021 362 997, croatiaairlines.com). Buses leave town 90min before domestic flights, 2hrs before international ones. A **taxi** from the airport costs 280kn-350kn – call 021 895 237.

There are three InterCity **trains** a day from Zagreb, journey time 6.5 to 8.5 hours. The **railway station** is on the Riva side of the bus station, diagonal to the port, with left luggage facilities. Frequent buses run from Zagreb (five hours) and Dubrovnik (four-and-a-half hours).

Split is a major **port**, with frequent services from Rijeka in the north, and Ancona in Italy. Hops to the islands of Hvar, Brač and Vis require a couple of hours and a nominal foot passenger fare from between 33kn and 60kn though rumours are of an imminent increase, at time of writing. The **ferry terminal** is a short walk from the Riva, a large building you can't miss diagonally opposite the bus station. Both **catamarans** and **hydrofoils** leave from the Riva, behind a building surrounded by cafés on the main waterfront. Tickets and information are available at the harbour terminal or at the Jadrolinija and Split Tours kiosks at the Riva end of the harbour front.

**Walking** is the only practical way to get around the town centre. To go to the hilly peninsula of Marjan or beyond Bačvice, take a city bus (11kn on board, 9kn from a kiosk) from either end of the Riva at Trg republike or Zagrebačka by the market. For timetable and route details, see www.promet-split.hr.

## RESOURCES

**Hospital** *Spinčićeva 1 (021 556 111).*

**Pharmacy** *24/7, Lučac, Pupačićeva 4 (021 533 188).* **Map** p175 F2.

**Internet** *Internet & Games Dencall, Obala kneza Domagoja (021 345 014, www.dencall.com).* **Open** *Summer* 8am-11pm daily. *Winter* 9am-8pm daily. **Map** p177 B2.
Internet café near the harbour. Dencall also issues cheap international phone cards.

**Police** *Pojišanska 2 (021 309 356).* **Map** p175 E2.

**Post office** *Obala Kneža Domagoja 3.* **Open** 7am-9pm Mon-Sat. **Map** p175 E2.

### Tourist information

**Split Tourist Office** *Peristil (021 345 606, www. visitsplit.com).* **Open** *Summer* 8am-8.30pm Mon-Sat; 8am-1pm Sun. *Winter* 9am-5pm Mon-Fri.

**Turist Biro** *Riva 12 (021 347 100, www.turistbiro-split.hr).* **Open** *Summer* 8am-9pm Mon-Fri; 8am-8pm Sat; 8am-1pm Sun. *Winter* 8am-8pm Mon-Fri; 8am-1pm Sat.
Handy travel agency with a booking service for private rooms. Pay the fee at the desk for a photocopied map and door key.

**EXPLORE**

**Hotel Luxe.** See p196.

EXPLORE

# Around Split

## TROGIR

Trogir was first settled by Greeks from Vis in 300 BC. Listed as a UNESCO World Heritage Site, the Old Town reflects the influence of subsequent periods of Roman, Hungarian, Venetian, French and Austrian rule. Its walled medieval centre is a warren of narrow cobbled streets, radiating from the cathedral square of **Trg Ivana Pavla II**, flanked by a wide seafront promenade, the **Riva**. In summer, the harbour wall is lined with luxury yachts and tripper boats, and the lively summer festival has entertainment on offer most evenings.

The **Old Town** stands on an islet, separated from the mainland by a man-made canal, and linked by another road bridge to **Čiovo island**. It's a fine setting but the two single-lane bridges will be choked every summer until a new bridge is built further east. Trogir's marina, with a cluster of bars and restaurants around it, lies on Čiovo. Just over Čiovo bridge are a couple of hotels, including, to the left, the Hotel Palace. By the mainland bridge is the bus station and the ever-busy, open-all-hours market.

Entering from the mainland, you pass through the Baroque **Land Gate**, guarded by a statue of local patron St John of Trogir. Here also is the **Town Museum** (Gradska vrata 4, 021 881 406). Set in the Garagnin Palace, it's a low-key display of archaeology, books, antique clothes and documents, but the courtyard is lovely and often used for traditional *klapa* concerts in the summer.

Ahead stands the 15th-century Venetian Čipiko Palace, built for a rich Croatian family who then spread their wealth in Kaštela. Alongside, the three-naved **Cathedral of St Lawrence** (Trg Ivana Pavla II, 021 881 426) took 300 years to build and is famed for the magnificent western portal, built in 1240. The 47m (154ft) **Bell Tower** affords magnificent views of the town and surrounds. Past it are the **Town Hall**, the **Loggia** and **Clock Tower**. The Loggia, with its reliefs and sculptures, dates to the 14th century though it was lovingly restored in the late 19th. Exiting the Old Town via the Sea Gate, and turning right on the Riva, you come to medieval **Kamerlengo Castle**, now used as an open-air cinema and events stage with a tower that offers more great views. The town walls once connected the castle to **St Mark's Tower**, at the other end of the lush football pitch. Unlike the crumbling castle, St Mark's has been painstakingly restored and the open top floor is now a café; the interior has been given over to a small museum of Dalmatian music. Turn left from the Sea Gate towards the bridge and you pass the 16th-century loggia that used to house the fish market, which has since moved to the mainland side of town.

## Restaurants

### Fontana
*Obrov 1 (021 885 744, www.fontana-trogir.com).* **Open** 7am-midnight daily. **€€**. **Dalmatian**
Fontana has a large terrace with a sea view, nestled between a school and a church, just in from the Riva. It serves quality traditional Dalmatian fish and meat. Prices are slightly above average but portions are ample and the view is lovely. Popular for special occasions and business lunches.
▶ *This venue is also a hotel and has 15 air-conditioned rooms. See website for details.*

### Kamerlengo
*Vukovarska 2 (021 884 772, www.kamerlengo.hr).* **Open** 9am-midnight daily. **€€**. **Dalmatian**
Of the more upmarket restaurants in the Old Town, Kamerlengo is a favourite. The terrace, with its charcoal oven, set between the stone walls of the building, provides a great setting in which to sample the Dalmatian treats – barbecued fish is the speciality.

### Konoba Škrapa
*Hrvatskih Mučenika 9 (091 784 2795).* **Open** *Summer* noon-11pm daily. *Winter* noon-11pm Mon-Sat. **No credit cards**. **€**. **Dalmatian**

Kamerlengo Castle.

Delightful staff, a cosy ambience and artistic table decorations tipify Škrapa. The restaurant is the home of honest, grilled Dalmatian food, provided at fair prices to locals and visitors alike. The house rakija comes round on a little tray with a bicycle bell. Seating inside and out.

### Pizzeria Mirkec

*Budislavićeva 15 (021 883 042, www.pizzeria-mirkec.hr).* **Open** 8am-11pm daily. **€. Pizzeria** Mirkec's summer terrace provides a prime spot on the Riva to enjoy tasty, good-value pizza and pasta. In the colder months, diners can climb the stairs for cosy indoor seating or use the halfway house just before the restaurant entrance. The experienced waiters are friendly and efficient.

### ★ Vanjaka

*Radnonov trg 7-9 (091 503 8734, restaurant-vanjaka.com).* **Open** 9am-midnight daily. **€€.** **Dalmatian** Set on a picturesque square in the centre of Trogir, Vanjaka is named after chef-owner Ljiljana, who also oversees three pleasant rooms offered as an affordable B&B deal. The restaurant comprises a large terrace and traditional, air-conditioned interior, where superior versions of Dalmatian favourites are served.

Grilled lamb comes on crushed new potatoes, spring onion and anchovies; fillet of sea bass on a creamy vegetable risotto with baked tomatoes. The fish platter for two lends itself to the perfect romantic evening. You'll find cheaper in Trogir but probably not better.

## Bars & Nightlife

The busy bars on the **Riva** and **Cathedral Square** often have live acts playing during the summer. **Big Daddy** and **Padre** are the first ones you find from the main road and they share a large open-air stage. They're the focal point for summer nightlife until they close at around midnight. People then either pile into taxis for **Hacienda** (*see p211*), or head for the mainstream disco **Stone Age**, which is in **Plano**, about five kilometres from the centre of Trogir. The more secluded **Radovanov trg**, behind the Cathedral, has bars with terraces for a quieter aperitif – try the secluded **Galion** or the lounge bar **Smokvica** (www.smokvica.com). If you're staying in Trogir later on, by the Land Gate as you arrive from the mainland bridge is busy late-opening lounge bar **Martinino** (Hrvatskih Mučenika 2). **Monaco** is a big disco bar, just to the right as you walk over the bridge to Čiovo.

EXPLORE

## Hotels

### Concordia

*Obala bana Berislavića 22 (021 885 400,*
*www.concordia-hotel.net). €.*
Set behind a 300-year-old facade, on the Riva near
Kamerlengo Castle, 11 rooms provide value for
money. The larger sea-facing ones have balconies
and there's a small restaurant and terrace downstairs where breakfast is served.

### Jadran

*Hrvatskih žrtava 147, Seget Donji (021 800 500,*
*www.hotel-jadran.com). €€.*
Of the 132 rooms at this comfortable hotel, most
have a sea-view – but perhaps not as stunning as
from the expansive terrace of the restaurant. There's
also an open-air pool, a bar and a car park. It's a bus
ride or half-an-hour's walk from Trogir.

### ★ Palace

*Put Gradine 8 (021 685 555, www.hotel-*
*palace.net). €€.*
The Palace opened its doors in 2008 and has since
added a spa with full facial and massage treatments.
Located over the bridge on Čiovo, a ten-minute walk
from the centre, it comprises 36 rooms and suites, all
with balconies and sea views. There's free parking
and a bar and restaurant too.
▶ *The Villa Meri (Splitska 1, 021 882 555,*
*www.villa-meri.com) is of comparable standard,*
*with six rooms and an apartment with a roof-*
*top terrace.*

### Vila Sikaa

*Obala kralja Zvonimira 13 (021 881 223,*
*www.vila-sikaa-r.com). €€.*
Run by the Runtić family, and just over the bridge
from the Old Town to Čiovo, this modern and well-
equipped establishment is set in a pretty building
dating back to the 19th century. The rooms are
comfortable – the more you pay, the bigger the
accommodation. All guests can take advantage of
the internet café area, travel agency and aperitif
bar of course.

## Getting there

From **Split airport**, the no.37 **bus** runs to Trogir
every 20mins (10kn). A **taxi** will cost about 150kn.
From June-Sept, the Bura Line (www.buraline.com)
runs **boats** several times a day from Split to Slatine
on Čiovo (19kn) and then on to Trogir (24kn).

## Resources

**Tourist information** *Trogir Tourist Office, Trg*
*Ivana Pavla II/1 (021 881 412, tztrogir.hr).* **Open**
*Summer* 8am-7pm Mon-Fri; 8am-3pm Sat. *Winter*
7.30am-3pm Mon-Fri; 7.30am-3pm 1st and 3rd Sat
in the mth.

## KAŠTELA

The seven villages of **Kaštela**, on the back road
from Split airport, remain one of Dalmatia's best-
kept secrets. Turn off towards the sea and, in a
very short space of time, you'll uncover, from
west to east: Štafelić, Novi, Stari, Lukšić,
Kambelovac, Gomilica and Sućurac. The number
37 bus between Trogir and Split links the villages;
sea quality is generally better towards the west.

The Kaštels are so named because each has at
least one castle, built for the Croatian nobility in
the 15th and 16th centuries. Koriolan Čipiko was
among the first of the Trogir gentry to move out
to Kaštela, in 1481. His village became **Kaštel**
**Stari** ('Old Castle') to differentiate it from the
parvenus; his nephew Pavao moved to **Kaštel**
**Novi** ('New Castle') a few years later.

Wide promenades hide decent restaurants and
bars. The sweeping **Kaštela bay**, with its clutch
of harbours and beaches, provides an idyllic
location for a leisurely afternoon's stroll. The old
stone houses, many of which are now renovated,
in the characterful village centres, were built close
together to maximise the protection afforded by
their castles. **Kaštel Lukšić** is the focal point
with a handful of trendy bars at its centre. Here,
inside the castle itself, is the Kaštela **tourist**
**office** (Dvorac Vitturi, Brce 1, 021 227 933,
www.kastela-info.hr). **Kastel Štafilić** claims
to have the only castle which was never actually
conquered by the Turks and one of the oldest
olive trees in the world, still going at over 1,500
years. The prettiest castle, in **Kaštel Gomilica**,
was built by Benedictine nuns.

## Restaurants

**Baletna Škola** (Kaštel Kambelovac, Don Frane
Bege 2, 021 220 208, www.restoran-baletnaskola.
com), on the site of an old ballet school, is a locals'
favourite with a diverse but essentially traditional
Dalmatian menu. The huge tree-shaded terrace
faces the sea and there's as much room again
inside. It also runs a hotel (www.hotel-baletna
skola.com). It's hard to beat **Konoba Intrada**
(Obala kralja Tomislava, Kaštel Novi, 021 231
301, www.konobaintrada.com) for atmosphere,
value for money across the menu and great
pizzas. **Odmor** (F Tudmana 532, 021 220 263,
restoranodmor.fullbusiness.com), on the north
side of the main Kaštela road – just east of a big
block of flats and supermarket in Kambelovac –
has a surprisingly secluded terrace, great chips
and low prices. **Bimbijana** (Marina Kaštela,
Kaštel Gomilica, 021 222 780, www.bimbijana.
com) is a spacious traditional restaurant and
large terrace serving hearty snacks and mains
to hungry sailors. These and others are open all
year round, though the promenades fill in summer
with seasonal venues.

EXPLORE

## Bars

Kaštela is an ideal place to go for a bar crawl. Start in Štafilić at the secluded modest beach-fronted bar **Nehaj**, which is a favourite with windsurfers. Following the delightful smells emanating from the bakery next door, weave your way, hopefully not too unsteadily, towards Novi and Stari via **Gabine** (www.facebook.com/caffebargabine), where there is live music most summer weekends. After the more genteel **Imaš** in Novi's small square, head for any of Stari's seafront bars. For the less energetic, wander around Lukšić and pick one of the wicker-chaired cafés by the castle; or **Bugsy's**, just to the east, with a twin terrace and a large interior full of Prohibition-era memorabilia.

## Hotels

The best bet is probably **Hotel Villa Zarko** (Obala kralja Tomislava 7A, Kaštel Lukšić, 021 228 160, 021 228 152, www.villa-zarko.com). It's on the edge of Lukšić, with 16 rooms, a terrace restaurant-bar and a tree-lined beach (shingle and concrete) mostly to itself. **Hotel Resnik** (Njiva Sv Petra 6, Kaštel Štafilić, 021 798 001, www.resnik-hotel.hr, open 15 Apr-15 Oct), by the airport, in a huge pine-wooded campus with its own beach, comprises a complex of bungalows, a sea-facing restaurant and five tennis courts. Keep an eye on the **Hotel Palace** (Obala kralja Tomislava, Kaštel Stari), a grand piece of beach-fronted, 1920s architecture on the road to modernisation, expected to open in 2016. For comfortable, affordable accommodation, **Sveti Jure** (Obala kralja Tomislava, Kaštel Novi, 021 232 759, www.sveti-jure.com) has a handful of rooms of wood and stone, with a traditional restaurant downstairs – park your car for free or moor your boat. **Hotel Tamaris** (Kralja Tomislava, Kaštel Kambelovac, 021 220 333, www.tamaris-hotel.hr) is cheap but pretty gloomy. **Villa Kristalia** (Gabine 9, Kaštel Štafilić, 021 234 920, www.villakristalia.com) is popular with French families and has its own outdoor pool. There's plenty of modern apartment accommodation for rent, particularly in Štafilić.

## OMIŠ & DUGI RAT

Past Split, towards Makarska, the area around **Omiš** and **Dugi Rat** is slowly beginning to attract visitors away from its tourist-friendly neighbours. Aside from Omiš itself, it is mostly a collection of small villages that developed inland, around the olive groves and vineyards that first brought people here, and then descended towards the sea as tourism and industry superseded agriculture.

Omiš, now probably best known for its annual *klapa* music festival, is stunningly photogenic. Craggy mountains rise up directly behind the old

stone houses, alleyways and squares that make up its compact centre, and around the mouth of the River Cetina; it's popular for rafting trips and climbing. Perched on the mountaintops, as the river gorge meets the sea, the ruined medieval defences built by the counts of Kačić and Bribir once made a safe haven for pirates. West of Omiš is Dugi Rat with its collection of beaches, cafés, bars and pizzerias. The much-vaunted Korenat Point Resort, however, remains at the planning stage.

Around Omiš and Dugi Rat, along the coast, is a collection of holiday settlements, some with stunning beaches, but many still making the transition from the package tourism of old: there are large boxy hotels in pink and white, and a plethora of apartment accommodation, some of it appealing, some less so. Inland, the Republic of Poljica ('Small Fields') was a polity of free peasants that endured from at least the 15th century to the beginning of the 19th. It just about survived the attentions of the Ottoman Empire but was finally laid waste by the forces of Napoleon. Residents of the small settlements here today are still uncovering relics from Poljica's past.

## Restaurants

For the view alone, **Milo** (Knezova Kačića 15, Omiš, 021 861 185) is worth a visit, although the food can be pretty hit-and-miss. More reliable is the long-established **Pod Odrnom** (Ivana Katušića 1, Omiš, 021 861 918, www.pod-odrnom.hr), where fish and meat are cooked on a wooden grill. It's not cheap but it should be worth it. The **Bastion** (Fošal 9, Omiš, 021 757 922) offers a similarly traditional experience with large platters of seafood.

In Dugi Rat, the **Konoba Bracera** (Glavica, Dugi Rat, 021 735 400, www.konobabracera.com)

**EXPLORE**

provides a fine setting for summer dining, its stepped terrace off the main road overlooking pine woods and a secluded pebble beach. Around a dark-wood interior, huge models of traditional sailboats adorn the rafters separating the ground floor from the gallery dining area. The extensive menu has a couple of surprises, such as spiny lobster, house-style. More traditionally, there's lamb ribs, grilled fish and meat and *peka* dishes.

## Hotels

### Plaža
*Trg kralja Tomislava 6, Omiš (021 755 260, www.hotelplaza.hr).* €€.
Opened in 2007, the centrally located Plaža overlooks the long, sandy beach at Omiš. Most of the 36 rooms and five apartments have sea-view balconies. A small spa contains a Finnish sauna and 'special adventure showers'. Note that in summer, this establishment sells to foreign travel firms – individuals wanting to stay need to book for a minimum of a week. In the quieter winter season, the restaurant terrace becomes a modest skating rink.

### ★ Villa Dvor
*Mosorska 13, Omiš (021 863 444, www.hotel-villadvor.hr).* €€.
High on the cliffs over the Cetina, reached by more than a hundred well-lit, stone steps, this completely renovated and partially rebuilt conversion of a family house provides guests with a spectacular setting and quality facilities. Inside is modern and tasteful, with attractive furnishings although rooms and balconies aren't huge. There's a cosy restaurant and bar in the unlikely event that you've had enough of the views from the bar on the roof-top terrace – beyond beckons the open sea. It's a 20-minute walk from town but there's ample parking for those who don't want to do that climb. Solar panels now power a newly installed lift.
▶ *Villa Dvor is a good base for river rafting – most of the agencies are on the nearby banks of the Cetina.*

## Getting there

Local buses run regularly from Split – allow 30 minutes for the journey.

## Resources

**Omiš Tourist Office** *Trg kneza Miroslava (021 861 350, www.tz-omis.hr).* **Open** *Summer* 8am-8pm Mon-Fri; 8am-noon Sat. *Winter* 8am-3pm Mon-Fri.

**Dugi Rat Tourist Office** *Poljika cesta 133 (021 735 244, www.tz-dugirat.hr).* **Open** *Summer* 7am-2pm Mon-Fri; 7am-1pm Sat. *Winter* 7am-2pm Mon-Fri.

# MAKARSKA RIVIERA

Heading south on the main coastal road from Split to Dubrovnik, just past Omiš, a big blue sign announces **Makarska Riviera**. Thus begins the 60 kilometre (37 mile) stretch of mainly purpose-built hotels with the nightlife hub of **Makarska** in the middle. Few historic monuments survived the Turkish occupation of the 16th century, or the earthquake of 1962, a decade after which a decision was taken to turn this section of the coast (some of it quite pretty, with palm-fringed pebble beaches) over to package tourism. Though some of the hotels are still quite bland, some have been improved; the spa-equipped **Hotel Horizont** in Baška Voda is probably the top pick.

Every few kilometres from **Brela** to **Gradac** along the dangerous coast road, the welcome and farewell signposts pop up in quick succession: Brela, revered by locals, **Baška Voda**, Makarska, **Tučepi**, **Podgora**, **Drvenik**, **Zaostrog**, **Brist** and Gradac. The islands of **Brač**, **Hvar** (both accessible by ferry) and **Pelješac** come into jaw-dropping view to your right. To your left rises the constant, imposing, grey façade of the **Biokovo mountain range**, site of the nature park. If you do find a tranquil spot, the natural backdrop is stunning in both directions. You are close to Bosnia here, its overwhelming coastal resort of Neum and a short drive away, the old Ottoman town of Mostar.

It's worth noting that the majority of bars, restaurants and hotels on the Riviera are seasonal. All those listed below open from late spring to early autumn, unless otherwise stated.

## Restaurants

Nearly all Makarska Riviera tourist hotels have restaurants – off-season half board rates can be attractive. Notable stand-alone venues include the upscale **Jeny** near Tučepi (Gornje Tučepi, Čovići 1, 091 587 8078, www.restaurant-jeny.hr) and **Jež** in Makarska town (Petra Kreimira IV 90, 021 611 741, www.facebook.com/JezRestaurant). Also in Makarska town, you'll also find the excellent **Stari Mlin** (Prvosvibanjska 43, 021 611 509). In Brela, at the end of the promenade, **Burin** (put Luke 8, 021 618 521) can provide decent fish and seafood, as can the sea-facing **Konoba Feral** (obala Kneza Domogoja 30, 021 618 909).

## Bars & Nightlife

Makarska town is the best place to be and one of Croatia's top party destinations. During the evening, head behind the waterfront to bar-lined Lištun, starting with **Bety** (No.1, 091 456 3355). Later on, much of the fun there centres around the **Buba Bar** (www.facebook.com/bubabar) which provides an enthusiastic crowd with after-beach parties, international guest DJs and dancing till dawn; it remains the most popular hangout by day as well. **Club Deep** (Šetalište fra Jure Radića 5A, www.facebook.com/deepmakarska), located in a cave, remains a focal point, though **Petar Pan** (Šetalište fra Jure Radića, 095 883 3899, www.petarpan-makarska.com), near the football stadium, is the place to see and be seen in. Tony Sanchez and other DJs helped filled an open-air space for 1,500 punters and VIPs in 2015.

## Hotels

### Aparthotel Milenij
*Šetalište kralja Petra Krešimira IV 5, Baška Voda (021 620 644, www.hotel-milenij.com). €€.*
The Aparthotel Milenij has 27 apartments spread over five floors, from small to spacious. There's 24-hour room service, a restaurant, two cocktail bars (one on the beach), a TV lounge with a pool table, gym, sauna, outdoor pool and an underground garage. It's popular with UK tour operators.

### Bacchus
*Obala sv Nikole 89, Baška Voda (021 695 190, www.hotel-bacchus.hr). €€.*
Near the beach and the centre of Baška Voda, the Bacchus is a renovated establishment whose rooms, suites and apartments contain king-size beds. Rates vary wildly; Apr and Oct are half the price of July. On site are a restaurant with a sea-facing terrace, an indoor pool and a sauna.

### Berulia
*Frankopanska 66, Brela (021 603 599, central reservations 01 384 42 88, www.brelahotelberulia.com). €€.*
Now in the dozen-strong local BlueSun group of hotels, the Berulia has had a significant upgrade. Set in pine trees opposite three other stablemates, it has an indoor pool, sauna and gym. Other activities provided on site include mini-golf, bowling and table tennis, and there are tennis courts available nearby.

### Horizont
*Stjepana Radića 2, Baška Voda (021 604 555, www.hoteli-baskavoda.hr). €€.*
Hotel Horizont, flagship of the Hoteli Baška Voda Group, is where contemporary design and spacious modern facilities extend to the labyrinthine spa complex. You'll have a huge range of treatments at your disposal, as well as an old-school masseur. Most of the 202-plus rooms, spread over five floors, have sea views, and there's a choice of restaurants.

### Meteor
*Kralja Petra Krešimira IV 19, Makarska town (021 564 200, www.hoteli-makarska.hr). €€.*
Reopened in 2006, this Socialist-era ziggurat has now become a decent hotel – foreign football clubs use it during the winter so you know the facilities must be top rate. It has a spa, pools outdoor and in, two restaurants

and the Tropicana disco. Rooms vary from boxy singles to quite spacious doubles with terrace.

### Park Hotel
*Kralja Petra Krešimira IV 23, Makarska town (021 608 200, www.parkhotel.hr). €€.*
Opened in 2007, this chic, modern venue has a spa, gym, the typical pair of pools (indoor and out), a restaurant and a cocktail bar. The see-through lift and room numbers dyed into the carpets add individuality. Good views, plenty of space in most rooms and luxurious suites also give it that extra edge. It shares a long, pineshaded beach with the Meteor (*see above*).

### ★ Porin
*Marineta 2, Makarska town (021 613 744, www.hotel-porin.hr). €€.*
Lovely, central establishment in a late 19th-century Renaissance-style palace-cum-fortress, once used as the town library. Repurposed as a hotel in 2002, this palace offers two dozen beds in seven rooms, with one duplex apartment. It's right by the sea, with terraces either side and a panoramic roof terrace too. In high season, it's affected by noise from the bars immediately downstairs. Come before the crowds, or flop here after a nearby barhop.

### ★ Riva
*Slakovac 8, Brist (021 610 165, 098 284 594). €.*
A lovely little place, its loggia-style restaurant terrace is lapped by a relatively secluded stretch of the Adriatic, below the balconies of each of its neat rooms. The half-board rates here are absolute bargains out of season, when the only sound you'll hear is the occasional fishing boat. Ask about weekly rates too – sometimes they offer seven nights for the price of six. The Riva is a short stroll downhill from the Zvijezda Mora bar, right by the southbound Brist bus stop, an easy beach walk from Gradac.

### Villa Andrea
*Kamena 46, Tučepi (021 695 240, www.villa-andrea.info). €.*
Opened in 2005, the Villa Andrea is trying to lift itself above the norm for the Makarska coast without pricing itself out of the market. To this end, its 18 rooms are comfortable and well furnished, its Olive Tree restaurant specialises in slow food, and it has a wine cellar, spa treatments using natural products from the region – and there's parking too.

## Getting there & around

The Riviera is served almost hourly by buses between Split and Dubrovnik, all year round. **Makarska town** is 75mins from Split (about 40kn) and three hours from Dubrovnik (just over 100kn). For short hops down the Riviera, simply flag down a passing bus – at the bus shelter on the coast road with the town's name on it – and pay the nominal fee once on board.

**EXPLORE**

## Resources

**Tourist information** Each resort on the Riviera (www.makarska-riviera.com) has its own modest tourist office: **Brela** (021 618 455, www.brela.hr), **Baška Voda** (tz-baska.hr), **Makarska** (Obala Kralja Tomislava 16, 021 612 002, www.makarska-info.hr), **Tučepi** (021 623 100, www.tucepi.com) and **Gradac** (021 697 511, www.gradac.hr)

# Brač

Despite being one of the closest islands to the mainland, less than an hour by ferry – and a prime candidate for the most popular – **Brač** lets you carouse with the hordes or get lost in solitude. In many ways, it's Croatia's 'every island'.

In **Bol**, it has a town where you can grab a lively cocktail and head to the island's picture postcard beach, the famous **Zlatni Rat**, windsurfing central. From Bol you can trek to the area's highest peak, the 778m **Vidova Gora** (2,552ft), or investigate remote and traditional villages, where donkeys still work the rugged landscape to transport grasses, grapes and olives.

And, because Brač is so close to Split, you can do it in a day trip. A ride in a bus or hire car from the northern entry port of **Supetar** – the other main tourist centre and family-friendly resort with sand-and-pebble beaches and package hotels – goes past pines, olive groves and marble quarries to the southern coast and Bol. When explored, Brač allows travellers to step off the tourist conveyor belt, take a break from the herd and gain a deeper sense of the island and its culture.

### INTRODUCING BRAČ

Brač, 40 kilometres long and 15 kilometres wide (24 miles by nine miles), is karst rock. This supple white stone has been used by Croatia's finest sculptors. Examples fill the cemetery near Supetar, with tombs of Byzantine and Art Nouveau fancy created by local sculptor Ivan Rendić (1849-1932). His contemporary Toma Rosandić made the **Petrinović Mausoleum**, the most impressive monument here.

The village of **Donji Humac**, south of Supetar and with views of the nearby quarry, provides an opportunity to observe the stone-carving tradition with a carefree ramble through an authentic settlement. It also contains one of the island's real gastronomic gems: **Kopačina**. Another easy excursion from Supetar is to the ancient hilltop settlement of **Škrip**, with the **Museum of Brač** (021 630 033) in the Radojković Tower. Supetar is also the setting-off point for buses to the old fishing village of **Milna** and the quieter beaches around it.

East of Supetar on the coast, **Splitska** is a pretty small town with a few restaurants and a

lovely quiet beach, and **Postira** is transforming itself from a tatty resort into something more attractive with hotel facilities to match and a shiny new man-made beach.

Inland, **Dol** is a historical treasure with a good restaurants, **Konoba Toni. Pučišća** is an often-overlooked coastal town with a quiet and protected harbour. There you will find the nicest hotel on the island in the boutique **Palace Dešković**. This is also the centre of the island's famous stone-carving tradition, with beautiful examples in its houses and churches dating back hundreds of years.

The dramatic clifftop **Blaca Hermitage** (021 637 092, 091 516 4671; open June-Oct 9am-6pm Tue-Sun, Nov-May 9am-3pm Tue-Sun; admission 40kn, 10kn reductions) is a four-hour hike or short walk from the boat service from Bol. It contains astronomical instruments, clocks and an atlas from 1623. On the way you pass **Murvica**, set below the **Dragon's Cave**, covered with pagan paintings of wild beasts from the 15th century.

East of Bol, at **Glavica**, stand the Dominican church and monastery (021 778 000; open May-June, Sept 10am-noon, 5-7pm daily; July, Aug 8am-noon, 5-9pm daily; 10kn), with a museum, featuring prehistoric finds, Greek coins and a Tintoretto. Overlooking Bol, Vidova Gora offers its magnificent views of the island and also across central Dalmatia. You should be able to make out Zlatni Rat, Hvar, Korčula, Biokovo and more. Allow two hours for the walk from the baroque **Church of Our Lady of Carmel** in the centre of Bol. Coach parties are an occasional hazard.

## Restaurants

### Bokuncin

*Obala kralja Tomislava 26, Sutivan (021 638 338, www.facebook.com/bokuncin).* **Open** noon-11pm daily. **€. No credit cards.** Dalmatian
One of the beauties of Brač is that there are many places besides the main touristy spots worth visiting. One of them is Sutivan, a few kilometres from the main ferry port, Supetar. Away from the seasonal fuss, one particular place to enjoy this small-town atmosphere is homely Bokuncin, at Sutivan's old port. At first sight, it's standard Dalmatian fare but there are a few twists. All the bread, pasta and pastries are homemade in the kitchen. Main dishes include plenty of vegetables, like courgette and aubergine.

### Konoba Dalmatino

*Radićeva 14, Bol (021 635 911, www.konoba dalmatino.com).* **Open** *Easter-Nov* noon-2am daily. **No credit cards.** Dalmatian
The interior of this rustic konoba, formerly Gust, off Bol's main square, is a collection of weathered green shutters, wine bottles, giant floor plants and wicker lampshades under a wooden-beamed ceiling. Tables

# SLOW FOOD DALMATIAN-STYLE
## *What is ispod peke*

*Ispod peke* is a classic feature on Dalmatian menus. Diners are requested to order it at least a day in advance, and ideally for at least four people. So what is this strange dish that you can't just order up and devour? *Ispod peke*, literally 'under the bell', is a way of slow cooking under a dome-shaped lid.

When Dalmatian mothers discovered their city cousins using ovens, this type of cooking bell was adopted as the country way to bake meat – and the successor to boiling food or roasting it on a spit. The age of electricity came relatively late to rural Croatia but still the popularity of this old cooking method survives.

In winter, a wood fire would be prepared on a stone slab in the most multifunctional area of the house – the place to get warm over a chat – and above the fire would be an array of meats in the course of being smoked. Chickens and turkeys were early *peke* favourites but, with the advent of refrigeration and the first butchers, small cuts of lamb and veal were added to the repertoire. Cooking *ispod peke* is also credited as being the first appetising Dalmatian way of cooking octopus.

Polite but knowing smiles will greet you when you ask for the secret of a good *peka* – everyone has their own tips and special ingredients. 'Know thy *peka*' also applies to the dome under which the meat is cooked. The fragile clay *pekas* were eventually replaced, in the early 20th century, with more robust iron ones – but no two ever produce quite the same result, although the distinctive succulent meat, delicious potatoes and all-round juicy flavours are unique to this type of cooking. Once the wood has turned into burning ashes on the hot stone slab, the iron bell is covered with the ashes and the contents start slowly cooking at a temperature of around 230 degrees centigrade, which goes down to about 170 degrees.

There are endless discussions about whether to turn the meat and when. The practicalities are that with so many factors having an input into the cooking temperature, you can never be sure exactly when it will be perfect. Having a peek inside the *peka* about 20 minutes before time gives the opportunity to assess the situation and perhaps turn the meat at the same time.

Classic *peka* restaurants include the **Konoba Tomić** (*see p208*) at Donji Humac and the **Konoba Dol** (*see p208*) at Dol, both on Brač, and **Konoba Roki** (*see p227*) on Vis.

**EXPLORE**

Petrinović Mausoleum. *See p206.*

Petrinović Mausoleum. *See p206.*

line the foyer, and also spread outside, all done up with traditional farm equipment and celebrity pictures. The homely atmosphere brings folks in but it's the food that brings them back. *Gregada* is the speciality (a stew with fish, scampi, potatoes, onions and herbs); Dalmatian *pašticada* is another. There are also steaks, lobster spaghetti and veal served over rice with a tomato, cream and cheese sauce. The wine list has a wonderful selection of top-end reds and whites.

### Konoba Dol - Kaštil Gospodnetić
*Dol (091 799 7182, www.konobadol.com).*
**Open** noon-11pm daily. **€€. Dalmatian**
This is another jewel off the beaten tourist path, in the village of Dol where other konobas offer authentic local food and mood. However, it's hard to beat Kaštil Gospodnetić with a history as rich as the island's. This big house overlooking Dol and the surrounding valley was built in the 16th century, and its furnishings date back to the 19th. The hosts will gladly give you a tour of the estate as you wait for your meal. Cooking method is a menu feature here so you can choose between octopus or meat, grilled or *ispod peke* (slow-cooked in coals). There's also grilled or roast lamb, and *pašticada* (Dalmatian beef stew with gnocchi). Mains come with an appetiser (pâtés,

cheese or prosciutto perhaps) then are followed by dessert and a glass of wine – it's all included in a single price. The property sits atop a small hill in Dol, so it should be easy to find, but do ask for directions if needs be when you call to book a table.

### Konoba Mlin
*Ante Starčevića 11, Bol (021 635 376).* **Open** *May-Oct* 5pm-midnight daily. **€€. Dalmatian**
This romantic old mill, in use as recently as 1900, is east of Bol's main harbour and has a secluded, tree-shaded terrace above the sea. The tiered terraces are great places to take in the sunset and enjoy the fabulous fish, which sizzle on an outdoor grill. The menu also offers good meat dishes and thinly sliced Dalmatian ham as an appetiser.

### ★ Konoba Tomić
*Gornji Humac (021 21 647 242, www. konobatomic.com).* **Open** *May-Oct* 5pm-midnight daily. **No credit cards. €€. Dalmatian**
This legendary konoba stands in the 800-year-old house of the Michieli-Tomić family, whose wines and brandies are sold all over Croatia. Practically everything served is home-made, grown or reared on the property, from *pršut* ham to lamb, plus – of

course – the wine and varied fruit spirits. If you visit in autumn, you may be lucky enough to watch the family make wine the old-fashioned way in a hand-turned press; you can visit the farm too. Prices are reasonable for the quality and authenticity. Succulent octopus is prepared *ispod peke* (under a cooking bell with hot coals). Order this, and your table, in advance. Tomić is near the airport, north-east of Bol.

## Konoba Toni

*Dol (021 632 693, www.toni-dol.info).* **Open** mid Apr-Oct 11am-midnight daily. €€. **Dalmatian**
This delightful inland village of old stone houses has two konobas close to each other: Stori Gusti offers honest local food in simple surroundings but Konoba Toni goes that little bit further. Dark wood benches and tables line the vine-covered terrace amid all manner of pots, presses, barrels and traditional cooking utensils. Inside, there's a huge open fire – normally with a lamb turning on a spit – and wine- and spirit-making equipment. All ingredients are sourced locally (the seafood supplied by fishermen from nearby Postira) and most are home-produced, including the signature Toni brandies. The konoba also has an apartment for rent in Postira.

## ★ Kopačina

*Donji Humac (021 647 707, www.konoba-kopacina.com).* **Open** 10am-midnight daily. €€. **Dalmatian**
If not the best restaurant on the island, certainly it has no rivals in the realm of lamb, served in every way imaginable. There's lamb soup, lamb on the spit, boiled lamb, lamb chops, lamb steak, lamb pâté and – the local favourite – lamb under the *peka*. The clientele includes well-heeled tourists pointed here by locals as well as workmen still dusty from the nearby marble quarry which is visible from the restaurant's shaded, multi-level terrace. Above, on the stone patio, with its wooden roof, you'll find owner Ivo working the grill and the mechanised spit (which turns with a bike chain). Beyond is an expansive, renovated indoor dining room. But back to the lamb… In July and August there's a lamb buffet; guests can try every variety mentioned above plus lamb liver, local cheese, salted anchovies and lentil soup with smoked ham. Don't leave without trying the *vitalac*, which one should do without the nuisance of vegetarians. It's an island speciality: lamb liver wrapped in the intestines of a lamb that has just drunk milk. There's also seafood and other *peka* dishes; bread is baked fresh here every day.

## Mali Raj

*Put Zlatnog rata, Bol (021 635 282, www.bol.hr/pages/konoba-mali-raj).* **Open** May-Oct noon-midnight daily. **No credit cards**. €€. **Dalmatian**
Around the corner from the car park for Zlatni Rat beach, this could easily be a tourist trap. In fact, prices are pretty reasonable and you get free parking thrown in. Along with the risotto with scampi and cognac, grilled langoustines, and the seafood salad, the menu offers genuinely good Dalmatian food. The setting sells it: an expansive terrace with the greenest grass you're ever likely to see in Croatia, divided by well trimmed hedges, manicured firs and stone troughs brimming with plants and flowers. *Photos pp210-211.*

## Nono Ban

*Gornji Humac (021 647 233, www.nonoban.com).* **Open** noon-midnight daily. **No credit cards**. €€. **Dalmatian**
This attractive restaurant is run by Jakša Versalović along the Supetar-Bol road, in a pleasant setting. With a charming view of Bol ten kilometres away, and its own car park, the Nono Ban is also popular because of its healthy food. The menu may be typically Dalmatian but here they catch their own fish and produce their own wine, brandies, cheese and meat products including chicken, ostrich, lamb, smoked ham and veal.

## Punta

*Punta 1, Supetar (021 631 507, www.vilapunta.com).* **Open** Apr-Nov 8am-midnight daily. €€. **Dalmatian**
On a secluded point right on the beach and away from the busy harbour terraces, this big house is a great place to grab a seaside table for breakfast, lunch or dinner. Watch windsurfers cavort as you choose from a konoba-style menu with a wider-than-average range of fresh seafood, including John Dory, grouper and mussels. Meat lovers can devour the usual Balkan grilled classics and there are vegetarian options among the pizza. Punta also offers rooms for rent.

## Restoran Lovrečina

*Postira (021 599 430).* **Open** noon-midnight daily. **No credit cards**. €€. **Dalmatian**
Lovrečina sits in a beautiful wooded and sandy little bay east of Postira. Its name derives from Sveti Lovre (St Lawrence), the old church here whose walls can still be seen. Later in the 11th century, this was probably the site of a Benedictine monastery. The extensive menu offers free-range lamb, tripe, *dolce garbo* (sweet-and-sour lamb liver), lamb prepared under a baking bell, octopus, sardines, *fritule* (sweet fritters) and *kroštule* (knotted sweet desserts).

## Ribarska kućica

*Ante Starčevića, Bol (098 938 0989, www.ribarska-kucica.com).* **Open** June-Oct 9am-1am daily. €€. **Dalmatian**
A beautiful old house on a rocky walkway offers views of a cosy cove beach and the sea. Each of the terraces has tables. It's somewhat pricey, but if you're going to have lobster on Brač, make it here. Sauces and side dishes are adventurous.

**Mali Raj.** *See p209.*

### Taverna Riva
*Frane Radića 5, Bol (021 635 236, www.*
*tavernariva-bol.com).* **Open** *Summer* noon-3pm,
6pm-midnight daily. **€€. Dalmatian**
There are very few places in and around Bol with a
location that can be compared to that of the Taverna
Riva, one of the oldest restaurants in this resort,
recently with menu and style changes. Slap bang on
the seaside promenade, this old, two-storey stone
house comprises a bar and pizzeria on ground level
and a restaurant upstairs. The terrace provides a
great view of Bol port and the island of Hvar. The
cooking is based on local tradition, with the usual
treats such as octopus or meat slow-cooked under
a cooking bell, roast lamb and seafood specialities.
But what makes this place different from so many
others is its more contemporary intrepretations of
Dalmatian culinary custom. You can always order
a plain, simple and delicious lamb (with potatoes
and tomato sauce) but also enjoy it as carpaccio or in
other dishes more suited to haute cuisine.

### Vinotoka
*Jobova 6, Supetar (021 630 969).* **Open** *May-Oct*
noon-midnight daily. **€€. Dalmatian**
This tranquil old building, on a steep street, offers
authentic Dalmatian food – primarily fish. The family
has a fishing boat, and produces its own olive oil and
wines (red and white). The dining space comprises
two rooms, one newly refurbished in modern style but
with elements of traditional Dalmatia, like a wooden
boat. There's also a new, more expansive menu to
match with dishes such as smoked tuna with olives
and lemon, also a larger list of premium wines.

## Cafés & Bars

### Caffè Bar Marina
*Porat, Supetar (021 630 557).* **Open** *Summer*
7am-2am daily. *Winter* 7am-midnight daily.
**No credit cards.**
This venue has a small terrace on the harbour with
an outdoor cocktail area and a large, elegant bar
indoors. After dining, a lively crowd of fun seekers
comes here for a quality cocktail or a shot of local
grappa. There's techno, pop and Croatian music,
and a lively staff, while warm local regulars give the
place a lived-in feel.

### Caffè Bar Pjerin
*Put Vele Luke, Supetar (091 580 1951).*
**Open** 6.30am-2am daily. **No credit cards.**
It's mainly locals that frequent Pjerin, where the neon
pulls you in off the crowded strip. The music is a mix
of disco, hip hop and Croatian. The young staff are
charming, if sometimes lost. You'll find it near the
busy corner of 1 Svibnja.

### Caffè Ben Quick
*Vlačića, Supetar (021 631 541).* **Open** 7am-2am
daily. **No credit cards.**
Between the port and the Vele Luke area, Ben Quick
is the choice of locals who seek a quiet cocktail – a
B52, Banana Colada or a Semafor ('Traffic Light')
– or some other mixed drink, to be enjoyed on the
terracotta-roofed terrace. Plop down in one of the
cane chairs, sip on your cocktails or a cold beer, listen
to relaxed pop tunes and drink in the sunset views
across the harbour.

**210 Time Out** Croatia

## Cocktail Bar Bolero

*Put Zlatnog Rata, Bol (no phone).* **Open** *May-Oct* 8am-1am daily. **No credit cards.**

At a scenic high point on the promenade, plush wicker chairs, sofas and meditative world music tempt you to this pine-shaded, terraced establishment to admire the view of windsurfers and Hvar beyond. It gets a good crowd by late afternoon and stays lively.

## Pivnica Moby Dick

*Loža 13, Bol (021 635 281).* **Open** noon-midnight daily. **No credit cards.**

Downstairs is an open-air, multi-terraced and stone-columned affair, with sea views. The bar inside has stone archways, a pool table and a boat hanging from above; the cavernous feel is livened by reliable reggae. Upstairs, over the harbour and Sv Ante chapel, there's a rooftop restaurant serving octopus salad, steak and grilled tuna – but most punters are here for the beer.

## Varadero Cocktail Bar

*Frane Radića, Bol (021 635 996, www.varadero-bol.com).* **Open** *May-Oct* 8am-2am daily. **No credit cards.**

In the main square, this open-air cocktail bar features wicker chairs on a stone patio, between pine trees that grow through the floor. By day, palm-frond umbrellas shade tables populated by coffee drinkers. By night, a DJ spins tunes from a music station with the venue name spelled out in giant wooden letters. The signature drinks are the mojito and daiquiri; the signature sport is football (shown on the flatscreen by the DJ perch).

## Nightlife

## Benny's Bar

*Banj put, Sv Roka, Supetar (091 543 7884).* **Open** *June-early Sept* 10am-2am daily. **No credit cards.**

Benny's Bar puts on regular DJs or live music all summer. Follow the beach around to the aqua park at Uvala Banj east of town, to find a contemporary, fashionable and large bar. It's the cool place to be, drinks are reasonably priced and there's plenty of fun to be had on the slide, in the pool, or down the helter skelter.

## Hacienda

*Selca (091 894 9996).* **Open** *May-Oct* 2pm-late Thur-Sat. **No credit cards.**

Between Selca and Gornji Humac, this hacienda-style spot offers seclusion and flexible nocturnal time-keeping. A young crowd jigs to house music until dawn amid the olive trees in the open air.

## Hotels

## Amor

*Put Vele Luke 10, Supetar (021 606 606, www.velaris.hr).* **€€.**

This part of Tourist Resort Velaris is set in Vela Luke Bay to the west of Supetar town centre. The whole resort was renovated in 2006 and Amor opened in 2007 after being reconstructed over the foundations of its predecessor, Hotel Lučića. Though modern, the exterior has a certain style and the interior is simple but elegant and provides all mod cons. The split-level apartments on the second floor provide some stunning views of Split and more luxury, with a balcony and hot tub.

## Bluesun Hotel Borak

*Put Zlatnog rata 42, Bol (021 306 202, www.brachotelborak.com).* **€€.**

When it comes to accommodation in Bol, there is one thing that matters – how close is it to Zlatni Rat, the best known beach in Croatia. This hotel, part of the Bluesun chain, fulfils that basic requirement. Furthermore, if you get tired of being part of the day-long fuss at Zlatni Rat, this hotel has its own beach, just 50m from the main building, as well as the swimming pool. The rooms are pretty comfortable, and recently refurbished, and rates are reasonable, considering the location. It also gives access to a nice promenade through the pine trees, by the sea, that takes you to the centre of Bol in 20 minutes or less.

## Bol

*Hrvatskih domobrana 19, Bol (021 635 660, www.hotel-bol.com).* **€€€.**

Most accommodation in Bol is set on the strip between town centre and Zlatni Rat beach. In recent years, a few venues have opened on the slopes overlooking the town. This is one of them, a boutique hotel with 18 stylish rooms, five deluxe suites, a

**EXPLORE**

restaurant, bar, gym, sauna, pool, garage and car park. Other extras include a shuttle service from the port where the catamarans come in from Split, or towards Zlatni Rat beach. The view is another plus, away from the summer frenzy of Bol, and across the channel between Brač and Hvar.

### ★ Bračka Perla
*Put Vele Luke 53, Supetar (021 755 530, www.perlacroatia.com).* **Open** Apr-Oct. €€€.
Associated with Marmont Hotel (*see p187*) in Split, Bračka Perla has similar ambitions in style. Describing itself as an art hotel, it offers individually decorated suites (eight) and rooms (three) – with a Mediterranean floral theme – around a courtyard and garden terrace with an open-air pool, hot tub, sauna, gym and massage rooms. A communal room for occasional rainy days, a restaurant with open fire and sea views complete the picture of luxury.

### Elaphusa
*Bračna cesta 13, Bol (01 384 4288, www.bluesunhotels.com).* €€.
Renovated and upgraded, this hotel – in the pines just off the walkway to Zlatni Rat – is the best of the Bluesun group. Its 300 rooms and six suites are standard but spacious, with wooden floors; half have sea views with terraces. The facility has swimming pools indoor and out, a rock-terraced sunbathing area, spa pool, children's pool, gym and numerous courts for ball games. There's a good spa centre, plus a restaurant with themed dinners. Throw in disco bar Ela, and disco bowling, and guests need never leave.

### Kaštil
*Frane Radića 1, Bol (021 635 995, www.kastil.hr).* **Open** May-Oct. €.
Thirty-two rooms, renovated in 2008, are set inside a pretty old stone building that backs on to the harbour. The Kaštil also contains the Vusio restaurant, Topolino pizzeria and Varadero cocktail bar. Many rooms have a sea view but they're above the terrace restaurant and busy harbour – noise might be an issue.

### ★ Lipa
*Porat 1, Postira (021 599 430, www.hotelpastura. hr).* **Open** May-Sept. €€.
Postira has moved upmarket lately, mainly thanks to the owners of the Hotel Lipa that opened in 2009. It has 28 rooms, most with a sea view, and six junior suites. The tasteful, purpose-built modern accommodation also comes with an outdoor pool, hot tub and sauna. As if he wasn't busy enough, the owner also has his own farm, ensuring home-grown vegetables, wine, olive oil and other produce finds its way to the hotel's restaurant and grill. Around the bay is a new artificial beach.

### ★ Palace Dešković
*Pučišća (021 778 240, www.palaca-deskovic.com).* **Open** Apr-Nov. €€€.
By far the loveliest option on Brač. It comes with all of the contemporary accoutrements: Wi-Fi, heated bathroom floors and massage bathtubs. But the 13 rooms also come with history as the hotel is older than the town's church next door – as its name implies, it's a renovated palace. A registered cultural monument, it has been in the family since it was built

Elaphusa.

in 1467. On the outside, the Renaissance feel has held pretty steady; inside, thanks to dedicated owner Ružica, each spacious room is unique, with antique furniture and beds. In number six for example, Secessionist furniture sits atop woven oriental rugs. Adorning the walls of the 13 doubles and two suites are Ružica's paintings. At street level, the restaurant offers dishes like angler fish wrapped in bacon. Out back, a leafy, walled garden is perfect for breakfast or relaxing after investigating the little, beautiful and town-hugging Pučišća Bay.

### Villa Giardino

*Novi put 2, Bol (021 635 900).* **Open** Mid May-mid Oct. **€€**.

This old, family-run villa is usually booked in high season – but snag one of the 14 rooms and you'll be a guest in someone's mansion. The interior is meticulously arranged yet comfortably renovated, with antiques furnishing many rooms, which have air con, ceiling fans and heating. Reserve number four and slumber in the bed Emperor Franz Josef slept in on a visit in 1875. Breakfast is served on the front terrace and there's a lovely garden at the back. Note the rave reviews in the visitors' book.

### Waterman Svpetrvs Resort

*Put Vele Luke 4, Supetar (021 640 253, www. watermanresorts.com).* **Open** May-Oct. **€€**.

Part of the Adriastar Hotels Group with interests as far afield as Montenegro, this package tourist complex of 566 units, and rooms for 1,500 people, is composed of several hotels under the same management near the main beaches in Supetar. Shared facilities include a spa and sports centre. Developments during 2014-15 included an adult-only hotel and a contemporary campsite.

## BEACHES

**Zlatni Rat** is the reason why many visit Brač and certainly why they visit **Bol**. The 'Golden Cape' is the money shot in every tourist brochure. To reach it, walk west from the harbour where buses and ferries drop you off, until you reach Put Zlatnog Rata, the promenade, a shaded walkway through a pine forest that follows a rise above the beach. The resort hotels are uphill from the promenade, among the pines, and the coast is below. The first big swimming area you come to is **Potočine** beach, about a kilometre outside town. This pretty cove with small, roundish pebbles draws windsurfers and sunbathers and is packed tight during the high season.

Further on is Zlatni Rat, altogether some 30 minutes from Bol, whose 500m finger of fine shingle sticks out into the sea like a natural pier. It is constantly in motion, its shape shifting with the tides. High waves and gentle winds combine to create ideal conditions for swimming and windsurfing, especially on the westward side,

where the waves come from the open Adriatic. The water is shallow and the seabed relatively smooth – equally ideal for kids. For more privacy, head west, past the nudist beach of **Paklina**, beyond which the coast gets rockier and you'll need to swim with sandals.

Further on is a secluded location with few other bathers. There is also a small cove with a beach of sand and small pebbles a short walk east of the harbour, right before the Dominican monastery. This is close to town and can fill with bathers.

If you're staying in **Supetar**, just west of the harbour, still in the middle of town, is a sizeable child-friendly, fine-pebble beach that draws scores of bathers from the nearby resorts. If you follow the beachside path west, past the park on a small peninsula, you find more smooth pebbly beaches. If you donit mind a rocky coast, put on a pair of swimming sandals and continue west for another couple of kilometres, along a tall stone wall. Here, you'll find isolated spots where you can sunbathe on flat rocks and swim, right next to an aromatic pine forest.

## GETTING THERE & AROUND

Brač is one of the few Adriatic islands to have its own **airport** (021 559 711, www.airport-brac.hr), 15km (nine miles) north-east of Bol. To get to Supetar, a **taxi** should cost around 300kn. Supetar is the island's main **port**. Jadrolinija (www. jadrolinija.hr) runs nine to 14 **ferries** a day from the harbour in Split (30kn, 50mins) all year round.

From Supetar **buses** run to most other destinations on Brač – in summer there are five a day to Bol or Milna. The **bus station** is located just east of the ferry port. In summer Jadrolinija runs a daily **catamaran** (50kn, 50mins) from Split to Bol, then on to Jelsa on Hvar. A catamaran also runs in summer from Split to Milna (40kn, 40min), then onto Hvar. On the east coast, Sumartin is linked with Makarska on the Croatian mainland, south of Split (30kn, 1hr).

## RESOURCES

**General** *Midea Rental Services, Stjepana Radića 2, Supetar.* **Open** *Summer* 9am-midnight daily. Apartments for rent, bike and boat hire, car hire, internet access, and scooter hire.

**Internet** *Interactiv Rudina 46, Bol (no phone).* **Open** *Summer* 9am-11pm daily. Ideally situated by the harbour.

## Tourist information

**Bol Tourist Office** *Porat bolskih Pomoraca (021 635 638, www.bol.hr).* **Open** *June-Aug* 8am-10pm daily. *Sept-May* 8.30am-3pm Mon-Fri. Helpful resource set in an old building by the port.

EXPLORE

EXPLORE

**Supetar Tourist Office** *Porat 10 (021 630 900, www.supetar.hr)*. **Open** *June-Aug* 8am-10pm daily. *Sept-May* 8.30am-3pm Mon-Fri.
By the ferry port, this office is laden with brochures and excursion information.

# Hvar

Outside of Dubrovnik, **Hvar** is the epicentre of the Dalmatian travel industry. Holidaymakers come to be around the yachts lining the harbour of the island's namesake capital and among the revellers forking out more than top dollar (in Croatian terms) to party into the night. A massive overhaul of key hotels here, in the Sunčani Hvar chain, has been followed by a slower stage of development as the town comes to terms with its stardom.

## INTRODUCING HVAR

The hub of it all is Hvar town's **harbour**. In high season this pretty, petite Venice-like capital of 3,000 locals on the island's south-west tip overflows with 30,000 daily visitors. They swarm the attractive waterfront and adjoining main square, **Pjaca**, doing coffee, the nearby **market** and the modest sights by morning, the beach by day and the bars by night. Prices now match those of fashionable hotspots elsewhere on the Med. Sunčani Hvar's Amfora Hotel broke new ground when it opened in 2008, its conference centre containing an outdoor meeting area and cascading pool area lined by bars, restaurants and gardens. Another new property, Villa Nora, provides Hotel Park with welcome competition.

The agricultural plain around **Stari Grad** was included on the UNESCO World Heritage list in 2008, throwing focus onto this hitherto sleepy but delightful town and surrounds. The plain is an almost unaltered and outstanding example of a Greek land parcel system (*chora*) dating back to the fourth century BC, and with its new status have come new walking and bike trails, and the likelihood of further investment in the infrastructure of a town which offers a complete contrast to its trendy neighbour.

A burgeoning café-and-gallery vibe fits well with the low-key attitudes of Stari Grad and **Jelsa**, further east along the coast. Both are fine examples of old neighbourhoods where stone houses, ornate colonnaded balconies and winding pedestrian promenades, polished by centuries of travellers, take top billing over discos and clubs. In Jelsa's serpentine alleyways, for instance, quality eateries have sprouted up. Nearby **Vrboska** is also a delight with its tiny stone bridges, marinas and just enough restaurants and bars to keep the yachties happy. There's a sense in these towns that, except for a few mad weeks, it's just you, the locals and ancient stone decor.

For a real insight into the complete history of this lavender-covered island – a thin strip extending east for 60 kilometres (36 miles) to the isolated but charming port of **Sućuraj** – go inland to **Humac, Dol, Malo Grabje, Velo Grabje** or **Vrbanj**. These are now mostly uninhabited except for the odd konoba. The original islanders built their old stone houses safe from the mainland pirates of **Omiš** and worked the land. In Humac you will find a delightful konoba of the same name; it runs tours of the nearby **Grapčeva cave** (099 577 1770).

In Dol you have **Konoba Kokot**, another gem of a traditional family restaurant and all around you will see the olives, grapes, lavender and aloe plants that go into producing some of Croatia's finest olive oil, wine and honey.

Stari Grad is also the point of entry for car ferries from Split. It was here that Greeks from Paros settled in 385 BC and named it Pharos – later bastardised to 'Hvar'. Invading Venetians then shifted the centre of power (and the name) to the west coast port of today's Hvar town. While the Venetians were building their capital, the island became the hub of an important Croatian cultural renaissance. The elegant loggias and main square in Hvar town owe their look to Venice.

The Venetians rebuilt the town of Hvar in the early 17th century. Its centrepiece is Pjaca, or **Trg sv Stjepana**, the rectangular main square lined with shops and restaurants, framed by the harbour and **Arsenal** at one end, the market and **St Stephen's Church** at the other.

The church contains a **treasury** (open summer 10am-noon, 5-7pm daily; winter 10am-noon daily; 10kn) containing two late Renaissance paintings. The Arsenal is used as a contemporary art gallery, as well as hosting sundry cultural and prestigious local events. In the same building is one of the oldest public theatres in Europe, dating back to 1612. Above stands the **Venetian Citadel** (Španjola, 021 741 608; open summer 8am-midnight daily; 25kn), with a display of Greek and Roman finds, and a view from the ramparts. All is a stroll from the terrace cafés on the square.

Today the most prominent sight in Stari Grad is the summer retreat of 16th-century poet Petar Hektorović, the **Tvrdalj** (021 765 068; open June-Sept 10am-1pm, 6-8pm daily, 10kn), known for its inscribed walls, gardens and fishpond. Nearby, a 15th-century Dominican monastery houses a **museum** (open summer 10am-noon, 4-7.30pm Mon-Sat; 10kn) containing other Hektorović artefacts, Greek gravestones and a Tintoretto, *The Mourning of Christ*, claimed to feature Hektorović himself.

More Greek, Roman and maritime items are on display at the **Bianchini Palace** (021 766 324, www.stari-grad-museum.net; open May, June, Sept 10am-1pm Mon-Sat; July-Aug 10am-noon

& 7-9pm Mon-Sat, 7-9pm Sun; 20kn) by the Tvrdalj. Hektorović never saw his Tvrdalj finished. As a preliminary to the crucial naval Battle of Lepanto near Corfu in 1571, the Turks attacked Stari Grad, Jelsa and Hvar town.

## Restaurants

### Alviž
*Dolac, Hvar town (021 742 797, www.hvar-alviz. com).* **Open** 6pm-midnight daily. €€. Dalmatian/pizzeria
Something of an upscale pizza and pasta joint beyond Hvar town's car park and bus station, Alviž also serves first-class fish, and risotto with shrimp and curry sauce. Find a table on the back patio under the 80-year-old grapevine that winds its way above your head and still provides grapes (used by the family for the restaurant's fruit, wine, dessert wine and grappa). This venue is friendly, welcoming and down-to-earth, with a laid-back atmosphere and the best pizzas in town.

### ★ Antika
*Donja Kola, Stari Grad (021 765 479).* **Open** *Feb-Oct* noon-3pm, 6pm-1am daily. **No credit cards.** €€. International
The heart of a growing funky scene in Stari Grad, Antika is part traditional, part laid-back modern. A hotchpotch of dining room furniture sits on the pinewood floors upstairs and stone tiles below; candlesticks overflow with years of coloured wax, under wooden beam ceilings; plaster walls with framed photos and faded paintings fill a house built in 1566. Outdoor tables line the alley and piazza round the corner. The food veers away from grilled fish without subjecting you to populist pizza. Starters include dishes like tuna carpaccio, or chicken breast salad. Mains might involve shark in a sour cream and chive sauce – or steak in a garlic, green pepper, or stroganoff sauce. Opposite, Antika's café-bar serves cocktails; White Russians are the speciality. Pull up a converted tractor seat downstairs or have the friendly staff 'pulley up' your drink to the breezy terrace as you lounge on the faded orange cushion of a brown wicker couch.

### Eremitaž
*Priko, Stari Grad (021 766 167).* **Open** *Apr-Nov* noon-3pm, 6pm-midnight daily. €€. Dalmatian
This 15th-century, sea-view stone house – between the harbour and the tourist hotels – offers well-made, reasonably priced Dalmatian standards on a pretty, shaded front terrace. The building used to house sick sailors in quarantine.

### Gariful
*Riva, Hvar town (021 742 999, www.hvar-gariful. hr).* **Open** 10am-2am. €€€. Dalmatian
Gariful ('Carnation' in local dialect) is on the waterfront promenade of the Riva, alongside the superyachts berthed in the port. Unsurprisingly, it's a top-class seafood establishment, its menu based on the catch of the day prepared in any given way known in Dalmatia: grilled, *brodetto*, baked in salt, and so on. You can also get Adriatic lobster and international items such as steak or caviar. The wine list has the best possible Croatian selection, with a few top foreign labels and champagnes thrown in. The service suits the surroundings, and

**EXPLORE**

Stari Grad.

if they can't show you to a table on the terrace, there's a glass-floored interior with an aquarium underneath. Gariful is a VIP magnet, attracting the likes of Prince Harry, Roman Abramovich and Giorgio Armani.

### ★ Giaxa

*Petra Hektorovića 3, Groda, Hvar town (021 741 073, www.giaxa.com)*. **Open** *Apr-Nov* noon-midnight daily. €€€. **Contemporary Dalmatian**
For Dalmatian food with a mercurial twist, there are few better places than Giaxa, a relatively new venture from the team responsible for the highly regarded Luna a few doors down the same alley. Transforming local dishes with a touch of contemporary invention is Giaxa's main strength. Creativity runs through the whole menu. Signature dishes include a grilled octopus salad flavoured with pine nuts and peppercorns, while the *pršut*-stuffed gnocchi in asparagus sauce represents a perfect marriage between tradition and invention. Mains feature dishes like poached sea bass stuffed with scampi and wild herbs, or lobster in tomato and white wine sauce. In summer, look out for the daily three-course tasting menus. The setting is as splendid as the food, a 15th-century Gothic palace that once belonged to the Jakša family. A trio of stone columns run down the centre of the dining room, overlooked by brightly coloured wooden animal sculptures courtesy of local artist Darko Šoša.

Giaxa.

### Huljić

*Banski Dolac (091 178 8880)*. **Open** *June-mid Sept* 6pm-midnight daily. **No credit cards**. €€. **Dalmatian**
Huljić is a real find. Guests are looked after – over red and white wines made by owner Teo Huljić – before a meal at the four-storey collection of terraces that is the restaurant proper. The design theme is handcrafted sturdy: wood and stone on stone tiles. An old wine press sits in the corner as world music wafts. The bar forming a centrepeice for the restaurant has a terracotta roof and a tree sprouting through it. The philosophy, according to Teo, is part Dalmatian and part New Age – grilled tuna with fruit sauce of figs, melon, wine and herbs for example. Booking is recommended.

### Humac

*Humac (091 523 9463, 021 768 108)*. **Open** *Summer* noon-10pm daily. **No credit cards**. €€. **Dalmatian**
In a deserted village of the same name surrounded by lavender fields some eight kilometres east of Jelsa, signposted on the bumpy main road to Sućuraj, this traditional konoba serves all the classic Dalmatian specialities by candlelight, cooked over an open flame. This is no gimmick – as well as no permanent inhabitants, Humac has no electricity. The restaurant is also where to gather for tours of the nearby Grapčeva Cave.

### Jurin Podrum

*Donja kola 11, Stari Grad (021 765 804)*. **Open** *Summer* noon-2.30pm, 6pm-midnight daily. €€. **Dalmatian**
Set in the tangle of streets in Stari Grad old town, this is a fine local bistro. There's seating outdoors and a picture of Tito on the wall inside under the beams and Christmas lights. To match the changing artwork, the food philosophy is slightly different. As well as the usual shellfish-in-sauces are handy diversions such as octopus, and courgette spaghetti.

### Konoba Gusarska Luka

*Sućuraj waterfront (021 773 214, 098 911 2342)*. **Open** *Mar-Dec* 6am-midnight daily. €€. **Dalmatian**
Sućuraj has a surprising number of good, traditional restaurants but Gusarska Luka is the one locals recommend. It's nearly always busy and usually the last one to close. Alongside the standard Dalmatian fish and meat offerings, *Gusarski ražnjić* consists of two skewers of roasted meat and vegetables. The view is good too but you're hard pushed to find a bad one around Sućuraj's lovely bay.

### Lucullus

*Petra Hektorovića, Groda, Hvar town (021 718 073, www.villanora.eu)*. **Open** 6pm-1am daily. €€. **Dalmatian**

a fireplace and modern art on display. The grilled fish, though pricey, is awfully good. Regulars swear by it, phoning owner Nikša Barišić ahead of time, during the day, to see what's fresh for them later on. Fishermen come every day to let Nikša plan his menu. But don't be frightened to go on a limb and try the Big Mama: steak stuffed with cheese, ham and olives.

### Me and Mrs Jones
*Mala banda, Jelsa (021 761 882).* **Open** *Summer* 8am-noon, 5pm-midnight daily. *Winter* 5-11pm Fri-Sun. €€. **Dalmatian**
Often overlooked on Hvar, Jelsa is now the only town on the island connected to the mainland by seaplane. It's a picturesque municipality with excellent beaches, and recently, the culinary highlight of Me and Mrs Jones. The former Konoba Napoleon is set in the middle of the old harbour, opposite the seaplane port; it's named after the owners' favourite song. The restaurant is equally selective when compared to the standard menus around the Dalmatian islands, still based on seafood, but with some non-traditional twists in the cooking and presentation. (Think shrimp and wild boar pasta.) Location is a major plus, with a view over the oldest part of Jelsa; no website but search for 'Me and mrs jones Jelsa' on Facebook.

### Passarola
*Mate Miličića 10, Hvar town (021 717 374, www. restaurant-passarola.eu).* **Open** 10am-midnight daily. €€. **Dalmatian**
The usual take on gastronomy on Hvar is that the waterfront restaurants should be your first port of call, but there is also a fine selection of spots in the narrow streets north of the cathedral. One such venue, with a good reputation, is Passarola. It's a seafood restaurant with more modern, slightly artistic, approach to cooking and plating. It also offers meat dishes you wouldn't ordinarily find nearby, such as beefsteak in truffle sauce, and duck breast à l'orange. There are classics, too: tuna steak, risotto with shrimp and asparagus, and various pasta dishes.

Under the same ownership as the Villa Nora (*see p223*), this celebrated restaurant with an atmospheric stone interior is presided over by jovial chef-owner Antun Matković, who frequently emerges from the kitchen to join customers at their table. His motto is, 'No food is good unless the cook preparing it does so with his own hands.' There is plenty of seafood, plus local specialities such as goat with potatoes roasted in a brick oven. Reservations recommended.

### Luviji
*Jurja Novaka 6, Hvar town (091 519 8444).* **Open** *May-Sept* 6pm-2am daily. **No credit cards**. €€. **Dalmatian**
This former basic wine cellar and family house behind the church on the main square now lead to a roof terrace restaurant. Actually, there are only three big tables and the menu is whatever is fresh that day (lobster spaghetti, ideally), but essentially this is a family-run eaterie serving age-old Dalmatian favourites – with a panoramic view.

### Macondo
*Groda, Hvar town (021 742 850).* **Open** *Apr-Oct* noon-2pm, 6.30pm-midnight Mon-Sat; 6.30pm-midnight Sun. €€€. **Dalmatian**
You'll be lucky to grab a table here, at the harbour end of Groda – but the interior is homely enough, with

### ★ Robinson
*Mekičevića Bay (091 383 5160, www.robinson-hvar.hr).* **Open** *June-mid Sept* 11am-nightfall daily. **No credit cards**. €€. **Dalmatian**
About a 45-minute trek from Hvar town towards Milna on a path along the sea, Robinson – without electricity or water, hence the name – sits on a secluded bay prized by sailboats. (If you would prefer, call Domagoj, owner, chef and waiter, to set you up with a boat.) After you get to the spot, you put in your order then take a swim in water even bluer than usual because the beach stones are bleached white. The beach empties when Domagoj offers lunch and a beer under a thatched roof. Specialities include *gregada, pašticada, brodetto*, grilled fish, lobster, lamb and octopus salad. What he doesn't catch or grow is shipped over every day.

EXPLORE

## San Marco
*Hotel Palace, Trg sv Stjepana, Hvar town (091 174 1500, www.suncanihvar.com).* **Open** *Apr-Oct* 11am-midnight daily. **€€€. Dalmatian**
The flagship restaurant of the oldest Hvar hotel, the Palace, is in keeping with the historic character of its surroundings. The food on offer is typically Dalmatian: fish grills, seafood delicacies and succulent meat dishes. It's served as a live band entertains with jazz and blues while a Venetian terrace helps provide the ideal formula for a romantic night out.

## Turan
*Jelsa (021 761 441).* **Open** *mid Apr-mid Oct* 5pm midnight daily. **€€. Dalmatian**
At the back of Jelsa old town and up a leafy and nameless incline, keep an eye out for Turan (the restaurant's current name) and for Dominko (its former name and that of its parent company). The venue is one and the same. The establishment is worth exploring for the friendly staff and the fabulous terrace, ideal for summer dining. Host Martin prides himself on *peka* specialities – producing meat and lobster from under the traditional coal-covered, bell-shaped metal lid – and flambé desserts.

## Zlatna Školjka
*Petra Hektorovića 8, Groda, Hvar town (098 168 8797, www.zlatna.skoljka.com).* **Open** *May-Oct* noon-3pm, 7-11pm Mon-Fri; noon-3pm, 7pm-midnight Sat, Sun. **€€. Dalmatian**
Billing itself as a slow food restaurant, the 'Golden Shell' at the church end of Hektorovića does a number of inventive dishes along with Dalmatian standards. Varieties of lamb stew are a house speciality as well as home-made gnocchi in wondrous sauces and cheese in olive oil. You eat on a simple shaded terrace with unpretentious checked tablecloths. Owner Ivo also offers a challenge menu: effectively a four-course tasting menu of either 'land' or 'sea' dishes.

## Zorače
*Uvala Zorače (021 745 638).* **Open** *Summer* 11am-11pm daily. **€€. Dalmatian**
Run by the Barišić family, this *konoba* in Zorače, six kilometres from Hvar town, is set in a small, quiet bay. Food is typical, local and good. Fresh fish and meat are grilled over an open fire or slow-cooked in the traditional way under the bell. You can order in advance when you reserve the best outside table, set on top of the cliff – great for a sunset beverage before dinner. Dining here is like going round a friend's house, relaxed and friendly, which is no bad thing when Hvar is so rapidly going upmarket. Access can be an adventure: Zorače is at the bottom of a steep narrow road, and parking is tight in high season.

## Zvijezda Mora
*Petra Zorinića, Hvar town (091 564 5487, www.zvijezdamora.com).* **Open** *Summer* noon-midnight daily. **€€. Dalmatian**

Zvijezda Mora brings the best local produce and Mediterranean cuisine to life – with flair – in a lovely setting close to the seafront. Choose the freshest fish or decide on stuffed squid or *brudet* (seafood stew). The desserts, including almond and red pepper semifreddo, or lavender and chilli panna cotta, blow you away. The wine list complements the various dishes well so relax and give your taste buds a treat.

# Cafés & Bars

## Adriana Top Bar
*Obala Fabrika 28, Hvar town (021 750 200, www.suncanihvar.com).* **Open** 10am-2am daily.
As its name suggests, the Adriana Top Bar sits atop one of the finest hotels in the luxurious Sunčani Hvar hotel chain, in the north-west corner of the old port. Prices take into account the panoramic view of the most beautiful parts of Hvar town, but for those who can afford to indulge in the summer fuss around the Hvar Riva, it's probably not a problem. Besides cocktails, food is available in the shape of salads, sandwiches and burgers. *Photos pp220-221.*

## BB Club featuring Shrimp House
*Hotel Riva, Hvar town (021 750 750).* **Open** 8am-2am daily.
In tune with Hvar town's new cosmopolitanism, the BB Club appeals to the party-minded fraternity whose yachts gently bob around the harbour outside the restaurant door. A DJ spins on the waterfront terrace while mixologists fix quality cocktails – note the Hvar Rose Martini (vodka, vermouth, grenadine and orange bitters). There are burgers, club sandwiches and Mexican dishes too.

## Café Nonica
*Kroz Burak 23, Hvar town (no phone).* **Open** 8am-2pm, 5-11pm Mon-Sat; 5-11pm Sun. **No credit cards.**
It's about time that Hvar town's stodgy-strudel bakery scene got a shake-up. Located on the narrow stone alley that threads its way through Burak, just uphill from the Riva, 'Granny's Cafe' is everything you might want from a cake shop, with muffins, brownies, thick slices of torte and good quality coffee. There's a lot of local fare here too, with traditional biscuits like *Hforski koloč* ('Hvar cake', a melt-in-the-mouth affair with a mild citrus flavour) piled up on the display counter. With limited space inside and a couple of chairs out in the alley, it's a shame there are so few tables.

## Colonnade Beach Bar
*Bonj les Bains, Amfora bay, Hvar town (091 452 4702, /www.suncanihvar.com).* **Open** *Summer* 11am-2am daily.
A palm beach club in the classic mould, the Colonnade suits the Riviera chic of its location, Bonj les Bains beach. It's not only the champagne cocktails, there's quality dining too.

## ★ Hula Hula Beach Bar

*Majerovića (no phone, www.hulahulahvar.com).*
**Open** *Mid May-late Sept* 9am-9pm daily.
**No credit cards.**
This is the place for daytime partying and après-beach relaxing. It's a short walk round the coast from the Hotel Amfora on a reasonably isolated jut of coastland called Majerovića. The decor is Bali-meets-Adriatic with comfy recliners, fringed umbrellas and a wooden bar. While lounging with a piña colada or margarita, listening to the soulful tunes and watching the sunset – in one of the few spots in town where it actually disappears into the sea – you can order food from the adjoining bistro. Dubbed Bubba Gump, it does salads, Thai curry or big snacks.

## Kiva Bar

*Fabrika, Hvar town (no phone, www.kivabarhvar. com).* **Open** *Summer* 9am-2.30am daily. *Winter* 9am-2.30am Fri, Sat. **No credit cards.**
When the competition all around is wicker and swizzle sticks, Kiva is an honest-to-goodness bar. It says so on the wall ('It's A Bar!') and sticks to its word, playing old rock 'n' roll faves, funk and jazz in a loud, intimate, stone room. It's true that it once displayed the lyrics to 'Imagine', a cheap toy guitar and peace signs – unforgivable trespasses anywhere else – but with music this good and drinking this serious, they must be having us on. Find it just behind the quay, in a narrow alley.

## Konoba Menego

*Groda, Hvar town (021 742 411, www.menego.hr).*
**Open** *Apr-Nov* noon-2pm, 6-10pm Mon-Sat.
**No credit cards.**
This wine bar is as close to traditional as downtown Hvar gets: candles in old holders, legs of ham hanging from the ceiling of a stone dining area, oars everywhere, ropes, nets, goat skins and farm implements, wicker lampshades above the wooden tables, and serious-looking ancestors in black and white photos. The menus are strapped to tools. Red wine from the family vineyard – on the island of Sveti Klement – is front and centre. This is accompanied by small dishes equivalent to tapas, but Croatian: *Pag* cheese, *pršut* from Drniš, marinated anchovies, and the hard-to-find *Forska pogača* (Hvar anchovy pie). Try figs with almonds steeped in rakija to finish.

## Libido

*Jelsa (no phone).* **Open** *Summer* 6pm-2am daily.
**No credit cards.**
This is a Jelsa cornerstone, located where the beach meets the harbour, above Gringo's pizzeria, under the same umbrella. (Look for the giant neon 'wine & cocktail bar' sign.) Bohemian artwork, beaded candleholders, African masks and panoramic seaside views provide the backdrop for jigging to clubby music and sipping on seriously strong cocktails like the Kick in the Balls (rum, melon liqueur, coconut, orange juice and cream).

## Loco Bar

*Trg sv Stjepana, Hvar town (no phone).*
**Open** *Summer* 9am-3am daily. *Winter* 8am-midnight daily. **No credit cards.**
The first thing Zoran, the bar owner, will tell you: Loco has the best coffee in town. It's definitely the least expensive, and it is good. This is one of the few places that doesn't automatically raise its prices every season – consequently, locals drink here. One of several venues lining the main square, the Loco Bar is a tremendous place to relax before submerging into – or emerging from – the crowded Hvar alleyways. Upstairs in the classic old stone-and-wood interior, Zoran's paintings are on display, and for sale in his atelier. Outside, striped lounge furniture, a happy and funky assortment of musical sounds and decent mixed drinks, plus various snacks, make this one of the brighter spots in the locality. On Facebook search for 'Loco Bar Hvar'.

## Pinetta

*Donjo Kolo (091 227 661).* **Open** *Summer* 6pm-1am daily. **No credit cards.**
While neighbouring Nautica themes on wood and white sails, Pinetta tends towards a wine-bar style with warm-coloured, comfy sofas on tiled or stone floors, surrounded by stone walls. It's ideal for sampling Hvar's autochthonous red Plavac wines from Svirće and Sveta Nedelja. Nibbles include anchovies, pâtés, cheese, cold cuts, bruschette and salads but most people pick Pinetta for its relaxing ambience. A few tables line the alley outside.

## Red Baron

*Riva, Hvar town (091 251 8212).* **Open** *May-Sept* 8am-2am daily.
Currently the busiest of the bars on the marina strip, Red Baron has an ideal location and you don't have to shell out too much to enjoy it – prices are reasonable. The other key to its success is its outdoor lounge feel, with chairs and tables pressed up against ancient stone walls on one side, an open awning providing clear views of fancy yachts on the other. Cocktails, Hvar wines and sweet, heady Dalmatian *prošek* are on the drinks list; music is uptempo but not club-volume-deafening. It's a great place for a refined – but not too refined – night out. On Facebook search for 'Red Baron Hvar'.

## Tarantela

*Pjaca, Jelsa (no phone).* **Open** *Summer* 8am-2pm, 4pm-2am daily. **No credit cards.**
On the main square, this Jelsa institution has a plain interior, and an expansive terrace where all the action happens. Named after the local snub-nosed lizard, Tarantela has generated a community of regulars over the last few years, a fine collection of CDs and peppy staff, crazy Mario and the crew, overseen by progressive bar owner Dominic. Chilled by day, cool for sundown cocktails and absolutely ideal pre-club.

**EXPLORE**

Adriana Top Bar. See p218.

### ★ Tri Pršuta Wine Bar
*Petra Hektorovića, Groda, Hvar town (098 969 6193).* **Open** *Summer* 6pm-2.30am daily. **No credit cards.**
Pršuta is your sanctuary when Groda is groaning elbow-to-elbow in high season; affable owner Vidan won't hesitate to discuss the history and culinary specialities of Croatia. Wood-beamed ceilings and antique furniture surround sofas; *pršut* hams hang from above. A glass of top-quality red like a Zlatan Plavac Grand Cru, goes perfectly with a plate of regional sheep cheese, or whatever Vidan decides to bring out that day and share with the room. It's not uncommon for perfect strangers to become friends and sample each other's tipples. The wine cabinet even contains a 1947 Bourgogne. There is, at any given moment, more than €1,000 worth of vino open behind the bar – and a guitar sitting in the corner for anyone who feels the inclination.

## Nightlife

### ★ Carpe Diem
*Riva, Hvar town (021 742 369, www.carpe-diem-hvar.com).* **Open** *Summer* 9am-2am daily. *Winter* 9am-midnight daily.
Opened in 1999, Carpe Diem is still the landmark cocktail-swigging hangout of celebs and the yachting fraternity. After daytime coffee, 'Sunset Grooves' greets the post-beach crowd from 5pm, there's a fashion show twice a week, DJs kick it at night. Behind a loggia facade, it's surprisingly ordinary inside however, with just higher-than-ordinary prices and standard music for the genre. Its reputation stems

from its VIP scene in high season, fuelling the Hvar hype. Its reservation-only policy in August (put your name on the list as you pass by in the day) means that the terrace, and separate bar, operates as a celebrity zone. Carpe Diem's other venue, Carpe Diem Beach, is a ten-minute boat ride from town. At Stipanska Bay, Marinkovac, amid pine forest and beach it has bars, terraces, restaurants and a spa area.

### Chuara
*Jelsa waterfront (no phone).* **Open** *Summer* 9am-1pm, 5pm-5am daily. *Winter* 8pm-3am daily. **No credit cards.**
This enclosed courtyard lounge, full of urban flair, gets marks for style: white cotton chair covers and red lights highlight a billowing white cotton awning above giant palms. A café by day and club by night, Chuara's main service to Jelsa is as a pulsating disco. There's also occasional live music.

### Pink Champagne Hvar
*Ive Miličića 4, Hvar town (021 742 283, www.pink champagnehvar.com).* **Open** midnight-dawn daily.
Hvar's nightspots attract the rich and famous to its beach and waterfront but Pink Champagne shows that it's possible to create a similar kind of buzz just outside the town centre. Partnered with another leading venue, Hula Hula, this luxurious and upscale club has a burlesque feel, hosting nightly cabaret and regular DJ parties. The real fun usually begins around 2am – when everywhere else is getting a little bit tired – with performers on stage and a packed dance floor, no matter if it's an 1980s night or electronica. VIP booths available by reservation only.

feel but boasts serious amenities: a big spa complex with all the treatments and classes, including yoga; a rooftop terrace with heated swimming pools indoor and out; and a panoramic bar. Rooms come in shades of lavender-purple in tribute to the island's most famous crop; those with sea views have excellent views of the old port.

### ★ Amfora, Hvar Grand Beach Resort

*Biskupa Jurja Dubokovića 5, Hvar town (021 750 300, www.suncanihvar.hr).* **Open** May-Oct. **€€€.**
The Amfora reopened its doors in the summer of 2008 as a swish holiday hotel that also has the best conference facilities on the island. Set in pine trees a ten-minute walk from the main square in Hvar town, it's Hvar's largest hotel, its sweeping concrete wings perched above a cascading pool ideal for paddlers, and a crescent of pebbly beach on the seafront below. The exclusive Bonj les Bains beach house and lounge bar is a few steps away, as is the Splash bar, for après-beach DJ parties. Rooms are decked out in pristine whites and feature well-chosen contemporary furniture. Classic views of the Pakleni islands open up from the sea-facing doubles. There is a gym on the top floor, and free Wi-Fi throughout. *Photo p222.*

### Hvar

*Racic, Jelsa (021 761 024, www.hotelhvar-adriatiq. com).* **Open** May-mid Oct. **€€.**
The best of the Adriatiq Hotels (formerly Jelsa Holiday) resorts on the island, Hotel Hvar is well equipped with indoor and outdoor swimming pools, an exercise room and a children's club. All 206 rooms have balconies, with sea or inland views. Beaches are a hop away. Rates are half-board.

### The Palace, Hvar Hotel

*Trg sv Stjepana 5, Hvar town (021 741 966, www.suncanihvar.hr).* **Open** May-mid Nov. **€€.**
This historic hotel right on the harbourfront was revamped in 2008. Occupying a section of Venetian loggia, it now features an indoor pool, upgraded rooms, and a restaurant with a Venetian terrace, offering quality Med dishes and live music. All this has been achieved without disturbing the protected historic exterior.

### ★ Pansion Meneghello

*Palmižana, Sv Klement, Pakleni islands (021 717 270, 091 478 3111, www.palmizana.hr).* **Open** Apr-Oct. **€€.**
This is a unique island retreat, a taxi-boat journey from Hvar town, dunked amid the exotic botanical garden of cacti, palms and Central American succulents planted by Eugen Meneghello in the years before World War I. Still run by the Meneghello family, the complex is designed for relaxation, with 13 bungalows stuffed with examples of the family's art collection, art shows on the veranda, and a stellar restaurant. Palmižana beach, just below the Meneghello's place, can be busy with day-trippers

### Veneranda Club Hvar

*Stipanska, Hvar town (no phone, www.facebook. com/Veneranda.hr).* **Open** *Summer* 10am-5am daily. **No credit cards.**
Set in a hillside Venetian fortress on the western side of Hvar town's harbour, the Veneranda is an open-air disco with DJs, of course, and dancers, who inevitably end up in the swimming pool around the dancefloor. Look out for flyers around town and be prepared to pay a premium, by local standards, at weekends.

### ★ Vila Verde

*Jelsa waterfront (www.vilaverde.info).*
**Open** *Summer* 7pm-2am daily. **No credit cards.**
Under bar chief Ivana Gamulin, VV is the liveliest spot away from Hvar town. In a vast garden terrace of pebbles surrounded by palms and oleanders, a crowd of locals and internationals soak in the night air and sip cocktails made of fresh ingredients, like mint picked on the premises. Designated drivers can still belly up to the bar and order from a bevy of milkshakes including the Bomba (banana, peaches, nuts, milk and sugar). As a bartender hand-crushes ice, and grinds brown sugar and lime before mixing in cachaça for a signature Caipirinha, a DJ blends acid funk on the portico of the once private hacienda. Occasional live acts.

## Hotels

### Adriana, Hvar Spa Hotel

*Fabrika 28, Hvar town (021 750 200, www.suncanihvar.com).* **€€€.**
This Sunčani makeover, overlooking the yacht harbour, is small enough to retain an intimate boutiquey

EXPLORE

during the day, but in the evenings and early mornings you have the whole of this uniquely calming island to yourself. You can also go diving, sailing or take an art workshop, all in one day. Stays of seven days are preferred in high season.

▶ *See also the more upscale Villa Meneghello in Hvar town, same website.*

### Pansion Murvica
*Sv Rok, Hvar town (021 761 405, 091 550 2596, www.murvica.net).* **No credit cards. €€.**
Set behind the bus station, and signposted on the right as you enter town, this comfortable family-run pension consists of three studio apartments (all with a kitchenette) and a double room. Its decent restaurant opens from Easter to Hallowe'en. There's not much of a view but if you prefer character to package hotels, choose this. Breakfast is a few euro extra.

### Park
*Bankete, Hvar town (021 718 337, www. hotelparkhvar.com).* **€€.**
Next to the Palace over the harbour, this is the alternative to the Sunčani Hvar hotels. Set in a Baroque building, the Park has 14 apartments of varying sizes and one room, tastefully kitted out with sleek white couches and modern wooden furniture against bare stone. All have plasma TVs, massage showers and views of the sea and Pakleni islands.

### Podstine
*Put Podstina 11, Podstine (021 740 400, www. podstine.com).* **Open** May-Oct. **€€.**
Also not tied to the Sunčani Hvar chain, the

family-run Podstine has 52 rooms and is tucked away by its own beach a 15-minute walk down the coast from Hvar town harbour. Prices for sea-view rooms increase gradually from May through to high season, but you'll also be getting a lovely terrace restaurant, spa centre, tennis courts, outdoor swimming pool and any number of rental and excursion options, including the hotel's own yacht.

### ★ Riva, Hvar Yacht Harbour Hotel
*Obala Riva 27, Hvar town (021 750 100, www. suncanihvar.hr).* **€€€.**
The Riva is a classy and pricey hotel set in a century-old building on Hvar town harbour front. The 54 rooms over three floors are seriously trendy – note the see-through shower doors and artsy pictures of Bardot, Dean or Hepburn. Strong reds, contemporary design and nude murals in the hallways give the hotel a hedonistic edge. The Riva also has its cosy nooks however – the sloping-ceilinged attic room (number 313) is one of the cutest on the island. All have flatscreen TVs and Wi-Fi. Amenities are also dictated by space – there's no room for a gym or a pool – but ample attention has been given to the upscale Roots Mediterranean restaurant and the terrace BB bar, where you can look forward to tasty cocktails and a summer of regular DJ appearances.

### ★ Vila Irming
*Put Veleg kamica 8, Sv Nedjelja, near Jelsa (no phone, www.irming.hr).* **Open** May-Oct. **No credit cards. €.**
A 15-minute drive from Stari Grad or Jelsa, through the Pitve-Zavala road tunnel, brings you to Sveta

Amfora, Hvar Grand Beach Resort. See p221.

Nedjelja, a romantic wine and fishing village at the bottom of Sveti Nikola hill. There are two good restaurants, Tamaris and Bilo Idro, and one shop. The Privoras' detached villa sits in the middle of a sheltered grove, imbued with the pure scent of pine and sea. Hammocks are hung in the garden, sun loungers just below, there's a pebble beach and marina a minute away. There's great climbing and a deserted lagoon five minutes away. Fire up the barbecue for freshly caught fish. The Privoras can organise everything, including transfers to and from Hvar town.

### Villa Meneghello

*Križni rat 26, Hvar town (021 717 270, www.villameneghello.com).* €€€.
The Meneghellos of Pansion Meneghello fame have opened a villa in the quiet Križni rat part of town, hosting a dozen or more people in two self-contained, family-sized apartments. The house is set in a huge garden overlooking the sea, 15 minutes' walk from the town centre. The apartments can be rented separately or together as a whole house. With fully-equipped kitchens, walls covered in contemporary Croatian artworks, a dinky outdoor pool and a summer kitchen in the garden, modern bohemian luxury in the Meneghello style is assured.

### Villa Nora

*Petra Hektorovića, Groda, Hvar town (021 742 498, www.villanora.eu).* €€.
The four rooms and five suites in a newly restored 14th-century palace in the heart of Hvar town provide a welcome choice. Independently owned Villa Nora, which also owns Restaurant Lucullus which provides breakfast, has set about making this venue as chic and individual as possible – the spacious superior rooms and suites are warm in their decor and as generous in mod cons as you would expect for the price. The relatively small building does not allow for much in the way of additional facilities but you're right in the centre of things.

## BEACHES

In **Hvar town**, the pebbly **Amfora Grand** beach is in front of the Hotel Amfora. Next door is **Bonj les Bains**, a bathing platform backed with renovated 1930s changing rooms, a Sensori C spa for massages, sun loungers and showers. Just two kilometres north-west is the beach of the **Hotel Sirena**, secluded amid pine and wild sage; there's a bar and grill too. A further two kilometres away is **Kamp Vira**, a pebble beach with a flat shore and good facilities.

**Stari Grad** features beaches lining each side of the bay, the southern one towards Borić less crowded; and **Jelsa** has child-friendly **Mina**. Other spots near Jelsa include **Grebišce**, 1.5 kilometres away, where you'll also find the bar-restaurant Corni Petar. Taxi boats run to the Glavića peninsula and the nudist beach on nearby **Zečevo island**.

On the undeveloped south coast, **Zavala**, **Dubovica** and **Sveta Nedjelja** are secluded and an easy taxi journey from the main three towns. A 45-minute hike east of Hvar town (before Milna) is rewarded with the crystal-clean, white-stone **Mekičevića Bay** frequented by naturists and known as **Robinson's Beach** – with the restaurant of the same name.

Get the boat taxi (30kn, 30mins) to the beaches of the **Pakleni islands**, in particular the sandy one at **Palmižana**. Naturists gather at **Jerolim** and **Stipanska** on **Marinkovac**, site of the renowned Carpe Diem Beach bar.

## EXCURSIONS

Public transport on Hvar island can be, at best, inconvenient, with an infrequent **bus route** between Hvar, Stari Grad and Jelsa. The best way to explore its coves and villages is by using a **hire car**, **bike** or **moped**. In Hvar town, Navigare (021 718 721, 099 447 0700, www.renthvar.com) on the main square rents out scooters, boats and cars, as does Luka Rent (021 742 946, 091 591 7111, www.lukarent.com) at the harbour.

Zvir (Križna Luka, 021 741 415, www.jkzvir.hr) is a renowned sailing club. **Marinas** include Adriatic Croatia International Vrboska (021 774 018, www.aci-club.hr) and the ACI Marina in Palmižana on the Pakleni islands just off the coast of Hvar town (021 744 995, www.aci-club.hr).

The best of the handful of **diving clubs** on Hvar is the Divecenter Hvar (aka Diving Center Jurgovan, 021 741 603, www.divecenter-hvar.com) by the Hotel Amfora, a short walk from the harbour from the action.

For **sea kayaking**, **sailing tuition**, **hiking**, **climbing** or a combination package, Hvar Adventure (021 717 813, 091 154 3072, www.hvar-adventure.com) just off the harbour behind the theatre, offers the best range. Secret Hvar (021 717 615, www.secrethvar.com) offers walking tours and jeep safaris taking in the best of the island's natural beauty, archaeological heritage and culinary culture.

## GETTING THERE & AROUND

Unlike Brač, Hvar has no airport. European Coastal Airlines (www.ec-air.eu) runs a **seaplane** service to Jelsa from Split airport.

**Car ferries** arrive at Stari Grad, 16km (ten miles) to the east of Hvar town, where traffic is barred from the centre. Seven a day run from Split in summer, three in winter (1hr 45mins, 45kn foot passengers, 265kn-588kn cars). Ferries running on the main coastal line down from Rijeka or up from Dubrovnik also call at Stari Grad, as do international lines from Ancona and Pescara on the Italian coast, run by Jadrolinija, Split Tours and SNAV. Another regular ferry option from the

**EXPLORE**

# BLUE NOON

*You'll rave about the cave on Bišev*

Every day, around midday, a small miracle takes place inside the sombre stone walls of Biševo island's half-submerged *Modra špilja* (Blue Cave). The water in the bottom of the chamber lights up from below, giving off an eerie blue glow. It's easy to imagine that ancient visitors might have regarded this as spiritual. Nowadays it is the site of regular pilgrimages, but by tourists. In summer, between the peak hours of 11am and 1.30pm, scores of boats take a 10-15 minute float through the cave, allowing passengers to gawp at the light show before they head to a nearby beach.

The Blue Cave is a natural hole carved into rock along the shore of Biševo island, which is the five-kilometre (three-mile) chunk of land you'll notice off to the south-west, as you look out to sea from Komiža on Vis island. The floor of the Blue Cave is submerged, and it has an underwater entrance on its seaward side. When the midday sun is right over, the light shines through this entrance, causing the stunning effect of blueness. Unfortunately, the cave is usually so full of boats – coming via a thoroughly unnatural

19th-century entrance – that you can't jump in for a swim in the magically lit water. Some scuba centres offer a diving tour of the cave, via the underwater portal, but you will have to stay submerged, as the boats make surfacing impossible.

Srebrna Tours (Ribarska 4, 021 713 668, www.srebrnatours.hr) and most other travel agencies in Komiža arrange day trips (around 100kn per head). You leave between 9am and 11am for the 45-minute boat ride between Komiža and a dock on Biševo island, where you'll have time to order drinks from the thatch-roofed bar. A smaller boat picks you up there and takes you on the round-trip cave tour.

While it's a long way to go for a quick peek at the cave, probably the best part of the day is still to come. On most trips, once the cave-touring boat drops you back at the dock, your original boat returns and takes you on to Porat, a secluded beach on the western side of Biševo. There's another thatch-roof snack bar and a decent seafood restaurant, Konoba Porat. All afternoon you can frolic on these lovely sands before the jaunt back to Komiža – you, and your fellow tourists.

mainland is at Drvenik on the Makarska Riviera to the isolated town of Sućuraj (40min, 15kn, 90kn-186kn cars) on Hvar's eastern tip. Sućuraj is practically isolated as far as local buses are concerned, so you need your own transport or arrange for someone to pick you up.

Hvar town and Jelsa are served by Jadrolinija **catamarans** on various routes from Split. There is also a privately-run catamaran (Krilo) from Split to Korčula that calls at Hvar town. These are busy in high season – try to buy tickets in advance.

Hvar **buses** are timed to coincide with incoming and departing ferries to Stari Grad harbour. About seven a day head from Hvar town to Stari Grad harbour ('trajekt' on timetables) and Stari Grad town (30mins), with a couple more on summer weekends. From Stari Grad harbour to Stari Grad town, the bus covers the 3km journey before calling at or linking with Vrboska and Jelsa.

A **taxi** between Hvar town and Stari Grad costs around 250kn. Agree on a price with reliable Tihi Taxis (098 894 825 and 098 338 824, www.tihi-hvar.com) beforehand.

## RESOURCES

### Tourist information

**Hvar Tourist Office** *Trg sv Stjepana, Hvar town (021 741 059, www.tzhvar.hr).* Open *June-Oct* 8am-2.30pm, 3.30-10pm daily. *Nov-May* 8am-2pm Mon-Sat.

**Hvar Turistik** *Jurja Škarpe 13, Stari Grad (021 717 580, 091 895 7733, www.hvar-touristik.com).* **Open** *May, Oct* 10.30am-12.30pm, 4.30-6.30pm Mon-Sat. *June, Sept* 10.30 am-1.30pm, 4.40-7pm Mon-Sat. *July, Aug* 10am-2pm, 4-8pm daily. Recommended room-booking service in Stari Grad.

**Jelsa Tourist Office** *Mala Banda (021 761 017, www.tzjelsa.hr).* **Open** *Summer* 8am-10pm Mon-Sat; 10am-noon, 7pm-9pm Sun. *Winter* 8am-1pm Mon-Fri.

**Stari Grad Tourist Office** *Obala Dr Franje Tudjmana (021 765 763, www.stari-grad-faros.hr).* **Open** *Summer* 8am-10pm Mon-Sat; 9am-noon, 6-8pm Sun. *Winter* 8am-2pm Mon-Fri; 9am-noon Sat.

# Vis

**Vis** island has a special place in the hearts of many Croatians, who consider this a truly unspoiled example of the best of the Dalmatian coast. Its designation as a military base under Tito froze development for more than 40 years, allowing farming and fishing to remain the dominant activities.

Now tourism is taking over this remote spot, one of the farthest islands from the mainland. Vis has become a hot destination among those in the know who want a quiet getaway amid a gorgeous patch of clear sea, which provides great fish, swimming and diving.

While the party scene here may not be as raucous as on Hvar, Vis island's gastronomy can compare with any Dalmatian destination. The natives, whose dialect is a Croatian-Venetian hybrid incomprehensible to many Croats, take real pride in their unique culture – and cuisine. Local fishermen and farmers provide the produce for native specialities like *viška pogača*, a sardine-stuffed bread, while vintners provide indigenous wines, such as the red Plavac and white Vugava.

Traditionally, the farmers and vintners are from around **Vis town**, the main port in the north-east, closest to the mainland. Fishing, though less intense than it once was, is still centred around the more secluded village of **Komiža**, on the seaward side of this 17-kilometre (ten-mile) long island. Between these two main settlements are smaller villages, some famous restaurants and wonderful beaches.

## INTRODUCING VIS

Vis town was created through the union of the seaside communities of **Luka**, the working harbour area, and **Kut**, the neighbourhood with more food, fun and night-time action. Both sides are relatively quiet during daytime beach hours, and a lot of the restaurants only open around 6pm. The marina brings in a sizeable yachting crowd who support a growing number of gourmet restaurants. Students also come here for the fantastic nearby beaches and bars.

Komiža feels slightly more bohemian. This is the place to enjoy an easy-going Mediterranean pace and excellent pebbly beaches. Many of Komiža's hospitality industry staff are year-round residents who tend to be more friendly and casual than summer workers, the latter more focused on tips.

Despite the relaxed atmosphere, the village has some fancy, formal restaurants. Refreshingly, there is no nightlife industry per se, with the recent exception of **Fort George**, in the stronghold of the same name built by the British in the early 19th century.

Obscure historic remains relate to the island's strategic importance since 500 BC. In Vis town, you can find Greek vessels, Roman baths and Baroque Austrian architecture. Ruled by the Venetians, then the Austrians, Vis passed to the Kingdom of Yugoslavia in 1920; from 1944 it was used as a base by Tito and his Partisans. It remained a military facility, off-limits to foreigners, until 1989. You can visit **Tito's cave** headquarters, halfway up Mount Hum – just ask at any local travel agency.

**EXPLORE**

The major historical sights in Vis town are the **Archaeological Museum** in the Austrian fortress, or Baterija (021 711 729; open May-Oct 10am-1pm, 5-9pm Mon-Fri, 10am-1pm Sat; 20kn), with pottery, jewellery and sculpture from the Greek and Roman eras, including a 400 BC bronze head of a Greek goddess; and, in Kut, **St Cyprian's church**, 18th-century Baroque with a campanile. The main tourist sight in Komiža is the stubby Venetian fortress and tower, **Kaštel**. It is home to the **Fishing Museum** (open summer 9am-noon, 6-10pm daily; 10kn), with memorabilia from Komiža's glory days as a busy hub of the industry. Just in the distance, you can see the islet of **Biševo** with its singular attraction, the **Blue Cave** (*see p224* **Blue Noon**).

## Restaurants

### Boccadoro

*Petra Hektorovića 2, just outside Vis town (021 711 362, www.hotelsangiorgiovis.com).* **Open** *Apr-Nov* 8am-11am, 6pm-midnight daily. **€€€**. **International**

The house restaurant of the Hotel San Giorgio, opposite across a narrow alley, Boccadoro completes its luxury atmosphere. Open to non-residents, this venue is a fusion of international and traditional. The Italian chef cooks up top quality fish, risotto with rosemary and cheese from Pag, and wonderful desserts made from carob flour (there's an abundance on the island). There is also a selection of excellent local reds and whites. Boccadoro is an ideal place to take breakfast – homemade breads and speciality coffees helping holidaymakers get ready for another day in paradise.

### ★ Kantun

*Biskupa Mihe Pušića 17, Vis town (092 285 4818).* **Open** *May-Oct* 6pm-midnight daily. **€€**. **Wine bar/Dalmatian**

Oenophile owner Ivan Ivičević Bakulić created this special venue, under a thick ceiling of grape vines in Luka, serving fine indigenous wines. Now Kantun also serves superb Med fare. Inside is a modern makeover of a traditional *konoba*, each table decked with a different cover, the low stone tables in the back room surrounded by local art. A jazz soundtrack adds to the bohemian feel, made more Croatian with the sizzle of lamb or amberjack on a huge open grill. Reserve a table here or on the patio, and sip an aperitif in the candlelit, vine-covered courtyard then get ready for huge servings of fish soup, accompanied by delicious dark bread with fresh herbs and garlic. Leave room for dessert though: rožata crème caramel, carob or chocolate cake. Search for 'Konoba Kantun' on Facebook.

### Karijola

*Šetalište Viškog Boja 4, Vis town (021 711 358, www.pizzeria-karijola.com).* **Open** *June, Sept* 5-11pm daily. *July, Aug* noon-late daily. **No credit cards**. **€**. **Pizzeria**

Konoba Bako.

This relaxed, friendly and hospitable pizzeria has an unbeatable location on a terrace over the Prirova pensinsula on the walk to Kut. The pizzas are the best to be had on Vis and the wine list has local labels Roki and Lipanović.

### ★ Konoba Bako

*Gundulićeva 1, Komiža (021 713 742, 098 360 469, www.konobabako.hr).* **Open** *Summer* 4pm-2am daily. *Winter* 5pm-midnight daily. **€€**. **Dalmatian**

On a terrace just above the sea, the friendly Bako provides some of the fancier meals in Komiža while exuding a relaxed atmosphere. There is gorgeous beachside seating, with tables intermingled with pine trees and tall lamps. Inside, sit amid ancient Greek and Roman artefacts recovered from the waters by restaurant founder Tonko Borčić Bako, who dived here for decades. A simple menu includes fresh langouste lobsters – grilled, broiled or served in *brodet* (Dalmatian stew).

### Konoba Golub

*Podselje (098 965 0327, www.facebook.com/konoba.golub).* **Open** *Apr-Nov* 1pm-1am daily. **No credit cards**. **€€**. **Dalmatian**

Located four kilometres behind Vis town on the old road to Komiža, just above the expanse of flat farmland that dominates the island's centre, Golub is a super little place to enjoy lamb, fish, squid, beef and home-grown vegetables, plus house-made olive oil, liqueurs and wine. The restaurant is every bit as simple and rustic as the village, which supports a population of 35. Grab a seat on the patio, under a terracotta roof, decorated with grape harvesting equipment. Owner Ivica delivers the food from a giant open grill.

### Konoba Jastožera

*Gundulićeva 6, Komiža (021 713 859).* **Open** *Mid Apr-mid Oct* 5pm-midnight daily. **No credit cards. €€€. Seafood**
At this old lobster pot house hoisted above the sea, dining tables are placed on a floor of planks, under which yachters can pole their tenders into the restaurant and rope off next to the cage from where dinners are plucked. Waiters happily discuss the ingredients, merits and history of every item on the menu – in particular the tantalising lobster dishes: langouste lobster with spaghetti au gratin, cream soup with lobster, or grilled lobster with four sauces. Other seafood includes crab, clams and fabulous octopus salad. There are also grills, steaks and an extensive selection of domestic wines. Celebs love it – note the pictures of John Malkovich and other notable Croatophiles who have visited. Not cheap, but worth the price. Book well ahead; search for 'Konoba Jastožera' on Facebook.

### ★ Konoba Roki

*Plisko Polje 17 (021 714 004, www.rokis.hr).* **Open** *Apr-Oct* noon-midnight daily. **No credit cards. €€. Dalmatian**
Offering a rural dining experience on a working vineyard, in an open courtyard next to Vis cricket ground (formerly the World War II airstrip), Roki's is high on any must-visit list. Book by calling or dropping into their wine shop near the Bejbi bar. They will arrange transport here – free for four or more, otherwise 60kn return per car – but if you just turn up, you may well be turned away. Dishes, from *peka* preparations to fresh fish, are served amid olive groves and vineyards, accompanied by Roki's own Plavac or Vugava wines.

### Konoba Stončica

*Stončica 1 (021 711 952, www.konoba-stoncica. com).* **Open** noon-2am daily. **€€. Dalmatian**
This is Croatia as it should be: a sandy bay, overlooked by somebody's house, not that there are many houses; a few tables placed randomly outside, perhaps five paces from the sea. At these tables, regulars neck drinks and wait for a plate of the usual: sardines that have been gutted, skewered, then sizzled on an open grill. Other dishes are available, all from the canon of Dalmatian favourites. Incongruously, a gaggle of jolly yachters may interrupt this timeless Adriatic tableau with demands for 'pints of beer' in plummy accents before sitting back to enjoy the experience as much as anyone.

### Konoba Vatrica

*Kralja Krešimira IV 13, Kut, Vis town (021 711 574).* **Open** *Summer* 8am-midnight daily. *Winter* varies. **€€. Dalmatian**
Deservedly popular, this local favourite in Kut sits under a vine-covered terrace on the waterfront, behind which is a cosy stone-and-wood interior tastefully filled with bric-a-brac. Black cuttlefish risotto, lobster, langoustines and pasta vongole are the specialities, with a daily-changing, fresh fish menu. The portions are more than generous, the steak cooked to perfection, and the atmosphere convivial. The friendly Vatrica family are happy to open in winter if there's a demand.

### Pojoda

*Don Cvjetka Marasovića 8, Kut, Vis town (021 711 575).* **Open** *Summer* noon-1am daily. *Winter* 5pm-midnight daily. **€€. Dalmatian**
Expect a fabulous setting, decent cuisine and fair prices at the best restaurant in Vis. On offer are Dalmatian standards plus standouts such as prawn and barley risotto, and lentil and squid *brodet.* Tempting appetisers include octopus salad and seafood cocktail. The service is genuinely friendly and very efficient.

### Villa Kaliopa

*Vladimira Nazora 32, Vis town (021 711 755).* **Open** *Apr-mid Nov* 1-4pm, 5pm-midnight daily. **No credit cards. €€€. Dalmatian**
Where the yachting crowd comes to splash out, aided by a handy anchorage. You'll pay 400kn per head all-in to enjoy the shade of the palm trees, bamboo and statues in this enclosed garden between Kut and Luka – attached to the 16th-century mansion of Milanese nobleman Francesco Garibaldi – but the location and the food are memorably worth it. The cuisine is Dalmatian and Goran Pečarević strives to use local ingredients; his menu changes according to what's fresh that day.

## Cafés & Bars

### ★ Caffè Bar Bejbi

*Šetalište Stare Isse 9, Vis town (021 711 083).* **Open** 6am-2am daily. **No credit cards.**
A comfortable dive in the working section of the harbour by the docks, Bejbi ('bay-bee') bustles day and night with people who like to drink and gab. The thatched terrace has its own bar and harbour view, and a new, retro-modern mural. Pool tables, moody jazz and bossa nova are found in the large indoor bar. Usually one of the last places to close, this is where all the other parties continue. A worthy stop on any serious bar crawl, it can offer quality cocktails and occasional live acts playing funky rock.

### Caffè Bar Biliba

*Korzo 13, Vis town (021 711 357).* **Open** 7am-11pm daily. **No credit cards.**

This convenient and convivial terrace, next to the Hotel Tamaris, fills trg Klapavica, on the sea in Luka. The indoor section is around the corner, and there is more outdoor seating along the steep, pleasantly shaded stone streets of the Old Town. The location and friendly service attract a large local crowd, even during the day, when most other places in Vis town are closed or nearly empty. Internet access is available from computers in the back of the building, while the widescreen TV is usually tuned to international sports events.

### Corto Maltese Cocktail Bar

*Riva 38, Komiža (no phone).* **Open** 8am-2am daily. **No credit cards.**

The place to grab a drink among young locals, the Corto Maltese Cocktail Bar is decorated with silhouettes of the comic-book adventurer of the same name. There are outdoor tables set up between pine trees on the promenade overlooking the sea – very romantic. Indoors, there's a dartboard, and a bank of red-booth seating and red walls surround a U-shaped bar, where owner Toni and his merry crew serve up cocktails you'd recommend to friends, and dispense standard beers and wines. Later on, as the crowd begins to weed out, make sure you hang around for the disco music and order a top-secret Corto Maltese.

### Fabrika

*Riva Sv Mikule 12, Komiža (021 713 155, www. facebook.com/Fabrika.hr).* **Open** June-Sept 7am-2am daily. **No credit cards.**

The brainchild of rock-pop singer Luka Nizetić, Fabrika is a well-thought-out exercise in hipster-glam and flea-market chic, furnished with a mix-and-match collection of odd chairs, tables, and disembowelled TV sets; all of which is backed by a suitably retro musical soundtrack. Great as a daytime café or night-time cocktail bar, Fabrika also provides 'fun food' that includes tapas-style nibbles (*pršut*, anchovies, smoked tuna), bruschetta sandwiches, and at least one lunchtime main course a day.

### Lambik

*Pod Ložu 2, Vis town (091 168 1952).* **Open** *Summer* 7am-2am daily. **No credit cards.**

This ancient-looking courtyard and grape arbour ← formerly the 16th-century villa of Croatian poet Hanibal Lučić – is one of the more entertaining and idiosyncratic bars on the island, ably run by a charming, young brother-and-sister team who enjoy partying late with their equally young guests. It is also one of the most attractive venues. Low tables and comfortable wicker chairs spill out on to a pleasant square in Kut, at night a place of drunken singing and snogging. An atmospheric, vine-draped arcade has tables and chairs scattered among dimly lit columns and arches, while an indoor bar area encourages mingling and dancing. The bar opens late, and you may be offered home-made grappa. Average dance music is often provided by local DJs.

## Nightlife

### Aquarius

*Kamenica beach, Komiža (095 902 7701, www.facebook.com/aquarius.komiza).* **Open** June-Aug 24hrs daily. **No credit cards.**

A real place to party on Vis island, Aquarius is an oasis where traditional island life and big-city rave intersect, by Kamenica beach. The husband-and-wife team of Tomislav and Marcela are Split natives who fell in love with Komiža and were determined to bring something special to this quiet fishing town. Projections beam in the sea while foreign acts and DJs turn this beach disco into an all-night jamboree lasting long past the break of day. A younger crowd is peppered with up-for-it boating types and occasional celebrities, who stick around after the music for a reviving coffee while overlooking the waves. The thatched roof bar, canvas-sheltered dance floor and low beach furniture help make sure that the lively atmosphere can also be relaxed when the music starts to fade.

### ★ Fort George

*Vis town (091 265 6041, www.fortgeorgecroatia. com).* **Open** 10am-2am daily.

The historically symbolic stronghold of Fort George was a military base for several different nations. Originally built by the British in 1813, and named after King George III, it was later used by the Austro-Hungarians and the Yugoslavs Now it has been remodelled into a bar and a music venue, with plans to open up a restaurant, at time of writing. All things considered, this probably makes it the most exciting nightspot on Vis right now. The closing party for the huge Ultra Europe festival was here in July 2015; the rest of the season's schedule involved live music every Friday, performed by Croatia's top stars, plus DJ parties several nights a week. The Fort also hosts art exhibitions and a permanent display of its history, with focus on the 19th century and World War II.

## Hotels

### Biševo

*Ribarska 72, Komiža (021 713 144, 021 713 279, www.hotel-bisevo.com).* **€.**

Komiža's one hotel is an adequate resort-style complex with 131 rooms, mostly doubles. Set on the harbour front, by a busy beach, the modern Biševo has its own parking, and air-conditioning in some rooms. The key attraction is the spa centre, with masseur, and sand volleyball court. The restaurant serves breakfast, included in the room price, and decent seafood.

### Dionis

*M Gubca 1, Vis town (021 711 963, www.dionis.hr).* **€.**

This family-run B&B in a refurbished building on the harbour has eight rooms, each with air con. They also run the downstairs pizzeria.

## Issa

*Šetalište A Zanelle 5, Vis town (021 711 124, 021 711 164, www.hotelsvis.com). €€.*
The Issa is a boxy, modern structure with 256 beds that offers low-frills resort-style digs. There are tennis and sports courts, and equipment rental nearby, including bikes and diving gear. It's right by the main downtown beach. Air-conditioning is only available in the pricier rooms – it is worth booking those during the summer. Phone, balcony and satellite TV are provided in each.

## Komiža Provita

*Obala pape Aleksandra III 5, Komiža (021 713 463, www.komiza-provita.com).* **No credit cards.** €€.
Friendly, family-run place right on the waterfront, with four rooms and two studio apartments, all sea-facing, and reasonable prices. Keep a careful lookout for the hand-painted *camere/zimmer* sign as you walk south along the Riva embankment.

## Kuća Visoka

*Obala sv Jurja 22, Vis town (+44 203 287 0015, www.thisisvis.com).* **No credit cards.** €€€.
This charming, four-storey stone house in Vis town centre has three bedrooms, two bathrooms, a kitchen and an extensive video library. It only accepts advance booking and the minimum stay is four nights.

## ★ San Giorgio

*Petra Hektorovića 2, Vis town (021 711 362, www. hotelsangiorgiovis.com).* **Open** May-Oct. €€.
The San Giorgio has ten rooms, three standard doubles, six junior suites, and a deluxe. When it opened in 2008 it instantly became one of the nicest lodging options on the island. Factor in friendly, English-speaking staff plus the wonderful restaurant Boccadoro (*see p226*) and the sum total is attractive for both new and returning island customers.

## Tamaris

*Obala sv Jurja 30, Vis town (021 711 350, www.hotelsvis.com). €€.*
The Tamaris, set in an old harbourside building, is more attractive than its sister Issa. With 50 beds, it's smaller and less institutional. All rooms have air-conditioning. There's a decent restaurant with a harbour-facing terrace where breakfast is served.

## Villa Nonna & Casa Nono

*Ribarska 50, Komiža (021 713 500, 098 380 046, www.villa-nonna.com).* **No credit cards.** €€.
Affordable, comfortable and central digs are available in this aged yet remodelled townhouse one block from Komiža harbour. Villa Nonna has seven apartments (six plus one suite), each more distinctive than a hotel room. Kitchenettes allow you to cook up the produce from the market on your doorstep. The tastefully finished wooden interiors and satellite TVs allow you to impress newly met friends. Across a stone garden courtyard from the main house, the Casa Nonna has

just undergone an extensive renovation and now offers three double rooms for groups of up to nine. There's a large dining room and kitchen, satellite TV and two bathrooms. Both are popular, so book early.

## BEACHES

Beaches, tucked into coves, or just a trek away, are sprinkled over Vis. North and west of Komiža, a hiking trail leads along the coast and then up and over a ridgeline to **Uvala Perna**. On the south side of Vis, halfway between Komiža and Vis town, **Uvala Stiniva** is reached via a steep downhill trek or by boat. Small downtown beaches lie just north of Komiža harbour. Further along, by the Hotel Biševo are busy **Uvala Pod Gospu** and **Bjažićevo**, both with small pebbles easy on the feet.

In the other direction are the quieter pebble beaches of **Lučica** and **Jurkovica**. South from town is popular **Kamenica**, a pleasant mix of sand and small pebbles, and further south are a nudist beach and secluded swimming spots with rocky beaches – remember to take sandals. On the west side of Vis harbour, you'll find a busy public beach near the Hotel Issa. Past the hotel are more rocky beaches, a nudist swimming area and wild, more private beaches beyond. Again, you'll need sandals. On the other side of the bay, past the British Naval Cemetery, there's a pebble beach at **Grandovac**.

Away from town, the beaches are only accessible by boat, car or moped. There are inviting sand beaches in the narrow inlet of **Stončica** and near **Milna**. There are stony ones south of Milna and along the whole southern coast of the island. These include **Srebrena**, located in an inlet near Rukavac, with flat, pale stones and the most beautiful views.

## RESOURCES

### Tourist information

**Komiža Tourist Office** *Riva sv Mikule 2, Komiža (021 713 455, www.tz-komiza.hr).* **Open** *Summer* 8am-10pm daily.
**Vis town Tourist Office** *Šetalište Stare Isse 5, Vis town (021 717 017, www.tz-vis.hr).* **Open** *Summer* 8am-10pm daily.

## GETTING THERE & AROUND

In summer Jadrolinija runs three **ferries** a day from Split to Vis town (2hrs). Out of season, it's daily. Also in high season, Jadrolinija catamarans (75mins) run the same route. Out of season the sea can be very choppy. **Ferries** and **hydrofoils** run from Ancona and Pescara in summer. It's a 20-minute **bus** ride from the ferry dock in Vis town to Komiža. For a **taxi**, call Ivo Pečarević on 098 740 315 mobile or Taxi Frone Trade: 098 932 1623; 091 558 6092; 099 355 1701.

**EXPLORE**

# Dubrovnik & Southern Dalmatia

**S**trikingly beautiful southern Dalmatia has the clearest waters and, in Dubrovnik, the lion's share of Croatia's high-end tourist industry. Yet the celebrated Old Town and pristine sea around it remain intact and open to all. Swamped in high season, Dubrovnik is best enjoyed, as much of Dalmatia, in the colder months, when hotel rates fall and the compact historic centre is bearable. In the north, Pelješac is an interesting diversion for windsurfers and wine buffs. In the south, towards the airport, waterfront Cavtat is relaxing. The accessible islands of Korčula and Mljet – one a mini-Dubrovnik, the other a wilderness – are holiday destinations in their own right. Little Lastovo, halfway out to Italy, feels appealingly lost – just the thing after the hurly-burly of Dubrovnik in high season.

**Vineyards of Pelješac.**

## Don't Miss

**1 Dubrovnik city walls**
Iconic, historic and panoramic (p236).

**2 Mljet National Park**
Home to nothing but wild nature (p271).

**3 Vineyards of Pelješac**
Home to Croatia's finest reds and welcoming rustic cellars (p268).

**4 Vela Spina** Stone Age finds by a Korčula seafront (p263).

**5 Lastovo** Remote island and pirate haunt (p272).

# Dubrovnik

Dubrovnik is a one-town tourist industry all on its own. As stunning as the clear blue sea around it, the former centre of the independent Republic of Ragusa (in existence from 1358 to 1808) invites superlatives and attracts the lion's share of year-round visitors. When foreigners think of Dubrovnik they think of the city's proud, pristine fortifications set against an azure background. And the travel brochure covers need little touching up: anti-clockwise currents running up the coast from Albania mean that the Adriatic is crystal clear here.

Dubrovnik has the cream of Croatia's five-star hotels and attracts the most notable celebrities. It also features a cablecar up Mount Srdj overlooking the Old Town and stages the most venerable cultural event in the country, the high-brow **Dubrovnik Summer Festival** (*see p250* **All Dubrovnik is a Stage**), in place since 1950.

## INTRODUCING THE CITY

The festival echoes the cultural, architectural and scientific wonder that was Ragusa, a state backed by lucrative maritime trading and a progressive urban infrastructure. Ragusa was the name given to it by refugees who established a settlement here after fleeing the Roman-Byzantine city of Epidaurum, today's Cavtat, in the seventh century. A wily maritime power run by an enlightened council of local noblemen, Ragusa vied with Venice for Adriatic trade. It eventually became a self-governing republic with its own currency and its institutions quickly blossomed. Although a rigid class system ensured that only the aristocracy was allowed to vote, Ragusa had its own public health service.

With no royal intrigue – the Old Town is free of grandiose statues – Ragusa thrived. Whenever the Turks threatened, Ragusa paid them off. Citizenship was bestowed upon the skilled and the entrepreneurial, Jews included. Buildings of marble and stone replaced wooden ones. Ragusa's sailors worked a profitable fleet of 300 ships. Some worked aboard Columbus's to the New World in 1492 – ironically, the first step in robbing Ragusa of its riches when Atlantic trade links began to replace Mediterranean ones in importance.

As the economic tide was turning, a great earthquake struck in 1667. The rebuilding programme called for height restrictions in case of further disaster. Just over a century later, Napoleon's forces entered Ragusa in 1806. The republic was abolished.

Short French rule saw a swift improvement in the urban infrastructure. After Napoleon's defeat, the Habsburgs moved in to control Ragusa until their demise in 1918. As a symbol of Slavic learning and culture, the city was central to the revival of Croatian national feeling. When it

became part of the new Yugoslav state, it took its Slav name of Dubrovnik. Ruled from Belgrade, Dubrovnik's lack of overland transport links and outdated trade saw economic decline and mass emigration to the Americas. At the same time, tourism took off, with the 1930s seeing an influx of Czech, German and British travellers.

With the post-war Tito regime throwing the doors wide open to foreign visitors, Dubrovnik became increasingly tourist friendly. However, in 1991 Dubrovnik was shelled day after day during a six-month siege. Painstakingly rebuilt, it has since reinvented itself as a high-end tourist destination, particularly with its hotels. Entrepreneurs have upped the ante on luxury lodging – Dubrovnik is now a similar price bracket to the French Riviera.

Meanwhile Dubrovnik's rich cultural scene is in a state of transformation: is the Summer Festival a mainstream tourist attraction, or should it celebrate ground-breaking contemporary culture? By far the biggest local talking point is the fate of Mount Srdj, the high plateau overlooking the town where a proposed golf-resort-cum-apartment mega-development has become the focus of impassioned for-and-against debate.

## OLD TOWN

Almost everything worth seeing is centred in the compact, crowded Old Town. To get the best view, and one of a stupendously clear, blue Adriatic lapping the rocks below and stretching way beyond, embark on a stroll round the **City Walls**. An hour should suffice but take as long as you like.

You'll be spending the bulk of your time within the 15th-century ring of fortifications, in the small square half-mile of gleaming medieval space bisected by 300-metre (985-foot) long **Stradun**, Dubrovnik's main street. As you flit between the main gates of **Pile** and **Ploče**, guided by the list of places on the maroon flags, each venue with its own logoed white lamp, barkers on every side-street corner entice you into the bland tourist restaurants on Prijeko and a cacophony of tour guides give their spiels. All is free of traffic until you reach the bus-choked hub outside the Pile Gate. Beyond, over the drawbridge, stands the Lovrijenac Fortress, used for productions of Shakespeare classics during the Summer Festival, and the permanently busy main road to the ferry port at Gruž and Lapad. Exiting the Old Town via the Ploče Gate takes you past the attractive old harbour, where taxi boats set off for the nearby island of **Lokrum** (*see p261* **Haunted Island**). Beyond the gate stretches Banje beach, then a string of luxury hotels.

Back inside the city walls is Dubrovnik's main square and crossing point of **Luža**, where you'll find the landmark astronomical clock tower

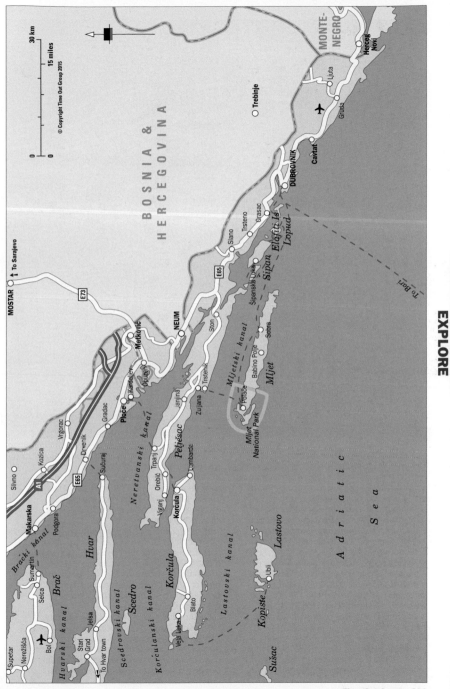

**EXPLORE**

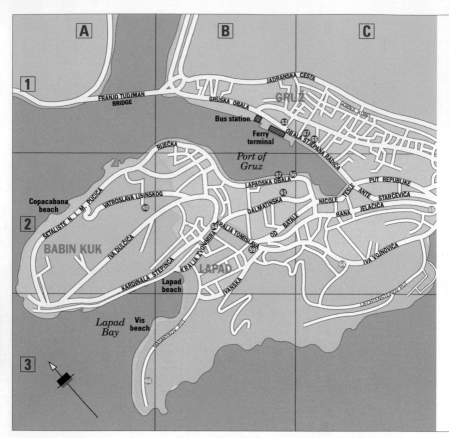

**EXPLORE**

(sadly, a modern rebuild of the 1444 original); **Orlando's Column**, where all state declarations were read; the smaller of Onofrio's fountains, and a prosaic statue of Shakespeare-era playwright Marin Držić. Surrounding Luža are the main historic attractions of the **Rector's Palace**; the **Cathedral** with its treasury; the **Sponza Palace** and the **Dominican Monastery**.

The other sights are within easy reach. On the south side of the harbour, round the corner from the Rector's Palace, **St John's Fortress** (Damjana Jude 2) houses both the **Maritime Museum** (+385 20 323 904; open summer 9am-6pm Tue-Sun, winter 9am-4pm Tue-Sun; 70kn) and the **Aquarium** (+385 20 323 978; open summer 9am-9pm daily, winter 9am-4pm Tue-Sun; 40kn). The former houses an attractive collection of ships' models, paintings and photographs detailing Dubrovnik's seafaring history; while the latter consists of a gloomy collection of tanks containing Adriatic sealife.

Walking round from the old harbour, along the rocks fringing the sea-lapped city walls, are spots used by bathers and divers. The most popular is by one of the **Buža** bars, its jagged stones planed flat for sunbathers. Metal steps cut into the rock to help you clamber back up.

In front of the clock tower, the **Baroque Church of St Blaise** (open 8am-noon, 4-6pm daily), named after the protector of Dubrovnik through the centuries of trade, torment and tourism, was rebuilt after the 1667 earthquake. Inside, the altar, with a statue of the saint, is the main draw. The stained-glass windows are a modern addition.

On the other side of St Blaise, the adjoining squares of **Gundulićeva poljana** and **Bunićeva poljana** are busy day and night. Market stalls cover the pavement in the morning, entertainment for diners and coffee drinkers at nearby terraces; bars kick into gear after dark.

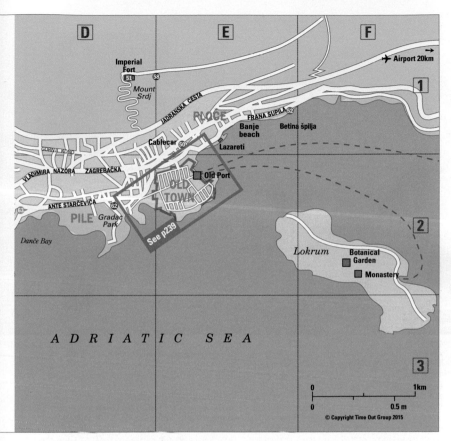

At the other end of Stradun, by the 15th-century Pile Gate, the main drawbridged entrance to the Old Town, stands Onofrio's **Great Fountain**, less ornate than how it looked before the 1667 earthquake. Behind the Franciscan church nearby, the **Franciscan Monastery**, embellished with beautiful cloisters, houses what is claimed to be the world's oldest pharmacy and a museum of religious artefacts. The best contemporary attraction is **War Photo Limited**, with changing exhibitions of conflict photography from around the world, with one room devoted to the 1991-95 war in Croatia.

On the dining front, Dubrovnik is beginning to offer the culinary quality and variety that should be expected of such a luxury resort. Enjoying the unparalleled setting of St Luke's Fortress, **360 Degrees** is one of the leading restaurants in Croatia, whose local hegemony may be soon be challenged by the revamped and long prestigious **Nautika** at the other end of the Old Town.

## Sights & Museums

### Cathedral

*Poljana Marina Držica (020 323 496)*. **Open** *Summer* 9am-5pm Mon-Sat; 11am-5pm Sun. *Winter* 9am-noon, 3-5pm Mon-Sat; 11am-noon Sun. **Admission** *treasury* 15kn. **No credit cards**. **Map** p239 D3 ❶
The original church, allegedly funded by Richard the Lionheart in recognition of the local hospitality

---

### IN THE KNOW DUBROVNIK CARD

The Dubrovnik Card (www.dubrovnikcard. com; 150kn/one day; 200kn/three days; 250kn/ one week) allows entrance to the City Walls, several museums and attractions and free rides on public transport. Accompanied children under 12 are free.

City Walls.

when shipwrecked on Lokrum in the 1190s, was lost to the 1667 earthquake. In its place was built a somewhat bland, Baroque affair, free but unenticing to walk around. The main draw is the treasury at one end, a somewhat grotesque collection of holy relics. The arm, skull and lower leg of city patron St Blaise are kept in jewel-encrusted casings, another box contains one of Christ's nappies, and wood from the Holy Cross is incorporated into a finely crafted crucifix from the 16th century. Perhaps the most bizarre artefact is the creepy dish and jug designed as a gift for the Hungarian King Mátyás Corvinus, who died before he could receive it.

### ★ City Walls
*Old Town (020 324 641, www.citywallsdubrovnik. hr).* **Open** *Summer* 9am-7pm daily. *Winter* 9am-3pm daily. **Admission** 100kn; 30kn reductions. **No credit cards**. **Map** p239 B2 ❷
The first thing any visitor should fork out for is entrance up to the City Walls. The main entrance is by the Pile Gate. With arrows up towards the Adriatic side, you're soon scaling staircases to allow you a sublime view of the blue, blue sea to one side and people's red-tiled roofs, terraces and washing lines to the other. There are a couple of cafés towards the harbour end, where you turn and head towards the thicker, inland-facing walls. You can also choose to leave the walls here, near the Old Port. As well as giving you a perspective on Dubrovnik, a stroll around the walls

reveals how intricate a job building them must have been. Remember to pack a hat and sun cream. Audio-guides are available at the main entrance.

### Dominican Monastery
*Sv Dominika 4 (020 321 423).* **Open** *Summer* 9am-6pm daily. *Winter* 9am-5pm daily. **Admission** 20kn. **No credit cards**. **Map** p239 E2 ❸
Between the Sponza Palace and the Ploče Gate, this monastery is best known for its late Gothic cloisters and late 15th-century Dubrovnik School paintings in the museum – in particular masterpieces by Nikola Božidarević, including his *Our Lady with the Saints*. On the walls of the monastery church are a beautiful wooden crucifix by Paolo Veneziano from 1358 and a painting by renowned fin-de-siècle artist Vlaho Bukovac from Cavtat, *The Mirade of St Dominic*.

### ★ Franciscan Monastery/ Old Pharmacy Museum
*Stradun 2 (020 321 410).* **Open** 9am-5pm daily. **Admission** 30kn. **No credit cards**. **Map** p239 C2 ❹
One of the oldest pharmacies in Europe is, quite remarkably, still a working chemist's, located in the complex of the Franciscan Monastery. In addition, beautiful cloisters lead to the Old Pharmacy Museum by a pretty courtyard. There you'll find disturbingly large grinders and implements used by the medical profession in the Ragusan era.

### ★ Rector's Palace

*Pred Dvorom 3 (020 321 497, www.dumus.hr).*
**Open** *Summer* 9am-6pm daily. *Winter* 9am-4pm daily. **Admission** 70kn. **No credit cards.**
**Map** p239 E3 ❺

The most historic monument in Dubrovnik, the Rector's Palace has been rebuilt twice. The first time, by Onofrio della Cava of fountain fame, was in Venetian-Gothic style, visible in the window design once you ascend the grand staircase to the Rector's living quarters. Damaged by an explosion in 1463, the palace was rebuilt again by Florentine architect Michelozzo Michelozzi, who was responsible for the loggia façade. On the ground floor, either side of a courtyard, are the prison and courtrooms of the Ragusa Republic, and a glittering display of medieval church art. Upstairs, where each Rector resided for a month's stint, is a strange assortment of items: sedan chairs, carriages, magistrates' robes and wigs, portraits of local notables and Ivo Rudenjak's beautifully carved bookcase. One curiosity is the clocks, some set at 5.45pm, the time when Napoleon's troops entered in 1806. The same ticket is valid for the Archeological Collection, a small but attractive collection of medieval carvings right by Ploče Gate.

### Sponza Palace

*Luža (020 321 032, www.dad.hr/sponza.php).*
**Open** *Summer* 9am-9pm daily. *Winter* 10am-3pm daily. **Admission** free. **No credit cards.**
**Map** p239 D2 ❻

The attractive, 16th-century former customs house and Ragusa mint is used to house the extensive state archives. Several rooms off the arcaded ground-floor courtyard are used to display photocopies of the archives' most treasured historical documents.

### ★ War Photo Limited

*Antuninska 6 (020 322 166, www.warphotoltd. com).* **Open** *June-Sept* 10am-10pm daily. *May, Oct* 10am-4pm Mon, Wed-Sun. **Admission** 40kn. **No credit cards. Map** p239 C2 ❼

Managed by conflict photographer Wade Goddard, who came here in the early 1990s, this gallery exhibits works by some of the world's leading exponents of this brave and often unrewarded art. See website for details of this year's principal exhibitions.

## Restaurants

### ★ 360 degrees

*Sv Dominika (020 322 222, www.360dubrovnik. com).* **Open** *Mar-Dec* noon-midnight daily. €€€€.
**Map** p239 E2 ❽ **Mediterranean/Dalmatian**
360 degrees offers both a top-drawer setting in the St Luke's Fortress bastion, and top-drawer cuisine that melds the best of contemporary Mediterranean food with Croatian culinary tradition. Meticulously sourced dishes are painstakingly created and immaculately presented, with stand-out mains including

sea bass with confit of artichokes and asparagus and steamed turbot with apricot purée, rabbit and pigeon. The restaurant also boasts what is quite possibly Croatia's longest (and most expensive) wine list, including a whole page of champagnes. The terrace bar has the best cocktails in town. If you can, beg for a booth in the gun chambers close to the sea.

### ★ Azur

*Pobijana 10 (020 324 806, www.azurvision.com).*
**Open** 12.30pm-11pm daily. **No credit cards.** €€.
**Map** p239 D4 ❾ **Global**
This superbly located newbie sits by the entrance of Buža I (*see p241*). Here you can tuck into a reasonably priced, Med- or Asian-influenced main – fragrant meatballs in a chicken and coconut broth, perhaps, or Adriatic prawn pouches on grilled aubergine in a red curry and coconut sauce – before an afternoon's sunbathing, or enjoy a nightcap overlooking the waves.

### Barba

*Boškovićeva 5 (091 205 3488, https://hr-hr. facebook.com/dubrovnik.barba).* **Open** *Apr-Dec* 9am-11pm daily. €. **Map** p239 D2 ❿ **Seafood**
Barba ('uncle', 'old man' or 'captain') is a streetfood fish restaurant based on a healthy concept. Fresh Mediterranean food is quickly prepared and thrown together in imaginative combinations: octopus sandwiches with mascarpone; marinated anchovies with cuttlefish salad and nectarines; shrimps with rocket and parmesan… You'll also find pasta with tuna and artichokes, and mussels and fava beans. Barba is always fast and warm-hearted, with great ideas.

### Dubravka 1836

*Brsalje 1 (020 426 319, www.dubravka1836.hr).*
**Open** *July, Aug* 8am-2am daily. *Sept-June* 8am-midnight daily. €€. **Map** p239 B3 ⓫
**Dalmatian**
By the Pile Gate, this landmark venue dating back to – yes – 1836, is now a modernised, sunken room brightened by old photos of the trams that terminated here when intellectuals, writers and the chess society were regulars. A spot on the seafacing terrace is ideal for the Dubrovnik Breakfast with ham and cheese, one of five morning options. Salads, pizzas and seafood dishes comprise the main offerings.

### ★ Kamenice

*Gundulićeva poljana 8 (020 323 682).* **Open** *July, Aug* 8am-1am daily. *May, June, Sept, Oct* 8am-11pm daily. *Nov-Mar* 8am-4pm daily. €. **Map** p239 D3 ⓬
**Seafood**
Timeless, traditional and tremendously cheap, this locals' favourite has hardly changed despite the new tourist traps around it. A prime site by the market has not affected prices, decor or staff dress. Waitresses in mules deliver piles of mussels, squid and oysters in white-tile surroundings. Watch out for early winter closing times.

**EXPLORE**

## Konoba Dalmatino

*Miha Pracata 6 (020 323 070, www.dalmatino-dubrovnik.com).* **Open** *Mar-Dec* noon-midnight daily. €€€. **Map** p239 D3 ⑬ **Dalmatian**
For traditional food, served with finesse, and with a reasonable price tag, Dalmatino takes some beating. It's located in an old house that has been renovated to show the original stonework at its exposed best. The menu is as straightforwardly Dalmatian as the name of the restaurant, featuring plenty of local fish and fowl, although there's creativity in the details – grilled fish might be served with a colour-coordinated array of Mediterranean vegetables instead of the usual *blitva*. Desserts are superb: the likes of cheesecake or chocolate mousse. The place is run by a South African of Korčulan descent, so it's no surprise that the wine list veers enthusiastically towards the fine whites from that island.

## Konoba Ribar

*Kneza Damjana Jude (020 323 194).* **Open** *Mar-Jan* 10am-midnight daily. €€. **No credit cards**. **Map** p239 E3 ⑭ **Dalmatian**
On the same street as the Aquarium, this is a local (mainly seafood) place for locals at local prices. It does a lovely grilled beef steak (90kn) too, plus home-made *pršut* ham and wonderful cheeses. The small interior is decorated with paintings by local artists; there are tables outside too. In winter, it offers 25kn-30kn *marenda* (snack) lunches: beans and sausages, tripe and cod, all home-style.

## ★ Kopun

*Poljana Rudjera Boškovića 7 (020 323 969, www. restaurantkopun.com).* **Open** *Feb-Dec* noon-1am daily. €€€. **Map** p239 D4 ⑮ **Dalmatian**
Kopun is local dialect for capon. And, not surprisingly, it's Croatian-raised capon that provides much of the inspiration behind the menu at this restaurant, with speciality dishes such as capon with oranges and honey. *Pièce de résistance*, however, is capon stuffed with a rich filling of herbs, meat and vegetables, a dish sufficient for a party of three or four – although you really ought to order it a day in advance. Kopun's menu also features some exquisite fish and seafood, alongside traditional Dubrovnik favourites such as *šporki makaruli* (locally made pasta with goulash sauce), accompanied by Istrian and Dalmatian wines. The interior is a breath of fresh air too, eschewing Dalmatian folksiness in favour of bright-white minimalism with artworks on the walls.

## Lady PI-PI

*Peline (020 321 154, www.facebook.com/LADY. PI.PI.Dubrovnik).* **Open** *July-Dec* 9am-midnight daily. €€. **Map** p239 D1 ⑯ **Dalmatian**
It's a strenuous climb up the steps from Stradun to reach the under-the-walls alley that harbours Lady PI-PI, and then you usually have to queue to get in (you can't reserve). However neither of these factors appear to have dented the popularity of this cult outdoor restaurant, its split-level terrace spread beneath a shady pergola. The recipe for success is simple: grill it, and grill it with affection. Fish, steaks and sausages all come off the coals in fragrant, succulent form. The grotesque street-facing sculpture poised above a stone bowl provides a clue to the name.

## Lokanda Peskarija

*Na Ponti (020 324 750).* **Open** 8am-midnight daily. **No credit cards**. €. **Map** p239 E3 ⑰ **Dalmatian**
Everyone's favourite cheapie ensures queues around the old harbour all summer. Nothing fancy here, just good domestic dishes at knockdown prices swiftly served by overworked staff. The management has somewhat overreached itself, placing tables in every available space, but few seem to be complaining.

## Lucin Kantun

*Od Sigurate (020 321 003).* **Open** *Apr-Nov* 11.30am-11pm daily. €€. **Map** p239 C2 ⑱ **Dalmatian**
'Clean and crisp' best describes the simple furnishings and mainly white interior. The food, however, is far from simple. Not quite a tapas bar, Lucin Kantun offers a full, sit-down meal comprised of lots of small, delicious dishes – marinades of salmon, lobster, octopus and the like, or a variety of hot concoctions, plus a large choice of cheeses, hams, dips and other tempting nibbles. Finish with the home-made cake.

## ★ Nautika

*Brsalje 3, Pile (020 442 526, www.nautika restaurant.com).* **Open** *Feb-Dec* 6pm-midnight daily. €€€€. **Map** p239 B2 ⑲ **Dalmatian**
Renovated and reopened in May 2015, Dubrovnik's most prestigious culinary spot offers two panoramic terraces of starched white-tablecloth formality. To get full value for your blow-out, book seaview tables on the Penatur terrace or on Lovrijenac. Chef Mario Bunda insists on fresh, locally sourced ingredients – shellfish features in dishes from the Elafiti isles such as Lopud *brodet* with polenta and Šipan fisherman's carpaccio, or there are lobster medallions from Vis.

## Nishta

*Prijeko 30 (020 322 088, www.nishtarestaurant. com).* **Open** *Mar-Dec* 11.30am-10pm Mon-Sat. €€. **Map** p239 C2 ⑳ **Vegetarian**
Opened by a Swiss-Croatian couple, Dubrovnik's first vegetarian restaurant offers miso and gazpacho soups, a superbly varied salad bar, and several exercises in veggie East–West fusion: try the *temperitos*, burrito-like treats with tempeh; or the health-restoring *orsotto* (barley cooked risotto-style with seaweed). Laško beer and good wines by the glass keep the mood bubbly. Success has led to another opening in Zagreb.

EXPLORE

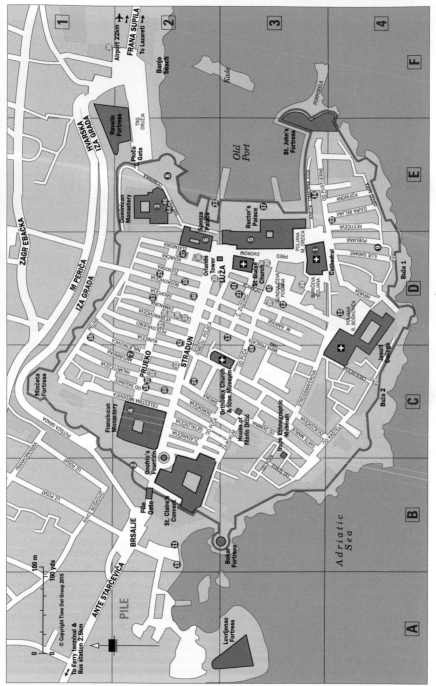

EXPLORE

**EXPLORE**

Poklisar.

### Oliva Gourmet
*Cvijete Zuzorić 2 (020 324 076, www.pizza-oliva. com).* **Open** *Mar-Dec* 10am-midnight daily. **€.**
**Map** p239 D3 ㉑ **Dalmatian**
Oliva Gourmet aims to inject a touch of 21st-century pizzazz into traditional Adriatic dining. The interior transforms a traditional stone-clad space into pop-art heaven, with a slate-grey floor, white and pink chairs and unabashedly loud purple tablecloths. The menu sticks to what the locals do best, with shellfish starters and fish mains predominating. Look out for traditional Dubrovnik staples that local grannies may still make but which have largely disappeared from restaurant menus: chickpea soup (a light affair best treated as a starter) and *šporki makaruli* (pasta tubes bathed in mixed-meat goulash).
▶ *For well-priced and decent pizzas, sister restaurant Oliva (Lučarica 5, 020 324 594, same website) is close by.*

### Oyster & Sushi Bar Bota
*Od Pustijerna (020 324 034, www.bota-sare.hr).* **Open** 9am-midnight daily. **€€€. Map** p239 E4 ㉒
**Seafood/Japanese**
Freshly farmed shellfish from the famed oyster beds of Ston are the star attraction at this open-air bar with high stools and high tables, beautifully situated on a raised terrace behind the cathedral. The oysters are served fresh, fried in tempura, or in a sushi roll. There is also a full sushi menu, with fishy Adriatic ingredients well to the fore and some creative

Adriatic-Japanese combinations. Fish carpaccios, tuna tartare and tempura-fried shrimps round out the menu.

### Poklisar
*Ribarnica 1 (020 322 176, www.poklisar.com).* **Open** *Mar-Dec* 9am-midnight daily. **€€. Map** p239 E2 ㉓ **Dalmatian**
With its terraces flanking a prominent square by the old harbour, the Poklisar fills up quickly in high season. Prices, given the setting, are reasonable and among the Croatian standards is the odd gem: shrimps in saffron sauce or home-made gnocchi with gorgonzola and rocket. Desserts include the likes of walnut pancakes or wild-fruit parfaits. Dine before the cheesy live music drowns out the lap of the sea.

### Proto
*Široka 1 (020 323 234, www.esculap-teo.hr).* **Open** 10am-11pm daily. **€€€€. Map** p239 C2 ㉔ **Seafood**
Edward VIII entertained Wallis Simpson at this long-established seafood restaurant. As well as squid and lobster in simple, superbly balanced sauces, there's fresh shellfish from Ston up the coast. You can spend an enjoyable hour over the fish platter for two, and the extensive wine list covers just about every quality wine that Croatia has to offer. Choose between restrained elegance in the 1930s-influenced dining room, or Old Town views from the first-floor terrace. Booking essential.

The more haphazard of the two open-air bars cut into the sea-facing rocks, Buža I welcomes sunbathers, divers, drinkers and film fans. Its entrance faces the terrace of the Azur (*see p237*); on the wall is daubed '8-20 Topless Nudist'. Down a stone staircase are bar tables and metal steps towards the sea. Films are also shown.

### ★ Buža II

*Crijevićeva 9 (098 361 934).* **Open** 10am-late daily. **No credit cards.** Map p239 C4 ㉘
The more well known of the cliff-face bars – follow the 'cold drinks' sign from the open square of Rudjera Boškovića. Prices are a little steeper but you get a thatched roof and table service. Buža II also has the same jaw-dropping view – if you can find a table in high season.

### Buzz Bar

*Prijeko 21 (020 321 025, thebuzzbar.wix.com/buzz).* **Open** 8am-2am daily. **No credit cards.** Map p239 D2 ㉙
The only bar in a street filled with restaurants, seconds away from Stradun, Buzz has won over a local crowd thanks to its good vibe, pleasant interior of colourful chairs and witty decor, craft beers such as Istria's San Servolo and reasonable prices – the latter not an epithet that could be attached to its neighbouring restaurants. There are also organic lemonades, cocktails, whiskies and cognacs, and carefully selected rock, pop and jazz.

### Casablanca

*Zamanjina 7 (098 854 954).* **Open** 8pm-2am daily. **No credit cards.** Map p239 D2 ㉚
Old film and beer ads brighten the space; posters promote long-forgotten Olympics and pool-table lightshades of coloured glass advertise Coors beer. Cocktails come in creamy or killer varieties, football or music videos are screened and staff buzz about in daft blue shirts with some bullshit motto on them. Recommended.

### ★ Cele Café

*Stradun 1 (099 423 0400, www.cele-dubrovnik. com).* **Open** 7am-midnight daily. Map p239 D2 ㉛
Opened in 1932 by a certain Celestin 'Cele' Šikić, this busy place is one of a gaggle of cafés grouped around the Stradun's bustling eastern end. Given a thorough refit in 2011, Cele was relaunched as a 'brunch&bar', serving all-day breakfasts (omelettes, croissants, cereals), salads, wok-fried dishes and burgers until 5pm, when it reverts to its primary function as a drinking venue. Cele's sizeable pavement terrace can be mobbed by tourists in high season, and the place only really comes into its own when the midsummer deluge has receded.

### D'Vino

*Palmotićeva 4A (020 321 130, www.dvino.net).* **Open** *Mar-Dec* 10am-2am daily. Map p239 C2 ㉜

### ★ Wanda

*Prijeko 8 (098 944 9317, www.wandarestaurant. com).* **Open** 11am-10pm daily. €€. Map p239 D2 ㉕
**Mediterranean**
The estimable Wanda has breathed life into staid Prijeko, offering top Mediterranean cuisine at reasonable prices. Local Goran Starčić worked in Los Angeles before setting up back home. His team regularly puts together simple, well-conceived dishes with fresh local ingredients: soups, appetisers, salads, risottos. Look out for the seasonal daily specials.

## Cafes & Bars

### B4 Revelin

*Vetranovićeva 3 (no phone).* **Open** 7.30am-2am daily. **No credit cards.** Map p239 D2 ㉖
This minimalist matte-grey café-bar just off the Stradun is the ideal big night out warm-up venue, with dance music on the sound system and disco lights casting shifting pools of colour across the ceiling. Graphics on the back wall present a traditionalist counterpoint to all this stylish modernity, with portraits of the Zelenci ('Greenies') – the weathered bronze figures that used to strike the bell of Dubrovnik's main city clock.

### ★ Buža I

*Accessed from Ilije Sarake (098 361 934).* **Open** *Summer* 8am-3am daily. *Winter* varies. **No credit cards.** Map p239 D4 ㉗

EXPLORE

Opened in 2008, Dubrovnik's first real wine bar is presided over by Australian-Croatian Sasha and his friendly and knowledgeable team. D'Vino manages to stock more than 100 varieties, 76 available by the glass. Every decent Istrian, Slavonian and Dalmatian label is here, including Grgić Plavac Mali and Zlatan Plavac. The house wine begins at 25kn and savoury meat-and-cheese platters are tailor-made to complement the wine. It's a comfortable, modern, intimate space to enjoy a drink – with a few seats outside in summer. The venue also lays on wine tours.

### Festival Café
*Stradun 28 (020 321 148, www.cafefestival.com).* **Open** *Mid Feb-mid Jan* 8am-midnight daily. **Map** p239 C2 ㉝
This landmark venue on Stradun is pricey even by Dubrovnik standards but popular all the same – everyone meets at the Festival. Breakfasts go for 60kn, dishes of the day 80kn and seasonal mixed drinks – for example a frozen cappuccino with Bailey's – 50kn. It's got a proper bar counter, a long interior brightened by vintage coffee ads and outdoor seating. Fruit frappés and home-made cakes complete the picture.

### Hard Jazz Caffe Troubadour
*Buničeva poljana 2 (020 323 476).* **Open** *Summer* 9am-3am daily. *Winter* 5-11pm daily. **No credit cards. Map** p239 D3 ㉞
The most famous bar in town, formerly run by Marko Brešković (1942-2010), one-time bass-player with the Dubrovački Trubaduri and an accomplished jazz musician to boot. Brešković used to preside over nightly jams on the Troubadour's terrace, and despite his demise the Troubadour remains its old self, with its commitment to live music intact and its traditional clientele still loyal. Drink prices are somewhat inflated on gig nights, and coffee isn't served after 8pm – but it's still hard to find a seat here on a summer evening.

### Laura
*Frana Supila 1, Ploče (098 428 278).* **Open** 7am-2am daily. **No credit cards. Map** p239 F1 ㉟
Ever wandered around the Old Town and wished there was a corner bar just for locals, in which everyone was a bit pissed up in a fun way, and where the music was half-decent? Welcome to Laura. Occupying a strategic corner by the Ploče Gate, with a right-angle of tables outside for perfect sundowners, Laura buzzes from breakfast to way past the witching hour. If there's no sport on the big TV screen, they'll put on either well-chosen electronica or guitar-driven sounds.

### Libertina
*Zlatarska 3 (020 321 526).* **Open** *Summer* 10am-midnight daily. *Winter* 10am-2pm, 7-11pm daily. **No credit cards. Map** p239 D2 ㊱

This characterful shoebox of a bar is known as 'Luci' after Luci Capurso, owner and ex-member of vintage beat combo Dubrovački Trubaduri. Shying away from his Eurovision Song Contest past, Luci serves the regulars, pleasingly oblivious to the piles of money being made at inferior bars on his doorstep.

### Ludwig
*Zamanjina 7 (no phone, kult.com.hr/clubbing/kult-patrola/101-ludig.html).* **Open** noon-midnight daily. **No credit cards. Map** p239 D2 ㊲
The walls of this grunge bar in a Stradun side street are decorated with a random mosaic of posters, book covers and pictures torn from magazines (Gogol, Mogwai, *Kill Bill* and Hendrix all get a decorative look-in). But it's the hard-living black-clad drinkers hunched around the counter that make the place.

### Nonenina Bar
*Pred Dvorom 4 (098 825 844, www.nonenina.com).* **Open** *Mar-Dec* 9am-1am daily. **Map** p239 D3 ㊳
Formerly part of the Hemingway chain and now sailing under its own flag, this prominent cocktail bar opposite the Rector's Palace offers mixed drinks by the glass or pitcher for four. There are no real surprises among the long selection: daiquiris and mojitos are mixed with Havana Club 3; a combination of Pernod and champagne in Death in the Afternoon, and a pleasant buzz around the bar and terrace.

### Razonoda
*Pucić Palace, Od Puča 1 (020 326 200, www.thepucicpalace.com).* **Open** 11am-midnight daily. **Map** p239 D3 ㊴
This fine wine bar is set in the five-star surroundings of the Pucić Palace (*see p245*). Dalmatian labels comprise the bulk of the extensive selection: Pelješac reds such as an excellent dry Dingač, a deep Miloš-Plavac and a gentle, flowery Grgić; a Pošip white from Korčula or Vugava from Vis. Istrian and Slavonian selections feature heavily too. Local pršut ham and cheeses can be ordered, plus pastries and desserts.

## Shops & Services

### Algoritam
*Stradun 8 (020 322 044, www.algoritam.hr).* **Open** 9am-8.30pm Mon-Fri; 9am-3pm Sat; 10am-1pm Sun. **Map** p239 D2 ㊵ **Books**.
Half the store is dedicated to English-language publications: from travel guides to bestsellers, classics to heavyweight volumes on politics, history, art and design. There's also an impressive stock of (pricey) English magazines (*Q*, *Arena*, *Vogue*), postcards, CDs and glossy photographic histories of Dubrovnik.

### Artur Gallery
*Lučarica 1 (020 323 773).* **Open** 9am-1pm, 5-7pm Mon-Fri. **Map** p239 D3 ㊶ **Gifts & souvenirs**
This little gallery puts on regular exhibitions by local artists, as well as art workshops. The gift shop

**Maria Boutique.**

sells tasteful souvenirs, jewellery and books related to Dubrovnik. Look out for books by Italian cartoonist Osvaldo Cavandoli. His drawings found inspiration in Dubrovnik thanks to gallery owner Tea Batinić, who invited him here a few years ago. The result was *Dubrovnik*, 35 stories written by Batinić, illustrated by Cavandoli.

### Atelier Secret
*Kunićeva 2 (no phone).* **Open** *Summer* 9.30am-midnight daily, *Winter* 9.30am-4pm Mon-Sat. **No credit cards. Map** p239 C2 ㊷
**Accessories**
Intriguing but affordable locally made accessories, including necklaces and earrings fashioned from Adriatic coral, and bauble-like pendants made to traditional Dubrovnik designs.

### Carmel
*Zamanjina 10 (091 577 7157).* **Open** *Mar-Dec* 10am-2pm, 6-10pm daily. **No credit cards.
Map** p239 D2 ㊸ **Gifts & souvenirs**
A few steps above restaurant-crammed Prijeko is this small photography gallery, hosting themed exhibitions over the summer and selling prints by leading Croatian photographers. It also sells jewellery manufactured by the nearby Atelier Secret.

### Dubrovačka kuća
*Od sv Dominika (020 322 092).* **Open** 9am-11pm daily. **Map** p239 E2 ㊹ **Gifts & souvenirs**

High-quality treats here include local spirits, sweets, posters, olive oils, regional wines and bath salts. A link with the Museum of Arts and Crafts in Zagreb means beautiful ceramics and glassware at affordable prices. There's more information on the Facebook page.

### ★ Gundulićeva poljana market
*Gundulićeva poljana (no phone).* **Open** 6am-1pm Mon-Sat. **No credit cards.** Map p239 D3 ㊺
**Food & drink**
A good place to pick up your beach picnic contents is this popular market in the heart of the Old Town. It mainly sells fruit and veg but you'll also find nuts, olive oil, lavender, honey and local spirits.

### ★ Maria Boutique
*Ulica Sv Dominika (020 321 330, www.mariastore. hr).* **Open** *Summer* 10am-midnight daily. *Winter* 10am-5pm Mon-Sat. **Map** p239 E2 ㊻ **Fashion**
Maria describes itself as a concept store but fashion is the focus here. Strategically located at the Ploče Gate, it's one of the few places in Croatia where you can find a battery of major international names such as Givenchy, Stella McCartney and Rick Owens, all laid out in an ample space – with prices to match the quality and atmosphere on offer. Staff are approachable, though, and in no way snobby.

### Modni Kantun
*Zlatarska 3 (020 321 241).* **Open** 9am-9pm daily. **Map** p239 E2 ㊼ **Accessories**

This tiny store sells fashion accessories by Croatian artisans, including plenty in the way of unique jewellery. Look out in particular for Ivana Bačura's hand-made rings and earrings – stylish, simple and understated exercises in silver and muted shades of stone.

### Uje
*Od Puča 9 (020 324 055, www.uje.hr).* **Open** 9am-9pm Mon-Sat; 9am-3pm Sun. **Map** p239 C3 ⓰ **Food & drink**
The Dubrovnik outlet for a Split-based deli outfit, selling jams, pickled capers, marinated seafood and all manner of Mediterranean goodies. It's also a good place to stock up on Brachia olive oil from the island of Brač.

### Vinoteka Miličić
*Od Sigurate (020 321 777).* **Open** *Summer* 10am-11pm daily. *Winter* 9am-6pm Mon-Sat. **Map** p239 C2 ⓰ **Food & drink**
Halfway along Stradun, this small, friendly shop contains a reasonable selection of local and international wines. A comprehensive list of the domestic varieties on offer in-store or by order is on the website. For a standard bottle to take to the beach, you'll find cheaper at one of the local groceries outside the Pile Gate.

## Nightlife

### ★ Culture Club Revelin
*Sv Dominika 3 (020 436 010, 098 533 531, www.dubrevelin.com).* **Open** *Summer* 11pm-7am daily. *Winter* Fri, Sat & special events. **Admission** 70kn-150kn. **Map** p239 E2.
The angular 16th-century fortress that marks the eastern end of Dubrovnik's Old Town has become the place to go after drinking-up time has been called in the town centre's bars. It's an ideal venue for a club: the stark interior of bare stone blocks, arched aisle spaces and lofty barrelled roofs provide the perfect backdrop for the state-of-the-art light show. What Renaissance Ragusans might have made of the lithe females dancing in cages is another question entirely. A lot of leading Croatian pop and rock acts perform here throughout the year. In summer, there'll probably be an international DJ appearing every weekend – Fatboy Slim and sundry others have lugged their record boxes up Revelin's stone steps.

## Hotels

In addition to the hotels and hostels listed below, apartments and villas can be rented through **Dubrovnik Apartment Source** (+353 86 024 1834, www.dubrovnikapartmentsource.com), established by American couple Andrew and Michelle Kehoe. The company deals with quality properties in and around the city.

### Apartments Amoret
*Ilije Sarake 4 (020 324 005, www.dubrovnik-amoret.com).* **€. No credit cards. Map** p239 D4.
Thirteen wonderfully decorated apartments at five different locations in the Old Town. All come with kitchenette, TV and free Wi-Fi. In summer, stays of under four nights are subject to a slight surcharge, but prices are still very good for the quality of the accommodation and the location.

### Celenga Apartments
*Svetoga Josipa 13 (020 362 900, 099 8070 760, www.pervanovo.com).* **€. Map** p239 C3.
These four-star apartments, for between two and four people, combine contemporary design and conveniences (including free Wi-Fi, spacious bath tubs, LCD TVs and air-con) with historic surroundings.

### Fresh Sheets
*Sv Šimuna 15 (091 799 2086, www. freshsheetshostel.com).* **€. Map** p239 C4.
Dubrovnik is surging with backpackers, although the only officially registered hostel within the Old Town walls for the past few seasons has been Fresh Sheets, run by an engaging Croatian-Canadian couple. Newly renovated, the hostel is squeezed into a tall thin house at the top of several flights of steps. It has three floors of (mostly bunk-bed) dorms, with a shower/WC on each floor. Doubles can also be arranged in one of the buildings nearby. The reception-cum-common room makes socialising easy, and you can forage for breakfast ingredients (included in the price) in the communal kitchenette. The hostel is open from mid March to the end of October. The same team has also launched Fresh Sheets B&B near the Cathedral (*see below*).

### Fresh Sheets B&B
*Bunićeva poljana 6 (091 799 2086, freshsheets bedandbreakfast.com).* **€€. Map** p239 D3.
The search for city-centre B&B accommodation that lives up to its promise is now made easier with Fresh Sheets B&B (run by the same team as the Fresh Sheets Hostel, *see above*). Squeezed into the second floor of a stone house just behind the Cathedral, it offers the kind of Dubrovnik views you dream about, with some rooms facing out towards the Rector's Palace, others overlooking the lively fruit and veg market of Gundulićeva poljana. Reached by a stone staircase, rooms (mostly doubles, although there is one studio apartment and one two-room family apartment) are furnished in simple but contemporary style, and have the added benefits of cable TV and air-con. Breakfast is served in a cosy communal kitchen, and help-yourself tea and coffee are available throughout the day.

### Hotel Stari Grad
*Od Sigurate 4 (020 322 244, www.hotelstarigrad. com).* **€€. Map** p239 C2.
The boutique Stari Grad is a rare find in the Old Town, in a quiet street off the main plaza. This 16th-century nobleman's house has been renovated (in 2013) and

EXPLORE

modernised without compromising its period features; the eight quiet, contemporary rooms are large and staff are eager to please. The Green & Purple Café bar is a funky place to sit for a drink, and the fifth-floor restaurant Above5 has a beautiful terrace overlooking the Old Town, sea and neighbouring islands.

### ★ Karmen Apartments
*Bandureva 1 (020 323 433, www.karmendu.com).*
**€€. No credit cards. Map p239 E3.**
Four comfortable year-round apartments at affordable prices not five minutes' walk from the old port. Bohemian touches reflect the past of genial host Marc van Bloemen, whose parents were movers and shakers in the 1960s – that's an original Marcel Marceau self-portrait propped against the wall.

### Pucić Palace
*Od Puča 1 (020 326 222, www.thepucicpalace.com).*
**€€€€. Map p239 D3.**
A beautiful five-star right in the Old Town, the Pucić Palace weaves old-world heritage with 21st-century convenience. Nineteen rooms are individually decorated, with ample beds and sumptuous linens. Large, soundproofed windows allow Old-Town views – most notably from the stand-out Gundulić suite, overlooking the market square of the same name. Note also the Defne restaurant on the roof terrace.

### ★ Vacation Suite Kashe
*Ribarnica 1 (099 219 4385).* **€. Map p239 E2.**
Right on the old port, this comfortable flat can sleep four, with two bedrooms, two bathrooms,

harbour views, all the mod cons one would expect and Wi-Fi. An extra two can be put up at the Studio Bruno downstairs.

## OUTSIDE THE OLD TOWN

**Ploče** is the picturesque stretch of coastline and sliver of land running east from the gate of the same name towards Cavtat and Dubrovnik airport. Until relatively recently, coast and land were pretty much all that were here. Traders would bring their wares over the hillsides by donkey to the Old Town and set up on open ground outside Ploče Gate. The view of Lokrum island, which lounges the length of Ploče, was enjoyed by these passing peasants from Konavle and Bosnia and the handful of nobles who built isolated villas overlooking the sea. The lure of tourism encouraged villa owners to convert their homes – this is now a row of luxury hotels. It is also a hub of culture: one mansion was converted into the Modern Art Gallery, while the old quarantine barracks of Lazareti is now the DJ spot of the same name. By day you can lounge on adjoining **Banje beach** (perhaps at East-West beach club), the nearest one to the Old Town, although locals prefer Sveti Jakov, a 20-minute walk along Frana Supila. Each hotel can also offer at least one decent restaurant – most have sea-view terraces.

**Pile** overlooks a beach, Penatur, flanked by the Lovrijenac fortress and Gradac park. Lookout post for the Ragusa Republic, Lovrijenac

Banje beach.

bears the motto, 'Liberty is not for sale, not even for gold', a proud summation of the city's independent spirit.

In similar vein, high above the hinterland, **Mount Srdj** witnessed brave defensive action by locals in 1991. It now contains the Homeland War Museum and the terminus for the restored cablecar, saving visitors the strenuous two-hour climb. At the top are a restaurant, the Panorama, the ruined Napoleonic fort, the hilltop cross you see illuminated at night from town – and that breathtaking view.

Shortly after Pile, main roads divide. One goes to the main harbour and bus station at Gruž; the other forks off for the twin-headed peninsula of **Lapad** and **Babin kuk**. Each is given over to leisure and relaxation, the hilly, verdant landscape sliced by roads accessed by Dubrovnik's vintage orange-and-white buses. Hotels dot the twisted shoreline, whose beaches include Lapad itself, beneath the Hotel Kompas; and the Copacabana near the Hotel Minceta, equipped for water activities.

## Sights & Museums

### ★ Cablecar

*Petra Krešimira IV (020 325 393, www.dubrovnik cablecar).* **Open** *June-Aug* 9am-midnight daily. *Sept* 9am-10pm daily. *Apr, May, Oct* 9am-8pm daily. *Feb, Mar, Nov* 9am-5pm daily. *Jan, Dec* 9am-4pm daily. **Tickets** 60kn; 30kn reductions. *Return* 108kn; 60kn 4-12s. **Map** p235 E1 (50)

This popular attraction whisks passengers up in a bright orange box high over the Old Town up to the top of Mount Srđ. It's a quick but thrilling journey, and well worth the steep fee. The cablecar offers the opportunity to see the Old Town nearly vanish as a panorama of Adriatic blue dominates the horizon. Expensive it might be, the cablecar is simply a must for a complete visit to Croatia's most beautiful city.

### Homeland War Museum

*Imperial Fort (020 321 497, www.dumus.hr/en/museum-of-contemporary-history).* **Open** *Summer* 8am-10pm daily. *Winter* 9am-4pm daily. **Admission** 30kn. **No credit cards. Map** p235 D1 (51)

The Homeland War is the Croatian term for the conflict of the 1990s that broke up Yugoslavia and gained Croatia its independence. The setting here is apt: a Napoleonic Fort, bravely defended by locals in 1991, now easily accessible by cablecar. Go straight up the two flights of stairs to the top terrace of the fortress in which the museum is housed and take in the view. The fort was built by the French in 1806-1812 then extended by the Austrians. Inside you see examples of the ammunition used to shell Dubrovnik, maps of the damage it caused, all manner of memorabilia and a video recording of Dubrovnik as it was being shelled.

### ★ Museum of Modern Art Dubrovnik

*Frana Supila 23 (020 426 590, www.ugdubrovnik.hr).* **Open** 10am-8pm Tue-Sun. **Admission** 30kn. **No credit cards. Map** p235 E1 (52)

Just a short walk from the Old Town, the wonderful former Banac Mansion has four floors and nine rooms of exhibition space, with a permanent collection that includes many works by Cavtat-born Vlaho Bukovac, alongside challenging contemporary shows. There is usually at least one major summer exhibition featuring a leading Croatian or international artist, and frequent contemporary-art happenings.

## Restaurants

### Amfora

*Obala Stjepana Radića 26, Gruž (020 419 419, amforadubrovnik.com).* **Open** 8am-midnight daily. **€€€. Map** p234 B1 (53) **Mediterranean**

Amfora is an excellent choice for both meat and fish lovers, its cuisine drawing its inspiration from all areas of the Mediterranean, with styles and influences from Morocco to Lebanon, and all the way to the Croatian coast. The menu might feature a house-style traditional *pašticada*, a stew cooked sous-vide for 48 hours. This technique is also used for some fish dishes. All pastas, gnocchi and breads are prepared in this kitchen. Fresh ingredients are provided by the local produce market – the blue-fin tuna is line-caught. The wine list is long, and mainly local, as is the olive oil – note the bottle of Torkul from Korčula on every table. Besides the modern interior, there is an outdoor area with views of an orchard. Reservations are recommended in high season.

### Ankora

*Zaton Veliki (020 891 031, www.restaurant-ankora-dubrovnik.com).* **Open** *May-Oct* 11am-midnight daily. **€€€. Dalmatian**

Sitting on the terrace of the Ankora, eight kilometres west of Dubrovnik, gives you the impression that you are on the deck of a boat. Not only is the sea within easy reach, all 80 seats by the water – an eastern wind brings fragrances of the Mediterranean herbs used to make home-made grappa, gladly served to you as you sit down. Since you are so close to the waves, it comes as no surprise that the menu is full of fresh fish, shellfish, scampi and lobster, prepared in the traditional Dalmatian way. A variation on this theme is seafood pasta and risotto. Reservations are recommended on balmy summer evenings.

### Chihuahua-Cantina Mexicana

*Šetalište kralja Zvonimira 2, Lapad (020 424 445).* **Open** 9am-midnight daily. **No credit cards. €€. Map** p234 B2 (54) **Mexican**

Having moved from its Old Town location to the upper end of the pedestrianised zone near Lapad beach, Chihuahua remains a lively place for decent

Mexican food, nasty margaritas and cool music. On offer are all the usual favourites: nachos, burritos, fajitas, enchiladas and quesadillas – a change from the generally staid international dining scene around Dubrovnik. Check the restaurant's Facebook page for more information.

### Glorijet
*Obala Stjepana Radića 16, Gruž (020 419 788).* **Open** 10am-midnight Mon-Sat. **€€. Map** p234 C1 ⑤ **Seafood**
There can't be a better location for a traditional seafood restaurant than right next to Dubrovnik's fish market in the harbourside suburb of Gruž. It's also an atmospheric place to eat, beneath the barrel-vaulted brick ceiling of a former boathouse, looking out on the quays where excursion boats are moored. It's the perfect place to work your way through the traditional Adriatic repertoire of grilled fish, shellfish and seafood risottos – standards are slightly higher (and prices slightly lower) than in the Old Town.

### ★ Gverović-Orsan
*Stikovića 43, Zaton Mali (020 891 267, www. gverovic-orsan.hr).* **Open** *Mar-Dec* noon-midnight Mon-Sat. **€€. Seafood**
In the fishing village of Zaton Mali, seven kilometres north-west of town, this old boathouse was converted into a restaurant by Niko Gverović in 1966. Beautifully located and family-run – Niko Jr runs it with his mother, Mira – its speciality is the black risotto Orsan, with four kinds of shells and shrimps sautéed in wine and lemon and mixed with rice soaked in black squid ink. The restaurant has its own beach (and shower), so you can swim while dinner is cooking.

### ★ Konavoski Komin
*Velji dol (020 479 607).* **Open** noon-midnight daily. **€€. Dalmatian**
Classic eaterie outside Dubrovnik towards Cavtat, well worth the effort of heading out of town for. Ham, lamb, cheese in olive oil and veal are the specialities, served by staff in traditional costumes. Phone to order a dish *ispod peke*: slow-cooked under hot coals, literally 'under a cooking bell'.

### Konoba Blidinje
*Lapadska obala 21, Lapad (020 358 794, konobablidinje.com).* **Open** 9am-midnight daily. **No credit cards. €€. Map** p234 B/C ⑤ **Dalmatian**
Facing Gruž harbour across the water, Blidinje comprises a rustic ground-floor space of two dozen covers, and two first-floor terraces with wonderful views of the marina and hills beyond. Carnivores should order veal, lamb or pork slow-cooked in the open oven – having given the kitchen a two-hour notice. The mixed grill for two, as good as any in town, would feed three. It's a pizzeria too, with plenty of choice. Considering the quality and location, prices are more than reasonable.

### Konoba Kasar
*Zaton (020 891 226, www.restaurant-kasar.hr).* **Open** *May-Oct* 11am-midnight daily. **€€. Seafood**
Set in the old boathouse of a 15th-century summer mansion, Kasar is a good choice for those who want to escape the crowds of Dubrovnik and enjoy home-style food by the sea. In fact, this restaurant is easier to find from the sea than after the ten-kilometre drive from Dubrovnik. Parking is also hard to find in Zaton, but the trip is worth it. By day, Kasar allows you a break from your swim – if you're arriving by yacht, there are two moorings at your disposal. Rustic cuisine is based on what the sea has to offer – and your fresh tuna steak or tasty lobster will be complemented with home-made bread with olive oil.

### ★ Orsan Yacht Club
*Marina Orsan, Ivana pl Zajca 2, Gruž (020 435 933).* **Open** 9.30am-11pm daily. **€€. Map** p234 B2 ⑤ **Dalmatian**
Here in Gruž Bay, a dozen tables sit on a sea-lapped terrace in the shade of a huge pine tree, making for a summer retreat that is enjoyed by cats and regular local diners alike. Menu highlights include oyster soup, octopus salad, lobster and Dalmatian rib-eye steak. Wine prices are more than reasonable.

### Panorama
*Mount Srđ (020 312 664).* **Open** *June-Sept* 9am-midnight daily. *Apr, May, Oct* 9am-8pm daily. *Nov-Mar* 9am-5pm daily. **€€. Map** p235 D1 ⑤
**Mediterranean**
Passengers arriving at the cablecar station at the top of Mount Srđ can take advantage of this café-restaurant complete with the jaw-dropping view down to the Old Town, Lokrum island and, off to the right, a stunning sunset. A lot of people stop by just for a coffee or beer but it also serves good-quality Mediterranean food. You can opt for a full Panorama plate, with swordfish, sea bass and calamari; Dalmatian ribsteak; or a simple pasta or salad. There are sandwiches (steak, club, ham and cheese), burgers and breakfasts too.

### Pantarul
*Kralja Tomislava 1 (020 333 486, www.pantarul. com).* **Open** noon-4pm, 6pm-midnight Thur-Sun. **€€€. Map** p234 B2 ⑤ **Contemporary Dalmatian**
Pantarul ('fork' in local dialect) is a new Dubrovnik success story. Here, unpretentious slow-food cuisine is based on seasonal ingredients. The vegetables arrive from the fields around Dubrovnik, the fish is what the local fishermen have caught that day and the meat is prime quality. In a simple, modern and yet cosy interior, you can opt for the creative five-course tasting menu of fish or meat, or choose from the concise à la carte selection. Fettuccine with veal tail and sage, gnocchi with octopus in arrabiata sauce or tender beef cheeks are stand-out dishes. *Photo p248.*

**EXPLORE**

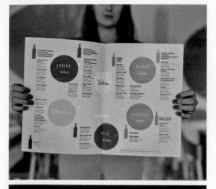

**Pantarul.** See p247.

**EXPLORE**

### Pivnica Dubrava
*Mali Stradun (020 448 354).* **Open** 11am-
midnight daily. €€. **Map** p234 A2 ❻ **Dalmatian**
Behind the pub sign hides a restaurant for lovers
of simple meat meals, prepared in a traditional
Dalmatian way: grilled or under an iron bell that's
covered with ashes and burning coal, locally
referred to as *sach* or *peka*. Grill is grill, but what
could really put a smile on your face is *peka*-cooked
veal, lamb or octopus. Its home-made bread is

prepared the same way. Reservations are a must at
weekends, when live Dalmatian music is a regular
fixture. Check the restaurant's Facebook page for
more information.

### Shizuku
*Kneza Domagoja 1F, Lapad (020 311 493,
www.facebook.com/ShizukuDubrovnik).* **Open**
5pm-midnight Tue-Sun. €€. **Map** p234 B2 ❻
**Japanese**
Opened by a Japanese couple in 2013, this pretty
much ticks all the boxes: fine sushi and sashimi
prepared with attention to both detail and authenticity; a good choice of Japanese meat dishes and
soups; and moderate prices. Located near the beach
in Lapad but slightly set back from the tourist areas
in a residential neighbourhood, it's popular with the
locals and also does a brisk take-out trade. Japanese
spirits and beers help to stretch out a long and
satisfying evening.

### Tovjerna Sesame
*Dante Alighieria (020 412 910, www.sesame.hr).*
**Open** 8am-11pm daily. €€. **Map** p235 D2 ❻
**Dalmatian**
Ideal for mid-priced meals, morning coffees and
evening drinks, the Tovjerna Sesame has a characterful front room that serves as a café-bar, and
a back room decked out in oriental carpets and oil
paintings that serves as a restaurant – the dining
area spreads to the upstairs veranda in summer.
Oyster soup, Šipan salad and the house risotto of
clams and squid feature among the starters and
light lunches, while main fish courses feature some
winningly inventive combinations.

## Cafés & Bars

### Art Café
*Branitelja Dubrovnika 25 (020 311 097).*
**Open** 10am-2am daily. **No credit cards**.
**Map** p235 D2 ❻
Something of a local favourite due to its outside-the-
Old-Town location, this pop-art masterpiece boasts
psychedelic comic-book murals, glow-in-the-dark
tables and gaudily coloured bar stools. Out on the
wedge-shaped terrace, sofas made from bathtubs
provide the perfect place to relax over a choice of
*rakijas* and a long menu of smoothies.

### Culto
*Iva Vojnovića 39A (no phone).* **Open** 8am-
midnight Mon-Thur, Sun; 8am-2am Fri, Sat.
**No credit cards**. **Map** p234 C2 ❻
This is probably the smartest and certainly the
largest of four adjoining bars. It needs its long bar
to accommodate the huge range of ingredients
for intriguing cocktails such as Flying Kangaroo
(rum, vodka, Galliano, coconut and pineapple juice).
Low slung black and chocolate sofas line the white
walls. A lower level at the front provides golden

bucket seats and there are video screens for daytime distraction. DJs take over at weekends. See the bar's Facebook page for more information.

## Roxy
*Bana Jelačića 9 (020 421 754).* **Open** 8am-midnight daily. **No credit cards.** **Map** p234 C2 ⑥⑤
Set on a small stretch lined with party bars, the Roxy has been Dubrovnik's prime musos' hangout for the past 25 years, with letters from the Beatles Fan Club, an old Animals album and an original Penny Lane 45, all framed and mounted. There's a Seeburg jukebox, too, just for show – chat-level sounds come from the CD player.

## Sunset Lounge
*Hotel Dubrovnik Palace, Masarykov put 20 (020 430 000, www.dubrovnikpalace.hr).* **Open** noon-1am daily. **Map** p234 A3 ⑥⑥
The sunset view is in full panorama here in the chic surroundings of the Hotel Dubrovnik Palace. On a clear day you can see Mljet. Afternoons mean happy-hour drinks, evenings a piano player. Cocktails comprise 35 standards, there are specialist Perković brandies (carob, fig, nut) and wines include the best local labels, rarely, as here, found by the glass.

## Shops & Services

### Gruž market
*Obala Stjepana Radića, Gruž (no phone).* **Open** 6am-6pm Mon-Sat; 6-11am Sun. *Fish market* 6am-noon Mon-Sat. **No credit cards. Map** p234 C1 ⑥⑦ **Market**
The main market in Dubrovnik for fruit, vegetables and fish. In a section of the ruined garden of the Gundulić summer villa, Gruž market is larger and cheaper than the one in the Old Town, Gundulićeva poljana (*see p243*). Shoppers and occasional restaurateurs arrive here, near the ferry terminal, from early in the morning, hoping to find the best merchandise. Prices are mostly fixed and haggling doesn't tend to happen. Finding a little discount might be easiest at the end of the working day, when vendors are looking to offload all their stock. If you are fond of fine fish, get here by 7am, when women traders arrive from the Elafiti islands. The stock varies from day to day, but Fridays is usually the best.

## Nightlife

### East-West
*Banje beach, Frana Supila (099 211 9666, www.ew-dubrovnik.com).* **Open** *Summer* 10am-6am daily. *Winter* varies. **Map** p239 F3.
A café-restaurant by day, by night this is a clubby beachside cocktail bar. The clientele is chic – it's hired for fashion parties – but the place is far from intimidating and prices are reasonable.

### ★ Lazareti
*Lazareti complex, Frana Supila 8 (020 324 633, www.lazareti.com).* **Open** varies. **No credit cards.**
This would be Dubrovnik's best year-round nightspot if it ran a regular programme – as things stand at time of writing gigs and DJ appearances come in flurries, and the website is not updated often enough to provide due notification. The club is set in an old stone former quarantine barracks. Pay your money at the gate, and head down to an open courtyard under the stars. The main building is at the bottom: a stage for DJ decks and live acts; a dancefloor, and a balcony area with bar.

## Hotels

### Bellevue
*Pera Čingrije 7 (020 330 000, www.adriatic luxuryhotels.com).* €€€€. **Map** p235 D2.
Dubrovnik has more than its fair share of cliff-hugging, sun-trap hotels and this particular feat of engineering is one of the more outstanding examples. The venue, cut into the cliff facing the sea, has been expensively refurbished to feature local woods and granite. All rooms have a sea view, as do the spa and highly rated Vapor restaurant. The Nevera Beach restaurant occupies a man-made cave right beside the private beach.

### Berkeley
*Andrije Hebranga 116A, Gruž (020 494 160, www.berkeleyhotel.hr).* €€. **Map** p234 C1.
This lovely aparthotel just across from the main ferry terminal, was conceived by ex-Sydney restaurateurs Nick and Marija and comprises 20 beautiful suites and one apartment. The small rooftop pool is a bonus.

### ★ Excelsior
*Frana Supila 12, Ploče (020 353 353, 020 353 000, www.adriaticluxuryhotels.com).* €€€€. **Map** p235 F1.
A €22-million refit of Dubrovnik's most prestigious hotel was followed by a grand reopening in 2008. Built in 1913 as a private villa, it became the Hotel Excelsior in 1930. Royals, writers, movie stars – they all stayed here. It now features four restaurants, three pools, a piano bar and spa. The adjoining Villa Rustica contains luxury lodging for six. The Satu sushi bar and the luxuriant wellness centre endow the hotel with additional kudos.

### Grand Hotel Park
*Šetalište kralja Zvonimira 39, Lapad (020 434 444, 020 434 888, www.grandhotel-park.hr).* €€. **Map** p234 B2.
A bold wedge of modern architecture set back slightly from the Lapad seafront, the 224-room Park was renovated in 2008 and its facilities upgraded to four-star standard. Rooms come in relaxing peachy-creamy colours and are fitted with hydromassage shower units. New facilities following the refit include sauna, steam bath, massage and beauty

**EXPLORE**

# ALL DUBROVNIK IS A STAGE

*The city's Summer Festival is Croatia's own Edinburgh.*

Shakespeare and his Croatian counterpart, Marin Držić, could not have wished for a better setting than the ones provided by the historic open-air venues of Dubrovnik's Old Town, moonlit and dramatically backdropped by the Adriatic. The long-established Dubrovnik Summer Festival provides top-notch classical music, theatre, opera and ballet – and there is ever more talk about introducing contemporary elements.

Reaching its 65th anniversary in 2015, the festival is Croatia's most important cultural event. For 47 days and nights, from 10 July to 25 August, the streets, churches, squares and famous buildings of Dubrovnik's celebrated Old Town are the stage for international and domestic names in the arts. Shows bring Dubrovnik's historic jewels to life – many come here for the atmosphere alone. Shakespeare is performed open-air at the Lovrijenac fortress, dancers prance after dark outside the Church of St Blaise and all kinds of events have the moonlit City Walls as a backdrop. The atrium of the Rector's Palace is particularly known for its ambience and acoustics. Even Lokrum island, 15 minutes across the sea and forbidden to visitors after 8pm, breaks its curfew to theatre-goers, ferried back in special boats to the mainland after the final curtain falls.

Locals are involved in every sense. Two costumed servants at the Old Town's gates welcome visitors to the teeming madness that is Stradun in festival time. A busking band led by famous flautist Žarko Hajdrarhodzić plays classical tunes from street corner to street corner as acrobats tumble, *klapa* folk singers boom out traditional Dalmatian tunes and artists offer open rehearsals. On the eve of opening night, midnight on 9 July, amateurs take the lead roles as artists, with politicians and the festival management the butt of their jokes.

It all harks back to the 1930s when *Dubravka*, by 17th-century Croatian writer Ivan Gundulić, was dramatised outdoors for those attending the PEN writers' congress. It set the tone for the slightly playful take on Renaissance literature still prevalent today. Things began in earnest in the early 1950s when director Marko Fotez set a production of *Hamlet* at the Lovrijenac fortress. As the event

evolved, the Old Town gradually became its stage. For a few days, one week and then two, Dubrovnik lived the festival year after year.

This same concept has been in place since and, unlike Edinburgh, Dubrovnik has kept the arts agenda mainly high-brow. When the Serbian bombardment of Dubrovnik destroyed much of the Old Town in late 1991 and into 1992, the festival took on a poignant aspect. In place of an opening ceremony, locals lit candles in the windows while Ivan Gundulić's 'Anthem to Freedom' played on the radio to a deserted Stradun.

In peacetime, the festival has expanded its schedule and its scope, inviting big international names; Derek Jacobi and Daniel Day Lewis have appeared as Hamlet, with the play still the festival mainstay. Locals wax lyrical about Peter Brook's English-language *Hamlet* set on Lokrum a few years ago. The festival's core programme remains the classical arts, with emphasis on Shakespeare and his Croatian counterpart Marin Držić. The bulk of theatrical performances are in Croatian and few are subtitled.

Some forward-thinking locals worry about the future of the festival, its agenda stuck with a standard, established repertoire, with little by way of underground or alternative arts. Many of Croatia's leading contemporary playwrights and actors have gone abroad, leaving the stage to the older generation, happy to take the applause for another professional rendering of wordsmiths from the 1500s. Perhaps, some argue, new ideas and new blood are needed at management level.

Despite this, and the fact that all high-end hotels fill up quickly (look for a private room or a package hotel in Lapad), foreign visitors flock here in droves at festival time: top-drawer classical music and ballet – 2015 saw appearances by Zoltán Kocsis and the Mozarteum Quartet – are universal. Around the main events, book launches, art exhibitions and other inclusive cultural events dot the Old Town. Folklore shows at the Revelin Fort also generally play to an international crowd. (The stage is exposed to the elements so if there's a strong wind that evening, take extra clothes.) Even in Croatian, Shakespeare set atop Lovrijenac, standing 37 metres (121 feet) above the open sea, is memorable.

Tickets for these major events sell out pretty quickly, having been on sale since St Blaise's Day (2 February) on the festival website, www.dubrovnik-festival.hr. If you're looking for tickets on the day, try the stall set up by the Festival Café (see *p242*) halfway along the main street. Most performances begin at 9.30pm.

treatments, and a small gym overlooking a dinky indoor pool. There's also a respectably sized outdoor pool, although family friendly Lapad beach is only two minutes' walk away.

### ★ Dubrovnik Palace
*Masarykov put 20, Lapad (020 300 300, www.dubrovnikpalace.hr)*. €€€. **Map** p234 A2.
This ten-floor, 308-room luxury hotel is set in woodland paths at the tip of Lapad, in full view of the Elafiti Isles. Following a reconfiguring a few years ago, this is what everyone sees from their balcony, from the four bars, three restaurants, four pools and gym. Saunas, massage treatments and beauty procedures are on offer at the energy clinic spa. Also of note are the Lanterna Glorijet poolside bar and the Sunset Lounge cocktail bar.

### ★ Grand Villa Argentina
*Frana Supila 14, Ploče (020 430 830, www.adriatic luxuryhotels.com)*. **Open** Mid Feb-mid Jan. €€€€. **Map** p235 F1.
This villa-and-hotel complex centres on the de luxe Hotel Argentina, opened in the 1950s and long considered one of Dubrovnik's most stylish addresses. Within the same complex and surrounded by lush seaside gardens are the Villa Argentina, housing intimate luxury apartments; and Villa Sheherezade, a mock-Oriental palace in which up to 12 people can relax in opulence for €6,000 a day. Indoor pool, gym, beauty centre and private beach are all part of the package.

### Lapad
*Lapadska obala 37, Lapad (020 455 555, www.hotel-lapad.hr)*. **Open** mid Mar-Oct. €€. **Map** p234 B2.
Overlooking Gruž harbour, this well-known hotel consists of three elements: a fin-de siècle façade facing the main road towards the Babin Kuk headland, containing the lobby and reception area; and, on the other side of an outdoor pool and a pleasant courtyard, the accommodation building, divided into two wings. Of the nearly 200 rooms, the ones in the older wing are cheaper. Despite an impressive recent refit, the Lapad still has a taste of times gone by, with an on-site hairdresser, as well as pool parties and musical entertainment in the summer. Handy for Lapad and the Old Town, and a ten-minute walk from the ferry port and bus station.

### More
*Kardinala Stepinca 33 (020 494 200, www.hotel-more.hr)*. €€€. **Map** p234 B2.
Built into the Babin kuk cliff-face, this lush, waterfront hotel comprises 34 luxurious rooms and three suites, most with a sea view. There's an outdoor pool, gym, lounge bar and the Molteni restaurant, which is of international standard.

### Petka
*Obala Stjepana Radića 38, Gruž (020 410 500, www.hotelpetka.hr)*. €€. **Map** p234 B1.

EXPLORE

A convenient place to flop after that long bus or ferry journey, the Petka now has a few extras after its recent upgrade. Most of the 100-plus rooms have a balcony overlooking Gruž bay and harbour, and access to a gym and good restaurant. The full-board supplement is a snip.

## Uvala
*Masarykov put 6, Lapad (020 433 608, www. dubrovnikhotels.travel/hotel-uvala-dubrovnik).* **Open** Apr-Nov. €€. **Map** p234 B3.
The Uvala has a spacious spa with full treatments, indoor and outdoor pools, a sauna and solarium. The other four Dubrovnik hotels owned by the Maestral group – Adriatic, Komodor, Splendid and Vis – are resort hotels on the same main road in Lapad.

## Importanne Resort
*Kardinala Stepinca 31, Lapad (020 440 100, www.importanneresort.com).* €€€. **Map** p234 A3.
This complex on the Lapad headland comprises two holiday hotels, the Neptun and the Ariston, and three upscale properties: the Royal Palm apartment hotel; the Royal Princess Apartment Hotel; and the intimate, 12-person Villa Elita. There is a Blue Flag beach and pine trees all around. The facilities (massage rooms, saunas, seawater pools, freshwater indoor and outdoor ones) are superb.

## Kazbek Hotel
*Lapadska obala 25, Lapad (020 362 900, www. kazbekdubrovnik.com).* €€€. **Map** p234 B2.
Opened in 2008, this conversion of the Zamanje family villa (1573) is now a luxury hotel of a dozen rooms, one suite, three restaurants and a beautiful outdoor pool with a bar beside it. A speedboat and yacht are on hand for guests' use.

## Maro & Baro Apartments
*Zrinsko-Frankopanska 12 (099 376 58 00, apartments-maro-baro.dubrovnikhotels croatia.net).* €. **Map** p235 D2.
In a quiet street, only ten minutes' walk from Dubrovnik's historic centre, is a house with one two-storey and two studio apartments, each with its own entrance. The larger one has a living room, kitchen and bedroom on the second floor – and its own terrace with a view of the Lovrijenac fortress. Two smaller apartments share a terrace and each have a living room, bathroom and kitchen. Dubrovnik is a city of many steps and you'll find this a bit of a climb – by consolation, a fridge full of welcome drinks, juices, beers and regional wines awaits. A private airport transfer and a discount in the restaurants of Orsan, Ankora and Pivnica Dubrava are also offered.

## Pervanovo Apartments
*Vatroslava Lisinskog 43-59, Lapad (020 362 900, www.pervanovo.com).* €€. **Map** p234 A2.
Set in Lapad, these 18 newly built apartments are contained within eight luxury villas, most with balconies, some of which have rather charming sea views and others facing inland. All are equipped with washing machines, air-con and HD TVs.

## Radisson Blu Resort & Spa, Dubrovnik Sun Gardens
*Na Moru 1, Orašac (020 361 500. www.dubrovniksungardens.com).* €€€.
Ten kilometres north of town, sprawling across the seafront just below the pleasingly rustic village of Orašac, this is a self-contained resort with rocky beach, wonderful views, well-tended gardens and pretty much everything you need for a hassle-free vacation. A cluster of bars and eateries around the forum-like 'Market Place' augment the main hotel restaurants, and there is a huge range of beauty treatments on offer at the spa centre. Accommodation is in immaculate hotel rooms or in 'residences': apartments ranging in size from one-bedroom to three-bedroom family affairs with kitchenette. The only possible drawback is location: public transport from Orašac to Dubrovnik is far from ideal (especially at night), and the shuttle boats and buses offered by the hotel don't run that often out of season.

## Rixos Libertas
*Liechensteinov put 3 (020 200 000, www.rixos.com).* €€€. **Map** p234 C2.
The Turkish-owned Rixos Libertas has long been one of Dubrovnik's architectural landmarks, originally built in the early 1970s when Croatian modernism was at its peak. Dramatically ranged across a steep hillside in a succession of curving terraces, the hotel was damaged during the 1991-2 siege and spent a long time awaiting reconstruction. Now restored to its former glory, it features superb views, a two-floor spa, two pools and the popular Golden Sun casino.

## ★ Valamar Dubrovnik President Hotel
*Iva Dulčića 142, Babin kuk (052 465 000, www. valamar.com/en/hotels-dubrovnik/valamar-dubrovnik-president-hotel).* €€€. **Map** p234 A2.
This leading lodging of the Valamar group has its own excellent section of beach; each of the 181 rooms has a balcony view of the sea and Elafiti islands beyond. There's also an indoor pool, children's entertainment and access to nearby tennis courts. The nearby sister hotel Valamar Club Dubrovnik is also geared for children, with water chutes, banana rides and pedalos, plus a small football pitch, minigolf and diving; the Valamar Lacroma Dubrovnik is a state-of-the-art hotel with the Ragusa spa and its dizzying array of treatments (free with a minimum four-night stay), pools indoor and out (and separate kids' pool) and fine dining at the Langosto luxury restaurant
**Other locations** Valamar Club Dubrovnik, Iva Dulčića 18; Valamar Lacroma Dubrovnik, Iva Dulčića 34 (same phone and website as above for both).

## Vila Micika
*Mata Vodopića 10, Lapad (020 437 332, www.vilamicika.hr)*. **€. Map** p234 B2.
You won't find cheaper accommodation anywhere in Dubrovnik than this compact, well-positioned two-storey property in Lapad. Triples are available and there are tennis courts are nearby. Breakfast is extra but there are also plenty of cafés nearby.

## ★ Villa Dubrovnik
*Vlaha Bukovca 6 (020 500 300, www.villadubrovnik.hr)*. **Open** Apr-Nov. **€€€€**.
The Villa Dubrovnik is a stunningly located, superbly appointed luxury hotel, set on a rocky outcrop, a complimentary boat journey from the Old Town (it's half a kilometre away and the handy water shuttle service operates five times a day). It's a wonderfully tranquil spot. Breakfasts and sunset cocktails take in the magnificent view – no wonder the hotel's slogan is 'romance forever'. All of the property's 56 rooms, set on descending terraces, have sea and Old Town views, and all are beautifully appointed with access to a stretch of private beach, and both indoor and outdoor pools. For many, the most attractive facility, at sunset at least, is the Bar Giardino, a verdant, panoramic terrace and the ideal spot for a cocktail before the last boat to town. The Mediterranean flavours of the Restaurant Pjerin may just force you to stay, though.

## BEACHES & EXCURSIONS

The city beach, **Banje**, is a short walk from the Ploče Gate. It's good for kids, pebbly and, at times, sandy, depending on the waves. It has showers, plus jet skis and inflatables. Most of the beach is run by the East-West restaurant club and bathers who want a deckchair or sunlounger will have to pay – as a result, Banje has evolved to become a hang-out for tourists, not locals. They head instead for **Sveti Jakov**, down the coast past the Villa Dubrovnik, a 20-minute walk along quiet, tree-lined Vlaha Bukovca. Bus Nos.5 and 8 run most of the way from north of the Old Town. Although this is everyone's favourite beach, it's rarely crowded. The sun stays warm until late in the evening, bathing the Old Town in a golden light. It's part shingle, part pebble, with showers, sunshades, and a bar and restaurant at beach level. It is accessed via a long stairway you'll be reluctant to climb back up. Between Banje and Sv Jakov are the hotel beaches, either exclusive or hired by the day. Each can offer a pool, a terrace and a fine Martini. Just east of the Grand Villa Argentina is **Betina špilja**, a cave with a fine white pebble beach, only accessible from the sea. Rent a taxi boat at the old harbour, arrange a pick-up time and get the captain's number. Do remember to take provisions with you.

Pile is not known for its beaches – but **Šulići** is one of Dubrovnik's cleanest, a handy short walk from the Pile Gate. On the other side of the promontory, the rocky beach of **Danče** stretches to an open, clear sea. The bay here isn't so sheltered, so waves can be rough.
**Lapad** (bus No.6 from Pile) has a family-friendly public beach complete with showers, sunloungers and shallow waters overseen by lifeguards. Behind, the pedestrianised shade of Šetalište kralja Tomislava has a bouncy play area and tennis courts are nearby. Immediately to the west, the rocks beside the Niki i Meda Pucića promenade allow for nude sunbathing.

Further north-west, the **Babin kuk peninsula** (also served by bus No. 6 or reached via the Niki i Meda Pucića promenade) is dotted with decent hotels, each of which has access to a beach of some sort. The best equipped is the **Copacabana**, a half-moon of pebbles and gravel set in **Seka Bay**. Although the water here isn't as pristine as elsewhere – Seka Bay also faces the Daksa Canal, through which ferries pass en route to Gruž – the Copacabana can be bags of fun. Parachute boat rides, water chutes, canoes, jet skis, pedalos and banana rides all provide for high-action entertainment. Nearby is a signposted path down to a far quieter, naturist beach, **Cava**.

There is also nude bathing at the island of **Lokrum**, 15 minutes by regular taxi boat from the Old Port, itself five minutes' walk from the main square in the Old Town. Outdoor adventure firm Adriatic Kayak Tours (Zrinsko-Frankopanska 6 (020 312 770, www.adriatic kayaktours.com) offer sea-kayaking jaunts to Lokrum as well as the Elafiti Islands.

Diving is also popular in and around Dubrovnik. Local clubs such as Blue Planet Diving (Hotel Dubrovnik Palace, Masarykov put 20, 091 899 0973, http://blueplanet-diving.com) and Navis Underwater Explorers (Copacabana beach, 020 356 501, 098 919 7402) offer both trips and a range of different diving courses for all levels and ages.

## GETTING THERE & AROUND

**Dubrovnik airport** is located 22km (14 miles) south-east of town, down the coast at Čilipi. Regular buses (30mins, 35kn) meet every scheduled flight, first stopping near the Pile Gate before going on to the bus station, 5km west of the Old Town at Kantafig. Buses from the bus station to the airport don't pass via Pile Gate – the stop at the Cablecar terminal on Petar Krešimir IV is the nearest one to the Old Town.
A **taxi** costs about 250kn, nearer to 350kn if you're at a hotel on the Lapad or Babin kook headland. Call one on +385 970.

Dubrovnik has no train link. The nearest main station is in Split, four-and-a-half hours away by regular bus. Half-a-dozen services arrive daily from Zagreb (ten hours). All the main **ferries** and **catamarans** arrive at Gruž harbour. The ferry from Bari in southern Italy runs six days a week in summer, twice a week in winter, leaving around 10pm, arriving in Dubrovnik around 7am the next day.

Libertas **city buses** link Gruž, Babin kuk, Lapad and Ploče to the Old Town. Buy a ticket (10kn) at any newsstand or in exact change (12kn) from the driver. Gruž is a deceptively long walk to and from town – allow 30 mins and don't count on easily making it by taxi if you're running late. Although there are cabs aplenty at the Pile Gate, the road to Gruž is always busy and often gridlocked.

**Taxis** start at 25kn and charge 8kn per km – expect a 50kn-70kn bill for Gruž. Bus Nos.1A, 3 and 8 do the same journey.

## RESOURCES

**Hospital** *Roka Mišetića, Lapad (020 431 777, www.bolnica-du.hr).* **Map** p234 C3.
Dubrovnik's main hospital is some 4km out of town in Lapad.

**Pharmacy** *Kod Zvonika, Ulica Kovacka (020 321 133).* **Open** 8am-8pm daily. **Map** p239 D2.
Located right in the Old Town, this is the main late-opening chemist.

**Post office** *Vukovarska 16 (020 362 068).* **Open** 7am-8pm Mon-Fri; 8am-3pm Sat; 8am-noon Sun. **Map** p234 C2.

**Tourist information** *Brsalje 5 (020 323 887, http://experience.dubrovnik.hr).* **Open** 8am-8pm daily. **Map** p235 D2.
Office near the Pile Gate with friendly, multi-lingual staff.

# Korčula

As you approach Korčula from the mainland nearby, the crowded little houses on the edge of the island seem to be pushing each other out of the way to see if you are friend or foe. Holding them in, stern medieval walls centrepieced by the slim belltower of **St Mark's Cathedral** stand guard over the narrow Pelješac Channel, protecting the riches contained on the sixth largest island in the Croatian Adriatic. So lush with dark pine forests, vineyards and olive groves the ancient Greek settlers called it Korkyra Melaina ('Black Corfu'), Korčula has managed to avoid the tourist trap tendencies of its original Greek namesake to the south.

No longer fought over by Turk or Venetian, by French or Austrian, by Partisan or German, Korčula is one of Dalmatia's most relaxing getaways. The main town of the same name, set on the north-eastern tip of the island opposite the Pelješac peninsula, has one of the best-preserved medieval centres in the Adriatic. Historic Korčula is therefore the most popular south-Dalmatian destination after the more crowded Dubrovnik, with which it is often compared.

And Korčula is undoubtedly a beautiful place in which to get stuck for a week or two, its woolly green covering of evergreen holm oak and prickly maquis punctuated by dark-green spears of cypress. The main road from the ferry port at Vela Luka to Korčula town switches from one side of the island's central spine to the other, offering majestic maritime views that take in the crisp grey-brown silhouettes of neighbouring islands **Hvar** and **Lastovo**. Throughout the interior, hillside-hugging villages hover above a patchwork of vineyards and vegetable plots.

The main attraction is Korčula town itself, with its historic centre of narrow alleys and crenellated walls. Superb beaches (including some genuinely sandy ones) are to be found at **Lumbarda**, and in the secluded coves of the south coast. The beautifully situated port of **Vela Luka** is the island's other major urban centre, although there's a lot to be said for the sleepy villages inland – it's here that the true heartland of Korčula's distinctive cuisine and unique wines is to be found.

Tourists with modern-day demands are at last catered for at the **Lešić-Dimitri Palace Korčula**, a five-star luxury retreat with a spa and restaurant to match. The refurbishment of the four-star **Marko Polo** is another boon. Recent additions to the Korčula festival calendar include the **Korkyra Baroque Music Festival** (www.korkyrabaroque.com), inaugurated in 2012, and the **Marco Polo Triathlon Challenge** (marco polochallenge.korcula.hr), first held in 2011.

Korčula's claimed connection with famed traveller Marco Polo is not as tenuous as you might think: it's possible he was born here, perhaps on the mainland in Šibenik, or in Venice. Polo certainly fought for the Venetians in the Battle of Korčula in 1298, and for centuries DePolo has been a common family name here. The **Marko Polo House**, frequently shown to tourists as Marco Polo's birthplace is actually a 17th-century structure that has no direct connection with the man – but today this is a proper museum attraction.

## KORČULA TOWN

Unlike Dubrovnik, Korčula was governed by the Venetians, responsible for the layout of Korčula Old Town, no more than a few hundred metres across. Within the oval walls, streets are laid out in a herringbone pattern. Those running west are straight to let in the cool westerly breeze on burning summer days; those running east are curved to keep out the chilly winter *bura* wind from the north-east. Those facing north allowed locals to rush up and quickly defend the Pelješac Channel.

Although Korčula's main claim to fame as the birthplace of Marco Polo may be urban myth, it does offer authentic historic attractions thanks to a medieval building programme begun by one of Polo's contemporaries, ruling Venetian nobleman Count Marsilije Zorzi. Entering the Old Town from the south, ascend the **Punat**, or stone bridge, and pass beneath the **Veliki Revelin Tower** (also sometimes called the Kopnena Vrata or Land Gate), bearing the Venetian coat of arms and erected to mark the island's gallant defence against the Turkish navy at the Battle of Lepanto. By the gate is a produce and souvenir market, and to one side is an open-air cinema, in summer the setting for performances of the Moreška sword dance.

Through the tower is the square of Sv Mihovil, lined with municipal buildings. A small chapel here, dedicated to the Miraculous Virgin of the Island, was built after Lepanto. Every 15 August a procession runs from the chapel to mark the Virgin's Ascension.

The main street, Ulica Korčulanskog Statuta, leads to **St Mark's Cathedral**, one of the finest examples of Dalmatian church architecture and design. Taking three centuries to build, it features several styles, including Gothic, Romanesque and Baroque. Beneath it is the sarcophagus of St

Theodore, the protector of Korčula. Here you can also see Tintoretto's *St Mark with St Bartholomew and St Jerome*; his *Annunciation* also stands in the south nave. Next door, the **Cathedral Treasury** contains a collection of Dalmatian art from the 15th and 16th centuries. Opposite the cathedral, the **Town Museum**, set in a 16th-century Venetian palace, contains a copy of a fourth-century Greek tablet from Lumbarda, the earliest evidence of civilisation on the island. Down a side street is the excellent **Icon Museum** and, entered through it, the 14th-century Church of All Saints.

The **Memorial Collection of Maksimilijan Vanka**, on the waterfront near the Monastery of St Nicholas, shows Vanka's works and also hosts temporary exhibitions by renowned Croatian artists.

## Sights & Museums

### Cathedral Treasury
*Trg svetog Marka (020 711 049, hvm.mdc.hr/opatska-riznica-sv.-marka,42/hr/crkvene-zbirke).* **Open** *Apr-Oct* 9am-2pm, 5-7pm daily. **Admission** 15kn. **No credit cards.**
Next to the Cathedral, the Cathedral Treasury is much more than just a collection of priestly vestments and church silver, containing a small but really quite exciting collection of religious art through the ages. Star attraction is the altarpiece by 15th-century Dalmatian painter Blaž Jurjev, showing a tender and radiant Madonna flanked by a collection of saints. Look out too for small but exquisite alabaster panels from 15th-century Nottingham depicting the Kiss of Judas and the Flagellation of Christ; and a 19th-century statuette of Mary Queen of Scots that opens its skirts to reveal a (wholly chaste, we hasten to emphasise) diorama within.

### Icon Museum
*Trg svih svetih (020 711 306).* **Open** *July-Aug* 10am-noon, 5-7pm daily. **Admission** 20kn. **No credit cards.**
Located down a narrow alley, the excellent Icon Museum contains religious images of mostly Cretan origin that ended up in Korčula when Christian forces evacuated ecclesiastical treasures from Aegean islands threatened by the Ottomans. A passageway leads from the museum to the 14th-century Church of All Saints.

### Memorial Collection of Maksimilijan Vanka
**FREE** *Put svetog Nikole (098 970 5334).* **Open** *Summer* 9am-noon, 6-9pm daily. **Admission** Free.
The Memorial Collection of Maksimilijan Vanka, on the waterfront near the Monastery of St Nicholas, shows art nouveau and Expressionist works by this 20th-century painter and hosts temporary exhibitions by renowned Croatian artists throughout the summer.

Korčula.

**EXPLORE**

### Marco Polo Exhibition

*Plokata 19, Travnja 33 (098 970 5334).*
**Open** *July, Aug* 9am-10pm daily; varies in
other summer months. **Admission** 30kn.
**No credit cards.**
Opened in 2012, this modern multimedia attraction
retraces the travels of Marco Polo using dioramas
and lifelike dummies clad in medieval costume. With
near life-size camels, monkeys and Chinese emper-
ors, it's visually very effective. Pick up the head-
phone audio guide and follow the story.

### Marko Polo House

*Ul Depolo (no phone).* **Open** *July, Aug* 9am-9pm daily.
*Apr-June, Sept, Oct* 9am-3pm daily. **Admission**
20kn. **No credit cards.**
The man who travelled along the Silk Road to Kublai
Khan's China was born around 1254, possibly in
Korčula – although other contended birthplaces are
Šibenik on the mainland or Venice. Fighting for the
Venetians in the famous Battle of Korčula in 1298, he
was captured by the Genoese and during his imprisonment dictated his famous memoirs to a literate fellow inmate. The house frequently shown to tourists
as Marco Polo's birthplace is actually a 17th-century
structure said to be built on the site of his former
home – that shouldn't take the romance out of what
remains a plausible story.

### ★ St Mark's Cathedral

*Trg svetog Marka (020 711 049.)* **Open**
*Apr-Oct 9am-7pm daily.* **Admission** 25kn.
**No credit cards.**
Set bang in the centre of the Old Town, Korčula's
cathedral is one of the finest examples of Dalmatian
church architecture. Taking three centuries to
build, it features several styles, including Gothic,
Romanesque and Baroque. Inside, 15th-century
stonemason Marko Andrijić is responsible for the

canopy set on four columns above the altar, or ciborium. Beneath it is the sarcophagus of St Theodore,
the protector of Korčula. Here you can also see *St
Mark with St Bartholomew and St Jerome*, an early
work by Tintoretto, whose *Annunciation* also
stands in the south nave. Cannonballs and weapons from wars with the Ottomans are also placed
here, along with a 13th-century icon of the Virgin,
prayed to for salvation when the Uluz Ali's corsairs
threatened in 1571.

### Town Museum

*Trg svetog Marka (020 711 420, www.gm-korcula.
com).* **Open** *July-Sept* 9am-9pm daily. *Apr-June*
10am-2pm daily. *Oct-Mar* 10am-1pm daily.
**Admission** 20kn. **No credit cards.**
Set in the 16th-century Gabrielis Palace, this small
but highly entertaining museum now sports
English-language documentation. Pride of place
on the ground floor belongs to ceramics dredged up
from ancient Greek and Roman shipwrecks. There
is also a replica of a fourth-century Greek tablet
from Lumbarda, announcing the establishment
of a Greek colony on the island. Among the knick-
knacks upstairs are furnishings through the ages,
photographs of World War II Partisans, and a reconstruction of a traditional Korčulan kitchen on the top
floor – in the old days, it was common for kitchens to
be situated up here in the attic.

## Restaurants

### Adio Mare

*Sv Roka 2 (020 711 253, www.konobaadiomare.
hr).* **Open** *Apr-Nov* noon-midnight Mon-Sat;
6pm-midnight Sun. **€€. Seafood**
A bit of an institution, Adio Mare is Korčula town's
oldest family-run restaurant and little has changed
since it opened in 1974. It's a friendly, buzzy, hearty

**St Mark's Cathedral.**

Dalmatian restaurant showcasing tradition rather than innovation. Book a table on the shaded terrace upstairs and enjoy the *brodet* fish stew with polenta, the grilled meats or the pasta with beans. There's a decent enough selection of local wines. Baby seats are available if needed.

### Filippi
*Šetalište Petra Kanavelića (020 711 690, restaurantfilippi.com).* **Open** *Apr* 10am-noon daily. *May-Oct* noon-3pm, 6pm-midnight daily. €€. **Dalmatian**
Ston oysters, traditional Korčula pasta and main courses of classic steak and fowl complement local seafood at this Croatian restaurant. The wine list concentrates on local quality, with the best Plavac Mali reds from the Pelješac peninsula, Grk and Pošip whites from Korčula.

### Gradski Podrum
*Trg Antuna/Kaporova (020 711 222).* **Open** *Apr-Oct* 11am-2pm, 6-10.30pm daily. €€€. **Dalmatian**
Extensive menu, a terrace on an open square by the Town Hall and St Michael's church, excellent service – there are reasons why the Gradski is just that bit more expensive than elsewhere. Try the fish stew with white wine, potatoes and parsley.

### Kanavelić
*Ulica Franje Tudjmana 1904 (020 711 800).* **Open** *May-Nov* 6pm-1am daily. €€€. **Dalmatian**
Until the Lešić-Dimitri Palace Korčula came along, this place was arguably the best in Korčula town. Chandeliers hang from high wooden-beamed ceilings, creating historic charm. Recommended are the fish stew – white fish boiled with white wine and olive oil, served around a moat of polenta – and lobster medallions in tomato sauce served with homemade noodles.

### Konoba Komin
*Šetalište Petra Kanavelića 26 (020 716 508).* **Open** *Summer* noon-midnight daily. *Winter* 5-11pm Mon-Sat. €€. **Dalmatian**
Having moved from its old position in an Old Town alleyway to a new site on the battlement-hugging promenade, Komin ('The Hearth') now features a small sea-facing terrace. The grilled meat and fish at this traditional Dalmatian *konoba* are hearty and fresh. The place is also a great haven out of season.

### ★ Lešić-Dimitri Palace Korčula
*Don Pavle Poše 1-6, (020 715 560, www.lesicdimitri.com)* **Open** 8am-midnight daily. €€€€. **Contemporary Dalmatian**
Befitting its historic, five-star hotel surroundings, the Lešić-Dimitri, with its panoramic terrace, has significantly raised the bar when it comes to fine dining in Korčula town. Under chef Toni Erceg, the restaurant celebrates local, seasonal produce and reproduces traditional dishes in a healthy and

modern way. Starters include monkfish soup with polenta, house cuttlefish and marinated monkfish on fennel salad. Mains might be fillets of sea bass or slow-roasted lamb. For dessert, there's the seductively smooth house chocolate cake. Informed staff will guide you through an extensive wine list that features international selections alongside some of the island's best Grk and Pošip – which can be tried by the glass.

### Marinero
*Marka Andrijića 13 (020 711 170).* **Open** *Apr-Nov* 11am-2pm, 6pm-midnight daily. €€. **Seafood**
In an alley in the Old Town, Marinero offers fine seafood in an authentic and warm setting. Mother is the chef, her sons catch the daily supply of fish and the local wine flows until the guests start singing. A favourite is fish cooked *à la gregada*: baked with potatoes and vegetables in a juicy sauce that's mopped up with hunks of bread. The lighter and less common version, *na lešo*, is fish gently boiled with vegetables to create a delectable and tender meal.

### Pizzeria Caenazzo
*Trg Sv Marka (098 244 012).* **Open** *May-Sept* 11am-midnight daily. **No credit cards.** €€. **Pizzas**
A decent pizzeria with perhaps the best location in the Old Town, its tables scattered around one corner of St Mark's Square in front of the imposing cathedral. Expect friendly service, good cold Laško beer, and fine prices.

### Pizzeria Tedeschi
*Ulica Don Iva Matijace Opata 26 (020 711 586).* **Open** *May-mid Oct* 9am-midnight daily. €€. **No credit cards. Pizzas**
This small, well-located spot turns out fine pizzas from its wood-stoked oven, and pastas made by the owner's aunt in Žrnovo. Tables view the Old Town walls.

### Planjak
*Plokata 19, Travnja (020 711 015).* **Open** *Summer* 9am-midnight daily. *Winter* 8am-3pm Mon-Sat. €. **Grilled meats**
On a shaded terrace in a square just behind the market, this is the place for cheap Balkan grilled meats – go elsewhere if you're in the mood for seafood. There are classic *ćevapčići* and *ražnjići* kebabs, and a daily menu for 60kn.

### Stupe
*Ksenija Raškić, Stupe (098 933 7611).* **Open** *Summer* noon-10pm daily. €€. **No credit cards. Dalmatian**
Stupe island, a short hop from Korčula town, is uninhabited but for this one restaurant that serves simple, tasty meals in summer. Arrange a pick-up time with the captain of your taxi boat and organise your day around swimming, sunbathing and dining.

**EXPLORE**

## Cafes & Bars

### Bili cvitak

*Hrvatske bratske zajednice 68 (020 711 630).*
**Open** *Summer* 9am-2am daily. *Winter*
9am-midnight daily. **No credit cards.**
Latest addition to the behind-the-bus-station bar
crawl, Bili cvitak ('Little White Flower') is a snazzy
café-bar decked out in cool blacks and greys, with
an outdoor terrace that swarms with drinkers on
warm evenings. With a pumping sound system,
disco lights and a mirrorball, its back room is your
best hope for a bop come the summer season. There's
a temptingly priced range of cocktails, and the list
of bottled beers includes Leffe. Check the bar's
Facebook page for more information.

### Cukarin

*Hrvatske bratske zajednice (020 711 055).* **Open**
*Mar-Nov* 8.30am-12.30pm, 5.30-8.30pm Mon-Sat.
Traditional local cakes are the mainstay of this landmark outlet, which is famous for and named after its
*cukarin*: whisper-light, crescent-shaped little biscuits traditionally dipped in Prošek wine. They also
make the irresistibly chocolatey Marko Polo *bom-
bice*, and several other own-brand cakes that are displayed in the glass cabinet below the counter. There's
a growing range of other speciality products too, so
you can stock up on Korčulan wine and olive oil.

### Dos Locos

*Šetalište Frana Kršinića 14 (091 528 8971).*
**Open** 4pm-2am daily. **No credit cards.**
On the other side of the street from Bili cvitak, wicker-
and-bamboo Dos Locos attracts partygoers with its
DJ beats and music vids, as well as sport or fashion
channels, projected on the wall. Scantily clad bar
employees dance to the rhythm to keep the atmosphere playful. The music runs the gamut from live
acoustic to raw hip hop.

### Massimo Cocktail Bar

*Kula Zakerjan, Šetalište Petra Kanavelića
(020 715 073).* **Open** *May-Oct* 6pm-2am daily.
**No credit cards.**
Set under the turrets of the 15th-century Zakerjan
Tower in the northern fortifications, Massimo is
accessible by stairs, then ladder. Standard cocktails
in lurid colours come to you by pulley as you take in
the view as far as Pelješac. Getting down afterwards
may be a problem.

### Servantes

*Hrvatske bratske zajednice (no phone).* **Open**
7am-midnight daily. **No credit cards.**
Hidden from the bus station by a cute wedge of park,
Servantes offers an eccentric interior of irregularly
shaped mirrors and pebble-dash effects, and a shady,
lawn-side outdoor terrace. As well as beers and wines
there's a decent list of spirits including *kruškovac*
(pear brandy), *orahovac* (walnut) and *medica* (honey).

### Vinum Bonum

*Sv Justina (020 715 014).* **Open** *May-Oct*
11am-2pm, 6pm-midnight daily. **No credit cards.**
You know when you walk in that you've come to the
right place for local wine and *rakija* grappa. The decor
is simple: a bar, bar stools, a wall of wine and a map
indicating where the labels come from. Regulars,
including the odd Moreška dancer, provide the atmosphere, catching up on gossip over a plate of sardines,
*pršut* ham or cheese with the knowledgeable staff. All
the wines are local, from Korčula and Pelješac.

### Zi Zi

*Šetalište Frana Kršinića (no phone).* **Open**
8am-midnight Mon-Sat; 4pm-midnight Sun.
**No credit cards.**
A tiny local bar, Zi Zi generates a genuine year-round
buzz whether tourists are in town or not. Beer from
the Ožujsko stable (including Tomislav porter and
Zagreb-brewed Staropramen) dominates the drinks
list; a dartboard, a Hajduk Split calendar and pictures of girls and cars provide the decor.

## Nightlife

### Boogie Jungle

*Put Lokve (095 537 3167, www.boogie-jungle.com).*
**Open** *June-Sept* 11pm-5am daily. **Admission**
from 40kn. **No credit cards.**
Korčula has been crying out for a proper nightclub
for years, and it has finally arrived in the form of
Boogie Jungle, a ranch-style agglomeration of
buildings on a terraced hillside three kilometres
from town on the Žrnovo road. The club comprises
a largely alfresco series of terraces and awnings
with VIP areas, three bars, and plenty of room
to circulate and mingle. Surrounded by dense
Mediterranean greenery and with the capacity for
1,500 people, it's the ideal venue for a long night of
revelry. There are palms, cacti, drapes and coloured
lights, plus a long list of wines, long drinks and
cocktails. International DJs, themed events and
festivals provide the peaks to a full summer programme. Expect a hike in admission prices when a
big-name DJ is here.

## Hotels

### ★ Korčula De La Ville Hotel

*Obala dr Franje Tudjmana 5 (020 726 336,
www.korcula-hotels.com).* **Open** Apr-Dec. €€.
Renovated and renamed ('De La Ville') in 2015, this
landmark originally opened in 1912, the first hotel
on Korčula. Behind its pristine, palm-lined exterior
are 20 rooms, all with a blue, grey and white colour scheme and most with a balcony and sea view.
There's air-con and Wi-Fi throughout and the restaurant has been upgraded. The location remains,
of course, a major selling point: a few steps from the
city beach and bathed in the last warming rays of
sunset. Half-board rates have been raised but book

EXPLORE

early enough, even in high season, and you may be pleasantly surprised – especially for a stay of three nights or more. Reception will be happy to help with cycle, scooter and even boat rental.

### ★ Lešić-Dimitri Palace Korčula
*Don Pavle Poše 1-6, (020 715 560, www.lesic-dimitri.com)* **Open** Apr-Oct. €€€€.
The pinnacle of luxury in Korčula, located in a beautifully renovated 18th-century bishop's palace and five medieval cottages, in the heart of the Old Town. Suites are named after stages on the Silk Road travelled by Korčula legend Marco Polo: Venice comes with a Venetian red ceiling and theatrically large chairs that look like something from *Alice in Wonderland*; Arabia is hung with flowing fabrics to give it the feel of a nomad's tent. A recurring theme is provided by cushion-piled divans and geometric-patterned wooden screens evocative of interiors from the Middle East to the Far East. The suites have sleek modern kitchens, espresso machines, free Wi-Fi and flat-screen TVs, although sensitive restoration has left much of the building's original stonework and wooden beams untouched. As well as being home to the swish LD restaurant, the Lešić-Dimitri also features a spa with a team of Thai therapists. This is pure honeymoon material – without the crowds of Dubrovnik.

### Marko Polo Hotel
*Šetalište Frana Kršinića 102 (020 726 336, www.korcula-hotels.com).* €€.
The Marko Polo offers a sea view from most of its 103 rooms. A two-phase renovation in the mid-2000s – which put it ahead of its disappointing surrounding properties – saw new bathrooms, indoor and outdoor pools, a gym and sauna centre. Guests also have access to tennis courts and a sailing and windsurfing school.

### Royal Apartments
*Trg Petra Segedina 4 (098 184 0444).* **Open** June-Oct. €. **No credit cards.**
Just west of the Old Town, Royal Apartments is a cluster of five units, the biggest with separate kitchens and living rooms. The lodgings, well marked with a green awning on the waterside square, are simple, fairly priced and comfortable, and everything is close at hand.

## Beaches & excursions

Going to the beach on Korčula is best done away from Korčula town. You'll find far fewer people and cleaner water. The spots in town, such as **Banje beach** by the Hotel Marko Polo, are crowded. The nicer, shingle one by the **Hotel Bon Repos** is a bit of a walk, while locals pack sandy **Luka Korčulanska**, 15 minutes away towards Dominče. For diving, the Dupin Dive Centre (020 711 342, 098 812 496 mobile,

www.croatiadiving.com) is a British-run school based at the Bon Repos.

An easy day trip – from Korčula town's smaller east harbour – is to the lovely pine-forested island of **Badija**. Regular taxi boats make the trip (journey time 15 minutes). The island is a haven for deer and naturists. Round the corner from the quay, in front of the 15th-century Franciscan monastery, paths lead to pebble beaches and hidden coves. The deer have roamed free here since being introduced a few decades ago.

**Vrnik** is the only inhabited island in the archipelago of islets east of Korčula Town. Famous for its Roman stone quarries, it has beaches fringed with pine forests, which are popular with locals. Sculptor Lujo Lozica has his workshop here – catch him in the right mood and he might show you around.

## Resources

**Tourist Information** *Obala Franje Tudjmana 4 (020 715 701, www.visitkorcula.eu).* **Open** *June-Oct* 8am-3pm, 4-10pm Mon-Sat; 8am-1.30pm Sun. *Nov-May* 8am-2pm Mon-Sat.
Located in an old customs house by the Hotel Korčula on the west quay, this enormously helpful office dispenses heaps of advice, free maps and details of accommodation.

## BLATO

Once the biggest settlement on the island (a status now enjoyed by Vela Luka), Blato was once an important agricultural centre, exporting its wine and olives throughout central Europe. The vine-pest outbreaks of the 1920s put paid to Blato's prosperity; thousands of locals emigrated to the Americas during the inter-war years. Nowadays, it's a prosperous if rather sleepy rural town, with a single, graceful tree-lined avenue running through the centre. Set amid the older parts of town just south of the main street, Blato's parish church overlooks a lovely Renaissance loggia. Unusually, Blato's streets have numbers instead of names. The **Barilo Ethnographic Collection** is an interesting record of local life.

## Sights & Museums

### Barilo Ethnographic Collection
*90 ulica 10 (020 851 623, www.korcula-barilo.com).* **Open** 9am-8pm daily. **Admission** 15kn; 10kn reductions. **No credit cards.**
Many of us have the odd family heirloom or antique displayed at home, but few have amassed such an impressive collection as the Barilo family, owners and curators of this absorbing private

museum. The Barilos have scoured the island to amass a riveting record of Korčulan life over the past hundred years or so – there's a living room stuffed with family photographs and reproduction prints, a pre-modern kitchen with traditional stove and homely textiles, and a bedroom decked out with examples of the kind of frilly nightgowns that people don't wear that often any more. At the end of the visit, you'll be offered local liqueurs in the parlour.

## Restaurants

### ★ Mala Kapja

*Blato (020 851 833)*. **Open** varies; phone ahead. **No credit cards**. €€. Dalmatian
Just off the main road from Blato to Korčula Town (the turn-off is signed by a picture of a fat chef in a stripy vest), Mala Kapja is a working farm that raises most of the meat that it cooks. Expertly grilled or baked under a *peka*, the freshest of flesh is served up on an open terrace looking out towards Blato's fertile strip of farmland.

## ČARA & SMOKVICA

Like near-neighbour Pupnat, the village of **Čara** hovers above a broad agricultural plain whose vineyards produce some of the island's best Pošip grapes. The question of whether it is Čara or neighbouring Smokvica that produces the best Pošip wine is the subject of much local debate. South of Čara, **Zavalatica** cove is home to a small seaside village whose pristine waters are ideal for splashing around in. **Luka Krajančić** (Zavalatica 313, 020 832 100) in Čara is one of Korčula's most enterprising contemporary wine makers, producing individually crafted Pošip wines that can hold their own with any of Mediterranean Europe's quality dry whites. A lot of Croatia's top restaurants stock Krajančić's Pošip – it would be foolish not to call in here to pick up a bottle or two.

**Smokvica** is one of the most picturesque of Korčula's inland settlements, its red-tiled houses spilling down a hillside overlooking fields that produce some of Korčula's best Pošip wine. South-west of Smokvica, a road descends towards the bay of **Brna**, which used to serve as Smokvica's port and is now a seaside village of predominantly modern houses and apartments. Family-run for at least four generations, the **Toreta winery** (Smokvica 165, 020 832 100) is just below the main street that leads through Smokvica. There's a display of wine-pressing equipment used in the old days, and a selection of wines to taste and buy. Pošip is Toreta's main product, although Rukatac is exceedingly good too. Toreta's *rakijas* and liqueurs are simply superb.

## Hotels

### Hotel Feral

*Brna (052 832 080, www.hotel-feral.hr)*. **Open** Apr-Sept. €€.
This hotel has 83 rooms, all with views over the sea and the harbour village of Brna. The rooms are tastefully decorated in warm colours, and most come with a small balcony. It has a small outdoor pool, a terrace restaurant and a private beach too. Staff can organise kayaking, sailing and local trips. Rates drop considerably if you fix your date and book through the hotel website – full-board is a steal, really.

## LUMBARDA

Arranged around a series of small bays, the village of **Lumbarda**, six kilometres to the south-east of Korčula town, is thought to be the oldest settlement on the island. A stone inscription dating from the fourth century BC (a replica of which can be seen in the Korčula Town Museum) refers to an ancient Greek colony at Lumbarda – however, no other evidence of a Greek city has ever been found here, suggesting that the Greeks never actually put down firm roots on Korčula. Nevertheless, the Greek presence lives on in the name of the local wine, Grk, which is a distinctive dry white that flourishes in the sandy soil of Lumbarda but which can't be grown successfully anywhere else.

Lumbarda's sandy beaches are arguably the best on the island. Head south from the village until you reach a fork in front of the small 18th-century Holy Cross Church (where the public Korčula-Lumbarda bus terminates) surrounded by vineyards; take the left-hand one for the rockier Bilin žal or continue south-east for the lovely, sandy **Vela Pržina**. Hidden behind a shaggy screen of agaves, vineyards and rushes, this modest but glorious crescent of sand is arguably the finest beach on the island. It gets busy in high summer but has everything you might want for a family day out – shallow waters for paddling, a beach volleyball court at the back and a well-organised bar with drinks and snacks.

North-facing **Bilin žal** beach has a tiny strip of sand bordered by lots of pebble and rock, but it is very shallow and reasonably smooth underfoot – making it the perfect paddling beach. The views of Pelješac across the water are magnificent, and there is a café and grill-restaurant in the semi-ruined 15th-century bishop's castle right on the beach.

Back in Lumbarda, there's a scuba-diving school, **MM Sub**, at Tatinja 65 (020 712 288, 098 285 011).

EXPLORE

# HAUNTED ISLAND

*Lokrum offers an easily accessible break – unless you're a cursed royal.*

Lokrum is for lovers and legends. This unspoiled island, lush with pines, palms and cypress trees, basks in the Adriatic less than a kilometre from the Old Town. Dotted with diverse ruins and remnants – medieval and ecclesiastical, Napoleonic, Habsburg – it has long been given over to nature. It's a UNESCO-protected nature reserve: no rubbish, no dogs, no fires, no smoking, no overnight stays.

Between April and October, the boat traffic from the mainland is constant. Little open taxi-boats make the short journey from the old harbour every half-hour (35kn return; www.lokrum.hr) yet those arriving first thing in the morning feel as if the whole island is theirs. A gecko, turtle or snake lizard might pop up. Buzzards, grey falcons and swifts nest here in spring or autumn. Man is free to frolic naked around Cape Skrinja, round the corner from Portoć, the jetty for the taxi boat. Lovers carve their names on the cactus leaves. In late summer, stunning fluorescent blue damselfish appear through seagrass brushed by starfish and sea urchins. A more idyllic setting so close to Dubrovnik you could not imagine.

Yet mention Lokrum to an older local and you will hear tales of curses and ill fortune. The liveliest of these legends surrounds the departure of the Benedictine monks, settled on Lokrum since 1023. On the fateful eve of their departure in 1798, the monks tramped around Lokrum in candlelit procession. A curse is said to have resulted from their solemn farewell. Soon afterwards, rich Ragusans who

bought the island suffered various strokes of misfortune – but nothing like as bad ias those ncurred by the Austrian nobility to whom they sold Lokrum, lock, stock and barrel, in 1859.

The buyer, Maximilian, brother of Austro-Hungarian Emperor Franz Josef, loved Lokrum. He turned the island into his own pleasure garden, building the summer residence you can still see mingled with the ruins of the medieval monastery complex a short walk from Portoć. Around it were his exotic gardens. Some 150 years later, imported plants blend with native ones. Maximilian's tree-lined walks run through the island; the Path of Paradise leads from the Napoleonic Fort Royal to his residence via an old olive grove planted by the Benedictines. Peacocks still roam here but not the parrots Maximilian also brought. His gardens may have been idylilic but his end certainly was not – he was famously shot by firing squad in Mexico and his beloved wife went mad.

The attraction of Lokrum for today's visitors remains. In its south-west corner, a lake of warm saltwater, the so-called Dead Sea, formed by tectonic fracture, is surrounded by rocky beaches. In the middle bloom botanical gardens beside a tranquil café-restaurant, handy if you haven't brought supplies with you.

The last boats leave for Dubrovnik around 7pm, depending on the time of year. Check f you're planning to spend a long day there. The service closes at the end of October and starts up again on the last day of March.

**EXPLORE**

## Restaurants & wineries

### ★ Bire
*Lumbarda (098 344 712, www.bire.hr).* Winery
Winemaker Frano Milina-Bire enjoys a growing
reputation for producing some of the best Grk on
Korčula, and his visitor-friendly winery, occupying
a hillside overlooking the village, is the best place to
taste it. Groups and individual tourists are welcome
to sample the wine in a rustic stone-clad room before
buying some of the bottles stacked like firewood
against the cellar's walls. The household also makes
its own goats' cheese and *pršut* to provide visitors
with tasty platters to go along with their Grk. In the
garden, tomato plants and broad beans sprout up
among the kitchen herbs.

### Cebalo
*Mala postrana (091 515 9932).* **No credit cards.**
Winery
Another place that sells Grk wine directly to callers
and also arranges tasting sessions, with a pleasant
terrace overlooking vineyards and vegetable gardens.

### More
*Lumbarda (098 427 843).* **Open** *Summer*
11am-3pm, 7-11pm daily. €€. Seafood
Feast-sized portions of fine seafood are served on a
small terrace covered with thick vines; dangle your
toes in the crystal-clear sea before enjoying arguably the best lobster in the Adriatic, with home-made
macaroni in tomato sauce.

### Vinarija Popić
*Mala postrana (091 884 6946).* **No credit cards.**
Winery
A family winery offering Lumbarda Grk to taste and
for sale, as well as an intriguing barrique Plavac.

## Hotels

### Borik
*Lumbarda (020 712 215, www.hotelborik.hr).*
**Open** mid May-mid Oct. €.
A good-value, clean and comfortable hotel above
the waterfront in Lumbarda, with its own restaurant and pizzeria, and low wicker tables and sofas
scattered on a pleasant, chilled-out terrace. Rooms
in the main hotel have air-con as opposed to those
in the annexe. Half-pension costs about 50kn per
person extra.

### Pansion Marinka
*Lumbarda (020 712 208, www.bire.hr).*
**Open** May-Nov. €. **No credit cards.**
With lodgings amid olive trees across from the sea,
owners Frano and Višnja run the best-value spot on
the island. Of the ten simple rooms, two have balconies. Meals are prepared with home-grown ingredients – the family runs Agroturizam Bire, making
wine, cheese, olive oil and spirits.

## PUPNAT

The village of **Pupnat** is a typical wine and
vegetable-growing community set at the side of a
small but fertile plain. To the south of Pupnat at
the bottom of a steep slope is **Pupnatska Luka**,
once the village's port. Accessible via a narrow
windy road, Pupnatska Luka is today a beautiful
crescent of fine pebble, and is arguably the best
of Korčula's south-coast beaches. There are a
couple of café-cum-snack bars at the back of
the beach, screened by outsized cacti. The only
problem with Pupnatska Luka is the lack of
parking spaces, and the constant danger that you
might meet a large and cumbersome car coming
in the opposite direction on the way up or down.

## Restaurants

### Konoba Mate
*Pupnat 28 (020 717 109).* **Open** 11am-midnight
Mon-Sat; 7-11pm Sun. **No credit cards.** €€.
Dalmatian
Slightly off the main Korčula–Vela Luka road is
this popular, family-run find. Ingredients are grown
on-site. The *pršut* ham comes from the smokehouse
behind the terrace; the pastas (such as the goats'
cheese ravioli) are hand-rolled and sun-dried, and
the lamb and pork are cooked under the *peka* lid. The
*pašticada*, a slow-cooked roast swimming in plums
and sweet wine, is excellent.

## RAČIŠĆE

Twelve kilometres (7.5 miles) west of Korčula
town, **Račišće** is a picturesque port spread around
a broad bay. Overlooking the shore is the **Church
of St Mary the Helper**, and a small village
loggia. Until World War II, Račišće was very much
a seafarers' settlement, its bay busy with medium-
sized cargo boats. Nowadays the harbour is so
quiet that you can swim and paddle to your heart's
content. Walk north-west of Račišće harbour for
15 minutes to find **Vaja**, a beach of gleaming white
pebbles lapped by an indigo sea.

## VELA LUKA

Occupying an irregular-shaped bay at the
western end of the island, **Vela Luka** is the
island's main port for car ferries to Split and
Lastovo. Founded by the inhabitants of Blato in
order to export their wine and oil, Vela Luka
doesn't have the vintage medieval appearance of
Korčula town, but its sea-facing row of
19th-century houses, bordered by palms and
lawns, is as handsome as any in Dalmatia. The
**Vela Spila** cave, and the off-shore sunbathing
paradise of **Proizd** provide the main excuses to
stick around. As in Blato, Vela Luka's streets don't
have names, but are numbered instead.

## Sights & Museums

### Museum Collections of the Vela Luka Cultural Centre

*Ulica 26/2 (020 813 602).* **Open** 9am-2pm, 6-11pm Mon-Sat. **Admission** 15kn. **No credit cards.**
This combined archaeological collection and art museum has two Henry Moores, and finds from nearby Vela Spila (*see below*), inhabited in Neolithic times. Summer art exhibitions frequently feature challenging stuff by contemporary Croatian artists.

### ★ Vela Spila

*Vela Luka (020 813 602, www.vela-spila.hr).* **Open** 5-8pm daily. **Admission** 10kn. **No credit cards.**
Hidden among olive groves above the town is Vela Spila ('the Great Cave'), a gaping limestone cavity with a sea-facing entrance and two large holes in its roof, producing an eerily atmospheric play of light. Inhabited since the Stone Age, the cave is the earliest known home of modern humans on the Adriatic, and has become a major centre for archaeological research. Coordinated by the local museum and an international team led by Cambridge University, digging seasons take place here every September. Fragments of ceramic cult objects found in recent years have produced something of a sensation in archaeological circles – thought to be around 17,500 years old, they are believed to be the earliest examples of clay craftsmanship in Europe. Visitors can peer into the excavation trenches and soak up the atmosphere of Indiana-Jones-style discovery, although there's no museum display inside the cave as yet. A mute brown stone marks the spot where 'Stanko', a 9,000-year-old skeleton (one of the oldest human skeletons yet excavated in the Mediterranean) was discovered a decade ago. Vela Spila is a five-minute walk uphill from Vela Luka's seafront.

### Zlokić Oil Press

*Vela Luka (098 929 5073, www.uljarazlokic.com).* **Open** varies; contact Vela Luka tourist office (Ulice 41/11, 020 813 619, www.tzvelaluka.hr) for information. **No credit cards.**
On the eastern fringes of town, just off the main road to Blato and Korčula town, the Zlokić Oil Press is an ideal place to get to grips with Vela Luka's growing reputation for top-quality olive oil. There's a museum display of olive presses through the ages, including some hard and heavy granite wheel-powered affairs that required a team of four men to turn. There's also the chance to taste local oils: Zlokić's principal blend is Velouje, made from the famously polyphemol-rich Lastovka olives that are unique to western Korčula. Zlokić also produces Veluoško oil, made from olives that have been preserved the old-fashioned way (under seawater) rather than sent straight to the presses. Veluoško oil loses a few of the health-giving natural substances common to other oils from the island, but has a highly individual taste.

## Restaurants

### Konoba Bata

*Ulica 56 (091 515 4261, www.gdje.hr/korcula/konoba-bata).* **Open** May-Oct noon-3pm, 5pm-midnight daily. €€. **Dalmatian**
If you are no stranger to Dalmatian cuisine, then forget about the menu and chat with the waiter. Before tourism, Vela Luka lived on fish, wine, and olive oil, so its cuisine hides tasty secrets that are worth discovering. *Popara na Veloluski*, a type of *brodetto*, would be a good choice, but if you want to play it safe and try everything the sea has to offer, then opt for the Bata fish platter.

## Hotels

### Korkyra

*Obala 3/21 (020 601 000, www.hotel-korkyra.com).* €€.
Vela Luka's old harbourside hotel has been more or less totally rebuilt to provide a home for this new, beautifully designed property, with cool, contemporary furniture setting the tone in both public areas and the rooms themselves. Rooms feature hardwood floors, flat-screen TVs and view-through bathrooms enclosed in glass windows. With a decent ground-floor restaurant and a kidney-shaped pool at the back, the hotel offers quality relaxation all round. The top-floor gym and spa centre overlooking the harbour are a major feature.

## Beaches & excursions

Of all the boat-trip getaways in the seas off Korčula, the island of **Proizd** is the one that attracts most in the way of superlatives. Twenty minutes in a taxi boat from Vela Luka harbour, Proizd features some of the Adriatic's most dramatic beaches – for the most part made up of smooth stone slabs that descend at a steep angle into the sea. All in all, it's perfect for sunbathing and swimming – the waters here are crystal clear. Tracks criss-cross the island, ensuring that you can visit more than one stretch of Proizd's coast in the space of a day. One area is clearly marked for naturists. There's a cafe-restaurant near Proizd's boat jetty but it soon gets busy – so bring your own supplies.

## Resources

### Atlas Tourist Agency *Obala 3/21 (020 812 078, atlas.com.hr).*

This friendly and obliging agency is happy to arrange private accommodation and hotels in Vela Luka and across the whole island. They also handle boat, car and bike rental, day trips to Dubrovnik, Mostar, around the island and more, fishing trips and licenses and insurance. Don't miss the intriguing donkey safari.

**EXPLORE**

**Tourist information** *Vela Luca Tourist Office, Ulice 41/11 (020 813 619, www.tzvelaluka.hr)*. Open *July, Aug* 8am-9pm Mon-Sat; 9am-2pm Sun. *June* 8am-2.30pm, 5.30-8pm Mon-Fri; 8am-12.30pm, 5.30-8pm Sat. *Sept* 8am-2pm & 5-8pm Mon-Sat. *Oct-May* 8am-3pm Mon-Fri.
Information on attractions, accommodation and public transport links, from a friendly and enthusiastic team.

## ŽRNOVO

Spread across the hills above Korčula town, **Žrnovo** is a sprawling settlement made up of several distinct villages, **Prvo Selo**, **Brdo**, **Postrana** and **Kampus**, each grouped around its own chapel. Occupying a hillock in between the villages is **St Martin's Church**, containing some delightful, locally carved Baroque altarpieces. **St Postrana** is the most picturesque of Žrnovo's quarters, with its stone houses and narrow stepped alleyways.

Lying at the bottom of the coastal slopes south of Žrnovo is one of Korčula's best known targets for bathing connoisseurs, **Bačva beach**, a peaceful small bay with a shingle beach and a hut selling refreshments. Be warned that the steep and narrow access road is not for the faint-hearted – a lot of people come by boat.

## Restaurants

### ★ Konoba Belin

*Žrnovo Prvo Selo (091 503 9258)*. Open *May-Sept* 10am-midnight daily. €€. **No credit cards.**
**Dalmatian**
A family-run *konoba* with multi-terraced outdoor seating, Belin serves superb, lovingly prepared local fare. Quality grilled fish, served with local Grk or Pošip in the open air, turns a summer evening into a memorable occasion. The home-made *žrnovski makaruni* – topped with either goulash or seafood – is a big deal here. The menu also includes local favourites such as breaded octopus, rabbit and grilled lamb.

### Konoba Gera

*Žrnovo Postrana (020 721 280)*. Open 6pm-midnight daily. €€. **No credit cards.**
**Dalmatian**
Set among the stone houses and alleys of Postrana, Gera is a traditional family *konoba* with wooden benches set out on a terrace overlooking a leafy garden. Its strong point is fish, meat and vegetables, simply grilled, washed down with local wine. It also serves the ubiquitous local favourite *žrnovski makaruni*.

### Ranč Maha

*Žrnovo-Pupnat road (098 494 389)*. Open *Summer* 1-11pm daily. *Winter* 1-11pm Mon-Sat. **No credit cards.** €€. **Dalmatian**

This ranch-style restaurant, run by the Mahelić family, is up in the hills eight kilometres from Korčula town. It's the place to eat *peka* – lamb or goat slow-cooked under smouldering charcoal, ordered in advance. Turning up on spec, try a grilled dish. Pretty much everything served is local, including the succulent home-cured *pršut*. Home-made grappas provide an aperitif. Seating is in a spacious garden planted with herbs and figs. It's a cosy retreat in winter with wood-burning fire – call ahead to see if they're open.

## Getting there & around

From Dubrovnik, two daily **buses** runs to Korčula town (currently leaving at 9.45am and 6.40pm; journey time 3hrs, 105kn), price of the Orebič ferry included.

A daily **catamaran** connects Korčula town with Split (2hrs 25mins, 60kn), and the twice-weekly coastal ferry (Rijeka–Split–Dubrovnik) stops at Korčula town too; a catamaran also connects Korčula town with Dubrovnik (2.5hrs, 55kn) four times a week in summer.

The quickest hop from the mainland for foot passengers to Korčula town is the **boat shuttle** from Orebić on the Pelješac peninsula (summer only, Mon-Fri, every 1-2hrs, 15mins, 15kn). The car ferry from Orebić lands at Dominče (daily every 1-2hrs, 20mins, 10kn) – a shuttle bus runs the 2km to Korčula town.

The other port is Vela Luka. A twice-daily **car ferry** docks from Split after calling at Hvar (3hrs 30mins, 55kn) and a **catamaran** arrives from Split once a day (1hr 45mins, 45kn). Between Vela Luka and Korčula town, a bus runs several times a day, usually coinciding with ferry arrivals and departures (80mins, 39kn).

## Resources

**Travel agency** *Plokata 19 Travnja 192, Korčula (020 711 282, www.kaleta.hr)*. Open *Apr-Oct* 8am-11pm daily.
Travel agency and internet café in the town centre. Cruises, wine tours, picnics, car hire.

**Hire company** *Rent a Đir, Obala Hrvatskih mornara (020 711 908, www.cro-rent.com)*. Bikes, scooters, cars and boats for rent, as well as diving lessons and diving equipment hire.

# Cavtat

Down the coast from Dubrovnik, **Cavtat** (*photo p266*) is an easy day trip, either by bus No.10 or boat from the old harbour. The southernmost resort in Croatia, Cavtat is built on the old Greek and Roman settlement of Epidaurum, which was sacked by invading barbarian tribes in the seventh century. Refugees flooded to Ragusa and built Dubrovnik.

Attracting holidaymakers here began in the early 1900s. Proximity to Dubrovnik airport means that their modern-day counterparts can breeze in, turn up at their friends' yacht lining the pretty, palm-fringed **Riva promenade**, and breeze out again – for relaxation and a bit of history, this is a Dubrovnik in miniature without the hassle.

The Riva also contains one of the town's leading attractions, the **Baltazar Bogišić Collection** (478 556, open 9.30am-1.30pm Mon-Sat, 15kn), housed in the former Rector's Palace, its garden dotted with Roman-era stones. Within are rows of books from the library of this prominent collector of the late 19th century, plus a large painting of the Cavtat Carnival from the same era by local realist painter Vlaho Bukovac, whose works bring thousands here every year.

**Bukovac's** own gallery (Bukovčeva 5, 020 478 646, open summer 9am-1pm, 5-9pm daily, winter 9am-1pm daily, 15kn), stands in a sidestreet just off the Riva , and presents a comprehensive overview of this prolific artist. Another key sight is the **Račić Mausoleum** (020 478 646, open summer 10am-noon, 6-8pm Mon-Sat, 10am-noon Sun), set on the hilltop tip of the peninsula – follow the path from the prosaic **Monastery of Our Lady of the Snow**, at the other end of the Riva from the Baltazar Bogišić Collection. Built in 1921, the mausoleum is one of the most famous works by Croatia's greatest sculptor, Ivan Meštrović, incorporating a mix of styles including Greek, Byzantine and Egyptian. The view alone is worth the climb.

The sea here is particularly clear. Just outside Cavtat is the Hotel Epidaurus, linked to one of Croatia's best diving centres, **Epidaurum** (020 471 386, 098 427 550 mobile, www.epidaurum. com). Roman ruins and sunken ships line the seabed nearby.

## Restaurants & hotels

The Riva is lined with bars and eateries but the best table in town is easily the **Taverna Galija** (Vuličevića 1, 020 478 566, www.galija.hr), a classy, imaginative (mainly) seafood restaurant with a prominent sea-view terrace. Its nearest challenger is **Leut** (Trumbićev put 11, 020 478 477, www.restaurant-leut.com, closed Jan), a fish restaurant with a leafy terrace. For drinks and snacks, **Ancora** (Obala Ante Starčevića 22, facebook.com/ancora.cavtat), offers tapas, cheap cocktails and internet access. More recently, gastronomic focus has fallen on **Bugenvila** (Obala Ante Starčevića 22, 020 479 949, www. bugenvila.eu), the kitchen run by Lukasz Widomski, former sous-chef at London's Le Caprice. Imaginative cuisine, using fresh and/ or organic and free-range ingredients, comes with a sea view. Cavtat has a number of classy hotels. The sea-view, five-star **Hotel Croatia**

(Frankopanska 10, 020 300 300, www.adriatic luxuryhotels.com/en/hotel-croatia-dubrovnik-cavtat, €€€) is now part of the high-end Adriatic Luxury Hotels Group, and remains a massive, multi-tiered year-round resort hotel with pools, tennis courts and two beaches. In the same group, the well-located **Hotel Supetar** (Obala Ante Starčevića 27, 020 300 300, www.adriatic luxuryhotels.com/en/hotel-supetar-dubrovnik-cavtat, €€) is its more modest cousin.

# Pelješac

**Pelješac** is passed over by most visitors to Dubrovnik but locals are drawn to its very lack of tourists, its fine wines, long shingle beaches and, most of all, the best mussels and oysters in Croatia. They are farmed at Ston, one of two key destinations on the Pelješac peninsula, which sticks out 90 kilometres (56 miles) towards Korčula. The other is Orebić, a resort in its own right, a quick hop and a quieter alternative to Korčula. A windsurfing scene nearby gives it the younger edge that Korčula lacks. One road runs the length of the peninsula and, unless you have a car, your best bet is to head for Ston, where Pelješac meets the mainland, by bus from Dubrovnik, or cross from Ploče to Trpanj.

With your own transport, you can drive the 65 kilometres (40 miles) of vineyard-lined road, calling at wineries serving the famed Postup and Dingač reds. *See p268* **Dalmatia's Wine Trail**.

Ston's natural lake-like bay has hosted mussel and oyster farms since Roman times. In summer, locals sell 5kn oysters by the side of the road. Renowned restaurants from here to Dubrovnik feature Ston oysters on their menus. The Ostrea Edulis variety can only be found in Ston. Smaller than its Atlantic counterpart, it is served open on its flat side. The meat is also firmer and richer flavoured. It is also not cut off from its shell, so don't tip it down your throat.

Excellent beaches stretch either side of the main road too. On the north side, **Divna**, near the tiny village of **Duba**, some six kilometres from Trpanj, is secluded and sandy. **Prapratno**, three kilometres west of Ston, is also sandy. On the south side, **Žuljana**, before Trstenik, is a lovely village in a bay where you'll find several beaches. The most beautiful is **Vučine**, 15 minutes' walk south.

**Ston** is really two towns in one, linked by hilltop fortifications. Ston, called Veliki ('Great') to distinguish it from its smaller sister of Mali Ston, has its own historic walls (now open to the public), built to protect the salt pans there. Half the 14th-century towers and walls remain, surviving the earthquake of 1996 that destroyed houses in both towns. Damage is still visible.

**Orebić** has hotels and restaurants and more to pack into a weekend. A major trading centre until the late 19th century, it contains grand villas festooned with greenery, built by retired sea captains. Its main sight is a **Franciscan monastery** (open summer 9am-noon, 4-7pm Mon-Sat, 4-7pm Sun; 15kn) on a hilltop 20 minutes' walk from the Hotel Bellevue. Built in the late 15th century, it houses *Our Lady of the Angels*, an icon said to protect sailors in the Pelješac Channel picturesquely spread below. Before you reach it, another trail leads to the summit of **Sv Ilija**, with views from 961 metres (3,153 feet) high.

Locals come to Orebić and nearby for its beaches. The nicest one is **Trstenica**, sandy, with a few bars and a section for naturists. It's a 20-minute stroll east of the ferry terminal. Boats make regular journeys to **Viganj**, a popular spot for windsurfing. Near here is **Poboduče**, a wine-producing and fishing village nestled in a secluded pebble-beach bay: a tranquil spot that's well worth a visit. **Campsite Liberan** (091 6171 666, www.liberan-camping.com) rents boards and has a windsurfing school; **Perna** (098 395 807 mobile, www.perna-surf.com), between Viganj and Orebić, specialises in kitesurfing. The main diving club, **OreBeach**, outside Orebić (Šetalište Kralja Krešimira 141, 020 713 985, 091 1543 5532 mobile), is a modern centre with a hotel and restaurant.

Viganj has three churches. The oldest, the 16th-century **St Liberan** – more a chapel, really – sits on the main spit of beach that is the windsurfing hub. The other two, **Our Lady of the Rosary** and 18th-century **St Michael's**, are on the way to a historic local point of interest: the **Nakovana archaeological site**, with evidence of the Stone Age.

## Restaurants

You can sample wine and snack at most of the wine cellars. For something more substantial, Mali Ston boasts the best tables. Picks are shellfish specialist **Bota Šare** on the waterfront (020 754 482, www.bota-sare.hr), from the same family as the venues at Bačvice, Split and Old Town Dubrovnik, and **Kapetanova Kuća**, a converted waterfront villa with modern seafood cuisine courtesy of chef Lidija Kralj.

At Viganj, try **Karmela** (020 719 097), overlooking the bay, outdoor **Forte** on the street leading to the village of Dol (020 611 187) or the more ramshackle **Bistro Ponta** (020 719 060) on Ponta beach.

### Mimbelli

*Trg Mimbelli 6, Orebić (020 713 636).*
**Open** noon-11pm. **€€**. **Seafood**
Set back only slightly from the shore, the restaurant of the Mimbelli guesthouse serves up local seafood

There are few better places to while away a warm Pelješac evening than the 'Three Palms', a welcoming wooden pavilion with removable canvas sides that sits right on the lip of Orebić's small-boat harbour. A big wicker lobster pot hanging from the ceiling helps to set a jolly seafaring tone – although there's also something of a pirate theme, with the staff clad in skull-and-crossbones T-shirts (and at least half of them sport black pointy beards). It's a quality coffee-sipping spot during the daytime. Otherwise, silky red Dingač and Postup wines are available by the glass; the cocktail menu is dusted off in summer.

## Cafes & Bars

Beach bars are ubiquitous. **Karmela 2** is the spiritual heart of Viganj and the place to go out and let your freak flag fly. DJs and live acts play in summer – look for the Karmela surfboard and yellow fence. In Orebić, **Mimbelli** (*see p266*) and **Tri Palme** (*see left*) are recommended.

## Hotels

Family-run **Indijan** (Škvar 2, 020 714 555, www.hotelindijan.hr, €€), is a delightful, mid-priced, beachfront venue in Orebić with a spa, pool, sauna, bar and restaurant.

Viganj has only one hotel: **Villa Mediterane** (No.224, 020 719 196, www.villamediterane.be, open June-Oct, €) at the far end of town. Campsites abound – the best is **Antony Boy** (020 719 330, www.antony-boy.com). Private rooms line the seaside road.

In Mali Ston, renowned **Kapetanova Kuća** restaurant (*see p266*) is attached to a decent hotel, the **Ostrea** (020 754 555, www.ostrea.hr, €). The **Vila Koruna** (020 754 999, www.vila-koruna.hr, €€) has a nice terrace restaurant.

In the middle of Pelješac, the **Hotel Faraon** (020 743 408, www.hotelfaraon-adriatiq.com, €) is set in Trpanj, close to a sandy beach and with plenty of outdoor activities on offer.

## GETTING THERE & AROUND

Pelješac is served by **bus** from Dubrovnik. Ston is 1.5hrs away, Orebić another hour. Three services a day run the whole length of the peninsula, one going over to Korčula, 2hrs from Ston. There are no other buses. The price of the bus ticket includes the ferry crossing.

From Korčula, there are regular foot passenger and ferry **boats** hopping the 30mins to Orebić. Marmo (020 701 137) lays on three boats a day between Viganj and Korčula (14kn). There is a regular Jadrolinija ferry from the transport hub of Ploče, just south of the Makarska Riviera on the mainland, to Trpanj on the north coast of Pelješac. The crossing lasts around 50mins. There is also a frequent service between Sobra on Mljet and Prapratno near Ston.

**Cavtat.**

with a touch of finesse, offering a range of fish cooked in interesting sauces as well as simply grilled or baked. Starters can make a good light lunch – seafood pastas and a choice of dishes cooked *buzara* style (mussels or shrimps cooked in wine sauce). Ask about daily specials – the menu may change to accommodate the fresh catch of the day. The wine list contains the best whites and reds of Pelješac. The cute, retro-style dining room is tiny, but there's a small scattering of tables out front and a much bigger area of courtyard seating at the back.

### Peninsula Wine Bar & Shop

*Donja Banda (www.peninsula.hr).* **Open** *Apr-Nov* 9am-11pm daily. €€. **Dalmatian** Beside the main road on Pelješac, at the heart of the local wine scene, just after Potomje in the direction of Orebić, is the Wine Bar and Shop Peninsula. A selection of over 60 wines from Pelješac and Korčula, hard to find elsewhere, makes the effort worthwhile. Aside from the famed Plavac reds and Pošip whites, from little boutique wineries and available by the glass, you can also pre-order some great fish or meat, prepared on an open fire behind the bar. Friendly service and reasonable prices. *See p268* **Dalmatia's Wine Trail**.

### Tri Palme

*Orebić harbour (no phone, www.facebook.com/ pages/Tri-Palme-Orebić).* **Open** *Summer* 8am-1am daily. *Winter* 8am-11pm daily. **No credit cards**. €€. **Dalmatian**

# DALMATIA'S WINE TRAIL

*Pelješac is the home of internationally celebrated Dingač*

Croatia has caused quite a stir with food-lovers in the last few years. Fresh seafood, truffles, wonderful cheeses and scrumptiously cured prosciutto are just a few delicacies on offer. But perhaps in no arena are folks as pleasantly surprised as with the wine. Croatia's improving viticulture is nationwide. But for red wine the place to go is the **Pelješac peninsula**: a mountainous sliver of land one hour north of Dubrovnik. And when one talks of red wine and Pelješac, the first word usually uttered is Dingač.

**Dingač** refers to a seven-kilometre-long stretch of seaside land where Plavac mali grapes – a varietal indigenous to Dalmatia – grow. Only grapes harvested in this small area, on the underbelly of the peninsula roughly between the towns of Podobuce and Trstenik, have the right to be called Dingač. And just like with any other patch of land

that's internationally celebrated for wine, the reason farmers cling proprietarily to this geographic distinction is because of the valuable convergence of conditions here.

First and foremost, the land faces south-west, which means grapes receive the full allowance of long, sunny Dalmatian days. Secondly, the soil the vines grow in is calcified and rocky, which provides two benefits to the plants: a second shot of sun due to the light's reflection from the rocks and an evolutionary advantage owing to the fact that only the heartiest grapes can grow here. Finally, the hillside upon which the fruit grows is incredibly steep, meaning harvest time is difficult but in return the land gets a third instalment of sunlight reflected right off the sea.

The result is a strong, full-bodied red (usually in the 14-per cent range) with a massive bouquet that resembles the great

wines of the genre: Sangiovese, Pinot Noir or Red Zinfandel. The difference being that the flavour of the best bottles of Dingač is, some would argue, more robust, both in taste and smell. According to one vintner from the peninsula, the trick isn't in growing great grapes here, the trick is learning how to control their strength without being too controlling. Another compared the grapes to wild horses, which you want to tame – a bit – but not so much that you destroy the innate qualities that make them wild.

The difference between simply wild versus wild-yet-refined is the fine line that separates local bragging rights from world acclaim. It is this struggle to find its own international identity that makes Dingač worthy of closer inspection. The question is how to meld distinctive natural resources with modern techniques to make a truly competitive product. For visitors and connoisseurs, this metamorphosis carries the excitement of watching potential excellence from inception. In 2007, a wine road linking 11 vineyards – including producers of Dingač and other masterful winemakers such as Vinarija Miloš in Ponikve – was signposted along the peninsula.

'People think only the French make good wine but the wine here is excellent,' said Goran Miličić of the Miličić Vineyard, which has its operations on the edge of Potomje, the heart of Dingač production. 'The biggest difference is that the French have four, five or more generations but we are only in our first generation, which means we have to start everything for ourselves.'

Linking Potomje to Dingač is a 400-metre (1,310-foot) tunnel, which cuts into the hill and connects the town to the grapes. It was actually built by residents with their own money during the communist era. Previously, growers had to lead donkeys up and over the hill to fill baskets and then go back again. On the other side, around the near cliff-face of Dingač, every square metre seems stuffed with vines hanging heavy with bunches of grapes. From atop the slope, the sea is a straight shot down 300 metres (985 feet). Were it not for wine, the area would seem incredibly forbidding. With the wine, it feels something like standing over a gold mine.

'Dingač is one of the rare positions in Europe where you can say, more or less, that every year is a good year,' says Vlado Borošić, a wine expert and the owner of the **Vinoteka Bornstein** (see p49) boutique in Zagreb. 'But the thing is, Dingač can be even better still. They have an excellent terroir. With some serious marketing and investment it can really be one of the top wines in the world.'

**EXPLORE**

# Mljet

**Mljet** is the nearest thing to having your own island. For complete silence, rest and relaxation, get the catamaran or ferry from Dubrovnik and leave the world behind.

Mljet is Dalmatia's most southern, most verdant and, some would argue, most beautiful isle. More than 70 per cent of this thin, 37-kilometre (22-mile) long one-road idyll is covered in pine forest. A third of it is national park. Before Tito chose Istria's Brijuni as his place for leisure, luxury and safari animals, Mljet was a prime candidate for the prestigious role. And though it never got to accommodate zebras, elephants and giraffes, Mljet remained a natural escape, underdeveloped and underpopulated.

According to legend, Odysseus was so enchanted by Mljet that he stayed here for seven years. Locals tend to stay for the day, arriving in someone's boat in the morning, spending the day cycling and swimming, before heading back for dinner in Dubrovnik. Tourists coming on the ferry are plonked at sombre **Sobra**, on the north-east coast. Those in the catamaran go on to the western tip and **Polače**, named after mildly interesting Roman ruins. This is your best arrival point, with private rooms and cycle hire (although there's a steep hill to start off with). It is five kilometres to the newer port of **Pomena**, where you'll find the island's only hotel, the Odisej, plus more private rooms, cycle hire places and restaurants. The hotel is the island's link with

civilisation, boasting a cashpoint and internet access. Note that it closes for the winter.

Halfway between Polače and Pomena is the main ticket office for the **national park** at Goveđari. Kiosks are also dotted elsewhere. If you're spending the night on the island, you do not pay for park entry.

Around the lakes, the little stone-house settlements of **Babine Kuće** and **Soline** are nice for a wander. From Veliko Jezera, a hiking path leads to the 253-metre (830-foot) high point of **Montokuc**, allowing fine views of Pelješac and Korčula. Hiking maps of the islands are sold at kiosks in Polače and Pomena. Other sports activities – windsurfing, diving – can be organised from the Hotel Odisej.

The rest of the island contains a few small settlements, headed by the administrative capital of **Babino Polje**, and nothing else but nature. As nearly all tourists hang around the lakes, this is pretty much yours. There's nothing by way of transport or refreshments but the reward is three sandy beaches near **Sapunara**, on Mljet's far eastern tip. The main one can get a little crowded, but the other two, **Podkućica** and the beautiful **Blace**, are quieter, the latter attracting nudists. Locals can find you a private room or there is apartment rental.

On the south coast, a hard walk from Babino Polje or an easy boat excursion from the Hotel Odisej is **Ulysses Cave**, where the nymph Calypos is said to have held Odysseus captive. Seven years stuck in paradise, maybe it was the itch that made him leave.

Lastovo. See p272.

## Sights & museums

### Mljet National Park

**Main office** *Pristanište 2, Govedari (020 744 041, np-mljet.hr).* **Open** *Apr-Oct* 24hrs daily. *Nov-Mar* 7am-3pm Mon-Fri. **Admission** 70kn-80kn; 30kn-40kn reductions. **No credit cards.**
Mljet's main draw is this national park covering the western third of the island. Many head first for the salt-water lakes of Veliko and Malo Jezero, linked by a channel of water. Malo Jezero is safe for children and its water is quite warm. Veliko Jezero, on the other hand, is connected to the Adriatic and has tidal flows – make sure you know which way the current is going and don't get swept out. In its centre is the islet of St Mary, with the church of the same name and a 12th-century monastery. An hourly boat links with the little bridge on Malo Jezero or you can hire a small canoe.

## Restaurants & hotels

Mljet's dining scene is modest but you can find fresh, local dishes at serene lakeside taverns. Note that virtually every establishment closes for the winter, usually by October, to re-open in the spring. Popular in high season, **Mali Raj** (Babine Kuce 3, Govedari 020 744 115) on the west of the island is a small *konoba* serving Dalmatian staples with gorgeous views of the lake. **Nine** (020 744 037) is the best of a handful of spots opposite the Hotel Odisej. This is the place to come for fresh lobster, kept in wells outside and fished out at your request. It's a favoured haunt of the yachting fraternity.

Another favourite is the **Melita** (020 744 145), set in the old monastery in the middle of Veliko Jezero, with a terrace by the water. You can eat fish or grilled meat while dipping your toes in the water. Although it's quite out of the way, the **Konoba Barba** (020 746 200), in the village of Prožura, between Sobra and the island's only petrol pumps, is like dining in somebody's house. Fresh fish and friendly conversation from the old lady are provided in equal measure.

Few tourists bother to stop in the administrative capital of Babino Polje – but this is where you'll find the wonderful, family-run terrace restaurant **Triton** (Sršenovici 43, 020 745 131, 091 205 3531) and the best bar anywhere on the island, Božo Hadjić's **Komarac** ('Mosquito', Sršenovići 44).

Along with the isolation and pristine beaches of Mljet's eastern tip, you can tuck into fish stew or slow-cooked octopus or goat at the **Stermasi** in Saplunara (098 939 0362, www.stermasi.hr), which also rents out cheap lodging. **Srsen Apartments** (020 747 025) in Soline stand out because the large limestone house contains sleek, modern flats of a good standard. The balconies have views of the lake and the sea. Private rooms are generally available in Polače and Pomena, although they can be scarce in Sobra. Expect to pay 200kn-250kn for a double. We recommend you phone ahead in high season – you can book at one of Dubrovnik's many travel agencies.

Mljet's only hotel, the **Odisej** (Pomena, 020 300 300, www.adriaticluxuryhotels.com/en/ hotel-odisej-dubrovnik-mljet, open Easter-Oct,

EXPLORE

€€€) is now part of the Adriatic Luxury Hotels group and has new spa facilities to complement its improved sea-view restaurant and children's pool. Staff are on hand to advise on a variety of water sports.

## GETTING THERE & AROUND

The *Nona Ana* **catamaran** leaves Gruž in Dubrovnik every morning for Sobra (about 30kn) then Polače (about 75kn). Allow an hour or so, nearly two for Polače. Some services also call at the Elafiti Islands. It leaves Polače for Gruž late afternoon, and early evening from Sobra. The service is run by G&V (www.gv-line.hr) which publishes a new timetable each summer.

Run by Jadrolinija (www.jadrolinija.hr), the Dubrovnik-Bari **ferry** calls at Sobra three times a week. There is a regular service to Sobra from Prapratno on Pelješac and in high season from Korčula.

A **bus** shuttles between Sobra, Polače and Pomena for arrivals and departures of Jadrolinija ferries – but it can be full in high season. There is no other public transport.

You can rent a **bike** from Polače harbour, the Hotel Odisej or the main ticket office for the national park. Mini Brum (020 745 084, 099 611 5574, www.rent-a-car-scooter-mljet.hr) rents out customised **cars** from Sobra or offices across the island.

# Lastovo

Located far out in the Adriatic between Croatia and Italy, the small island of **Lastovo** (*photos pp270-272*) is not an easy destination. Served by a single daily ferry from Split in season, this is a holdover outpost of the Med as it used to be: spare, barren and decidedly untouristy. Its unforgiving isolation, which protected it against pirates, today offers the same respite from the mad march of tourist development sweeping Croatia's coast.

Seemingly cut off from the world by steep cliffs plunging directly into the sea, Lastovo was settled as a safe redoubt against the unending raids of Ushak, Turkish and Genoese pirates. Unlike most Adriatic port towns, Lastovo village is situated beyond the crest of the cliffs, smack in the crater of a dead volcano, its Venetian church spires entirely invisible from the sea. The whole island served as an impregnable defence from sea raiders during the centuries of warfare between the Venetian Republic and Ottoman Empire.

Lastovo's stormy history has seen it claimed by Venetians, Ragusans, French, British, and eventually Habsburg rulers before being granted to Italy from World War I until 1945 – it was never a part of the Kingdom of Yugoslavia. Mussolini hoped to make Lastovo the site of his ambitious if soft-brained resettlement programme to relocate the poor of overcrowded Naples to a sunny new island home in Dalmatia. Almost all of the Italians were repatriated to Italy after 1945, but the Lastovans still speak a Croatian heavily peppered with Italian words and phrases.

Lastovo was declared a National Nature Park in 2006 but tourists are still precious enough to be greeted with a smile and an invitation to a glass of home-brewed *travarica* spirit. Cars pick up pedestrians. Grab a fishing rod and catch your dinner. Swim in a bay all to yourself. Kick off your shoes and really relax. This isn't tourism. This is way-out-thereness, an antidote to the crowds. Think Robinson Crusoe, only with fine wine, seafood risotto and maybe a rented moped.

**Lastovo village**, at the other end of the island from the port of **Ubli**, is a vertical maze of old stone houses and flower-covered, walled alleys clinging to the inner crater of an extinct volcano. The tiny centre at the top of the hill offers a bar, two markets, tourist information and a restaurant. A path leads down to a small beach at **Sv Mihovil**.

During the winter carnival, Poklad, the cigarette-smoking effigy of a medieval Turk is submitted to various creative indignities while hoisted on a rope 300 metres (985 feet) above the town before being burned by costumed villagers dancing to traditional Moreška music shouting 'UVO! UVO! UVO!'. Obviously, alcohol consumption is deeply involved.

## Restaurants & hotels

The seasonal **Hotel Solitudo** (Uvala Pasadur, 020 802 100, 098 424 552, www.hotel-solitudo. com, €€), near Ubli, has singles, doubles and suites. Some have sea views, as does its decent terrace restaurant. Recently upgraded, it now also has as a gym and jacuzzi, and staff can lay on diving and boat excursions. The **Konoba Augusta Insula** (Zaklopatica, www.augustainsula.com) offers excellent home-made wine and seafood, including delicious lobsters that are seemingly kept by the dock as pets.

## GETTING THERE

In season, daily **ferries** to Lastovo from Split, Hvar town and Vela Luka on Korčula arrive at Ubli, an undistinguished hamlet and former military base on the south-west coast, where taxis can be found. Moped rental is the best way to see the island.

# DUBROVNIK'S OTHER ISLANDS
### *Archipelago escapes.*

An easy getaway from Dubrovnik is to take a boat for the three (barely) inhabited islands of the 14-isle **Elafiti archipelago**: Koločep, Lopud and Šipan. Ferries from the main harbour at Gruž are geared for islanders and workers – super-cheap but infrequent. To do all three islands, head to Dubrovnik's old harbour and find a fish picnic trip. Prices (250kn, 180kn without the picnic) and departure times (10am out, 6pm back) are pretty standard. Unlimited free drink for the three hours at sea is part of the package, so don't opt for a rowdy crowd if you're after peace and quiet – it's an eight-hour day and there's no escape. Given the right passengers, though, it's the ideal way to see the islands, and the fish is fresh and plentiful.

The first stop, **Koločep**, home to 150 people, offers steep cliffs, wind-carved caves and shaded walking trails for an hour. You then get three hours on the sandy beaches and sea promenade of **Lopud**. A path near the Grand Hotel here leads over the hill to the other side of the island, and the lovely sandy beach of Šunj, 15 minutes away. It faces **Šipan**, the largest of the islands, similarly dotted with a few old churches, noblemen's villas, Roman remains and two villages: Šipanska Luka and Suđurađ. This unspoiled island has its own dialect, spoken by locals who still live from growing melons. The final hour here should be longer – you'll get the boat back to Dubrovnik with a heavy heart.

**EXPLORE**

# In Context

# History

*Competing sovereignties have
been behind many conflicts.*

Scholars have yet to resolve the etymology and meaning of the word Croat, with clues as to its origins sought variously in the Greek words for 'people who have a lot of land', 'tree', 'a dance', and the phrase 'inhabitants of the island of Krk'. The word may also have distant Iranian roots meaning 'friend' or 'protector'.

Arriving at the shores of the Adriatic at the start of the seventh century, Croats were among a wave of Slav invaders that reached their most western point of conquest in Istria at the gates of Italy. The Slav tribes also pressed south, destroying Salona in AD 614, the magnificent capital of Roman Dalmatia.

What later developed into Croatia became dominated by Habsburgs and Hungarians; meanwhile the independent city-state of Ragusa, today's Dubrovnik, flourished. A painful and bloody path to unity in the 20th century culminated in a new, independent nation and EU accession – but only after two world wars and the brutal conflict with Serbia in the 1990s.

The crowning of Croat King Tomislav.

## ROMANS, ILLYRIANS AND CROATS

In the face of the barbarian onslaught on the mainland, the Romans and other Romanised peoples of Illyria moved to the islands, later returning to their cities when it became clear that the Slavs were not interested – at this stage – in urban living. This resulted in two quite different civilisations co-existing in close proximity during the seventh century. The Romans kept to the towns of Split, Trogir and Zadar while, in the Dalmatian hinterland, Slav tribes maintained their own language, religion and social systems. There was a pragmatic exchange between the two societies, with the Romans ready to trade commercial services and crafts for the livestock and other agricultural products of the Slavs. Over time, the two cultures intermixed. Rulers of the pagan Slavs came under the influence of the Christian civilisation of the cities, and the urban population became progressively less distinct from the more numerous ethnic Slavs living in the surrounding countryside.

In a pattern that was to be repeated over the centuries, the ups and downs of distant empires gradually changed the political complexion of the Adriatic coast. The struggle between the Franks and the Byzantines in the age of Charlemagne, crowned Emperor of the Holy Roman Empire in AD 800, had

direct repercussions for Dalmatia. When Charlemagne and the Byzantine Emperor made peace in Aachen in AD 812, the Byzantines were allotted the Roman cities; the Franks got the rural hinterland, founding a dukedom centred on Sisak.

The first historical document referring to Croatian state institutions dates from AD 852, when Trpimir (AD 845-864) styled himself 'Dux Croatorum'. The small territory of this Croatian dukedom extended across the hinterlands of Zadar, Trogir and Split, but did not include the coastal cities themselves. Interestingly, there was also a fledgling Pannonian Croatian state, positioned along the river Drava, in an area that in the Middle Ages became known as Slavonia. Cautious progress by the Croat rulers was suggested by an agreement made between Byzantium and the Croatian state, according to which the cities on the Adriatic seaboard would pay a fee to the Croatians in exchange for the right to work their own fields. The Venetians also paid the Croats for the right of their ships to pass through.

## BALKAN THREAT AND MAGYAR RULE

The Croat ruler Tomislav (910-928) succeeded by 925 in becoming a full-blown king. The Byzantine empire allowed him to control the cities of the Adriatic as the Emperor's pro-consul. During his rule, there were two Church assemblies in Split in which vital questions facing the early medieval Church were discussed. Militarily, Tomislav kept the Hungarians in the north at bay and stopped Bulgarian Emperor Symeon's attempt to conquer the country. He was an administrative innovator, bringing the machinery of feudal government up to date, with the division of Croatia into 11 administrative districts.

Culture and religion in the kingdom were marked by the division between the users of Latin and the users of the Slavic alphabet, Glagolica. In the early years, inland Croatian priests knew no Latin, could marry, and wore their hair long like the Byzantine clergy. By the 12th century, the papal authorities and the mostly Latin-speaking coastal nobility had brought the Croatian Church firmly within the established order of Roman Catholicism. Glagolitic survived as the secular alphabet for Croatian literature from the 14th to 16th centuries, and was to enjoy a partial revival in the 19th century, thanks to the influence of Romantic literary nationalists.

In a fateful accident of royal marriage and inheritance, the Croatian crown passed in 1102 to King Kálmán of Hungary. He assumed the Croatian throne under a joint agreement that was to guarantee the separate but unequal existence of Croatia within the Hungarian kingdom until 1918. According to the Pacta conventa the Croatian nobility kept their Sabor (assembly) and local authority in the country. While Croatia continued to exist as a separate political entity, the process of state building was blocked for almost 900 years by the interests and competing sovereignties of the Ottomans, the Venetians, the Hungarians and the Habsburg Empire.

The decline of the medieval Croatian kingdom was hastened by the rise of Venice, which in the 14th century consolidated its hold on Dalmatia. One low point was the sale of Dalmatia to the Venetians for 100,000 ducats, with the result that the Venetians ruled both the cities and islands of Dalmatia, with only the rump of Croatia in Slavonia left. After the fall of Bosnia in 1463, Croatian lands were more vulnerable to Turkish attacks, and defeat at the Battle of Krbavsko Polje, in Lika, in 1493, ushered in a century of chaos and destruction. The situation was just as serious for the Habsburgs, who trembled as the Ottomans

drew nearer and nearer to Vienna, crushing the Hungarians at the Battle of Mohács in 1526. With the King of Hungary fallen, the following year the Croatian nobility chose to put their faith in the Habsburg ruler King Ferdinand, in the hope that he would protect them from the depredations of the Turks.

## OTTOMANS AND HABSBURGS

Croatian trust in the Habsburgs was not very generously rewarded. The Emperor Ferdinand I carved another slice off what was left of the Kingdom of Croatia with the establishment of a broad military zone, controlled from Vienna, along the border with the Ottoman Empire. This was the *Vojna Krajina*, or Military Border. After the fort at Bihać fell in 1592, only small parts of Croatia remained unconquered. The remaining 16,800 square kilometres (6,486 square miles) were referred to as the 'remnants of the remnants of the once great Croatian kingdom'. The 16th century in Croatia was also the era of Matija Gubec's bloodily suppressed peasant uprising, and the Uskok pirate state in Senj, which had managed to harass the Venetians, Habsburgs and the Turks from its stronghold on the inhospitable coastline nearby.

The exception in this story of hardship and imperial domination is provided by Dubrovnik.

IN CONTEXT

Miniature of King Kálmán of Hungary

Known as Ragusa, and recognised as a sovereign republic, the city was the main Mediterranean centre for trade with the Ottoman Empire by the 16th century, and maintained its independence until the Napoleonic Wars. Despite the difficult political situation, Dalmatia in the 15th and 16th centuries saw a flourishing of Renaissance culture. In this period, hundreds of Croat humanists studied at universities abroad.

## 'The eventual reversal of Ottoman fortunes followed their defeat at the Battle of Sisak in 1593.'

The strong cultural identity of the coastal cities of Dalmatia was as much connected to their sense of belonging to a cultural heritage going back to the Romans and Greeks, as to their Latin scholarship and the development of Croat vernacular literature. Italian humanists, along with painters, sculptors and architects, who came to work on the magnificent building projects of Renaissance Dalmatia, must have felt very much at home here.

The eventual reversal of Ottoman fortunes followed their defeat at the Battle of Sisak in 1593. But instead of relaxing Habsburg control of the country, Ferdinand II consolidated the imperial organisation of the Military Border, taking it completely out of the hands of the Croatian Parliament. The noble Zrinski and Frankopan families plotted to eject the Habsburgs from Croatia, in an unlikely and desperate-sounding coalition with Louis XIV of France, the King of Poland, the Venetians and even the Turks. Unfortunately, word of the plot leaked out, and Peter Zrinski and his brother-in-law Franjo Frankopan were beheaded in Vienna Neustadt in 1671. The 17th and 18th centuries saw the power of the Croatian nobles in the Habsburg lands decline, with the Croatian *Sabor* in an increasingly weak position relative to the Vienna-appointed Governor, or *Ban*.

Following the Ottoman retreat after their second failed advance on Vienna in 1683,

southern Slavonia was also brought into the Vojna Krajina. From the mid-16th century onwards, the Habsburgs had attracted border guards to the area with offers of free land without manorial obligations and by allowing freedom for Serbs to practise the Orthodox religion. Consequently, according to the first census of 1819 over half the population of the Military Border were Serbs, whose large presence in historic Croatia was to become a source of tension. The economy of the Military Border stagnated thanks to bureaucratic restrictions on the size and transfer of agricultural holdings, a complex customs regime and the fact that all men of military age had to spend much of the year on exercises.

When the Hungarians tried under Ferenc Rákóczi to rid themselves of the Habsburgs, the Croatian nobility opted to collaborate with Vienna, signing the 'pragmatic sanction' that made possible Maria Theresa's accession to the throne in 1740. This turned out to be a mistake, as during her 40-year rule she further centralised power, shutting down the Croatian *Sabor*. Her son, the enlightened despot Josef II, made some small improvements in the conditions of the peasantry, but was even more determined than his mother to carry out the Germanisation of the Habsburg empire.

### NAPOLEON AND GROWING NATIONALISM

After Venice fell to revolutionary France in 1797, her possessions in Dalmatia also came under French control. French rule brought a number of advanced but short-lived administrative reforms, which included Napoleon's innovative establishment of an Illyrian kingdom, embracing Dalmatia and much of modern Slovenia. After Napoleon's defeat, Dalmatia passed into the control of the Habsburgs. At the same time, the growing strength of nationalism in Hungary was felt in Croatia, which many Hungarians treated as a province and attempted to 'magyarise'. It was against this background that a new direction in Croatian politics was defined, with the emergence of the Illyrian movement.

The fragmentation of the lands of the medieval Kingdom of Croatia had long been bemoaned, triggering calls for the 'Triune Kingdom of Croatia, Slavonia and Dalmatia' to be reunited under the House of Habsburg. However, the Slav activists of the early 19th century, fearing the term 'Croat' was too narrow, and following the example of the writer Ljudevit Gaj, instead described themselves as Illyrians, thereby hoping to bring under one umbrella the Habsburg empire's Croat, Slovene and Serb inhabitants.

Political Illyrianism ended after 1848. Although the Croatian *Ban*, Josip Jelačić, had helped the Habsburg monarchy suppress the Hungarian uprising, it earned him no favours from Vienna. Instead, during the authoritarian backlash against national independence movements between 1849 and 1860, the *Sabor* was not allowed to meet, and the Austrians ruled Croatia even more directly than before. Jelačić died a bitter man.

In the latter half of the 19th century, the Illyrian movement split. The heirs of Ljudevit Gaj continued to champion a broad alliance with other Slavs, notably the Serbs. Now describing themselves as Jugoslavs (South Slavs) rather than Illyrians, their leader for many decades was the redoubtable scholar-Bishop of Đakovo, Josip Strossmayer. Their opponents, under Ante Starčević, rejecting the pan-Slav alliance with the Serbs as unworkable and as detrimental to Croat interest, gathered under the banner of the Party of Rights. A struggle between Strossmayer and Starčević for hearts and minds dominated Croat politics in the late 19th century.

While the political situation resembled stalemate, the economic development of the country advanced apace. The ejection of the Ottomans from Bosnia in 1878 removed the purpose of having a Military Border, and opened up new opportunities for trade and mineral exploitation. The building of strategic railways made possible the industrial development of Slavonian cities such as Osijek and Slavonski Brod. The inland towns, which had stagnated for centuries, enjoyed an urban renaissance, with the transformation of Zagreb a case in point. A major earthquake provided an opportunity to remodel the city according to the civic ideals of the *fin de siècle*, creating a distinctive green horseshoe of squares and parks.

### INDEPENDENCE – BUT NOT FROM BELGRADE

Not surprisingly, the beginning and, even more, the long continuation of World War I tested the Croats' loyalty to the old order to its limits. At first, most Croats fought loyally for the octogenarian Emperor Franz Josef but, as the fighting dragged on and the prospect of defeat loomed, many Croats began pondering their future without the Habsburgs. The leaking of the terms of the secret London Treaty of 1915, by which the Entente Powers promised Italy most of Dalmatia if it were to come into the war on their side, shocked Croats into action. Alarmed by the possibility of partition between Italy in the west and Serbia in the east, opinion swung towards the establishment of a South Slav state embracing Serbia and Montenegro in order to guarantee the integrity of Croat lands.

The first Croats to advance this programme were three Dalmatians, Supilo, Trumbić and the sculptor and architect Ivan Meštrović, who set up the Yugoslav Committee for this purpose in 1915. The campaigners for Yugoslavia envisaged Croatian autonomy and equality within the new framework. But the state formed in 1918, after Austria-Hungary collapsed,

**Josip Jelačić.**

disappointed them. It became clear that Yugoslavia's Serbian rulers saw Yugoslavia as an extension of Serbia and the imposition of a centralised constitution in 1921 discredited the Yugoslav cause in Croatia.

Opinion now rallied to the separatist Stjepan Radić, leader of the Croat Republican Peasant Party, who had never supported the Yugoslav project. Having warned the Croats that 'they were rushing into union with Serbia like a band of drunken geese in a fog', he campaigned for an independent Croatian republic. The young Yugoslav state was immediately faced with fierce opposition from Radić's party, which only became more radical and intransigent following his assassination in the Belgrade Parliament in 1928.

His successor as leader was Vladko Maček, who maintained the Peasant Party's policy of non-violent struggle against Serb domination. Alongside this popular movement, which usually won the elections in Croatia, a more extremist opposition movement grew up on the far right under Ante Pavelić. His Ustashe movement traced its descent from Starčević's Party of Rights. But unlike the latter, it was prepared to engage in violence to achieve the goal of independence. An extreme solution on the left was offered by the Communist Party, destined to take control of the country later on, but in the 1920s and '30s a minority group.

**Soviets in Vis, 1944.**

### ASSASSINATION, FASCISM AND WAR

While in politics, the Kingdom of Yugoslavia drifted in the 1930s towards authoritarianism, in the cultural sphere there was a resurgence of opposition to parochialism and right-wing politics. The leading figure in Croatian literature in this period was Miroslav Krleža, who opposed the clerical right and the political dominance of the Peasant Party. He was aligned politically with the underground Communist Party, but in cultural matters he struggled against the confines of Socialist Realism.

The assassination of Yugoslavia's authoritarian King Alexander in Marseille in 1934 put an end to the political stalemate. Because the new King Peter was a minor, power passed to a regent, Prince Paul, an Anglophile liberal who was bent on solving Croat grievances without, however, conceding independence. Maček was brought in from the cold and after tortuous negotiations over borders and competencies, an autonomous Croat unit – the Banovina – was established within Yugoslavia in 1939. Dismissed as a façade by Pavelić's now-exiled Ustashe, the Banovina managed to alleviate Croat frustration – a necessity for the whole of Yugoslavia now that Nazi Germany and Fascist Italy were threatening the balance of power within Europe.

However, the Banovina had no time to establish itself. After a pro-British faction in the Yugoslav army overthrew Prince Paul in 1941, Hitler invaded Yugoslavia and rapidly conquered the country. In Zagreb, Mussolini hurriedly installed Pavelić and his Ustashe cronies as lords of the new Independent State of Croatia (NDH), a name that belied its real status as an Italian dependency.

The NDH co-operated wholeheartedly with Nazi plans to exterminate the Jews and other minorities. Its agenda also included forcing Serbs to convert to Catholicism or be killed; many simply fled. As the Axis powers awarded the NDH the whole of Bosnia-Herzegovina, where Serbs made up the single largest ethnic group, the NDH was locked into civil war from the moment it was established in April 1941.

As World War II intensified, a frightful three-cornered conflict developed over Croatia between Communists, Serbian royalists, known

RAF driver with young Partisans, 1944

as Chetniks, and the Ustashe, who claimed the support of Nazi Germany and Fascist Italy. In reality, Italy was an ambivalent godparent of the NDH, making no secret of its eventual ambition to annex Dalmatia and realise Mussolini's goal of turning the Adriatic Sea into an Italian lake. Pavelić's poorly equipped army was no match for its opponents, and especially the well-organised Communist Partisans, led by Josip 'Tito' Broz (see p287 **Tito and Croatia**). The Partisans showed their strength by holding two congresses inside the NDH in 1942 and '43 at Bihać and Jajce, where they sketched out the foundations of a new Yugoslav state. This was to be a truly federal arrangement, with Serbs sharing power not only with Croats and Slovenes but with Macedonians, Montenegrins and Bosnians.

### SOCIALIST YUGOSLAVIA

With the defeat of the Nazis in 1945, Ustashe leader Ante Pavelić fled and it was the turn of the Communists to rule Croatia. Once more, Croatia was back inside Yugoslavia as one of six federal units. Its borders were smaller than those of the Banovina, owing to the Communists' decision to resurrect Bosnia as a federal unit. Those losses were partially offset by the inclusion in Croatia of the cities

of Rijeka and Zadar and of most of Istria, which Italy had obtained from the Habsburg Empire after 1918.

While there was little nostalgia for the bloodstained rule of Pavelić, now in exile in Argentina, the imposition of full-blown Soviet-style Communism under Tito grated on Croats, most of whom resented the persecution of the Catholic Church, symbolised by the trial and imprisonment of the Archbishop of Zagreb, Alojzije Stepinac, in 1946. A hate figure to Serbs for his initial collaboration with the NDH, Stepinac was correspondingly admired by Croats, especially in the countryside, and an official campaign against him merely fuelled a cult of Stepinac as a national martyr.

The tense atmosphere felt in Croatia lessened after Stepinac's death in 1960, which Tito cleverly exploited to bring about a rapprochement with the Church, allowing Stepinac a grand funeral in Zagreb to which foreign diplomats were invited. The Church took the proffered olive branch at face value and under Stepinac's successor, Cardinal Šeper, Church-State relations lost their bitterness.

The development of mass tourism in the 1960s also brought new life to the Croatian economy, especially in Dalmatia and Istria. It was helped by market reforms, accompanied by a considerable degree of local autonomy, allowing Croatia to become the second-most prosperous republic within Yugoslavia. Domestic production and Western imports led to an improved supply of both food and consumer goods. And Croatians took advantage of going abroad as 'guest workers', bringing back their hard-earned Deutschmarks to fuel a boom in Communist consumerism.

In several republics and provinces, including Macedonia and Kosovo, the post-war generation of leaders was challenged by relative youngsters offering a heady mix of liberalism and local nationalism. In Croatia, the standard bearer for change was the Croatian Spring, or Maspok, short for *masovni pokret*, 'mass movement'. Its broad aims were economic and political reforms to secure Croatia a greater share of the wealth it generated and to increase Croatia's autonomy – and that of the other republics – within Yugoslavia. It was seen by many Serbs as a device to reduce their influence as an ethnic group in Yugoslavia, as well as to marginalise the role of the Communist Party.

The most pressing economic issues included the fact that although Croatia brought half the foreign capital into the country, it disposed of only 15 per cent of it. The centralisation of decision-making and budgetary considerations in Belgrade worked to the disadvantage of Croatia, and led to the widespread perception that Croatia was being economically exploited within the federation.

### CRUSHING THE CROATIAN SPRING
The crunch came in 1971, as the demands of the Croatian nationalists became increasingly radical, with calls for a separate Croatian currency and seat at the UN, as well as frontier changes with Bosnia. Croatia's 12 per cent Serb minority were concentrated in the old Military Border region. That December, Tito moved to crush the Croatian Spring. With tanks revving ominously at their army barracks, he summoned the leaders of the Croatian Party to his hunting lodge at Karađorđevo, in Serbia, and ordered them to resign. They duly quit without demur, though their quiet exit did not save Croatia from a wide-ranging purge. The Croatian cultural organisation Matica Hrvatska was closed, hundreds of prison sentences were handed out and thousands of Party members were expelled. It was the end of an experiment

in a democratic form of Communism and its failure led to a great silence falling over Croatia, which gave rise to its new nickname in the late 1980s: 'the silent republic'.

The mute discontent of Tito's last years was alleviated by rising living standards, based largely on foreign credits. But after Tito's death in 1980, the credits dried up and the economic situation worsened rapidly. As foreign debts spiralled and inflation spun out of control, the Communists rapidly lost prestige and the power to successfully suppress criticism. The old ideology of 'brotherhood and unity' became an object of general ridicule as the six republics fought openly over economic policy.

New Communist leader Slobodan Milošević began to tear up the ground rules that had existed in Yugoslavia since 1945, openly promoting a violent and aggressive brand of Serb nationalism that paid no heed to the rights of Croats, Albanians, Bosnians or anyone else.

Milošević's first target was Kosovo, the Albanian-dominated province in southern Yugoslavia that Serbs regarded as the cradle of their medieval state. With the army behind him, in 1989 Milošević quelled Kosovo, gunning down dozens of Albanian protesters in the streets. An internal coup then delivered Montenegro peacefully into his hands.

### THE HOMELAND WAR
The rise of Milošević forced other Communist leaders to look to their constituencies and concede democratic reforms. A plethora of parties appeared on the political scene, and with that, the prospect of multi-party elections. In Croatia the Communist Party leader Ivica Račan called a poll in April 1990, but he profoundly miscalculated the depth of Croat resentment against Communist rule and victory went instead to the nationalist Croatian Democratic Union (HDZ) whose leader, a former general, Franjo Tuđman, had served prison terms after the Croatian Spring.

Tuđman at first confined himself to arguing for a confederation and greater Croatian self-rule. But growing violence dictated its own course of events. No sooner was the election over than armed Serbs based in the hilly north Dalmatian town of Knin threw up roadblocks and proclaimed a separate Serb state within Croatia – the Republic of Serbian Krajina (RSK).

Yugoslavians pay final respects to Tito, 1980.

With Milošević's energetic backing and Yugoslav tanks, the RSK rapidly annexed as much of the republic as possible. Facing a clamour from a panicked population, Tuđman edged towards proclaiming total independence – risking the threat of open war. The Croats also had to march in step with their Slovene neighbours, who were also busily proceeding towards independence anyway. The two republics agreed to jump ship together on 25 June 1991. But whereas Slovenia shrugged off Yugoslav control without effort, after a ten-day shoot-out with the Yugoslav army, Croatia faced determined opposition from Milošević, the army and the 600,000 Croatian Serbs.

In the second half of 1991, the RSK mopped up one district after another, at its highpoint controlling one-third of the republic, including most of northern Dalmatia, eastern Lika, Kordun and Banija, parts of western Slavonia and the regions of Baranja and Srijem in eastern Slavonia. The eastern border town of Vukovar came under especially prolonged joint RSK and army siege, reducing the graceful Baroque streets to rubble. When the town fell on 17 November, the victorious Serbs committed one of the worst atrocities of the conflict, butchering more than 200 wounded soldiers lying in Vukovar hospital. With less success, hundreds of miles away, the army

pounded away at the historic city of Dubrovnik. However, the blaze of international publicity intimidated them from repeating the tactics in Vukovar and the town stayed in Croat hands.

The horrific scenes screened all over the world fed a clamour to punish Belgrade through recognising Croatian independence. France and Britain, Serbia's traditional allies, held out to the end but bowed to the inevitable after Germany – the destination of many Croat refugees – threatened to recognise Slovenia and Croatia unilaterally, if need be. Fearing an ugly open rupture in the European Union, its member states agreed jointly to recognise the two states at Christmas 1991, a decision that took effect in January 1992.

Tuđman perceived recognition as an historic victory and the fulfilment of what he called the '1,000-year-old dream' of a Croat state. Nevertheless, at first the victory seemed hollow. The 'Homeland War' had cost thousands of lives and inflicted massive infrastructural damage. Towns, railways and factories lay in ruins, hundreds of thousands of people had been made homeless and the once lucrative tourist industry had collapsed. The RSK was also still in control of one-third of Croatia's territory, its gains seemingly cemented by a UN-brokered peace plan and by the deployment of peacekeepers along the frontline. Problems worsened in 1993-94, when Tuđman hurled the infant Croatian army on to the side of the ethnic Croats in Bosnia's own messy civil war – a fateful decision that led to Croatia's virtual international isolation. Under strong pressure from the US in 1994, Tuđman executed a humiliating retreat from the Bosnian arena.

By 1995, the US was desperate to roll back the Serb juggernaut in Bosnia, end the war there and rescue the hard-pressed Muslim-led government in Sarajevo. Croatia was brought in from the cold as the US gave the green light for armament supplies, which made the Croatian army a significant regional force. Thus reinvigorated, Tuđman determined to reverse Serb gains in Croatia at the same time as doing US bidding in Bosnia. A *casus belli* presented itself in July when the Bosnian Serbs threatened to overrun the large but isolated Bosnian city of Bihać, near the Croatian border. As Bosnia appealed for foreign aid, Tuđman obligingly sent his army racing over the border, where, much to the outside world's surprise, they rapidly routed the supposedly invincible Serbs, relieving Bihać before doubling back south to sever the RSK's supply lines through Bosnia to Serbia. In Knin, Tuđman ordered an all-out attack on the RSK, Operation Storm. The RSK crumbled and the next morning Croat soldiers were hosting their red-and-white flag over the battlements of Knin whose inhabitants, along with about 150,000 other Serb inhabitants of the RSK, fled to Serbia in a long column. Victory was complete. The remaining Serbian-controlled territories in eastern Slavonia, including Vukovar, were returned to Croatia in 1998 under UN supervision. Tuđman had only a short time to savour these triumphs before he succumbed to cancer in December 1999.

Thousands attended Tuđman's cold funeral in Zagreb, though few international leaders joined the throng. While most Croats mourned the man, they did not mourn the HDZ's increasingly corrupt and authoritarian style of government, turfing out Tuđman's henchmen at the next elections and putting back in the driving seat Ivica Račan, the old Communist leader recast as a social democrat.

## TOURIST EUROS AND EU ACCESSION

The Račan government acted fast to mend fences with Europe. The president's almost monarchical powers were massively trimmed, state interference with the media was curbed by law, the path was cleared for exiled Serbs to reclaim property and return, and Zagreb pledged never again to meddle in Bosnia.

The progress was not all plain sailing, as Europe made any serious rapprochement conditional on Croatia's absolute co-operation with the Hague war crimes tribunal. And the court's demand for the extradition of key military figures was deeply unpopular in a country still not recovered from the trauma of the Homeland War.

Yet, with Tuđman and Milošević gone, there was a distinct feeling that Croatia had turned a corner and passed key tests. The war had not delivered political extremism nor the return from the grave of the Ustashe. The tourists were back in bigger numbers than ever and even buying up holiday homes. In 2005 the arrest of alleged war criminal Ante Gotovina, after years on the run, won brownie points with the West – although the event polarised the locals.

At the same time, the Zagreb–Split motorway opened, linking the capital to Dalmatia. With routes opened from the UK and Germany, the airports of Split, Dubrovnik and Zadar saw busy traffic and Croatia became the destination of the moment. New luxury hotels were built, particularly on Hvar and in Dubrovnik. Shopping malls sprang up around Zagreb.

Compulsory military service ended in 2007 but the decade ended with a series of unsolved murders allegedly linked to organised crime, politics and the media. In 2009, after six years as prime minister, Ivo Sanader resigned with little clear explanation as to why. He was replaced by fellow HDZ politician Jadranka Kosor, who led a series of anti-corruption measures and attempted to address the economic crisis.

The presidential elections of 2010 saw the near collapse of the HDZ and a landslide victory for the Social Democratic Party under Ivo Josipović, though public protests marked the start of the new decade. With a new coalition government under Zoran Milanović in 2011, Croatia neared ever closer to EU accession. A vote of 66 per cent in a national referendum saw the European Union welcome its newest member in July 2013. With the young, progressive Milanović still in power, Croatia was enjoying a period of relative liberalisation through 2014 and 2015.

# TITO AND CROATIA

### Croatia's uneasy relationship with its old overlord.

Born in 1892 in the village of Kumrovec, Josip Broz Tito, ruler of Yugoslavia from 1945 to his death in 1980, remains a paradoxical figure in contemporary Croatian culture. He is seen as a Communist dictator, who kept Croatia in Yugoslavia, crushed the Croatian Spring independence movement in 1971 and built the notorious Goli Otok island prison camp to punish his enemies. He was also a Croatian hero from the hilly region of Zagorje, the only World War II resistance leader who managed to liberate his own country and tread a difficult third way between Stalin and the West. At home, he was the preserver of Brotherhood and Unity.

A wave of Tito nostalgia has seen a best-selling cookery book of his favourite recipes; the marketing of the Tito cult on the Brijuni Islands (location of his summer residence); several films about his life; a photo exhibition about his travels, and the planned restoration of his yacht *Galeb* as a tourist attraction in Rijeka. Over the border in Serbia, an optimistic entrepreneur proposed setting up a Yugoland theme park in Subotica.

Tito's life story is an extraordinary one. Raised on the Slovene-Croatian border, he left his peasant background to become an engineering worker, ending up in Vienna. In World War I he was taken prisoner by the Russians but freed after the Bolshevik Revolution, staying on as a Red Guard during the Civil War. After returning home, he worked in a flour mill, shipyard and foundry, and was made head of the Zagreb Communist Party in 1928. He was then arrested and spent six years in prison. After his release he went to Moscow and became a leading Communist functionary under the name Comrade Walter. Avoiding the Stalinist purges, he was appointed leader of the Yugoslav Communist Party in 1939. The origins of his new name, Tito, lie either in his abrupt style of giving orders 'Ti… to!' ('You… that!') or in the initials of a Soviet-made pistol, the TT-30.

From 1941 he led the Yugoslav Partisan resistance against the Nazi invasion, narrowly escaping death or capture on several occasions. He secured the support of both the RAF Balkan Air Force and Stalin's Red Army, whose pincer movement north tied up the Nazis and opened the way for the Partisans to liberate first Belgrade, then Zagreb.

Head of a new six-republic Yugoslavia from 1945, Tito indulged his taste for palaces and conspicuous expenditure. He wore a gold-edged uniform with a belt buckle of pure gold, he dyed his hair and he changed his clothes several times a day. He had Brijuni transformed into an elite residence and playground, where he entertained world leaders, film stars and other celebrities. Constantly on the move, he stayed in luxurious residencies across Yugoslavia, on *Galeb* ('*Seagull*') and his specially kitted-out Blue Train. As the economy gradually ground to a halt, Tito strutted the world stage as a leading figure of the non-aligned movement.

Following his death in May 1980, huge crowds packed the stations between Ljubljana where he died and Belgrade where he was buried, to watch the funeral train go past. It was the end of an era for the country.

Today, the towns that bore his name have been renamed, but many street signs remain. All the wealth and property he amassed, in accordance with the principles of the Communist system, reverted to the state on his death. The presidents of independent Croatia have found themselves sleeping in his bedrooms, from the official Zagreb residency of Pantovčak to Brijuni.

The village of Kumrovec is now an ethnographic museum and a visitor attraction. Forty houses from the old village have been restored, each featuring staged scenes of traditional rural culture. However, the main attraction remains the house were Josip Broz was born.

**IN CONTEXT**

# Food & Wine

*As fresh as it gets, and diverse too.*

**TEXT: ALISON RADOVANOVIC**

The landscape, climate and history of Croatia dictate what's put on the dinner table. In a space less than half the size of England, you've got alluvial plains, mountain ranges and 2,000km (1,240 miles) of coastline, as well as the two major rivers. Add in three distinct climatic regions – Alpine, Continental and Mediterranean – plus cultural and political incursions by Turks, Venetians, Austrians, French and Hungarians, and it's no wonder that Croatia's cuisine is so varied. Visitors can miss out on much of this diversity however, a hangover from the package-tour days of the 1980s. Dalmatia, Dubrovnik in particular, can disappoint. By happy contrast, Split has enjoyed a new wave of modern bistros. Elsewhere, notably in Istria and mainland Kvarner, a new generation of Croatian chefs use imaginative and advanced techniques to create something truly special. Domestic wines, too, have improved enormously. Although little is exported, there is much to enjoy in situ, particularly from Pelješac and Slavonia.

PASKI SIR  248,90  MLADI 2014

## THE REGIONS

Croatian cuisine can be divided between the Central European tradition and that of the Central Mediterranean. For centuries the region was ruled by either the Austro-Hungarian Empire or the Venetian Republic and both cultures have left their culinary mark. Each region of Croatia also contributes its own specialities but it should be borne in mind that today these are regarded as national dishes and can be found all over the country.

Istria is considered to be Croatia's culinary temple – its peasant traditions, fresh and seasonal ingredients, and inventive chefs all combining to make this small peninsula the destination of choice for visiting gastronomes. Italians flood across the border on Sundays to sample the best of it. The celebrated use of truffles, to season steaks, or added to chocolate cake, is only one indication of the sophistication of the dishes on offer. Dalmatia, on the other hand, does the simple things right, relying on the high quality of the local olive oil, wine, garlic, tomatoes – and on the freshness of its seafood. Constant across the entire country, though, is this love of fresh ingredients, whether for meat-based dishes or piscine cuisine.

## FROM SEA AND RIVERS

The Adriatic boasts more than 400 species of fish, but with limited quantities of each kind. This is different from the North Sea, where some of the same species can be found in abundance, whereas others are not found at all – such as the renowned *zubatac* (dentex), common in the Mediterranean and Adriatic, and popular in local cooking.

Dalmatia has a seafood tradition dating to Greek, Roman and Byzantine times – its waters are famously clean. Oysters from Mali Ston were first farmed by the Romans after Augustus conquered the Illyrian tribes. These days Dalmatian tuna is prized by the Japanese.

Mass tourism has seen some types become rare. Sea dates (*prstaci*), once commonplace, are now a protected species in Croatia, and are smuggled in from the adjoining tiny coastline of Bosnia and Herzegovina. Cooked in white wine and garlic, they are a delicacy beyond compare. Fish farms for striped sea bass (*lubin* or *brancin*) and gilthead sea bream (*orada*) have been set up in Ston and on Brač.

Seafood is prepared in a few set, simple ways, the most common being *buzara*, where the fish is gently poached in a tomato-based sauce. Fish is often just cooked on the grill,

**Istria.**

*na žaru*. Red mullet (*trilja*) is considered perfect for this. *Brodet*, fish stew, is also popular. Seafood risottos are another standard feature, especially *crni rižot* using dark squid ink. If there is any made from cuttlefish, *od sipe*, it has stronger, tastier ink.

Don't be afraid to ask if the fish on offer is fresh, frozen or farmed. You will usually be shown the fresh fish on offer for you to choose from. Fish is priced by the kilo, on average in the 300kn-350kn range, sometimes sold as the pricier 'first class' rather than 'second class' varieties. About half a kilo should be enough for one person. You can ask how much it weighs, or have it weighed.

*Škrpina*, scorpion fish, has deliciously tender meat but it's the devil's own job to pick through the bones. John Dory (*kovač*), golden grey mullet (*cipal*) and the bream family (*pagar*, *arbun* and *pic*) are also common – just ask what's fresh. Dentex is usually excellent.

You'll find grilled squid (*lignje na žaru*) on almost every menu. Octopus (*hobotnica*) is often used as a salad, chopped portions mixed with onion and herbs. The most popular shellfish are scampi (*škampi*), served in their shells, and invariably *buzara* style. Warn children that it won't be neatly packaged in

breadcrumbs. Use your fingers and expect it be pretty messy. Lobster (*jastog*) is invariably the most expensive item on the menu, 500kn a kilo or more.

Continental Croatia – with its two major rivers, the Danube and the Sava – is well known for its freshwater fish, including *šaran* (carp) and *štuka* (pike). *Fiš paprikaš*, freshwater fish stewed in a paprika broth, is a particular favourite. If you're inland but don't want fish, then *čobanac*, a meaty, paprika goulash, is also a regular find.

The classic accompaniment to fish is *blitva*, a local kale dish mixed with potatoes. A simple side salad also goes well.

### THE BOUNTY OF THE LAND

Croatians love their meat. Prime cuts such as *ombolo* (medallion of pork) and beefsteak are cooked quickly, often over an open fire, and served very simply. A favourite is a mixed grill, Balkan *ćevapčići* (minced meatballs) and kebabs, together with typical central European sausages and cutlets. *Pljeskavica* is like a Balkan hamburger. Look for the little jars of Ajvar (paprika and aubergine relish), to garnish your meat – it's on most restaurant tables.

Dishes, such as *Zagrebački odrezak*, a schnitzel stuffed with cheese and ham,

Dalmatia.

reflects a strong Austrian influence, while the hot, spicy *kulen* is a superb salami liberally permeated with paprika, showing the Hungarian influence. Cured meats are a great tradition too, with each region producing their own slightly different versions. *Pršut*, air-cured ham, is a delicacy in Istria and Dalmatia.

You may see roadside spits, roasting whole lambs or pigs, placed outside restaurants as an enticement to passers-by. This practice is typical of the mountainous Gorski Kotar region, which produces some of the finest lamb in Croatia.

Beef is also used in a slow-cooked stew, *pašticada*. *Peka* or *od peke* is the cast-iron dome used to cover meat slow-roasted with hot coals – to get the real deal you often need to order a day in advance. Octopus is also excellent when prepared in this manner.

The saline climate of the islands of Pag and Cres produces exquisite lamb, raised on salty wild herbs – also *paški sir*, sharp sheep's cheese from Pag, dried, matured and prepared with olive oil.

More than 30 per cent of Croatia is covered in forest and hunting is a national pastime. The game widely available is mostly venison and wild boar. This meat is normally slow cooked either by braising on top of the stove

or in rich, meaty goulashes. They are frequently served with Italian-style gnocchi or polenta.

### AND TO DRINK

Wine is either red (*crno*), white (*bijelo*) or rosé (*crveno*), dry (*suho*) or sweet (*slatko*). In Dalmatia, the deep reds are mixed with water as a *bevanda*, the whites in the north with mineral water (*gemišt*). Of the coastal reds, the most renowned (and most expensive) is Dingač. Deep ruby red in colour, and a superb accompaniment to grilled fish (the tradition in Dalmatia), Dingač is produced in the restricted area of the same name on the steep south slopes of the Pelješac peninsula. The grape variety there is Plavac Mali, a cousin of Zinfandel. Native Croatian wine maker Miljenko Grgić, who gained his reputation in Napa Valley, California, came back to his homeland to produce quality wines of the Plavac Mali variety. Postup, also from Pelješac, is equally reputed. Babić from Šibenik is a popular and reasonably priced alternative.

Because of the rocky, limestone soil, southern white wines are mostly dry, such as the golden yellow Pošip, strong in alcohol and from the Čara vineyards of Korčula island. Grk, its name ('Greek') echoing its ancient tradition, is another white from Korčula, from

IN CONTEXT

Lumbarda. Vis is known for Vugava, from the grape of the same name, Krk for Vrbnička Žlahtina. Inland, whites are dominated by the lightweight Graševina.

The primary wine of Istria is Malvasia. Possibly one of the oldest types in Europe, this white grape is grown in over two-thirds of Istria's vineyards. Malvasia is usually dry and it is best drunk young. Because Istria has two distinctive soil types, Malvasia produced near the coast tends to be more robust; grapes from the hinterland provide a more delicate bouquet. Istria's indigenous red wine is Teran, a rich red tipple with a strong, fruity flavour.

Many of Istria's best wines are being produced by a new generation of vintners, who formed Vin Istra (www.vinistra.hr), dedicated to improving the quality of local production and to the promotion of Istrian wines. A Wine Roads trail makes it easy for visitors to find the best cellars and taste these wines first-hand.

Clear fruit brandy (rakija) is the common spirit, and is akin to grappa. Grape brandy is loza. Regional varieties include mistletoe, biska, from Istria. If it grows then some Istrian will have popped it into grappa. Fruits, berries, nuts, herbs, even truffles, the range is truly staggering. Orahovac (walnut) grappa and any number of fruit brandies are sold from small, roadside stalls. In most restaurants you will be offered a complimentary shot of the spirit on settling your bill.

In a recent and welcome development, craft beers such as San Servolo from Istria and Zmajska from Zagreb have been seen in more and more outlets across Croatia, challenging the near duopoly of domestic lagers Ožujsko and Karlovačko.

## VENUES AND MENUS

Dining venues fall into general categories of a standard restoran, a more informal and often family-run gostionica and, best of all, a konoba. The traditional konoba is defined by its rustic atmosphere and authentic approach. Before these popular venues became public, konobas were private cellars with wine barrels, hams hung out to dry, vats of pickled vegetables and fireplaces for preparing food. Today, konobas are the cornerstone of the Adriatic dining experience – old stone houses with heavy wooden tables, fishing nets and perhaps a few traditional implements on display. It feels like dining in someone's living room.

Rather than an elaborate menu, konobas offer no-frills, freshly prepared dishes and a selection of well preserved products. Everything offered should be home-made or locally sourced. The table wine will be universally acceptable – Croatians wouldn't go there otherwise – and various kinds of rakija (brandy) made with herbs, flowers or fruits, will also be on offer.

The jelovnik (menu) is divided rather differently from its British counterpart. First on the list will probably be hladna jela (cold food), the starter or antipasti. Typical dishes might be thin slices of pršut, ovčiji sir (sheep's cheese) or kozji sir (goat's cheese) or perhaps a carpaccio of meat or fish. Then there are the soups, juhe, such as riblja juha (fish) or govdja juha (beef). Mineštra/manistra is a hearty pulse soup, based on pork stock.

Gotova jela – 'finished food' – are the dishes that are pre-prepared in quantity and therefore fast. Gulaš (goulash) would be a typical example, a rich stew usually served with pasta, gnocchi or polenta. Local fuži, pasta twists, are a popular form. Divljač gulaš is game goulash, quite often crna (venison) or svinja (wild boar).

Jela sa roštilja is grilled meat (meso) or fish (riba), also rendered as na žaru. Jela po narudžbi are the house specialities, also known as specijaliteti. These are main courses and the ingredients will depend on which region of Croatia you are dining in. Istria will inevitably offer tartufi (truffles), while in Dalmatia it's likely to be a form of buzara sauce.

Prilozi i salate are side dishes and salads. This will include krumpir (potatoes), blitva (local kale), mješana salata (mixed salad), rajčica (tomato), zelena (green salad) and rokula (rocket). Kruh (bread) may also feature on the menu.

Kolači means cakes and this section of the menu covers puddings in general. As well as pancakes, there's pita od jabuka (apple strudel) and kroštuli, which are tiny, deep-fried doughnuts without the jam. Sladoled is ice-cream. The better establishments offer a digestif at the end of your meal, perhaps a herb grappa (travarica) or fruit brandy (rakija). Coffee (kava) is always strong.

For more menu vocabulary, see p313.

# Nature & Wildlife

Croatia is blessed with 20 national parks and nature parks, from Kopački rit at the country's far eastern border down to Mljet at its southern tip. They take in spectacular waterfalls, challenging mountain climbs and an archipelago of 140 deserted islands. Equally impressive is their wildlife – hundreds of species of birds, bats, plants and reptiles, plus brown bears, lynx, wild boars, snow voles, water shrews and a little community of mongooses that are as much a part of Mljet's identity as its tranquil saltwater lakes or abandoned medieval monastery. On top of this, Croatia's unspoiled landscape and surrounding waters attract an exotic range of creatures whose activities are protected as part of conservation projects or reserves. Dolphins at Blue World in Veli Lošinj and rare griffon vultures on Cres are cared for and monitored in their natural habitat. Visitors may observe them while volunteers can gain experience working close to them. Visitors can also spend a day with falcons at the Dubrava Centre near Šibenik or go on a five-day course in falconry.

## THE PARKS

Since 1949, Croatia has created eight national parks and a dozen nature parks. The oldest, **Plitvice**, is perhaps the most spectacular, with 16 lakes connected by waterfalls. **Krka National Park** (*see p167* **Watery Wonders**) has waterfalls too, as well as plunging rapids and a collection of remote villages. The nature park of **Kopački rit** contains the most prolific birdlife in the region, while **Kornati** (*see p168* **Island Life**), **Mljet** (see p270) and **Brijuni** (*see p76* **Tito's Xanadu**) all offer away-from-it-all diversion. At Brijuni you can even see footprints of creatures who came before: dinosaurs.

## PLITVICE

Just off the motorway between Zagreb and Split, an easy drive from the coast, **Plitvice Lakes** (053 751 015, www.np-plitvice-jezera.

hr) are the crown jewel of Croatia's National Parks, the oldest, most visited and most spectacular. Every year, upwards of a million tourists head past the road sign marked 'NP Plitvicka Jezera' – but don't let this deter you.

Set in the Lika region, known for its war-time hardships in the 1990s and fantastic lamb, Plitvice is home to 1,146 species of plants, 140 types of birds and more than 50 mammals. Most of all, though, people flock here for the series of continually changing, cascading waterfalls and crystal-clear lakes. The dimensions of the 16 lakes have been created from centuries of calcium carbonate deposits, which find home in and on algae, moss and bacteria. This deposit-and-plant combination creates a travertine barrier, a natural dam, which is growing by a couple of centimetres a year. This process, a singular occurrence and the reason Plitvice is included on UNESCO's World Heritage List, means the bodies of water and the waterfalls linking them are always evolving.

Atop these morphing conditions, boardwalks – tasteful enough to appear natural – follow the contours of and criss-cross over the fantastically turquoise water. These walkways, set amid the surrounding beech, spruce and fir forests, give you a fish-eye view of the lakes and falls. Regular trams travel the length of the most visited part of the park, a two-square-kilometre fraction of its near 300 square kilometres (115 square miles), from the upper lakes to the lower ones, and the Veliki slap, or big waterfall. If you start early, you can easily see the area in a day. There are also electric-powered boats to transport visitors across the larger lakes. Although the water looks divine, swimming is strictly forbidden.

A handful of tourist-friendly eateries dot the park. The best known is **Lička kuća** (Entrance 1, 053 751 024, open April to October), a sprawling terrace offering the house speciality of Lička juha sausage stew. Three hotels stand near Entrance 2, including the three-star **Jezero** (Velika poljana, 053 751 500), with doubles around €100. Cheaper still is the nearby **Plitvice** (053 751 100), renovated after the Yugoslav war whose first victim worked here at the park headquarters.

The lake area has two entrances, with parking a few kilometres apart on the old main road between Zagreb and Dalmatia, the E59/ E71. The A1 motorway running parallel to it has turn-offs at Otočac and Gornja Ploča. Buses from Zagreb or Zadar take about three hours and cost about 75kn.

### KOPAČKI RIT

Ten kilometres north-east of Osijek is the Kopački rit nature reserve (031 445 445, pp-kopacki-rit.hr), one of the biggest areas of wetland in Europe and home to more than 200 species of birds. This 23,000-hectare (57-acre) site is a natural maze of

IN CONTEXT

Plitvice.

inter-connected lakes, reeds, woodland and pasture, with a swamp-like atmosphere. The park is at its most spectacular during the spring and autumn floods, when a vast area remains under water for weeks at a time, creating a uniquely soggy habitat for birds and small animals. The lakes support a large population of carp, pike, catfish and perch, alongside an abundance of frogs, snails and insects, preyed on by those higher up the food chain, notably herons and cormorants.

The main entrance is at the Visitor's Centre outside the village of **Kopačevo**, in a traditional thatched hut. Reaching it is difficult without your own transport – it's a good four-kilometre walk from the nearest bus stop in Bilje. From the entrance, there's a pleasant two-kilometre walk to the first dyke, from which you can see a partially sunken forest – you half-expect to see a crocodile hiding in the marshes. This is also the start of the boat trip on *Eagle One* around the park that leaves from a well-signposted jetty (enquire at the entrance for departure times). Other attractions accessible by bike, jeep tour or car include the **Tikveš Hunting Lodge**. This was built for the Archduke Franz Ferdinand, then taken over by Serbian royalty between the wars, before becoming the favourite hunting resort of Tito.

Back in Kopačevo, the **Zeleni zabac** restaurant (Ribarska 3, 031 752 212) has a view of the park. In the park itself, **Kormoran** (031 753 099) is the best known of the eateries. Perch, carp and *fiš paprikaš* are the local specialities. Accommodation options nearby are a small number of bed & breakfasts in traditional peasant houses. **Vaš** (Ribarska 82, 031 752 179) in Kopačevo has two rooms for rent in a scenic courtyard.

**North Velebit.**

The owner, Tibor, is also happy to take you on an unofficial boat tour of the nature reserve, which is right outside the bedroom window, and to lay on home-made food for his guests.

Kopački rit is ten kilometres north-east of Osijek. Most tour agencies in town can arrange trips. **Generalturist** (Kapucinska 39, 031 211 500, www.generalturist.com) and **Cetratour** (Ivana Gundulićeva 61A, 031 372 920, www.cetratour.hr) are two of them.

### NORTH VELEBIT

In many ways, the lesser-known National Park of North Velebit (053 665 380, www. np-sjeverni-velebit.hr) provides the ideal Croatian outdoor experience. You can be atop mountains you've just hiked, enjoying fantastic views of the peninsular, and then be swimming in the Adriatic down below within the hour.

An easy drive from Rijeka or Zadar, Velebit is much wilder and more remote than nearby Plitvice, covering 110 square kilometres (42.5 square miles) of the mountain range of the same name. In the foothills nestle the remote village of Kuterevo and its **bear sanctuary** (Pod crikvom 109, 053 799 001, kuterevo.wordpress.com/bears), designed for brown bears separated from their mothers who would not cope in the wild. Some 70,000 visitors a year come to coo at the orphan cubs – there is a bear trail too.

Velebit is known for its staggering beauty and its unpredictable weather, sudden storms and freezing winds. Prepare yourself and your efforts will be rewarded.

From the North Velebit Information Centre at **Krasno**, a mountain village halfway between the motorway and the coast, the park entrance is a 45-minute slow climb along a bone-shaking and nerve-wracking thoroughfare through the trees. When you emerge on to the plateau, the sheer scale and beauty of your surroundings is surreal. From here, hiking options include the three peaks (each 1,676 metres – 5,500 feet – high) or a trek to the botanical gardens with its 2,000 plant species. Afterwards reward yourself with a hot drink or a warming schnapps at the **Dom Zavizan** lodge. Check for availability of dorm accommodation.

For the more adventurous, the **Premužić trail** is well-trodden but at 57 kilometres (35 miles) can take up to a week to complete. Sleeping huts line the route but there is no food available.

## PAKLENICA

On the southern slopes of the Velebit range, the stark karst river canyon of Paklenica attracts climbers of all ages and abilities. It is easily accessed from the Zagreb–Split motorway. The quality of the minor roads can be a bit hit and miss – an adventure in itself. This part of the Croatian interior is lacking in mass tourism – and infrastructure. You might have trouble finding last-minute accommodation or hiring a bike, but plan it right and you'll enjoy stunning scenery without the hordes.

Smaller than its counterparts Velebit and Plitvice further north, Paklenica National Park

(Dr Franje Tuđmana 14A, 023 369 155, www.np-paklenica.hr) is famous for the canyons of Velika and Mala Paklenica that reach from the sea right up to the mountain peaks. If Velebit is for committed hikers and hardy mountaineers, then Paklenica, with its warmer climate and weird rock formations, attracts casual walkers and amateur rock climbers. Easy, hour-long strolls take you from the sea's edge to a mountain hut. Located near Zadar, Paklenica is perfect for those who don't want to exert themselves or stray too far from the sun-lounger.

The wildlife you will encounter might not be as spectacular as around Plitvice but you could still see a golden eagle, a peregrine falcon or a chamois. Reptiles include the rare, poisonous Orsini's viper. Some 230 species of bird have been recorded, many nesting in the rocks and cliffs around the canyon.

Hikers can look forward to some 200 kilometres (124 miles) of trails, climbers nearly 370 routes with degrees of difficulty from easy to challenging. Casual visitors can stroll around the half-dozen watermills, built in the early 1800s, one restored to full working order.

The park has a camping site (open mid March-mid November) by the main office building. Zadar is a short drive away for those who would prefer to stay in town.

IN CONTEXT

**Paklenica.**

# Sailing

To explore Croatia by sea is to reveal its true secrets. Croatia has it all – the range of sailing options, the spectacular scenery, the unspoiled bays, the myriad islands and, most importantly, clear, calm and clean waters around them. Europe's finest sailing playground is a little over two hours from London. It's affordable, relatively safe (at sea and on shore) and contains a diversity of destinations for sailing routes that are amenable to all. Novice sailors can charter a boat with a qualified skipper, potter round the islands, and find out as much, or as little, about sailing as they'd like. Those who are serious about learning to sail, or improving their skills, can take a course at one of the sailing schools. Sailors of varying abilities, wanting the security and bonhomie of a group, can join a flotilla holiday. If your party includes someone with a skipper's ticket there's a multitude of charter options, with yachts and motorboats, while high rollers can take a fully crewed luxury yacht, classic or contemporary, and cruise the party hotspots.

## WHERE TO GO

It's surprising how much you can see in a week. The diverse appeal of Croatia's 2,000 islands, islets and reefs, together with the varied mainland ports and anchorages, will leave you wanting to come back for more.

In the north, the Istrian peninsula and Kvarner Bay have a high concentration of marinas and a more cosmopolitan feel than Dalmatia, due to the pervasive Italian influence. If gastronomy and culture are important, this may be your cruising area. Stunning and newly popular islands such as Lošinj, Rab and Brijuni are a magnet for luxury yachts. What is lacking is Dalmatia's diversity and sheer number of islands – exploration has fewer surprises than down south.

Kornati is easily reached from the marinas at Zadar, Biograd and Murter. For tranquil wilderness, start from here. With its 152 islands, islets and rocks, the Kornati archipelago is the densest group of islands in the Med. It can be tricky sailing, and the navigator will be working hard counting off the islands and watching out for rocks, but for peace and quiet, it's hard to beat the rugged lunar landscape and deserted bays. It's also something of a gourmet's paradise, with some notable restaurants geared to provide passing sailors and their passengers with good grilled sea bass or steak. The islands around Šibenik are pretty special too – less barren and remote but still largely undiscovered.

On the mainland, Skradin's ACI marina, 12 kilometres (seven miles) upstream from Šibenik, on the River Krka, is a favourite for sailors who want to explore the waterfalls. Tribunj Marina near Vodice and Marina Frapa are two of Croatia's classier marinas, situated in quiet fishing villages. Croatia's first

Hvar.

dedicated superyacht marina and resort area near Šibenik, Turkish-owned D-Resort, opened in summer 2015.

Central Dalmatia meets the requirements of most holidaymakers, starting with the marinas and charter bases within easy reach of Split airport. Brač and Hvar are an easy sail away from Split. Scores of picturesque anchorages and village harbours lie peacefully between the busier and more discovered towns. For a longer sail there's the more remote but gentle island of Vis, and for a Dalmatian time warp try Šolta. High rollers should head to Trogir and Hvar town. After partying all night in Hvar, relax at the neighbouring Pakleni islands, the perfect anchorage to soothe the spirits.

Further south towards Montenegro, Cavtat, on the mainland close to Dubrovnik airport, is another regular superyacht destination. Pelješac is a favourite with experienced sailors for its weather conditions. The picturesque town of Korčula is a popular land-based tourist destination but the island has plenty more to offer. Mljet's saltwater lakes and large bays make for popular anchorages in summer; remote Lastovo has good berthing facilities for passing yachts and a number of restaurants. Close to Dubrovnik, Lopud and Šipan are islands to escape from the metropolis – for both sailors and ferry passengers.

## WHEN TO GO

Avoid late July and August if you can. Italians sail over en masse at the beginning of August and popular marinas and ports can be hard to access in the evening. Charter prices are at their peak and most marinas add ten per cent to mooring fees. May and June can be warm and sunny, with relatively calm weather; however the sea is still warming up so can be a little bracing at times. September is great for sea temperatures but, as with May and June, you may well find that some of the restaurants in the more remote destinations are closed. Serious sailors may prefer the more challenging weather conditions in April and October or perhaps want to join in a winter sailing regatta.

Marina Dalmacija, Sukošan.

## HARBOURS AND MARINAS

Most boats are surprisingly luxurious, with toilets, showers, electricity, gas, usually ample kitchen/diner space, comfortable cabins and plenty of room on deck to eat, drink, sunbathe and be merry. But where do you park? Do you choose marinas, village harbours or anchorages? Most people opt for a mixture.

There are more than 50 marinas in Croatia, about half of them state-owned, recognisable by the acronym ACI. Planned and built ahead of its time, the ACI network ensured you could always find a safe haven almost wherever you were in the Croatian Adriatic. Now you're spoiled for choice but the demand for space is still high. Overnighting in a marina is great for improving the confidence of inexperienced crew and for a little extra comfort. You'll be moored on lazy lines (see p302) and protected by a breakwater that reduces the motion of the boat to a very gentle sway. You'll always have access to toilets, showers, shore power and water, though the electricity and water supply may be restricted on the more remote islands.

Often there'll be a restaurant, shop and café, and sometimes you'll find nightclubs, swimming pools and other entertainment. Comfort costs money and most of the marinas have hiked their prices in recent years by between five and 15 per cent. That said, Croatia is still good value compared with Greece and Turkey. The intangible cost is the change in atmosphere: one minute the waves are lapping against the sides of the boat, the wind is blowing out the sails and there's no one in sight; the next the skipper is wedging your floating hotel into a tight space between two loud boats full of partygoers. Be prepared.

On the other hand, there's nothing like being lulled to sleep by nature and waking up in the morning in glorious sunshine to have a quick dip, off the back of the diving platform, in your own bay. Your charter boat will have a tender (a rubber dinghy) to get you to the shop or restaurant ashore without getting wet. You'll have the choice of paying extra for an outboard motor if you don't have the energy to row. Anchoring can be idyllic but occasionally novices find it hard to get used to. A local skipper will know the best bays given the prevailing conditions and your preferences. Otherwise, consult a good cruising guide and check the charts. In some anchorages, particularly Kornati and the Zadar area, someone will come round and collect a fee. Very occasionally, a local entrepreneur may also try to charge for anchoring, so politely check credentials.

Berthing in a village or town harbour can give you the best of both worlds. You'll normally pay less than at a marina, many have shore power and water, some have toilets and showers, and you'll generally get the protection of a breakwater and the stability of lazy-line moorings. Depending on location, you probably won't be berthed like sardines, as in a marina, and you'll be able to walk off the boat to the nearest restaurant. Some restaurants in otherwise deserted bays also have lazy-line berthing on pontoons, sometimes with electricity and water.

## TIDES AND LINES

Croatia has practically no tidal differences to worry about and only occasional strong currents, in channels or at river mouths. Summer weather is normally calm and sunny, though you will get the odd thunderstorm roughing up the sea. Croatia's Meteorological and Hydrological site (meteo.hr) has detailed weather forecasts on the Adriatic in English. The mighty Bura wind from the north-east is usually only a problem in winter but deserves respect year round. Weather forecasts in English are easily available at marinas, from the harbourmaster or on the radio, and locals are always happy to fill you in on climate tips. The cooling Maestral wind is predominant in summer but you may end up motor sailing for a few days if winds are light.

At most marinas and ports and in many bays with piers, using the lazy line is the standard method of berthing. Normally, when you approach a destination with lazy-line berths, someone comes to meet you on the quay or pontoon and holds up a rope. Heading in forwards allows for a little more privacy on deck but most prefer reversing in – it's easier to get on and off for a start. So, heading in backwards, someone stands at the back with a boat hook (normally supplied), picks up the raised rope, walks with it along to the front of

the boat, pulls it in and secures it to the cleat on the front. Simultaneously, two other members of crew should be ready at the back of the boat with coiled ropes, already tied to the cleats on both sides of the back end. The ropes should be passed under the bottom rail and back over the top rail towards you so that when you throw the rope, it pulls directly on the cleat and not over or under a rail. As the boat reverses in, throw one rope to the person on land who's helping you berth and he will secure it; then throw the other rope. It's worth practising the throw a little to measure the weight of the ropes and to avoid hitting anyone in the face or chucking the ropes straight in the water. Don't worry though if you make a mistake – the locals have seen it all.

## PRACTICALITIES

Book early, shop around and avoid the peak months of July and August. Check the charter company small print for extras – final clean, outboard motor for the dinghy, extra sails, towels, and so on – and make absolutely sure your boat has a bimini, a cockpit cover for protection against the sun. You also need to budget for fuel, onboard provisions, flights, transfers, eating out and the odd night at a hotel if you can't get your flights to coincide with the charter period, which normally runs from Saturday to Friday.

For novices, a basic one week's charter of a Bavaria 46, from **BavAdria Charter** (www. bavadria.com), with plenty of room for four people and a skipper, will cost around €2,500 in late September and around €3,500 in late July/early August. A skipper will cost €125 per day plus food and if you stay in a marina every night, allow around €70 per day (double for a catamaran), though some of the town and village ports are well equipped and much cheaper. Only some anchorages charge a fee.

**One Stop Sailing** (www.onestopsailing. co.uk) offers RYA courses at Split and caters for singles as well as families and groups. Depending on the level and the time of year, the price per person per week starts from around €650. Flights, transfers and evening meals are excluded but you won't need to dig into your wallet for much else.

**Sunsail** (www.sunsail.com) organises regular flotilla getaways around Dalmatia. The price goes up or down according to the size of yacht and how many are sharing it. If you don't need a skipper, take your pick from the yachts and motorboats. An Elan 333, just over ten metres in length, provides ample space for two and is relatively easy to manage. A week in early September, chartering from **Feral Tours** (feral-tours.com) in Zadar, costs around €1,250 before discounts; €1,600 in August.

In a recent development, **Sail Croatia** (www.sail-croatia.com) has instigated party boats for the 21-35 age group, with disco lights, fog machine and outdoor bar. Its 44-passenger Maestral calls in at club hubs down the coast.

For jet setters there's even more choice, with many charter companies offering larger yachts and motorboats. **Ocean Blue** (www. oceanblueyachts.com) can charter you a Sunseeker Predator 95 in an all-inclusive weekly package but you'll be looking at something approaching €90,000. For yacht and crew only, it's nearer €65,000. A classic Galatea yacht is around €40,000 a week

in peak season from **Exclusive Travel** (exclusivetravelcroatia.com). **Dalmatian Destinations** (www. dalmatiandestinations. com) has some of the largest yachts in Croatia for charter.

Modern yachts and motorboats are designed to maximise storage space but leave your rigid suitcases behind and pack everything in fold-away bags. Sunscreen, shades and a hat are essential; long sleeved shirts and a warm jumper are advisable; waterproofs hopefully won't be necessary but can be a godsend if you're unlucky with the weather. Plastic, rubber or jelly shoes protect against stony beaches and sea urchins, whose spikes are painful but not life-threatening. Charts and guides are provided but check if snorkelling gear is on board. Most charter boats will have a CD player. Lifejackets and other essential safety equipment are supplied, as are kitchen essentials.

Sail Croatia.

# Essential Information

# Getting Around

ESSENTIAL INFORMATION

## ARRIVING BY AIR

The main international airports are **Dubrovnik**, **Pula**, **Rijeka**, **Split**, **Zadar** and **Zagreb**. **Brač** is used for charters, domestic internal and budget central European and Scandinavian services. **Osijek** has also just joined the budget rosters. All airports except Pula have transfers into town, usually a bus costing around 35kn.

Since 2014, a seaplane service has run from Split, currently running to Jelsa on Hvar and Mali Lošinj. Operators European Coastal Airlines (www.ec-air.eu) is hoping to expand its roster in the near future.

## ARRIVING BY BOAT

Croatia is accessible from Italy by sea. There are a number of routes, the main ones being from Ancona, Pescara and Bari to Split, Hvar, Zadar and Dubrovnik.

Croatia's main passenger line is **Jadrolinija** (051 666 111, www.jadrolinija.hr). Other companies operating routes between Italy and Croatia are **SNAV** (Ancona to Split; Pescara to Hvar, Bol and Vela Luka; snav.it); **Blue Line** (Ancona to Split and Hvar; www.blueline-ferries.com), and **Venezia Lines** (Venice to Poreč, Pula, Rovinj and Umag; 052 422 896; www.venezialines.com). All inhabited Croatian islands are well connected either with ferries or fast boats. Most are operated by Jadrolinija, while local companies include **Bura Line** (www.buraline.com) that serves Trogir.

## ARRIVING BY TRAIN

Croatia has direct train connections with Austria, Bosnia-Hercegovina, Germany, Hungary, Italy, Serbia, Slovenia and Switzerland. The domestic rail network is not very developed, so while Zagreb, Rijeka and Split are linked by train, you cannot get to Dubrovnik.

On the routes it does run, the train service is slow but affordable. A first-class ticket on the InterCity service from Zagreb to Split costs around 250kn, second-class 170kn, with three trains a day, and overnight trains in season.

Information on rail links between Croatia and other countries, as well as on internal routes, can be obtained from **Croatian Railways** (060 333 444, www.hzpp.hr).

If you intend visiting Croatia on an Inter-rail pass, you can choose between the Interrail Global Pass and the One Country Pass. See www.interrail.eu. Getting to Croatia from the UK involves three or four changes but you can book this route online.

## DRIVING

The rules of the road are stringent: seat belts must be used front and rear, and using a mobile while driving is forbidden. No under-12s are allowed in the front seat. In winter, you must drive with your lights on. Croatia has a permitted blood alcohol level of 0.05%, except if you are responsible for any traffic accident, in which case any alcohol level in blood is a violation.

The speed limit is 50km/h (30mph) in built up areas, 90km/h (56mph) outside built up areas, 110km/h (70mph) on major routes designed for motor vehicles, and 130km/h (80mph) on motorways. Croatia has an excellent network of motorways, those with tolls are marked with green signs. Tolls are paid at the end of the journey, and routes and prices are available online: www.hac.hr; www.arz.hr; www.bina-istra.com; www.azm.hr.

In the event of an accident, you must contact the police on 192, or general emergency number 112.

English-language traffic reports are given on radio HR2 throughout the day. Frequencies for different parts of Croatia are available on www.radio.hrt.hr/drugi-program/frekvencije. Updates are also posted on the website of the Croatian Automobile Club (072 777 777, www.hak.hr), or call for information. Road assistance is available on 1987.

To enter Croatia by car you need a valid driving licence with a photograph, vehicle registration documents and insurance documents. The Green Card is not needed for vehicles from the EU.

### Car hire

Car hire in Croatia is expensive – about 500kn a day for an average family car. Try and get some quotes online before you travel to avoid any nasty surprises when you arrive. Drivers must be over 21 and must have held their driving licence for at least one year.

**Dollar** 021 399 000, www.subrosa.hr.
**Hertz** 062 727 277, www.hertz.hr.
**Oryx** 01 29 00 333, www.oryx-rent.hr.
**Thrifty Croatia** 021 398 800, www.subrosa.hr.

## BUSES

Croatia is part of the **Eurolines** network but journey times can be immense; London to Croatia takes more than 36 hours. For more details contact Eurolines' UK partner **National Express** (08705 143 219, www.nationalexpress.com). For travel from elsewhere in Europe v isit www.eurolines.com.

Within Croatia, many private companies run frequent services between the main towns, either on local roads or via the motorway, especially between Zagreb and Split, and further to Dubrovnik. Leading companies include **AutoTrans** (www.autotrans.hr) and **Promet Makarska** (www.promet-makarska.hr). Good resources are the timetable on the websites for Zagreb www.akz.hr and Split bus stations www.ak-split.hr.

Note that a nominal fee is charged for luggage – keep small change to give to the driver as you board.

## TAXIS

Taxis can be found in all towns and resorts. They are not cheap but can be a lifeline if you've missed the last bus on an island. A tip is expected.

## CYCLING

Cycling isn't big with the locals and the main roads are not particularly cycle friendly. Cycling for tourists is growing, as is mountain biking, with agencies organising tours. Information on bike tracks and mountain biking in central Dalmatia can be found at www.dalmatia.hr. Istria is also better developed for cyclists – see www.istria-bike.com. Try also www.findcroatia.com for a list of links for agencies and websites.

## WALKING

Cicerone (www.cicerone.co.uk) publishes *Walking in Croatia*, while Sunflower books (www.sunflowerbooks.co.uk), issues the hiking guide *Landscapes of Croatia*. For hiking and other active tourism in central Dalmatia see www.dalmatia.hr.

# Resources A-Z

## AGE RESTRICTIONS

The age of consent in Croatia is 18. You must be 18 to buy cigarettes or drink alcohol.

## BUSINESS

Croatia has readily embraced market capitalism. Some of the inefficiencies of the old system remain, but Croats are in fact natural-born capitalists.

Personal relationships are important – getting to know people over meals or simply coffee goes a long way to ensuring smooth business relations.

There are a number of organisations offering advice and contacts including, in Zagreb, the **British Croatian Business Club** (www.bcbc.org.uk) and the **American Chamber of Commerce** (01 48 36 777, www.amcham.hr). In London a good point of first contact is the **British Croatian Chamber of Commerce** (www.britishchambercroatia.com).

Other sources of information are the subscription-only *Croatia Business Report* (www.croatia businessreport.com) and the book *Doing Business with Croatia* published by Global Market Briefings (www.globalmarket briefings.com).

## CHILDREN

Croatians have a very Mediterranean attitude towards children and treat them as little grown-ups. They are generally allowed into restaurants and cafés without any fuss. Croatia may be a major holiday destination, with famously clean seas, but be warned that its beaches are mainly stony and children should wear plastic sandals to avoid sharp rocks or lurking, spiky sea urchins.

## CUSTOMS

Croatia is a member of the European Union, and all EU rules and regulations now apply. The import and export of Croatian currency is limited to 15,000kn. The import and export of foreign currency is unlimited but it's compulsory to declare amounts exceeding the equivalent of €10,000.

If you are travelling within the EU, there is no limit on the amount or value of goods for personal consumption. Importing goods for commercial purposes, the limits are 800 cigarettes, 400 cigarillos, 200 cigars or 1kg of tobacco; ten litres of spirits stronger than 22 per cent; 20 litres of alcoholic beverage under 22 per-cent strength; 90 litres of wine (no more than 60 litres of sparkling wine) and 110 litres of beer.

If arriving from a non-EU country, passengers older than 17 can import 200 cigarettes, 100 cigarillos, 50 cigars or 250g of tobacco; four litres of wine; 16 litres of beer; one litre of spirits over 22 per cent or two litres of alcoholic beverages under. Other goods are allowed up to the value of 3,200kn for air and sea passengers; 2,200kn for others and 1,100kn for children under 15.

Valuable professional and technical equipment needs to be declared at the border (just to be sure that it leaves with you again).

Anything that might be considered a cultural artefact, art or archaeological finds, can only be exported with official approval. For more information visit the customs website at www.carina.hr.

## DISABLED TRAVELLERS

Croatia is not as enlightened as other countries when it comes to providing facilities for the disabled. That is changing as a result of the large number of people left handicapped by the fighting in the 1990s.

It's vital that prior to travel you ask your hotel whether it has disabled access and facilities – a number of hotels do, but not all. **Hrvatski savez udruga tjelesnih invalida** *Šoštarićeva 8, Zagreb (01 481 2004, www.hsuti.hr).* Croatian Union of Physically Disabled Persons Associations.

## DRUGS

Croatia is a transit point for drug smuggling. Penalties for use, possession and trafficking of drugs are severe. Offenders can expect prison sentences and/or large fines. Since the war, Croatia has had to cope with a significant drugs problem among its youth.

## ELECTRICITY

Croatia uses a 220V, 50Hz voltage and continental two-pin plugs. Visitors from the UK require an adaptor.

## EMBASSIES & CONSULATES

**Australian Embassy**
*Kaptol Centar, Nova Ves 11, Zagreb (01 48 91 200, www.croatia.embassy. gov.au).* **Open** 8.30am-4.30pm Mon-Fri.

**British Embassy**
*Ivana Lučića 4, Zagreb (01 60 09 100, www.gov.uk/government/world/ croatia).* **Open** 8.30am-5pm Mon-Thur; 8.30am-2pm Fri.

**British Consulates**
*Obala Hrvatskog Narodnog Preporoda 10/III, Split (021 346 007, british-consulat-st@ st.htnet.hr); Vukovarska 22/1, Dubrovnik (020 324 597, zagreb. consular@fco.gov.uk).*

**Canadian Embassy**
*Prilaz Gjure Deželića 4, Zagreb
(01 48 81 200, www.canada
international.gc.ca/croatia-croatie).*
**Open** *May-Sept* 10am-noon, 1-3pm
Mon-Thur; 10am-1pm Fri. *Apr-Oct*
10am-noon, 1-3pm Mon-Fri.

**Irish Embassy**
*Miramarska 23, Zagreb (01 631
0025, www.dfa.ie/irish-embassy/
croatia).* **Open** 8am-noon, 2-3pm
Mon-Fri.

**New Zealand Consulate**
*Vlaška ulica 50A, Zagreb (01
4612 060, nzealandconsulate@
email.t-com.hr).* **Open** 8am-noon,
1.30-3pm Mon-Fri.

**US Embassy**
*Ulica Thomas Jeffersona 2,
Zagreb (01 66 12 200, www.zagreb.
usembassy.gov).* **Open** 8am-4.30pm
Mon-Fri.

Details of other embassies and
consulates can be found on the
website of the Croatian Ministry
for Foreign Affairs at www.mvep.
hr/en/diplomatic-directory/
diplomatic-missions-and-consular-
offices-to-croatia).

## EMERGENCIES

In case of an emergency the
numbers to call are: **112** for general
emergencies; **192** for the police;
**193** for the fire brigade; **194** for
an ambulance; and **195** for search
and rescue at sea.

## GAY & LESBIAN

Homosexuality was decriminalised
in Croatia in 1977, and it is forbidden
to discriminate against anyone on
the grounds of their sexuality.
However, it's only in the last few
years that gay and lesbian groups
have had any sort of profile and
begun to make assertions of their
rights – and not without opposition.
In June 2011, the first Gay Pride
march took place in Split and was
fiercely attacked by homophobic
groups. As a reaction, more
participants gathered in 2012,
since when there have been no
further incidents. The group Queer
Zagreb (www.queerzagreb.org)
organises a festival of gay art in
Zagreb every April, and screenings
of gay films every third weekend of
the month at the Tuškanac cinema
(Tuškanac 1, Zagreb, www.
queerzagreb.org/film).

For an excellent web-based
gay guide to Croatia, with all gay-
friendly locations and venues go to
www.friendlycroatia.com. The
International Gay and Lesbian

Travel Association (www.iglta.org)
offers an online directory of gay- and
lesbian-friendly travel businesses.
British travellers can check Travel at
www.thegayuk.com.

## HEALTH

Croatia has a reciprocal medical
agreement with the United Kingdom
that means – in theory at least – that
British passport holders are entitled
to free hospital and dental treatment
during their stay in Croatia. Even so,
we recommend investing in travel
insurance because public facilities
are not always available and,
particularly in the case of an
emergency, you may need to go
private. Since Croatia joined the EU,
the European Health Insurance Card
(EHIC) is valid in all member states,
meaning that citizens can receive
certain medical treatment in another
member state for free or at a reduced
cost. It is not, however, a substitute
for full travel insurance. Details
about the card, who can have it,
where you can get treatment, and
what it covers, can be found here:
www.nhs.uk/NHSEngland/
Healthcareabroad/EHIC/Pages/
about-the-ehic.aspx. Non-EU visitors
must pay for any treatment, so travel
insurance is strongly recommended.
The standard of medical care in
Croatia is generally good.

### Contraception

Condoms are available from
pharmacies, kiosks and groceries.

### Dentists & doctors

Pharmacists (*see right*) are usually
able to help with minor complaints,
but for proper medical care your
best bet is to go to the local hospital
or emergency unit where a duty
doctor can have a look at you.
*See above* for medical insurance.

The address and telephone
numbers of general hospitals in
Dubrovnik (*see p252*), Split (*see
p200*) and Zagreb (*see p69*) are
given in their relevant chapters
in this guide.

### Opticians

You will need to pay for optical care.
Every main town centre has optician
stores (look for *optičar* or *optika*), and
you should be able to get replacement
lenses and frames easily, usually
within a day. Some only sell glasses
but even those usually have contracts
with surgeries where they can send
you to have your sight checked.

### Pharmacies

Pharmacies are usually open from
7am to 8pm during the week, and
until 2 or 2.30pm on Saturdays. In
larger towns there will normally
be some pharmacies that are
open 24hrs, seven days a week.
Prescriptions need to be paid for.

### STDs, HIV & AIDS

Croatia has one of the lowest rates
of HIV/AIDS in Europe. There are
ten facilities for free testing in the
country. Contact the Ministry of
Health on 01 46 07 555, www.
zdravlje.hr.

## HOTELS

The Croatian tourist board website
(www.croatia.hr) has a decent
accommodation search facility that
includes both hotels and private
rooms. Website www.goadriatica.
com offers similar facilities. Most
local tourist offices will not book a
hotel (or private) room for you, but
will provide you with a list of places
and phone numbers. Private travel
agencies, set up in all main towns,
should be able to accommodate. The
most obvious choice for a unique and
memorable place to stay is in a
lighthouse (www.lighthouses-
croatia.com). Some dozen such
remote settings have been converted
into three-star accommodation units.
Villa rental is slowly taking off, led
by Istria's Villas Forum (www.
villasforum.com), which set the
benchmark on how to renovate
run-down regional properties.

## ID

Although it's unlikely that you will
ever be asked to show it, you are
supposed to carry some form of
picture ID on your person while in
Croatia. Rather than risk losing
your passport, UK residents are
recommended to get the credit-
card style photo driving licence.

## INSURANCE

Travellers should take out
comprehensive travel insurance,
especially if you are going to indulge
in any risky sports – climbing,
skiing, mountain biking – although
check the small print first to see if
such activities are covered by your
policy. If you are going to take
expensive equipment make sure that
it's also covered. If you need to claim,
make sure you get all the paperwork
from medical staff or police.

## INTERNET ACCESS

Most towns have a handful of internet cafés and rates are usually reasonable. However, their number is decreasing thanks to free Wi-Fi access becoming almost standard everywhere – not only in hotels, restaurants, bars, and airports, but in entire towns, such as Rijeka.

## LANGUAGE

English is widely spoken, and not only by Croats in the tourist industry. Most, if not all, tourist offices will have an English speaker and tourist information material is usually also available in English. Many people in Istria and on the coast speak Italian as well.

## LEGAL ADVICE

If you get in trouble with the authorities you should get in touch immediately with your local embassy or consulate (see p307).

## LOST PROPERTY

Every airport has a lost-luggage office. Croatia's main national bus company, Autotrans, provides a lost-luggage request form at https://www.autotrans.hr/en-us/luggage.

## MEDIA

Croatian newspapers and magazines are available from kiosks. The best-selling national daily paper is *Večernji List* followed by *Jutarnji List*. Both are European-owned and follow the line of their publishers. The third best-seller is *Slobodna Dalmacija*, a Dalmatia-based paper with news from the coast.

*Sportske Novosti* is the main sports daily, carrying the football results from across Europe including the top two divisions in England.

Croatia also has a number of weeklies. The most significant is *Nacional*, which has pulled off some major scoops in recent times. Most notable was an interview with Croat general Ante Gotovina, while he was a fugitive from UN prosecutors. Another weekly, *Globus*, competes with *Nacional* on stories. Other weeklies include more tabloid-oriented *Gloria* and *Story*.

Croatian papers tend to be less prudish than similar mid-range British ones – expect bare flesh to be on display now and then. Pornographic magazines are more openly on display in Croatia than would be expected in Britain.

Many British and European newspapers and magazines are also available from Tisak kiosks, usually one, sometimes two days late.

## Radio

There are some 200 licensed radio stations in Croatia. Of the three main state-run stations, HR1 and HR2 broadcast politics, documentaries, entertainment music and sport. HR3 has a cultural and spiritual agenda. HR1 also carries occasional English-language broadcasts and HR2 has news, weather reports and road reports in several languages during the summer season. Some of these are also available on Glas Hrvatska, HRT's external service. There are plenty of commercial alternatives.

## Television

There are four main TV stations. HRT1, HRT2, HRT3 and HRT4 are state-run and screen news, drama, documentaries and sports programmes. Nova TV and RTL are privately owned with national reach and there are also a number of local TV stations. Most of Croatia is covered with cable TV, from several providers, and many international channels are widely available.

Croatian TV shows a lot of TV series and films from the US and Britain. These are always subtitled.

## MONEY

The Croatian **kuna** (kn) is divided into 100 lipa. Coins are issued in denominations of 10, 20 and 50 lipa, and 1, 2 and 5kn. Notes come in denominations of 10, 20, 50, 100, 200, 500 and 1,000kn. Euros are not generally accepted – Croatia is a member of the EU but not the eurozone – but some hotels, restaurants and bars in tourist areas accept them.

Prices in Croatia can roughly be compared to Western Europe. Local goods and those from neighbouring states are a little cheaper; those imported from the West are more expensive. Public transport, cinema, cultural institutions, and drinking and dining in local places generally cost less here than in the West.

Foreign currency may be exchanged in banks, post offices, most tourist agencies, bureaux de change and at some hotels. Usually, there is no commission, but check a couple of places before changing, especially at small exchange offices. Don't ever accept offers from people approaching you on the street.

## ATMs

ATMs are easy enough to find in main towns but are sometimes scarcer in the provinces. Instructions appear in English and all major cards are covered.

## Banks

Banks are usually open 8am-7pm Monday to Friday, and 8am-noon on Saturdays.

## Credit & debit cards

Most hotels, shops and restaurants accept Eurocard, MasterCard, Diners Club, American Express and Visa, as well as debit cards. However, do ask, especially in bars and restaurants.

## NATURAL HAZARDS

There are mosquitoes in Croatia, so it's a good idea to pack repellent. Croatia also has two species of poisonous snake, the horned viper and the common adder. In the unlikely event of being bitten, try not to panic, keep the bitten area as still as possible and get to a hospital immediately. Far more rare are scorpions and Mediterranean black widow spiders. If you're stung, the advice is the same as with snakes.

In fact, the only regular hazard you're likely to encounter are sea urchins, the small spiky black creatures who sit on the rocks just below the water surface of the shore. waiting for the unwary. They are not poisonous but their spikes can be painful. Wear sandals or flip-flops.

Apart from that, by far the most common natural hazard is tourists being too adventurous. Follow instructions for hiking, climbing, kayaking and the other outdoor activities that are becoming increasingly popular in Croatia. This means you should bring enough water and wear appropriate shoes and clothes. In case of emergency, dial 112, and the Croatia Mountain Rescue Service (HGSS) or some other organisation will come to your aid. However, the very first rule is: don't put yourself in a position where you have to call out the Croatia Mountain Rescue Service.

## OPENING TIMES

Public sector offices and most businesses usually operate from 8am to 4pm Mondays to Fridays. Post offices are open from 7am to 7pm, and generally close at weekends, except the larger ones on Saturday mornings. Shops open from 8am to 8pm weekdays and until 2 or 3pm on Saturdays, although in summer some stay open much longer, usually until 9 or 10pm. Shopping malls are open at least till 9pm.

## POSTAL SERVICES

Stamps are available from post offices, and from newspaper and tobacco kiosks. Mail across Europe takes less than a week; to the US it's about seven to ten days. International postcards and letters should cost about 10kn.

## RELIGION

Croatia is 87.8% Roman Catholic (4.4% Orthodox, 0.4% other Christian and 1.3% Muslim).

Most towns and villages have a patron saint whose day will be celebrated once a year, usually with a procession and festival.

## SAFETY

Croatia has a low crime rate. Even so, don't be too showy with expensive possessions and don't wander around poorly lit city areas. Follow the same rules that you would at home and you'll be OK.

Foreign women may not appreciate the amount of attention they get from local men, especially those in coastal areas. If it's in danger of crossing the line between flirtation and harrassment don't be shy of making your displeasure clearly known.

### Landmines

Landmines are a problem in parts of the countryside close to former frontlines. Look out for signs bearing a skull and crossbones and stay well clear. However, not all minefields are marked and it is definitely not advisable to wander around any abandoned villages or across any uncultivated fields. In war-affected areas such as eastern and western Slavonia, the area between Karlovac and Knin or Drniš, and in inland parts of the Zadar area, do not stray away from the main roads or clearly marked footpaths.

## SMOKING

Many Croats smoke and it is a far more socially acceptable habit than in the UK or US. Smoking is not permitted in public buildings and cinemas, and on public transport. Smoking is prohibited indoors in restaurants, but allowed in cafés

and bars with a terrace or indoor ventilation. Completely smoke-free cafés and bars are rare. Cigarettes are bought from kiosks, news-stands, groceries and gas stations. Most major Western brands of cigarettes are available.

## STUDY

If you are looking to study Croatian, many local universities offer summer schools and short courses, including the University of Zagreb (www. unizg.hr). The Croatian Heritage Foundation (01 6115 116, www.matis. hr) also runs summer schools in conjunction with the university.

In London, the Croatian Language School (020 8948 5771, www. easycroatian.com) runs intensive immersion courses.

**University of Osijek** *Trg Sv Trojstva 3, Osijek (031 224 102, www.unios.hr).*

**University of Rijeka** *Trg braće Mažuranića 10, Rijeka (051 406 500, www.uniri.hr).*

**University of Split** *Livanjska 5, Split (021 558 222, www.unist.hr).*

**University of Zadar** *Ulica Mihovila Pavlinovica 1, Zadar (023 200 665, www.unizd.hr).*

**University of Zagreb** *Trg maršala Tita 14, Zagreb (01 45 64 111, www. unizg.hr).*

## TELEPHONES

The dialling code for Croatia is +385. Croatian town and city codes have a zero in front of them that must be left off when calling from overseas.

When calling overseas from Croatia, the prefix 00 is the international access code.

### Public phones

Public telephones use cards bought from post offices, kiosks, petrol stations and stores. They come in values of 15kn, 30kn, 50kn and 100kn, and can be used for local and international calls. Local calls cost 0.80kn per minute, 3kn per minute to neighbouring countries, 3.50kn to the rest of Europe and 5kn per minute to Australia and the USA. Calls elsewhere cost 10kn per minute.

It may be more convenient to place a call from one of the booths that you'll find set up at most post offices.

### Mobile phones

Croatia relies on the mobile. After Croatia joined the EU, roaming prices for EU citizens went down sharply – now it's almost equal to

local rates. Other countries are still subjected to roaming agreements with foreign companies, with significant expenses. You can purchase a local SIM card with a pre-paid subscription; cards with some starter airtime are available, although you should make sure your mobile is unlocked. Several operators still offer pre-paid cards, most notably: T-mobile (www.hrvatskitelekom.hr); Tele2 (www.tele2.hr); and Vipnet (www.vipnet.hr). Their stores are usually centrally positioned in most major towns, and cards can be upgraded at every kiosk or a petrol station where you can buy a voucher for any provider. Vouchers are available in values anywhere between 25kn and 200kn, depending on the operator.

## TIME

Croatia is in the Central European time zone (CET), an hour ahead of GMT and six hours ahead of Eastern Standard Time. The clocks go forward an hour in spring and back an hour in autumn.

## TIPPING

Tipping is expected by taxi drivers and waiters in restaurants. Round up bills to the next 10kn-20kn, or by about ten per cent. You don't need to tip in pubs and cafés, unless you have received special service and have been there for a while.

## TOILETS

Most cafés and bars have toilets – although the staff would probably prefer it if you bought a drink before or after using them. Toilets in train stations, airports and other public areas will sometimes have a lady stationed at the door to collect a user fee of around 2-4kn – keep a few coins handy on long bus journeys. Universal signs will be placed on the toilet doors to indicate men's and ladies', or look out for M (men's) and Ž (ladies'). Shopping malls and larger department stores also have toilets. Most tourist towns have a handful of public toilets, usually accessed for a couple of coins.

## TOURIST INFORMATION

All cities, towns and even a number of villages have tourist information offices. There will usually be at least one person who speaks English. Levels and quality of service are variable, but all of them work under the umbrella of the Croatian National Tourist Board. Its main website, www.croatia.hr, is reasonably comprehensive and has links to all local tourist boards.

### Croatian National Tourist Office (UK) *Suite 4C, Elsinore House, 77 Fulham Palace Road, London W6 8JA (020 8563 7979, www. gb.croatia.hr).* Open 10am-4pm Mon-Fri.

## TOUR OPERATORS

There are literally hundreds of tour operators selling all kinds of holidays in Croatia. The Croatian National Tourist Office in London (*see above*) has a more extensive register, and many of them are available via the Croatian Tourist Board (www.croatia.hr).
**Adventure Company** *(01420 541 007, www.adventurecompany.co.uk).* Active breaks around Dalmatia: rafting; diving; canoeing; mountain biking and horse riding.
**Andante Travels** *(01722 713 800, www.andantetravels.co.uk).* Archaeological tours of Dalmatia including Split, Salona and Brač.
**Arblaster & Clarke Wine Tours** *(01730 893 244, www.winetours. co.uk).* Wine tours.
**Bond Tours** *(01372 745 300, www. bondtours.com).* Includes tailor-made trips, apartments, fly-drive and adventure tours.
**Bosere Travel** *(0143 834 094, www. bosmeretravel.co.uk).* Specialist trips to Croatia including naturist, diving, painting and trekking.
**goadriatica.com** *(01 24 15 614, www.goadriatica.com).* Zagreb-based company specialising in lighthouse holidays and trips for special events.
**Hidden Croatia** *(0871 208 0075, www.hiddencroatia.com).* Breaks and tailor-made holidays.
**Holiday Options** *(0870 0130 450, www.holidayoptions.co.uk).* Large range of holidays in Croatia.
**Nautilus Yachting** *(01732 867 445, www.nautilus-yachting.com).* Sailing holidays.
**Peng Travel** *(0845 345 8345, www.pengtravel.co.uk).* Naturist breaks in Istria.
**Saga Holidays** *(0800 300 500, www.saga.co.uk).* Large list of destinations in Croatia.
**Sail Croatia** *(020 7751 9988/0871 733 8686, www.sailcroatia.net).* Specialists in sailing holidays for beginners upwards.
**Scuba En Cuba** *(01895 624 100, www.scuba-en-cuba).* Since moved into Croatia, offering diving holidays in Dubrovnik and on Korčula island.

**Simply Croatia** *(020 8541 2214, www.simplytravel.com).* Flights from Bristol, London and Manchester to properties in rural Istria, Kvarner and Dalmatia.
**Thomson Holidays** *(0870 060 0847, www.thomson.co.uk).* Large range of holidays in Croatia.
**Travelsphere** *(01858 410 818, www.travelsphere.co.uk).* Coach travel.
**2 Wheel Treks Cycling** *(0845 612 6106, www.2wheeltreks.co.uk).* Cycling and cruise trips to Istria and Dalmatia.

## VISAS

Visitors from the European Union, Canada, USA, Australia and New Zealand do not need a visa if staying in Croatia for less than 90 days. Since 2014, citizens of countries already with a visa for a Schengen country can enter Croatia. If you're travelling between Split and Dubrovnik, you have to pass a small stretch of coastline around **Neum**, in the territory of Bosnia-Hercegovina. Buses and cars are stopped and identity documents checked.

## WEIGHTS & MEASURES

Croatia uses the metric system.

## WHEN TO GO

Croatia's Adriatic coast benefits from a typically Mediterranean climate, with hot summers. The average summer temperature is about 25C and in winter 12C. To avoid the crowds go in May, early June or September and early October, when the weather is slightly cooler and hotels are much cheaper. On the coast, winters and early spring and autumn are usually mild, with quite a lot of sunny days, so it can be pleasant to travel in March and April as well – and ever more resorts and hotels are gearing themselves to business year-round.

### Public holidays

The following are all national public holidays:
**1 Jan** New Year's Day; **6 Jan** Epiphany; **Easter Sunday** and **Easter Monday; 1 May** Labour Day; **Corpus Christi** (moveable feast); **22 June** Anti-Fascist Resistance Day; **25 June** Statehood Day; **5 Aug** Victory Day/National Thanksgiving Day; **15 Aug** Assumption; **8 Oct** Independence Day; **1 Nov** All Saints' Day; **25, 26 Dec** Christmas holidays.

## WORKING IN CROATIA

Croatia is a highly desirable place to live and an increasing number of people are settling here and setting up businesses. Aside from tourism, in which you will find a number of expats in sailing and diving clubs, there's also the property sector and the old stand-by of English-language teaching. With Croatia becoming an EU member, this procedure has become much easier. For job openings, check www.moj-posao.net/EN, with limited material in English, and the state-run Office of Employment (www.hzz.hr), with no English option. Although both are aimed primarily at Croats, with a little translation help it's worth a look as you will find bilingual job opportunities posted from international or Croatian employers.

### Work permits

The regulations on working in Croatia have completely changed since it became a member of the EU. Detailed instructions are available at www.mvep.hr/en/consular-information/stay-of-aliens/granting-stay-in-croatia. In short, there are three categories of foreigners:

1. Nationals of the European Economic Area (EEA), members of the Swiss Confederation and their family members, and family members of Croatian nationals.
2. Nationals of third countries with permanent residence in an EEA member state and their family members.
3. Nationals of third countries (out of the EEA).

Those from the first category, including UK nationals, need to register their temporary residence if they stay longer than three months. Nationals of EU member states and their family members can work in Croatia with no residence or work permit and no work registration certificate. However, there are restrictions for citizens of countries that have limited access for Croatian nationals to their labour market.
A list of those countries can be found on the website of the Ministry of Labour and Pension System (www.mrms.hr). For United Kingdom nationals, this means that they can work in Croatia without a work permit after two years of Croatia's accession to the EU, that is, from 2016 onwards. Citizens of other countries should check www. mvpei.hr for detailed information.

# Vocabulary

The official language of Croatia is Croatian. It has dialects in Dalmatia, Istria, Zagreb and Zagorje, and Slavonia, but there is a standardised version used in official documents. Road signs are given in Croatian. In Istria they are often in Italian and Croatian. English is widely spoken in holiday areas but less so in the interior, where if you learn a few phrases, it is likely to be appreciated.

## PRONUNCIATION

Croatian is a phonetic language and has no silent letters. For English speakers, the difficulty comes with some of the sibilant consonants, which have different sounds to the English ones:

c is 'ts' as in 'hats'
ć is a light 'ch' as 'future'
č is 'ch' as in 'church'
š is a soft 'sh' as in 'shoe'
ž is 'zh' as in 'pleasure'

Other letters are lj, as in the 'lli' of million, nj as in the 'ny' of canyon and đ, as in the j of jury. This is often rendered in English as 'dj' (as in Tudjman), a practice we follow in this guide. The Croatian letter j is pronounced as an English 'y'.

## BASICS

yes da
no ne
hello/good day dobar dan
goodbye do vidjenja
hello (on phone) molim
hello! (familiar) bok!
good morning dobro jutro
good evening dobra večer
good night laku noć
please molim
thank you (very much) hvala (lijepo)
great/OK dobro
I don't know ne znam
do you speak English? govorite li engleski?
I'm sorry, I don't speak Croatian Izvinite, ne govorim hrvatski
I don't understand ne razumijem
what's your name? (polite) kako se zovete?
what's your name? (familiar) kako se zoveš?
my name is... zovem se...

excuse me/sorry oprostite
where are you from? (polite) odakle ste?
where are you from? (familiar) odakle si?
when? kada?
how much is it? koliko košta?
large veliko
small malo
more više
less manje
expensive skupo
cheap jeftino
hot (food, drink) toplo
cold hladno
with/without sa/bez
open otvoreno
closed zatvoreno
can I book a room? mogu li rezervirati sobu?

## GETTING AROUND

where is...? Gdje je...?
where to? kamo?
here ovdje
there tamo
left lijevo
right desno
straight on pravo
backwards natrag
a ticket to... jednu kartu za...
single u jednom pravcu
return povratnu kartu
when does the next bus/ferry/train leave for...? kada polazi sljedeći autobus/trajekt/vlak za...?
I'm lost Izgubio same se (masc)/Izgubila sam se (fem)
how far is it? koliko je daleko?
arrival polazak
departure odlazak
station kolodvor
airport zračna luka/aerodrom
port luka
ferry terminal trajektna luka

## BOOKING A ROOM

do you have...? Imati li vi...?
reservation rezervacija
I have a reservation Imam rezervaciju
full board pansion
half board polupansion
single room jednokrevetna soba
double room dvokrevetna soba
shower tuš
bath banja/kupanje
balcony balkon
sea view pogled na more

## TIME

In Croatian, half-hours mean half to the next hour, so it may be easier to say *deset i trideset* ('10.30') instead of *pola jedanaest* ('half-to-eleven').

what time is it? koliko je sati?
ten o'clock deset sati
day dan
week tjedan
today danas
tomorrow sutra
yesterday jučer
in the morning ujutro
in the evening uvečer
early rano
late kasno

## NUMBERS

1 jedan; 2 dva; 3 tri; 4 četiri; 5 pet; 6 šest; 7 sedam; 8 osam; 9 devet; 10 deset; 11 jedanaest; 12 dvanaest; 13 trinaest; 14 četrnaest; 15 petnaest; 16 šestnaest; 17 sedamnaest; 18 osamnaest; 19 devetnaest; 20 dvadeset; 21 dvadeset i jedan.

30 trideset; 40 četrdeset; 50 pedeset; 60 šezdeset; 70 sedamdeset; 80 osamdeset; 90 devedeset; 100 sto.

200 dvjesta; 1,000 tisuća

## DAYS, MONTHS

Monday ponedjeljak
Tuesday utorak
Wednesday srijeda
Thursday četvrtak
Friday petak
Saturday subota
Sunday nedjelja

January siječanj
February veljača
March ožujak
April travanj
May svibanj
June lipanj
July srpanj
August kolovoz
September rujan
October listopad
November studeni
December prosinac

spring proljeće
summer ljeto
autumn jesen
winter zima

# The Menu

## EATING OUT
### Useful phrases

**are these seats taken?**
da li je slobodno?
**bon appetit! dobar tek!**
**do you have...? Imate li...?**
**I'm a vegetarian**
Ja sam vegetarijanac
**I'm diabetic**
Ja sam dijabetičar
**I'd like a table for two**
molim stol za dvoje
**the menu, please**
molim vas jelovnik
**I didn't order this**
nisam ovo naručio
**the bill (please)**
račun (molim)

### Basics (osnovno)

**ashtray** pepeljara
**bill** račun
**bread** kruh
**cup** šalica
**fork** vilica
**glass** čaša
**knife** nož
**milk** mlijeko
**napkin** ubrus
**oil** ulje
**pepper** biber
**plate** tanjur
**salt** sol
**spoon** žlica
**sugar** šećer
**teaspoon** žličica
**vinegar** ocat
**water** voda

### Meat (meso)

**but** leg
**ćevapčići/ćevapi** mincemeat
rissoles
**čobanac** spicy meat stew
**govedina** beef
**grah sa svinjskom koljenicom**
bean soup with pork knuckle
**guska** goose
**gusta juha** thick goulash soup
**janjetina** lamb
**jetra** liver
**koljenica** pork knuckle
**kunić/zec** rabbit
**odrezak** escalope (usually veal
or pork)
**panceta** bacon
**pašticada** stew of beef marinated
in wine
**patka** duck
**piletina** chicken

**pljeskavica** meat patty
**prsa** breast
**purica/tuka** turkey
**ražnjići** skewered meats
**srnetina** venison
**šunka** ham
**svinjetina** pork
**teletina** veal
**zagrebački odrezak** stuffed
breaded meat chop

### Fish/seafood
### (riba/plodovi mora)

**riba sa roštilja/na žaru**
grilled fish
**bakalar** cod
**barbun** mullet
**brancin/lubin** sea bass
**brodet** fish stew
**cipal** golden grey mullet
**crni rižot** black risotto (with squid
ink)
**dagnje/mušule/školjke** mussels
**girice** whitebait
**hobotnica** octopus
**jastog** lobster
**jegulja** eel
**kamenice/ostrige** oysters
**kapica** clam
**kovač** john dory
**lignje** squid
**list** sole
**losos** salmon
**orada** gilthead sea bream
**oslić** hake
**pastrva** trout
**rak** crab
**šaran** carp
**sipa** cuttlefish
**škampi** scampi
**škrpina** sea scorpion
**skuša** mackerel
**štuka** pike
**trilja** red mullet
**tuna** tuna
**žablji kraci** frogs' legs
**zubatac** dentex

### Accompaniments
### (prilozi)

**kruh** bread
**krumpir** potatoes
**prženi krumpir** chips
**riža** rice
**tjestenina** pasta

### Salads (salate)

**cikla** beetroot
**krastavac** cucumber
**mješana salata** mixed salad
**rajčica** tomato

**rokula** rocket
**zelena salata** green
(lettuce) salad

### Vegetables
### (povrće)

**cvjetača** cauliflower
**gljive** mushrooms
**grašak** peas
**kuhani kukuruz** sweetcorn
**leća** lentils
**mahune** green beans
**mrkva** carrot
**paprika** pepper
**šparoge** asparagus
**špinat** spinach

### Fruit & nuts
### (voće & orasi)

**ananas** pineapple
**banana** banana
**dinja** melon
**jabuka** apple
**jagoda** strawberry
**kruška** pear
**lubenica** watermelon
**malina** raspberry
**marelica** apricot
**naranča** orange
**orah** walnut
**šljiva** plum
**smokva** fig
**trešnja** cherry

### Desserts
### (deserti)

**kolač** cake
**kremšnita** cream cake
**kroštule** fried pastry twists
**palačinke** pancakes
**rožata** crème caramel
**sladoled** ice-cream
**torta** gateau

### Drinks (pića)

**mineralna voda** mineral water
**sok (od naranče)** (orange) juice
**led** ice
**čaj** tea
**kava** coffee
**pivo** beer
**tamno pivo** dark beer
**rakija** brandy
**vino** wine
**bijelo vino** white wine
**crno vino** red wine
**crveno vino** rosé wine
**pjenušac** sparkling wine
**gemišt** spritzer
**bevanda** wine & water

ESSENTIAL INFORMATION

# Further Reference

## BOOKS

### Fiction

**Ivo Andrić**
*The Days of the Consuls*
Tales of 19th-century Ottoman-ruled Travnik, by the man both Serbs and Croats claim as their own. Ivo Andrić is best known for his masterpiece *Bridge over the Drina*.

**Slavenka Drakulić**
*As If I Am Not There*
Harrowing story of a Bosnian rape victim from the Yugoslav war, by one of Croatia's leading contemporary writers

**Branko Franolić**
*An Historical Survey of Literary Croatian*
Offers precisely what it says on the cover.

**Miroslav Krleža**
*The Return of Philip Latinovicz*
A classic work, and thus often a set novel in schools, by the acknowledged master of 20th-century Croatian literature.

**Miroslav Krleža**
*The Banquet in Blitva*
Satire of Europe in the Age of the Dictators, written in the 1930s.

**Olja Savičević**
*Farewell, Cowboy*
Published in 2015, a vivid tale of small-town Croatia set around a murder mystery.

**Dubravka Ugrešić**
*Fording the Stream of Consciousness*
The most striking work of this exiled Croatian writer, also known for *In the Jaws of Life*. Ugrešić is criticised in Croatia for her neutral stance in the 1990s.

### History

**Ivo Banać**
*The National Question in Yugoslavia*
In-depth exploration of national identities.

**Catherine Bracewell**
*The Uskoks of Senj*
History of the pirate sea-kings of the Adriatic in the 16th century.

**Elinor Despalatović**
*Ljudevit Gaj and the Illyrian Movement*
The story of Croatia's national awakening in the turbulent 1830s and 1840s.

**Misha Glenny**
*The Fall of Yugoslavia*

Colourful account of how it all ended in carnage, and why, by the BBC's man on the spot.

**Ivo Goldstein**
*Croatia, A History*
Goldstein is a Zagreb historian, and this book is an overview of the country from the earliest times.

**Brian Hall**
*The Impossible Country*
Touching travelogue of Hall's journey around Yugoslavia in the build-up to war, 1991.

**Robin Harris**
*Dubrovnik, A History*
Large volume on the Pearl of the Adriatic.

**Barbara Jelavich**
*History of the Balkans*
Sets the convuluted history of the region in a broader context.

**Allan Little & Laura Silber**
*The Death of Yugoslavia*
Fly-on-the-wall account to accompany the BBC TV series of the break-up of Yugoslavia.

**Jasper Ridley**
*Tito – A Biography*
A rather sympathetic portrayal of Yugoslavia's long-time Communist dictator

**Mark Thompson**
*Forging War – The Media in Serbia, Croatia and Bosnia-Hercegovina*
Thompson looks in particular at the role played by the local press in manipulating the population. Look out also for Thompson's *A Paper House*, one of the better travelogue histories as Yugoslavia was collapsing.

### Travelogue

**Michael Donley**
*Marco Polo's Isle*
Impressions from a year spent on Korčula.

**Rebecca West**
*Black Lamb and Grey Falcon: A Journey through Yugoslavia*
The benchmark for all Balkan travelogues, the book was researched in the late 1930s but its insights remain valid in the same way de Tocqueville's observations on democracy in the US are still worth reading; Rebecca West saw through to the Balkan soul.

### Religion

**Stella Alexander**
*The Triple Myth – A Life of Archbishop Alojzije Stepinac*

Fair account of the rise and fall of Croatia's war-time primate.

**Stella Alexander**
*Church and State in Yugoslavia Since 1945*
Well researched account of confessional relations, written before the killing began again.

## WEBSITES

**www.croatia.hr**
Official tourist website – excellent hotel database.

**www.croatiabusiness report.com**
An English-language website devoted to Croatia's economic and business affairs.

**www.croatia-holiday andhome.co.uk**
Property and rental offers across Croatia

**www.croatiaonline.blogspot.hu**
Interesting and pertinent features from around Croatia.

**www.croatiaweek.com**
Useful news portal in English.

**dalje.com/en/croatia**
Regularly updated news source.

**www.hic.hr**
Croatian news in English.

**www.hina.hr**
Croatian state news agency, with English items.

**www.istra.hr**
The Istrian Regional Tourist Board's official site.

**www.klubskascena.hr**
Clubbing and DJ news and listings.

**www.kvarner.hr**
The Kvarner Regional Tourist Board's official site.

**www.split.hr**
The website of the city's municipal authority.

**www.timeout.com/croatia**
Newly revamped guide to getting the best out of Croatia.

**www.titoville.com**
A cult site dedicated to the memory of the old leader.

**www.visit-croatia.co.uk**
A large website devoted to Croatian tourism.

**www.zadar.hr**
The Zadar Regional Tourist Board's official site.

**www.zagreb.hr**
The website of the Zagreb municipal authority.

**www.zagreb-touristinfo.hr**
A great source of useful information on Zagreb.

# Index

-Love, Ana 62
101 Dalmatinac Design Hostel 195
1492 Cockitail Bar 131
22,000 milja pod morem 59
360 Degrees 235, 237
5/4 55

## A

Academia Ghetto Club 179
Adio Mare 256
Adria 128
Adriana, Split 185
Adriana, Hvar Spa Hotel 221
Adriana Top Bar 218
Adriatic, Rovinj 84
Adriatic Grašo 188
Adriatic Kayak Tours 254
Advent Zagreb 62
Agava 120
age restrictions 307
AKC Medika 62
Algoritam 242
Alviž 215
Amarin 84
Ambrela 78
Amfora, Dubrovnik 246
Amfora, Hvar Grand Beach Resort 221
Amor 211
Ancora 265
Ankora 246
Antika 215
Antony Boy 267
Aparthotel Lekavski 151
Aparthotel Milenij 205
Apartmani Jerko 166
Apartmani Silvija 166
Apartments Amoret 244
Apetit 175
Apoksiomen 136
Aquarium, Dubrovnik 234
Aquarium, Vodice 159
Aquarius, Zagreb 68
Aquarius, Vis 228
Arausa 159
Arbiana Hotel 132
Arch of Sergians 72
Archaeological Museum, Split 188
Archaeological Museum, Vis 226
Archaeological Museum, Zadar 144
Archaeological Museum, Zagreb 54
Archaeological Museum of Istria 72
Arcotel Allegra 63
Aruba 78
Amfiteatar 74
Arsenal Zadar 148

Art Café 248
Art Hotel 195
Art Hotel Kalelarga 151
Art Pavillion 54
Art Public Bar 83
Art Studio Naranča 183
Artur Gallery 242
Astoria 130
Atelier Devescovi 84
Atelier Secret 243
Atelier Sottomuro 84
Atelijer Galerija Brek 84
ATMs 309
Atrij 144
Atrium Hotel 195
Atrium Residence Baška 129
Aurora 166
Azur 237

## B

B4 Revelin 241
Babin kuk peninsula 246, 253
Babine Kuće 270
Babino Polje 270
Bacchus 205
Bacchus Jazz Bar 59
Back-Door Bar 148
Bačva beach 264
Bačvice 172
Badi 94
Badija 259
Baltazar 46
Baltazar Bogišić Collection 265
Baletna Škola 202
Banje 253, 259
banks 309
Banova Vila Beach Bar 131
Barba 237
BarBar 111
Baredine Cave 90
Barilo Ethnographic Collection 259
Baroque Church of St Blaise 234
Barun 162
Batana House 81
Batelina 80
Baška Aquarium 127
Baška Voda 204
Bass 77
Bastia 99
Bastion 203
BB Club featuring Shrimp House 218
Beertija, Zagreb 59
Beertija & Klub 111
Belgian Beer Café Brasserie 111
Bellevue 249
Benčić Truffles, 97, 98

Benny's Bar 211
Berkeley 249
Berulia 205
Best Western Hotel Astoria 64
Best Western Hotel Jadran 113
Betina 155
Betina špilja 253
Bety 204
Bevanda 116, 120
Bevanda Bar 118
Bifora 179
Bijeca 79
Bikers Beer Factory 59
Bili cvitak 258
Bilin žal 260
Bimbijana 202
bio&bio 183
Biograd 157
Biokovo Nature Park 204
Bire 262
Biševo 228
Bistro Apetit 46
Bistro Dar dot 55
Bistro Fotić 56
Bistro Karlo 56
Bistro La Rose 106
Bistro Pizzeria Moho 116
Bistro Ponta 266
Bistro Trattoria Franica 127
Bistro Yacht Club 116
Bistroteka 56
Blaca Hermitage 206
Blace 270
Blato 259
Blu 81
Blue Cave, Biševo 224
Blue Planet Diving 254
Blue Waves Resort 129
Bluesun Hotel Borak 211
Boa 113
Boban 189
Bobis Riva 183
Boccadoro 226
Bokeria Kitchen&Wine 175
Bokuncin 206
Bol 206
Bol, Hotel 211
Donji Humac 206
Boogaloo 63
Boogie Jungle 258
Booze and Blues 51
Bora Bar Trattoria/ Tartufferia 135
Borik 152, 262
Bornstein 49
Boškinac 138
Bota Šare 266
Botanical Gardens 54
Boutique Hostel Forum 151
Boutique Hotel No.9 64

Brač 204, 206-214
Bračka Perla 212
Brasserie on 7 175
Brela 204
Brijuni 76
Brijuni archipelago 76
Brijuni National Park 76, 79
Brist 204
Brna 260
Brokul&Ž 61
Brtonigla 93
Bruschetta 147
Buba Bar 204
Buffet Stubica 125
Bugenvila 265
Bugsy's 203
Buje 93
Bukovac, Vlaho gallery 265
Bunari, Šibenik 161
Bunarina 77
Burin 204
business 307
Buža I 241
Buža II 241
Buzz Bar 241
Byblos 88

## C

Cablecar 246
Café Brazil 149
Café Dalmatino 159
Café del Mar 87
Café Nonica 218
Café Wagner 119
Caffé Bar Bejbi 227
Caffé Bar Biblia 227
Caffé Bar Galerija 179
Caffé Bar Guc 125
Caffé Bar Kon-Tiki 119
Caffé Bar Lanterna 159
Caffé Bar Leonardo 119
Caffé Bar Marina 210
Caffé Bar Montona Gallery 96
Caffé Bar Nautika 77
Caffé Bar Orange 125
Caffé Bar Pjerin 210
Caffé Bar Sun & Fun 127
Caffé Bar Virada 160
Caffé Bar XL 83
Caffé Ben Quick 210
Caffé Biser 131
Caffé Cinema 83
Caffé Diana 77
Caffé Libar 180
Caffé Uliks 77
Čajoteka Natura 180
Calisona 81
Camp Slanica 156
Camping Split 196
Campsite Liberan 266

Index

Cantinetta Sveti Jakov 116
Cape Eve 86
Čara 260
Cardo 189
Carmel 243
Carpaccio 57
Carpe Diem 220
Casa Garzotto 84
Casa Vecchia 157
Casablanca 241
Cathedral, Dubrovnik 235
Cathedral, Zagreb 43
Cathedral of St Euphemia 80
Cathedral of St James, Šibenik 161
Cathedral of St Lawrence, Trogir 200
Cathedral of the Assumption 126
Cathedral Treasury 255
Cava 253
Cavtat 264-265
Cebalo 262
Cele Café 241
Celenga Apartments 244
Celtic Caffè Bard 112
Charlie's Bar 180
Chihuahua-Cantina Mexicana 246
children 307
Choco Bar 119
Chocolat 041 59
Chops-Grill Steak&Seafood 176
Chuara 220
Church of St Anastasia 157
Church of St Anthony 157
Church of St Blaise 250
Church of St Cross 159
Church of St George 165
Church of St Mary the Helper 262
Church of St Stephen 96
Church of the Exalted and Blessed Virgin Mary, Hum 100
Cicibela 127
Cioccolata, La 87
Cittar 93
City Garden 92
City Heritage Museum, Rovinj 80
City Museum, Rijeka 104
City Museum, Šibenik 161
City Walls, Dubrovnik 236, 268
Clo Bar 191
Club Boa 128
Club Deep 205
Club Nina 2 113
Club Uljanik 78
Cocktail Bar Bolero 211
Cocktail Bar Code 92
Cocktail Bar Volsonis 128
Cogito Coffee 60
Colonnade Beach Bar 218
Colosseum Beach Bar 119
Comitium Cocktail Bar 87

Concordia 202
Consul 196
Continental 113
contraception 308
Copacabana 253
Coric Tower 159
Cornaro 185
Corto Maltese, Split 176
Corto Maltese Cocktail Bar, Vis 228
Courtyards, The 54
credit & debit cards 309
Crème de la Crème 183
Cres 132-134
Croatian Association of Artists 54
Croatian Design Superstore 61
Croatian Museum of Naive Art, Zagreb 43
Croatian Museum of Natural History 46
Crveni Island 86
CukariKafè 112
Cukarin 258
Culto 248
Culture Club Revelin 244
Ćušpajz 57
customs 307
Cvajner 77

D

Dalmatian Villas 186
Damir i Ornella 91
Dance 253
dentists 308
Design Hotel Astoria 120
Dimensions 78
Dingač 268
Diocletian Heritage Hotel 186
Diocletian's Palace 172
Diocletian's Wine House 176
Dioklecijan 180
Dioklecijan Hotel & Residence 196
Dionis 228
disabled travelers 307
Disco Bar Jungle 128
Divna 265
Divota Apartment Hotel 196
Djina 149
Dobar Zvuk 60
Dolac 49, 50
Dominican Monastery 236
Dos Locos 258
DoubleTree by Hilton 64
Draga di Lovrana 123
Dragon's Cave 206
drugs 307
Društveni Centar Rojc 78
Drvenik 204
Držić, Marin 268
Duba 265
Dubrava Sokolarski Center for Falconry 161

Dubravka 1836 237
Dubravkin put 47
Dubrovačka kuća 243
Dubrovnik 230-254
Dubrovnik Airport 254
Dubrovnik Apartment Source 244
Dubrovnik Card 235
Dubrovnik Palace 251
Dubrovnik Summer Festival 250
Dugi otok 152
Dugi Rat 203-204
Dupin Dive Centre 260
Dva Ribara 147
Dvi Murve 87
Dvor 189

E

E&D 77
East-West 249
Elafiti Archipelago 273
Elaphusa 212
electricity 307
ELFS 61
Eli's Caffé 60
Emanuel 196
embassies & consulates 307-308
emergencies 308
Epario 132
Epidaurum 265
Epoca 87
Eremitaž 215
Escape Lounge Bar 131
Esplanade Zagreb 65
Ethnographic Museum, Split 172
Ethnographic Museum, Zagreb 54
Etnobutiga Ča 97
Etnoland, Šibenik 161
Euphrasian Basilica & Bishop's Palace 86
European Costal Airlines 203
Excelsior 249
Exit 160

F

F-Marine 192
Fabrika 228
Face 77
Factory Bar 149
Falkensteiner Punta Skala Resort: Hotel Diadora & Hotel & Spa Iadera 151
Family Hotel Vespera 136
Farabuto 74
Festival Café 242, 251
Figa 180
Filippi 257
Filodrammatica Bookshop Cafe 112
Filomena Spa & Lifestyle Club 196
Firule 187

Fjord 86
Fontana 200
Fonticus City Gallery 98
Fort Bourguignon 78
Fort George 228
Fort Punta Christo 78
Forte 267
Fortuna 130
Forum 131
Foša 147
Franciscan Monastery, Orebić 266
Franciscan Monastery/Old Pharmacy Museum 235, 236
Frankopan 127
Fratarski island 79
Fresh Sheets 244
Fresh Sheets B&B 244
Fro 180
Fulir Hostel 51

G

Gabine 203
Gaga 180
gajeta 155
Galerija Klovićevi Dvori 46
Galerija Makina 74
Galerija Nova 54
Galevac 154
Galija 176
Gallerion Naval Museum 91
Gallery, Zagreb 68
Gallery Rigo 91
Gallileo 155
Gallo 57
Garden, the 149
Gariful 215
gay & lesbian 308
GetGetGet 183
Giannino 81
Giaxa 216
Gina 74
Giro Espresso 163
Gjuro II 51
Gliptoteka 46
Globo 196
Glorijet 247
Godimento 164
Goli & Bosi Design Hostel 186
Governor's Palace 104
Gostionica Bukaleta 133
Gostionica Feral 130
Gostionica Istranka 117
Gostionica Labirint 130
Gostionica Marina 136
Gostionica Tip-Top 57
Gradac 42, 204
Gradska Kavana 125
Gradska Vijećnica 162
Gradski Podrum 257
Grand Hotel 4 Opatijska cvijeta 120
Grand Hotel Adriatic 121
Grand Hotel Bonavia 113
Grand Hotel Imperial 132

Grand Hotel Park 249
Grand Villa Argentina 251
Great Fountain 235
Grožnjan 98-99
Grožnjan Musical Summer
  98
Gruž market 249
Gundulićeva poljana
  market 243
Gverović-Orsan 247

**H**

Hacienda, Brač 211
Hacienda, Vodice 159
Hard Jazz Caffe
  Troubadour 242
Havana 127
hazards, natural 309
health 308
Hedonist 194
Hemingway Bar Split 194
Hemingway Lounge Bar 60
Hemingway Medveja 119
Hemingway Opatija 119
Hilltop Retreat, The 97
history 276-287
History & Maritime
  Museum, Rijeka 106
Hitch Bar 150
holidays, public 311
Homeland War Museum
  2461
Hookah Bar 160
Horizont 204, 205
Hostel Krk 129
Hotel Amfiteatar 78
Hotel Amfora 101
Hotel Antunović 65
Hotel AS 52
Hotel Bastion 152
Hotel Borovnik 156
Hotel Central 65
Hotel Club Funimation
  Borik 152
Hotel Colentum 156
Hotel Croatia 265
Hotel Delfin 88
Hotel Dubrovnik 65
Hotel Faraon 267
Hotel Feral 260
Hotel Filipini 88
Hotel Flores 89
Hotel Imperial 160
Hotel Jadran 164
Hotel Kaštel 97
Hotel Kolovare 152
Hotel Lovran 126
Hotel Milan 78
Hotel Miramar Restaurant
  117
Hotel Mozart Piano Bar
  119
Hotel Olympia 160
Hotel Omir 78
Hotel Orion 160
Hotel Palace, Zagreb 65
Hotel Palace, Kaštela 203
Hotel Palazzo 89

Hotel Panorama 164
Hotel Park 126
Hotel Pipištrelo 78
Hotel Poreč 89
Hotel Punta 160
Hotel Resnik 203
Hotel Riviera 78
Hotel Solitudo 272
Hotel Stari Grad 244
Hotel Supetar 265
Hotel Tamaris 203
Hotel Ugljan 154
Hotel Venera 152
Hotel Villa Zarko 203
Hotel Zora 169
hotels 308
Hrvatske divote 51
Hula Hula Beach Bar 219
Huljić 216
Hum 99-100
Hum Museum 100
Humac 216
Hvar 204, 214-225
Hvar, Hotel 221

**I**

I-GLE 61
Icon Museum 255
ID 308
Ilirija Group 158
Illy Bar 150
Imaš 203
Imperium 194
Importanne Resort 252
Indijan 267
insurance 308
International 132
internet access 309
ispod peke 207
Issa 229
Istra 132
Istra, Hotel 84
Istralandia 91
Istria 70-101
Ivo 154

**J**

Jabuka 51
Jadran 202
Jelsa 214
Jeny 204
Jež 204
Jezera 155
Jezera Village Holiday
  Resort 156
Johnson 117
Judino drvo 194
Judita Gourmet & Wine
  Shop 184
Jungla Club 194
Jupiter Luxury Hotel 186
Jurin Podrum 216

**K**

Kadena 189
Kali 154

Kamenar 169
Kamenice 237
Kamenjak peninsula 79
Kamerlengo 200
Kamerlengo Castle 200
Kanajt 129
Kanavelić 257
Kantina 74
Kantinon 81
Kantun 226
Kapetanova Kuća 266
Kaptol 42
Karijola 226
Karma Record Store 62
Karmela 266
Karmela 2 267
Karmen Apartments 245
Karolina 113
Kaštel 186
Kaštela 202-203
Kaštelet 188
Kaštil 212
Katarina Hotel 196
Katedrala 174
Kava Tava Tkalčićeva
  48
Kavana Ovčice 192
Kavana-Restoran
  Bajamonti 180
Kaya Energy Bar 99
Kazbek Hotel 252
Kebap & Meze bar İştah
  189
Kempinski Hotel Adriatic
  95
Kerempuh 47
Kimen 134
Kiva Bar 219
Kobaje 192
Kocka 194
Kolaž 60
KOLO 93
Koločep 273
Komiža Provita 229
Komiža, Viz 225
Konavoski Komin 247
Konoba, Split 189
Konoba Astarea 94
Konoba Augusta Insula 272
Konoba B&B 165
Konoba Bako 226
Konoba Barba, Biograd
  157
Konoba Barba, Mljet 271
Konoba Bata 263
Konoba Bazilika 157
Konoba Bepo 159
Konoba Berlin 264
Konoba Bile 138
Konoba Blato 106
Konoba Blidinje 247
Konoba Bracera 203
Konoba Čiho 57
Konoba Čok 92
Konoba Corsaro 127
Konoba Cotonum 158
Konoba da Lorenzo 94
Konoba Dalmatino, Brač
  206

Konoba Dalmatino,
  Dubrovnik 238
Konoba Didov San 47
Konoba Dol - Kaštil
  Gospodnetić 208
Konoba Dolina 96
Konoba Dorjana 96
Konoba Feral 204
Konoba Flume 108
Konoba Gera 264
Konoba Golub 226
Konoba Gusarska Luka
  216
Konoba Hum 100
Konoba Hvaranin 190
Konoba Intrada 202
Konoba Jastožera 227
Konoba Kandela 155
Konoba Kasar 247
Konoba Kod Joze 176
Konoba Komin 257
Konoba Marjan 190
Konoba Marul 176
Konoba Marun 124
Konoba Mate 262
Konoba Matejuška 190
Konoba Menego 219
Konoba Mlin 208
Konoba Mondo 96
Konoba Morgan 94
Konoba Nebuloza 108
Konoba Nino 127
Konoba Nono 94
Konoba Papec 165
Konoba Ribar 238
Konoba Roki's 227
Konoba Rustika 159
Konoba Škrapa 200
Konoba Šimun 159
Konoba Skoblar 147
Konoba Stončica 227
Konoba Tomić 208
Konoba Toni 209
Konoba Torkul 166
Konoba Tramerka 117
Konoba Vatrica 227
Konoba-Pizzeria Bukaleta
  136
Kopačina 209
Kopački rit 295-297
Kopun 238
Korčula 254-264
Korčula, Zagreb 58
Korčula De La Ville Hotel
  258
Korkyra 263
Korkyra Baroque Music
  Festival 255
Kormarac 271
Kornat 147
Kornati National Park 152,
  168
Koromašna Bay 155
Kosi Toranj 112
Kosirina 156
Kraš 184
Krk 126
Krka National Park 167
Kruščić 184

**INDEX**

KSet 63
Kuća Istarskog pršuta 112
Kuća Visoka 229
Kukljica 154
Kukuriku 108
Kvarner 102-139

**L**

L at Hotel Lone 81
Labin 100-101
Labin Art Republic 100
Labin Museum 100
Lady PI-PI 238
Laguna 131
Lambik 228
landmines 310
language 309
Lapad Hotel 251
Lapad peninsula 246, 250, 253
Lastovo 272
Lastovo village 272
Laura 242
Laurus 118
Laval Caffè 112
Lavender Bed Bar 158
Lazareti 249
Ledana Bar 150
legal advice 309
Legends Bar 194
Legends Pub 166
Lešić-Dimitri Palace Korčula 254
Leut 265
Libertina 242
Libido 219
lighthouses 99
Limb 60
Limski kanal 86
Lino Restaurant 101
Lipa 212
Loco Bar 219
Lokanda Peskarija 238
Lokrum 253, 261, 268
Lone 85
Lopud 273
Lošinj 134-137
Lošinj Hotels & Villas 137
Lošinjsko Jidro 136
lost property 309
Lovran 122-126
Lovranski Pub 125
Lovrijenac Fortress 250
Lucin Kantun 238
Lucullus 216
Ludwig 242
Luka Ice Cream & Cakes 184
Luka Korčulanska 259
Luka Krajančić 260
Lumbarda 254, 260-262
Luna Hotel 139
Luna Rossa 58
Lungo Mare 147
Lungomare, beach 79

Luviji 217
Luxe 196
Lvxor 180

**M**

ma:Toni 190
Macondo 217
Maestral 93
Makarska Riviera 204-206
Makin 93
Makina 159
Makrovega 176
Maksimir Park & Zoo 66
Mala Kapja 260
Male Madlene 82
Mali dućan-Matejuška 193
Mali Raj, Brač 209
Mali Raj, Mljet 271
Mali Raj, Opatija 118
Mali Raj, Rovinj 82
Mali Ston 266
Malin 128
Mandrać, Novigrad 92
Mandrać, Le 118
Mano 47 Maraschino 150
Maraschino, Zagreb 61
Maraska 146
Marco Polo Triathlon Challenge 255
Marcvs Marvivs Spalatensis Library Bar 181
Mare Mare Suites 136
Maria 62
Maria Boutique 243
Marina, Krk 129
Marina, Novigrad 92
Marina Frapa 166
Marina Kornati Restaurant 157
Marine Education Centre 135
Marinero 257
Maritime Museum 234
Marko Polo Hotel 255, 259
Marko Polo Exhibition 256
Marko Polo House 255, 256
Marmont Hotel 187
Maro & Baro Apartments 252
Martinino 201
Marul 197
Mašklin i Iata 58
Massimo Cocktail Bar 258
Mazzgoon 177
Me and Mrs Jones 217
media 309
Medieval Mediterranean Garden of St Lawrence's Monastery 161
Mediterranean Sculpture Symposium 100
Medulin Riviera 79-80
Medvednica 68
Melià Coral 94
Melin 49
Melita 271

Memorial Collection of Maksimilijan Vanka, Korčula 255
Méridien Lav, Le 197
Meštrović Atelijer, Zagreb 46
Meštrović Gallery 188
Meteor 205
Mihovil's Fortress 161
Milan 74
Milenij 121
Mimara Museum, Zagreb 54
Mimbelli 266
Milo 203
Miramar 121
Mirogoj 66
MK Bar 49
Mljet 270-272
Mljet National Park 271
MM Gallery 99
MM Sub 260
mobile phones 310
Močvara 68
Moderato Cantabile 164
Modern & Contemporary Art Museum, Rijeka 106
Modern Galerija 55
Modni Kantun 243
Modra špilja 224
Monastery of Our Lady of the Snow 265
Monde, Le 190
money 309
Monokini 119
Monte 82
Monte Mulini 85
Montokuc 270
More 251, 262
More, Split 198
Mornar 110
Motovun 95-97
Motovun Film Festival 95
Mount Srdj 246
Mount St Michael 153
Movie Resort Apart Hotel 159
Mozart 121
Mozart Caffé 87
Mulino 95
Municipal Gradska Galerija Labin 100
Municipium 110
Murter 154-156
Museum Collections of the Vela Luka Cultural Centre 263
Museum Lapidarium 91
Museum of Arts & Crafts, Zagreb 55
Museum of Brač 206
Museum of Broken Relationships 46
Museum of Contemporary Art, Zagreb 67
Museum of Contemporary Art of Istria 74

Museum of Modern Art Dubrovnik 246
Museum of Sacred Art 161

**N**

Na Kantunu, Rijeka 104 110
Na Kantunu, Split 181
Na Tale 138
Nadalina 185
Nakovana Archaeological Site 266
Natura Croatica 62
Natural History Museum, Rijeka 106
Nautica 93
Nautika 238
Navigare 92
Navis Underwater Explorers 254
Neboder 114
Nehaj 203
Niko 147
Nin 153
Nine 271
Nishta, Dubrovnik 238
Nishta, Zagreb 58
Nonenina Bar 242
Nono Ban 209
North Velebit 297-298
North-west Istria 93-95
NoStress Bistro 177
Nostromo, Rijeka 101
Noštromo, Split 178
Novi Zagreb 42
Novigrad 90-93
No.4/Četvorka 162

**O**

O'Hara Music Club 194
Obojena Svjetlost 195
Octopus Bowling 195
Odisej 271
Odmor 202
Okrugljak 47
Oliva 90
Oliva Gourmet 240
Olive Island Marina 153
Omiš 203-204
Opatija 115-122
opening times 309
Opium 160
opticians 308
OreBeach 266
Orebić 266
Orlando's Column 234
Orsan Yacht Club 247
Oštarija U Vidjakovi 190
Ostrea 267
Our Lady of the Rosary 266
Outlook 78
Oxbo Urban Bar & Grill 58

Oyster & Sushi Bar Bota, Dubrovnik 240
Oyster & Sushi Bar Bota, Split 178
oysters 266

## P

P1477
Pag 137-139
Paklenica National Park 298
Paklina beach 213
Palace, Trogir 202
Palace Hvar Hotel, The 221
Palace Deškovic 212
Palma 158
Panorama, Dubrovnik 247
Panorama Hotel Zagreb 52
Pansion Marinka 262
Pansion Meneghello 221
Pansion Murvica 222
Pansion Saturn 137
Pansion Stanger 126
Pantarul 247
Paradiso Beach Bar 88
Parentino Wine Bar 87
Park, Rovinj 85
Park, Hvar 222
Park Hotel, Makarska 205
Park, Split 198
Park Plaza Histria Pula 79
Passarola 217
Pauza 58
Peek&Poke Museum of Informatics & Technology 106
Pelegrini 162
Pelješac 265-267, 268
Peninsula Wine Bar & Shop 267
Pepenero 92
Peppermint 63
Perna 266
Perstil 187
Pervanovo Apartments 252
Peškarija 162
Pet Bunara 148
Petar Pan 205
Peterokutna kula 87
Petka 251
Petrinović Mausoleum 206
Phanas Pub 113
pharmacies 308
Pharos 99
phones, public 310
Piassa Granda 83
Piazza Luxury Suites 187
picigin 182
Pietas Julia 77
Pile 245
Pile Gate 235
Pimpinella 190
Pinetta 219
Pinia 128
Pink Chamoagne Hvar 220
Pintur 99

Pivnica Dubrava 248
Pivnica Moby Dick 211
Pivnica Pinta 49
Pizza Delfino 124
Pizzeria Caenazzo 257
Pizzeria Ex 110
Pizzeria Mirkec 201
Pizzeria Skipper 190
Pizzeria Spalato 159
Pizzeria Tedeschi 257
Pizzeria Tri Bunara 148
Planjak 257
Plava Club 88
Plava Laguna 90
Plavi Podrum 118
Plavi Val 159
Plaža, Omiš 204
Plaža, Pag 138
Pleso Airport, Zagreb 68
Plitvice Lakes National Park 294-295
Ploče 245
Po Bota 181
Poboduče 266
Pocco Locco 158
Pod Gričkim Topom 47
Pod Odrnom 203
Pod starim krovovima/ Kod Žnidaršića 49
Pod Voltom 96
Pod Zidom 49
Podgora 204
Podkućica 316
Podstine 222
Pojoda 227
Poklad 272
Poklisar 240
Polače 270
Polari Bay 86
Pomena 270
Poreč 86-90
Porin 205
Portić 127
postal services 310
Potočine beach 213
Prapratno 265
Preko 154
Preko Marina 153
Premantura 79
Preradovićeva flower market 53
President, Split 187
President Pantovčak 52
President Solin 198
Primošten 165-169
ProCaffe 192
Proizd 262, 263
Proto 240
Pucić Palace 245
Pula 72-79
Pula Amphitheatre 72
Punta, Brač 209
Punat, Korčula 255
Puntulina 82
Pupnat 262
Pupnatska Luka 262

## Q

Q Bar 150
Quasimodo 195
Quasimodo Hostel 198

## R

Rab 130-132
Rabac 101
Račić Mausoleum 265
Račišće 262
radio 309
Radisson Blu Hotel, Split 198
Radisson Blu Resort & Spa, Dubrovnik Sun Gardens 252
Rakhia Bar 49
Ranč Maha 264
Razonoda 242
Re di mare 191
Rector's Palace 237, 268
Red Baron 219
Regina del Formaggio, la 185
Regional Museum, Biograd 157
religion 310
Remisens Hotel Excelsior 126
Remisens Premium Hotel Ambasador 121
Remisens Premium Hotel Kvarner Amalia 123
resources 307-311
Restaurant Ariston 118
Restaurant Kamenar 166
Restaurant Kvaner 100
Restaurant Santa Lucia 133
Restaurant Sidro 92
Restoran Galeb 128
Restoran Knezgrad 124
Restoran Lovrečina 209
Restoran Najade 124
Restoran Paradigma 178
Restorarn Panorama 166
Ribarnica Brač 193
Ribarska Koliba 74
Ribarska Kućica 209
Ribice i Tri Točkice 58
Rijeka 104-115
Rijeka International Carnival 109
Ristorante Spagho 110
Ritam 154
Riva, Hvar Yacht Harbour Hotel 222
Riva, Makarska Riviera 205
Riva Cavtat 265
Riva, the, Split 172
Rivica 128
River Pub 112
Rixos Libertas 252
Robinson 217
Rock Caffe 78

Rovinj 80-86
Rovinj Aquarium 81
Royal Apartments 259
Roxy 249

## S

Sabor 42
Sabrage 112
safety 310
sailing 299-303
St Catherine's Church 42
St Donat's Church, Zadar 144
St John the Evangelist's Basilica 157
St John's Fortress 234
St Liberan 2676St Martin's Church, Žrnovo 264
St Mark's Cathedral, Korčula 254, 255, 256
St Mark's Church, Zagreb 46
St Mary's Church & Treasury, Zadar 144
St Michael's 266
St Pelagius 91
St Postrana 264
St Vitus's Church 106
Saint & Sinner 88
Samurai 178
San Antonio 198
San Giorgio 229
San Marco 218
San Rocco 95
Santa Maria, Rab 131
Santa Maria, Vodice 159
Santos Beach Club 131
Sapunara 270
Savudrija 94
Savudrija Lighthouse 94, 99
Scandal Express 78
seaplane 203
Seasplash 78
Sedmica 61
Seka Bay 253
Servantes 258
Šetalište San Marco 100
Shamballa 63
Sheraton Zagreb Hotel 65
Sheriff & Cherry 84
Shizuku 248
Šibenik 161-165
Šipan 273
Sirup 63
Škrip 206
Slanica 155
Slavija 187
Sljeme 68
smoking 310
Smokvica 260
Smokvica, Trogir 201
Sobe Simoni 187
Sobra 270
Soline 270
Šolta island 176
Šperun 191
Split 170-199

INDEX

Split, Hotel 198
Split Circus 181
Split City Museum 174
Split Gallery of Fine Arts 174
Sponza Palace 237
Spunk 67
Srsen Apartments 271
ST Riva 183
Šta da?! 112
Štala 133
Stare Grede 191
Stari Mlin 204
Stari Podrum 95
STDs, HIV & AIDS 308
Stellon 191
Stermasi 271
Stoja 79
Ston 265
Što čitaš/Sapunoteka 62
Strossmayer's Gallery of Old Masters 55
Štruk, La 48
Studio Kairos 52
study 310
Stupe 257
Šulići 253
Sunset Lounge 249
Sv Ilija 266
Sv Katarina Island 86
Sv Mihovil 272
Sveta Srca 74
Sveti Jakov 253
Sveti Jure 203
Sveti Nikola 87

T

Taban Hostel 53
Tajana 128
Take Me Home 51
Tamaris, Krk 129
Tamaris, Vis 229
Tarantela 219
Taverna Galija 265
Taverna Riva 210
Taverna Sergio 92
Teak 183
Tears of St Lucia 101
Technical Museum 55
telephones 310
television 309
tennis 94
Tic Tac 155
time 310
Tinel 162
tipping 310
Tito, Josip Broz 76
To je to SPLIT! 183
Toć 191
toilets 310
Tony, Murter 155
Tony, Pag 139
Top Pick Hotel & Casa Valamar Sanflor 101
Torci 1893
Torcida 163
Toreta winery 260

tour operators 311
tourist information 310
Tovjerna Sesame 248
Town Museum, Korčula 255, 256
Town Museum, Trogir 200
Trattoria Al Gastaldo 82
Trattoria Dream 82
Trattoria Riva's 110
Trattoria Tinel 191
Treće Poluvrijeme (Kuka) 192
Tri Palme 267
Tri Pršuta Wine Bar 220
Tri Tiffany 128
Tribunj 158
Trilogija 48
Triton 271
Trogir 200-202
Tropic Club 195
Trsat Castle, Rijeka 106
Trsatika 110
Trstenica 266
truffles 98
Tučepi 204
Tunel 113
Turan 218
Tvornica kulture 63

U

Ubli 272
Ugljan 152, 153-154
Uje 244
Uji Oil Bar 179
Ulixes 97
Ulysses Cave 270
Umag 94
Uvala 252
Uzorita 163

V

Vacation Suite Kashe 245
Vaja 262
Valamar Club Tamaris 89
Valamar Bellevue Hotel & Residence 101
Valamar Diamant Hotel 89
Valamar Dubrovnik President Hotel 252
Valamar Riviera Hotel & Valamar Villa Parentino 90
Valentino 84
Valle Losca 118
Valsabbion 79
Vanga 138
Vanilla 195
Vanjaka 201
Varadero Cocktail Bar 211
Vela Luka 254, 262-264
Vela Nera 75
Vela Pržina 260
Vela Spila 263
Veli Jože 83

Veliki Revelin Tower 255
Velo, Labin 100
Velo Misto 191
Veneranda Club Hvar 221
Venetian Citadel 214
Venezia Lines 90
Vešmašina 51
Vestibul Palace 187
Vidilica 192
Vidova Gora 206
Viecia Batana 84
Viganj 266, 267
Viking 86
Vila Irming 222
Vila Koruna 267
Vila Lili 85
Vila Sikaa 202
Vila Verde 221
Villa Andrea 205
Villa Angelica 97
Villa Annette 101
Villa Ariston 122
Villa Beller 122
Villa Club 88
Villa Diana 159
Villa Dobrić 187
Villa Dubrovnik 253
Villa Dvor 204
Villa Eden 154
Villa Giardino 213
Villa Kaliopa 227
Villa Kapetanović 122
Villa Koša 169
Villa Kristalia 203
Villa Mai Mare 158
Villa Matejuška 198
Villa Mediterane 267
Villa Meneghello 223
Villa Micika 253
Villa Nonna & Casa Nono 229
Villa Nora 223
Villa Rosetta 95
Villa Spiza 179
Villa Stari Dvor 154
Villa Valdibora 86
Villa Varoš 198
Vinarija Popić 262
Vino, D' 241
Vino & Ino 164
Vinoteka Bornstein 268
Vinoteka Miličić 244
Vinotoka 210
Vintage Industrial Bar 63
Vinum Bonum 258
Vinyl 61
Vinyl Bar 151
Vis 225-229
visas 311
Višnjan Observatory 91
Vitality Hotel Punta 137
Vitriol 92
vocabulary 312
Vodice 159-160
Vodnjanka 75
Volta 15 110
Vrata Krke 167 Vrbroska 214

Vrnik 259
Vučine 265

W

Wanda 241
War Photo Limited 235, 237
Waterman Svpetrvs Resort 213
weights & measures 311
Wellness Hotel Aurora 137
Westin Zagreb 65
wildlife 294-298
wine 39, 288-293
Wine & Cheese Bar Paradox 193
Wine Vault 83
work permits 311
working in Croatia 311

Y

Yesterday 88
Youth Hostel Rijeka 114

Z

Zadar 142-153
Zadar Cathedral 144
Zadar Museum of Ancient Glass 144
Zagreb 40-69
Zagreb Card 42
Zagreb City Museum 46
Zameo ih vjetar 155
Zaostrog 204
Zavalatica 260
Žbirac 193
Zelena Laguna 90
Zen Club 78
Zeneta 187
Zi Zi 258
Žibrac 193
Zigante 96
Zinfandel, Split 183
Zinfandel's 59
Zlatna Ribica, Šibenik 163
Zlatna Ribica, Split 179
Zlatna Školjka, Hvar 218
Zlatna Školjka, Rijeka 111
Zlatni Lav 134
Zlatni Rat 206
Zlatni Rt 86
Zlokić Oil Press 263
Zorače 218
Žrnovo 264
Zuljana 265
Zvijezda Mora 218